Acclaim for Russell S. Bonds's

STEALING THE GENERAL

"The Great Locomotive Chase has been the stuff of legend and the darling of Hollywood. Now we have a solid history of the Andrews Raid. Russell S. Bonds's stirring account makes clear why the raid failed and what happened to the raiders."—*James M. McPherson*

"A major contribution to the literature of American history and Civil War history."—*Railroad History*

"The first major study in decades, thoroughly worthy of an expedition that, 'had the wildness of a romance.'"—*The New Yorker*

"The best study of the raid. . . . a tale of daring and adventure made all the more remarkable because its events are true."
—*Fredericksburg Free-Lance Star*

"Definitive."—*Charlotte Observer*

"A solid read that is also magnificent storytelling."
—*Civil War Bookshelf*

"Excellent."—*Trains Magazine*

"Bonds writes with flair and skill that adds to the inherent drama of the story. . . . It seems hardly likely that anyone will need to write a book on this episode again."—*William C. Davis*

"In this gripping, smooth-running account of the raid and its aftermath, Bonds zooms effortlessly from broad-stroke overviews of Civil War strategy to minute-by-minute scrutiny of unfolding events on the ground. He sets up the story with a quick, punchy outline of the first year of the war. What follows is a fast-paced, extremely well-told tale of espionage, capture, trial and escape."
—*Publishers Weekly (starred review)*

"One of the Civil War's most celebrated events has at last found its historian."—*Blue and Gray*

"Robert Penn Warren once wrote that Americans should remember the Civil War because the stories of the men who fought it, "may affirm for us the possibility of the dignity of life." Such dignity is often accompanied by great bravery, but it can also come at a tragic price. Mr. Bonds's magnificent and definitive 'Stealing the General' reminds us of the tragic dignity of the bold young men who stole a train in an attempt to win their war and of those who gave chase in an attempt to avert the loss of theirs."—*The Wall Street Journal*

"Excellent history, and never less than gripping entertainment. The men and the times are brought vividly to light."
—*Bennington (Vt.) Banner*

"Phenomenally well written, organized, and presented."
—*Civil War Books and Authors*

"Outstanding. . . . A story of bravery and cowardice, brilliance and foolishness, good luck and misfortune. Climb aboard."
—*Hawaii Marine*

"Russell S. Bonds's riveting, page-turning account. . . . brings the story back to life in superior fashion."—*Tennessee Bar Journal*

"A very well-written and accurate account of one of the most thrilling episodes of the Civil War. Russell S. Bonds's research is impeccable, and the wonderful results are within these covers."
—*James G. Bogle, author of The General and the Texas*

"Readers can use this account to benchmark the kind of effort a definitive work does so well."—*Midwest Book Review*

Bonds does a great job of placing the raid into the wider context of the war, describing how it was hoped the raid would impact the strategic situation. . . . A story of personal courage and endurance and a volume to add to your bookshelf.—*Civil War News*

Stealing
the General

Stealing
the General

The Great Locomotive Chase
and the
First Medal of Honor

★

RUSSELL S. BONDS

WESTHOLME
Yardley

Frontispiece: The *General* at the 1939 New York World's Fair. (*Colonel James G. Bogle Collection*)

First Westholme Paperback Copyright © 2008

Text © 2007 Russell S. Bonds

Maps © 2007 Westholme Publishing, LLC

Maps by Joseph John Clark

Illustrations credited to the Colonel James G. Bogle Collection may not be reproduced without permission.

Westholme Publishing, LLC

Eight Harvey Avenue

Yardley, Pennsylvania 19067

Visit our Web site at www.westholmepublishing.com

First Paperback Printing: September 2008

10 9 8 7 6 5 4 3 2 1

ISBN: 978-1-59416-078-3

(ISBN 10: 1-59416-078-3)

Printed in United States of America

To the memory of my father,

Gary C. Bonds

. . . And I will overthrow the chariots, and those that ride in them; and the horses and their riders shall come down, every one by the sword of his brother.

Haggai 2:22, King James Bible

Because this was it: an interval, a space, in which the toad-squatting guns, the panting men and the trembling horses paused, amphitheatric about the embattled land, beneath the fading fury of the smoke and the puny yelling, and permitted the sorry business which had dragged on for three years now to be congealed into an irrevocable instant and put to an irrevocable gambit, not by two regiments or two batteries or even two generals, but by two locomotives.

William Faulkner, The Unvanquished

RAILROAD, n. The chief of many mechanical devices enabling us to get away from where we are to where we are no better off.

Ambrose Bierce, The Devil's Dictionary

Contents

Maps & Table

The Andrews Raiders

James J. Andrews	Civilian
Pvt. William Bensinger	*Co. G, 21st Ohio Infantry*
Pvt. Wilson W. Brown	*Co. F, 21st Ohio Infantry*
Pvt. Robert Buffum	*Co. H, 21st Ohio Infantry*
William Campbell	Civilian
Cpl. Daniel Dorsey	*Co. H, 33rd Ohio Infantry*
*Cpl. Martin Jones Hawkins**	*Co. A, 33rd Ohio Infantry*
Pvt. William Knight	*Co. E, 21st Ohio Infantry*
Cpl. Samuel Llewellyn**	Co. F, 10th Ohio Infantry
Sgt. Elihu H. Mason	*Co. K, 21st Ohio Infantry*
Pvt. Jacob Parrott	*Co. K, 33rd Ohio Infantry*
Cpl. William Pittenger	*Co. G, 2nd Ohio Infantry*
*Pvt. John Reed Porter**	*Co. G, 21st Ohio Infantry*
Cpl. William Reddick	*Co. B, 33rd Ohio Infantry*
Pvt. Samuel Robertson	*Co. G, 33rd Ohio Infantry*
Sgt. Maj. Marion Ross	*2nd Ohio Infantry*
Sgt. John M. Scott	*Co. F, 21st Ohio Infantry*
Pvt. Charles Perry Shadrach	Co. K, 2nd Ohio Infantry
Pvt. Samuel Slavens	*Co. E, 33rd Ohio Infantry*
*Pvt. James (Ovid Wellford) Smith***	*Co. I, 2nd Ohio Infantry*
Pvt. George D. Wilson	Co. B, 2nd Ohio Infantry
Pvt. J. Alfred Wilson	*Co. C, 21st Ohio Infantry*
Pvt. John Wollam	*Co. C, 33rd Ohio Infantry*
Pvt. Mark Wood	*Co. C, 21st Ohio Infantry*

Names of Medal of Honor recipients appear in italics.

*Overslept and missed the train at Marietta, did not participate in theft of the *General*

**Enlisted in Confederate units near Jasper, Tennessee, to escape arrest, did not participate in theft of the *General*

Preface

★

"The Boldest Adventure of the War"

At the intersection of Juniper and Third Streets in Midtown Atlanta stands a historical marker placed by the State of Georgia in 1982 to honor, of all things, a Yankee spy. Tourist guidebooks for the city make no mention of the place, and in fact there is nothing at all to see there apart from the fading sign itself, wedged between a utility pole and a nondescript yellow-brick apartment building. The monument attracts no tour buses or school field trips and draws little attention from passersby, perhaps because its only heading is an unremarkable name: JAMES J. ANDREWS. Civil War buffs pass up the quiet corner in favor of the battle murals at the Atlanta Cyclorama or the grassy fields at Kennesaw Mountain, twenty miles to the north. Even the most diligent *Gone with the Wind* fans visiting the Margaret Mitchell House, at the nearby intersection of Peachtree and Tenth Streets, apparently lack either the information or the enthusiasm to hike the eight blocks to this spot. (They more likely stroll in the other direction, looking for the place on Peachtree Street where a jaywalking Ms. Mitchell was struck and killed by a taxicab on her way to the theater in 1949. No marker there, as it happens.)

But the Andrews marker is unusual not only because of the person it honors, but also for where it stands—not at a birthplace or on a battlefield, but at the site of an execution. A few feet from this street corner on the otherwise beautiful afternoon of June 7, 1862, James Andrews was hanged as a Union spy. Or perhaps hanging is too kind a word for it. Andrews, thirty-three years old at the time and six feet tall, was "strangled to death," according to one account of the incident, "for the tree on which they hung him was so low that when his head touched the limb his toes touched the ground, and it was necessary to dig the sand away in order that he could be choked." The provost marshal buried him in the red clay under a nearby pine tree, his ankles still bound by iron shackles and the frayed rope still snug around his neck.[1]

Though his ultimate and grisly punishment may suggest otherwise, James Andrews was more common thief than secret agent. Eight weeks earlier, on April 12, 1862—one year to the day after Confederate guns opened on Fort Sumter and started the Civil War—Andrews and nineteen volunteers, all but one drawn from Ohio infantry regiments, infiltrated north Georgia wearing civilian clothes and stole a steam engine called the *General*. The raiders uncoupled the gleaming locomotive, tender, and three boxcars from the rest of the train during a breakfast stop north of Atlanta, then raced northward up the Western & Atlantic Railroad into the North Georgia mountains at speeds approaching and possibly exceeding sixty miles an hour, cutting telegraph lines and destroying track along the way. Andrews' plan was to drive the stolen train to Chattanooga and wreck the critical rail connection with Atlanta behind him, thus isolating East Tennessee and blocking supplies and reinforcements from the south. The sabotage would, in theory, open East Tennessee to the Union army and cut off men and materiel from Georgia, Alabama, and the West from reaching Confederate forces in Virginia. In essence, Andrews planned to facilitate with a handful of men the same result Generals Ulysses S. Grant and William T. Sherman would require an army to achieve two years later—the reduction of Chattanooga, the seizure of Georgia's railroads, and the ensuing strangulation of the Deep South. If they succeeded, Andrews and his handful of Ohio boys could change the course of the war.

Unfortunately for the band of Northern soldiers, they did not count on the determination of the *General's* young conductor, William A. Fuller, who left a breakfast of steaming eggs and biscuits and chased the stolen train for more than two miles on foot before jumping on a handcar to continue the pursuit. Fuller and several compatriots then drove a series of engines through station after station, biting at the heels of the fleeing raiders and preventing serious damage to the railroad until, running out of wood and water a few miles shy of Chattanooga, Andrews and his men abandoned the *General* and took to the woods. The Great Locomotive Chase, as it came to be known, quite literally ran out of steam.

In the hours and days that followed, "the engine thieves," as the Southern newspapers ungenerously called them, were hunted down in North Georgia, North Alabama, and East Tennessee, where they were finally captured. But their story was just beginning. Eight of the raiders were tried by a

Confederate court-martial and executed as Union spies. Eight others made a daring escape from an Atlanta prison—their pleas for clemency having been coldly dismissed by Confederate President Jefferson Davis—and the remainder were released in a prisoner exchange in the spring of 1863. In recognition of their actions, six of the raiders would become the first men in American history to be awarded the newly created Medal of Honor—commonly though incorrectly known today as the Congressional Medal of Honor—and they would be hailed in the North as heroes at a time of the war when, frustrated by sluggish, bumbling generals and battered by unexpectedly defiant Confederate armies, the Union desperately needed something to cheer about. Georgia's most famous storyteller Joel Chandler Harris would call the theft of the *General* and the subsequent pursuit "the boldest adventure of the war."[2]

The Great Locomotive Chase captured the imagination of many Americans during and after the Civil War, its story romanticized and retold down the years in articles, speeches, books, paintings, and ultimately on film. Several of the surviving participants in the raid wrote and published their own accounts or gave public lectures on the subject. Raider William Pittenger milked the tale more than anyone, publishing four full-length books and numerous articles on the adventure—even though he was terribly nearsighted and spent the entire chase in a closed boxcar. Wilbur G. Kurtz, a commercial artist and historical consultant on the film *Gone with the Wind* who happened to marry William Fuller's daughter, conducted interviews of many of the participants and collected extensive research on the Andrews Raid for more than fifty years, now archived at the Atlanta History Center and at the Academy of Motion Picture Arts and Sciences in Los Angeles. Local historians and railroad enthusiasts alike have compiled impressive collections of photographs and documents. The locomotive *General* is the main attraction at the Southern Museum of Civil War and Locomotive History in Kennesaw, Georgia. And, of course, the story has been famously if inaccurately told in a swashbuckling 1956 Disney movie starring Fess Parker, in addition to inspiring the 1927 Buster Keaton classic, *The General*.

Yet despite the story's fame in the annals of the Civil War and its enduring cultural popularity, no modern narrative history of the Great Locomotive Chase exists. The last book-length treatment was Charles O'Neill's *Wild Train: The Story of the Andrews Raiders*—for the most part a compilation of lengthy quotes and descriptions from other sources—and it was published half a century ago, in 1956. Many of the characters involved, from the ambitious

Union astronomer-general who approved the mission to the enigmatic Andrews himself, are largely unknown. Most accounts of the raid, including those written by the participants themselves, are filled with inaccuracies, exaggerations, and self-serving descriptions. Oft-repeated myths about the Great Locomotive Chase—trains jumping over gaps in the rails, locomotives racing across bridges engulfed in flame—have become widely accepted as fact. "Never has a story been so badly mauled and twisted," Wilbur Kurtz wrote, pitching the idea of a movie based on the raid in a 1952 letter to Walt Disney. "Anything, however outrageous, was considered meet and proper to heighten the thrills; seemingly, a story already high in heroic content needed a shot in the arm, despite the fact that what is known to have actually transpired makes it a thriller without any embellishment."

There has been little effort among historians to clarify the record or correct these persistent errors. Indeed, professional Civil War historians largely overlook the Andrews Raid, regarding it as a sort of flashy sideshow in the early days of the war, as perhaps it was. One recent military history dismisses the raid as "a mere distraction in the Confederate war effort," and it is true that the episode had no lasting effect on the state of military affairs in Georgia and Tennessee, and in fact provided little distraction at all, except to the Southern newspapers and the citizens of north Georgia for a time.[3] Those few histories of the raid that have been written—perhaps driven by a desire for cinematic adventure and by widespread fascination with the golden age of railroad transportation and the steam locomotive—tend to narrowly focus on the minute-by-minute circumstances of the five-hour iron horse race itself. As a result, the strategic inspiration and military context of the raid is given short shrift, as is its aftermath, a compelling tale of courts-martial, torture and imprisonment, daring escapes, grisly executions, bungled military opportunities, and—for a few fortunate survivors—newly minted medals for heroism and a personal audience in Washington with President Lincoln himself.

This book is my effort to tell the story of the Great Locomotive Chase and to reexamine its place in the war and its lasting legacy: the highest military citation for valor given by this nation—an honor first bestowed upon six soldiers who never fired a shot, all of whom had offered in writing to lay down their arms and sacrifice their loyalty to the Union in exchange for a reprieve from the gallows. I have endeavored to place the raid in the larger context of the war in the spring of 1862, to illuminate little-known actors on the war's great stage, and to broaden the lens to tell the entire story. I have also tried to avoid being influenced by the romantic adventure that has surrounded the story and take a clear-eyed look at the Andrews Raid, which has been hailed for decades as a brilliant, daring scheme, doomed by bad weather and worse luck, but may in fact have been a fool's errand—ill-conceived, poorly planned, badly manned, and clumsily executed. Even if the raid had been carried out flawlessly, it is by no means certain whether the actions of twenty men on a single day in April 1862—the wrecking of a single rail line in north Georgia—could have hastened the war's conclusion and avoided the carnage still to come.

But whatever its merits as a military operation, the Andrews Raid drew the admiration not only of President Abraham Lincoln and Secretary of War Edwin M. Stanton, who awarded the raiders the Medal of Honor despite their failure, but also of the people of the South, many of whom would regard the foiling of the scheme to be more important to the young Confederacy than even the victory at Manassas the summer before. Moreover, the thrilling contest between iron horses, along with the bloodbath at Shiloh and the historic clash of the ironclads *Monitor* and *Virginia* that same spring, in retrospect seemed to herald the arrival of a new era of warfare in the dawning industrial age.

Most of all, like many Civil War stories, the history of the Andrews Raid is a story of ordinary men, far from home, called to do extraordinary things in service of their country. It is a story of boldness, adventure, determination, hardship, and heroism on all sides. "This is an epic without villains," one historian would later note, "and one in which there was glory and pain enough to be shared by all those in it, without diminishing the common supply."

Part I

The Plan

Strawberry Plains Bridge, Tennessee. (*Library of Congress*)

CHAPTER ONE

The Bridge Burners

East Tennessee

Bridge-burners and destroyers of railroad tracks are excepted from among those pardonable. They will be tried by drum-head court-martial and hung on the spot.

—Colonel Danville Leadbetter, CSA
Proclamation to the Citizens of East Tennessee
November 30, 1861

FOR RALPH WALDO EMERSON, lecturing at the Mercantile Library Association in Boston in 1844, the steam locomotive was a machine with almost mystical powers. He spoke of trains annihilating distance and likened railroad iron to "a magician's rod, in its power to evoke the sleeping energies of land and water." Emerson saw the railroad as a great instrument of trade and unity for young America, stating that "the great political promise of the invention is to hold the Union staunch." He was confident that the thousands of miles of railroad track already crisscrossing the country would establish "an American sentiment" and stitch the disparate regions together as one nation. "Not only is distance annihilated," Emerson said, "but when, as now, the locomotive and the steamboat, like enormous shuttles, shoot every day across the thousand various threads of national descent and employment, and bind them fast in one web, an hourly assimilation goes forward, and there is no danger that local peculiarities and hostilities should be preserved." Emerson was a visionary and a sage, but on the peacemaking capabilities of the railroad, he was wrong. Seventeen years later, when

America's "local peculiarities" grew into stark political and cultural differences and then exploded into hostilities beyond imagining, the steam locomotive changed from a tool of commerce and peace to, as railroad historian George Edgar Turner put it, a "machine which was to work a greater change in warfare and its methods than had been wrought by any other instrument since the invention of gunpowder." From 1861 to 1865, America's railroads at the same time unified the nation and contributed to tearing it apart.[1]

In the years following Emerson's Boston lecture, railroads spread across the American landscape like summer ivy on a garden wall, the total miles of track more than trebling during the 1850s to cover every state east of the Mississippi River. By 1860, the American rail network was larger than that of the rest of the world combined. With the outbreak of the Civil War, trains, rail lines, and rail centers were transformed from instruments of commerce into important tactical and strategic assets, and quickly became primary military objectives as well. For the first time in history, military maps were laced with thin lines denoting rail connections between cities, armies, and strategic points, and commanders struggled to master the complicated logistical and financial task of railroad management while working to capture the railroads in their front and protect and effectively employ those in their rear. The railroad had changed forever not only the practical considerations of military transport and supply but also the broader conceptual thinking of military strategy.[2]

This development was not lost on the officers of both armies, most of whom, according to historian Gary Gallagher, "grasped the importance of railroads from the very beginning of the conflict." In an August 1861 letter explaining his strategy to President Abraham Lincoln, Union General George B. McClellan, who was himself a former vice president of the Illinois Central Railroad, emphasized that "the construction of railroads has introduced a new and very important element into war, by the great facilities thus given for concentrating at particular positions large masses of troops from remote sections, and by creating new strategic points and lines of operations." Considerable early evidence supported the young general's assessment. Indeed, some two years before the first shot was fired, a train on the Baltimore & Ohio Railroad had carried a detachment of United States Marines under Robert E. Lee—in those days a brown-bearded, blue-uniformed colonel—to put down an uprising at Harper's Ferry led by the abolitionist John Brown. From the first days of the Civil War, trains were used similarly, but on a much larger scale, to mobilize troops for battle. The day after the Confederates shelled Fort Sumter, Secretary of War Simon Cameron sent a telegram urging the Governor of Massachusetts to rush newly enlisted volunteers to Washington by rail. Three months later, the curtain-raising battle of the war was fought on July 21, 1861, in the rolling fields and railroad yards of Manassas Junction, Virginia, with Rebel reinforcements delivered to the front in boxcars and flatcars on the Manassas Gap Railroad. And early the following spring, the eccentric Virginia commander and former college professor Thomas J. Jackson, already known as Stonewall for his rock-solid stand at Manassas, employed a system of roads and railroad lines to mystify and defeat superior Union forces in the Shenandoah Valley. The tight-lipped Jackson closed the campaign with a rapid movement of his army kept secret even from his own subordinate commanders, shifting his corps by rail from Staunton in the Shenandoah Valley to Beaver Dam Station near Richmond, in position to land with both feet upon McClellan's right flank on the York-James Peninsula. As the war approached its first anniversary, there was, in short, no question that the railroad would be an essential tool—and primary target—in the campaigns yet to come.[3]

In this, the South was at a distinct disadvantage. More than two-thirds of the total miles of railroad track lay in the North, and the Confederacy had fewer engines and rolling stock and far less industrial capability and raw materials from which to produce them. The scarcity of trains and track made the railroads of the South even more precious than their Northern counterparts, and their importance would only grow as the Federals seized control of ports, rivers, and waterways early in the war. As a result, although some battles would be fought on open ground by happenstance wherever two great armies happened to come to blows, many of the strategic movements in the Southern states would come to be directed toward, and major battles fought around, key railroad centers or rail lines—as at Manassas, Harper's Ferry, Corinth, Chattanooga, and Atlanta.[4]

One of these key railroad arteries, or "trunk lines," as they were called, ran southwest from the Confederate capital at Richmond through the Cumberland Gap and Knoxville, Tennessee, to Chattanooga, where it split in two: the Memphis & Charleston Railroad, running westward through Bridgeport and Huntsville, Alabama, before curving north to Memphis; and the Western & Atlantic Railroad, which meandered southward through the mountains of North Georgia to Atlanta. The railroads intersected in Chattanooga, a village of 5,000 cradled on three sides by imposing mountain ridges and lassoed by a bend of the Tennessee River. In the deadly game of strategic tic-tac-toe then unfolding, the junction at Chattanooga was center square, and whoever held it could block railroad transport and military supply across and down. If a Union force could capture Chattanooga and either break or hold the trunk lines that met there, it could sever Confederate forces in the East from those in the West and stop munitions, troops, and supplies from Georgia and Alabama from reaching the gray army in Virginia. Destruction or isolation of the center of the South's rickety system of rail transport would be a hard blow to the sternum of the Confederacy that might knock out its breath for good.[5]

No one was more acutely aware of this than the President of the United States. Abraham Lincoln's only previous military service was a brief and uneventful stint as a young militia captain in the 1832 Black Hawk War, where, as he put it, he "had a good many bloody struggles with the musquetoes." Now the fractured nation's commander-in-chief, Lincoln had spent countless hours in the early days of the war poring over maps and reading textbooks on strategy and tactics in an effort to shore up his limited military experience and develop a strategy that would win the war. The new president was self-deprecating about his ability and always deferential to his generals, but he could read a map as well as anyone, and he viewed the Union's military objectives to be very straightforward. No one could doubt the immediate priority of protecting Washington and threatening Richmond and the main Rebel army nearby, but Lincoln also worried constantly—and disproportionately, some would say—over the mountainous eastern portion of the state of Tennessee.

On the brown and curling maps tacked to the walls of his office, the Confederate strategic line of defense gently curved southwest from Richmond in the east to Memphis in the west, with its thinly defended center in the heart of the Volunteer State, which Lincoln referred to as "the keystone of the Southern arch." In addition to its location at center stage of the theater of war, the 400-mile-wide state was embroidered with winding rivers and railroads that were of considerable and obvious strategic importance to even the most casual military observer, as they linked the Eastern theater of military operations with the Mississippi River and the increasingly critical armies in the West. As early as July 1861, hard on the heels of the defeat at Bull Run, Lincoln had offered a memorandum of proposed strategic steps to be taken by Union forces in the West, ending the list by proposing "a joint movement from Cairo on Memphis; and from Cincinnati on East Tennessee."

Federal armies were on the move to implement the former of these sugges-tions, inching southward from Illinois under the leadership of an unproven and as-yet unknown brigadier named Ulysses S. Grant, but as the divided nation marked the new year, East Tennessee remained unthreatened by Union forces.[6]

What was worse, much of the population of these Southern highlands was staunchly pro-Union, and it was this fact, as much as the region's strate-gic value, that kept the chief executive up at night. Tennessee, like the nation, was a house divided. Although the state had a star in the Confederate flag and would furnish more soldiers for the Southern cause than any other state save Virginia, Tennessee also would supply some 40,000 men to the Federal armies during the war, more than all the other Southern states combined. Tennesseans had refused to leave the Union on their first referendum on the issue in February 1861, finally becoming the last state to secede and join the Confederacy in June—with citizens of East Tennessee still opposing seces-sion more than two to one. The residents of the East Tennessee hills had always been staunchly patriotic and politically independent, in many respects isolated from the economy and the social structure of the plantation South. Slaves were few and far between in highland villages and on hillside farms. As one historian of the region noted, "most East Tennesseans saw little future in joining a rebellion of southern states in which they had little at stake and much to lose." As a result, the majority of the population held true to the Old Flag, and Confederate authorities were embarrassed by and openly con-cerned about the large numbers of outspoken "Tories" and "Lincolnites" in their midst. Writing from his headquarters in Knoxville, Confederate Major General E. Kirby Smith, in command of Rebel forces in East Tennessee, described the region as "an enemy's country; its people beyond the influence and control of our troops and in open rebellion." Union-loyal East Tennesseans "look confidently for the re-establishment of the Federal authority in the South with as much confidence as the Jews look for the com-ing of the Messiah," one correspondent reported to Confederate President Jefferson Davis, "and I feel quite sure when I assert that no event or circum-stance can change or modify their hopes."[7]

In the fall of 1861, it had been this "hostile element" of Tennessee mountain men that made the first effort to break the Confederate railroad lifeline that connected Virginia and the battlefields of the Eastern Theater with the Deep South and the Mississippi Valley. William Blount Carter, a native Tennessean and former Presbyterian minister, approached Union

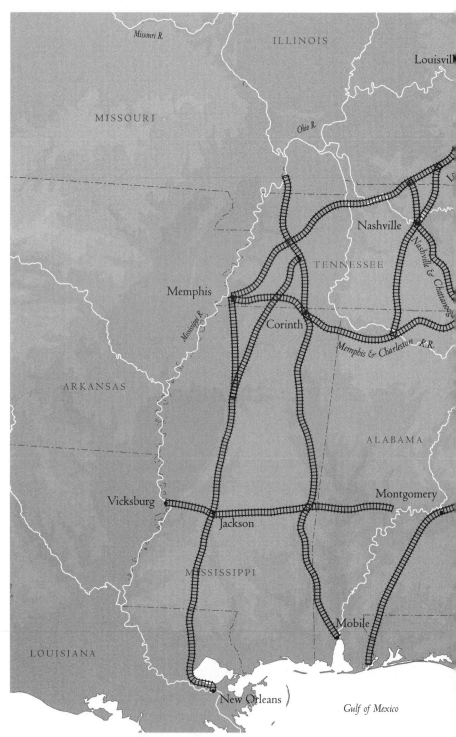

Principal railroads of the Confederacy, 1862.

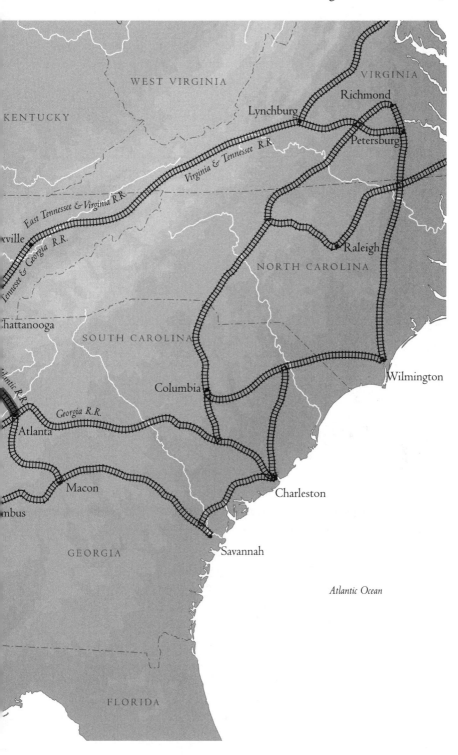

General George H. Thomas with a plan for a campaign of bridge burning to be conducted by insurgent civilians. The midnight attacks he proposed would cut critical rail lines in the region and hopefully paralyze the occupying gray army. Supporting Union forces in Kentucky could then spill through the rugged mountain pass at Cumberland Gap into Tennessee and overwhelm the small Confederate detachments at Knoxville and Chattanooga. East Tennessee would be instantly relieved, Rebel armies in Virginia cut off, and the Confederacy shorn in two. Thomas liked the sound of that and, with Lincoln's enthusiastic blessing and a modest fund to finance the operation, assigned Captain David Fry of the Second Tennessee (U.S.) Volunteer Infantry Regiment—one of those 40,000 Union volunteers from Tennessee—to assist Carter with finalizing and executing the contemplated sabotage.

Born in the foothills of the Smoky Mountains near Greenville, Tennessee—just a country mile from the birthplace of another stalwart mountaineer named Davy Crockett—Captain Fry had fled his home north to Kentucky to enlist in the Union Army, reporting to Camp Dick Robinson near Lexington in September 1861, where he was promptly commissioned an officer and company commander. A veteran of the Mexican War, Fry was, according to one fellow soldier, "a man of fine stature and great muscular power, brave as a lion, yet sympathetic as a child to those in need or distress." Another comrade would pronounce him "one of the noblest men in the world." He looked forward to returning to his home state to take personal action to loosen the grip of the secessionists he viewed as an insurgent minority, and he would soon gain considerable notoriety for leading raids into Tennessee, "taking money, powder, threatening death, and on occasion beating Southern men." Fry began by recruiting several dozen civilian volunteers for his new bridge burning mission and worked out a plan for crossings across the region to be assaulted and destroyed simultaneously.[8]

The surprise attacks worked spectacularly, with local volunteer saboteurs overpowering sentries and seriously damaging bridges across East Tennessee and into North Georgia and Alabama on the night of November 8, 1861. The crippled bridges—at Strawberry Plains, Lick Creek, Hiawassee, and six other crossings—halted rail traffic throughout the region, and the attacks themselves terrified pro-Southern residents and shocked Confederate authorities. "The Confederacy was startled and stirred from end to end," Knoxville lawyer Oliver P. Temple reported. "Men awoke frightened as if by a horrible dream. Universal consternation prevailed in East Tennessee." As a result of this sudden and violent rebellion against the rebellion, the mountains of East

Tennessee became a sort of upside-down Wonderland where black was white and where loyal blue seemed rebel gray. Confederate leaders breathlessly reported the outbreak of "Civil War," secessionists panicked over the "rebellion" in their midst, and Union men were arrested and jailed as "rebels" and "traitors." "The burning of railroad bridges in East Tennessee shows a deep-seated spirit of rebellion in that section," Tennessee Governor Isham G. Harris warned Confederate President Jefferson Davis on November 12. "Union men are organizing. This rebellion must be crushed out instantly, the leaders arrested, and summarily punished."[9]

Colonel Danville Leadbetter. (*USMHI*)

The Confederate high command responded swiftly, assigning a transplanted Yankee, Colonel Danville Leadbetter, "to assume the command of the troops necessary for guarding the line and dispersing the insurrectionists and bridge-burners." A native of Leeds, Maine, Leadbetter graduated from West Point in 1836 and spent his military career in the Corps of Engineers, working in the U.S. Coast Survey and becoming an accomplished designer and builder of lighthouses—several of which still stand, dark and rusting, to this day. Leaving the army in 1858, he became the chief engineer of the State of Alabama, moving to Mobile and constructing lighthouses and fortifications along the Gulf Coast, including the imposing forts protecting Mobile Bay itself. When the war began, Leadbetter sided with his adopted home of Alabama and received a colonel's commission in the Confederate Army. Now fifty years old, the new Rebel sheriff in town was a solid man with stern, tired eyes and a persistent, enigmatic smirk surrounded by an impressive rampart of thick brown whiskers. His adversaries would remember him as a villain of almost Shakespearean proportion, "nothing more or less than a contemptible drunken bully, a profane, blustering braggart, and withal a most arrant coward." Leadbetter would soon demonstrate a cold-blooded willingness to use any means to carry out his assignment, and would in time be absolutely despised by the locals, one of whom would later describe him as "the worst man, the greatest coward, and the blackest-hearted villain that ever made a track in East Tennessee."[10]

The bridge burners Leadbetter was charged with dispersing were, as it turned out, as inept at evading subsequent capture as they had been successful in accomplishing the destruction assigned to them in the first place. While the actual sabotage of the bridges went off without a hitch, squabbling and uncertainty among Union generals stopped the supporting military effort before it even got started. General Thomas's interest in a planned offensive built around the railroad sabotage was particularly short-lived. Having promised the support of his troops mere weeks before, the future "Rock of Chickamauga" now bristled at those who pressed him to advance, refusing to budge and insisting in the days before the operation that if the civilian saboteurs "are not content and must go, then the risk of disaster must remain with them." Apparently, however, no one bothered to inform the bridge burners themselves that they had lost both the enthusiasm of the Union command and the possibility of any supporting Federal infantry arriving from Kentucky. This left Leadbetter's Confederate patrols and local secessionist militia unmolested, able to repair the damaged bridges at their leisure and free to round up the insurgents, many of whom had been recognized by bridge guards who were also their longtime neighbors.

The manhunt was by no means easy, however. East Tennessee was a roughed-up country, its ridges and gorges dotted with country homesteads and backwoods cabins whose residents were all too eager to offer sanctuary to the fugitive bridge burners. "That country consists of a tumultuous mass of steep hills, wooded to the top, with execrable roads winding through the ravines and often occupying the beds of water-courses," Colonel Leadbetter reported. Fearing retribution, many young men literally took to the hills, regardless of whether they had been involved in the sabotage. "At the farm houses along the more open valleys no men were to be seen and it is believed that nearly the whole male population of the country were lurking in the hills on account of disaffection or fear," Leadbetter's report continued. "The women in some cases were greatly alarmed throwing themselves on the ground and wailing like savages. Indeed the population is savage." These lamentations would only increase when punishment was doled out to those who were caught.[11]

When local authorities inquired of Richmond as to what to do with the captured bridge burners, Confederate Secretary of War Judah P. Benjamin ordered that they were to be "tried summarily by drum-head court-martial, and, if found guilty, executed on the spot by hanging." He urged the "vigilant execution" of this order, adding coldly: "It would be well to leave their bodies hanging in the vicinity of the burned bridges." Colonel Leadbetter carried out the order vigilantly indeed, and five Tennessee civilians were promptly and unceremoniously hanged. According to "Parson" W.G. Brownlow, the editor of the *Knoxville Whig*, and local folklore, Leadbetter saw to the hangings personally and tied the nooses with his own hands. Brownlow later described the execution of Jacob Harmon, Jr., and his young son Henry:

> Old Mr. Harmon was seated in one cart upon his coffin, and his son in the other, and each cart was surrounded by a strong guard of Rebel bayonets and driven down the hill to a scaffold. The young man was hung first, and the father was compelled to look upon his death-struggles. Then he was told to mount the scaffold; but, being feeble and overpowered by his feelings, two of the ruffians took hold of him, one of them saying, "Get up there, you damned old traitor!" and the poor old man was launched into eternity after his son.

In accordance with Benjamin's instructions, Leadbetter ordered those executed to be left hanging by the railroad tracks for four days and four nights, directing local engineers to run their trains slowly past, "in order that the Secessionists on board might feast their eyes upon the ghastly spectacle." Unseasonably warm days in early December caused the colonel to modify this last after some thirty-six hours, however, as "the corpses were becoming somewhat offensive."[12]

The intrepid Captain Fry, the operation's erstwhile leader, escaped the Confederate posses scouring the wooded hilltops and would in the months to come continue to lead raids and gather recruits in the rough country—at least until Confederate authorities finally tracked him down. "Had he been promptly helped, as seemed possible at that time, he would have saved much of the suffering and persecution endured by the people of that State, and given a strong element to the Union cause," a fellow soldier later said of Captain Fry. "As it was, he was left to his fate almost unaided." But that comes later in our story.

Lincoln's first effort to weaken the gray army in East Tennessee and push Union men through the Cumberland Gap had been unsuccessful, but hardly unnoticed. Two of the nine bridges attacked in the uprising were below Chattanooga on the railroad to the rail center and arsenal of Atlanta, 138 winding miles to the south. For several days, the sidings and platforms of Chattanooga's railyard were quiet, as not a single rail car arrived up the line from Atlanta. Elsewhere in Tennessee, a novice quinine smuggler and self-appointed Union "scout"—a common euphemism of the day for the dishonorable and distasteful term "spy"—probably took note of this interruption in Southern supply in the course of his travels. For it was about this time that his thoughts began to turn from smuggling to sabotage, and he began gathering intelligence in support of a plan to replicate the effort of the East Tennessee bridge burners, in spectacular fashion, and to greater effect.

The spy's name was James J. Andrews.[13]

*T*he railroad bridge burnings in November 1861 brought harsh recriminations against Union loyalists throughout the hill towns and hardscrabble country of East Tennessee. In addition to the gruesome hangings of the bridge burners themselves, Rebel troops resorted to an iron hand to keep other Union sympathizers held in check, including a declaration of martial law in Knoxville and an order from the Confederate War Department that dozens of influential Union-loyal citizens, including a judge and several state legislators, were to be imprisoned without trial "till the end of the war." In all, some four hundred Unionists were arrested and jailed. On November 30, Colonel Leadbetter issued an ominous public proclamation to the citizens of East Tennessee demanding allegiance to the Confederate States and promising the "invasion of your homes and the wasting of your substance" so long as the "insurrectionary tumult" persisted. "No man's life or property is safe, no woman or child can sleep in quiet," the Rebel colonel warned, ending the pronouncement with an explicit threat of swift capital punishment to anyone who attacked the railroad tracks or bridges.

An uneasy, fearful calm ensued. "The execution of the bridge-burners is producing the happiest effect," Leadbetter reported to Richmond a week later. "Insurgents will continue for yet a while in the mountains, but I trust that we have secured the outward obedience of the people." Additional railroad guards were posted at bridges and trestles, and the railroad companies themselves became more cautious and vigilant. These precautions and his stern proclamation convinced Leadbetter that the situation, though still volatile, was under control. The former coastal engineer was confident that no one would dare to attack the railroads leading to Chattanooga again.[14]

The draconian reprisals and martial law in the Tennessee hills increased the Northern outcry for a substantial Union force to come to the aid of the loyalists in the region, an effort led in Washington by U.S. Representative Horace Maynard and Senator Andrew Johnson, formerly the governor of

Tennessee and the only Southern U.S. Senator who held his seat after secession. They found a sympathetic ear in Abraham Lincoln. More than ever, the
president thought it crucial, even with all the other demands being made on
the still-green Federal armies, to break the South's strategic keystone and bring
relief to the people of East Tennessee as soon as possible. He had in mind
something far grander than the eventual capture or isolated destruction of
railroad tracks and trestles. Lincoln's dearest hope was to secure and protect in
the mountains of Tennessee a bastion of Union loyalty to mirror the one
established a year before in the mountains of western Virginia, whose population had refused to secede from the Union by an overwhelming margin.[15]

Unfortunately, the president faced the same problem in conducting offensive operations in Kentucky and Tennessee as he faced in Virginia: a stubborn
and sluggish army commander at the head of the forces that would be called
on to strike the blow. The Army of the Ohio was led by General Don Carlos
Buell, a forty-one-year-old West Pointer and native son of the Buckeye State
who was known as a gruff and demanding officer and a harsh disciplinarian,
having once been court-martialed for thrashing a delinquent soldier with the
flat of his sword. After brave and distinguished service in the Mexican War,
Buell had taken his place in the dramatis personae of the present conflict
months before the first cannon was fired. In December 1860, as a major
attached to the Adjutant General's office in Washington, it had been Buell
who personally delivered a message to Major Robert Anderson at Fort
Moultrie outside Charleston, South Carolina, authorizing him to move his
command to nearby Fort Sumter and directing him if attacked to "defend
yourself to the last extremity."[16]

Buell had organized the army into its present state in November after suc-
ceeding another obscure brigadier named William Tecumseh Sherman, who
had been transferred to St. Louis and then quietly relieved of command after
suffering what would in modern terms be considered a nervous breakdown.
Immediately after he took command, Buell was directed by President Lincoln
and General-in-Chief George B. McClellan to liberate East Tennessee at the
earliest possible opportunity, capturing Nashville if possible while continuing to protect Louisville to the north. But Buell, who was stout of form and
standoffish in manner, was a character who seemed to be made for staying
put, his theatrical name notwithstanding. Even the slow-moving McClellan,
throwing stones from the glass house of his own long-stationary headquarters near Washington, became increasingly impatient with Buell's persistent
lack of progress, imploring him in dispatches throughout the winter to move

on East Tennessee "unless it is impossible." McClellan encouraged his friend Buell, "If you gain and retain possession of Eastern Tennessee you will have won brighter laurels than any I hope to gain." The Tennessee congressmen Johnson and Maynard added their own strident appeals to the Ohio general, despairing that "our people are oppressed and pursued as beasts of the forest. The Government must come to their relief. We are looking to you with anxious solicitude to move in that direction."[17]

But neither emotional pleas nor military directives could incite action from Buell, who seemed by his manner altogether more likely to gather dark clouds than bright laurels. He dispersed his forces haphazardly and seemed to concentrate most of all on not drawing the attention of his gray adversaries. "Thus far, I have studiously avoided any movements which to the enemy would have any appearance of activity or method," he proudly reported to McClellan several weeks after assuming command. He sat idle into December, assuring his superiors in Washington, "I have by no means been unmindful of your wishes in regard to East Tennessee and I think I can both appreciate and unite in your sympathy for a people who have shown so much constancy. Their constancy will sustain them until the hour of deliverance." That hour, however, seemed far away as the men of the Army of the Ohio celebrated Christmas around their campfires on the outskirts of Louisville, while their commander offered the persecuted Unionists of East Tennessee nothing more than his confidence in their own constancy. "Armies travel slowly indeed," Colonel John Beatty of the Third Ohio lamented in his diary. "Within fifteen miles of the enemy and rotting in the mud."

After the first of the year, Lincoln had had quite enough of being stuck in the mud, and he wrote Buell directly to prod him to move.

WASHINGTON, January 4, 1862.

GENERAL BUELL:

Have arms gone forward for East Tennessee? Please tell me the progress and condition of the movement in that direction. Answer.

A. LINCOLN.

Buell, however, was no more concerned by pointed inquiries from Lincoln than he had been by the general-in-chief's earlier stream of urgent dispatches. He replied to the president promptly the next day, explaining that "arms can only go forward for east Tennessee under the protection of an army," seemingly oblivious to the 60,000 men he had at his disposal. He continued, "While my preparations have had this movement constantly in view, I will

confess to your excellency that I have
been bound to it more by sympathy for
the people of East Tennessee and the
anxiety with which you and the general-
in-chief have desired it than by my
opinion of its wisdom as an uncondi-
tional measure."[18]

Buell preferred instead to move due
south from Louisville to capture
Nashville, a worthy objective, but one
of comparatively little strategic value to
McClellan and Lincoln. Indeed, a
thrust at the thinly defended Tennessee
capital at the extreme northern edge of
the state seemed to Lincoln to be an
effort by Buell simply to grasp the low-
hanging military fruit, rather than daring to make true progress by seizing

General Don Carlos Buell (*Library of Congress*)

Knoxville and Chattanooga and breaking the Confederate line at its center.
In a responsive letter the next day, Lincoln made clear his preference that
Buell capture a point on the railroad in East Tennessee rather than Nashville.
"First," he explained, "because it cuts a great artery of the enemy's communication, which Nashville does not; and secondly, because it is in the midst
of loyal people who would rally around it, while Nashville is not." The plight
of the East Tennessee Union loyalists was never far from Lincoln's mind, and
Buell's indifference to the region disappointed and upset the chief executive.
"My distress is that our friends in East Tennessee are being hanged and driv-
en to despair and even now I fear are thinking of taking rebel arms for the
sake of personal protection," he wrote. "In this we lose the most valuable
stake we have in the South."[19]

McClellan agreed, expressing his own frustration and regret that the Ohio
general had "from the beginning attached little or no importance to a movement in East Tennessee." He advised Buell that his own "general plan for the
prosecution of the war make the speedy occupation of East Tennessee and
its lines of railway matters of absolute necessity," with Buell's suggested move
on Nashville being of "very secondary importance." In fact, Buell's inaction
seemed to McClellan to offer a ready excuse for his own. He told Buell that
he could not possibly advance on Richmond with his massive Army of the

Potomac until the Ohioan's forces were "solidly established in the eastern portion of Tennessee." Buell remained unmoved, and unmoving, the officers and men of his army shivering in their camps. "We are mud-bound," one of his brigadiers wrote. "It rains a little, then snows a little, then thaws a good deal, and finally everything on the surface of the ground seems liquid earth, and our cavalry horses have the scratches to such a degree that half of them are this day unfit for service. All this from being compelled to remain in the same spot." [20]

On January 7, Lincoln followed with a wire to Buell requiring that he name a date certain on which he would be ready to move southward in concert with Major General Henry W. Halleck, in command of forces in Western Tennessee. "Delay is ruining us," Lincoln said plainly, "and it is indispensable for me to have something definite." Not only did the president receive no date certain for any movement from either general, however, but he received something else altogether from the soft and timorous Halleck: a lengthy letter sent the day before that explained all the many reasons why an advance was not only impracticable, but foolish. Voicing the all-too-prevalent complaint among Union generals early in the war—that he lacked sufficient men and materiel to take action—Halleck complained, "I am in the condition of a carpenter who is required to build a bridge with a dull axe, a broken saw, and rotten timber." Receiving this latest excuse for the army's inertia, the crestfallen commander-in-chief added his own handwritten comment to the letter before filing it away. Lincoln scrawled: "The within is a copy of a letter received from General Halleck. It is exceedingly discouraging. As everywhere else, nothing can be done." [21]

*B*uell finally moved on his chosen objective of Nashville at the end of February, creeping southward from Bowling Green, Kentucky, as slowly as the springtime thaw—which in fact seemed a long time coming, as the southward march was delayed one morning when the Federals awoke to find their artillery pieces and limbers sunk to their axles and frozen solid in the mud. This halting, long overdue advance on the Tennessee capital was not at all uncharacteristic of the crusty Ohioan. "Buell always made haste slowly," one subordinate later said. In fact, Buell's army—some 73,000 strong by now—did not so much capture the city as accept it when offered by the mayor, who crossed the Cumberland River in a wobbly rowboat to capitulate and save his city from destruction. Even then, Buell dawdled on the north bank of the river for days, receiving from Lincoln a welcome promotion to major general, along with a backhanded compliment for his "cautious vigor." Following the promotion, however, vigor seemed to depart entirely and undue caution again prevailed, as Buell struggled with the touchy politics of commanding an occupying force in a hostile capital, pleading for reinforcements and resisting calls from Halleck for him to advance and consolidate his army with Grant's to the southwest. This resumption of the Northern army's inertia gave Confederate troops under General William J. Hardee the opportunity not only to save themselves by retiring southward, but also sufficient time to set up further obstacles to the invading army by wrecking railroad track and burning bridges and trestles in their wake. Buell's critics howled at his inaction, including several subordinate officers under his charge. Months after he was first urged to advance on East Tennessee, Buell's divisions remained some 140 miles from Chattanooga. One of his division commanders, Brigadier General Ormsby M. Mitchel, a Republican and staunch abolitionist, chafed under Buell's frustrating timidity and was outraged by his conciliatory stance toward the residents of Nashville, including his policy of returning fugitive slaves who fled to the occupying blue army seeking refuge from their oppressors.[22]

In mid-March, Buell was finally ordered outright by a newly promoted General Halleck—placed by Lincoln on March 11 in command of all the western armies, including Grant's and Buell's forces—to immediately march west to join up with Grant and oppose the Confederate army now consolidating its strength under Generals Albert Sidney Johnston and P.G.T. Beauregard at Corinth, Mississippi. To comply with this order while protecting his modest gains, Buell divided the Army of the Ohio into several parts. He left a garrison of 18,000 men at Nashville to secure middle Tennessee, sent a detachment under Brigadier General George W. Morgan east to threaten Cumberland Gap, and assigned Mitchel's 10,000-man force—which was known as the Third Division—to march south across Tennessee into north Alabama in an effort to "occupy the Memphis & Charleston Railroad when the opportunity offered."[23]

The aggressive and ambitious General Mitchel—who would have flatly disagreed with Lincoln's recent lament that "nothing can be done"—had been champing at the bit for weeks to advance. Unleashed at last, he intended to make the most of the opportunity of what was now, for all intents and purposes, an independent command. He knew that the railroad that was his target—the "M&C"—led east, where it twisted through the mountains to the linchpin intersection at Chattanooga. With the dispersion of the Union's western armies, the broad discretion afforded to Mitchel, and the temptation to move on sparsely defended East Tennessee and its railroads, the stage was now set for one of the most dramatic adventures of the war. On March 18, Mitchel broke camp outside Nashville and put his men on the road heading due south toward Alabama. For the first time in their lives, the Ohio and Indiana boys of the Third Division saw fields of cotton, their white bolls dusting the landscape like unmelting snow.[24]

As for the main body of the Army of the Ohio under Buell, some 37,000 strong, they struck out to the southwest on turnpikes lined with greening meadows and early budding trees, marching to rendezvous with three divisions under Grant then encamped on the banks of the Tennessee River, in the quiet fields and woods around a tiny log chapel called Shiloh.

Brigadier General Ormsby MacKnight Mitchel. (*Library of Congress*)

CHAPTER TWO

Old Stars

Shelbyville, Tennessee

I have but one trouble, and that is my dependence on others, who are too slow. The entire war has moved too slowly.
—Brigadier General O.M. Mitchel, US
Letter to George S. Coe, April 2, 1862

ORMSBY MacKNIGHT MITCHEL, brigadier general commanding the Third Division in the Union Army of the Ohio under Buell, was a genius. Some of his contemporaries would have balked at this description—he had been called a damned fool and a self-important ass by men above and below him in the ranks, from the firesides of the army to the halls of the War Department—but the fact of his intelligence was undeniable. He had not yet had a chance to demonstrate his talent in the military sense, though he had graduated a respectable fifteenth out of forty-six cadets in the West Point class of 1829, along with such future Confederate heroes as Robert E. Lee and Joseph E. Johnston, and was showing considerable promise in moving his blue-clad troops toward and into the Deep South in the early spring of 1862. It was not this plodding forward progress that gave proof of his intelligence, however, but his prewar career as a nationally renowned astronomer, lawyer, engineer, and professor of mathematics back in his adopted hometown of Cincinnati. Mitchel was ambitious to move up in the still-fluctuating hierarchy of Union generals and perhaps conscious of those that perceived him as an overbearing egghead rather than a bold commander—his own men called him "Old Stars." He had taken command in early September and was determined to make a strong showing and cement his growing reputation at the head of a division of Midwesterners, most of them farmers back home, that would in the coming weeks achieve the deepest penetration of Southern territory to date by any Union force.

Mitchel was born on a farm in Union County, Kentucky, in the summer of 1809, just five months after and 150 miles from his fellow native Kentuckian and future commander-in-chief, Abraham Lincoln. Mitchel's father died when he was only three, and his family moved to Ohio four years later. There, young Ormsby began his education and at age twelve worked as a mercantile clerk in the towns of Piqua, Lebanon, and Xenia to support himself and his mother. A bright boy who was said by one early biographer to be reading Virgil at age nine and "progressing in Greek" at twelve, Ormsby "soon found the plodding and menial duties of a country store tame, painful, and unsatisfactory." Searching for a future beyond what he could see from behind the counter of a general store, he discovered that a fine technical education and monthly stipend were available to young men who were admitted to the national military academy at West Point. The boy secured an appointment through the aid of one of his mother's relatives, Postmaster General John McLean, who would later become an Associate Justice of the Supreme Court best known for his dissenting opinion in the *Dred Scott* case. Entering the academy at age fifteen, the youngest member of his class, Ormsby Mitchel quickly gained a reputation as an above-average cadet but a truly gifted mathematician. Along the way, he befriended an upperclassman named Jefferson Davis, who was said to have "taken a fancy to the little fellow in the class below him, and to have often made him his companion." Mitchel returned to West Point after graduation as a professor of mathematics and astronomy. He was just twenty years old.[1]

Moving to Cincinnati two years later, Mitchel passed the bar and practiced law for two years before joining the faculty at Cincinnati City College, where for the next ten years he taught mathematics, philosophy, and astronomy. In 1843, Mitchel founded the city's observatory, its cornerstone laid with considerable ceremony by venerable former President John Quincy Adams who marked the occasion with a three-hour speech delivered in a driving rain. Mitchel established a thriving astronomical society and raised funds from its membership to travel to Europe, where he purchased for the new observatory a Merz & Mahler telescope with an eleven-inch aperture, an instrument unmatched at that time in the Western Hemisphere. Peering through that lens on a starry night in 1846, he discovered an ice-capped geological formation on Mars known to astronomers even today as the Mountains of Mitchel.[2] Even as he secured the respect of his scientific peers through such discoveries and his prolific writings on the subject, including the acclaimed works *The Planetary and Stellar Worlds*, *Orbs of Heaven*, and *Astronomy of the Bible*, Mitchel gained broader popular renown through a series of public lectures on the stars and planets throughout the eastern United States. One of his lectures in New York was attended by a young reporter and sometime poet named Walt Whitman, who would immortalize Mitchel as the unnamed inspiration for the "learn'd astronomer" described in one of his most famous verses.[3]

Not that Professor Mitchel had his head in the clouds, by any means. Quite the opposite, in fact, as his considerable accomplishments in the pure science of astronomy were neatly balanced by his practical legal training and his experience in the leading technology of the dawning industrial age: the railroad. His first job out after leaving his assistant professorship at West Point in 1831 was as a surveyor for the Philadelphia & Madison and the Pennsylvania & Ohio railroads. Even during his lengthy tenure at Cincinnati City College, he worked for a year on the Little Miami Railroad, where he was chief engineer of the road at age twenty-six, and just before the Civil War began, he held the same office for the Ohio & Mississippi Railroad. Meanwhile, his reputation as a scientist, lecturer, and inventor of astronomical instruments continued to grow. He was elected to membership in the American Philosophical Society and the Royal Astronomical Society of England, was awarded an honorary master of arts degree from Harvard, and in 1856 accepted an appointment as the head of the Dudley Observatory in Albany, New York. As he approached age fifty and the dark clouds of war began to gather, Mitchel, according to one observer, was "an inexhaustible Roman candle of varied enterprise," not only dabbling but excelling in the broadest possible array of vocations. The only experience he seemed to lack was the command of troops in the field.[4]

When war broke out, Ormsby Mitchel, like thousands of former officers across the country, volunteered his services. He was initially rebuffed—after all, the rebellion was no more than a nuisance. The war would only be a thirty-day affair, sixty or ninety at most. But after the upstart Rebels bloodied the nose of the Union Grand Army of the Republic on the banks of a Virginia creek called Bull Run and sent them stumbling back to Washington, Mitchel tried again. On July 27, 1861, he wrote directly to President Lincoln to plead for an appointment to a command position, noting that he had been offered by the governor of Ohio a colonelcy, but stating confidently (if

immodestly) his belief that his "age, education and experience" should enti-
tle him to a higher rank and post. "I am no office seeker, but a plain patriot
desirous to do my duty," he assured the president, who promptly appointed
him a brigadier general of volunteers.[5]

Mitchel's service began with personal tragedy. The day after he left home
for his new post, his wife Louisa suffered a stroke and died before he could
return to her side. Stricken with grief but undaunted, Mitchel saw to the care
of his two young daughters, brought his sons Edwin and Frederick on his
staff, and returned to the field as soon as possible. Sadness soon gave way to
frustration as Mitchel first spent months in Cincinnati building fortifications
for the city and training green recruits and then stalled in the field for
months under the lethargic Buell, whom Mitchel would later call, unkindly
though probably not unfairly, "the slowest person I ever had the misfortune
to be associated with." But now, with the issuance of the mid-March order
detaching his division from the main body of the army, Buell's grip on the
reins of his division was relaxed, and Old Stars moved with alacrity.

Leaving Nashville on March 18, "with banners waving and the sun shining brightly on the glittering muskets," as one soldier remembered the scene,
Mitchel's division covered the 45 miles south to Murfreesboro in two days of
hard marching. As they tramped southward into what one soldier would call
"the heart of the slaveholding South," the men of the Third Division became
some of the first Union soldiers to witness a scene that would repeat itself
on country roads across the Southern states in the three years to come. Slaves
from neighboring farms and cotton plantations—their skin "many shades of
color, varying from pure African black to oily white"—came out in droves to
hail the great blue army as it marched past. "As our column advanced, regardless of sex, and in families, they abandoned the fields and their houses, turning their backs on master and mistress, many bearing their bedding, clothing,
and other effects on their heads and backs, and came to the roadsides, shouting and singing a medley of songs of freedom and religion, confidently
expecting to follow the army to immediate liberty. Their numbers were so
great we marched for a good part of a day between almost continuous lines
of them," one officer wrote. "They shouted 'Glory' in seeing the Stars and
Stripes, as though it had been a banner of protection and liberty, instead of
the emblem of a power which hitherto had kept them and their ancestors in
bondage."

The spirited initial advance of the 10,000 bluecoats soon stalled in the
face of three railroad bridges and track over Stones River that had been

reduced to ashes by retreating Confederates while Buell idly awaited reinforcements in Nashville. The southbound flight of the departed Rebels was
confirmed by a young fugitive slave who stole into the lines of the advancing
Federals. When a Union major inquired whether the boy felt bad to have run
away from his masters, he replied, "Oh, no, massa. Dey is gone too."[6]

Determined to open the southbound road for further advancement,
Mitchel set his troops to work repairing some twelve hundred feet of broken
bridges and trestles that stood between him and the otherwise open and
apparently undefended road to northern Alabama. Now fifty-two years old,
Old Stars was small and slender—"not over five feet six inches tall," according to a subordinate, "but every inch a soldier and a disciplinarian"—with a
mane of graying hair swept back from an angular, clean-shaven face and
piercing, darting eyes. Though he had the impassioned appearance and fiery
temperament of a European composer, Mitchel was a devout Presbyterian
and a man for rule and regulation, both in professional action and personal
behavior. "General Mitchell never drinks and never swears," one officer noted
in his diary. "Occasionally he uses the words 'confound it' in rather savage
style; but further than this I have never heard him go." Mitchel not only
imposed sharp, by-the-book discipline among his troops but also spread
infectious enthusiasm and engendered respect for his intelligence, drive, and
military bearing. "Gen. Mitchell is the man, in him we have confidence," one
soldier confided in his journal. But the general's fervid enthusiasm, according
to Cincinnati journalist Whitelaw Reid, also "led to an appearance of eccen-
tricity and nervous excitability that, outside the range of his personal influence, engendered distrust of his stability and judgment." Compounding the
problem was the general's bristling, arrogant personality and an undisguised
thirst for glory and advancement—his nickname, after all, was derived not
only from his astronomical background, but also from the campsite rumor
that he even slept at night with his gold insignia pinned to his shoulders.
Subordinates and peers alike consistently described the Cincinnati general as
ambitious—sometimes meant as a compliment, and sometimes not.[7]

For the bridge repair project, Mitchel's boundless energy was exactly what
was called for. He jumped into the challenging task with aplomb, selecting
men from the army with experience in construction to lead gangs of framers
and directing the design and construction of the new spans personally.
Working in shirtsleeves and high-top boots in the coffee-colored river, his
blue tunic cast aside on the bank, the general looked more like a jobsite foreman than a learned university professor, sloshing down in the muddy water

among the crews and "stimulating them by word and example." According to one observer, Old Stars "worked like a beaver, and chafed and fretted, and caused the men of his command to perform more hard labor than was agreeable." The construction proceeded quickly, and within days two of the bridges were completed, with the third merely awaiting the addition of the track on top of the stoutly constructed timbers. "Thus in ten days a work had been accomplished which has no parallel in the histories of bridge-building," Mitchel immodestly declared in a letter home, "and which General Buell pronounced absolutely impossible." Mitchel was not only proud of his repairmen-soldiers, but believed them better for the effort. The hard work and considerable accomplishment of the past two weeks had "brought up their health and spirits," he wrote, and his men were now "ready for any service."[8]

Notwithstanding the newly opened road heading south, Mitchel's division continued to hold in place, hamstrung by the slower repair of several smaller railroad trestles close to Nashville. In the meantime, spring had finally broken through, and soldiers passing time in camp noted in their diaries and letters home the blooming peach trees, redbuds, and early flowers. "Tennessee is a beautiful state," one Northern officer conceded in his journal. "All it lacks are free schools and freemen." For his part, however, Mitchel wrote home to express his continued frustration at the delays brought on, as he saw it, by his unresponsive superior, who had not responded to Old Stars's request to take charge of the railroad. "Here now, I shall be compelled to wait! wait!! wait!!!" the astronomer-general fumed. At last, Mitchel received new orders that not only detached him even further from the oversight and restraint of General Buell, but also seemed to contain a considerable element of discretion. On March 27, a rambling dispatch from Buell stated that Mitchel's force could be "concentrated for an advance or for defense, if necessary," and listed several possible objectives scattered across Middle Tennessee and North Alabama. "I do not think it necessary to do more than suggest these general factors to you. You will understand well how to take advantage of them, or guard against them, according to circumstances," Buell wrote.[9]

Mitchel took this vague direction to mean that he was, at last, permitted to use the 8,000 effectives under his command as he saw fit. With the bridges complete and supply lines extended southward, the Third Division resumed its advance, arriving during the first week of April on the outskirts of Shelbyville, Tennessee, a lovely and resilient little community on the banks of the curling Duck River. The town had in recent years survived a devastating tornado and an outbreak of Asiatic cholera, as well as more recent plundering of provisions, wagons, and slaves by retreating Confederates. Here the

Yankee army "met with a reception such as we had not experienced anywhere south of the Ohio River," as one among the arriving soldiers would recall. Cheering crowds lined the streets, and the Old Flag waved from doors and windows. "The young men shouted for joy, the maidens blessed us with their sweet smiles, the old men wept, and the old ladies clasped their hands, exclaiming, 'Bless God, our day of deliverance has come.' The bright eyed urchins sang 'Yankee Doodle' on the street; the songs of auld lang syne were heard in almost every house," a war correspondent from the *Cincinnati Commercial* reported. That night, an impromptu choir of the town's citizens arrived in camp to serenade the troops with a chorus of "O, Columbia! the Gem of the Ocean."

Mitchel, in high spirits from this warm welcome and his division's progress, established his headquarters in a building on the town square overlooking the army's encampment on the banks of the Duck River. Sending his outriders to scout the terrain to the south, he spread his maps and began to plot his advance, hoping to do nothing less than drive a stake into the heart of Dixie. "I hope to be placed in command of the entire railroad to Chattanooga, and then my troubles will be over," he wrote to a friend back home on April 2, "for with a clear field and plenty of room in which to operate, and no one to depend on but myself, I ask no odds of anyone." He closed the letter: "I hope one of these days to address you from Decatur, or, possibly, from Chattanooga."[10]

The first week of April 1862 saw great armies on the move at the eastern and western ends of the strategic lines dividing North and South. In the east, on April 2, General McClellan finally set in motion the long-stagnant Army of the Potomac, moving 100,000 men to the York-James Peninsula of Virginia to begin a long-overdue drive to the gates of Richmond. After months of preparation, drilling, reinforcement, and delay, the torpid McClellan had simply run out of excuses to move. "Napoleon himself could not stand still any longer with such an army," Lincoln said. Standing between McClellan and the Confederate capital were 60,000 Rebel soldiers that would soon be reconstituted as the Army of Northern Virginia, setting up the first in a series of epic battles that would over the next three years decide the fate of the Great Republic. Eight hundred miles to the west, the 44,000-man Confederate Army of Mississippi under General Albert Sidney Johnston consolidated its strength and began creeping forward to swamp the unsuspecting army of Major General Ulysses S. Grant. Just before dawn on Sunday, April 6, Johnston's Rebels attacked and surprised the Union army, many of them cooking breakfast or still asleep in their tents, and sent them into a scrambling retreat toward the Tennessee River, opening the bloodiest battle in American history at Shiloh—from a Hebrew word meaning "place of peace." By the end of the next day, more than 23,000 Americans, blue and gray alike, would be killed or wounded, and the country's view of the war and its cost would be changed forever.[11]

Two hundred miles to the east of Shiloh, left out of these epic battles and grand strategic movements, the Third Division passed a quiet and delightful Sunday in camp outside Shelbyville, card games and chaplains competing for the attention of the men. "The spring of 1862 opened very early, and now the meadows were verdant and the birds singing," one soldier wrote, remembering the "calm, quiet and beauty of that Sabbath, with the white tents dotting the level fields, and the soldiers luxuriating in one day of rest after the hard march." The early part of the day was spent in religious devotionals and sun-drenched dress parades, well-attended by the locals, who were "most cordial" to their Northern visitors and extended dinner invitations to various officers of the division. "Our troops have conducted themselves with the greatest propriety and are winning golden opinions from even the Seceshs," Colonel William H. Lytle proudly recorded. Many soldiers spent the evening writing letters home, as a particularly accomplished regimental band gave an "elegant serenade" outside the colonel's tent, playing among other pieces Verdi's "Anvil Chorus" and an air from the opera *Lucia di Lammermoor*.[12]

Later that night, as the musicians packed their instruments and the army's campfires burned down to glowing coals, a contraband smuggler and scout by the name of Andrews arrived in camp. He obtained an audience with General Mitchel at his headquarters to propose a secret assault on the railroad in north Georgia. No record was made of the meeting, and no written orders were issued as a result. Neither the general nor the spy would live long enough to chronicle the discussion in retrospect—Mitchel would die of disease six months hence, while Andrews would face the gallows in Atlanta in just a few weeks. But that night, neither man knew what fate held in store for them, and they huddled at length over lamplit maps and crafted a raid behind enemy lines that in time one Southern newspaper would call "THE MOST EXTRAORDINARY AND ASTOUNDING ADVENTURE OF THE WAR" and "THE MOST DARING UNDERTAKING THAT YANKEES EVER PLANNED."[13]

Nobody knew very much about James Andrews. He was born in Hancock County in the western part of Virginia in 1829, but nothing is known of his childhood or his education. He called the hamlet of Flemingsburg, Kentucky

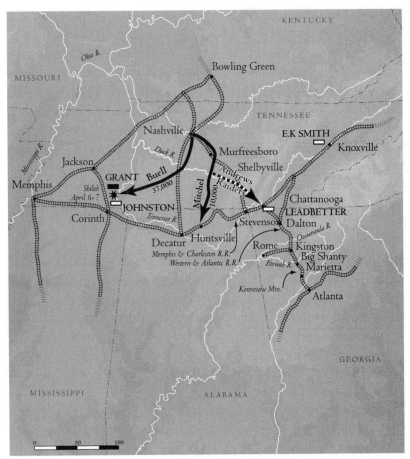

Military situation in the West, April 1862.

home, but even the folks back in Flemingsburg would have had little to say about him. Andrews simply came walking up the road into town one day in 1859, asking for odd jobs and eventually finding steady work in town as a house painter and music teacher, known for his kindly manner and his excellent singing voice. He was a quiet young man, but handsome and social—well-regarded among the young ladies in town—and in time was said to be engaged to one Elizabeth Layton, who had set their wedding date for the forthcoming June. "They were affectionate and happy together till the war came on," a neighbor would later say. Notwithstanding his commitment to Miss Layton, Andrews had a reputation as a bit of a ladies' man, as evidenced by one of the few surviving letters in his hand: a December 6, 1861, note addressed to the "Ladies' Soldiers Aid Society of Flemingsburgh." The almost flirtatious letter, asking that the ladies "excuse the impertinence, and intrusion," is filled with descriptions of the northern Kentucky village as "*that town* where the *ladys* are so *clever*" and other flattery. (Months later, in a letter written to a friend back home in the hours before he would face the gallows, Andrews would ask, "Remember me also to the young ladies of Flemingsburgh, especially to Miss Kate Wallingford and Miss Nannie Baxter.") Despite this apparent sociability, Andrews seemed somehow distant, perhaps even melancholy, and far from familiar—no one in town, for example, was known to have ever called him "Jim."[14]

Andrews never made mention of any military background or passionate political sentiment—he was no fire-breathing abolitionist, though he claimed to be for the undivided Union and the Old Flag, first and last. In the fall of 1861, he traveled south and began smuggling quinine through the lines, supposedly in order to gain the confidence of the Rebels—though it was, no doubt, a very profitable enterprise as well. Quinine, used widely to prevent malaria and treat a host of other ailments, was a scarce and valuable commodity in the South, thanks in large part to the Northern blockade. In 1862, an ounce of quinine that sold for five dollars in New York could bring fifty or sixty dollars in Charleston or elsewhere in the bug-ridden South, where malaria was rampant and the mosquitoes were said to move not in platoons, but in regiments.[15]

Capitalizing on the trust he engendered through his supply of drugs, needles, harness buckles, and other contraband, Andrews began gathering information from behind Confederate lines to trade the other way, and thereby built a substantial and not-so-covert reputation as a covert agent. "I didn't know Andrews, but I had heard of him—everyone had," one soldier in the Third Division would later remark. "His fame as a scout went everywhere before him." One rumor had it that Andrews had actually been inside the Confederate fortifications at Fort Donelson in January 1862, sneaking vital information out to General Grant—a farfetched tale that, if true, would have been a remarkable intelligence coup and a huge contribution to one of the first Federal triumphs in the war. Although it is speculation, it is reasonable to assume that, like many of the questionable characters who traveled and traded across the lines, Andrews could be characterized as a "double agent," engaged at least in part in playing both sides to achieve a profitable middle. His adversary William Fuller would later write that Andrews was "a convenient, useful and good friend (?) of both the north and south, according to the latitude of his place at any given time, but his last service was intended for the Federals." In short, for all the praise lavished on the gallant secret agent as a Union hero, it seems that he was in fact entirely for sale. "Andrews was in the business of a spy and a contraband agent for the money," his compatriot William Knight confirmed in an interview years later.

In recent weeks, Andrews had offered his services to General Buell during the occupation of Nashville. Writing years after the war and attempting to distance himself from a failed raid he regarded as a debacle, a typically sour Don Carlos Buell would claim that he had had small use for Andrews as a spy, and that the mysterious

James J. Andrews. (*Colonel James G. Bogle Collection*)

Kentuckian had seldom come through with anything more than outdated information. "I had little confidence in his usefulness," Buell wrote, "apprehending that he thought more of his [quinine] traffic than of the object for which he was engaged." So he said looking back. But at the time, Andrews had impressed Buell sufficiently for the miserly general not only to approve his activities but also to order manpower and resources devoted to supporting his efforts. Andrews likewise seemed to have little trouble convincing General Mitchel to go along with his plans.[16]

The railroad raid Andrews proposed to Old Stars that night at Shelbyville would not be his first attempt. Just a few weeks before in Nashville, he had peddled a similar though less ambitious plan to General Buell. In late March, with Buell's express or tacit consent, Andrews had led a squad of eight men down to Atlanta with plans for a covert rendezvous with a traitorous Southern railroad engineer who was to assist with the hijacking of a southern train. The operation, however, was snakebit from the start, hampered by bad weather and poor planning, and then scrapped altogether when the turncoat engineer simply failed to show up at the agreed place and time. After spending several days in Georgia studying the train schedules, meeting with his contacts, and gathering information, Andrews returned to Tennessee, disappointed but apparently not at all dissuaded. The men who accompanied him on his first foray south, however, were by no means keen to try again. "Never!" one of the volunteer infiltrators said when asked if he would be willing to join another such effort. "If Andrews and Mitchel want bridges burned, they can go themselves and burn them!" Another soldier who returned to camp was heard to say that "he wouldn't undertake it again for anything," and that "he felt all the time he was in the enemy's country as though he had a rope around his neck."[17]

Arriving back in middle Tennessee in April and finding the Army of the Ohio well dispersed and on the move, Andrews elected not to return to Buell, but reported to Old Stars instead. His decision to do so was either savvy or fortuitous, for the energetic Mitchel would be much more likely to bet against the house and support Andrews's longshot plan for a second try. The revamped scheme Andrews presented to Mitchel was more detailed and more ambitious. This time, he proposed to sneak behind enemy lines, again going almost as far south as Atlanta, where he would seize a train and drive it north up the Western & Atlantic Railroad toward Chattanooga. One can imagine the tall, dark-bearded spy leaning over the map shoulder-to-shoulder with the fidgety, intense astronomer-general, tracing the curving line from Atlanta to Chattanooga with his finger. The W&A wound through the broken, rugged terrain of north Georgia and crossed no fewer than seventeen bridges, including the Etowah River Bridge near Allatoona, the Oostanaula River covered bridge near Resaca, and eleven covered bridges across the twisted ribbon of Chickamauga Creek. Andrews proposed to burn the bridges north of the Etowah River, destroy track elsewhere as opportunity offered, and cut the telegraph lines along the way. A larger group than before—twenty-four soldiers this time—would provide the muscle needed to wreck the railroad and enable the operation to overcome any upstart resistance from civilians or local militia. After arrival in Chattanooga, the raiders would throw the switch at the Market Street crossing, turn the engine westward onto the Nashville & Chattanooga and thence to the Memphis & Charleston Railroad, where they would meet up with Mitchel's advancing forces, the door left wide open behind them for Union forces to capture the city. Coordination of movements between the railroad raid and the Third Division was crucial, and this aspect almost certainly hooked Mitchel, who was rigidly punctual and had a scientist's love of absolute precision and a railroader's devotion to schedules.

Andrews's proposal probably appealed to Mitchel on a number of different levels. Mitchel was a former railroad man himself, and he regarded the control and use of the railroads as critically important in this and any other campaign. Had he heard the remark, Old Stars would have agreed with the Confederate brigadier who had said, "Railroads are at one and the same time the legs and stomach of an army." Mitchel had in fact proposed his own bridge burning operation near Knoxville back in September, and the plan had drawn considerable interest before being derailed by the objections of a prickly red-haired brigadier named Sherman, who had taken exception to the proposal to march Mitchel's troops across his department. Now here was Andrews, with a similar but stronger movement in mind. Andrews's plan to paralyze the rails in north Georgia was bold, required little initial investment in terms of men or materiel, and depended upon rapid advancement and careful synchronization of scheduled movements. There seemed, in fact, very little to lose except the lives of the few volunteer infiltrators the raid would require.

On the other side of the ledger, the potential rewards of the operation were considerable, perhaps even tremendous. At a minimum, the theft of a train and the destruction of railroad track so far behind Rebel lines would sow confusion and uncertainty as the Third Division advanced to the south and east. At best, the raid could starve the meager Confederate garrison at Chattanooga of supplies and reinforcements, making the rail center suscep-tible to capture and occupation. Mitchel may well have envisioned himself, some two weeks hence, delivering an ultimatum of surrender to the town fathers of Chattanooga, much as the suddenly famous U.S. Grant had done two months before at Fort Donelson. Promotion, acclaim, and national headlines were sure to follow.

Convinced that the raid was worth a try and no doubt impressed, as oth-ers had been before and would be later, by Andrews's quiet self-confidence and imposing presence, Mitchel approved the effort, and the two spent con-siderable time overnight finalizing details from coordination of the move-ments to financing—and possibly financial rewards—for the effort. On this, accounts differ sharply: some would later maintain that Andrews was to be paid $20,000 for his work; others said $50,000 in gold; yet another claimed the spy had told him that he was to have an unspecified but large sum, along with the right to trade across the lines without interference to the extent of $5,000 per month. Whatever the ultimate incentive, arrangements were made for small, up-front amounts to be furnished for civilian clothes, small arms, and other accoutrements, and with that, the secret meeting between the eccentric general and his mysterious new agent was adjourned. Word-of-mouth instructions were given that same night to the captains of Colonel Joshua W. Sill's brigade to hand-pick soldiers, spread across the various com-panies of the 2nd, 21st, and 33rd Ohio regiments, to take part in a secret mission. The criteria for this selection were not spelled out in any written order. Though some would later maintain that the raiders were an impressive group of "picked men, chosen because of their soldierly qualities," one might disagree with this assessment, given the haphazard collection of privates and corporals that was ultimately assembled for the effort.[18]

The detail of volunteers needed for the dangerous raid, as it turned out, would not be difficult to come by. The young Midwesterners of Mitchel's division were brash and enthusiastic, full of boasting for themselves and cheers for the Union and their general, the war still a lad's adventure to them. They had spent but one brief winter encamped, and that one on the banks of the Ohio River, close to home. The soldiers in the Third Division had done little more than drill, march, stand guard, and skirmish. No one had yet heard of places called Antietam, or Gettysburg, or Chickamauga, or Andersonville. But it was the nature of their leadership, not just naïveté, that made privates and corporals quick to step forward for an unknown and dangerous purpose. "General Mitchel was an energetic and enthusiastic commander," one of the volunteers would recall, "and had so thoroughly instilled in our minds the importance of soldiers doing their duty under any and all circumstances that we were ready to go wherever he saw fit to lead, or wherever duty called."[19]

Recruitment for the newly conceived mission began through fireside conversations that same night. Corporal Daniel Allen "Al" Dorsey, twenty-three, a schoolteacher before the war, recalled one such scene in the camp of the 33rd Ohio Regiment. "After roll call on Sunday evening, April 6th, 1862, a group of some half dozen of our company were standing around the camp fire pleasantly chatting about army matters, the salubrious climate, the budding spring time, etc., when we were joined by our company commander, Lieut. A.L. Waddle, who joined in the conversation a few moments, and then quietly informed us that one man was wanted from this company to go, in company with others from our brigade, on 'a secret expedition attended with much peril.'" Other men were pulled aside for more discreet entreaties from their officers. Eighteen-year-old farm boy Private Jacob Parrott was summoned from his tent by his captain and asked if he would go on an unknown expedition—"he only knew that it was a secret one"—and Private William Bensinger, twenty-two, was likewise singled out by his captain to report to the colonel the next morning. "He said he supposed it was for a secret expedition, but he could not tell me what," Bensinger remembered. "I told him I would go." Also selected from Bensinger's regiment, the 21st Ohio, was Sergeant

Raiders, left to right, top to bottom: Marion A. Ross, William Bensinger, William Henry Harrison Reddick, Wilson Wright Brown. (*Colonel James G. Bogle Collection*)

Elihu Harlam Mason, a handsome Indiana-born farmer, with blue eyes, blond hair and beard, who was two weeks past his thirty-first birthday. Mason had enlisted just after Fort Sumter, leaving his wife of nine years and a young child back home in Pemberville, Ohio.[20]

Teachers and farmers would not suffice—the mission would also require certain specialized expertise. James Andrews had learned his lesson from his failed operation the month before—this time, he would take his own railroad engineers, as well as skilled machinists, along with him. Private William Knight's brigade was addressed on the parade ground, their colonel asking those men capable of running a locomotive to take two steps forward. Only two men did. "I stepped out, thinking I was going to get some soft snap, such as running a saw or a grist mill," Knight remembered, "but it turned out to be not so very soft." Instead, he was taken to Andrews, who quizzed him on his competency to drive an engine and traced their planned destination on a borrowed map spread out on the colonel's table. Knight thought the operation seemed "plausible enough," though he observed, "It looked much better on paper than I later found it on land." Andrews warned Knight that "if we were caught in the enemy's lines, and they knew us, we would be treated as spies." Knight was quick-witted and good with tools, having spent his adolescence working in his grandfather's sawmill before moving on to the railroad shops at Logansport, Indiana, by the time he was eighteen. He was running trains to Chicago and back as an engineer when the war began, and he had enlisted in the 21st Ohio at Defiance, along with his brother James. He responded, like the others, without hesitation: "I said I would go."[21] A second and more senior railroader, Corporal Martin Jones Hawkins, also volunteered for the expedition. A native Pennsylvanian, he was thirty-one, tall and lean, and moved with the easy, languid posture and catlike grace of an acrobat, which he had been for a short time. He would come to be recognized by the other raiders as the most experienced railroad man in the group.[22]

Another engineer, twenty-four-year-old Private Wilson Brown, was pulled from formation and sent to report directly to General Mitchel. Brown's uncorroborated conversation with the general, described some years after the war, is the only firsthand account of any discussion by Old Stars of the planned raid. Mitchel questioned Brown extensively on his ability to handle a locomotive—work that the good general understood very well from his engineering days—and examined papers the young man had with him reflecting his earlier experience on the Mobile & Ohio Railroad. Brown then received permission to ask questions of the commanding general, starting with a request for an explanation of the object of the raid. "To destroy the bridges over one of the main lines of the enemy's communications," Mitchel replied, an action he believed would "go far to separate their armies, and put them at our mercy." Asked his view of the operation's chance of success, the normally confident general seemed to hedge. "If the enterprise can be carried out as planned by Mr. Andrews, I think the chances are very good

Raiders, left to right, top to bottom: Samuel Slavens, Daniel Allen Dorsey, William James Knight, Elihu Harlam Mason. (*Colonel James G. Bogle Collection*)

indeed; but if any delay happens, the difficulty will be increased." With considerable prescience, Old Stars explained that as the Union army approached, "the roads will be more occupied with troops and stores moving back and forth, and these will be in your way."

Mitchel closed the meeting with a comment on the need for the daring effort and the attendant risk involved. "Your mission is very hazardous," he told Private Brown. "It is not pleasant for me to send such a number of picked men into the enemy's power; but in war risks must be run, and we are engaged in a war of right and wrong; armed treason must be met and conquered; and if you fail, you die in a glorious cause." The pious astronomer-general then expressed his confidence in Andrews and in the protection of "the Ruler of destinies."

"He grasped my hand and terminated the interview," Brown remembered. "I never saw him again."[23]

*T*he volunteer infiltrators were instructed to obtain civilian clothes and given passes to Shelbyville, a mile from camp, to buy provisions. There were only two or three general stores in the little town that carried these items, and Corporal William Pittenger later remarked that "the proprietors must have wondered to see the Yankees take such a sudden liking to their goods." The men selected for the raid began to run across one another in the shops and taverns, each one guessing at the other's purpose for being in town. "Among those who were purchasing I noticed with pleasure Marion Ross, Sergeant Major of the 2nd Ohio," Pittenger recalled. "I put a few cautious questions to him and answered as many in return, when we both became convinced that we were on the same errand."

Marion Andrew Ross was raised on a farm in Christianburg, Ohio, the third of twelve children born to Levi and Mary Ross. The young man attended prep school at Antioch College, where he was an accomplished musician, serving as president of the Antioch Musical Society and playing the flute in the academy's orchestra, the Campagnolians. He enlisted on April 15, 1861, the day after President Lincoln's first call for volunteers, and was impressive enough in his first months of service to earn a promotion to regimental sergeant major in December. Ross's military acumen and his later adventures behind enemy lines may have seemed out of character to those who knew him as a soft-spoken student and delicate flautist—a classmate would remember him as "a farmer boy of more than ordinary retiring modesty, with no element of reckless danger in his nature." Pittenger described the twenty-nine-year-old Ross as being "of sentimental character, very fastidious, neat and almost dandyish in dress, fond of parades and generally of the pomp and glitter of war, and was often teased for these qualities." Solid, with a thick beard and flaxen blond hair as fine as corn silk, Ross was a formidable presence, but apparently no hard-as-nails sergeant—so much so that Pittenger, for one, was surprised to see him involved in the endeavor at all.[24]

Back in camp, others selected for the raid were scrounging for clothes and supplies and dodging the considerable output of the ever-grinding rumor mill, for which the mysterious meetings, musterings, and preparations had provided considerable grist. Private William Henry Harrison Reddick, a fair-haired, twenty-one-year-old farmer, began by scrounging clothes from his tentmates, getting "two checked shirts of one of our boys who had just returned to camp, and a pair of jeans from the cook in the hospital." For his part, Al Dorsey had mixed success going tent-to-tent, borrowing a coat, vest, and cap from his friends, but finding no replacement for his blue uniform pants. And his buddies in camp were relentless in their teasing of the young corporal—"many were the twits and jests that were gotten off at my expense, as it was understood that I was selected for the raid," he said. His comrades were merciless: "Dorsey, you're a goner!" they said. "That's the last we'll see of Dorsey!" "Good-bye, Dorsey!" "Say, Dorsey, they'll hang you sure as hell!" "Leave us a lock of your hair, Dorsey!"[25]

For others, their parting from camp was more solemn. Samuel Slavens, described by one acquaintance as a "frank, open-faced, jolly fellow," was a plump thirty-one-year-old private and a solid family man. He had rosy cheeks, sparkling eyes, a curling mustache, and a dark bushy beard that combined to make him look for all the world like a young Saint Nick, not yet gone gray. He volunteered for the raid and then sat down to write a letter home to his wife, Rachel, and three young sons that would turn out to be his last. It was his second letter of the day. He had written one earlier that morning that told of the recent march south from Nashville—"It is warm and nice, and we had a good turnpike, and had our knapsacks hauled," he said—and passed along his love to all. His second letter was one filled with worry and foreboding:

> April 6, 1862
> Shelbyville, Tenn.
>
> P.S.
> Dear Wife Rachel:
> Since I wrote this morning I received your kind letter dated Feb. 18th, and was sorry to hear that you weren't very well, and sorry to think that the children will have the measles when you are by yourself. If I was at home it would be all right, but as it is I cannot help you. You will have to do the best you can until I get home, which I hope will not be long.

I don't want you to give yourself any uneasiness, any more than you can help, about me; but if anything happens to me that we never meet again on earth, I hope we will meet in heaven. Life is uncertain in war. Train up our babies in the way they should go. Give them all the education you can, but live as comfortably as you can under the present circumstances. I know that you will have your hands more than full if the boys get the measles.

I would like to be there to help you take care of them the best in the world, but all I can do is to wish you well, and think of you, which is very often.

Good-bye.

Samuel Slavens

Wrapping up his correspondence, Slavens headed out to the regimental parade ground, where he encountered and introduced himself to Dorsey. "Corporal, I understand you are going south on this secret expedition. I am going [too], and we will go together," he said, quite as if the pairing had been specifically ordered by division headquarters. Dorsey, who was no doubt delighted that he would not have to embark upon such a frightening odyssey alone, "cheerfully accepted" the invitation, and the two men henceforth became almost "inseparable companions."

At dusk, an ambulance pulled up outside the colonel's tent to pick up Slavens and the other men from the 33rd Ohio who had volunteered to go with Andrews. The group consisted of Dorsey, Slavens, Hawkins, Reddick, and Parrott, along with Corporal Samuel Llewellyn and Privates John Wollam and Samuel Robertson. The wagon creaked and rolled past the long, white ranks of tents and down the road toward Shelbyville, where they were to meet up with men from the 2nd and 21st Ohio Regiments, who would fill out the balance of the roster for the expedition. "Some of us had not completed our disguise before leaving camp," Dorsey would later note, "and further exchanges of civilian clothes—which were generally of cotton goods—were made here. I failed, however, to get a pair of trousers, and went of our lines in my blue ones, hoping to change them by a purchase at some country store before going far." The departure from camp on a secret mission while still wearing his uniform pants was not an auspicious start for Corporal Dorsey.[26]

Across the way in camp of the 2nd Ohio, William Pittenger spent the quiet Monday writing letters, "with the faint impression," he later said, "that I might not soon again have the opportunity." About this he turned out to be correct: his next letter, written from a prison cell months later, would be one pleading for the mercy of Confederate President Jefferson Davis. Looking back, a modern observer would perhaps be forgiven for wondering why the captain in command of Company G of the 2nd Ohio had approached Pittenger to take part in a daring expedition behind enemy lines. A twenty-two-year-old corporal from Steubenville, Ohio, he was a country schoolmaster before the war and looked the part: pale, thin, nearsighted, and stoop-shouldered, with curly light brown hair and fancy oval spectacles pinched atop a prominent nose. Pittenger was bright and exceedingly talkative, a trait which, along with his glasses, would draw marked attention to him and would later provoke dislike and eventual distrust among a number of his compatriots. One fellow soldier would later comment that Pittenger talked "for the same reason that a timid boy out at night whistles—to keep off 'spooks' by appearing to be brave." The former teacher was serving as a war correspondent for his hometown paper, the *Steubenville Herald,* and one fellow raider would later suggest that he was "allowed to go with the expedition in order to write up an account of it—more as a newspaper correspondent than as a soldier." There is no official or even credible truth to this rumor (which seems in fact more like an after-the-fact cheap shot), though Pittenger would indeed come to spend the rest of his long life writing accounts of the Andrews Raid.

Along toward evening, Pittenger changed into his new outfit of civilian clothes, carefully folded his uniform, and stepped from his tent into the company street, his changed appearance causing a "sensation" in the camp. Deflecting questions about whether he had received a furlough or been discharged, Pittenger shook the hands of his buddies in Company G as he prepared to go. He found the parting from his messmates to be an emotional one. "I had tramped with them over Kentucky and half of Tennessee; had stood guard on many a dark and wintry night; had slept by their side in the open air when our heads were whitened with frost; had floated with them down a mountain stream on rafts and logs," the young corporal recalled. "It was not easy to leave them, for most of them did not expect to see me again," he said, "and I half feared they were right."[27]

*T*he twenty-four men who would make history as the Andrews Raiders first convened just after dusk on Monday night, April 7, on a knoll west of Shelbyville on the farm of a man named Holland. "Never before, for so extraordinary an attempt was so incongruous a band assembled," one

Third Division officer later wrote of the party. The volunteers were for the most part native Ohioans, sons and grandsons of pioneer families who had struck out west to find their fortunes, but the similarity ended there. The oldest man present was thirty-three; the youngest seventeen. There were four railroad engineers, several farmers, two machinists, and a cobbler. Two were civilians, and one was an Englishman. Three—Ross, Dorsey, and Pittenger—had taught school. One, improbably, had at one time been a circus performer. Five of the men had volunteered for the army within a week of the Confederate firing on Fort Sumter. Having been picked from eighteen companies spread across three infantry regiments of the Third Division, the raiders were not a cohesive military unit or even friends. "We were unacquainted, at that time, with each other," one said. From that night forward, however, they would be linked together in history, first by Southern newspapers as the notorious "Train-Stealers" or "Engine Thieves," then as the so-called Mitchel Raiders, and later and more famously as the Andrews Raiders.[28]

For most of the men, the meeting provided the first opportunity for them to meet one another and to look over their new leader, a man whose "meditative air as well as impressive personal appearance made him a man impossible to forget." James Andrews "was a large, well-proportioned gentleman with a long, black silken beard, black hair, Roman features, and rather effeminate voice," Corporal Dorsey recalled. Pittenger wrote that Andrews was "in the prime of manhood, being about 33 years of age, six feet in height, weighing 180 or 190 pounds, with strong regular features, very clear complexion, very abundant black hair, a fine long silken beard slightly waved, and eye dark gray and penetrating." Several among the assembled commented favorably on Andrews's calm, gentlemanly manner and his commanding presence. He seemed to Pittenger "more like a dreamer, a poet, or a martyr, than a military leader or a dauntless adventurer, yet there was something of each of these in his composition." If there was any reluctance to submitting without question to the direction and authority of an enigmatic civilian they had never seen before, no one said so, either then or later.[29]

The men gathered around their mysterious captain a few paces off the road in a grove of gnarled and withered trees, leaning close to hear their instructions and trying their best to ignore the persistent, ominous howling of a dog somewhere across the valley. "A thunder-storm was rising, the wind moaned through their naked branches, and the lightning revealed white eager faces, not one of which I knew," Jacob Parrott recalled years later. "At each peal of thunder Andrews paused and then quietly went on."

"Now, my lads," Andrews began, "you have been chosen by your officers to perform a most important service, which, if successful, will change the whole aspect of the war, and aid materially in bringing an early peace to our distracted country. Chattanooga is the objective point." He then described how their small force would go about cutting off the Mountain City from all hope of relief and reinforcement, leaving it vulnerable to General Mitchel's approaching army. Andrews's explanation of his plan was quiet and informal, one among the listeners remembered, "far more like a talk than a set speech, and hardly so loud as an ordinary conversation." The Kentuckian told the men up front about the risks involved, emphasizing that if they were captured in disguise behind enemy lines, they would "in all probability be massacred at once or hung as spies"——but no one present accepted the offer to back out of the operation and return to camp, no questions asked. He then turned to practical instructions of how they would proceed. "There was explanation, repetition, and enlargement of parts not fully understood, with frequent question and answer," Pittenger recalled.[30]

The men were to break up into small groups for their travels, first proceeding east to the Tennessee River and Chattanooga, where they would board a train south to Marietta, Georgia four days hence, on Thursday afternoon. Andrews would give them money, with which they could purchase food, pay for lodging, and hire conveyances if available. He acknowledged that traveling would be difficult, especially going through the rugged terrain to the east, and he emphasized that they only had three days and three nights to reach their destination. He would travel the same route, sometimes ahead of the others and sometimes behind, and would join them in Marietta, where they would spend Thursday night at a hotel. One soldier asked what they were to do if they were closely questioned as to their identity and their purpose. "The most plausible thing will be to tell them that you are Kentuckians escaping from the rule of the Yankees; that you expect to join some Southern regiment," Andrews replied. "Say just as little as will carry you through, and always have some reason for not joining just then." He added, "if you should be closely questioned it will be safe to say that you are from Fleming County, Kentucky, for I happen to know that no Southern soldiers hail from that place, and you will not be confronted by anyone who knows you are not." As a last resort, the infiltrators could always enlist in a Confederate unit and then desert at the earliest opportunity. "The difficulty is to keep out of the Southern army, not to get into it," Andrews said.[31]

On Friday morning, April 11, the men would commandeer a northbound train and drive it up the Chattanooga line, wreaking havoc on the road behind them. "We are to destroy the telegraph line, tear up the track, and burn bridges, preventing Confederate reinforcements from being rushed to the front from the south," Andrews explained. His plan was ambitious, to say the least—one student of the raid would later surmise that the Kentuckian intended to burn the covered bridge over the Oostanaula River at Resaca, all eleven bridges over the snaking turns of Chickamauga Creek, as well as a bridge of the East Tennessee, Virginia & Georgia Railroad a short distance off the main line of the Western & Atlantic. The skinny former teacher Bill Pittenger, for one, was apprehensive about what might happen if they succeeded in sneaking south but failed to make the northbound return. Because of his terrible vision, he "greatly disliked the thought of being left alone under any circumstances," especially a scenario where he might end up stranded so far behind enemy lines. Andrews reassured the bespectacled corporal that the twenty-four men would cling together in a group, and would "come through in a body or die together."

The bearded spy also spelled out his plans for coordination with the movement contemplated by Old Stars. "General Mitchel starts south in the morning for a forced march with all his energy, and he will surprise and capture Huntsville on Friday, the very day were are to capture the train; so that when we get back to that point we will find him ready to receive us." The anticipation of such a triumphal return to their units thrilled the volunteers. "This was glorious! The thought of coming into camp after piercing the heart of the Confederacy set every nerve on fire," Pittenger remembered. Any skepticism and worry among the little company now seemed to disappear in a buzz of excitement and expectation. "Boys, we're going into danger, but for results that can be tremendous," Andrews said in parting. "If we burn those bridges, General Mitchel can take and hold Chattanooga. But we'll have to be prompt. The last train for Marietta leaves Chattanooga at five in the afternoon. Be sure to catch it not later than Thursday, and I'll either be on it, or on an earlier one. Good-bye till then."

With that, the conference broke up, and the sky opened in a steady rain that soon became a downpour. Andrews distributed substantial sums of Confederate money among the small squads of men that were forming up. The soldiers began to leave the thicket of trees, mostly in twos and threes, with Andrews grasping the hand of each man as he departed.[32]

As the evening thickened into night and the thunderstorm rumbled behind them like a distant cannonade, the two dozen disguised Union infantrymen set out along the railroad headed east, stumbling over the crossties as they plodded silently toward the Confederate lines. Pittenger took one last look back and saw their bearded leader Andrews. "He was looking after us," the former schoolmaster recalled, "his head bent slightly forward in the pensive attitude habitual with him, and a broad stream of lightning made him at that moment stand out as clearly as the mid-day; the next moment he disappeared in utter darkness, and the crash of thunder overhead drowned every other sound."

The rain would fall for the next ten days.[33]

The Tennessee River with Chattanooga in the distance. (*Library of Congress*)

CHAPTER THREE

The Heart of Dixie

The Roads to Chattanooga and Huntsville

We found the people generally accommodating, confiding, and easily deceived.

—Corporal Daniel A. Dorsey, 33rd Ohio

"To START ON A LONG JOURNEY could have been less promising than ours," William Pittenger wrote years later. "The night was pitchy dark, and the rain poured down. The Tennessee mud, which we had pretty fully tested on our many marches, was now almost unfathomable." The vicious storms seemed to march right along with them eastward, lashing them with sheets of rain accompanied by booming thunder and relentless lightning. "Only those that have been down in that country knows how it can rain down there and thunder and lightning," William Knight recalled. "I sometimes thought the good Lord was going to thunder us out of existence." Foul weather notwithstanding, the men were determined to cover as many miles as possible under cover of darkness. According to Andrews's plan, they would have to travel almost 200 miles in less than four days—with the first ninety or so from Shelbyville to Chattanooga to be covered on foot, or as one of them put it, "as best we could." This initial leg of the journey would involve not only passing out of Federal lines—hopefully avoiding the need to explain themselves to Union soldiers standing guard—but also crossing into Confederate territory, which meant that Rebel pickets, local militia, and inquisitive civilians would have to be either avoided entirely or fooled by the cover story Andrews had suggested. The tale was certainly plausible on its face. Young men from border states like Kentucky frequently migrated in the early months of the war to join up with far-flung military units, blue and gray, and the roads and pikes of the central South were often crowded with would-be volunteers, drifters, merchants, skulkers, refugees, vagrants, and dusty travelers of all types. Moreover, because the closest Union army was known to be more than 200 miles from Atlanta, the deeper the men penetrated into Georgia, the less suspicion they were likely to arouse. But maintaining their civilian disguise and selling their false identities as bluegrass Confederates would be up to the individual raiders, all of whom were Midwestern- or New England-born Yankees, and none of whom had ever engaged in such deception before. Whether Ohio farmers, teachers, and machinists could pass for Southern army recruits remained to be seen.[1]

Setting out on the road eastward toward the Cumberland Mountains and Chattanooga, Pittenger fell in step with three of his new compatriots, none of whom he had ever met before tonight, but each of whom made a quick and definite impression. One was, like Andrews, an enigmatic civilian. His name was William Campbell, and he was described by more than one witness as "a giant," standing several inches over six feet and weighing almost 250 pounds. One historian would later sum him up as "a hulking, fairly good-natured bullying type of man, with a background of not very much to his credit." Born near Salineville, Ohio, in 1839, Campbell was one of six ne'er-do-well brothers who were said by a neighbor to have inherited from their father "a very irreligious disposition." If the later testimony of those who knew them can be credited, the Campbell boys were a rough lot indeed—according to one local legend, when their father was struck and killed by a wagon while crossing the street with a keg of beer, the brothers immediately sat down and consumed the barrel's contents before seeing to the old man's arrangements. As a boy, William seemed to be bright but found school irksome, and soon had "as little use for a schoolmaster as for a preacher." He worked on river barges as a young man, developing considerable strength and a taste for hard drinking and rambling adventure. With the outbreak of the war, Campbell avoided soldiering and moved to Louisville, Kentucky, where for several months he had been keeping a "house of ill fame." In early April 1862, he was in the camp of the 2nd Ohio, supposedly there to visit friends serving in that regiment, along with his brothers James and Harvey in the 3rd Ohio across the way, though an unverifiable and considerably less charitable story maintains that Campbell had been drawn into a knife fight in Louisville and had killed a man, escaping prosecution by going to the front and finding refuge among his many friends (and sometime clients) in the ranks.

Whatever his reason for being there, when the call for volunteers for the railroad raid went out, the big man asked to come along, motivated by reasons that apparently did not include fervent loyalty to the Union cause. One acquaintance would later suggest that the big man volunteered "partly from a love of adventure and daring—partly from a desire for notoriety—largely from a hope of reward or gain in case of success, but most of all to get rid of other fears and troubles." Perhaps in light of his formidable stature, like a schoolyard tough picked first for the ball game, he was readily accepted into the enterprise.[2]

The next member of Pittenger's newfound grouping was a member of the 2nd Ohio, Company K named Perry Shadrach, an apparent buddy of Campbell's who may well have gotten to know him at his "establishment" in Louisville. Born in Somerset County, Pennsylvania, his real name was Philip Gephart Shadrach, though he hated the name, in part because his brother Oliver teased him relentlessly by calling him "Flip." He was named for the Shadrach's family doctor, and his parents earnestly hoped that the boy would follow in their physician's professional footsteps, so much so that they tagged him with the nickname "Doc"—which he didn't like either, though it sure beat "Flip." A mischievous, playful youth, he showed every sign of falling well short of family expectations, when enlistment gave him the opportunity to escape to the life of a soldier and at the same time choose his own *nom de guerre*. The young man signed on with Uncle Sam down at the local salt works, under the name Charles P. Shadrach, introducing himself to his new comrades as "Perry." He became the fourth generation of Shadrach men to serve in the United States Army—his great-grandfather fought in the Revolution, and his father and grandfather in the War of 1812.

Pittenger described the twenty-one-year-old private—who would be listed alternately on company rolls as Perry G., Charles P., or Philip Gephart Shadrach (sometimes with an –h, and sometimes with a –k)—as "plump, solidly built, merry and reckless, with an inexhaustible store of good nature." He was short and pudgy, with thick blond hair swept back over impish brows and blue eyes, which "sparkled with mischief at the slightest provocation." His other compatriots would have agreed with this description, finding the young man likeable enough but unremarkable—"he had no special accomplishments that I remember," one would ungenerously remark. A more critical acquaintance from back home described Shadrach as "a rather good harded young man but certainly not very intelligent," finding him not only reckless, but vulgar, profane, and "in every way unfitted for the work before him."[3]

The fourth member of the group, Private George Davenport Wilson, seemed exactly the opposite in almost every way. Tall and slender, with receding brown hair and sleepy gray eyes, Wilson struck Pittenger almost immediately as a natural leader and the most remarkable man of the entire group, one who had "traveled and observed much and forgotten nothing." A journeyman shoemaker back in Ohio, Wilson had indeed not only seen but also suffered much in recent years, having endured the deaths of his young daughter and his father in 1861, and enlisting in the army shortly thereafter. Now thirty-two years old, Wilson wore a gold ring and a distinctive pin containing an ambrotype of his wife. All in all, civilian disguises notwithstanding, they were a conspicuous little platoon—the huge giant; his rumpled, playful sidekick; the handsome, dark-bearded man with a gold pin; and the bespectacled, slump-shouldered teacher—and they would not be long in arousing suspicion among the Southerners they would encounter to the east and south.[4]

The balance of the raiders broke down into similar groups, though several decided against the risk of larger numbers and chose to travel in pairs, at least for now. Bill Reddick found a traveling companion in Private John Wollam, twenty-two, like him a member of the 33rd Ohio and a fellow farmer back home. Wollam was described by a compatriot as "a raw-boned, thin-faced fellow," neither slender nor heavy-set, but "merely angular and as lively as a tiger." Private J. Alfred Wilson—no relation to George D. Wilson—joined up with Private Mark Wood, and they were a mismatched pair. "Alf" Wilson, as he preferred to be called, was twenty-nine, "of rather slender, but wiry build, of nervous temperament, light hair and bluish gray eyes," according to an acquaintance. "He is a man somewhat after the old John Brown make-up, at least in this one respect of tenacity of resolution, belief and purpose." Wilson hailed from the still-tangled frontier of northwestern Ohio, where he worked his family's farm before enlisting at Perrysburg in August 1861. His new compatriot Wood, aged twenty-three, was born in Nottingham, England, a machinist by trade who had emigrated to the United States some four years earlier. He was one of the few raiders who had heard a shot fired in anger in the war, his regiment having seen limited action in the Battle of Ivy Mountain, Kentucky, back in November. He would see more fields of battle, and many other trials besides, before the war was over. Wood is perhaps best described by his friend Alf Wilson, who called him "a bright, free, thoughtless, rollicking Englishman; good-humored, impulsive, generous and brave, and had much of the spirit of adventure in his composition so characteristic of his countrymen." Like

Raiders, left to right, top to bottom: William Hunter Campbell, William C. Pittenger, Philip Gephart Shadrach, George Davenport Wilson. (*Colonel James G. Bogle Collection*)

Pittenger and the others, Alf Wilson would remember a harsh first day on the road. "The whole face of the country was a vast sheet of water," he said.[5]

Also traveling together were Corporal Samuel Llewellyn, a twenty-year-old sometime coal miner from Pomeroy, Ohio, and Private James Ovid Wellford Smith, a Virginia-born machinist who at seventeen was the youngest member of the party. Smith had a soft, round face heretofore unthreatened by whiskers, black eyes like deep pools, and a head of thick black hair, all of which combined to give him a boyish appearance that made him look even younger than he was in fact. He had joined the blue ranks back in August 1861 at Circleville, Ohio, without the knowledge or permission of his parents. Another young raider, Private Jacob Parrott, paired up with Private Samuel Robertson, a scraggly former sawmill worker. Both were only eighteen. Like the Pittenger group, each of these pairings managed to slog a few miles eastward in the darkness, finding shelter that first soggy night in sheds, barns, or slave quarters along the way. Parrott and Robertson's experience was typical. "That night we stumbled ten miles in the darkness, knee-deep in mud and soaked to the skin," Parrott recalled. "We slept in a shed, breakfasted in a farmhouse, and struck into the mountains Tuesday night."[6]

A few miles away, a larger gathering of men coalesced around Andrews himself, including the engineer Will Knight; plump, bearded Samuel Slavens; Al Dorsey—still wearing his blue uniform pants—and Robert Buffum. The latter was a comparative old man among this group—thirty-three years old, a Massachusetts-born farmer, small, dark, and bony, with thick black hair and beard, blue eyes, a missing upper front tooth, and an unpredictable temperament that suggested that other parts may have shaken loose at some point as well. To be fair, Buffum was hardly the pride of the 21st Ohio—muster rolls and regimental correspondence show him often insubordinate, drunk, or entirely unaccounted for. The commanding officer of his regiment would later describe his personal character as being "that of a jayhawker, fillibuster and guerilla, with a slight sprinkle of the horse thief." Argumentative, stubborn, fond of whiskey and Shakespeare, Buffum was sometimes morose and sometimes downright garrulous. He would spend hours in absurd, pointless arguments with his companions—trying to convince them that a black hat was white, for example—and would sometimes be heard to "pray & swear almost in the same breath." Buffum's history is not well documented, though he was involved with antislavery forces in the "Bleeding Kansas" conflicts of the mid-1850s. But despite his past transgressions and his present lack of discipline, the belligerent little New Englander would make his mark on the expedition and repeatedly demonstrate his courage, resourcefulness, and nerve in the days to come.[7]

The five men traveled all night through relentless curtains of rain and had breakfast in the hamlet of Wartrace, which the previous day was held by the graybacks but was by now and for now occupied by Federal cavalry. Upon leaving that place, they encountered interference from a diligent Union cavalryman, who was not inclined to let them pass, but a quiet word from Andrews cleared the way, and they moved on eastward without incident. "The mild-mannered Andrews soon convinced us that as a leader he knew his business, and could be an autocrat or desperado, if need be," Dorsey recalled. He felt that the departure from the little Union-occupied settlement seemed to mark a point of no return, and indeed that turned out to be the case. "This was the last we saw of the boys in blue for many months, and alas, for some, it was the last they ever saw of them," he said.[8]

Andrews then separated from the others for the journey eastward. They took their noontime meal at a farmhouse by the road and hired a wagon to take them as far to the east as the team could go and return before dark. "A negro boy of probably the age of 16 years was detailed for the purpose," Dorsey said, "and we started out gay and happy." The roads were rough, however, and the wagon rickety in the extreme—nothing more than a benchless woodrack box hitched by an old-fashioned harness to four small mules, which were guided by a haphazard system of jerklines and a blacksnake whip that seemed to be the only quality piece of equipment in the entire outfit. But they made good time nevertheless, as the young boy mounted the lead mule and "whipped right ahead as if he didn't care whether the wagon followed or not." Late in the afternoon, the men arrived at a ferry on a swollen stream outside the country village of Manchester, just in time to cross with Andrews, who had reappeared riding a fine gray horse.

Andrews's mount—which some later surmised may have belonged to W.S. Whiteman, a Nashville-based paper mill owner and business partner in the contraband trade—enabled him to ride ahead of the men to make "all necessary inquiries," as Alf Wilson said, to keep track of the progress of the scattered groups of wayfaring Ohioans, and perhaps to scout for any danger. "Passing out of sight," Wilson said, "he would allow us to go by, when he would mount and overtake us in some safe place where he would give us instructions, and then ride on, as though we were entire strangers to him." When they were within earshot of any "Southrons," Andrews engaged in a little theater to establish the Rebel credentials of the raiders, asking them where they were going and whether they were soldiers. "No sir," they would reply, "but we expect to be as soon as we can get to one of the Kentucky regiments. We've got so disgusted with the cussed Yankees since they came into Kentucky that we can't stand it any longer." Wilson, for one, believed that this charade had the desired effect and thought the Southerners who heard these exchanges "seemed to think we were as good Confederates as ever lived."[9]

Arriving in Manchester, Dorsey, Slavens, Knight, and Buffum sought to address the problem of Dorsey's still-incomplete civilian disguise. Buffum slipped into a general store and bought a pair of yellow-and-white-striped cotton pants. The Massachusetts private passed the bundle over to Dorsey, who tucked it under his arm as they walked briskly out of town, "quite content with our success in having passed the village without interruption." No sooner had this self-congratulatory thought passed through their heads, however, when they came upon a Rebel guard post at a bend in the road. The four mounted graybacks "were armed with double-barreled shotguns and weren't slow in bringing them to bear on us, and demanded that we should give an account of ourselves or be blown through," Knight recalled. Here was their first test. Dorsey was extremely anxious in his blue trousers, and though he tried to look unconcerned, his heart was thumping so hard he would later swear he thought that it could be heard by the others. He would recount years later the ensuing dialogue with the grayback pickets—complete with his characterization of the real and affected Southern accents involved—and the raiders' almost comical efforts to put on what Knight would refer to as "a bold front."

"Good evenin', gentlemen, good evenin,'" the guards said. "Whar yo gentlemen bound for?"

"We're bound fo' Geo'gia, sir; to Ma'ietta, Geo'gia, sir, to jine the Confede'ate a'my," the Ohioans answered.

"Whar did ye cum frum?"

"Cum frum Kaintucky; frum Flemin' County, Kaintucky, sir, left thar to git rid o'Yankee rule, sir. Them Yankees is a mighty bad set; they're just tearin' up things awful; stealin' every thing they can git thar han's on, and runnin' all the niggahs off no'th, an' tryin' to fo'ce our people into their a'my, an' we jis woudn' stan' it, so we left thar. If we got to fight on ary side, we fight fo' the south; we're SECESH, WE are!"

If this sounds to the modern ear like the disguised Federals were protesting too much, it must not have seemed so at the time, for Dorsey and the others quickly found themselves fending off invitations from the Tennessee soldiers to join their ranks. "Gentlemen, we're mighty glad to see our friends from old Kaintucky cumin' to jine us in fightin' for our rights," one of the horsemen said. "We been fallin' back, and lettin' on like we was afeard on 'em; but we're just drawin' 'em on, gittin' 'em sort o' scattered out like, but d'rectly we'll pounce on 'em an' whup hell outen 'em. One southe'neh kin whup fo' Yankees any day."

"But what's the use fo' you gentlemen to go way down to Geo'gia to enlist? We got a mighty fine company heah, and would like to have youens jine us. We'll treat you mighty well; come, go back with us to the village, an' jine our company."

"Very much obliged to you genlemen," the raiders responded, "but we have friends in a Kaintucky regiment near Marietta, and of co'se we would prefer to be with them."

Throughout this twangy exchange, Dorsey stood smiling blandly, sure that he saw the rebel sentries cast an "occasional glance" at his blue uniform pants. "A dogon good hoss you a ridin', sir," he offered meekly to one of the graybacks, trying to divert the horseman's attention and thinking that "a little flattery would not be amiss." One of the Confederate scouts thrust his hand in his pocket, apparently tiring of the discussion and reaching for a weapon to dispatch the intruders. But much to Dorsey's relief, the gray trooper instead "produced a bottle of whiskey, and proposed that before we separated we drink to Jeff Davis and the Confederacy." Or as Knight put it, "as our story proved satisfactory, they dropped the guns and presented a quart bottle, which, being less formidable, we didn't refuse."[10]

Buffum raised the bottle and cried—presumably muffling his accustomed nasally New England tones—"Success to the Confederacy; defeat and death to the blue-bellied Yankees!" The Northern infiltrators and the Confederate guards passed the whiskey around, laughing and exchanging hearty toasts to the health of ol' Jeff Davis. The raiders had passed their first test at deception behind the enemy lines, and their confidence grew. Shortly thereafter, Dorsey discarded his army blue under a pile of brush by the roadside and changed into the new nankeen britches, feeling "more comfortable, though a little cool." This was perhaps the first and only time in history when a pair of yellow striped pants was donned by a spy behind enemy lines in an effort to look inconspicuous.[11]

Another party had passed through Manchester long before. Sergeant Major Marion Ross's group—which included the engineers Hawkins and Brown, John Reed Porter, and William Bensinger—had made good time despite the downpour and arrived in Manchester about four o'clock on Tuesday. Parched from their travels, the group purchased two pints of corn juice and fended off inquiries by claiming to be Kentuckians headed south to join the army. "The town seemed to be alive with secesh citizens who seemed to be very inquisitive as to who we were and where 'you all gwyn,'" Bensinger remembered. Called "Ben" by his companions, William Bensinger had grown

up on a farm in Wayne County, Ohio. He was of average height but strongly built—the result of years spent with an axe and maul clearing thick woods
back on the farm—with dark hair and blue eyes. He wore a simple brown
coat and vest topped off with a jaunty straw hat. Bensinger had enlisted in
August 1861 and would remain in the army until after the war, with much
gallant service to his country still to come. His companion John Reed Porter
hailed from Wood County, Ohio, and was a devout Methodist, the only one
of the group "who had a clear religious faith and seemed to be happy in it."
Porter was a scarecrow in a square-cut butternut coat, five foot ten but weighing only 135 pounds, with a smooth face, brown hair, and brown eyes. The
five men ate supper four miles past the town, at the home of an old chap who
was accommodating though suspicious. Noticing a stopped clock on the
wall, Wilson Brown, an incurable tinkerer, offered to repair it. "Ah," the old
man declared, "you are a Yankee then." Undaunted, Brown said he had
learned from a northern man who had worked in Flemingsburg, and he
promptly fixed the man's timepiece. Finishing up their evening meal, the men
moved on, telling their host they could not stay for fear of pursuing
Yankees.[12]

A few miles away, Pittenger's group spent a disconcerting Tuesday night
lodged with a slavehunter who tracked runaway Negroes with bloodhounds
for money. "He said that he had caught a great number, and regarded them
as perfectly fair game, and the business as highly profitable," Pittenger
recalled. "The idea that there was anything cruel or dishonorable about it had
not occurred to him." The next morning, determined to make better time in
the wet conditions, the group happened upon a teamster who for an "exorbi-
tant" price agreed to take them eastward in his wagon. The man dropped them
off in sight of the Cumberland Mountains, and they plodded on, stopping to
eat a meager dinner of half-baked bread and salt pork at a "miserable hut"
inhabited by an owner Pittenger described as belonging to the class of poor
white trash. "They owned no property of their own, seemed devoid of any
ambition to better their condition in life, and eked out a scanty subsistence by
hunting or fishing, only working for a day or two occasionally when driven to
it by hunger," he said. "Even the Negroes looked down upon them."[13]

By Wednesday afternoon, disparate squads of raiders began to join
together, less cautious about traveling in small groups since they were far
beyond the lines by now—though one might question whether they were ever
that concerned at all, since Andrews himself traveled at times with four or
five other men. In any event, Knight, Brown, Slavens, Dorsey, and Buffum,

Raiders, left to right, top to bottom: Samuel Llewellyn, Ovid Wellford Smith, Jacob Parrott, Robert Buffum. (*Colonel James G. Bogle Collection*)

after an earlier stop at a cabin where they had a drink of whiskey and then purchased a round for the rough men present—to discourage pursuit, they said—soon joined up with Pittenger, Campbell, Shadrack, and George Wilson and began climbing the mountain range. On their way up the slope, the raiders caught up with a talkative Confederate soldier home on furlough from back east. He was very gratified that such a large number of Kentuckians were coming out in favor of the Southern Cause. The Rebel claimed to have been in a number of the war's early battles, among them the opening fight at Bull Run. It was an odd conversation for Pittenger, whose company had arrived on the field at Manassas late in the day, just in time to catch a glimpse of the Union collapse. "Little did he think that I too had been there," Pittenger said, "as we laughed at the wild panic of the Yankees."

*M*itchel and Andrews had agreed on Friday as the critical day when the spy would commence his destruction of the Western & Atlantic Railroad and Mitchel would seize Huntsville and begin pressing eastward toward Chattanooga. Old Stars saw the deadline as immovable, however, where Andrews, unaccustomed to strict schedules and comfortable with adapting to changing circumstances, would see no harm in a brief postponement due to the dreadful weather. Indeed, if Andrews had formed his impression of the speed with which Union generals could be expected to move from his previous sponsor General Buell, then his assumption of a delay was a logical one. By late Wednesday, he had decided that the persistent rain and high water would have almost certainly forced a delay of Mitchel's advance on Huntsville. The weather had certainly led to creeping progress of Andrews's own men working their way through the mountains toward the depot at Chattanooga. "In our instructions we were allowed just four days, not only to reach Chattanooga, but to accomplish the work," Alf Wilson said. "The continued rains and bad roads made this schedule a near-impossibility." Andrews thought so too. Spreading the word among the scattered groups of raiders, he decided on Wednesday afternoon to call for a one-day postponement of the plan. "Towards evening Andrews came riding up and quietly told us that owing to the swollen condition of the streams, Mitchel would be delayed in his movements, and we would take another day," Dorsey recalled. This was, according to Pittenger, "a considerable relief," for the sun was setting behind the mountains, and most of the raiders were still more than a hard day's journey from Chattanooga.[14]

It was a critical mistake. Andrews was wrong about General Mitchel, underestimating the Ohioan's determination to advance, and was dead wrong about the harmlessness of a one-day delay. Mitchel's three regiments of infantry and cavalry had broken camp in the soggy predawn darkness and fell in columns facing south on the muddy road before daybreak that same Wednesday, April 9. The relentless rain had been "almost tropical," one soldier would recall, and it showed no sign of letting up. Men in the long blue ranks stood with shoulders slumped, their heads bent against the downpour, the cold water trickling down their necks and dripping from the brims of their caps in an almost constant stream. Regimental flags remained furled, dark and dripping, on their staffs. Cavalry horses chuffed and steamed in the cool spring morning, and waterlogged soldiers cursed and slipped in the deepening mud. Bill Pittenger would later express his admiration for the determined action of his comrades back in Shelbyville. "No soldier is likely to forget the discomfort of moving camp in the midst of a rainstorm," he wrote. "The tents are wet through as soon as struck, uniforms are soon in the same condition; the three days' rations carried in the haversacks tend to melt into a pastelike mass. The forty rounds of ammunition and the loaded musket must be kept dry at any cost. Then the slow plowing of the wagons through the mud, the sticking fast of cannon, the roads soon trodden into jelly—these are but ordinary discomforts."[15]

The Third Division would endure these and other hardships in the days to come, the price to be paid for the accolades that would come for their drive southward into Alabama. Old Stars had planned on advancing as far as possible toward the state line this day, and he intended to follow that plan as scheduled, rain or no rain. His destination was the Memphis & Charleston Railroad at Huntsville, nearly sixty miles due south, and if he was to make it there by Friday morning, as he had arranged with Andrews, he figured that his division had better get started. Not only was the weather not cooperating, but Mitchel also had no way of knowing what sort of resistance he might encounter from Confederate soldiers or local militiamen defending hearth and home.

Mitchel's decision to press forward notwithstanding the adverse conditions was entirely characteristic of the energetic general. There was nothing in the world he despised more than tardiness, and this natural predilection was only intensified by his lengthy service under the slothful Buell. Accordingly, the brainy Ohioan consistently demanded punctuality and strict adherence to plans and schedules throughout his command in matters large and small. One story in this regard not only made the rounds in camp but was published in the press, later recounted by a *Harper's Monthly* reporter in an article called, with refreshing candor, "Gossip About Our Generals."

It was said that Old Stars demanded a reveille that was not only bright, early, and timely, but also was exactly coordinated across the companies and regiments of his division. His first general order to that effect failed miserably, however, as the pocket watch of every general officer in the ranks showed a different time. Mitchel therefore summoned the commander of one of his batteries and instructed him to fire a cannon each morning at six o'clock, whereupon buglers and drummers throughout the camp would sound reveille. The next morning, the artillerist rose well before the appointed time, taking breakfast and leisurely dressing himself while the gun was manned. "He had failed, however, to catch the spirit of Mitchel's order," the *Harper's* correspondent wrote, "and at a minute or two of six o'clock, instead of the precise moment, he ordered the gun to be fired." Within minutes, one of the general's aides dashed up and breathlessly and indignantly informed the flustered captain that he had fired the gun ninety seconds too soon, and that "the General was very much dissatisfied." The next morning, the exasperated Mitchel made sure the operation ran quite literally like clockwork, this time planning to give the signal himself to fire the morning cannon by dropping a handkerchief. He did so exactly at six o'clock, the gun was fired, and "throughout the camp, with admirable promptness, the bugles and drums sounded the call, and for a minute or two the hills and valleys about Huntsville resounded to that most exquisite of martial music, the bugle in camp."

Old Stars was delighted. "Beautiful, Captain, beautiful!" he cried. "That's the way to do it. We'll have it so every morning. Be prompt to a minute— exact to a second," he added, flushed with excitement and scarcely able to contain himself. "Bless me, my dear Sir, I've been used to calculating time to the tenth of a second."[16]

This obsession with timeliness, along with the Cincinnatian's long-suffering ordeal under the dilatory Buell, combined to make prompt action a watchword of Mitchel's command. Indeed, one Northern newspaper would describe the movements of Old Stars's division as "being made with the regularity of clock-work." And so, the officers and men of the Third Division were not surprised to be in columns on the road as ordered on the morning of April 9, though no one in the ranks knew where they were going or why. "There was not a man in the division except himself, not even one of his staff, who knew the destination of the command," his son and aide F.A. Mitchel wrote. The *Cincinnati Commercial* reporter traveling with the troops wrote that inquiries as to their destination were answered by nothing more than "pleasant smiles beaming forth on Mitchel's countenance." The division marched rapidly to and past Fayetteville, a "secesh hole" twenty-six miles to the south that presented a stark contrast to the friendly environs at Shelbyville. The advance had been difficult, to say the least, in the wet conditions. "Roads sloppy, and in many places overflowed," Colonel John Beatty recorded in his diary.[17]

The men were on the road again by six o'clock the next morning, by now suspecting "that this continued tramping meant a forced march, and that something was to be done." After another day-long march, halt was called at dusk some ten miles north of Huntsville. Cavalry patrols intercepted and brought to camp anyone found on the roads, so that no one could warn of the blue army's approach. Mitchel divided his cavalry forces into three bodies, giving each a specific assignment for the movement on Huntsville in the morning. One was to swing southeast, or left, to a point on the Memphis & Charleston Railroad, cut the telegraph wires, and intercept any trains or troops attempting to escape from the town in that direction. A second body of horsemen would swing southwest, or to the right, and perform the same work. The remaining blue troopers were to ride straight into town and seize the station and the telegraph office. The infantry would follow close behind.[18]

Mitchel was ready, and he was determined. He would take Huntsville as planned, at first light Friday morning.

For two of the Andrews Raiders, their career as secret agents would be both short-lived and decidedly short on glory and adventure. Sam Llewellyn and the young pup James Smith had walked together through the Cumberland Mountains on the road to Chattanooga, making good time through the hilly country, only to be confronted by Confederate guards near the town of Jasper. As instructed, the two Ohioans stuck to the script and recited their excuse of being displaced Kentuckians en route to Georgia to enlist—but there would be no bottle of whiskey passed around this time. The gray soldiers were unimpressed with the cover story and threatened Llewellyn and Smith with arrest, seemingly not believing that the two travelers were who they said they were. Why were they out in this weather, traveling at night, without so much as a knapsack and a change of clothes? What Kentuckian in his right mind would travel all the way to Georgia to join the Confederate army? After all, if the two strangers wanted to enlist, there were perfectly admirable grayback units in need of new blood right here in East Tennessee. It appeared that Andrews had been right—it was not easy to stay out of the Confederate Army. Llewellyn and Smith, seeing no alternative, signed on as Rebel soldiers then and there. They soon found themselves assigned, somewhat ironically, to a field artillery unit posted in defense of Chattanooga.

Llewellyn's stint as a Rebel artilleryman would be almost as brief as his experience as a Yankee spy. He promptly deserted his new unit. Later accounts would vary in the degree of drama surrounding this departure—one story had him racing across a burning bridge toward the Union lines, crying for the bluecoats to hold their fire, while another said simply that he slipped out of the Confederate lines and was picked up as an apparent Rebel prisoner, dripping wet in his new gray uniform. As for young Smith, he decided for whatever reason not to make a break for it when Llewellyn did. He continued his unwanted and uncomfortable service as a cannoneer, until subsequent events cast suspicion on him and his story.

But that would come later. For now, whatever the personal fates and futures of Llewellyn and Smith, the meaning for the rest of the raiders was simple: two soldiers had been subtracted from their number as surely as if they had never joined the enterprise at all, and now twenty-two men were left to continue the southbound trek to Marietta.[19]

Closing out their second full day on the road, the raiders continued to make slow progress in the muck and mire of the mountain roads of East Tennessee. The newly formed combination of Dorsey's and Pittenger's squads found shelter Wednesday night in Battle Creek Valley outside Jasper at the home of a "rabid secessionist" named James Clepper. The fiery old man, who was pleased to see such a mass of volunteers on their way south to enlist, called himself a colonel (perhaps of his own commissioning) and claimed to have no less than twelve sons in the Confederate army—a boast that finds no support in army rolls or pension records. He took in the entire group, giving up his own sleeping quarters for their comfort, though the Ohioans paid for their hostelry in the form of a painful evening spent listening to old Clepper loudly denouncing the abolitionists. "It would not have been safe for him to say what he did against Union soldiers if we had been sailing under our own colors," William Knight said, "but now he had the advantage, and we took it meekly."

It was a disheartening end to a long and miserable day. Feet were sore and legs ached from the long hike up and over the mountains. The incessant rain, which had given the men a daylong drenching in the cool mountain air, and the fact that the men had meager butternut or brown clothes instead of their warm army blue, resulted in sniffles and colds for several of the men—though the ever-resourceful Robert Buffum came up with a heavy dose of quinine for the afflicted (probably chased with a swallow of whiskey for good measure). They picked up the next morning where they had left off the night before in this regard, as the colonel offered them a nip of applejack just before breakfast. "We told him we would," Knight remembered. "We was like the fellow that was out after dark and he kept whistling and they asked him what he whistled all the time for. He said he whistled to keep Spirits up and keep Spirits away; we took Spirits down to keep Spirits up."[20]

The rain continued without slackening on Thursday. "While it is impossible to follow the different groups as they found their way along the road, from the information picked up along the route," wrote Frank Gregg, a reporter who tried to track the raiders' path from Shelbyville to Chattanooga years after the war, "further along they were seen to pass at no great distance apart." Many of the men came on through the town of Jasper, where Smith and Llewellyn came to grief, and several almost suffered the same fate. The little mountain village was occupied by rebel cavalry (armed with a brass gun, no less) and peopled with suspicious citizens, perhaps still skittish from the bridge burnings during the November just past. In particular, the locals cast a wary eye on Pittenger and his companions—though for the most part their suspicions were voiced long after the fact, much as a murderer's neighbors will insist they knew all along there was something wrong with the boy, only after the constable has led him away. The Ohioans stopped in a grocery to buy tobacco, and it was said that "they beat 'em all talking secesh." The townsfolk later claimed to be unimpressed with this bluster, however, being "doubtful whether the South produced such a Yankee face as the man with the spectacles had," and noting that the big man in the party wore a "pair of shoes with perforated tips, never seen before, and not made south of the Ohio River." The Confederate captain in command closely questioned the Ohioans, who gave a sufficient account of themselves and were allowed to continue on their way. (It is unclear why the cover story that had failed to pardon Smith and Llewellyn seemed to work just fine in excusing Pittenger and the others.)

By Thursday afternoon, the bulk of the raiders were clear of Jasper, apparently so effective in their bumpkin disguises that one soldier overheard Dorsey's party referred to as a "lot of country fellows, who scarcely knew enough to come in when it rained." The ungainly mannerisms and affected accents of the disguised Yankees make clear, in retrospect, that they did not hold a high opinion of Southern recruits. "We made it a point to appear as insignificant or uneducated as possible," Dorsey recalled. "I know that I purposely mispronounced words; always said goin' or gwyn' instead of going; comin' instead of coming; called a horse, hoss; whip, whup; tobacco, tobacker; a negro servant, boy, etc. I doubt if any with whom I talked could have been made to believe that fellow had ever seen the 'no'th side of the Ohio rivah.'" The rag-tag collection of "country Jakes" still had some twenty-five miles to go, with more rough terrain and a rain-swollen river still to cross.[21]

Some among the infiltrating Federals made good time through improvisation. Sam Slavens and Al Dorsey were sitting on a fence rail about midday Thursday when two horsemen approached from the west. The two men became anxious, as one of the riders trotting down the muddy track appeared to be a Confederate officer. Their worry changed to "amazement, or more properly amusement, that the supposed officer was our own Buffum," Dorsey recalled. "He had borrowed a Confederate colonel's overcoat, and hired a man to take him on horseback to Jasper, a few miles farther on." Others hitched a ride as well. Beyond the town that afternoon, Ross, Bensinger, Brown, Porter, and Hawkins traveled five miles due south and crossed the Tennessee River. They then flagged down a train loaded with wounded Confederates returning from the field at Shiloh, and soon arrived in Chattanooga, registering for the night in a comfortable room at the Crutchfield House hotel.[22]

Most of the others remained some distance away, spending the night in a roadside boardinghouse some twelve miles past Jasper and owned by the Widow Hall. The little hostel was so well established that its location, nestled in the hills across the Tennessee River to the west of Chattanooga, would be recorded by Union topographers and noted in the *Atlas to Accompany the Official Records of the War of the Rebellion*, compiled by the U.S. government more than thirty years later. Although the men still pretended to be strangers to one another, any pretense of scattering or traveling separately had been entirely abandoned by now. James Andrews, along with Dorsey, Slavens, Pittenger, Campbell, Shadrach, and Buffum, all stayed at Widow Hall's, "and a merry crowd we were," Dorsey remembered. Following a "bountiful supper," the men stayed up late in the sitting room, gathered around a crackling fire and swapping stories, few of which were true. (Pittenger—who would become a minister after the war—claimed there was no drinking that evening, but it could be that the bottle simply passed him by.) The men sang songs, and the conversation ranged to "serious and political matters," where George Wilson took the lead, to sport and humor, dominated by the wit of Perry Shadrach, "which seemed to pour forth in an unending stream." Their dark-bearded chief did not join in the conversation, though he seemed to enjoy it, sitting quietly by himself a short distance from the group gathered around the hearth. "Our gaieties were prolonged to a very late hour," Pittenger recalled.[23]

The next morning, Andrews rose before the others, the sky again a cold Confederate gray. He swung up into the saddle of his gray horse and rode off before breakfast. The other guests of the Widow Hall moved south of the boardinghouse to a nearby private ferry over the Tennessee River. There they found the hapless ferryman bailing out his flatboat, under orders not to allow anyone to cross for three days, so he said, because of a vague report that "the Yankees are coming." The river was wide and deep, well beyond fording, and there were no nearby bridges—they had no choice but to push on along the west bank in hopes of crossing directly below Chattanooga. It was a difficult home stretch, as one journalist later measured, covering "fourteen miles across the mountains by a steep trail," and they were running out of time.

But they were close. After three full days—and some long nights as well—of slogging through pouring rain and ubiquitous, sole-sucking mud, the raiders were at last nearing their goal. The river was the last remaining obstacle to their boarding a train in Chattanooga for the easy train ride south to their rendezvous point at Marietta, Georgia. For the most part, with the exception of the one-day postponement and the loss of Smith and Llewellyn—which no one was aware of as yet—everything had gone as planned. In point of fact, the infiltration into Southern territory had been much easier and less eventful than they had expected, so much so that Pittenger, who would spend hundreds of pages chronicling the adventure, would note that "there are but few incidents of this downward journey upon which it is worth while to linger."

Best of all, as far as they could tell, the raiders continued to move into the heart of Dixie entirely undetected. The two youngest members of the expedition, Jacob Parrott and Sam Robertson, were feeling rather good about their progress that Friday morning, having found out from their compatriots that they now had, as Parrott later put it, "a day to spare." They trudged upstream toward the Tennessee River ferry below Chattanooga and on their way met a friendly civilian they had seen a short ways back downriver. The man turned to them with a broad and knowing smile.

"Hello, Yanks," he said.[24]

Henry Greene Cole. (*Marietta Museum of History*)

CHAPTER FOUR

An Uncompromising and Violent Union Man

Huntsville, Alabama, and Marietta, Georgia

We were now almost directly in the centre of the Confederacy, with our deadly enemies all around us . . . .
—Corporal William Pittenger, 2nd Ohio

A T TWO O'CLOCK IN THE MORNING on Friday, April 11, after a rest halt of just a few hours, a silent reveille roused the soldiers of Mitchel's Third Division, their bedrolls spread along the roadside some ten miles north of Huntsville. Old Stars himself had slept only two hours, napping in his rumpled uniform against an old log. The men shouldered arms, slung knapsacks and cartridge boxes, and quietly took up the line of march, drowsy and stiff but no doubt excited by the apparent urgency and secrecy of their southward advance. "For the rest of the night they marched like an army of specters toward the city, where they hoped, at least, slept peacefully its inhabitants," the general's son and aide Frank Mitchel wrote. The army passed without stopping through the sleeping hamlet of Meridianville, where "not a light or a head appeared at the window." A few miles out from Huntsville, three detachments of Ohio cavalry commanded by Colonel John Kennett shook loose from the column and swung out to their assignments along the railroad, as General Mitchel had directed the day before. The Third Division had covered almost forty miles in forty hours of marching. "By six in the morning," a journalist later wrote, "the spires of Huntsville and the groves of cedar that surround them were in sight."[1]

Huntsville, the third-largest city in Alabama and the seat of Madison County, was a thriving and prosperous town of nearly 4,000 residents. The city owed its success to its prominence as a cotton market and its key position astride the primary east-west railroad, just a few miles north of the banks of the Tennessee River. Lieutenant Harrison Millard of the 86th Indiana would describe Huntsville as a "delightful and sympathetic little city, with a large stream of the purest water running through its center." In addition to the plantation-style homes of the wealthy cotton planters and an impressive domed and colonnaded courthouse in the town square, Huntsville boasted a new three-story brick depot, built in 1860, which housed the superintendent's office for the eastern division of the Memphis & Charleston Railroad. As reported by a New York newspaper that same week, visitors to the town would also find "a Bank, a Theatre building, two female Colleges, one male college (unfinished), many handsome stores, several iron foundries, saw and grist mills, &c., also ten churches—three of which are exclusively for the colored population." The paper went on to praise Huntsville unreservedly as "one of the handsomest cities in the Union."

Nestled in the Tennessee Valley among rolling mesas and hills, Huntsville was more than 110 miles from Nashville, where most residents believed the closest Union force to be. One of the locals said simply that "it had not been generally believed that the enemy would come here." John Withers Clay, the editor of the *Huntsville Democrat*, agreed with this assessment. "Every one seemed so incredulous of the enemy's approach & so unconcerned that I yielded to the general fatuity," he admitted. There had of course been talk of Union forces up here and over yonder, but the populace had in recent days been discounting these reports as nothing more than rumormongering by the faint of heart. "For weeks, we had had rumors of the approach of the enemy—that they were in such & such numbers at Pulaski, at Elkton, at Madison X-Roads, at Fayetteville, at Winchester &c.—would be in Huntsville on a certain day, at a certain hour—& facts had as often contradicted rumors," Clay wrote in a letter to his brother. "So, we only illustrated the old fable of the shepherd's boy and wolf, when the enemy did come."[2]

At six o'clock, horsemen from the 4th Ohio Cavalry galloped southward down the tree-lined streets into the city, seizing the post office and the telegraph without a struggle. (Huntsvillians would later see treachery in this regard, as Mitchel thereafter appointed the telegraph operator J. Howard Larcombe, considered by many to be "not sound on the Southern question," as the new superintendent of the railroad.) To the east and west, blue troopers blocked the railroad to prevent the escape of any engines or rolling stock. Hard on the heels of the cavalry, the lead infantry brigade under the Russian-born Colonel John Basil Turchin—who had left his former name (Ivan Vasilevich Turchininov) behind him and had dark notoriety as a callous pillager still ahead—marched into the town square. The residents of Huntsville, many of them peering out of shuttered windows and cracked doorways but offering no resistance, could scarcely believe their eyes. They had gone to sleep in perfect security just hours before and now awoke to the sound of Union regimental bands playing "Yankee Doodle" as thousands of Federal soldiers swarmed the streets of their hometown. As it turned out, the city was entirely undefended—though the Union troops quickly found some 170 Rebel soldiers who happened to be passing through the town by train "still sleeping about the cars at the depot, and incontinently captured the lot." Apart from a cannon discharged by the cavalry to stop a fleeing locomotive to the east of the town, the Third Division had captured Huntsville without firing a shot, and without suffering a single casualty.[3]

The spoils were great. In addition to bagging several hundred Confederate officers and men, the Third Division seized fifteen locomotives—all but one in working order—between 80 and 150 rail cars, huge amounts of cotton and other stores, and, last but certainly not least, a desperate encoded telegraph from Confederate General P.G.T. Beauregard near Corinth, Mississippi, to General Robert E. Lee's adjutant in Virginia, advising him that Beauregard's position was precarious and his gray army, still licking its wounds from the clash at Shiloh, was undermanned and overmatched. Sitting at a pine mess-table, Mitchel the mathematician promptly deciphered the coded message himself—"with an occasional hint from some member of his personal staff," one aide noted—and forwarded it to Buell and Halleck, both of whom characteristically chose not to act on the information. Reading reports of the intercepted dispatch in the newspapers, Lee calmly advised Beauregard to change his cipher a few days later.[4]

The conquering Union soldiers were not only proud of these tangible rewards, they quickly became fond of the city itself, which for many would become a base of operations in the weeks and months to come. "Huntsville is one of the most beautiful cities in America," Colonel William Haines Lytle wrote in a letter to his sisters back in Cincinnati. "There is a great deal of wealth here. The private residences very elegant & embowered in shrubbery & surrounded with fine gardens. The air is so laden with perfume they called it I am told the 'Happy Valley,'" he wrote. "Alas! It is no Happy Valley now," his letter continued. "The desolate footstep of the war has gone over it and it will tell with pallid lips in years to come the bloody history of this accursed rebellion."⁵

Residents of the town felt the hard hand of war immediately, as Union soldiers went door-to-door in search of arms and Confederate soldiers and sympathizers. "Truly our town is full of the enemy," Huntsville diarist Mary Chadick wrote. "There is a sentinel at every corner." The *Cincinnati Commercial* would later report a scene of "perfect terror" in the streets of the town: "men rushed into the streets almost naked, the women fainted, the children screamed, the darkies laughed," the paper said. General Mitchel rode in alongside the infantry and sought out the city's mayor, Robert "Bob" Coltart, who was no doubt stunned by the morning's developments. Mitchel imperiously demanded of the mayor that the men of his army—whose supply wagons had been left far behind by their rapid march—were to be furnished breakfast immediately, or they would go door-to-door and take it from private homes. "Bob, accordingly (& properly, I think—to prevent private pillage) bought at City expense $500's worth of bacon, beef, flour, meal &c., for the Vandals—and had them cooked by distribution," editor John Clay wrote.

Old Stars established his headquarters in the parlor of the hotel at the railroad depot, where Mary Chadick and other ladies of the town asked his permission to visit the wounded Confederate soldiers who were now in his custody. Mrs. Chadick, the wife of a local Presbyterian minister who would keep a diary of life in wartime Huntsville beginning on that day, wrote that General Mitchel initially brushed off their request and instead took the opportunity to hold forth to his captive and genteel Southern audience. "Instead of a direct reply, he went on to speak of the very great surprise he had given us that morning, and expressing great surprise on his part that we had no reception prepared for him!" Mrs. Chadick wrote. "He went on to enumerate the towns he had taken in his route, saying that he did not know how much farther he should go. He expressed surprise that we had so few provisions here (all our government stores had been removed), and said that we should be compelled to call on the North for help." All in all, Mrs. Chadick's party came away from the meeting filled with contempt for the preening general, mocking his appearance as a great conqueror "where he had no armed force to oppose him."⁶

General Mitchel reported the day's work not only to his immediate superior General Buell, but also directly to Washington, fearing, so he claimed, that communications to Buell and Halleck may be unreliable.

HEADQUARTERS THIRD DIVISION
Huntsville, Ala., April 11, 1862.

SIR:

After a forced march of incredible difficulty, leaving Fayetteville yesterday at 12 m., my advanced guard, consisting of Turchin's brigade, Kennett's cavalry, and Simonson's battery, entered Huntsville this morning at 6 o'clock.

The city was taken completely by surprise, no one having considered the march practicable in the time. We have captured about 200 prisoners, 15 locomotives, a large amount of passenger, box and platform cars, the telegraphic apparatus and offices, and two Southern mails. We have at length succeeded in cutting the great artery of railway intercommunication between the Southern States.

Very respectfully, your obedient servant,

O. M. MITCHEL,
Brigadier-General, Commanding.[7]

A number of critics would later accuse Old Stars of embroidering his successes—Buell, for example, complained that in Mitchel's reports, "everywhere the pleasing impression of an apparently vigorous action is marred by exaggeration and false coloring, and inconsistency and self-seeking." But this initial report from Huntsville, if a tad triumphal in tone, was accurate enough—the city and its residents had indeed been surprised, substantial numbers of prisoners and equipment seized, and the all-important Memphis & Charleston Railroad was now in the hands of the bluecoats. True, he had not faced any meaningful opposition and had not fought and won a battle, but there was no denying the importance of Mitchel's achievement. He had captured a Southern city without losing a man, and more important, he had broken, perhaps for good, one of the critical railroad lines of the Confederacy. More than two years before Sherman marched through Georgia, Old Stars had come to Alabama.[8]

That same Friday, almost 120 miles to the east-northeast, at about the same time as General Mitchel was scrawling his self-congratulatory report of the capture of Huntsville, the bulk of the railroad saboteurs sent out under his authority finally laid eyes on Chattanooga. "The little city was nestled among the mountains, with the black brow of Lookout frowning down upon us, the broad Tennessee lying across our path with no bridge or visible means of crossing, [and] a knowledge of the fact that it was occupied by the enemy in force . . . presented a scene at once awful and sublime," Daniel Allen Dorsey remembered. The Tennessee River looped around Chattanooga like a great moat, several hundred feet wide, with its waters high and its current rushing fast from the week of rainfall. As the raiders made their way down the valley toward the river, they encountered a great number of other travelers, many of whom had news of the progress of the war, including further particulars of the battle to the west. "Glorious news frum Shiloh, gentlemen!" a man driving a few head of cattle eagerly reported. "We've had a big battle thar, and jist whupped hell out o' the Yankees; whupped 'em all out; gained a glorious victory!" The Ohioans took all this in stride, finding these and other accounts of the fight to be "rose-tinted for the Confederates." Gossips along the road also described an epic naval battle back east between the ironclad warships U.S.S. *Monitor* and C.S.S. *Virginia* (formerly the U.S.S. *Merrimack*). One Southerner reported confidently that the Rebel ironclad had towed the *Monitor* ashore with grappling hooks, and that the South now had the two best gunboats in the world, which would soon be steaming north to burn New York and Boston. "I need not say," Pittenger later wrote, "that the histories of the war have all neglected to record this capture."

The teenage privates Parrott and Robertson also made their way to the ferry, arriving along with the man who had spooked them up the road by greeting them as Yanks. The young soldiers had responded forcefully, drawing their revolvers and accusing the friendly traveler of being a Yankee spy—"We've come a long way to fight such fellows as you," they snarled—but he took back his comment immediately. He was a resident of Chattanooga, he said, and would accompany them to the Mountain City and vouch for them at the river crossing.[9]

They arrived at the upper Chattanooga ferry and found Andrews already waiting there on the riverbank, trying to convince the ferryman, W.L. Dugger, to make the crossing on his little boat despite the rough water and a rising windstorm. At last, Dugger relented, the party having badgered him and questioned his mettle to such an extent that the poor boatman said at last that he would put them across or drown in the attempt, and for his part, he didn't much care which. The ferry was horse-drawn and rickety, "a little, crazy, frail affair," one raider would later say. Perhaps the reluctant Dugger well knew the limitations of his conveyance—he agreed to make the crossing only after the raiders promised to help push the boat with long poles through the rushing current. "The rough water was nothing," Parrott would recall, "it was the guard on the other side we feared, but, strange to say, we stepped ashore unchallenged in Chattanooga." Unchallenged, but not unnoticed. Captain William Israel Standifer, a retired army officer and hardline Confederate who had served in the Mexican War, took note of the party as they stepped off the ferry. "They were a motley-looking set," he said. "If you had met one or two together, you would never have noticed them, but when seen together, there was an evident attempt to deceive in their appearance; some wore long coats, one had one coat-tail gone, straw hats and felt hats of the oldest kind were worn; in fact, they would have aroused suspicion at once if they had not been so far inside the lines." But Standifer, like all the other loyal Confederate civilians who would later claim they were suspicious of the Union raiders, did not raise an alarm or make any report to the local authorities.[10]

Established by Cherokee Chief John Ross as a riverside trading post in 1816, the town of Ross's Landing was renamed Chattanooga, from the Creek Indian word meaning "rock coming to a point," about the same time the Cherokees were driven west by way of the Trail of Tears. Not long after that, Chattanooga was selected as the terminating point of the Western & Atlantic Railroad up from Atlanta, and the future of the young town seemed assured. The W&A commenced operations in 1849, and iron roads reaching out to Nashville, Knoxville, and Memphis were completed in the decade that followed. Having once been a second-rate Indian trading village, the town, with a population of 2,546 in 1860, soon became the "gateway to the South," its economy and its military importance now centered on the railroad.

By 1862, Chattanooga had become far more than a flatboat landing or a mountain whistle stop. Geographic circumstance had placed the little city at the intersection of the nation's vast net of railroads that extended from the Mississippi Valley to the Eastern Seaboard. Every day and well into the night, trains passed through, heavy laden with men and materiel, transporting arms from the arsenals in Georgia to supply Confederate forces to the northeast up the East Tennessee & Georgia Railroad, or carrying troops along the Nashville & Chattanooga and the Memphis & Charleston to the west or the Western & Atlantic to the south. Wedged between the curl of the river and the imposing heights of Missionary Ridge and Lookout Mountain, the town appeared to be more crowded than it was—"populous as an ant-hill," one Northerner would say of the place. "But never think you have seen the town at one glance," he continued, "it is down here and up there and over yonder;

the little hills swell beneath it like billows; you will gain the idea if I say it is a town gone to pieces in a heavy sea." The population of the former Indian village was rough, to say the least. "I think there are more *squalid* dirty ragged looking ordinary men and women in this country than I have seen this side of *heathendom*," a traveling doctor wrote in his diary. "The boys here I think are pretty good fellows, but if they have any good-looking women here I have not seen them." All in all, Chattanooga was a muddy, chaotic collision of frontier and city, river and railroad, the rustic past and the industrial future. Arriving in 1863, General Ulysses S. Grant would call the rugged Mountain City "one of the wildest places you ever saw."11

The raiders crossing at Dugger's ferry landed on the south bank of the Tennessee and wasted no time in making their way up through the Friday commotion of Market Street toward the railroad station. The muddy streets were filled with wagons moving goods and people from the river landings to the terminal and the Crutchfield Hotel directly across the street. A writer making the same walk to the depot just before the war described the scene:

> The hotel swarmed with people, arriving and departing with the trains, east, west, north, and south, hurrying to and fro with eager and excited looks, as if lives, fortunes, and sacred honor hung upon the events of the next hour. All the corners and byplaces were filled with groups in earnest conversation, some were handling bundles of paper, others examining maps. Rolls of banknotes were exhibited, and net purses with red gold gleaming through their silken meshes. In the confusion of tongues the ear could catch words, Lots— Stocks—Quarter-section—Depot—Dividends—Township— Railroads—Terminus—Ten thousands—Hundred thousands— Million.

After days of rain, the blotted sun protested weakly through an ironclad, overcast sky. The raiders who had stayed at Widow Hall's discovered on their arrival that they were bringing up the rear, as it were: they had been preceded by most of their party, including engineer Knight and his companions, who arrived early on Friday and "strolled around the streets of the village— for at that time Chattanooga was nothing more—and saw whatever we thought worth looking at." Others, including Bensinger, Ross, Hawkins, Porter, and Brown, had already caught an earlier train south. The balance of the group convened at the colonnaded brick Union Depot, lining up to catch the last southbound train. Knight, who had been in town most of the day, recalled seeing his companions coming in. "I didn't know them personally," he said, "as I hadn't yet had an opportunity of becoming acquainted, but I could have picked them out from the whole Southern army."

The raiders found the railroad station in chaos, with long lines at the ticket office and a crush of worried travelers and wayward Confederate soldiers crowding the waiting rooms and platforms. Pittenger would recall a feeling of intense panic—"the attention of the enemy was about equally divided between preparing to resist, and preparing to evacuate," he said, "either of which called for the employment of every disposable soldier." The men soon discovered through conversations with the townsfolk that Mitchel had already captured Huntsville and cut off transportation and communication with Memphis, Corinth, and other points west—"unwelcome news to us," Dorsey thought. As a result, Rebel soldiers who were to have traveled westward on the Memphis & Charleston Railroad to join Beauregard's army near Corinth were held in place or redirected south, and the less stalwart among Chattanooga's civilian population rushed to the depot seeking deliverance from the gathering blue host.[12]

This reaction was not entirely unreasonable. The Mountain City was relatively lightly defended by just a handful of Confederates, as the citizens who lived there must have known all too well. Writing in late March, commanding Confederate General E. Kirby Smith had complained to Richmond about the troops under his command and "their insufficiency for the defense of this district." The general explained that Chattanooga was threatened by blue armies from three different directions, not to mention the violent insurgency still active from time to time in the East Tennessee hills. "Chattanooga is defenseless," he wrote, responsibility for its security resting entirely in the hands of a newly reassigned battalion that could not be reinforced and the remnant of a furloughed brigade, "some 260 broken-down men, who decline re-enlisting." Smith closed by pleading that the command be "immediately and largely" reinforced. "Besides its military resources and strategic importance, East Tennessee, if it falls into the hands of the enemy, will give 20,000 recruits to his army. The road is open either to Chattanooga or Kingston. Should [the enemy] push a column in either direction I have no adequate force to oppose him." Of course, the river and the natural fortifications of the mountainous terrain made the city a tough military nut to crack in any event, as other commanders would discover later in the war. A newspaper reporter in town from Alabama would note that, if the gaps were properly defended, even an undersized occupying force could hold the city indefinitely and "make a Thermopylae of it." But there could be no question that Chattanooga was occupied by little more than a skeleton force of gray soldiers, all of whom were "lightly armed or indifferently armed," according to one description. (Knight, for one, would not have agreed with this military assessment, no matter what the Confederate headcount may have been. "We found the town alive with Rebel soldiers," he recalled. "And there were a rough-looking set of soldiers, I can tell you. They were clothed in all kinds of clothing and were armed with guns of all patterns, especially all old patterns, from a pistol up to a twelve-pounder.")[13]

The Ohio soldiers secured tickets for the five o'clock train headed south, 118 miles to Marietta, Georgia. "Everything thus far appeared to work finely," Alf Wilson said. Despite the war and the widespread Union sentiment in this part of the country, there was no passport system or other travel restriction in place on the Western & Atlantic at the time. "When we had all secured our tickets, we went aboard the train, and to our great relief, no one seemed to pay any attention to us," Wilson wrote. "We took seats in the cars and were soon moving off into Dixie at a good rate of speed. I felt that this was a much easier and more expeditious way of getting on than the tedious, tiresome march of the previous four days."

Passenger cars of the era were similar to those used today—entered up steps into open vestibules at either end, with rows of rather uncomfortable bench seating flanking a center aisle. For Henry David Thoreau, the locomotives of the day brought to mind a "boiling, sizzling kettle," and the travelers cooped up in the coaches, he wrote, "make me think of potatoes, which a fork would show to be done by this time." Spittoons were often standard equipment, though the cars lacked other modern amenities, like water, lighting, and adequate ventilation. The thick air in the compartment smelled of whiskey, tobacco, and pitch-pine smoke from the engine. White faces peered out through the small square windows, the darkened landscape and fogged-in glass affording little view beyond their own reflections and an occasional shower of glowing sparks thrown back from the smokestack like falling stars. On this night, the cars were "jammed full," Pittenger said. "There was scarcely room to stand." Many of the passengers on the crowded train were Confederate soldiers on furlough, on their way to new postings, or redirected due to the blocked railroad to the west, and many of them, if the biased accounts of the Ohioans are to be credited, were "very much intoxicated" and full of typical bluster. "The way they talked about being ready to eat up every 'Yank' in the Union made it hard for us to keep from starting a free-

Raiders Martin Jones Hawkins, left, and John Reed Porter. (*Colonel James G. Bogle Collection*)

for-all fight then and there," Knight recalled, "but we bided our time." The Rebel braggadocio made for lively conversation, much of it centered on the recent great battle at Shiloh, which the Confederates still maintained was a Southern victory—though the raiders found that "the accounts were by no means so glowing as they had been at first."[14]

The train was still within whistling distance of Chattanooga, where the tracks turned hard to the northeast, skirting the steep incline of Missionary Ridge before curling back to the south toward the Chickamauga Valley and the mountains of North Georgia. This region of limestone and granite hills and caverns, north-south ridges and valleys, and winding creeks and rivers had been until shortly before the war depicted on maps of the state as a featureless expanse of green labeled "Cherokee Indians." Wartime visitors from the flatlands of the Upper Midwest were awestruck by the rocky, thickly wooded landscape, including an Illinois soldier who wrote in a letter home, "I think God Almighty might have made the world in four days if he had not ruffed it up so." But the seemingly impenetrable wilderness of the Indian country had been broken by the sinuous iron rails of the W&A and the map-dot stations that sprung up along the line. The railroad slithered like a moccasin through the broken terrain and across the winding Chickamauga Creek, crossing no less than eleven bridges within thirty miles. "As we ran southward over these," Pittenger said, "we couldn't help picturing our proposed return on the morrow, and the destruction we hoped to contrive."[15]

Progress was slow as the train inched along the sloping, twisting road in the growing darkness. The average speed of a train on the W&A was about sixteen miles per hour, though the rate of travel was considerably slower during this most mountainous portion of the route. This was not at all unusual in that era—railroad travel was certainly a great improvement over horse-drawn transportation, but it was nonetheless uncomfortable and often agonizingly slow. (Travelers in those early days were sometimes heard to complain that the engine's cowcatcher was improperly named: "This train can never overtake a cow," they would note, suggesting to the conductor that the cowcatcher should instead be attached to the rear of the train to discourage the cows from climbing aboard the coaches and disturbing the passengers.) The train's creeping rate of travel was not the result of any lack of capability on the part of the locomotives on the road. All of the W&A's iron horses, at least as a matter of engine capacity and tractive power, were able to run at speeds at least two or three times the sixteen-mile-per-hour average indicated on the schedule. Any slowness resulted instead from caution in navigating the steep, winding route, as well as heavy loads, inclement weather, fear of collision or derailment, and ever-present traffic delays on the single-line road.[16]

The southbound passenger train crossed the Georgia state line and passed through Graysville, Ringgold, and Tunnel Hill before making a brief stop for supper at the junction town of Dalton, thirty-eight miles south of Chattanooga. There was a frantic rush for seats in the undersized dining hall, and several of the raiders had to wait for a second seating or missed out entirely on what Jake Parrott would recall as "the last regular meal I had for eight months." Dorsey caught up with the landlady between tables and persuaded her to spare him a piece of pie, which she delivered with a pleasant smile that reminded the soldier of his mother and home. The enterprising Robert Buffum deftly slid under the arm of a Rebel officer as he stood up after finishing his plate to take the newly open seat. "There was some laughing, and Buffum was applauded for his 'Yankee trick,'" Pittenger recalled, "much more so than he would have been if it had been known that he was actually a native of Massachusetts, and then engaged in the Federal service." Buffum also persuaded someone to refill his ever-present bottle of whiskey, which "was indulged in as we felt the need of it, that night and the next day," Dorsey reported, grateful for his comrade's resourcefulness. "Buffum knew the ropes," he said admiringly.[17]

The conductor patiently herded the passengers back aboard the train after the second dinner seating, and the southbound trip resumed. Full darkness closed in around the raiders, giving them some small comfort as they sat in the close railcars shoulder-to-shoulder with Southern strangers and Rebel officers and men. Dorsey would later recall that nightfall was "very welcome indeed, for we were ill at ease among our enemies, well knowing that if they should become aware of our intentions, our lives would pay the penalty in short order. We were greatly fatigued, and dozed and slept with one eye open as the train rolled over the road we were to destroy on the morrow." The train chuffed across the Oostanaula River covered bridge—another target for the next day—and through and beyond the large station at Kingston, leaving the mountains behind them. The road then turned east-southeast to cross the Etowah River. Along the way, the Buckeye soldiers noticed "great traffic" on the railroad. "We saw many freight trains standing at the stations," Pittenger said, "and everything indicated that the capacity of this line was being pressed to the utmost, which would make the running of an unscheduled train—if we should capture one—that much more difficult."[18]

The hour was late when the train approached the station known as Big Shanty, a name that the raiders—those still awake, anyhow—would have recognized as the spot they were to make their move the following morning. Through the darkened windows of the passenger cars, the Ohioans saw not only a short, parallel siding, two wells, and a handsome two-story white house next to the tracks—but also swarms of Rebel soldiers, and dozens of flickering campfires, stacked arms and seemingly endless ranks of white army tents, stretching in rows like tombstones away from the tracks into the night.

Andrews had said there would be no telegraph at Big Shanty, but he had not told them this: they would steal the train tomorrow right here, in the middle of a Confederate army camp.[19]

*T*he raiders awoke around midnight to the train's whistle and the hoarse cry of the conductor: "Marietta! Marietta!" They looked through bleary eyes at the lovely resort town where they would spend a few precious hours before starting their adventure north. Back in 1838, the chief engineer of the Western & Atlantic, Lieutenant Colonel Stephen H. Long, had selected Marietta as his base of operations during the survey and construction of the new state railroad from its southern terminus, on a gently rolling wooded ridge on the south bank of the Chattahoochee River, north through the mountains to Chattanooga. As a result, though it is considered a suburb of Atlanta today, Marietta was an adolescent boomtown as early as the 1840s, its commerce established and its population rapidly growing when the streets of the backwoods settlement that would later become Atlanta were still no more than wagon tracks in the red dirt. In 1844, a lanky, twenty-four-year-old red-haired U.S. Army lieutenant by the name of Sherman spent six weeks in Marietta, sorting out a scandal over misappropriations in the Seminole War and riding along the grade of the then-unfinished railroad. (He would return to Marietta twenty years later.)

By the spring of 1862, Marietta had grown to a population of almost 3,000 and built a considerable reputation as a resort destination free from the ice and chill wind of the North and the oppressive heat and relentless bugs of the South. Planters from the flatlands and the coast came by the droves to enjoy the fine hotels, shady streets, and cool natural springs north of town, and their dollars, along with the substantial business brought by the railroad, gave Marietta an air of wealth and aristocracy that one would not have expected given the modest family farms that surrounded it. The merchants were prosperous, the churches handsome and well-established and the citizens respectable—a local editor would point out later that year that there were only two barrooms in Marietta—the same number, he said without apparent mirth, that there were before they were closed by the city. The town was laid out much as it is today—a pretty courthouse square guarded by oaks and surrounded by hotels and shops, with the north-south railroad line a block to the west, and steeples of the Baptist, Presbyterian, and Episcopal churches outlined in sharp relief against the hulking green backdrop of Kennesaw Mountain, just two miles northwest of the square. Later in the war, Union Major General Oliver Otis Howard would liken his arrival in Marietta from the north Georgia mountains to "coming out of the woods and desert places into the brightness of civilization."[20]

Andrews and his men, arriving around midnight after four days of rain-drenched travel on foot followed by a seven-hour train ride south, probably felt much the same way as they stumbled onto the platform at the depot in Marietta. They had only a few hours to get some much-needed rest. Fortunately, the town boasted two fine hotels: the Marietta Hotel on the south side of the town square, and the Fletcher House, facing the railroad tracks next to the depot. Even more fortunately, though perhaps not coincidentally, both were owned by transplanted Yankees. The proprietor of the former place was New York-born Henry Greene Cole, a forty-six-year-old civil engineer by training who had come to Georgia in 1838 and worked under Colonel Long designing the route and constructing the railroad bed for the W&A. He had used his wages from the work to purchase tracts of land in a number of counties across north Georgia, and before long had accumulated considerable wealth. In 1856, Cole built the Marietta Hotel on the south side of the town square, joining in the hotel business his friend, father-in-law, and fellow displaced Northerner, Massachusetts-born Dix Fletcher, who owned the Fletcher House hotel adjacent to the railroad station. Cole's hotel—which featured elegantly appointed rooms with feather beds and Marseilles quilts—was later praised by the *Savannah Republican* as "one of the most elegant and commodious in the State, and would do credit to any city in the South." Cole himself was likewise well-regarded, considered one of the wealthiest, most prominent, and respected citizens of Cobb County.

He was also a staunch Republican, an unapologetic Unionist, and an active and intrepid Yankee spy. Wiry and youthful, with hard eyes deep-set in a handsome face framed by receding hair that curled long back behind his ears, Cole would be described by a witness before a Federal commission convened years later as "an uncompromising & in some respects violent Union man." Another acquaintance would remember that the innkeeper's dislike of secession and secessionists was so intense that he hated handling Confederate money, refusing to ever carry it in his purse, spitting contemptuously that the Southern scrip was "worth no more than brown paper."[21]

There is no hard documentary evidence to link Cole to the Andrews Raid. Unlike other participants, who would publicize and inflate their contributions to the episode in future years, the Marietta hotelier never claimed any connection with the raid in any correspondence or in the course of his later efforts to obtain financial compensation from the U.S. government for his wartime losses. Still, a fairly substantial circumstantial case can be assembled that he knew James Andrews, and that he had indeed provided information to the Kentucky agent before his arrival on the night of April 11. Cole himself and a number of attesting witnesses swore to his unstinting allegiance to the United States and his diligent efforts to help the Union cause whenever and however he could. "I did all in my power to advance the Federal armies and was active by frequently going to the lines and sending through information," he would later testify. "His loyalty & devotion to the Union was of that marked & decided character that leaves no doubt on the subject," a Federal commissioner reviewing Cole's case would adjudge. Indeed, he would later be arrested and charged with bridge burning and spying after passing information on the north Georgia's routes and passes to the invading army of General Sherman.

Moreover, Cole not only knew the Western & Atlantic Railroad; he had helped to lay it out in the 1840s. Henry Cole was intimately familiar with the bridges, tunnels, gaps, and passes, perhaps as well as those who drove trains on the road. "I knew more about the country than all of them together," he would brag after the war. Cole would have had information not only on train schedules and stops, but on the line's bridges and stations, as well as telegraphs, equipment, personnel, and traffic on the road. Andrews, who had traveled south to Marietta and Atlanta on several previous occasions, had all this information and more in hand. It is logical to conclude that he got at least some of these details from Cole, who historian Thomas G. Dyer would later describe as "clearly a prime contact for Union agents operating around Atlanta."

And of course, another piece of the circumstantial case against Henry Cole is the undeniable fact that a contingent of the raiders stayed at his hotel the night before their northbound adventure. Although there is no record of any meeting between Cole and Andrews or any of the Yankees with him, it would be a remarkable coincidence indeed if a Kentucky spy leading twenty Federal soldiers more than 150 miles into enemy territory would just happen to select overnight lodging at a hotel run by a New Yorker who would later be revealed as perhaps the most notorious Union spy and contact for Union spies in all of Georgia.[22]

Most of the raiders bunked nearby at the Fletcher House, a four-story former cotton warehouse within spitting distance of the railroad tracks. More than two years hence, on July 3, 1864, the same hotel would serve as General Sherman's headquarters for the final stages of his approach to Atlanta. For now, it would serve just as well as the headquarters of a number of other, less famous Ohioans. "Before retiring, arrangements were made to have the hotel men awake us in time for the northbound train in the morning, which they promised to do without fail," Alf Wilson said. The hotel was filled to capacity, and the raiders slept three or four to a bed in rooms on the second floor, facing west out over the railroad tracks. Dorsey piled in with Slavens and Pittenger, and "catnapped it until morning." The quarters were cramped and the hours were short, but they had clean sheets and a roof over their heads. The raiders would look back longingly on that night—the last time any of them would sleep in a bed for months to come. They were 200 miles from their comrades up in Huntsville, the closest substantial Union force. "The goal was reached," Pittenger said. "We were now almost directly in the centre of the Confederacy, with our deadly enemies all around us.

Before we could return many miles toward our own lines, we were to strike a blow that would either make all rebeldom vibrate to its centre, or be ourselves at the mercy of the merciless."[23]

Andrews slept little that night, and any final arrangements he made in the last hours before the raid are unknown. As his men bedded down for the night, the Kentucky smuggler disappeared for a while without explanation. He may well have met with Cole or some other Union contact, or perhaps he checked at the nearby depot or in the latest papers for any news or change in the train schedules. Some have suggested that he could have stayed on the southbound train and continued down the line into Atlanta, though there is scant evidence to support such a further foray south and little reason for it at this late hour. Pittenger would later surmise that their leader left the Fletcher House and walked across the town square to Cole's Marietta Hotel, presumably to check on engineers Knight and Brown and be sure they were set for an early start in the morning. If so, he failed to do the same with engineer Martin Hawkins and his traveling companion John Reed Porter, who were the first to arrive in Marietta and had turned in much earlier that night.

Unlike their fellow soldiers, Hawkins and Porter had apparently failed to tip a bellman to rouse them in time for the early morning train. None of the Ohioans knew it yet, but their plans for tomorrow were becoming unraveled before the day even began.[24]

Part II

The Chase

William Allen Fuller. (*Colonel James G. Bogle Collection*)

CHAPTER FIVE

All Aboard

Atlanta, Marietta, Big Shanty

O the engineer's joys!
To go with a locomotive!
To hear the hiss of steam—the merry shriek——the steam-whistle—the
laughing locomotive!
To push with resistless way, and speed off in the distance!

—Walt Whitman, "Poem of Joys" (1860)

A LITTLE AFTER THREE A.M., AS the Yankee soldiers spooned and snored in their hotel rooms up in Marietta, train conductor William Allen Fuller stepped out of the front door of Washington Hall, the two-story red brick hotel where he lived, onto Lloyd Street in downtown Atlanta. He turned left and hurried down the gaslit street and past the new green city park toward the railroad depot. Fuller was three days shy of his twenty-sixth birthday but seemed quite a bit older—a steady, reliable sort, prematurely balding, clean-shaven except for an unimpressive mustache and a whisper of brown whiskers on his chin. He was fairly tall for those days, just a shade under six feet, his longish black hair swept back so that it nearly touched his collar. Despite the early hour, he looked fresh and sharp in a classic conductor's uniform: checkered pants, black boots, and a dark indigo coat with gleaming metal buttons. Beneath, he wore a dark plush vest, double-breasted and cut rather low, with a ruffled linen shirt and tie. In his left vest pocket, he carried a large gold watch, its chain dangling in plain sight across his front. Rather than a classic short-brimmed conductor's cap, he wore a slouch hat—though "not of the rakish sort," he would later insist, "as I have ever been conservative and not loud." Apart from the distinguished uniform, he was a plain-looking man, an unremarkable figure, and no one noticed him now, though the streets near the station were already buzzing with activity in the misty predawn darkness. But the young man's days of anonymity were about to end: he would soon be a Confederate hero, his gallant deeds described in newspapers across the South and his fame and reputation in the state of Georgia ensured for life.

Bill Fuller had worked for the Western & Atlantic Railroad since leaving his family's small cotton farm in Henry County, twenty-odd miles to the south, at the age of nineteen. He started out as a train hand, at times running for miles along the tracks in advance of freight trains as a flagman on twisting sections of the road, before moving up to the hard and thankless job of brakeman. Within two years, he had been promoted to conductor, one of the youngest then working on the state road, perhaps in part because of his diligent work ethic and serious, authoritative manner. The job involved much more than calling out stations and taking tickets—as one historian noted, Fuller "was kept busy balancing the daily accounts . . . checking consignment deliveries and pick-ups on mixed freights, and—among numerous other duties—trying to keep order on Saturdays when countrymen delighted to come exuberantly to town." He was more experienced than his youth would suggest, now with five years and several hundred runs up and down the line to his credit. Today, the young conductor would have in his charge his typical assignment, a mixed mail-passenger train heading north to Chattanooga—the opposite of the southbound run his older brother James, a fellow conductor still sleeping in the apartment he left behind, had completed late the night before.[1]

Fuller was a Confederate true believer, a hard-boiled "Southron" who had drilled with and almost joined a hometown militia company when the war broke out the year before. Soon after, however, Georgia's governor proclaimed that experienced railroaders could best serve the state and the Confederacy by staying at their posts on the W&A. Most of the men working on the road welcomed this free pass from the army. "The fighting commenced, and railroad men were exempted, for which I was truly glad," one freight railroader wrote, "for I was not mad enough to fight, and I always had to be awful mad to fight any way." This is not to say that men like Fuller had it easy—quite the contrary. Sure, the pay was good for railroaders, they managed to avoid the long marches and the campsite drudgery of a soldier—and no one shot at them—but if you were looking for a tough place to work in 1862, there was no better career than the W&A. Many jobs on the road were filled with backbreaking labor and all manner of industrial dangers; others with noise, heat, smoke, and long, bone-rattling rides up and down the still-primitive rails. Since the war began, the trains had run day and night, Sundays included, often meaning fifteen-hour workdays and more. "I have gone into Atlanta many times and got off of one train and stepped right on another to go back to Chattanooga," Western & Atlantic brakeman N.J. Bell remembered. Fuller worked hard, indeed, and he took his responsibility as conductor—essentially the on-board commander of the train and its crew—as seriously as any sea captain of a ship of the line.[2]

The city Fuller now called home was even younger than he was. By the early 1860s, Atlanta was the key connecting point for a sprawling network of railroads covering the lower South like a creeping vine, but it had started out, quite literally, as the end of the road. Twenty-five years earlier, after the Georgia legislature passed a bill appropriating funds for a state-owned railroad to be constructed between central Georgia northward to Tennessee, the chief engineer of the railroad, Stephen H. Long, selected a point on a low wooded ridge on the south bank of the Chattahoochee River as the terminating point of the line. The little settlement that sprung up there—unimaginatively called Terminus—attracted a handful of residents and businesses as construction proceeded on the State Road, but few envisioned a metropolis in the making. Indeed, when Long was replaced as chief engineer in 1840, he declined a half share of land along the young town's central street offered in parting compensation, departing with a condescending prediction: "Terminus will be a good location for one tavern, a blacksmith shop, a grocery store and nothing else."[3]

But as the railroad lengthened and Terminus became not an endpoint, but a promising intersection, it began to blossom into a small town, incorporated in 1843 and named Marthasville, after the daughter of former Governor Wilson Lumpkin. This folksy name did not last long, political namesakes notwithstanding, and the town in 1845 was renamed Atlanta, a change the *Atlanta Constitution* would later admit was made "with more taste than gallantry . . . by some ambitious railroad men." (Poor Martha Lumpkin, it seems, was profoundly hurt by this insult.) J. Edgar Thomson, then the chief engineer of the Georgia Railroad, had suggested the new name, which he presented as nothing more than a feminine version of the word Atlantic. "Eureka," he wrote in a letter to Richard Peters, the road's superintendent, "Atlanta—the terminus of the Western and Atlantic rail-road—Atlantic masculine, Atlanta feminine—a coined word, and if you think it will suit, adopt it." (His suggestion apparently did not originate from any altered spelling, intentional or unintentional, of the heroine Atalanta of ancient Greek myth, though some folks would later believe that to be the case—in part because Martha Lumpkin's middle name happened to be Atalanta.) The town fathers took a shine to this new name immediately—it sounded established, formidable, and eminently marketable. Besides, Atlanta was much shorter than Marthasville and could be printed more easily on railway tickets.[4]

Within a few years, Atlanta not only had far more taverns, smithies, and stores than Colonel Long would have imagined, but much industry, commerce, and society besides, its population swelling to 2,572 in 1850 and then more than trebling to 9,554 in 1860. Well-constructed brick-front buildings began lining its streets and surrounding Five Points, the central business district near the depot named for the haphazard collision of five streets. Churches were established to minister to the ever-increasing numbers of wayward sinners in town, and fine colonnaded homes began appearing along the dirt streets and avenues. The greatest explosion, however, was in manufacturing and commerce, thanks to the war's insatiable appetite for raw material, finished goods, and ordnance. Arsenals, factories, machine shops, rolling mills, tanneries, and other facilities strained to supply the needs of the Southern armies, producing armor plate, cavalry swords, harnesses and saddles, uniforms, boots, Bowie knives, gun caissons, and most important, all manner of guns and ammunition. An influx of workers to man these industries swelled the city's population, which would nearly double during the war, though in 1862 Atlanta remained a stumbling toddler in the family of Southern cities—Nashville was more than three times and Charleston more than five times as large. And like its neighbor Chattanooga to the north, Atlanta was still in many ways a hard-edged frontier town. (Roughly 60 percent of the cases prosecuted in the Mayor's Court of Atlanta involved disorderly conduct, and the court also saw widespread gambling, drunkenness, prostitution, larceny, and acts of rowdiness ranging from firing pistols at all hours to riding horses into hotel lobbies.)

The city's frantic, war-fueled commerce, its high society and its criminal element, and the ever-present scramble around the railroad station provoked a wide variety of reactions from visitors. One reporter was duly impressed by Atlanta's persistent air of "goaheadativeness," but others seemed daunted and overwhelmed. "Atlanta! ha! That's the place to get your money back!" exclaimed a visiting *Mobile Register* correspondent. "That is, if you wished to invest in dust, heat, and noise, and get so cuffed about and beplucked as to wonder if you ain't some other man." Still another reporter wrote that he detected a "slight perceptible odor of Yankeedom" in the city and was thoroughly convinced that the place was crawling with Yankee spies. (The fellow was a little paranoid, but he wasn't at all wrong, as it turned out.)[5]

The railroad remained the focal point of Atlanta's geography, government, and commerce and dominated the daily life and atmosphere of the young city. The city limits themselves were defined as a one-mile radius from the zero-mile post that marked the terminating point of the Western & Atlantic. The city's seal—which in the postwar era would feature a phoenix rising from the ashes—at that time depicted a locomotive. Atlanta's most impressive civic space and architectural feature was not a cathedral or courthouse but the 400-foot long, red brick railroad passenger depot, which the locals referred to matter-of-factly as the Car Shed. "It is a great railroad whirlpool and auction mart," one newspaperman observed of the young city, "in which something less than a million people plunge and splash about daily; where locomotives are eternally shrieking; and the auctioneers incessantly shouting . . . where the side walks are paved with goober-shells and apple peelings and the plays at the theater nightly joined in by the audience; where the all-pervading spirit of the people is trade, trade, trade, and where the only material thing is the news boys who merely run as fast as they can, and sell their papers in the usual way." By 1860, Atlanta's predominant horse was an iron one: the census that year listed more railroad engineers than blacksmiths.[6]

Fuller skirted the early morning chaos of wagons and arriving passengers in the streets outside the station and arrived at the Car Shed somewhere around a quarter to four, just in time to see the train he would conduct that day slowly backing in next to the platform. Inspecting the train from back to front, he saw first the two passenger coaches; then the mail and baggage car; then three empty boxcars, their doors unlocked and standing wide open, awaiting cargo to be loaded in Tennessee and brought back to Atlanta; then the striped, dark green-painted tender, filled with 1,750 gallons of water and piled high with nearly two cords of wood, with "W. & A. R. R." stenciled in gold on its side; and, finally, the magnificent steam-powered locomotive. Fuller looked the engine over admiringly, the onetime farm boy never tiring of the excitement of working with such magnificent machines.

An engine builder of the time would describe steam locomotives as nothing less than "melodies cast and wrought in metal"—and so it was with this one, an elegant, well-proportioned beauty with no vices except smoking and drinking. Up close, the eight-wheel, wood-burning engine seemed huge, some twenty-seven feet long from end to end and weighing more than 50,000 pounds, its finish glistening from the morning mist that had begun to thicken and drift down outside. Later made famous in movie scenes and lithographs as a shining, red-and-black engine with gold trim and an iconic, circumscribed gold numeral 3, the locomotive was in fact painted dark green with red-orange accents at the time, with the long cylindrical boiler of the engine silver metallic and the valves and domes atop it gleaming brass. The engine's number, stenciled on the sand-box atop the boiler, was 39. At the front, a spindly, cross-hatched and oversized red-orange cowcatcher (or pilot) pointed the way, with a boxy, tin-plated front oil lantern, some two feet in diameter, mounted above. Up top, a large balloon-style Radley & Hunter smoke-arrestor smokestack chuffed steam and smoke into the damp morning air as wood in the firebox was lit and the boiler began to heat up. The engine rested on a swiveling cart of four wheels in the front and four large, five-foot diameter orange-painted cast iron driving wheels in the back—a configuration known to railroad men as a 4-4-0. Centered just above these wheels on the side of the engine, just in front of the cab, was a gold-lettered plaque with the locomotive's name: GENERAL.[7]

Like most Southern locomotives, the *General* was a Yankee by birth, having been constructed for the W&A by the Paterson, New Jersey, firm of Rogers, Ketchum & Grosvenor at a cost of $8,850 and placed in service in January 1856. The engine's origin was hardly unusual—almost all of the South's locomotives were built up north. Many Southern engines had been named in accordance with their Yankee construction—a circumstance that became somewhat embarrassing when secession came and the stable was filled with iron horses with names like *Pennsylvania* and *United States*. The names of the W&A's forty-six locomotives ran the gamut from geographic (*New Jersey* and *Kentucky*, for example) to biographic (*Joel Crawford, R.C. Jackson*) to fanciful (including the *Flying Nelly* and the *Gazelle*). A number of engines bore names of Indian tribes, or words or place-names with Indian roots—*Cherokee, Choctaw, Coosawattee, Carahee*. The inspiration for the *General*'s moniker is not known—if a particular military hero was meant to be honored by the name, no one recorded the fact. With the coming of the war, the *General* would prove herself one of the great workhorses of the W&A—from October 1861

The *General* in her wartime character. Illustration by Wilbur G. Kurtz. (*Colonel James G. Bogle Collection*)

through the end of September 1862, she would pile up 29,692 miles pulling freight and passenger trains through north Georgia—more mileage than any other engine on the road except one. (Railroad men of the era often referred to their locomotives using feminine pronouns, much like the traditional and even affectionate terms employed by sailors in speaking of their ships.)

Already up in the cab of the locomotive was engineer E. Jefferson Cain, a transplanted Pennsylvanian who had come down to Georgia in 1857 to work on the state railroad. He was a fragile, almost elderly figure though only thirty-five, "physically frail and tubercular," according to one description, with a thin face bearing up under the burden of a thick mustache, which served to balance, or at least distract from, a set of ears as big as angel's wings. Fireman Andrew Anderson would stand post in the cab next to Cain, feeding and stoking by hand the cramped firebox that rested between the two rear driving wheels. The two men ran through their usual tasks to prepare for the day's run, lighting the lantern, checking wood and water in the tender, tightening bolts, and oiling journals as the locomotive hissed and smoked like a dragon in its cave.[8]

In all likelihood, the crew was giving a little extra spit and polish to the engine that morning, as they knew that their supervisor would be coming along for the ride. Anthony Murphy was the foreman of motive and machine power on the Western & Atlantic Railroad. In addition to oversight of the road's engineers, Murphy was responsible for the operation of locomotives and equipment, inspecting engines and rolling stock, and directing repairs as needed. That day, he was assigned to travel north to the station at Allatoona, about forty miles from Atlanta, to take a look at a new engine that would power machinery to pump water and cut wood for the road's thirsty locomotives. Operation of the W&A required a constant supply of cordwood and fresh water spaced at stations up and down the line. The *General*, for example, could travel only thirty-five miles or so on a cord of wood—making the trip to Chattanooga a "five-cord run"—and the water in the tender would be quickly consumed as the massive Wagon Top boiler heated up and provided steam to the cylinders. Accordingly, wood and water were a considerable source of logistical trouble and expense for the W&A, and any improvement to the delivery of either material would be a great asset to the operation and the bottom line of the state road.[9]

One of eight children, Murphy was born in Wicklow County, Ireland, in 1829, moving with his family to Schuylkill County, Pennsylvania, as a boy of nine. He moved on to Trenton, New Jersey, at age eighteen and embarked upon a career as a railroad man, starting out as a machinist's apprentice and then working in the machine shops on the Erie Railroad in New York and later on the Pennsylvania Railroad at Pittsburgh. In 1854, he headed south to Atlanta, one of the many skilled Northerners who would find work on the new and growing Georgia state road. Murphy spent four years as a machinist and then eighteen months as an engineer driving locomotives on the W&A before being promoted to his current position as foreman. (Some would later refer to him as a superintendent of the road—not entirely accurate, but at least a title that captured the supervisory nature of his post.) For Murphy, secession had not sparked any reexamination of life or loyalty, his time spent up north notwithstanding—he had married a beautiful brunette Georgia girl named Adelia McConnell four years earlier, and chose to stick by his new southern family and his colleagues on the state railroad.

Now thirty-two, Murphy was tall and trim, a purposeful character with dark, twinkling eyes, a droop mustache, and more than a hint of his childhood Irish brogue remaining. He was dressed for rough travel and hard work that day, wearing a dark vest and coat, brown pants, and a soft, broadbrimmed hat on a head of brown hair cut long. An interviewer meeting him years after the war would be well impressed by the foreman. "His head is cool, his heart is warm, and a more evenly balanced mind is never found," Wallace Reed wrote in the *Atlanta Constitution*. "Quiet, reticent and undemonstrative, Anthony Murphy is yet an almost invincible power when brought

E. Jefferson Cain, left, and Anthony Murphy. (*Colonel James G. Bogle Collection*)

into action." And for Murphy and his crew, there was much action ahead on that spring day.[10]

Promptly on schedule at four o'clock, Jeff Cain released the tender brake, nudged the throttle, and with a shriek of the whistle and a chuff of smoke from the stack, the *General* rolled forward out of the shadowy mouth of the depot. The schedule called for an almost twelve-hour trip northward up the crooked, 138-mile route through the mountains to Chattanooga, with a 3:40 P.M. arrival expected. The fare for the full trip from Atlanta to Chattanooga was five dollars, though there would be a number of interim stops during the course of the day. Murphy took a seat in the second passenger coach, among a crowd of civilian travelers dotted here and there with a few gray uniforms. The locomotive, tender, and six trailing cars rolled out of the western end of the Car Shed into the mist, the rails ahead gleaming like bayonets in the diffused lamplight and the ghost of the morning still to come. The *General* crept past the crossing at Whitehall Street, the city park and the three-story balconied Concert Hall standing to the right and the storefronts of Whitehall and then Peachtree Streets stretching out at right angles to the track. The signs of downtown Atlanta's various businesses were barely visible in the weak predawn light: the Trout House hotel, the *Daily Intelligencer* newspaper, M. Wittgenstein ("Wholesale Dealer in Imported Wines Liquors & Spirits"), F. Geuterbruck Tobacco, Atlanta Cigar Manufactory, and, at No. 8 Whitehall Street, Crawford, Frazer & Company's so-called "trading company," with its sign advertising "Auction & Negro Sales." The train chugged past the switch for the Macon & Western Railroad and then under the Market (later Broad) Street bridge, picking up speed as it left behind the sidings and roundhouse of the W&A, the shadows of the forest to the north now visible on the horizon beyond.

The *General* crossed the bridge over the Chattahoochee River at about 4:30 A.M., stopping for wood and water near the river and then at Vinings Station to pick up more passengers. It was Saturday morning, April 12, 1862. At that hour, exactly one year before, Confederate guns had opened fire on Fort Sumter. The Atlanta papers made no mention of the anniversary.[11]

*A*t the same time the *General* was making its way north from Atlanta, the raiders were awakened by the hotel men as promised. They had gotten no more than four hours of sleep and perhaps a good bit less—"the two or three hours soon slipped by," Alf Wilson later wrote. The soldiers dressed quietly and hastily in the dark, cramped hotel rooms, hitching up pants and belts, pulling on boots and checking their revolvers. If any prodding was needed, it was provided in a harsh whisper: "Hurry up or you'll be left!" Word was passed that a final meeting—an "informal council of war"— would be held in Andrews's room, its windows overlooking the railroad tracks. William Knight and Wilson Brown arrived right on time from the Marietta Hotel down the street, but Martin Hawkins and John Porter, the other Ohio soldiers who had bunked at Cole's hotel, didn't show. Andrews and the others surely would have noticed this, but apparently their absence was not discussed in the meeting, and no effort was made to rouse and round up the missing men. After all, Hawkins and Porter knew as well as the others what the departure time was that morning, and surely they would be there at the station. For now, a total of eighteen soldiers, plus the giant civilian William Campbell, crowded in with Andrews and leaned close to hear his final instructions. "There was suppressed fire in his low, almost whispered words, a calm confidence in his tone that was contagious," Pittenger later wrote. "There seemed to be no doubt, hesitation or shrinking on his part, but, on the contrary, an eagerness and joy that the time was so near at hand."

"Get seats near each other in the same car," Andrews said, "and of course say nothing of our business on the way up. When the train makes the Big Shanty breakfast stop, keep your places till I tell you to go. If anything unexpected happens, look to me for the lead." He selected the three men with railroad experience—engineers Knight and Brown, along with Alf Wilson—to

Western & Atlantic Railroad Stations in 1862

STATION	DISTANCE FROM ATLANTA
Atlanta	--
Vinings	11 miles
Marietta	20
Big Shanty	28
Acworth	35
Allatoona	40
Etowah	43
Cartersville	47
Rogers	49
Cass	52
Kingston	59
Adairsville	69
Calhoun	78
Resaca	84
Tilton	91
Dalton	100
Tunnel Hill	107
Catoosa	111
Ringgold	115
Johnson	120
Chickamauga	128
Boyce	133
Chattanooga	138

join him on the engine. "The rest of you will go on the left of the train, forward of where we'll uncouple it. Climb into the cars as quickly as you can when the order is given. If anyone interferes, shoot him, but don't fire unless you have to."

Andrews "went on to lay out every action with the nicest accuracy," Pittenger recalled. He explained the signals he would give to the engineers and instructed the firemen and brakemen on what was expected of them. "The rest of us were constituted a guard to shoot down anyone attempting to interfere with the work," Pittenger said. "Any man not aboard when the signal to go was given was to be left, since a delay of thirty seconds after our designs became clearly known could result in the slaughter of the whole party."[12]

Andrews asked whether there were any other questions or items of discussion. "At this point, Sergeant Major Marion Ross, the ranking soldier of the party, and as brave a man as we had, offered a respectful protest against going further," Pittenger recalled. The big, bearded sergeant probably stood to make his case. It was true, most of their party had succeeded in infiltrating south to Marietta, but the situation had changed, he said. They were a full day behind schedule. Mitchel's advance to the south had caused a panic, alerted Confederate authorities, and driven rail traffic southward. The raiders had seen with their own eyes the crowded road and stations the day before, and the operation of the railroad would probably be even more irregular today, the tracks filled with soldiers and unscheduled trains. Ross also reminded the group of the thousands of Confederate soldiers they had seen encamped at Big Shanty—there would no doubt be a heavy guard posted at the station and around the train. "On these counts, Ross thought it better to postpone the attempt or give it up altogether," Pittenger said. The mission was certain to fail, Ross believed, and would cost the life of every man engaged in it.

Andrews listened thoughtfully and responded quietly. He acknowledged the facts as Ross had stated, but said that he believed that the change in circumstances actually worked in their favor. The large number of trains already on the road and the "military excitement and commotion" would cause their own unscheduled train to be less likely to be suspected. As for the troops at Big Shanty, if the raiders did their work properly, they would have no chance to interfere. In fact, Andrews said in earnest but wishful thinking, it would be easier to steal the train there than anywhere else, simply because no one would believe it could be done. "Andrews could always find a reason for everything," Pittenger said, "but these plausible arguments were not entirely convincing." A brief debate followed, and others among the party, including stalwart members of the group like Alf Wilson, joined in Ross's objection to proceeding.

In response, "Andrews made plain that he wanted no man to come against his better judgment," Pittenger recalled. "Anyone in the room who thought the attempt too hazardous to try was still at liberty to switch to the down train to Atlanta and thereafter work his way to the Union lines as best he could." But the black-bearded Kentuckian's mind was made up. Andrews lowered his voice. "Boys, I tried this once before and failed," he said. "Now, I will succeed or leave my bones in Dixie." His words were in retrospect filled with grim prophecy.[13]

Yet there it was; the decision was made. There would be no turning back. Moved by these words of determination, the raiders assured Andrews that they would stand by him, and if need be, die with him. "Never was there such a leader," Jacob Parrott later wrote. "We would have trusted them to the ends of the earth." Ross, Wilson, and the others apparently did not press their objections any further, and no one accepted the invitation to back out, though many would later wish that they had.

The twenty men shook hands all around, clambered down the stairs, and hurried next door to the station, as the train was almost due. They stepped to the depot and bought tickets to various points along the line as the train, "very long and apparently well-filled," pulled up next to the platform, drawn by what immediately struck Alf Wilson as "a fine-looking locomotive." Seated in the second passenger coach, railroad foreman Anthony Murphy noticed the large group of men boarding the first. "They were dressed like citizens from the country, and I supposed they were volunteers for the army, going to Big Shanty," Murphy remembered. He was half right—the strangers were headed to Big Shanty. Conductor Fuller also later claimed that he took particular note of the large number of passengers boarding at Marietta, and the fact that most of the travelers were men.[14]

As he stepped onto the train, James Andrews may have smiled grimly to himself, noticing with satisfaction the three empty boxcars hitched just behind the tender. This was perfect—he could not have ordered the train configured any better for his purposes. In all likelihood, he was already formulating the cover story he would use as a bluff if need be once they had taken the train—an idea about an "emergency ammunition train" he would claim to be rushing to Corinth via Chattanooga under urgent direction from General Beauregard himself. The bearded spy probably gave a long, last glance around the platform and back toward the town square and the Marietta Hotel, looking for any sign of the two missing men, Hawkins and Porter. At last, he swung up onto the coach and chose a bench near the front as the train began to move. "We took our seats in a sleepy, drowsy manner, and to all observers must have appeared indifferent to all surroundings, our feelings to the contrary notwithstanding," Dorsey said. It was fifteen minutes after five o'clock.

The raiders probably did not see that day's edition of Atlanta's only morning paper, the *Daily Intelligencer*, and even if they did, they might not have noticed the small report from the field buried on the second page, just above the letters to the editor. The item read:

It is reported, by a dispatch to a gentleman in this city, that the Federal Cavalry have taken possession of Huntsville, Alabama. If so, then the Memphis & Charleston Railroad is in possession of the enemy.[15]

*M*artin Hawkins and John Porter had overslept. They would later blame "some mistake or negligence of the hotel porter" in failing to wake them in time for the train, and Porter would point out by way of excuse, accurately but rather lamely, that the train "left quite early." The two men almost made it anyway, running the two blocks from the Marietta Hotel to the depot and arriving on the platform just in time to look to the north and see the train getting smaller and smaller as the passenger and mail cars curled around a bend out of sight. "We gazed intently until the smoke of the locomotive disappeared in the morning twilight," Porter remembered. "I can't describe my feelings at that moment. I glanced at Hawkins, who appeared to be as much bewildered as myself. There we were in the heart of the Confederacy, knowing that if we were suspected of anything wrong we could expect death." Knight carried a Colt revolver under his coat, but the weapon gave them little comfort under the circumstances. At a loss for what to do next, the two men left the station, walked back to the Marietta Square, and began strolling aimlessly around the town, killing time and trying their best not to look like Yankees.

Two more soldiers had been subtracted from the group of raiders. Twenty men, including Andrews, were left. Hawkins and Porter being left that morning was "a serious loss, for Hawkins was the most experienced engineer of the party, and he was the one selected to take charge of the engine," Alf Wilson later wrote, though he admitted, "but it is not likely that the result of the expedition would have been different, even with his practice and experience." It was the first stroke of bad luck that day, but it would not be the last.[16]

*T*he *General* and its train of cars clattered up the long, low grade from Marietta, driving northward through the thickening mist of the April morning. The train passed through a tiny station called Elizabeth and then turned hard to the east before curling back west in a sweeping arc around the imposing hulk of Kennesaw Mountain. The mountain's name was taken from the Cherokee word *Gah-nee-sah*, meaning burial ground—which it would become two years later, when more than 3,000 Americans would fall in battle there. The Buckeye soldiers sat quietly as they rocked gently back and forth with the movement of the train, impatient for the moment for action to arrive. "There was many an anxious gaze from one to another of our party after we had taken our seats in the cars that morning, as if to read the thoughts of each, as men will sometimes do when drawn up in line on the eve of a great battle when the skirmishers are slowly retreating before the advancing columns of the enemy," Alf Wilson said. But he detected no fear or nervousness among the men, remembering that each seemed "cool, decided, and resolute." Knight, sitting toward the front of the coach near Andrews, looked back over his shoulder and searched the faces of his comrades, finding them steady, though he thought "they looked a little paler than common." Reflecting on the suspense years later, he said: "As for myself, I don't know just how I looked. But I think I felt a little like if there had been a little ice water run down my back. And it made me think of what my grandmother told me when she took my hand to bid me goodbye when I was leaving home. Says she, 'Now, Will, you know that you have always been very daring and reckless, but don't venture too far.' I did not know but what I had got a little too far."

About this time, the conductor, who struck Parrott as a "genial young man, almost a boy," began to make his way down the aisle to take tickets. Fuller "passed through the car, took up our fares apparently without noticing that we were strangers, and asked no questions," Dorsey said. Fuller later claimed that he did indeed notice the "considerable party of strangers, dressed in citizen's clothes, [who] got aboard and paid their fare, some to one point and some to another." He also recognized Andrews, though he did not know his name. The tall, dark-bearded businessman with the long overcoat and the saddlebags was a frequent traveler on the road, and Fuller would recall finding him "very courteous and engaging." Fuller checked tickets closely, as he always did, and he eyed the passengers carefully—"he looked narrowly at us," one raider said—but he had no reason for any particular suspicions. "Deserters had been reported as slipping out from the camp [at Big Shanty], and the commanding officer had asked me and the other W&A conductors to be on the lookout and to arrest any soldier who got on the train without a pass," Fuller said. "On men going to the camp, as anyone from below Big Shanty could be, we weren't keeping such a close watch."[17]

For all the secret meetings and instructions from Andrews, it occurred to Pittenger that he was not sure exactly how the raiders would go about taking the train. As the train rolled northward, he and the others wondered how much of a fight they would have at Big Shanty. "I thought we would probably have to fight, and compel the conductor, train-hands, and passengers to get off," Pittenger said. The plan, or at least the sincere hope, was that passengers and crew would all disembark for a morning meal—but this was by no means certain. What if one of the crew stayed behind? What if some of the passengers interfered? What if a guard was posted at the cab? Would they have to draw their guns? Shoot the engineer and fireman? "Aside from considerations of humanity, it was our wish to avoid any collision or delay," Wilson said, "for there were thousands of Confederates camped within sight of the station."[18]

Day was finally breaking behind the heavy gray curtain of clouds as the train completed the seven-mile stretch from Marietta and began to slow for the stop at Big Shanty. As they came around the gentle curve, the raiders could see out the right side of the coach the picket fence surrounding the two-story trackside hotel where breakfast would be served. Out the windows to the left, the Confederate encampment they had seen late the previous night came into view on the west side of the tracks, though the camp seemed quiet, as the buglers had not yet sounded the morning's reveille. In the strengthening light, they could get a better idea of the size of the place. Hundreds of tents were pitched in three large sections arranged in a broad arc, with drill fields, an orchard, and several small sheds closer to the railroad track. Several raiders would later note that the number of Rebel recruits present had been greatly increased since Andrews's last visit, but they found it difficult to ascertain just how many graybacks there were. Some among the Ohioans would later estimate the size of the Confederate post at more than 10,000 officers and men; though the actual number was considerably less than 3,000. But the camp looked sizable enough. In addition to the amenities provided by the hotel just across the tracks, the camp had three parade grounds, stables, a cornfield, a garden, and a small camp hospital—but it did not have a telegraph.

The *General* clattered and chuffed up the long, low hill into Big Shanty right on schedule. A singsong cry went out from the conductor: "Big Shanty! Twenty minutes for breakfast!" In the cab, the engineer Jeff Cain tugged the cord to ring the engine's bell as the train squealed to a stop with the passenger coaches directly opposite the hotel. As he stepped down from his post, the fireman Anderson opened the door of the *General*'s firebox to vent some steam and prevent excess pressure from building up as the train sat idling. Just a few feet away, the raiders saw Rebel guards pacing back and forth, so close to the tracks that the Ohioans could hear the clink and rattle of their tin cups and bayonets. In the camp beyond, they could see soldiers beginning to emerge from their mud-spattered tents, hitching suspenders, banging kettles, and pounding rye coffee.

The usual pell-mell rush to grab a seat at the breakfast table began, and the passengers crowded toward the doors to disembark on the right side of the train. The Ohio infantrymen, their hearts in their throats, kept their seats and waited to see what Andrews would do, but he wasted no time. He stood, picked up his saddlebags, and joined the tail end of the crowd filing out of the coach. Knight, the engineer, immediately rose and followed. They shuffled down the aisle to the open door and stepped off on the opposite side of the train, just a few feet from the armed sentries.

No one paid them any mind.[19]

Western & Atlantic Railroad bridge over the Etowah River. (*Colonel James G. Bogle Collection*)

CHAPTER SIX

"Someone is Running Off with Your Train!"

Big Shanty to Etowah

The whistle had already sounded, and the conductor had called out, "Big Shanty! 20 minutes for refreshment!" The time had come for one of the boldest dashes that has ever been recorded in the annals of History . . . .

—Private William Knight, 21st Ohio

THE WHISTLE STOP AT BIG SHANTY was, according to a visiting newspaperman with an apparent fondness for tall tales, "one of the pleasantest places in all Georgia; a high, airy country, where the cool breezes blow and the crystal springs bubble—where the potatoes and the babies are the biggest, and the girls and peaches the sweetest in all this Confederacy." The little trackside settlement, known today as Kennesaw, was named for the jumbled collection of railroad shacks that stood at the top of the steep grade up from the Etowah River when the road was under construction—at some point, "the big grade to the shanties" was shortened to "Big Shanty." A recent addition to the place was Camp McDonald, organized in June 1861 and named for a recently deceased former governor of the state, where two regiments and three battalions of local volunteers were mustered into the service and taught the rudiments of military drill, often by babyfaced cadets from the nearby Georgia Military Institute. "You will find in some squads old gray-headed men drilled by a boy fifteen years old," an Atlanta correspondent reported.

The thirty-five companies in camp gave themselves romantic names like the Cherokee Dragoons, the Cobb Mountaineers, the Carroll Gold Diggers, and the Rowland Highlanders. Armaments were hard to come by, and many of the boys in the ranks brought their own muskets or squirrel guns from home, or made their way through marching and drill armed with improvised and presumably ineffectual retractable-blade lances they referred to as "Joe Brown Pikes," after the state's wartime governor.

The exploits of local regiments on the battlefields of Virginia in 1861 had resulted in glorious reports of their valor and the progress of their arms in the Atlanta newspapers, but as the weather turned colder and the casualty lists began to appear, the sweet taste of victory began to turn bitter for residents of the county. The winter had brought soldiers' letters and with them tales of hunger, sickness, and sore feet on the march. "The Yankees say that we have a new general in command of our army and say his name is Gen. Starvation," one local Johnny Reb wrote, "and I think for once they are about right." Another summed up the sentiments of many in the ranks in a letter to his sister: "I am mity tired of this wicked war," he wrote. Home front morale and enthusiasm waned, as did the number of recruits present on the drill fields at Camp McDonald. Then, in February 1862, Confederate President Jefferson Davis called for the formation of twelve additional regiments from Georgia, and Colonel William Phillips arrived at Camp McDonald looking to muster and train several new companies of infantry and one of artillery. The early spring brought warmer weather and brightened spirits, with citizens hopeful that the coming campaigns in Virginia and the West would bring total victory and recognition of the Confederate government. It also brought thousands of new gray recruits to the sixty acres of campsites and drillfields at Big Shanty.[1]

This meant business was booming at Mr. and Mrs. George Lacy's hotel, a pretty white two-story house with a tall-columned porch and green shutters, directly across from Camp McDonald on the east side of the railroad tracks. A favorite stopover for travelers in need of a meal or a break from the winding, bone-rattling ride on the coaches of the W&A, the Lacy Hotel was renowned for its comfortable beds and good Southern cooking. "Many a tale is still told in Cobb County concerning Mrs. Lacy's biscuits, waffles, and chicken," a local historian wrote years after the war, "and no less well remembered are her flock of ducks, which became so permanent a feature of the landscape that people accustomed to riding up and down the W. and A. used to look out of the windows of the trains and say, 'Well, there are Mrs. Lacy's

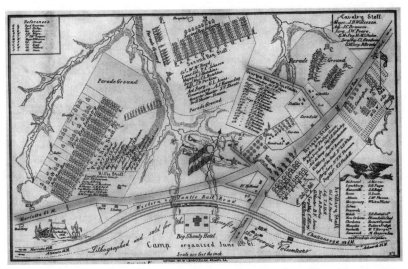

Camp McDonald, Big Shanty, Georgia. Note the railroad tracks and Lacy's hotel at bottom center. (*Library of Congress*)

ducks,' and then compute the distance remaining to their destination." The founding of Camp McDonald and the arrival of thousands of Rebel recruits was great for Mr. and Mrs. Lacy's business, but it was damned hard on the ducks, which often became the target of the pranks if not the cookpots of the soldiers encamped nearby.[2]

The gray sentries posted on the other side of the tracks from the hotel that Saturday morning in April 1862 looked bored and more than a little damp, pacing with their muskets at right shoulder shift in the cool, heavy air. The on-time arrival of the train up from Atlanta that morning caused no particular excitement in the camp. Locomotives arrived at Big Shanty several times a day, and whatever fascination the gleaming iron horses may have held initially for country boys new to the ranks of the army and the marvels of the railroad, the novelty had worn off long ago. There was little bustle or commotion about the station, apart from the stream of passengers disembarking from the right side of the coaches to head for the breakfast table. They stepped past the muddy flock of ducks, which were quacking and flapping about in standing water next to the siding, and filed through the gate in the picket fence. Mr. Lacy sat in a chair at the front door, a bag of silver held in his lap for making change. The passengers looked forward to the hearty breakfast—twenty-five cents for eggs, grits, biscuits with gravy, flapjacks with butter and sorghum, and hot coffee.[3]

James Andrews stepped down from the left side of the train—the side away from the hotel, facing the army camp—and he had dressed for the occasion. He wore dark slacks and vest under a black Prince Albert coat, his long black beard partially concealing a scarf tied neatly at the clean, wide collar of his white shirt. A heavy gold watch chain stretched across his vest. Emerging from the doorway of the coach, he placed a black stovepipe hat, Abe Lincoln-style, atop his head, and slung a pair of saddlebags—their contents unknown that day and down the years—over his left forearm. The overall impression was that of a Southern gentleman, a man of wealth and authority, a planter perhaps, or a distinguished lawyer riding the circuit, who had left his horse and was continuing his important journey by rail.[4]

Andrews walked slowly but purposefully forward past the three boxcars and the tender to the engine. There was no one in the cab. He turned to William Knight, who was trailing along behind him, and directed him to uncouple the train between the third boxcar and the mail and baggage coach. Knight promptly did so, detaching the mail car and the two passenger coaches to be left behind, laying the coupling pin carefully on the draw bar, and then strolling "leisurely" back up to the engine. "The guard was walking his beat within ten feet of where I pulled the pin," Knight remembered. Meanwhile, Andrews strode forward a few feet past the front of the train to check the railroad ahead and be sure that they were clear to depart. The switches were open, and the tracks were clear to the north as far as he could see, shining in the morning light like the road to glory. That done, Andrews walked back, still unchallenged, to the passenger coach where the other men were anxiously waiting. "The tension was frightful," one would recall. Though it had only been a few moments, it seemed to them that Andrews had been gone an age. He stuck his head into the car and said softly, "Well, boys, I guess it's time to go."[5]

The remaining men stepped off the left side of the train—just as if they were a gaggle of new recruits headed over to the camp to report—but instead walked quietly forward to the boxcars, their doors still standing open. "There was no running, no excitement," Dorsey recalled. The young Ohioan, who had been in the army for eight months but had never been in battle, had promised himself that he would never kill another unless in self-defense or some other justifiable cause. "But now I found myself placed in a position where, if need be, I felt that I could have no regard for any man who might put himself in our way," he wrote years later, reflecting back on the decisive moment at Big Shanty. "We were there to get that engine and meant to have it. As I walked up along the side of that train with my hand on my revolver, for the first time in my life I felt that if a man opposed me, I could shoot him with perfect deliberation." They arrived at the open door of the rearmost boxcar—which would soon be the last car on the now-abbreviated train— and clambered in, "the hindmost shoved and lifted the foremost and were themselves pulled up in turn." All of this unusual activity—the detachment of the passenger cars, the manning of the engine by a crew of strangers, the checking of the tracks and switches forward, and the spectacle of sixteen men climbing into an open boxcar—was done in full view of the Confederate sentries and the camp beyond, yet no one made a challenge, asked a question, or raised an alarm. "The rebel guards who were on duty about the platform did not at first seem to comprehend what was up," Wilson said, "and when it was, alas, too late, looked after us in blank amazement."[6]

Andrews told Knight to take the engine. Knight pulled himself up into the cab, checked the tender—which was nearly full, he noted with satisfaction—drew his knife to cut the conductor's bell-rope running back to the passenger cars, and released the tender brake. He glanced at the circular steam gauge, front center in the cab, and saw that it indicated plenty of pressure. He then took his place at the throttle, leaning out the right-side window to look past the smokestack and check the tracks ahead. Andrews and Wilson Brown joined Knight in the cab of the *General*; Alf Wilson climbed up on one of the forward boxcars to serve as a brakeman. (Locomotives of the era had no brakes per se—trains were slowed and stopped by a combination of engaging a link motion reversing gear on the engine and muscling a hand-brake on the tender or the other cars in the train.) The rest of the men pulled the door to their boxcar shut to guard against any stray musket shots that might be forthcoming.

The *General* stood hissing and ready. "All right," Andrews said to his engineer. "Let her go."

Knight pulled the throttle to the engine wide open. "It seemed for a second that everything stood still," he said.[7]

*T*he Western & Atlantic railroaders had jumped down off the engine and walked the forty feet to Lacy's Hotel, stopping on the front porch to wash their oily hands with soap and water in battered pans, drying off on large roller towels flanking the doorway. The schedule was tight; there was no time to lose if they wanted to get something to eat. They each handed a quarter to Mr. Lacy at the door and no doubt received a kind word in return as they entered the dining room, where "Mrs. Lacy presided at the head of the table in a most home-like fashion." Breakfast had been made ready for the train's arrival, and hungry passengers and crew sat right down to eat. Coffee was poured, eggs and grits ladled, and gravy spooned on still-steaming biscuits. "The meals were invariably tabled hot," Mr. Lacy's daughter Mrs. J.B. Seawell would remember fondly, "and grace was always said."[8]

But the blessing's "Amen" had hardly been spoken when the morning began to come unraveled for the crew of the *General*. They sat at a table with a view through the front window toward the railroad track—Fuller near the end of the table, with Cain and Anderson on his right and Murphy directly across from them. The four men had just started to eat when they heard a sudden hard *chuff!* from the engine outside. "This did not attract our attention particularly, but happening to glance out the window at the end of the room, I saw the engine going down the road," Murphy later said. "I yelled to Fuller, 'Someone is running off with your train!'" And here, at the outset of what would come to be known as the Great Locomotive Chase, begins an undisguised and somewhat unseemly battle for credit for the accomplishment of chasing and capturing Andrews and his men. For Fuller would recall the situation differently—the conductor would claim that it was he, not Murphy, who "heard the engine 'exhaust' very rapidly and suddenly," and that he alerted Cain and Murphy: "Someone who has no right to has gone off with our train!" (In another interview, Fuller would claim that he simply told his coworkers that something was wrong with the engine.) This would be the first of many conflicts of recollection between Murphy, who would regard his role as substantial but view the entire episode as a collaborative effort, and Fuller, who would in the years to come increasingly view himself as the sole hero of the day, with all others playing supporting and subordinate roles.[9]

Whoever first saw the train departing and raised the alarm, a great commotion ensued, according to Murphy, and "consternation reigned" in the little dining room. Passengers and crewmen crowded to the door and saw that the train had been divided, the mail car and two passenger cars standing idle before them on the tracks, the faces of a few forlorn passengers who had stayed in the coaches peering out the windows. "What was the cause, and by whom was the engine moved? was asked by many voices," Murphy recalled. He immediately asked Fuller about the large number of men who had embarked at Marietta, and the conductor confirmed that the men had tickets to Big Shanty or points beyond. Fuller rushed out the door to the tracks and asked one of the guards who had taken the train. The bewildered sentry replied that he did not know, but that he was a tall man with a thick dark beard, wearing a black military overcoat and a cape. Thinking of the warnings they had had about deserters from Camp McDonald, Fuller and Murphy immediately supposed that the thieves were nothing more than fugitives from the camp, who would run the engine until it ran out of steam and then abandon it.[10]

The two railroaders quickly agreed that under the circumstances, it was their duty to go after the engine as best they could. Their options at that point, however, seemed somewhat limited. The nearest telegraph office was more than seven miles away, back in Marietta. The nearest locomotive was probably more than twenty miles off. Still, they were determined to act. "We didn't know what to do at first, but it wouldn't do to stand there," Murphy said.

About that time, Lemuel Kendrick, a railroad contractor who also happened to be the local postmaster and the wealthiest landowner in the Big Shanty area—it was Kendrick who had owned the trackside hotel that was now under lease to George Lacy—came down the hill and joined the milling confusion. Murphy asked Kendrick to get a horse and ride south to Marietta and telegraph the superintendent of the road in Atlanta to let him know what had happened. Kendrick mounted up quickly and was soon galloping southward to raise the alarm.

In the meantime, Bill Fuller had broken into a run, heading north up the tracks from the station. "This seemed to be funny to some of the crowd standing around by the hotel there," the conductor remembered, "but it wasn't so to me." He didn't see what else he could do—as the conductor, the engine was his responsibility—and by the time he had reached the switch a hundred yards away, he had made up his mind to chase the train down on foot or to give out trying. Looking back, he saw the two older men, Murphy and Cain, following behind him. (The fireman Andrew Anderson, for whatever reason, remained behind; no explanation or excuse for his nonparticipation has ever been given.) Numerous witnesses would record the scene, more a slapstick comedy than a suspenseful drama—the three desperate railroad men sprinting off amid the laughter and jeers of the crowd, chasing after a train that had "shot out lively" and disappeared from sight some minutes before. As for assistance, other than Kendrick's run southward on horseback, there was little aid to be had. The large numbers of uniformed men and other spectators standing around the tracks by that time were more full of suggestions than of actual help. "Get a horse," one among the crowd yelled after Fuller. "Telegraph for an engine," said another. One of the soldiers asked in amazement as the conductor ran past, "What? Are you going after that train on foot?"

"Yes," Fuller called back over his shoulder.

He heard the reply as he left Big Shanty and its useless guards behind him. "What a damned fool," the soldier said.[11]

*I*n his enthusiasm, Will Knight had yanked the throttle too hard, causing the wheels of the *General*, with an initial puff of smoke and hiss of steam, to spin and slip on the wet rails before the locomotive lurched into motion. "But this was an instant only," Pittenger said. "None of the nearby soldiers had time to raise their muskets or give an alarm before the wheels 'bit' and the train shot away." Rolling out past the switches and sidings and out of Big Shanty, Knight stuck his head out the window of the cab for a look back. "I could see the trainmen and passengers coming out pell mell," he remembered, "but I can say they got out just in time to be left behind." Alf Wilson would infuse the scene with even more drama, writing later that "several squads of soldiers, with their guns, started for us on the dead run, yelling like wild Comanches." The soldiers, when they saw that the train was pulling away, "came to a halt and opened a lively musketry fire on us," according to Wilson. This apocryphal story—the first of many elaborations that would surround the day's events—was not true; in fact, no body of Rebel soldiers gave chase, no shots were fired at all, and the prevailing reaction back at Big Shanty was abject confusion rather than maniacal pursuit.[12]

After boarding the boxcar, the sixteen raiders sitting in the dark in the back of the train suffered a long moment of "intense suspense" as they waited for the train to move. "Then came a pull, a jar, a clang, and we were flying away on our perilous journey," Pittenger recalled. For the group of Federal raiders, this was a giddy moment. They had been told by Andrews that the theft of the train itself would be the greatest difficulty, and that the rest of the day's work would be easy. "It was a moment of rapture such as will never return," Pittenger said. "To seize a train of cars in an enemy's camp, surrounded by thousands of soldiers, and carry it off without a shot fired or an angry gesture, was a marvellous achievement." Al Dorsey's spirits were equally high as they rolled out of range of any possible gunfire. "All nature smiled in sympathy with us," he later wrote. "The trees by the roadside seemed to wave us Godspeed, and to clap their hands for joy, while the scream of our engine seemed to be a shout for the Union!" He literally jumped for joy, drawing his revolver and waving it over his head.

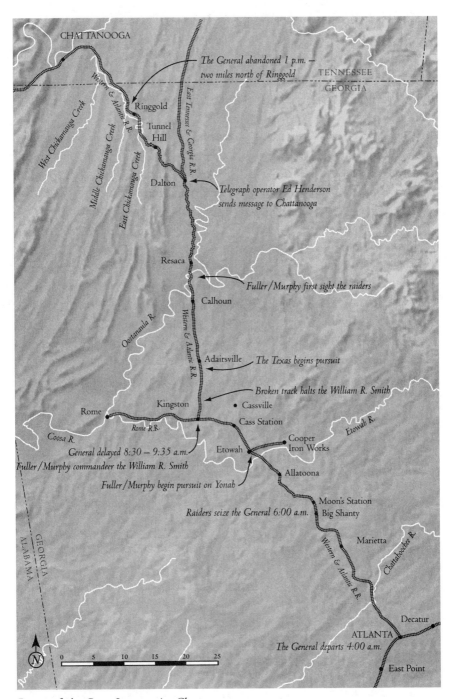

Route of the Great Locomotive Chase.

"Thank God, boys! We're done playing Reb!" he cried. "We're blue-bellied Yankees again!"

George Wilson, the oldest and maybe the wisest of the party, put a stop to this. He too was pleased with the clean getaway thus far, but saw no reason to get carried away. "Don't be so fast, now," he chided the younger man. "We are not out of the woods yet."

No sooner had the elder Wilson said those words when the engine began to lose steam, and the train slowly lost momentum and rolled to a full and unexplained stop. "We were not yet far from camp," Pittenger noted. "There had been just one burst of speed, and then this sickening and alarming failure of power." The worried men in the boxcar asked those posted on the engine what was going on, and were told that the steam had gone down. There was, for a moment, general and understandable consternation as the crew scrambled about the stalled *General* attempting to diagnose its ailment. "This engine gave us wings," Pittenger said, remembering the moment years later, "but if it should be disabled no valor of ours could beat back the hosts about us, no skill could elude their rage." A quick check revealed a simple cause—a damper had been left open, causing a leak of steam and commensurate loss of power with every stroke of the cylinders. Closing the damper and stoking the fire to rapidly address this lack of pressure, Knight soon had the *General* under way again.[13]

A little less than two and a half miles north of Big Shanty, the raiders soon came to a solitary freight platform known to W&A railroaders as Moon's Station. Nearby, a section gang of track hands was at work repairing a siding switch. The crew's foreman Jackson Bond heard a train approaching ahead of the established timetable, and he immediately checked his watch. "Something must be wrong," he told his crew. He was puzzled by the ahead-of-schedule arrival of the *General*, conspicuously lacking any passenger coaches behind it, and was downright concerned by the lack of familiar faces in the cab. He was well acquainted with Andy Anderson and Jeff Cain, who always greeted him when the train passed, but neither man was visible that day. Instead, a blond man he did not know stood at the throttle, with a tall, black-bearded man next to him. In later years, Bond would assert that the strangers on the train simply "turned their backs and did not stop," but other accounts make clear that the raiders paused just long enough to borrow some tools from the section gang before proceeding unhindered on their way. Wilson Brown jumped down from the engine and asked one of the track hands for a crowbar, which the man promptly and gullibly handed over.[14]

Raiders, John Morehead Scott, left, and John Alfred Wilson. (*Colonel James G. Bogle Collection*)

Shortly after passing Bond's work crew, James Andrews ordered the train stopped so that they could inspect the engine, stick close to the train's regular schedule, and cut the telegraph wires running parallel to the railroad line. Sergeant John M. Scott was detailed for the destruction of the wires, which stood a few feet from the tracks on twenty-foot-high wooden poles. Born in Stark County, Ohio, Scott was a handsome, athletic man of twenty-three, having married his sweetheart Rachel Davis back in September, just three days before he enlisted along with his younger brother James. Alf Wilson later wrote that Scott was "one of the best men in our party . . . a good soldier, quiet, determined, persevering and brave." Although he was one of only three sergeants among the group of Third Division volunteers for the secret mission—the rest were privates and corporals—Scott may well have been a fairly reserved fellow, the kind who seems to glide through events without making much of an impression. None of the surviving raiders, including those who would spend the rest of their lives writing about the episode, discuss Sergeant Scott in detail at any point before, during, or after the raid itself—except for his part in cutting the railroad wires. This he accomplished with all the "agility, intrepidity, and daring for which he was noted," according to a fellow soldier. Scott scampered up the pole lickety-split, like a squirrel up a tree, knocking the insulating box off the pole and then swinging down to the ground. His comrades found a small saw on the engine, which they used to sever the wire. At a later point that day, Scott would instead tie the telegraph wires fast to the rear boxcar as the train resumed its travel north. "The way we yanked down the telegraph poles and tore the wire loose when we started up, was frightful to behold," Wilson recalled.[15]

Meanwhile, the engineers Knight and Brown closely inspected the engine, and found it well-oiled and in excellent running condition. Andrews, beaming in triumph and excitement, walked among the raiders pumping their hands and crowing, somewhat uncharacteristically, about the advantage they now held. "When we've passed one more train," he declared, "the coast will be all clear for burning the bridges and running on through to Chattanooga and around. For once, boys, we've got the upper hand on the Rebels." The men dragged and piled a number of cross-ties across the track, partly to obstruct anyone trying to follow; but also because at this early stage, they felt that they had time to kill.

Despite all the later fame surrounding the speedy, reckless, desperate locomotive chase, Andrews in fact was in no particular hurry in the first few hours following the theft of the *General*. On the contrary, he thought it important—even imperative—that the raiders not exceed the average speed of sixteen miles per hour and that they adhere as closely as possible to the train's regular northbound schedule. Realizing his engineer's natural and understandable desire to run the locomotive all-out, Andrews specifically directed Knight to keep his speed down. After all, he had nothing to fear from pursuit behind—there was no telegraph and no locomotive available in that direction, he believed, and any effort to pursue on foot or on horseback would be a ragtag effort through rough terrain and would be too slow to catch the retreating train in any event. The obstacles he feared were those ahead. Except for the sidings available at certain stations, the Western & Atlantic was a single-track line for its entire distance—essentially a one-lane street with two-way traffic. By sticking to the regular schedule as they drove the *General* up the line, Andrews hoped to pass a "down" freight train on the sidings at the large station at Kingston and avoid drawing the suspicion of station masters and other trains until they were north of the Etowah River. The two other southbound trains he expected to encounter further up the line could be dealt with later—some would later say that Andrews had specific plans for passing these, as he knew their schedule and could ascertain their position at any given time; while others supposed he simply planned to "try his luck" once he got past the Etowah. In any event, instead of hurrying, Andrews and his men took their sweet time in the morning mist as they made this first deliberate stop. "We seemed to have things all our own way," Dorsey later wrote, "calmly moving along as if we were to have no opposition, little dreaming of the awful storm that was gathering around us."[16]

*B*ack in Marietta, Lem Kendrick clattered up to the depot on a lathered horse, delivering the news from Big Shanty like a Peach State Paul Revere. There he saw that a northbound freight train, drawn by the locomotive *Pennsylvania*, had not yet left the station. Kendrick shouted to the conductor Franklin Crawford, calling for him to hold the train while he ran inside the telegraph office and sent an urgent message to Atlanta. His wire reached E.B. Walker, superintendent of the W&A, informing him of the shocking theft of the *General*. Walker immediately responded by directing Crawford to take the *Pennsylvania* to Big Shanty, load up with soldiers there, and pursue the stolen train. Nothing would come of this—for whatever reason, it took most of the morning to get the train to Big Shanty and organize a group of soldiers to undertake what turned out to be a rather lackadaisical pursuit. (This was just as well, since the train could not have made it past the Etowah River anyway unless and until track broken by the raiders could be repaired.) In any event, it was after noon that day before they were ready to move out. By that time, the Great Locomotive Chase would already be over.

Word of the mysterious theft of a train spread quickly through the station and then the streets of Marietta, and John Porter and Martin Hawkins, still biding their time near the depot, soon heard the news. The townsfolk said that the feat had been accomplished "so quickly and easily that they could not imagine who did the deed or what it meant," Porter recalled. "Soon everything was wild with excitement, and the town was thronged with excited rebels, waiting to hear further developments regarding the 'wild train,' as it was termed." The two wayward Ohioans agreed to head out into the countryside. "In this we succeeded," Porter said, "and after reaching a piece of woods we came together, congratulated ourselves upon our success thus far, but what to do next we hardly knew."[17]

*T*he raiders reboarded the train after severing the telegraph wires and resumed their progress, gently turning to the northwest, descending the downgrade from Big Shanty and clattering on past the little depot in the village of Acworth. "Those on the engine were very much amused, as we ran by station after station, to see the passengers come up with their satchels in their hands, and then shrink back in dismay as we sped past without a sign of halting," Pittenger recalled. Six more miles and a broad curve back to due north, threading its way along a ridgeline between Crocker's and Pumpkin Vine Creeks, brought the train to the imposing mountain pass at Allatoona. The railroad stretched past an unimpressive depot, a little white grocery, and several wooden outbuildings before slicing through the high ridge in a deep V cut in the rock. (Two years later, Sherman would take one look at this formidable position and immediately decide to outflank rather than attack the place.) Alf Wilson would recall a small station engine standing on the siding at Allatoona, its crew eyeing the *General* and its boxcars suspiciously as it rolled through the gap without stopping.

It may have been the sight of this unidentified engine that caused Andrews to decide to take steps to ensure once and for all that no train could follow the *General* from the south. Shortly after Allatoona, he called another halt, and the men disembarked to again cut the wire—and this time, to pry up a rail from the tracks. This turned out to be a tall order. In what Southerners would later point to as a prime example of Yankee foresight and planning, the Union soldiers on the brilliant secret mission to destroy the Western & Atlantic Railroad had brought no equipment whatsoever with which to tear up railroad track. The raiders lacked pinch-bars, hammers, or any other tools for pulling spikes and had to make do with their borrowed crowbar, wooden cross-ties, and their bare hands. Several men lined up to work at a single rail. They pulled, pried, battered, and bent the rail, taking more than a few minutes to loosen it from the ties and yank it free. The effort, Pittenger later admitted, was "far from easy," and he thought that "it required no prophet to foretell that if we did not procure better tools rail-lifting would have to be used very sparingly in our programme." Despite the difficulty, however, the resulting break in the road made the raiders feel even more secure in themselves and confident in their future prospects. The gap they created would present a barrier to pursuing trains "as absolute as a burnt bridge," Pittenger believed. "The feeling of security after such obstruction was very delightful and not unwarranted."[18]

In the meantime, Knight borrowed a red handkerchief from Andrews and tied it to a small staff on the right side of the cowcatcher to make a serviceable flag. The red flag was a universal signal for danger, usually indicating that another "extra" train was following behind or that the rail was otherwise obstructed. This would hopefully provide some excuse for the *General's* progress slightly ahead of the schedule of the morning train, and might offer some unspoken explanation for the lack of passenger and baggage cars in the shortened train. This done, Knight returned to his post up in the cab. Back behind, the other soldiers loaded their liberated rail onto one of the boxcars and climbed back aboard to continue on their way.[19]

The road from Allatoona slanted in a steep downgrade to the banks of the Etowah River about five miles ahead. The *General* click-clacked easily down the slope and around a sweeping turn known as McGuire's Curve before coming in sight of the broad river. With headwaters in the north Georgia mountains near Dahlonega, the Etowah flows in a sidewinder's path 140 miles to the southwest through the highlands to Rome, where it joins the Oostenaula River to form the Coosa. Writing in his diary two years later, Sherman would describe the Etowah River as "the Rubicon of Georgia." The tracks of the W&A crossed the broad river on an impressive 620-foot span, a bridge William Fuller would later describe as "one of the best and most important bridges on the road." Deep wooden trusses bridged the rushing waters below on five large stone piers, the ruins of which still stand in the river today. The *General* and its shortened train glided smoothly across the great bridge, slowing as it reached the other side.

As they rolled across the Etowah, Andrews had to be pleased with his progress to this point. The bold Kentuckian and his men had stolen the train unhindered, had suffered no casualties, had severed the telegraph, had blocked and broken the track behind them, and had encountered no opposition whatsoever, apart from curious gazes of the train crews and track hands they had passed along the way. They were already almost twenty miles from Big Shanty and had reached and crossed the first of two major rivers on the line. It was not yet eight o'clock in the morning; it seemed that time, like everything else, was on their side. "Hitherto everything had worked exactly as we had calculated," Pittenger recalled, "and our confidence in our leader and in ultimate success was correspondingly increased." But Andrews's look of satisfaction faded to a frown as the train chugged over the bridge and reached the opposite bank. There on a side track in the mist stood an unscheduled and unexpected locomotive.

The siding peeled off to the right of the main line and led to a five-mile spur running east to the Etowah Manufacturing and Mining Company, known to the locals as Cooper's Iron Works. Mark Anthony Cooper was a sad-eyed, sixty-one-year-old pioneer industrialist and reformed politician who had been struck by the "grand scenery and water power" of the Etowah district when he came through on a campaign visit years before. Not only was the landscape beautiful, with rushing waters and a thick, verdant forest of poplar, hickory, pine, elm, and sweet gum trees, but it also rested upon one of the great iron ore deposits in the United States. Cooper bought an interest in a small furnace in the late 1840s and established the so-called Etowah Railroad running from the W&A to his mills in 1858. His business thrived, and by the start of the Civil War, Cooper was renowned as the "Iron Man of Georgia," employing approximately 600 people in his iron works, nail factory, rolling mill, and flour mill, most of them living in the nearby town of Etowah. Having produced iron for the rails of the Western & Atlantic, the Macon & Western, and the Georgia Railroad in prewar years—as well as for the bars of the state penitentiary—Cooper's furnaces and mills now not only produced several tons per week of pig and bar iron, nails, and railroad implements, but also were under contract to provide arms for the Confederacy. In recent months, the works had been forging steel for fearsome "war knives," as well as the heads of the pikes shouldered by recruits back at Big Shanty. Cooper was a prescient businessman—he would sell his mills and foundries to the Confederate government in 1863, just in time for them to be captured and burned by Sherman's army a year later. Unfortunately, ignoring the advice of his banker, he accepted the $400,000 purchase price in soon-to-be-worthless Confederate bonds. "I was not willing to speculate on the misfortunes of the country, nor was I willing to place my affairs in such a condition as would make it appear that I doubted the Confederacy," he later said in defense of this decision.

Cooper had recently leased from the stables of the Western & Atlantic a yard engine to use in running iron, coal, and other materials up and down the tap line from his works and in switching boxcars to and from the main road. Transportation of goods via this railroad spur was a considerable improvement over the old days, when some twenty tons of freight per day had to be hauled by horse-drawn wagons from the mills to the depot. The rented locomotive was old No. 10, the *Yonah*—from the Cherokee word for "bear"—and it was hard at work that Saturday morning on the siding near the river, a column of smoke billowing up from the stack into the slate-gray sky. Like the *General*, the *Yonah* was a Rogers-built 4-4-0, a rusty but comparable engine, and though it was one of the oldest engines in service in the state, it had compiled a solid record of reliable runs up and down the W&A before being passed into private service.[20]

For the raiders, this potential rival presented what they would later remember as "the first serious cause for anxiety" that day. For here was a locomotive, already under steam and apparently similar to their own, that was not reflected on the W&A's regular schedules and was entirely unknown to Andrews—yet there it stood, apparently conjured up in the mist, "looking as if it were ready to enter upon a race with our *General* on equal terms." A small group of men milled about the engine—a couple there to man the engine itself, others probably loaders, foundry men, or millworkers down from the iron works. This gathering was probably insufficient to give battle if it should come to that, but the smattering of men certainly seemed capable of running the engine to give chase or raise an alarm.

Knight cast a glance at the *Yonah* as he rolled the *General* on past without stopping, and like the others he was concerned, no matter how old and worn the switch engine looked. The engineer was always one to speak his mind, and today would be no different. Jerking his head at the locomotive hissing on the siding next to them, he said to Andrews, "We had better destroy that engine, and that bridge with it."

No one knows what Andrews was thinking at that moment. Perhaps he was still flush with the excitement of the morning's earlier triumphs; or maybe he envisioned further damage to the track ahead that would render any locomotive pursuit impossible. Or maybe he simply believed what he had told the Ohio volunteers: that the greatest challenge of the day would be to reach and take the engine—after that, success was certain. "It would have been," Pittenger would later assert, "but for unforeseen contingencies." When it came down to it, the bearded spy was much more concerned with obstacles up the road than he was with being run down from behind. Stealth and stifled communications had worked well to this point, and he planned to keep up appearances for as long as possible. Having avoided any argument, alarm, or clash of arms thus far, Andrews saw no reason to reveal his intentions for the sole purpose of disabling a locomotive that would soon be left behind in any event. Whatever his reasoning, he chose to avoid confrontation and to continue on their way.

Andrews looked back at the *Yonah*, turned to his engineer and shook his head. "It won't make any difference," he said.

"But we found out before night," Knight recalled years later, "that it made all the difference in the world."[21]

The Western & Atlantic Railroad at Allatoona Pass, Georgia. (*Colonel James G. Bogle Collection*)

CHAPTER SEVEN

The Crookedest Road Under the Sun

Etowah to Kingston

> While they were in ecstacies of joy at their good fortune, I was plodding along after them through the mud on foot.
>
> —William A. Fuller

FOR WILLIAM FULLER, ANTHONY MURPHY, and Jeff Cain, the Great Locomotive Chase started out as an arduous trial of footspeed, endurance, and shoe leather. Perhaps embarrassed that someone had taken the train under his charge without so much as an angry word of protest, the young conductor gave the effort all he had. "I ran two and a half miles," he later wrote, "and when I say run, I don't mean trot, gallop or pace. I mean run." The mist was hardening by now into a soft but definite rain, and the limestone mud between the tracks clung heavily to Fuller's boots as he plodded up the line. He was well aware of the long odds against him—he knew, of course, that he had no chance of chasing down a speeding engine on foot and taking it away from a large detachment of desperate and presumably armed men. (It was probably just as well that he failed to catch up with the stalled raiders when their steam went down just north of Big Shanty, as they presumably would have filled him full of lead.) Yet several things went through his mind that gave him comfort, if not confidence, as he started off in pursuit. Years later, he would remember analyzing the situation as he started out, his mind working as fast as his legs—"as I ran, I thought, and I thought as fast as I ran, and I ran as fast as I could," he said.

First of all, Fuller was in excellent physical condition for the trial ahead, and he knew it. He had run miles and miles of railroad line in his time as a flagman and brakeman on the W&A, so he was certain that his lungs and legs would hold out until he could enlist some help. Second, he was intimately familiar with the road, its stations, and its repair crews—and he knew that Jackson Bond's section gang was working less than three miles to the north at Moon's Station. (And happily, the route from here to there was almost all downhill.) Failing that, he would try to find a horse that he could mount and ride to Etowah, eighteen miles up the line. Finally, he supposed that the men who took the train were cowardly and inexperienced skulkers who wanted nothing more than to run the train away from Camp McDonald so they could escape from the ranks. He would probably come upon the abandoned train any minute, standing idle and empty.[1]

What he found instead at Moon's Station, after a run of more than two miles, was Bond's work crew, milling about with their hands in their pockets and their mouths agape, still in surprise and confusion at the conduct of the group of strangers that had passed almost a half hour before.

Bond would remember Fuller coming up in "breathless haste," asking, "How long has that train been gone?"

"Thirty minutes," Bond replied.

"In a hurry," Fuller recalled, "they told me that the captors of the train had stopped there and taken their tools from them, and that there were about twenty of them, all strangers, and working in great haste." For Fuller, this news dispelled any notion that the thieves were deserters hoping to dash past the guards and make their way home without leave. At that point, he remembered years later, he became fully convinced of the "true character" of the men who had stolen the *General*. "I knew it must be a Yankee trick," he said, "and from thence forward I doubled my determination."[2]

Fuller first mentioned getting a horse to continue his chase, but the foreman Jackson Bond pointed out another alternative. One valuable piece of the section gang's equipment was still nearby—a hand car used by the workers to move cross ties, spikes, and other materials up and down the road. The little maintenance vehicle is more accurately described as a pole-car. There were no crank or lever "seesaw"-type cars in those days on the W&A; instead, hand cars were propelled using long poles. The track hands would stand on either side of the cart and push off the ties in a manner not unlike a boatman in a Venetian gondola. After a quick explanation, Fuller and Bond's men lifted the car onto the main track for the pursuit northward.

Joining Fuller for the continued chase up the road were Anthony Murphy and Jeff Cain, just now coming up from Big Shanty. Here again, there is a minor but telling discrepancy between Fuller's and Murphy's accounts of what happened. Fuller would contend that he had to backtrack southward with the hand car to pick up his two lagging companions, going so far as to claim that he found them "walking along rather unconcernedly." Murphy, however, while acknowledging that Fuller "was ahead," would maintain that the men for the most part stuck together as they proceeded north—"we jogged along, and various opinions were expressed by each," he said. The contrast is also stark between the first-person-singular account of the conductor (Fuller would later write, "*I* found a gang of track hands" and "*I* put the hand-car on the track") and Murphy's description of a collaborative effort ("*We* pressed into service their car").[3]

In any event, they were now rolling instead of plodding, and the hopes of the railroaders lifted. They knew, of course, that the *General* and its captors were miles away by now—Fuller would tell an Atlanta newspaper just after the chase, "you know I could not have expected, with a hand-car, to overtake the raiders, now desperate and in the possession of a first-class engine and many miles ahead"—but he now felt they had a chance. Their next goal would be the station at the Etowah River and the spur line up to Cooper's ironworks. Fuller and Murphy were aware of the yard engine there; they knew that if it was at the station and under steam, they could improve their time. "This, in fact, was my only hope," Fuller admitted. Meanwhile, the *General* was still a few minutes ahead of the regular schedule. As a result, opposite rail traffic coming down from the north may slow the captured engine long enough for the pursuers to make up some ground. They would then have a locomotive of their own; they could gather reinforcements, try to telegraph an alarm, perhaps even arm themselves. But all of this would be possible and meaningful only if the engine turned out to be there; "if she was down from the works we would have means of following on," Fuller said, "if not, we were too near fagged out to have gone further." Etowah was a one-horse town, and the only horse was the *Yonah*.[4]

Bond and at least one of his crewmen joined Fuller, Murphy, and Cain on the hand car, and the trainmen, still winded from their two-mile run, were content to let the muscular rail workers provide the propulsion for awhile. Foregoing poles, the track hands sat at the corners of the car and pushed with their feet against the railroad ties, switching sides when their legs began to throb. The rhythmic kicking and the predominant downhill grade allowed the men to build up a "lively rate of speed," which soon brought them just short of Acworth, where they found several dozen crossties piled on the track and a telegraph pole and wires torn down and sliced through. "This changed our minds as to the deserters, for if they were, they meant more than we first expected," Murphy recalled.[5]

Coming to the station at Acworth, the W&A men learned from witnesses that the engine had paused but a moment there, as the engineer examined the journals, carefully oiled the engine, and then "moved off lively." Fuller and Murphy called a brief halt at the depot, catching their breath while they sought out arms and reinforcements. They were able to scrounge up two old double-barreled shotguns. Borrowing these rusty guns perhaps engendered some renewed confidence and boldness among the pursuers, though they would provide little in the way of actual help. The two men would never have an occasion to fire them that day—indeed, Fuller would later admit, "I didn't have time all day to examine mine to see whether or not she was loaded." The railroaders also rounded up additional manpower, in the form of Steven Stokely and Martin Rainey, two local men who stopped off to grab their rifles before squeezing onto the crowded platform of the push-car. Concerned that the raiders may have destroyed a small bridge coming up between Acworth and Allatoona, Fuller also dispatched a man named White Smith to ride up ahead on horseback in an effort to cut off the raiders and spread the alarm. The ragtag posse then reboarded the little pole-car and resumed the northward chase, soon passing Allatoona—where Smith gave up his horse and rejoined the others—and on toward the Etowah River. "On we pressed and pushed, every now and then being thrown in a ditch by the absence of a rail taken up by the raiders," Fuller said. Others along for the ride agree this happened once, sending the *General*'s crew and the track hands tumbling off the track. Years later, Fuller would claim rails were taken up at three or more points between Big Shanty and Etowah, though this recollection does not square with the accounts of the raiders—who claimed that they dislodged only one rail at this stage—or the recollection of Murphy and Bond, who would describe only one derailment of the handcar.[6]

This unwelcome interruption occurred as the car crested the hill within sight of Etowah, picking up speed as it rolled down the long grade to the river below. "Working and pushing and hurrying and overcoming all difficulties and hindrances, we finally came in sight of the station," Fuller wrote. To their great delight, the railroaders could see the *Yonah* standing at the station on the other side of the river, smoke boiling from its stack. The engine had not yet departed for the ironworks—they had made it to Etowah just in time. "God bless her," Fuller cried, "she is a fast one!" Just then, however, they noticed a break in the rails ahead—but it was too late to stop. "We were making good time as we neared the place where we intended to bid farewell to our little friend, the pole car, when suddenly we beheld an open space in the track," Murphy recalled. The primitive handcar had no brake to slow it down, and it plunged "pell-mell" into the gap. Some of the crew were able to jump clear at the last minute, but the others aboard tumbled painfully off the grade and into a ditch, which was partially filled with water from the week's worth of rain. Steve Stokely fell headlong from the car, burying the barrel of his long rifle nine inches deep in the mud. The railroaders and their little posse scrambled up the muddy bank, wet and shaken, but unhurt. "We were too much elated at the sight of the engine, not more than a mile distant, to be deterred by a catastrophe so insignificant," Fuller said. They heaved the car out of the ditch, carried it across the gap, and placed it back on the tracks, leaving one of the track hands to run back to the next section gang to warn them of the break and to see to its repair. "We pushed with a vim," Fuller recalled.[7]

The pursuers clacked down the hill and crossed the bridge "without incident"—without further incident, anyhow—and came to the station on the other side. The *Yonah* was on the turntable, its tender standing nearby on a side track. Fuller and the others abandoned the pole car and hastily explained themselves to the engineer and crew of the *Yonah*. All the men then began the laborious process of rotating the engine on the turntable and hitching it up to the tender, all of which had to be done by human hands. As the locomotive was made ready, Murphy saw that railroad ties, rails, tools, and other implements were loaded up on a flatcar to bring along with them.

The railroaders bent to their work with renewed purpose. Fuller would proudly remember this first stretch of the pursuit, which he would later describe as an effort made "on foot, for more than twenty-three miles, save the poor assistance of an old timber car, which cost more labor to push it up grade than was recompensed in the run down grade." This characterization of the chase thus far was a bit inflated—the distance from Big Shanty to Etowah was sixteen miles, not twenty-three; of that, only a little over two miles had been covered "on foot"; and much of the "labor" to push the pole car had been provided by strong-legged track workers. Despite the temptation in later years to gild the lily, however, no one could doubt that it was Fuller's determination alone that had put the pursuers in a position to run down the thieves who had stolen his engine. Fuller, Murphy, and Cain swung aboard the *Yonah*, taking along a few scattered Confederates who had been waiting at the station, ready to continue their chase on something close to equal terms. "I took charge of the *Yonah*," Fuller later wrote, and "in three minutes she was literally flying over the track in pursuit of the Raiders."[8]

Some folks must have thought Wilson Lumpkin was crazy, when in the 1820s the well-known Georgia congressman started talking about his desire to build a railroad from the banks of the Chattahoochee River up to southeastern Tennessee—essentially, from nowhere to nowhere. Born in Virginia at the tail end of the Revolutionary War, Lumpkin had moved as a child to Wilkes (soon to be Oglethorpe) County in northeast Georgia and an early life marked by frontier hardships and clashes with what he called "hostile and savage Indian neighbors." Following in the footsteps of his attorney father, Lumpkin farmed and taught school before passing the bar and then winning a seat in the state legislature in 1804. He was elected to the U.S. Congress four times in the eighteen-teens and -twenties before resigning to run for governor of Georgia. A Democrat and a self-described political moderate, he became most active on and famous (or infamous) for what he regarded as two key issues for the growing state: removal of the Cherokee Indians and improvement of the state's fledgling transportation system.

In his travels, Lumpkin had seen much of the broken country of north Georgia and, undaunted by its granite and limestone ridges, deep defiles, and ubiquitous creeks and runs, reported as early as 1826 his belief that "an excellent route over the rolling hills and through depressions in the mountain range might be had for a railroad to Tennessee at the northwestern corner of Georgia." During his service as Georgia's governor from 1831 to 1835, he continually stressed the importance of "a direct railroad communication connecting the Mississippi and the Atlantic. Such a railroad, if speedily executed, could not fail to give our State a great commercial emporium surpassed by few, if any one, on the entire Atlantic." In the meantime, a passion for railroad building had swept the young nation, and Governor Lumpkin went from being scorned as an impractical dreamer to being hailed as the father of Georgia's railroads. The idea of building a state-owned road gained political momentum throughout Lumpkin's gubernatorial term, and on December 21, 1836, the Georgia legislature passed a joint resolution establishing the Western & Atlantic Railroad—the name of the road reflecting the connection they hoped to achieve.[9]

Passing a law was one thing, but getting a route designed, track laid, bridges built, and locomotives steaming through the mountains was something else. Famed explorer, engineer, and inventor Lieutenant Colonel Stephen H. Long, who had surveyed the routes for the already famous Baltimore & Ohio Railroad ten years before, was immediately engaged by the governor as the W&A's first chief engineer. Long and his assistants soon completed a "special examination and survey of the very complicated and multiform region situated between the Chattahoochee and Etowah Rivers," as well as an initial plan for the route continuing through the mountains to the north. A beautiful 1837 map drawn by J.F. Cooper and prepared under Colonel Long's direction depicted the thin dark line of the proposed railroad running from the Chattahoochee River to the Tennessee state line, the route twisting around, across and through a topographical labyrinth spread across Cobb, Cass, Murray, and Walker counties. Long believed that the project held great promise. "The Western & Atlantic Railroad, when viewed in its relation to the natural and artificial channels of trade, and intercourse above considered, is to be regarded as the main connecting link, in the chain or system of internal improvements, more splendid and imposing than any other that has ever been devised in this or any other country," he wrote.

Construction on the line began in 1838 and would continue for the next twelve years, at times interrupted by financial problems, bureaucratic mismanagement, and challenges posed by the daunting terrain. Work crews, consisting of both hired and slave labor, graded the route through an almost pristine wilderness, thousands of acres of woodlands held sacred by the Cherokees until their removal, conducted with the hard-handed support of Governor Lumpkin, a few years before. As construction proceeded, endpoints were established and renamed at each end of the line—Ross's Landing became Chattanooga in 1838, and Marthasville became Atlanta in 1847. By that time, workers were building bridges and steadily laying rails, with rail service being extended as far and as fast as possible upon the completion of sections of the road.

The final result was a true marvel of engineering and railroad construction. The 138-mile route from Atlanta to Chattanooga maintained a ruling grade of less than one percent as it wound through the rocky landscape. To accomplish this, the pathway laid out by Colonel Long was necessarily tortured, the total curvature of the line exceeding 10,000 degrees—or twenty-eight complete circles all told. In his annual report of 1860, Superintendent John W. Lewis proudly described the W&A as "the crookedest road under the sun."[10]

The sixteen Yankees cooped up in the boxcar being pulled by the *General* would have agreed with the superintendent's description as they click-clacked up the road, "scouring past field and village and woodland." The *General* left the banks of the Etowah River behind and drove steadily northward into the thickening forest. Next up was the town of Cartersville, followed by a small wood-and-water station at Cass, and then the junction at Kingston, one of the largest stations on the line, some thirteen miles farther along. The raiders sat uncomfortably on the floor of the boxcar or stood and leaned against the sides, swaying first one way and then the other and struggling to keep their balance as the train frequently slowed for the route's many sharp turns. "We seemed to be running towards every point in the compass," Bill Pittenger recalled. Engineering wonder or not, the Buckeye soldiers found the railroad to be "of the roughest and most difficult character," the track "uneven and in generally bad condition."[11]

Two years later, the north Georgia wilderness was to become a ravaged, fought-over wasteland, the landscape stripped and scarred with trenches and redoubts and the trees cleared by the acre to create fields of fire, as tens of thousands of blue and gray soldiers swarmed southward and picked clean the land like devouring insects. But in the early days of the war, the Cherokee forest was dense and lush, the early golden-green of spring made more vivid that morning by a damp prism of falling mist. The thick blanket of trees around them—a mixture of pine, oak, hickory, maple, poplar, sweet gum, blushed here and there with blooming cherries and dogwoods—was largely unbroken except for an occasional hardscrabble farm and the sinuous river of iron trickling northward. Although they could not see them, the raiders passed close by the Etowah Indian Mounds, a sacred burial place for ancient tribal chiefs hidden in the woods not far from the railroad.

The *General* and its bobtail train rolled into the station at Cartersville, still ahead of schedule, and again chuffed on past the platform without stopping. Cartersville appeared to be a town of "considerable size," and a large number of disappointed passengers were left standing at the depot. "We could hear the engineers chuckling at the chapfallen faces of persons waiting for the train; and we laughed, too," Parrott later said. (The original Cartersville depot still stands today, one of the few original W&A stations still in existence.) Five miles farther on, Knight eased off the steam and tugged the reverse lever, Alf Wilson engaged the brake, and the *General* slowed to a stop at the lonely wood-and-water post at Cass Station.[12]

The nearby town of Cassville was the county seat of Cass County (later Bartow), one of ten original counties carved from former Cherokee Indian territory in the 1830s and populated by white settlers who acquired their parcels through the Cherokee land lottery. Adding insult to the injury suffered by the relocated Cherokees, the new county was named for General Lewis Cass, a renowned Indian fighter who later served as secretary of war under President Andrew Jackson. Cassville soon flourished and by 1850 was not only the largest and most prosperous town in Cherokee Georgia, but was also considered by many to be the cultural center of the entire state. The town boasted a fine courthouse (where many of the legal battles over the fate of the Cherokee Nation took place), two four-year colleges, a well-regarded newspaper, four large churches, several hotels, numerous businesses, and many stately homes. The little railroad station stood two miles outside of the handsome town, more of a trackside woodpile than a full-fledged freight or passenger terminal. The well-to-do citizens of Cassville—concerned about the prospect of steam trains bringing smoke, noise, soot, and questionable characters into their town—had protested the planned route as the railroad was being laid out in the 1840s, and the train station was accordingly moved to the southwest, the tracks then sweeping wide around the village itself. This decision would amount to municipal shortsightedness, however, for as railroad towns across Georgia—from Atlanta to Macon to Augusta to Columbus—would explode in growth and commerce during and after the war, the once-prominent community of Cassville would wither and die, cut off from the railroad vine. Two years later, some three hundred troopers from Sherman's 5th Ohio Cavalry burned Cassville to the ground, leaving only a handful of houses and the town's churches still standing. After the war, with the railroad and seemingly the world passing them by, the city's residents simply saw no reason to rebuild. They voted to move the county seat—and many of them moved themselves and their families—from Cassville to nearby Cartersville.[13]

All of that, of course, was still to come. For now, in early 1862, the little stop at Cass was an important one for engines running on the W&A, as it provided wood and water for the journey further northward into the mountains. Knight handed the appropriate ticket to the stationmaster, and he, Brown and Wilson stepped over to the stacked cords and began to "wood up" in the softly falling rain. The stationmaster's name was William Russell, and he was understandably curious at the unexplained arrival of the abbreviated train, "with no passengers, and none of the regular hands," running well ahead of the regular schedule.

"I don't recollect ever seeing you fellows before," Russell said, gnawing thoughtfully on the stem of his pipe. "What have you got in *there?*" he asked, pointing at the three closed boxcars.

"You just drop a few sparks from that pipe of yours inside and you'll find out soon enough," Andrews replied. He calmly and confidently went on to explain the situation.

Lying like a backwoods politician, the Kentucky spy told the frowning station tender that he had been ordered by no less a personage than Confederate General Pierre Gustave Toutant Beauregard, in command of the gray army at Corinth, Mississippi, in the aftermath of the great battle of Shiloh, to impress a train and load it with ammunition and gunpowder to resupply the desperate Rebel troops. This explained the deviation from the schedule, the absence of passenger cars and the regular crew, the three closed boxcars, and the apparent haste of the strangers who were now refilling the tender. "The very appearance of Andrews, tall, commanding and perfectly self possessed, speaking like one who had long been accustomed to authority, was so much like the ideal Southern officer that Russell's credence was won at once," Pittenger later wrote. The station man, who regularly received news of the war along with batches of other gossip from the crewmen on trains passing up and down the road, was aware of the bloody battle out west and thought it made perfect sense that the hard-pressed Confederate army would need provisions from the arsenals of Georgia under the circumstances. (In fact, as the telegram deciphered by General Mitchel at Huntsville the day before had shown, Beauregard was indeed in dire straits at Corinth needing far more help than a single train could provide.)

Andrews, ever bold, went one step further and asked for a schedule for the Western & Atlantic. Russell cheerfully took down his own timecard and handed it over, saying he would give General Beauregard the shirt off his back if it would do any good. Andrews's cover story had worked and worked well. Russell would later be heard to say, "I would have as soon suspected Mr. Jefferson Davis himself as one who talked with the assurance that Andrews did."[14]

Their tender full and their engine oiled, the disguised Yankees reboarded their train and chugged out of the station. If anyone thought of the possibility of someone following them at this point, no one mentioned it. No obstructions were left on the tracks, and no rails were taken up. They were just seven miles from Kingston, where the regular train coming over from Rome would be waiting for their scheduled passing, and where they would have to wait briefly for a southbound train to come through. The crowded intersection there, the raiders knew, would be "no small obstacle." Still, they were confident in their leader, who had to this point seemed to bypass every challenge with ease and with style. "Andrews had made himself familiar with the minutest working of the road at this point, and also at Dalton and Chattanooga, and we'd soon be able to see how he'd overcome the hindrances in his way," Pittenger said.[15]

The twenty men who stole the *General* were not the only Yankees headed toward Chattanooga that morning on a commandeered Southern train. Unlike Buell following the surrender of Nashville a few months before, General Mitchel had not rested on his laurels after capturing the city that was his initial goal, but instead moved quickly to broaden his gains and take advantage of the open rail line and the locomotives and rolling stock he now controlled. By Friday evening, he had fully outfitted a two-pronged expedition to drive both east and west from Huntsville along the Memphis & Charleston Railroad. The goal to the west was to seize the railroad bridge across the Tennessee River at Decatur, twenty-five miles away. This would secure his flank in that direction and would bring his division close enough to coordinate with Buell's army near Corinth. To the east, the plan was to proceed at least as far as the junction at Stevenson, seventy miles away and within striking distance of the ultimate prize—Chattanooga. What was more, if Andrews's mission worked out as Mitchel hoped and planned, then the astronomer-general could conceivably expect to find the Confederate defenders cut off and paralyzed and the Mountain City ripe for the picking. In any event, on the morning of April 12, 1862, Union soldiers aboard captured trains were driving toward Chattanooga from both the west and the south.

Old Stars and his officers had worked tirelessly on Friday afternoon to get two captured trains assembled and units detailed for the assignment, but it was clear by dusk that at least the eastward run to Stevenson would have to wait until morning. Colonel Joshua Sill's brigade was "placed in cars the same evening, but not being able to secure a trusty engineer, the men were compelled to remain closely packed in these uncomfortable quarters the entire night in that disagreeable state of uncertainty which always exists when one is expecting to start at any moment, but never goes," Lieutenant Angus L. Waddle wrote. "Soon after daylight on Saturday, however, we were off, and a novel train it was." A prominent feature of the train bound east for Stevenson was a platform car on which were placed two cannon, pointing diagonally ahead on each side of the engine——a daunting armament one soldier would remember as formidable in appearance if not in fact. General Mitchel rode in the cab of the locomotive, and Colonel Sill stood on the platform car next to the artillery pieces. Following behind was "a motley collection of passenger, freight and construction cars, all filled with armed men," Waddle recalled. Mitchel considered the movement east to be a hazardous one—first because it was over a longer distance, and second because he knew that civilians and military forces in that direction had been alerted to his approach by a single runaway locomotive that managed to escape the vise at Huntsville the day before. The road wound through a landscape filled with hills and cuts and wooded passes that could easily have concealed any number of gray soldiers in ambush. Accordingly, his train, crowded with soldiers and bristling with guns, moved gingerly down the track at a pace of only seven or eight miles per hour.[16]

Despite this supposed warning and the cautious progress of Mitchel's troop-train, citizens and soldiers in the villages and depots seemed shocked by the sudden and rapid arrival of this blue horde. "When we pulled into a town or station, it was amusing to see the expressions on the inhabitants' faces when they saw the train loaded with Yankee soldiers, as well as interesting to see the drilling squads of enemy soldiers and citizens break up and take to the hills," Private Jacob Adams of the 21st Ohio remembered. The train rolled through Brownsboro, Woodville, Larkinsville, Scottsboro, Bellefonte, and Oak Grove before arriving at Stevenson late on Saturday afternoon. Mitchel and his officers secured the junction, along with five additional locomotives to add to the bounty seized at Huntsville, and then adjourned to a local hotel for coffee and a supper of fried pork and cornbread.[17]

The other mission heading out to the west was conducted by the 24th and 19th Illinois Regiments under the command of Colonel John Basil Turchin. This smaller detail had departed about dusk on Friday night, and arrived near Decatur just before dawn on Saturday. The train rolled across a broad expanse of cotton fields, broken here and there by woods or sparkling creeks, their banks splashed with flowers. Slaves from neighboring farms and plantations soon flocked to the railroad to cheer the Union army and marvel at the spectacle of a train covered in indigo-clad soldiers and prickling with muskets and bayonets. "The negroes were gathered in masses all along the road," one man on the expedition wrote. "As the cars passed they bowed, they scraped, they grinned, they pulled on their hats, and in every way tried to secure a recognition from those they considered their friends. Occasionally a generous hearted soldier would wave his hand or flourish his sword to them, and then their child-like manifestations of delight literally knew no bounds."

Arriving at the impressive railroad bridge across the Tennessee River, just short of Decatur, the blue soldiers drove off a surprised detachment of railroad guards, who attempted to set fire to the bridge as they fled. The Illinois men, "deciding instinctively that it was always proper to do just the opposite of what these scoundrels were about," quickly determined to put out the flames and save the bridge for their purposes. Describing this action in a letter to his fellow Cincinnatian Secretary of the Treasury Salmon P. Chase in Washington—quite as if he had been there in person—Mitchel wrote that "the enemy fired a bridge in our very faces. The flames were extinguished, and rushing across the great Tennessee bridge we drove them from their tents, which they abandoned, leaving their breakfast smoking on the table." Turchin's force pressed on past the Rebel camp and seized the town beyond, driving off the battalion of Confederate cavalry posted there. According to a reporter on the scene, the gray horsemen had recently and frantically departed, "flying helter skelter toward Tuscambia, leaving tents, provisions, sabers and everything, except their precious carcasses, behind them." An old black gentleman standing nearby marveled at the Rebel skedaddle. "Golly, massa," he said to the reporter. "I've seed fast races afore, but neber anyting to equal dat!"[18]

Again suffering no casualties, the Illinoisans had captured the bridge, the railroad junction, the Confederate camp, and the town intact—though the latter was thought to be no great prize. "Decatur is a dilapidated old concern, as ugly as Huntsville is handsome," one underwhelmed Federal soldier wrote in his diary. The men secured the road, posted guards, and set up camp near the river to wait for further instructions. A large canebrake nearby soon provided fishing poles for every soldier in the regiment, who would in the days to come enjoy dinners of fine, large fish pulled from the Tennessee River.

General Mitchel reported his further successes to Buell, again sending a copy to the War Department in Washington, just to be sure that the president and the secretary of war were aware of his continued progress. "The work so happily commenced on yesterday has been completed to-day upon a train of cars captured from the enemy at Huntsville," he wrote. Describing the twin advances east and west from the city, he reported, "Both expeditions proved eminently successful. I accompanied the most difficult one to

Stevenson in person, from which place 2,000 of the enemy fled as usual at our approach without firing a gun, leaving behind five locomotives and a large amount of rolling stock." He noted that he had destroyed the small bridge over Widden's Creek to seal off his flank and keep the enemy from taking advantage of the line north to Nashville. If need be, the span could be replaced in short order, once he had been reinforced and was ready to advance to Chattanooga. "Thus in a single day we have taken and now hold a hundred miles of the great railway line of the rebel Confederacy. We have nothing more to do in this region, having fully accomplished all that was ordered," he wrote. Mitchel made no mention of the secret expedition he had sent down into Georgia early that week, nor did his destruction of the Widden's Creek bridge near Bridgeport seem to suggest that he had any confidence at all that Andrews and his men would soon be arriving from that direction. It was almost Saturday evening—a full day after the date the general and the spy had agreed upon for the planned raid—by the time Mitchel got to Stevenson and Widden's Creek. Andrews should have been here by now—if he was coming at all.[19]

Kingston was the largest station on the Western & Atlantic between Atlanta and Chattanooga and a critical junction on the road. The main line of the W&A curved in a broad lefthand bend to come into the station from the southeast, and a branch road then peeled off in a slow curve to the left, forming a "Y" where the railroad down from Rome, fourteen miles distant, came into the main line. Between the two lines, just after the split, stood the depot, a rustic stone and wood structure, about sixty by twenty feet, with a broad, three-foot-high platform around it on all four sides and a roof overhang that jutted out even with the platform. The building housed the agent's office, a ticket window, and a small waiting room. A few paces beyond the depot was a smaller, rectangular wood structure that contained a modest restaurant, as well as space for storing baggage. Four sidings ran parallel to the main track of the W&A—two on each side of the depot. Past the station buildings, the main line began to curl gently back toward due north, headed into the mountains toward Chattanooga. A couple of hundred yards to the northwest of the station, a disorganized rabble of local militiamen were marching and drilling that Saturday, "busily engaged in mastering the tactics."[20]

The intersection was crowded with men and cars that morning, the early train down from Rome having already arrived. Its engineer was Oliver Wiley

Harbin—"Wiley" to his friends. He was a big man, six foot two, with a thick beard and shining blue eyes—"their frankness," an interviewer later noted, "with his native geniality, at once commend him as one of God's honest men." Now twenty-seven, he had been railroading since the age of fourteen. He had signed on with the Rome Railroad Company in 1859 and would serve as an engineer on the short run from Rome to Kingston for almost thirty years to come. Harbin's regular engine was called the *Albert Shorter*, but that day he was running the *William R. Smith*, named for the wealthy and eccentric president of the road. The *Smith* was a Norris-built locomotive, with a cylinder nine inches in diameter with an eighteen-inch stroke, four-foot six-inch driving wheels, and a large, Radley & Hunter balloon-style stack atop the boiler. The rest of the crew included Cicero Smith, the conductor, William Kernodle, the fireman, and Joe Lassiter, a free black man, who was the train's brakeman and baggage man. Harbin's modest train—the engine, a tender, one baggage car, and one passenger coach—was stopped on the left or south side of the depot, standing partly on one of the sidings and partly on the tail of the "Y" toward Rome. Arriving about shortly after eight o'clock, he had run his train out the north end of the "Y" and backed down to his present position, so that his train was headed north, ready to start the return trip back to Rome. The schedule called for him to wait for the arrival of Bill Fuller's train, which would be bringing the day's mail and perhaps a few passengers up from Atlanta.[21]

Harbin was standing over by the depot, just outside the agent's window, when the *General* pulled in on the main track from the southeast. Something seemed amiss, and then Harbin realized what it was—the train had only boxcars, no mail car and no passenger coaches at all. A blaze of concern and conversation began to spread among the men at the junction. The arrival of this curtailed train instead of the scheduled mixed mail-passenger run was puzzling indeed to the regulars at Kingston station. The engine stopped a short distance past the depot, and a tall, thickly bearded man in a frock coat and a black top hat stepped down from the engine and strode toward the depot. He walked directly up to Harbin and asked if he had a switch key, as he wanted to take a siding to await the local freight from the north. "I have taken this train by government authority to run ammunition through to General Beauregard, who must have it at once," he said. Harbin pointed Andrews to the agent, Uriah Stephens. The spy stepped into Stephens's office, again deploying the tale that he was running ordnance north and then west to Beauregard. The regular passenger train would be along presently, he said.

Andrews inquired why the scheduled down freight had not yet arrived. By way of response, he was handed a telegram, which reported that the freight had been delayed and directed Fuller's train to wait. Andrews emerged from the office with the switch keys in hand. Returning to the *General*, he directed Knight to pull forward, threw the switch, and watched as the train backed down on the siding to the left of the main track. There, he stood on the locomotive with Knight and Brown, and waited.[22]

Some among the raiders would later claim that the engineer of the Rome train at Kingston—Wiley Harbin—had seemed upset and suspicious, muttering an oath and wondering aloud why Cain's engine had arrived with none of its regular crew on board. Interviewed many years later, Harbin would reject this account, saying that if that had happened, he had no memory of it. On the contrary, he pronounced himself entirely "satisfied with what explanations Andrews vouchsafed, and gave him and his train very little notice." Although a number of the raiders would later claim that the powder story "was not well-received by some" and that the station men and train crews at Kingston "seemed to think something was not right," Andrews and his men waited on their siding, uneasy but undisturbed.[23]

It was now about eight-thirty, two hours since Andrews and his men had taken the *General* and fled from Big Shanty. The down freight train was scheduled to pass by soon. Andrews expected that they would be delayed no more than a few minutes.

For the sixteen men cooped up in the dark one of the closed boxcars, sitting silently and doing their best imitation of a load of gunpowder, it was a puzzling and stressful delay. "We could hear low murmurs outside, we knew we were at a station, and alongside another train, and could hear the tread of feet; but we could not learn why we did not press on," Pittenger recalled. "A thousand conjectures will spring up at such times; and the possibilities of our situation were ample enough for all kinds of imagining." Andrews had neglected to appoint any lieutenant or second-in-command to direct the soldiers back behind while he was dealing with obstacles or managing the progress of the train—Pittenger, for one, would later complain of this oversight. In retrospect, he said, this may have been useful in case of a fight, going so far as to retroactively suggest George D. Wilson for the position of "authorized second" (a curious choice, since Wilson was a private and there were three sergeants and one regimental sergeant major present in the boxcar as well).[24]

After almost half an hour, the raiders heard the welcome shriek of the whistle of a train approaching from the northwest, and the local down freight

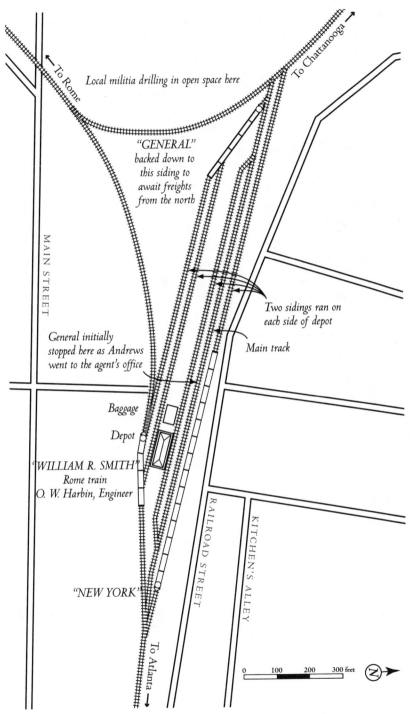

To Rome

To Chattanooga

Local militia drilling in open space here

"GENERAL" backed down to this siding to await freights from the north

MAIN STREET

Two sidings ran on each side of depot

Main track

General initially stopped here as Andrews went to the agent's office

Baggage

Depot

"WILLIAM R. SMITH" Rome train O. W. Harbin, Engineer

RAILROAD STREET

KITCHEN'S ALLEY

"NEW YORK"

To Atlanta

0   100   200   300 feet

N

Traffic at Kingston Station, 8:30 to 9:30 A.M., April 12, 1862.

rumbled in, stopping on the main line next to the depot. The engine was the *New York*—like the *General* a Rogers-built 4-4-0—and it pulled behind it a lengthy train of a dozen or more cars. Andrews immediately walked over from the siding and spoke with the conductor, repeating his story and requesting that the train be pulled to a siding so the *General* could pass. "This conductor saw that Andrews was treated with marked deference by the people about the station, and did not hesitate to believe his story and obey the order," Pittenger said. This would clear the main track—they would soon be on their way. But as the *New York* began grumbling forward to move toward a siding, Andrews noticed a red flag posted on the last car of the train.

"What does this mean?" he demanded of the conductor. "I am ordered to get this powder through to Beauregard at the earliest possible moment, and now you are signaling for another train on the track!"

The trainman apologized, but said that it could not be helped, and he explained why. This Yankee general by the name of Mitchel, you see, had captured Huntsville, and was reportedly moving by forced marches toward Chattanooga with a body of Union troops. There was little force to oppose him, so the railroad was running extra trains southward to move goods and rolling stock out of the threatened city. This was, according to Pittenger, a "startling piece of intelligence"—though it certainly should not have been. Andrews and each of the men along with him knew good and well that the plan had been for Mitchel to do just as he had done. The spy thanked the *New York's* conductor and asked him to move on past, saying emphatically: "I must be off the very first minute that is possible." The conductor pointed out, however, that with Union troops holding Huntsville, the Memphis & Charleston Railroad was blocked and there was no way to get a train through to Corinth and Beauregard.

Andrews replied to the effect that he did not believe the story. "Mitchel would not be fool enough to run down there, but if he is, Beauregard will soon sweep him out of the road," he said. "At any rate, I have my orders."[25]

With that, the *New York* was pulled to a siding to clear the main track, and the raiders resumed their wait for the extra train from the north. Nine o'clock came and went. Up on the engine, William Knight and Wilson Brown kept busy checking the engine and maintaining a good head of steam so they could move on as soon as the track was open. Back in the boxcar, the soldiers sat silent and nervous. "We waited a long time here in awful suspense, we in the box car not daring to speak, move, or scarcely breathe, lest those whom we heard tramping around our train should hear us, and thus explode

Andrews' powder story," Al Dorsey later wrote. "It seemed we waited for hours," Jacob Parrott remembered.[26]

Though Andrews exuded composure and confidence—stalking about the rail yard, even chatting with the men gathered around about his time in Beauregard's camp—the enthusiasm from earlier that morning had slowly waned, replaced by growing uneasiness and grim frustration. "Our precious time was being consumed with these delays," Alf Wilson said. "We felt and knew it." Finally, after a delay of nearly an hour, the screech of a second whistle was heard. The extra squealed to stop on the main line next to the depot. Andrews stared in disbelief.

On the last car of the train was posted another red flag.[27]

The *Texas* in 1903, the only known photograph of the engine in use. (*Colonel James G. Bogle Collection*)

CHAPTER EIGHT

The *Texas*

Kingston, Adairsville, Calhoun

But in a moment the tables were turned! Nor far behind we heard the
scream of a locomotive bearing down upon us at lightning speed!
—Corporal William Pittenger, 2nd Ohio

CIRCUMSTANCES HAD CHANGED considerably for Andrews and his volunteers in the past hour. The twenty disguised Union men had stolen the
General without interference, and their train had rolled unhindered and slightly ahead of schedule for the thirty-one miles from Big Shanty to Moon's to
Allatoona to Etowah to Kingston. But the *General* had been sitting idle and
steaming on a side track at Kingston for a full hour, not moving an inch as
an increasing crowd of Georgia railroad men gathered at the depot, eyeing the
strangers, chewing tobacco, smoking, talking, wondering what was going on.

As the minutes ticked by, Andrews became angry and frustrated, and the
men in the junction around him groused and complained, growing more rest-
less and doubtful. Why had Fuller not yet arrived with the passenger train?
Why were no telegraphs coming through from the south? Why hadn't the
Western & Atlantic office in Atlanta informed them of this special ammunition train? The spy, who seemed entirely unfazed by this cross-examination,
answered all questioners directly and confidently. "Andrews occupied attention by complaining of the delay, and declaring that the road ought to be
kept clear of freight trains when so much needed for the transportation of
army supplies, when the fate of the whole army of the West might depend
upon the celerity with which it received its ammunition," Pittenger wrote.

The big Kentuckian's aristocratic bearing and commanding presence seemed to assuage the suspicions of most of those present, though some of the raiders would later describe a crusty old switch tender, who kept grumbling that "something was wrong with that stylish looking fellow, who ordered everybody around as if the whole road belonged to him."[1]

Andrews sent Knight back to warn the others of the worsening situation. The engineer sauntered alongside the train, looking bored, hands tucked in his pockets, and leaned nonchalantly against the boxcar. "Boys, we have to wait for a train that is a little behind time, and the folks around are getting mighty uneasy and suspicious," he said softly. "Be ready to jump out, if you are called, and let them have it hot and fast." The soldiers checked their pistols in the dim light of the car, patting their pockets to be sure that extra rounds were near at hand. "We had a tolerably high estimate of our fighting power, and did not doubt that we could capture any ordinary train, or the usual crowd around a village station. But to be shut up in the dark, while—for aught we knew—the enemy might be concentrating an overwhelming force against us, was exceedingly trying, and put the implicit confidence we had in our leader to a very severe test," Pittenger admitted. Knight summed up the trying delay in an interview years later: Kingston was, he remembered, "an uneasy place."[2]

At long last, the raiders heard another whistle and the third train from the north pulled into the station. It had been an hour and five minutes since the *General* arrived at Kingston—though according to Jacob Parrott, it "seemed to those shut up in the box-car nearer half a day!" Andrews immediately ordered the crew of the new train to have it draw down the road and let his ammunition train out. The conductor promptly obeyed, and the track was finally open. Andrews again asked for the keys to change the switch and let the *General* back onto the main line, but according to the raiders, the old switch tender was having none of it. They could hear the man shouting through the walls of the boxcar. He had hung up his keys, the switchman said hotly, and he would not be taking them down again until Andrews explained by what authority he was ordering around everyone on the road. The raiders tensed, listening for an order to spring out from the car and fight for their lives.

But Andrews only laughed at the switchman's temper. "I've no time to waste with you, old fellow," he said, and walked past him into the office, where he grabbed the keys off the peg himself and went to change the switch. "The tender's wrath knew no bounds at this," Pittenger later wrote, "he stormed, declared he would have Andrews arrested, would report him, and many other things." Andrews waved, tucked the switch keys in his pocket, and swung himself back up onto the *General* as the engine crept forward off the siding. They were free, on their way again. "It had been a fearful ordeal, but it was well met," Pittenger would later write of the delay.[3]

As the train pulled out of Kingston, the track ahead curving right from west to north, the silver drizzle began to thicken into a steady, soaking rain.

Growling like the bear that was its Cherokee namesake, the *Yonah* ran the fourteen miles from Etowah to Kingston in fifteen minutes. "In these days, while we have heavy steel rail and good track, a good engine can easily run 60 miles per hour," William Fuller would write almost forty years later. "But in those times when the track was in a terrible condition, to run more than a mile a minute and make two full stops, and halt at Cartersville to six miles per hour [in order to pass by the crowded platform], is quite a different thing." Indeed, this speed run on the old switch engine was an impressive and somewhat reckless feat—not only because of the rocky state of the road and the age of the *Yonah*, but also because the fleeing saboteurs ahead could have taken up another rail at any point and caused a catastrophic derailment. Fuller would recall making two quick stops on this stretch to clear ties thrown on the track by the raiders—but as a practical matter the engine probably would not have been able to stop in time if the track had been broken instead of just obstructed. For some reason, however, although several of the Yankees had recognized the threat posed by the *Yonah* when they passed it at Etowah, the raiders did not make any effort to dislodge a rail and sever the tracks between Etowah and Kingston.[4]

Fuller positioned himself at the front of his new train, looking ahead for further obstacles on the track. Jeff Cain, who was somewhat frazzled and worried out from the day's ordeal, rode on the tender; Anthony Murphy stood in the cab, hard by the throttle. Now that they were making better time and might be closing in on the raiders, a new and disturbing thought crossed their minds—the possibility of an "ambuscade." After all, they surmised, these were vicious Yankee soldiers they were dealing with, and if they became desperate, they would likely try to kill their pursuers and, as Fuller said, "capture two instead of one engine." Passing by Rogers and then Cass stations, the pursuers learned that their quarry had refueled at that point and told the befuddled stationmaster that they were under special military orders and that the regular train crew would be following along behind. Andrews had no way of knowing that this part of his cover story was true—the regular crew was following behind, indeed.[5]

The *Yonah's* sprint up from Etowah was soon interrupted. "When we arrived at Kingston, greatly to our annoyance and chagrin, we found many heavy freight trains, which, by the request and demands of the raiders had been run past the station in order to let them out at the further or north end of the siding," Fuller recalled. The rail yard was jammed with trains and cars, on the main line, the sidings, and the branch curving off toward Rome. The *New York* was dead ahead, blocking the main track with its long train of cars. The *William R. Smith* still stood where Harbin left it near the depot, poised to make the return run westward to Rome. The extra trains that had caused so much chagrin for the raiders had pulled forward and now waited on sidings. On and around the platform and the depot, a congregation of train crews, station hands, and passengers milled about, some of them no doubt arguing over how to unravel the snarl of rail traffic that clogged the junction. In point of fact, Fuller and Murphy now were confronted with the same problem that Andrews had faced the hour before—a single line track to the north and a number of trains blocking the way. The experienced railroad men immediately recognized that would take far too much time to move the various trains and clear a path for the *Yonah* to proceed northward past the junction. They could go no farther with the rusty switch engine—they would have to change to another train.[6]

William Fuller jumped off the *Yonah* and ran forward toward the depot, "giving the news" to all assembled and causing "great excitement" among the small crowd gathered around the platform. An effort was made to send a message north by telegraph, but it was no use—the line was already dead. Meanwhile, Anthony Murphy immediately headed up to the *New York*. Knowing the capabilities of the available engines, Murphy would later say that he had no further use for the *Yonah*, and none for the *William R. Smith*, for that matter. "*New York* was best and larger than either," he said. The W&A foreman began barking orders and soon had the train's crew hard at work, dropping their freight cars and coupling to the flatcar with supplies that he had run with the *Yonah* from Kingston.[7]

There are substantial discrepancies in the accounts of the details of the railroad traffic jam at Kingston. First, witnesses over the years would disagree as to just how many trains Andrews had to wait for before the *General* resumed its flight. At least two trains—the regularly scheduled but tardy freight and one "extra"—came in from the north as the raiders waited. Most witnesses, including Pittenger, agree that there were three (the regular and two extras), though others would contend that there were no less than four trains running southward. Whatever the number, there is no question that the raiders were delayed considerably—even fatally—by the southbound traffic that had been dislodged from the north by Mitchel's capture of Huntsville and threatened advance on Chattanooga. Another unsettled factual question is one of timing; that is, just how far behind the raiders Fuller and Murphy were when they finally arrived at Kingston station. A large number of witnesses—and the preponderance of Andrews Raid lore and legend—maintained that the pursuers arrived in Kingston just *four minutes* after Andrews pulled away. Others thought it much longer—Wiley Harbin, for example, would state that Fuller did not arrive until "nearly three quarters of an hour" after the *General* departed.[8]

Harbin was oiling his engine when Fuller and Cain came running up. The Rome engineer was well acquainted with both men from his time on the road. They told him that their train had been stolen at Big Shanty, explained their subsequent pursuit on foot, by pole-car, and on the *Yonah*, and immediately requested that he take the *William R. Smith* and carry them on northward after the captured train. "In ten seconds I had told him of my situation, and of the importance of an immediate pursuit," Fuller later wrote. Harbin readily agreed, and immediately directed that the pin be pulled to leave his passenger coach behind, taking with him only the tender and the mail and baggage car. Fuller seemed to regard the engineer of the *Smith* as a definite upgrade over his own—he would later praise Harbin unreservedly, calling him "brave, loyal, true, and in every sense of the word, faithful and competent."[9]

The commotion at the depot drew the attention not only of the train crews and station men, but also of the company of militia drilling northwest of the junction. They came clomping into the rail yard and up to the depot, their equipment jingling, cartridge boxes and canteens flapping, muskets and squirrel guns pointed in all directions. A local man named Duncan Murchison, a veteran of the Indian Wars, was their volunteer drillmaster, and he was plainly thrilled with the developing chase and the prospect of doing some actual fighting. According to historian Wilbur Kurtz, Murchison, "with boisterous appeal to the valor of the crowd, and his own ostentatious example," immediately rallied his force of thirty or forty men and soon had them scrambling into Harbin's baggage car. "This mob was a rather unstable contingency in the pursuit," Kurtz noted, "as they had been interviewing sundry jugs of corn juice for the greater part of the morning."

Anthony Murphy, finishing his preparations to depart on the muscular *New York*, had just sent one of its crewmen forward to tell Fuller to move the *William R. Smith* out of the way, when he saw the *Smith* beginning to roll forward out of the station. He had no idea that Fuller intended to push on north with the *Smith* until he saw the engine start to move, and apparently the conductor had no intention of waiting for Murphy to come along. This "made me run and swear," Murphy wrote in a letter long after the war, especially "after the trouble I had been to, getting our *New York* ready." He caught up to the *Smith* as it swung onto the main track and pulled himself aboard the moving engine. In the baggage car, he heard the rabble of militiamen whooping and hollering as a boring day of drill had suddenly turned into a free train ride and a chance to shoot some Yankees. "We had no control over this crew," Murphy said, his disappointment still palpable years later. "Everyone was wild, the engine was small, with very low driving wheels, and there were several cars loaded with people, so that we made slow time, and I feared the day was lost."[10]

The *General* fled north from Kingston like a beast sprung from its cage. In the cab of the engine, James Andrews made no further mention of going slow or keeping to the schedule. "Push her, boys, push her. Let her do her best," the spy urged Knight and Brown. The train was run just a short distance out from the junction when Andrews ordered a halt. Each man was by now well aware of the work that must be done—John Scott, "with a man at each foot to give him a good start," quickly ascended a pole to sever the telegraph wire, while others threw down cross-ties to obstruct the track. The raiders climbed back into their car, noticing "a quickening of speed that after our long rest was delightful." Andrews was pushing forward for Adairsville, ten miles north of Kingston, where he hoped to meet and pass two trains: the through freight and the southbound passenger train. Along the way, they would have more destructive work to do. Cutting wire and dropping obstacles was all well and good, but with the large stable of iron horses they had just left behind, as Jacob Parrott recognized, "it would never do to make the run without tearing up track." Or as Pittenger said with considerable understatement, if the enemy decided to make up a pursuing train from Kingston, "it might be very embarrassing."[11]

Andrews therefore ordered a second halt about six miles north of Kingston, and the raiders went back to work. Again they found themselves hamstrung by their lack of equipment. "Lifting a rail seems easy enough, but it was far from easy in practice," Pittenger wrote. "The rail is long and heavy; it is securely bolted to other rails, and fastened with great spikes driven into solid oak ties, which in turn are deeply inbedded in the ground." Eight men bent to work on removing the rail, while the remainder loaded cross-ties onto the boxcars, for later use as obstructions or as kindling for the bridges to the north. The soldiers worked with greater urgency than before—though they still believed themselves more than an hour ahead of any possible pursuit. "Slowly we drew out spike after spike, battering out the great nails as rapidly as possible with our one iron bar," Pittenger recalled. The rail had been loosened for about two-thirds of its length, and the men started trying to pull it free. They were about to give up and take out some more spikes, when they heard the sound—"faintly but unmistakably"—of the whistle of a locomotive from the south.[12]

This put a new face on things—"we lifted again and with every particle of strength, as men lift for life," Pittenger said. "The strong rail bent under the terrible pressure and snapped with a dull *twang!*" The raiders climbed back in the boxcar with their broken piece of rail, and the *General* was quickly under way again. "For the time we were saved," Pittenger believed. But the situation was now dire: they clearly had a train now chasing behind them—though the broken track should halt that pursuit—and two trains still ahead they had to pass before they could get to the Oostanaula River and Chickamauga Creek bridges. Making it to those bridges was their only chance. "When we found that we were pursued we knew that the destruction of a bridge was the only thing that would save us and to do this we must outrun them far enough to burn the bridge before they came up," Alf Wilson recalled. They had to get past the trains at Adairsville and put some distance between them and the locomotive following behind.[13]

It was late morning when the *General* approached Adairsville, a trackside village nestled in the Oothcalooga Valley. The raiders probably were not aware of the fact, but the station stood exactly at the halfway point between Atlanta and Chattanooga—sixty-nine miles from each place. The four men on the engine—Knight, Brown, Alf Wilson, and Andrews—saw a very long train standing on the siding, the locomotive facing toward them. This would be the "Down Day Freight," waiting for Fuller's train to pass as usual—the *General* now being well behind its regular schedule. Slackening their speed, the raiders pulled to a sidetrack and eased up alongside the freight, which consisted of the engine, tender, and twenty-one cars. On the boiler of the locomotive, they could see its brass nameplate: TEXAS. Andrews spoke with the crew and conductor, responding to "the usual storm of questions" with his ammunition train story. He then asked a few questions of his own, inquiring about the latest news from Chattanooga and any word of the Federal army's operations in north Alabama. Telegrams were now being interrupted along the Memphis & Charleston Railroad well east of Huntsville, he was told, so everyone supposed that the Yankee army was moving ever closer to Chattanooga.[14]

Both trains here at Adairsville—the northbound *General* and the southbound *Texas*, panting next to each other on the sidings like two thoroughbreds on a hitching post—would now have to await the arrival of the fast passenger train down from Chattanooga. That train, too, was late, the panic and traffic in Chattanooga apparently playing hell with the regular schedule. In any event, the *Texas's* unusually long train of freight cars blocked the exit to the north. Andrews could not leave the station unless the conductor of the *Texas* would agree to pull forward and open the road.

The passenger train was already more than half an hour overdue, and the freight conductor, now that the *General* had arrived, was inclined to resume his southbound journey. After all, he had waited a good bit longer than the standard fifteen minutes that the rules of the road called for when an expected train was delayed. Andrews heartily agreed with the freight conductor running his train on southward—toward the break in the rail the raiders had just made. But when the conductor suggested to Andrews that he continue to wait the passenger train's arrival from the north, he disagreed. "I'll do no such thing," he said. "I must go at once! The fate of the army hangs on my getting promptly through with these carloads of ammunition." General Beauregard, he continued, did not have enough power for three hours' fight.

The conductor of the *Texas's* train was persuaded by this. "Get through by all means; but you will have to run very slow and put a flag-man out at every curve, or you will have a collision," he said. Andrews agreed to do so, and the two men parted. Climbing back into the cab of the *General*, he gave the signal, and Knight gently eased the engine forward out of the station. As the stolen train left the stone depot and whitewashed buildings of Adairsville behind, the *Texas* and its 700-foot-long train slithered off southward like a great serpent, headed toward Kingston and the gap in the rails four miles ahead.[15]

Andrews's decision to continue the run northward from Adairsville despite his knowledge of a southbound express up ahead was extremely dangerous. Railroad travel in those days was somewhat hazardous even under the best of conditions (the United States had railroad accidents at a rate forty times higher per passenger mile than England)—and these vehicular disasters were a new and frightening phenomenon of the industrial era. Of course, the horse-drawn transportation of the day saw the occasional minor accident— an overturned wagon or runaway coach, perhaps—but the derailed trains and railroad collisions reported in the papers these days were more frequent and more deadly. (Indeed, before the week was out, Georgia newspapers would report a fatal derailment on the Atlanta & West Point Railroad to the south-west, which "completely wrecked" nine cars and claimed the lives of a Tennessee soldier and six horses.) By the end of the Civil War, the number of fatalities in railroad accidents would skyrocket, and the popular press would trumpet the sensational stories and lurid images and express extreme concern, if not outright panic, over the growing danger. "Everyday the record of mortality is continued," the pages of *Harper's Weekly* would lament later on in the war. "Now it is a collision; now the explosion of a locomotive, and then again the sudden precipitation of an entire train down a steep embank-ment or perhaps into some river." By far the most feared of these dangers was the prospect of a head-on crash, which single lines of track (like the W&A) made possible, and which were avoided by prudent safety precautions and strict adherence to the schedule of the road.[16]

But Andrews was not running on any schedule at this point, and despite the suggestion of the freight conductor, he would neither run his engine slowly nor put out a flagman at all—he simply had no time. The only pre-caution he took was to have his engineers blow the *General's* whistle almost constantly, sounding a persistent warning as they sped up the line. Fortunately, the route of the W&A from Adairsville to the next station at Calhoun ran almost due north, straight and level for almost the entire stretch. Rolling out of the station, Andrews turned to his engineers and cut them loose. "Let's see how fast she can go," he said.[17]

Alf Wilson, still serving as brakeman, would vividly describe this all-out stretch of the race years later:

> Our locomotive was under a full head of steam. The engineer stood with his hand on the lever with the valve wide open. It was frightful to see how the powerful iron monster under us would leap forward under the revolutions of her great wheels. Brown would scream to me ever and anon, "Give her more wood, Alf!" which command was promptly obeyed. She rocked and reeled like a drunken man, while we tumbled from side to side like grains of

popcorn in a hot frying pan. It was bewildering to look at the ground, or objects on the road-side. A constant stream of fire ran from the rims of the great wheels and to this day I shudder when I reflect on that, my first and last locomotive ride.

We sped past stations, houses and fields and out of sight almost like a meteor, while the bystanders who barely caught a glimpse of us as we passed, looked on as if in fear and amazement. It has always been a wonder with me that our locomotive and cars kept the track at all, or how they could possibly stay on the track. At times the iron horse seemed literally to fly over the course, the driving-wheels of one side being lifted from the rails much of the distance over which we now sped with a velocity fearful to contemplate. We took little thought of the matter then. Death in a railroad smash-up was preferable to us to capture.[18]

The train sped north at what Parrott would call "a frightful rate," and the soldiers back in the boxcar were "thrown from side to side and jerked about in a manner that baffles description." It seemed to Bill Pittenger that "the engine seemed to be not so much running as coursing with great lion-like bounds along the track, and the spectacle from the locomotive as it rose and fell in its ceaseless rapid motion, while houses, fields and woods rushed by, was wonderful and glorious, almost worth the risk to enjoy!" Daniel Dorsey later wrote: "Sometimes it seemed that our car was off the track, or literally jumping along. We were tossed from side to side almost like beans in a gourd."

Up front on the locomotive, Alf Wilson began pouring copious amounts of oil on the wood to increase the flames in the firebox. Andrews stood in the cab nearby, his pocket watch held tightly in hand. He and Knight would later maintain that they had run the nine miles between Adairsville and Calhoun in seven and a half minutes—an almost unbelievable rate of seventy-two miles per hour—though Pittenger would later throw cold water on this somewhat, supposing that Andrews probably measured the time from the point when he was out of sight from Adairsville to the point when Calhoun first came into view. Still, the *General* was flying northward at a rate of a mile a minute or faster, trying to reach Calhoun before the passenger train departed. "We took awful chances" on this stretch, Dorsey admitted.[19]

The southbound passenger train had just started to roll forward out of the station when the *General* came rushing up the track, its whistle blaring insistently as it came into view, just in time. "If she had been coming down,"

Knight later said of the southbound train, "at the rate we were running, we would of run clear through them. There would have been Union and Rebel blood mixed." No doubt startled by the sudden appearance of this shrieking locomotive barreling toward them, the engineer reversed his engine and backed the train, pulled by the locomotive *Catoosa*, to the depot at Calhoun. Here, a standoff developed. The *Catoosa* only backed far enough to allow Andrews and his train to take a siding; the long string of coaches on the passenger train blocked the exit north, however, hemming in the raiders. Yet again, the *General* could not leave the station unless and until the crew of the passenger train agreed to pull ahead. But they refused to clear the way without a damned good explanation. After all, this sawed-off, unscheduled train from the south, which had none of its regular crew, had almost run into them head-on. Andrews told his powder train story and kindly requested that the conductor let the *General* pass. The conductor, a man by the name of Frank Watts, though he seemed to accept the explanation as far as it went, was reluctant to pull out southward and possibly face another train coming north. Andrews tried to persuade Watts and his engineer Joe Renard that they had plenty of time to make Adairsville before the next train came up—but the crew of the *Catoosa*, angry with Andrews's apparent recklessness and perhaps shaken by the near-collision with the *General*, still hesitated. (Jacob Parrott would later suggest that Andrews was the one who was a little unnerved by the near "smash-up," claiming that the spy told the ammunition train story, but "did not tell it so well" this time.) Sensing time slipping past, Andrews soon changed his tactics from slick persuasion to stern, direct orders. "I must press on without more delay," he said firmly. "Pull your engine ahead and let me out."[20]

Faced with such a peremptory direction, the conductor folded. (This was probably just as well for the crew of the *Catoosa*, as Andrews's next request presumably would have been made at gunpoint.) The *Catoosa* and its train of passenger coaches pulled forward and cleared the exit behind it to the north. As the *General* chuffed out of Calhoun, Andrews and the men on the engine waved cheerfully to the crowd gathered on the platform.

The Northerners again found their anxiety dispelled and their excitement and exultation renewed. They could now turn to their true mission of bridge-burning; there would be no more of the "hard drudgery of track raising and still more terrible work of sitting silent and housed in a dark car." They had traveled more than fifty miles from Big Shanty, had run through nine stations, and had passed no less than five southbound trains on the single-line railroad. The *Catoosa* should be the last scheduled train until Chattanooga, and the train they had heard behind them north of Kingston would surely have been halted by the broken track and would have to make repairs. They were clear of traffic, with "an open road ahead and scores of miles of obstructed and broken track behind us!"

Nothing could stop them now.

As the *General* hurtled from Adairsville up to Calhoun, tooting its whistle all the way, the posse of pursuing trainmen and would-be soldiers was rolling north from Kingston on the *William R. Smith*. Neither the raiders nor the pursuers knew it yet, but the delays were indeed costing Andrews and his men—the railroaders behind them were steadily gaining ground. Wiley Harbin stood at the throttle of the *William R. Smith*, his fireman William Kernodle at the firebox just behind, with the freeman Joe Lassiter on the brake, which was seeing very little use as the train barreled up the curving road. (The *Smith*'s train conductor Cicero Smith—though the local newspapers would commend him in the days to come for his role in the noble pursuit—actually stayed behind at Kingston and took no part in the chase.) Murphy and Cain were crowded into the cab, with Fuller standing on the running board looking ahead for obstructions on the track or any sign of his stolen train. Running around a broad curve, the *Smith* soon came upon the pile of crossties, and she was moving too fast to stop. The iron cowcatcher drove right through the wooden ties, scattering them to the sides like bowling pins—according to Harbin, "one sailed aloft nearly as high as the headlight." The engine was undamaged and no one injured, so the *Smith* continued on her way. A mile or so later, another pile of ties blocked the road; this time, Harbin was able to slow the locomotive and gently push the obstruction off the tracks.[21]

Despite its faithful service, it would be a short day for the *William R. Smith*. About six miles up from Kingston—four miles from Adairsville—the pursuers came to the place where the raiders had broken the track. The *Smith* squealed to a stop, no more than "ten or twelve feet from the gap," Harbin would recall. There was a moment of anger and confusion, especially among Murchison's militia in the baggage car, who saw their prospects for glory slipping away. "What'll we do now?" someone cried out in dismay.

Murphy, for one, was pleased at the necessity of abandoning the *Smith*. "To me this was a relief—to get rid of our small engine and a crowd so wild," he later wrote. He and Fuller both knew that they would soon meet the *Texas* and its southbound freight, and that another passenger train farther up the line might serve to delay the *General* even further. The two men, leaving the *Smith* behind, again ran north in the rain. Also left behind was Jeff Cain, the *General*'s regular engineer, who had had quite enough running for one day. His part in the chase was now concluded, and in Fuller's mind, the frail engineer had done little except costing precious time when Fuller had to run the handcar back from Moon's Station to pick him up. "In point of fact, he was of no service," Fuller later said harshly. "He was frail and unserviceable in times when the need of great physical strength and effort were brought into requisition." Murchison's Saturday soldiers turned out to be of just as little use.[22]

For his part, engineer Harbin took steps to ensure that the *Smith* might continue up the road and perhaps be present later, along with the few soldiers it carried, to make some small contribution whenever and wherever the chase came to an end. The engineer pulled his train as close to the gap as possible. Then, rails were taken up from behind the train, and placed in front, filling the gap. The raiders had failed to remove all the spikes, so the replacement track, while a little wobbly, seemed to be stable enough to bear the weight of the train. "Over this improvised piece of tracking crawled the *Smith*, its tender, and the baggage car," historian Wilbur Kurtz wrote. "It required fifteen or twenty minutes to accomplish this and when all was ready, those that had remained scrambled aboard."[23]

Up ahead, Fuller and Murphy hailed the *Texas* as it rolled toward them, about two miles south of Adairsville. The two men had by now added another two or three miles on foot to the distance they had logged that day—though the railbed had grown so wet and the mud so thick that it was difficult to move at anything faster than a brisk walk. At the throttle of the *Texas*, engineer Peter J. Bracken recognized the two men plodding toward him, guns in hand, and he immediately reversed his engine and brought the train to a stop. Bracken was of trim build and average height, dressed in a gray flannel shirt and dark gray vest, with thick dark hair, a mustache, and "chin whiskers a little too large to be considered a goatee." Like many of the engineers and machinists on the road, Bracken was northern-born, a native of Philadelphia, twenty-eight years old. He was, according to Fuller, "a first rate man." Yet upon seeing him, a flicker of doubt, like the passing shadow of a cloud, would cross Anthony Murphy's mind. "I knew there was a strong Union sentiment in the W. & A. R. R. shops," Murphy later wrote, an understandable situation given the birth and raising of the overwhelming majority of the road's engineers and machinists. "Most of the Mechanicks were northern men—as was Mr. Bracken," Murphy wrote. Decades after the war, he would recall wondering whether the Pennsylvania-born engineer would agree to do it—whether he would run his engine wide open in pursuit of fellow Yankees. But the worry passed almost as soon as it occurred—after all, Murphy had been an engineer himself, and could run the engine if it came to that.[24]

Bracken had been on his regular assignment that morning, running freight down from Dalton, where the East Tennessee & Georgia Railroad branched off, threading northeast to Cleveland and eventually Knoxville, Tennessee. He was accompanied on the *Texas* by his fireman, fifteen-year-old Henry Haney, and by a wood-passer named Alonzo Martin, a thick-set, auburn-haired man of twenty-three. Their formidable engine, the *Texas*, was Western & Atlantic No. 49, and she was an equal to the *General* in almost every respect, a twin born from another manufacturing womb. She was built in Paterson, New Jersey, by Danforth, Cooke & Company, a competitor of the Rogers shops across town that had built the *General*. The *Texas* too was a 4-4-0, with five-foot driving wheels and a fifteen-inch cylinder with a twenty-two-inch stroke—specifications identical to those of the *General*. The two engines even looked alike, right down to the ornamentation on the cover between the drivers—though the *Texas* added a signature Lone Star just above the scrollwork. The engine had been purchased for $9,050 ($200 more than the *General*) and placed in service on the Western & Atlantic in October 1856. Whatever concern he may have had about Bracken, Murphy was absolutely delighted with their latest locomotive. "It was a God-send to us," he recalled. "The *Texas* was the same class of engine as the *General*, and was in fine order," the foreman wrote years later, noting the engine's large driving wheels and the fact that it had been "recently out of the shop, where a thorough repairing had been given it under my own supervision. Driving wheels, truck and tender wheels were in fine shape, and it was almost as safe to run backward as forward, and backward we had to run it."[25]

Murphy need not have worried about Pete Bracken. The native Pennsylvanian did not hesitate in agreeing to push his engine back to chase after the raiders. "Bracken, we must catch them at all hazards," Fuller told him. Many years after the war, as he sat on the wide front porch of his house in Macon on a rainy afternoon and told the story of the chase to his wide-eyed grandchildren, Bracken would relate how Fuller asked him if he would pursue the stolen train, and his prompt response: "Indeed I will." The dark-haired engineer quickly reversed the *Texas* and pushed the long train some two miles back up to Adairsville, where he dropped the twenty-one freight cars

The *Texas* in her wartime character. Illustration by Wilbur G. Kurtz. (*Colonel James G. Bogle Collection*)

on a siding in order to continue the chase with only the *Texas* and its tender. This maneuver was executed with such skill that the freight cars were still rolling on the siding, "slacking speed while the *Texas* was gaining," as Bracken pushed his locomotive northward. The station had no turntable or other means of turning the engine around, however—as Murphy had noted, the *Texas* would have to make the northbound run after the *General* in reverse.[26]

The *Texas* roared off, leaving the depot and village of Adairsville behind. For the residents of the little station town, all the activity of the morning to this point—the runs on foot, the pole-car, the short trips on the *Yonah* and the *Smith*—would be nothing more than prologue. Now it was down to two equally matched locomotives, the *General* and the *Texas*, and the town of Adairsville—the first community in Georgia to be listed in its entirety on the National Register of Historic Places—would in the future proudly claim itself as the site of the start of the Great Locomotive Chase.[27]

Tunnel Hill. (*Colonel James G. Bogle Collection*)

CHAPTER NINE

A Trial of Speed

Resaca, Dalton, Tunnel Hill

It was like a meeting between two iron knights of the old time, not for material gain or principle—honor denied with honor, courage denied with courage—the deed not done for the end but for the sake of doing, put to the ultimate test and proving nothing save the finality of death and the vanity of all endeavor.

—William Faulkner
The Unvanquished (1938)

"Now FOLLOWED A TRIAL OF SPEED between locomotives—a race which for desperate, dare-devil recklessness, velocity and the high stakes at issue was never equaled on land or water on the American continent," Alf Wilson wrote. The *Texas* made the nine-mile run from Adairsville to Calhoun in twelve minutes, rattling up the line in reverse at about fifty miles per hour. Fuller was impressed with engineer Peter Bracken's willingness to throw caution to the wind and run his powerful locomotive all-out, despite the considerable risk of collision, derailment or ambush. "Like all locomotive runners," Fuller later wrote, "he was very much in love with his engine, but in this case, he showed that he preferred success even at the expense or the possibility of the loss of the *Texas*." Fuller took his usual post up front—in this case, perched on the tail end of the tender—looking ahead for trouble. "I would swing from the corner of the tender, hanging on with one hand, the other uplifted for a danger signal, thus keeping on the corner of the tender that gave me the longest view around the curves," the conductor recalled. Again, the pursuers encountered no break in the track and no obstacles to slow them down. Just as Andrews had been, Fuller and Murphy were worried about a possible collision with the scheduled passenger train ahead, and they began to sound their locomotive's whistle as they came closer to Calhoun. They saw a large crowd of people gathered around the station, presumably a mixture of passengers stretching their legs and locals puzzled at all the whistling, smoking commotion. Folks stared wide-eyed and gaping as the *Texas* and its tender pulled in, strangely unadorned by freight or coaches and running backward.[1]

The *Texas* slowed at the platform as Fuller again hollered a terse and alarming explanation to the railroaders and bystanders. The *Catoosa's* conductor Frank Watts replied that he had thought something was amiss, but said that "the fellow with the big beard told such a good story about the ammunition train, I had to pull out of the way." Meanwhile, Fuller and Murphy noticed a familiar face among the gathering. Edward Henderson was the telegraph operator at Dalton, thirteen miles farther up the line. Smooth-faced and almost painfully thin, wearing a black hat with a low crown and stiff brim, he was only seventeen, but had been working as a telegraph man in both Dalton and Atlanta since the age of twelve. He had hitched a ride on the southbound passenger train that morning to look for a break in the wires, since the telegraph was entirely and inexplicably dead in that direction. Fuller, hoping to find a place up the road where they could get a message out, reached out a hand and swung young Henderson up onto the train. The young lad sat up front on the tender, leaning close to the conductor to hear his instructions.[2]

The pursuers also picked up some useful and experienced muscle to work the firebox. Fleming Cox was an engineer employed by the Memphis & Charleston Railroad and a passenger on the train stalled there at Calhoun. Abandoning his trip south to Atlanta, where he was headed on leave, he climbed aboard the *Texas* and took over for Henry Haney as fireman for the miles to come. Slender but solid, six feet tall, with a thin face adorned with a neat black mustache and goatee, Cox was "a magnificent specimen of manhood and just in the prime of life," Fuller wrote. With these two valuable additions to their party, the pursuers continued on northward, their train never even coming to a full stop.[3]

Another passenger on the *Catoosa's* southbound train standing at Calhoun that day was Captain W.J. Whitsitt of the First Georgia Volunteer Infantry Regiment, who along with ten of his soldiers was returning south to his post at Mobile, Alabama. Hearing of the Yankee treachery that had passed him by just minutes before, Whitsitt had his small command assemble near the platform, ready to assist in the pursuit. This squad of Confederate infantrymen—a considerable improvement over the drunken rabble of militiamen back at Kingston—soon crowded aboard the tender of the *Catoosa*, as its engineer Joe Renard cut the engine loose from its train and started rolling northward in the wake of the *Texas*. (The *Catoosa's* engineer had initially protested this interruption of her southbound trip, but Whitsitt drew his revolver and persuaded him otherwise.)

There were now two trains coming after the *General*.[4]

*A*t long last, after a flight of more than fifty miles, the twenty Northern men on the stolen train were nearing the town of Resaca and the steep banks of the Oostanaula River. Formed about five miles northeast of Calhoun by the confluence of the Conasauga and Coosawattee Rivers, the Oostanaula (from the Cherokee meaning "shoally river" or "rock that bars your way") flows swiftly in a southwesterly direction, winding some 45 miles through the hills to Rome. Once the raiders crossed the Oostanaula and reduced its long covered bridge to smoldering timbers, they would be entirely protected from any threats from behind, with myriad opportunities to wreak further havoc ahead. From that point on, the increasingly tortured curves of the W&A would be punctuated over and over again with little bridges, most of them made of wood, crossing the snaking branches of Chickamauga Creek and other tributaries, gorges, and runs.[5]

But first, the Federal raiders needed to buy themselves a little more time. Andrews ordered a stop in a swale just a mile and a half north of Calhoun, and the raiders quickly set to work cutting the wire, loading crossties, and loosening another rail. Knight and Brown inspected and oiled the engine, finding it to be in fine condition, though they were running somewhat low on wood and water. "We worked cheerfully," Parrott remembered. "Scott was more agile than ever on the poles." The sergeant quickly severed the telegraph wire, as his comrades below painstakingly drove out the spikes—*clink! clink! clink!*—one by one. The Yankees straining to break the track leaned into their work, prying at the rail with their crowbar, a lever of green wood, and a fence rail. Andrews stood nearby, watching his men hammering away. He had taken off his cape and traded his distinguished top hat for a small and nondescript cap. "Here I saw Andrews show real impatience for the first—I am not sure but I may say the only—time," Pittenger recalled. The spy snatched the crowbar from the hands of one of the raiders and began working at the rail himself—and some of the raiders would remember him swearing and cursing as he did so.

Just then, the sharp cry of a train's whistle ripped through the air, and the raiders whipped their heads around to look back behind them to the south. "The roll of a thousand thunders could not have startled us more," Pittenger said. "Greater surprise would not have been created in our ranks had the locomotive, to whose scream we unwillingly listened, dropped from the sky!" Behind them in the distance they could see an engine moving rapidly toward them, tender first, at what one among the group would later describe as "lightning speed." The soldiers looked to their civilian leader for direction—should they stand and fight? But Andrews, continuing to favor retreat and obstruction over armed conflict, immediately ordered them back aboard the train. The raiders abandoned their work, the rail behind them loosened and perhaps a little bent, but still in place. They wedged the fence rail up under the track, hoping to force a derailment—or at least a pause for repair and adjustment—and remounted the train. The soldiers crowded in the boxcar were thrown from their feet as Knight threw open the valve, and the *General* picked up speed as it pulled away and disappeared around a curve.[6]

Andrews, who seemed to be entirely undismayed, coolly directed that one of his three boxcars be left behind to block the way of the pursuing engine. The sixteen soldiers abandoned the rearmost boxcar and moved much of their supply of crossties and other fuel they had gathered to the next car forward. They pulled the coupling pin, and the *General* again sped off northward, the boxcar left behind to block the track. Some thought was given to reversing the engine and kicking the freight car back at the trailing *Texas*, but the uphill grade dampened the effectiveness of this attempt.

The Ohioans, who were "greatly perplexed by the unexpected appearance of this pursuing train," debated among themselves where it could have come from. Was it one of the trains they had passed at Calhoun, or Adairsville? How had anyone passed the break in the tracks they had made? Who had raised the alarm? What had given them away? They discussed the possibility that a telegraph message been sent in some roundabout fashion, "around the whole circuit of the Confederacy back to Chattanooga," and orders sent to give chase until a force could be sent out from Chattanooga to head them off. If this had happened, the raiders agreed, "our race was almost run."[7]

A short distance behind them, for the first time since her startling abduction at Big Shanty, Fuller and Murphy laid eyes on the *General*. "They had stopped to remove another rail, and were in the act of trying to get it out when we hove in sight," Murphy remembered. "This, to them, no doubt, was a revelation." Fuller recalled seeing "the whole number" of the raiders—certainly more men than they had expected to encounter, as most had been concealed on the run thus far—prying diligently at the rails, with the telegraph lines already cut and lying on the ground. "A Yankee can work very fast and is full of resources when he is in fear of punishment or has hope of reward," he said. As the raiders disappeared around a curve up ahead, Peter Bracken eased off the throttle and slowed the *Texas* so that Fuller could disembark and check the track to determine the extent of the damage. He found the rail unspiked for much of its length, but "still in place and substantial." Fuller had to be tremendously relieved, for the *Texas* was his last train and his last chance. Any further pursuit on foot would have been fruitless—there were no additional trains he could run for farther up the line. If the raiders had succeeded in removing the rail this time, the chase would have ended, then and there.[8]

Rounding a curve, the pursuers soon came upon the empty yellow freight car standing suspiciously before them. Approaching the orphaned car, Bracken slowed the *Texas* to a crawl, fearing that the Yankees had set an ambush. But all was quiet. At this point, the fact that the *Texas* was running backward became a happy accident rather than a liability. Bracken rolled gently forward, eased the back of the tender up to the boxcar, and coupled to it. Fuller would later describe inspecting the car and finding it undamaged and full of crossties, fence rails, and brush. The presence of these combustibles confirmed the pursuers' suspicion—that the men ahead of them planned to burn the bridges on the road—but the boxcar itself would cause no more than a momentary delay. They would simply push the obstruction to the next siding and move it out of the way. The *Texas* was soon under way again, the yellow boxcar now in the lead, with Fuller perched atop it, holding on to the brake wheel with one hand.

Up ahead, the raiders adopted a new tactic. They punched a hole through the boards in the rear wall of their boxcar—completing some demolition they had started earlier as they moved from one car to another—and began to throw crossties out on the track behind them. "So great was our speed," Alf Wilson said, "that sometimes when one of these ties struck the track it bounded twenty or thirty feet high and came whirling end over end after the train as if shot from a cannon." These improvised missiles forced the *Texas* to abandon its initial rush forward and slow down, though the ties seemed to show, to the Ohioans' frustration, "a most perverse disposition to get off the track." The lengthening gap between the two engines provided a sigh of relief to the panicked raiders, who had already decided that the men behind them "had a faster engine than ours, or better fuel, or both."9

What the pursuers had in fact was an equal engine, an abundance of fuel, an open track, and the adrenaline rush of having flushed their game at last. What they lacked, of course, was manpower and firepower. The twenty armed and trained Federal soldiers aboard the *General* were fleeing frantically from a posse of seven civilians—two of whom were not yet eighteen years old—who were armed with two old shotguns, one of which would turn out to be unloaded. The Yankees had no way of knowing this, of course—and in fact, they had seen Confederate soldiers and Georgia militia all day as they ran up the line, from Big Shanty to Kingston to Adairsville, and were certainly justified in assuming that the force behind them was a strong one. "Andrews believed that, as a matter of course, the pursuing party was numerous and well-armed, a very natural conclusion," Dorsey later wrote.

The seven men on board the *Texas* each stood to his post: Fuller dangling up front and watching for obstructions; young Henderson, clinging to the rocking tender and probably hoping he lived long enough to deliver the telegraph message Fuller had dictated to him; Pete Bracken standing at the lever, with Murphy assisting in reversing the engine and yelling instructions to the crew; Fleming Cox stoking the firebox with wood passed from the tender by Alonzo Martin; and Henry Haney at the wheel of the tender brake, having tied a wooden rod through the spokes of the brakewheel to increase his leverage. "It is impossible for me or for anyone else, to describe accurately and with sufficient strength of words, this exciting race and chase," Fuller would recall. "The eye, the muscle, the nerve and the brain were all straining to their utmost tensions. There was nothing left undone by either the raiders or the pursuers that could be done."

The *Texas* wound through the rocky landscape, halting from time to time for Martin and Fuller to scramble down and clear a crosstie from the tracks. On the occasional straightaway, Fuller would signal Bracken that the way was clear, and he would pull the throttle lever wide open. The pace was at times almost terrifying—Fuller would recall that Bracken would "sometimes turn a little pale." The dripping woods rushed past them in a blur. "We ran so fast the telegraph poles looked like a fine tooth comb," Fuller wrote.10

*I*t was on this stretch of the Great Locomotive Chase that three of its greatest falsehoods were born. The first and most fanciful of these was the miracle of the flying locomotive. William Pittenger and others would later mistakenly believe that they had succeeded in taking up a rail and break-ing the railroad track above Calhoun, causing them to wonder for years how it was that an engine from farther south could have cleared the gap and come after them. Absent any other explanation for the locomotive that had appeared like a whistling specter in the mist behind them, Pittenger supposed that the *Texas* had actually been running so fast that it had *jumped* over a gap in the rails, a claim apparently advanced at times by William Fuller himself. In conducting research for his 1881 book *Capturing a Locomotive*, Pittenger dis-cussed the issue with Fuller:

> He [Fuller] said that when he saw our engine start on from this point he could see no obstruction, and allowed the train to contin-ue at high speed. A moment after he noticed a short blank in one of the rails. A terrible fear swept over him, for it was now too late to stop. But quick as a lightning-flash he noticed another fact— that the place of the missing rail was on the inside of a sharp curve. He explained to me that a train at very high speed throws the most of its weight on the outside rail of a curve, which is always made a little higher than the other. Had an outside rail been broken the destruction of the train would have been inevitable, but the break was on the inside. With that rapid decision which the better class of railroad men learn to exercise, he signalled to the engineer, "Faster, faster yet!" There was a sharp jolt, and the loco-motive and the cars attached were on the other side of the obstruc-tion with their speed not even abated.

There it was—a firsthand claim that the *Texas* had flown across the yawn-ing gap in the tracks, suffering nothing more than a "sharp jolt" as it jumped safely from rail to rail. Pittenger's books were very popular in their day, and the explanation soon became legend, shored up here and there by other remarks by Fuller. The conductor told one reporter, for example, that the *Texas* had encountered a loose rail and "jumped clear up off the track, we thought it was gone, but it careened back all right and we were safe." Other witnesses, not to be outdone, would tell their own variations on this story. Dorsey would suggest that the raiders, "in our unskillfulness," took up a rail on the inside of a curve rather than the outside; and since a train going around a curve throws its weight against the outside rail, the break could still be passed. (Dorsey would acknowledge, however, that the account of an engine jumping a break in the rails was "hardly possible—and is denied by others.") For his part, Jacob Parrott would claim that the raiders left a bent rail on the track in an effort to throw their pursuers off the rails. "But they did not even slow up near it, and we saw them jounced a foot in the air as they ran over it safely," he said. "What a race!"[11]

The leaping locomotive is, of course, an impossibility, ridiculed years later by Anthony Murphy and eventually corrected by Pittenger in his later writings. "The story of the missing rail was a mistake, a gross error, to speak mildly," Murphy wrote. But Pittenger's memory of this would harden as time passed—in no small part because of his consultation with Fuller. In fact, the Ohioan was probably mistaking the earlier removal of a rail (perhaps the one that had snapped with a "twang" south of Adairsville) for an unsuccessful attempt farther up the road (north of Calhoun), or perhaps thinking that the rail they had merely loosened had actually been removed entirely. Twenty-five years after the fact, in an exchange of correspondence in 1887-88, Murphy would finally convince Pittenger that the amazing flight of the *Texas* had never happened, nor could it have happened.

Adding to the confusion, the Atlanta newspapers reported that on multiple occasions, the pursuers aboard the *Texas* had mended the severed track by pulling up rails from behind them and spiking them down in front. This, too, was not accurate, at least so far as the *Texas* was concerned. The tactic of borrowing rails from behind to pave the iron road in front had indeed been suggested by Murphy and employed by Wiley Harbin in bringing the *William R. Smith* past the break north of Kingston, and it is possible that a reporter heard of that action and simply attributed it to the wrong place and the wrong locomotive.[12]

The second prevalent myth is the dramatic but apocryphal tale of the flaming boxcar on the bridge. In this version of events, after the raiders dropped their rearmost car north of Calhoun, they succeeded in setting a fire in one of their other cars (some say it was the second one and some the third), sparking it with kindling and coals from the firebox and then nursing the flame with brush, sticks, and oil-doused crossties. This car, smoking and crackling, was reportedly left in the middle of one of the covered bridges on the line. Some accounts have it on one of the bridges that cross the many branches of Chickamauga Creek, while others place the incident on the Oostanaula River bridge itself. It was said that the raiders watched breathlessly as smoke poured from the car, hoping to see the flames begin to gnaw into the beams and curl around the eaves of the rain-soaked roof. Jacob Parrott described the suspense: "The blazing car stopped in the middle of the bridge. We came to rest beyond and watched it. This was the crisis. Everything depended on how soon the fire caught the structure. We had only a handful of wood left. Would the flames never lick up into the rafters?" According to the story, the pursuers dashed up to the flaming car and, undaunted by the heat, coupled to it and pushed it free, saving the bridge and continuing the chase.

Peter James Bracken. (*Colonel James G. Bogle Collection*)

A compelling tale, to be sure—but again, it did not happen. "True, they *intended* to do this, but it never came off," a historian of the raid concluded years later, "however, the item was too good to write off; it stayed *on*, and no amount of debunking will ever eradicate it." In reality, the raiders dropped their second boxcar well short of the covered bridge, and Bracken again handled the obstruction with ease. He coupled to the second boxcar as he had the first, and pushed it on in front of the *Texas*. Other than serving to lighten the *General's* load, as the engine continued up the line with only the tender and a single freight car left, the abandonment of the two boxcars had served no purpose. "The time lost in dropping the cars was about as long as that lost in coupling to them," Pittenger admitted. The *Texas* pushed the two discarded boxcars through the bridge and deposited them on a siding shortly beyond. (The second boxcar may have been smoldering as it passed through the structure, kicking up a good deal of smoke and sparking the legend that the boxcar was in flames on the bridge as the *Texas* cleared it out of the way.)[13]

The idea apparently did not occur to the raiders that the covered bridge offered a ready-made roadblock, even if they could not burn it. Murphy, for one, feared that the thieves ahead of him would not only drop but derail a car, perhaps on the trestle approaching the river or in the confines of the bridge itself, and thus create a hindrance that could not be displaced without a large number of men, horses, and equipment. "On reaching the bridge, we found they had dropped the car on the trestle, but did not throw it off the rail, nor was it fired, as stated by some people," Murphy wrote. "Andrews was too anxious to escape." Murphy thought that an experienced railroad man would have known to attempt such a move, but apparently none of the railroaders along with Andrews ever suggested it.[14]

A third and final myth, perpetuated by books and eventually motion pictures over the years, was the tale that the *General* fled from the *Texas* in a "hail of gunfire." This story originated largely from the raider Alf Wilson, imaginative as ever, who had likewise claimed that the raiders had been shot at back at Big Shanty. "They opened on us at long range with musketry. The bullets rattled around us like hail, but fortunately none of our party was hit," Wilson wrote. "This is the only instance I have ever heard of where troops were put in to action on a moving railroad train, and I am clear in my mind that this kind of warfare will never become popular if everyone regards it from my standpoint." Other Yankees, such as William Knight, would also recall that some of the pursuing party "tried to pick us off with their rifles." In fact, Fuller, Murphy and their men just had the two old shotguns between them—which they never fired—and the only soldiers in pursuit (at least for now) were miles behind, with Captain Whitsitt on board the *Catoosa*. Still, popular depictions of gunfire in the course of the chase would endure, from the pages of comic books to the scenes of Disney's 1956 movie, which would add for good measure whooping Confederate cavalry and other cinematic derring-do.[15]

In addition to these legends, the story of the Andrews Raid was later sprinkled here and there with self-serving and sometimes almost preposterous claims of individual action and initiative. Fuller, for example, would later describe the raiders dropping a rail across the track as the *Texas* nipped at their heels. The following engine was unable to reverse in time, and the *Texas*'s tender "got over before we could stop." Fuller claimed that he removed the obstruction. "I pulled it out," he said, "though it weighed nine hundred pounds." The conductor would later ascribe to himself other improbable physical feats—such as when he grabbed Henderson by the hand as the *Texas* rolled past Calhoun and "literally threw the boy over into the tender"—as well as over-the-top descriptions of the hardships he endured, such as his claim that he was bleeding from the nose and the ears from his exertions.

On the other side, some among the Union enlisted men would ascribe to themselves boldness and foresight that exceeded that of their intrepid leader.

Several, including Knight, Pittenger, and Parrott, claimed that they urged Andrews to halt and fight. Pittenger's plan of attack, proposed to his bearded chief at one of the refueling stops, was to "let our engineer take our engine on out of sight, while we hid on a curve after putting a tie on the track, and waited for the pursuing train to come up; then, when they checked to remove the obstruction, we could rush on them, shoot every person on the engine, reverse it, and let it drive at will back as it came." Not only would this take care of the train behind them, it would have blocked or wrecked any others further back down the line. "Andrews said it was a good plan," Pittenger recalled; but he merely "looked all around, then hurried to the engine, and I had no further opportunity of discussing the subject." The Kentucky spy may well have considered the odds of success in an armed fight to be against them—he had seen armed soldiers drilling along the route, and he knew they were still deep in Southern territory—but many of his men would later suggest he lacked the nerve. (It is striking to think of the skittish, bespectacled Corporal Pittenger standing in the rain and urging the bold and formidable Andrews to have a little backbone.) Still, as Parrott would note, quite accurately, James Andrews "was not a soldier and had never been in battle." He was bold and effective operating on his own hook, as a smuggler or spy, but as a military leader, he was lacking. "Not saying anything against the man, but I don't think he was intended to take charge of a lot of men in a case like that," Knight concluded. Though some Southern accounts would later suggest a near-mutiny, none of the surviving raiders ever spoke of such a thing, either then or later. Andrews was in charge, and their course of action would be flight rather than fight.[16]

*T*he raiders, who were by now experiencing what one would call "the first feeling of despondency of the whole route," continued their run northward, leaving the Oostanaula River bridge intact and undamaged. A reporter would describe this as "the turning point of the contest; before, it was an offensive movement, from now on it was defensive, and all energy was applied towards making their escape from an enemy's country." With the two boxcars pushed off onto a siding just past the bridge and the track now clear ahead, the *Texas* chuffed through and beyond Resaca, closing to within a stone's throw of the *General*. The chase was truly on. "From this instant the race became one of life or death," Fuller told a spellbound audience in a speech years later. "Imagine two engines, one a Rogers and the other a Danforth & Cook, both five feet ten inch drivers, with 160 pounds of steam, and throttle wide open! No such race has ever been run, either before or since." The two locomotives ran at high speeds, the *General* rushing headlong through the rain and the *Texas* pressing close behind it in reverse. "Looking back at it now, our whole course seems reckless in the extreme," Murphy said, "but we were young then, and youth takes chances that are appalling to old age." Continuing to hurl crossties out behind them onto the track, the raiders would often pull away, their pursuers disappearing from view, but at every straight stretch of track, the trailing locomotive was clearly visible behind them. "First we drew away from them, then they caught up," Parrott recalled. "Over and over again this happened."[17]

The *General* hurtled up the W&A, which stretched north in comparatively gentle curves on this section, roughly parallel to the rippling banks of the nearby Connasauga River. "We crammed the furnace with every combustible we could lay our hands on," Wilson later wrote. "Again she plunged ahead at frightful speed, reeling and rocking on the rough track like a drunken man." Above the treetops behind them, Andrews could see the relentless black smoke of the pursuing engine, but they would soon have no choice but to make a stop, as the supply of wood in the tender was running out. (They had traveled almost forty miles since the stop at Cass Station and were therefore a good bit beyond the maximum distance the *General* typically ran on a cord of wood.) They soon came to the wood-and-water station near Tilton, seven miles north of Resaca, and the train slid to a stop on the wet rails. The raiders first drew water from the tank, leaving the tap open, and then rolled forward to the woodyard. The Ohio soldiers scurried desperately back and forth to the woodpile as the *Texas* again appeared in the distance, "thundering after us like a roaring storm-cloud before a furious wind," Wilson remembered. The tender was far from full, and the raiders continued their replenishment until the last possible moment, with the pursuers closing in. "The great characteristic of the members of this expedition, and one which gained the admiration of all, is the persistency with which they fought against odds, worked amidst the thousand dangers, and never abandoned the ultimate hope of carrying out their plans," a Chattanooga reporter later wrote of the desperate effort to refuel at Tilton, "though they had long passed the time when the work could have been successfully concluded." The *General* shot off up the tracks and away from the woodyard, its tender maybe two-thirds full of wood. Murphy remembered catching sight of the speeding locomotive up ahead. "We could see the top of the smokestack," he wrote. "It looked as though the *General* was sailing as it rounded the curve majestically and as fast as steam could force it."[18]

Now just ahead for the two rival engines was the important junction town of Dalton, the largest city on the line north of Marietta. Formerly a tiny mountain hamlet known first as Froglevel and then as Cross Plains, Dalton had been established in 1847, its limits defined as a one-mile radius from its new geographic, economic, and social center: the depot of the Western & Atlantic Railroad. (The historic red-brick depot building still stands, a plaque set in the hardwood floor marking the spot considered to be the center of Dalton.) Five years after the town's founding, a second line known as the East Tennessee & Georgia Railroad was completed, forming the right branch of a "Y" (or "wye," to use the railroad term) running northeast to Cleveland and Knoxville, Tennessee, where it connected on to Lynchburg, Virginia, and points north. The junction town was in 1862 one of the largest communities in Cherokee Georgia, and it would see a great deal of action in the war, beginning with the passage of the dueling locomotives on April 12, 1862. Two years later, Confederate General James Longstreet would disembark here at the depot in Dalton before leading his corps westward to the Battle of Chickamauga.

James Andrews seemed to give little consideration to the suggestions that his Union boys stop and fight it out, and this may have been in part because he was preoccupied with getting past the tangle of branches, switches, and sidings at Dalton. The junction up ahead posed a number of potential problems. First, they would have to slow or stop their train completely to check the switch ahead to be sure that it was set for the left-hand fork to the W&A and not the right to the East Tennessee & Georgia Railroad—they could hardly afford to make a wrong turn at this stage of the proceedings. Second, the tracks in Dalton actually ran through the passenger shed before passing a maintenance building and a turntable and then diving off to the left coming out of the station—a dangerous stretch to run at high speed. Finally, as at Kingston earlier that morning, the junction might well be crowded with cars, passengers, crews, and extra trains—but the Yankees would have no time, this time, for any explanations or delays.

Knight and Brown stopped the *General* a few hundred feet short of the depot at Dalton. Andrews dismounted and ran forward to check the switch and the track ahead. He was back in "an exceedingly short time" and offered a clipped and stern explanation as the train again lurched forward and picked up speed. "I am running this train through to Corinth, and I have no time to spare," he called out over the loud chuffs of the engine. Numerous sidings split off from the main line right and left, and the double tracks—one for the W&A, the other branching off to the East Tennessee & Georgia line—ran side-by-side under the peaked roof of the passenger shelter up ahead. The train, consisting by now of only the engine, tender, and a single boxcar, the latter almost ripped to shreds front and rear by its inhabitants, rushed "with frightful speed" under the roof, still accelerating, much to the astonishment of the passengers crowded in the pavilion to escape the falling rain. (Watching as the *General* came barreling headlong through the station, one nearby railroad man remarked that the superintendent would surely discharge the train's engineer if he saw him running like that.) The rails ahead curved sharply to the left as the abbreviated train darted out of the partial darkness of the shed, the bend so tight and sudden that, for an instant, William Knight thought the tracks came to an end and that he had mistakenly taken a dead-end siding. The engineer vividly recalled his fright more than forty years later, telling a visitor "that a terrible sensation was his, when the engine shot around the sharp curve—he could see no track ahead, and that sudden swirl made him think of open switches and siding collisions." He squeezed his eyes shut tight as the *General* hit the turn, lunging hard left without slowing. The raiders riding behind were sent tumbling against the right wall of the boxcar, and the crew on the engine clung desperately to handgrips and fought to keep their feet. "Knight thought it was the last of him and us, but kept a tight grip on the lever," Dorsey later wrote.[19]

Back behind, the *Texas* was rushing up the last two miles of the line into Dalton—for the most part an open, level piece of straightaway—and Fuller took the opportunity to scratch out a message to the recently promoted Brigadier General Danville Leadbetter at Chattanooga. Minutes later, the *Texas* sprinted into the station, slowing just long enough for Edward Henderson to jump off at the depot. He ran along the platform and into the telegraph office, Fuller's damp, scribbled note clutched tightly in his hand. The young, thin operator stooped over the key and began tapping out a message. At about the same time, a short distance up the line to the northwest, Andrews had ordered another halt, and Sergeant John Scott was scaling a pole to cut the telegraph wires.

As instructed, Henderson sent Fuller's warning off to the authorities in Chattanooga, but he received no confirmation and had no way of knowing if it had gotten through.

As the engineers laid out the crooked line of the Western & Atlantic in the 1840s, the imposing hulk of the high, north-south ridge of

Chetoogeta Mountain presented their greatest obstacle. While the other hills and ridges along the proposed route presented the designers with softer grades or welcome gaps along which the railroad bed could be laid, the rocky slope of Chetoogeta shot upward at a daunting angle, unbroken for miles in either direction, quite as if the Almighty had constructed a stone wall for the express purpose of keeping trains out of His mountains. The engineers soon decided that they would go under this mountain, not over or around it, and in 1847 construction began on what would become the first railroad tunnel to be built south of the Mason-Dixon Line. The site's Indian name would soon fade into disuse and a new name proudly applied to the ridge—Tunnel Hill.

Like many early Southern industrial achievements, the tunnel was constructed in large part with slave labor, drawn from surrounding farms and plantations. Work crews began the hard and dangerous excavation in early 1848, burrowing through the mountain inch by inch at either end, headed for a meeting in the middle. They broke through on the morning of October 31, 1849, and "met with an exactness creditable to the engineering of Messrs. Morse and Wells," Chief Engineer William L. Mitchell reported with pride. "The centre lines from the opposite ends varied from each other less than the sixteenth of an inch." Over the following months, the twelve-foot-wide tunnel was cleared and leveled, the top shored up with a solid clay brick arch and the sides lined with large limestone blocks. In the meantime, the railroad connection between Atlanta and Chattanooga was otherwise complete. During the two years the tunnel was under construction, the small number of passengers on the line would ride the train up from Atlanta, disembark in the shadow of Chetoogeta, board a stagecoach for a bumpy, circuitous ride around the mountain, and then catch a second train for the rest of the journey to Tennessee.

On May 9, 1850, the 1,447-foot-long tunnel was completed, and the first train was run over the entire 138-mile length of the W&A. The tunnel was considered one of the great engineering marvels of the South, and a grand ceremony was held at Tunnel Hill to commemorate the occasion. A number of dignitaries were in attendance, including John Pendleton King, former United States Senator and now president of the Georgia Railroad & Banking Company, the "Iron King" Mark A. Cooper, and the chief engineer, chief contractor, chief mason, and chief tunneler on the project. Called on to give a speech, Cooper lauded the completion of the first connection between the Atlantic Ocean and the Mississippi—"the chain is now complete," he said. A procession marched from east to west through the length of the tunnel, led by "a band of Sable musicians who belonged on the work and seemed to have sprung up spontaneously for the purpose." A cannon forged at Cooper's works was muscled to the summit of the mountain and seven salutes fired for the occasion. The tunnel was then dedicated by means of the application of the contents of several bottles of Madeira wine, a bottle of grape brandy, a bottle of port, and a bottle of a Georgia wine called scuppernong. The crowning touch was a generous sprinkle of water said to be from the River Jordan, presented by the Reverend John Jones of Marietta, a gift from the Reverend Lanneau, late missionary to Jerusalem. The water, "after being handed around the crowd for the inspection of the curious," was poured out on the rails by the chief engineer.[20]

Arriving at the tunnel a month short of twelve years later, James Andrews and his men could have used a little magic water themselves. Leaving Dalton behind, they had crossed Mill Creek and run by Buzzard's Roost Gap before curling back north and then hard to the west approaching Tunnel Hill. The route was bent and tortuous on this stretch, and the speed of the chase on the slick and twisting rails much less dramatic. The *Texas* was still pressing them, close behind, and the raiders' supply of wood from their hasty stop near Tilton, sixteen miles back, was already considerably depleted. The *General* sped toward the mouth of the tunnel and under the arched stone entrance into the blackness.

Jacob Parrott, along with many of the other raiders, thought the tunnel presented an "ideal place" to set up an ambush. "With the smoke of our train filling the space, with our party concealed along the sides in the darkness, success would be likely even if they had twice our number," Pittenger wrote. But again, no orders were given to stop and fight. The *General* "pitched on through the darkness," back out into the rain, and on past the trackside village of Tunnel Hill just beyond.

Approaching the tunnel behind them, the men aboard the *Texas* were watchful and wary, if not fearful. "I knew it would be dangerous to enter the south end until the Raiders had cleared the north end," William Fuller wrote in his account of the pursuit. He was concerned not only about an ambush, but also about obstructions placed on the track in the darkness, certain that the Yankees had reserved some crossties or other objects to place on the track in the tunnel. Anthony Murphy, for his part, was looking for something else as they rolled closer to the imposing face of the ridge. For a while now, he had thought that the thieves ahead might be running short of wood, as their speed had dropped considerably since the trains passed Dalton. It occurred to the Irishman that the tunnel would provide a sort of fuel gauge. If there were thick black smoke hanging in the tunnel—as typically occurred as a train passed through—that would mean the *General* had a blazing firebox and plenty of wood. Clear air in the tunnel, on the other hand, would suggest a lack of steam.

The *Texas* crawled forward slowly as it approached the tunnel, when to their satisfaction, Fuller, Murphy, and the others saw the dim gray light of day reflected off the unbroken surface of the rails throughout the length of the tunnel. A bright half-moon speck of light at the tunnel's exit was visible in the darkness far ahead. The road was unbroken and unobstructed—both the air and the tracks were clear. The engine thieves were running out of fuel and time.

The *Texas* sped out of the tunnel and back into the falling rain as Bracken pulled the throttle wide.

"Boys, we've got 'em now!" he cried.[21]

Raider Samuel Robertson. (*Colonel James G. Bogle Collection*)

CHAPTER TEN

"Every Man for Himself!"

Two Miles North of Ringgold

Fire on the mountain—run boys, run.
—The Charlie Daniels Band,
"The Devil Went Down to Georgia" (1979)

*T*HE RAIDERS CONTINUED TO struggle desperately to escape as they left the
tunnel behind and pushed on through the rain toward Catoosa and
Ringgold. They were low on fuel with the *Texas* close behind—we were "hot
on 'em," Murphy would recall—and though destruction of any bridges now
seemed impossible, they had not given up hope of saving themselves. After
all, they were now within thirty curving railroad miles of Chattanooga—even
closer as the crow flies—and they expected that General Mitchel was drawing close to the Mountain City with his division as well. They did not know
that, whatever now happened in their duel with the locomotive behind them,
their ultimate failure was now assured. For the young lad Ed Henderson,
bending over the telegraph key at Dalton, had managed to get Fuller's message through to Chattanooga just before the Yankees cut the wires. The telegraph read:

> Dalton, Ga.
> 12 April, 1862
> To GEN. DANVILLE LEADBETTER,
> Commander at Chattanooga:
>
> My train was captured this A.M. at Big Shanty, evidently by Federal
> soldiers in disguise. They are making rapidly for Chattanooga,

possibly with the idea of burning the railroad bridges in their rear. If I do not capture them in the meantime, see that they do not pass Chattanooga.

William A. Fuller[1]

For Brigadier General Leadbetter, this jarring missive—sent by some Georgia ticket-taker he had never heard of, who seemed to be issuing orders, no less—was yet another piece of bad news in what had been a terrible past couple of days. The apostate Northerner had enjoyed a relatively uneventful winter in comfortable quarters in Chattanooga, and the East Tennessee insurgency had been for the most part quiet—chastened, he believed, by his enforcement of hard-handed justice in the region and his diligent safeguarding of the railroads. He spent January and February happily laying out fortifications and defenses, improving railroad security, and interrogating the occasional prisoner, with the war seemingly far away to the north and the west. On February 28, 1862, he had been promoted to brigadier general, continuing a rapid advance up the military ladder. On the November night when David Fry and his men burned the East Tennessee bridges, Leadbetter was still an undistinguished major; just three and a half months later, his prospects seemed to shine as bright as the newly pinned gold stars that adorned his collar.

Then came spring, and with it, crisis seemed to be blooming in all directions. Chattanooga had been in a panic since early the day before, April 11, when word came from the west that a large Union force under General Mitchel had taken Huntsville in a surprise advance and were now coming east along the Memphis & Charleston Railroad. The junction town was in an uproar, citizens fleeing their homes while the officers of the overmatched Confederate forces tried to keep their composure as they scrambled to organize a defense and begged the powers that be for reinforcements.

And now this: a threat from the south as well. The news was heralded over town "quick as thought," according to a newspaper correspondent, "that the 'Yanks' had possession of the road; that all the bridges between here and Dalton were burned; that Cleveland, Tenn., had fallen into the hands of the enemy; and that they were in a few miles of Chattanooga." Bedlam ensued in the Mountain City. Tongue planted in cheek, the reporter continued: "There was no flag of truce sent out, no bacon burned, nor any precipitous stampeding; but nothing else was wanting to make the scene sublimely ridiculous. Some men cursed, others laughed; some grew pale, others discovered them-

selves subject to an infinitude of bodily distempers; some became quite attentive to their 'sick families;' while others, being slightly under the influence of
spirits more *ardent* than their own, gallantly seized defensive weapons, and
assisted upon marching against the foe."

General Leadbetter—who was himself regularly accused of everything
from drunkenness to cowardice, and who would be saddled with charges of
both in the Atlanta papers before the month was out—immediately dispatched a company of soldiers under the temporary command of a Major
Butler to meet the approaching Yankees. The "Moccasin Rangers," as they
were called, hastily assembled at the depot, loaded up on four or five platform cars, and sallied forth down the W&A to meet the advancing blue
horde. The local cavalry was denied a part in the chase, perhaps due to the
foul weather—the papers would also report, rather mockingly, that a "cavalry company was also ordered out, but upon arriving at a small creek a few
miles from town, which looked a little *muddy*, they were ordered back and
exhorted to resign whatever glory might be won in the coming conflict to the
infantry which had just departed in the train." Eleven miles south of
Chattanooga, in a shallow cut past the station at Chickamauga, the
Confederate soldiers disembarked from their flatcars, tore up the iron rails,
and took a position on the banks on each side of the track. They sent a flagman ahead and hunkered down in the rain to wait, hoping to bag the entire
platoon of Yankees, and their train along with them. Pittenger would later
attribute both extensive preparations and evil intentions to Leadbetter's gray
blocking force: he imagined them felling trees across the track and preparing
artillery emplacements to meet the approaching raiders, claiming, "Their
orders were for them to make a general massacre—not to spare a single man."
This unsupported charge hardly seems true given the ultimate outcome, but
in any event, the railroad ahead of the northbound raiders was now hopelessly blocked.

The stolen train would never make it to the Market Street crossing in
Chattanooga.[2]

"Our situation was becoming more unpleasant every moment," Alf
Wilson later wrote, with a considerable degree of understatement.
The *General's* thinning smoke did indeed tell the tale: the raiders were by now
almost out of wood to feed the furnace. The water in the tank was low, the
oil cans all but empty, the engineers, fireman, and brakeman all battling
exhaustion. Passing the little station at Tunnel Hill with their pursuers in

plain sight behind them, the boxcar-riders found they had no more crossties to throw out onto the track behind them. Front center in the cab, the needle on the steam gauge was falling rapidly. Desperate to rally their flagging engine, the raiders now stuffed anything remotely combustible into the firebox, along with the last scraps and splinters of wood. The oil cans went in, as did Andrews's hat and saddlebags, along with a number of pages of unidentified and presumably secret papers of some sort. Still hopeful that one of the small bridges up ahead could be ignited, Andrews ordered that the last boxcar be set afire, but the rain by now was falling in buckets, and there was little more than bark and splinters in the tender. The rain blew in the open end of the car, and it took careful nursing and a number of coals from the firebox to get a flame going at all. The car itself would not catch, and the would-be fire, smoldering and sputtering on the floorboards, ultimately served only to smoke the sixteen Federal soldiers out of the boxcar and up onto the tender, which by now had plenty of room to accommodate them.

The train, no longer careening along at breakneck speed, limped four miles to and past the town of Catoosa, and then managed another four miles hence to Ringgold, a mountain crossroads just beyond where the road curled to the west through the thousand-foot-wide gap between Taylor's Ridge and White Oak Mountain. But it was increasingly clear that time was running out. The *General* was failing, chuffing ever slower despite her minimal load of an almost empty tender and a single freight car that carried no freight. "She was shaken loose in every joint, at least she seemed so; the brass on her journals and boxes was melted by the heat; her great steel tires almost red hot, while she smoked and sizzled at every joint," Alf Wilson remembered. "I could liken her condition to nothing else than the last struggles of a faithful horse, whose heartless master has driven and lashed him until he is gasping for breath and literally dying in the harness."

Andrews then called a council of war (if a hasty discussion among a civilian and three privates could qualify as such) among the four men on the engine—Knight, Brown, Wilson, and himself—and discussed the course they should follow. They quickly concluded that the action that would give them best chance of survival was to separate, flee into the countryside, and head for the Federal lines, each man on his own. To try to escape as a group, or to fight it out at this late stage, seemed mere folly, "with the great number of rebel troops in the front and in our rear, and, in fact, on all sides of us," as Wilson put it. The twenty Yankees at this point would have been far from formidable as an organized military unit—exhausted, waterlogged, lacking any military leader, trapped front and rear in rugged territory, and armed with only pocket pistols. Andrews instructed the entire party: "Scatter in small parties and escape the best way you can." Bill Pittenger would later criticize this decision—"Andrews' presence of mind, for a time, seemed to desert him," he said—but this was, to be sure, more a result of the young corporal's fear of abandonment than an objective consideration of the circumstances.[3]

The old Ringgold depot still stands today, its original fourteen-inch stacked sandstone walls shored up here and there by limestone blocks. The station was constructed in 1849 and has been in continuous use on the road since May 9, 1850, the day the first train ran over the entire length of the W&A—though the building suffered considerable damage from artillery fire from Major General Joseph Hooker's guns at the Battle of Ringgold in November 1863. (A stern General U.S. Grant would confer with Hooker just behind the depot the morning of the battle.) The *General* rattled past the long, low roof of the depot and pulled around a broad curve before encountering a relentless upgrade, the woods again thickening on either side as the town disappeared behind. The wheezing engine slowed perceptibly as it came into the straightaway and started up the hill. Her five-foot drivers spun slower and slower, until it was clear that there was no way she would ever reach the crest.

Andrews gave his final command: "Jump off and scatter!" he cried. "Every man for himself!" Notwithstanding the spy's earlier (alleged) promise to Pittenger that the raiders would "come through in a body or die together," when the moment arrived, the twenty men leapt off the train in ones and twos and skedaddled in all directions. "They swung off one by one from the steps of the '*General*,' and from the car, in the midst of foes, their plans thwarted, efforts failed, and dangers just begun," a reporter later wrote of the scene. The sight of the thieves dropping off of the ragged, smoking train ahead would create an indelible memory for Anthony Murphy, who would write decades later: "The impression left on my mind then is such that I imagine I can now see them as they flee for safety, not knowing which way to go."[4]

Knight and Brown, the engineers, were the last two men off, the latter pulling the reverse lever in hopes of driving the engine back down the hill and colliding it into the *Texas*, which was following cautiously some two or three hundred yards behind. This final attempt at railroad havoc came to naught—the lethargic *General* lacked the steam to undertake such a rush, even downhill. Peter Bracken, who had been keeping a respectable distance as the locomotive ahead lost momentum, plainly on its last legs, simply reversed his engine too—that is, started it gently forward, since he had been driving backward all along—and gave room for the dying *General* to come to an uneventful halt behind him.[5]

The determined conductor William Fuller immediately jumped from the *Texas* and sprinted off into the woods after the raiders, rusty shotgun in hand. "We had saved the bridges and preserved the railroad—recaptured our engine, and now I wanted the Raiders," he recalled. Minutes later, the *Catoosa* arrived, carrying Captain Whitsitt's squad of Confederate soldiers, who likewise disappeared into the trees. As it happened, Whitsitt's infantrymen ultimately contributed little to the manhunt; they soon found themselves stalled by a high ridge nearby and then sidetracked altogether as one soldier accidentally discharged his musket, wounding one of his comrades.[6]

As the foreman of machine power for the state road, Murphy, for now, was more interested in checking on the stolen engine. He trotted a few steps up the hill and swung aboard the *General*. There was no wood in the engine's furnace and none in the tender behind, though there was still some water in the tank. On the footboard, Murphy found the switch keys Andrews had taken from Kingston, fifty-eight miles and several hours ago. The makeshift red flag hung damp and limp on its staff up front on the pilot. Apart from that, there was nothing unusual, nothing damaged or broken. Despite being pushed to her mechanical limits, the hissing locomotive seemed to be "all right," as Murphy put it, completely unharmed except for a single truck brass that had overheated for want of oil. "Those damned Yankees," one among the railroaders reportedly said, "they can run an engine as good as any of us."[7]

The two shining locomotives had come to a stop a short distance apart, standing in the drizzle in a dense thicket of pine and cedar trees. In his report made to the road's superintendent in the days that followed, Murphy would record the spot as about a half mile beyond mile post 116, some two miles north of Ringgold. A granite marker stands at the site today. James Andrews and his men had run the *General* nearly 89 miles from Big Shanty. Bill Fuller, Anthony Murphy, Peter Bracken, and the crew of the *Texas* had chased her down over the past forty-eight miles—every inch of it running backward.

The Western & Atlantic railroaders coupled the *Texas* to the *General* and, running forward now, began to tow her back down the line toward Ringgold. It was shortly after one o'clock in the afternoon, a little more than six hours after the theft at Big Shanty. The Great Locomotive Chase was over.[8]

*T*he raiders' sorry luck that day was even worse than they knew. Andrews's one-day postponement of the raid had put the action over to Saturday, and that meant it was "muster day" in the nearby town of Ringgold and other communities across the state. Throughout the countryside of Cherokee Georgia, men and boys left their farms and homesteads and hiked in the morning mist to the nearest villages and towns, often with wives, children, or siblings tagging along to visit the general store or to hear the latest gossip or news of the war. Dozens of would-be recruits headed to town to enlist, while home guardsmen met on village greens and courthouse squares to stumble their way through the unfamiliar manual of drill. Some plodded in on damp, sullen horses—most of these short-legged sorrels built for hauling and plowing, not for cavalry charges. Most men carried whatever sort of firearm they owned.

All of these homespun Rebels, men and boys, young and old, had one thing in common—they wanted to shoot some Yankees. Word soon arrived in Ringgold from the engineer of one of the strangely shortened trains that had just passed by that some Yankee fugitive spies were on the loose, scattered in the woods just to the north of town. One can imagine this exciting news was greeted with whatever early form of the Rebel yell may have existed in the North Georgia mountains at that time. "Then was organized the most stupendous man-hunt that ever took place in the South," Pittenger later reported, probably fairly accurately. The showers did nothing to extinguish the alarming news, which spread through the countryside like a windblown brushfire. The dirt roads and footpaths were soon filled with men on horseback and afoot, and the forest soon rang with the yelping of dogs and the whoops and yells of the locals. Crossroads, rivers, and ferries were guarded by homespun cavalry, made from scratch; rumors of sinister plots and huge rewards swept through the populace. Not everyone was sure who they were looking for or why, but that seemed to matter very little to the men beating the bushes and straining at the leashes of their barking hounds. "The only partially known object of the expedition imparted a tone of romantic exaggeration to it," Pittenger wrote, "and made the people doubly anxious to solve the mystery."[9]

Jump off and scatter, Andrews had said, and scatter they did, disappearing in small groups into the dense thicket of pine trees east and west of the railroad. "The boys lit out like a flock of quail," Knight remembered. Daniel Allen Dorsey, William Bensinger, Robert Buffum, and George Wilson sprinted into the woods to the right of the failing engine, heading off at a "rapid rate" in a direction they thought to be northeast. Poor Buffum was forced to relinquish two of his prized possessions at the outset. First, he had not had time to retrieve his whiskey bottle, heretofore a constant companion, from the smoking boxcar; and second, he soon shed his fine gray Confederate overcoat, "throwing his arms back and literally running out of it," as his friend Dorsey would recall. As the four scuffed their way through the sodden carpet of pinestraw and wet leaves, they encountered a number of women and children who had fled their homes in alarm at the exaggerated reports of an enemy invasion. The frightened locals hid in the woods and screamed to the passing raiders, "Run, for God's sake—the country's alive with Yankees!" The dim afternoon soon faded into darkness, and the quartet fled without direction—"we simply wandered," Dorsey admitted.[10]

The train engineers Knight and Brown, along with John Scott, Elihu Mason, and William Reddick, ran exactly the opposite way—to the southwest, toward the middle branch of Chickamauga Creek. They soon reached the stream, which they would understandably recall as a river, "bankfull" from the days of rain. Looking left and right for a place to cross, they saw no ford more favorable than where they stood, so they plunged in, holding their revolvers over their heads to keep their powder dry and "expecting a shot any minute from the rear." They made it across, no worse for wear and not that much wetter than they had been already, and hid themselves in the brush just on the opposite bank. A breathless, bumbling posse soon came up on the opposite side but were distracted by the sight of other fugitives from the Federal party farther up the river, and they headed off that way instead. "We lay where we first hid till dark," Knight remembered, "and to say it was dark would not express it."

Other groups of raiders plunged elsewhere through the rugged terrain, their clothes soon soaked from the rain and their faces striped by low-slung green branches. William Campbell, Samuel Slavens, and Perry Shadrach, none of whom were built for speed, may have been the first raiders captured despite being among the first men off the train. Tired, heavy, and laden with wet clothes and boots, the three fled more like ducks than quail and were soon chased down by a group of men and dogs a short distance from the railroad tracks. The three Yankees at first tried giving the time-tested Kentucky story, though they were caught too close to the train for the tale to have any plausibility (some would later suggest that the trio were spotted even as they jumped from the train and tracked down from that point). Thinking they might fare better as prisoners of war rather than civilian spies, the three then abandoned the cover story, identified themselves as Union soldiers and gave their regiments—Campbell falsely claiming to be a member Shadrach's Company K of the 2nd Ohio. The Flemingsburg alibi was thereby instantly transformed from a cover story into a brand that would serve to identify the raiders as they were captured. "Not the slightest blame can be attached to these captives for revealing themselves," Pittenger wrote, "but, unfortunately, they first told the old Kentucky story which had already served us so well that we forgot that it might wear out. After that, whenever a man was found hailing from Kentucky's Fleming County, he was set down as one of us, and no denial would even be listened to." Campbell, Shadrach, and Slavens were placed in irons and chained together before being taken in the midst of a "howling mob" to Ringgold and then on to Dalton.[11]

Their companions were making better progress, though most if not all of the fleeing Yankees had no idea which way they were headed. "Fast and blindly we traveled, not knowing where we were or what direction we took," Jacob Parrott remembered. The eighteen-year-old private found himself paired up with his friend Samuel Robertson, and the two young soldiers climbed a ridge and hid under a log until the next morning. Heading down the valley hoping to find their way northward, the two foolishly made their way back to the railroad tracks, where they soon encountered a patrol of local citizens. "We told the Flemingsburg, Kentucky story, and they nodded at each other wisely," Parrott recalled.

The two were taken to Ringgold for interrogation, which started out as merely harsh but soon turned brutal. Parrott was by appearance the younger and softer of the two—nearly five-foot ten, he weighed just 140 pounds, and was nattily dressed in a coat, vest, white broad-brimmed hat and black bow tie. "I was counted a Dude of the party," he proudly said years later, though to the Georgia mountain men, his attire may have suggested a Northern, big-city fragility they thought they could easily crack. Whatever the reason, Parrott would be the only raider singled out by the Rebel authorities for rough treatment. What followed is best described in Parrott's own words, given under oath in a deposition at the Judge Advocate General's office in Washington the following March:

Question. Will you state the circumstances of your capture and the treatment you received?

Answer. There was a man named Robinson, of our party, who was captured with me. We took to the woods after we left the train, and after a time we came out of the woods. When we came out on the railroad there were four citizens there, who saw us and took us. We were taken to Ringgold, where a company of Confederate soldiers was stationed. When we got into the hands of an officer, one of them took me out and questioned me, but I would not tell them anything.

An officer and four soldiers took me out and stripped me, and bent me over a stone and whipped me. They stood by me with two pistols, and said if I resisted they would blow me through. I was whipped by an officer, a lieutenant, who was with the party, and who had on the uniform. He gave me over one hundred lashes with a raw hide.

He stopped three different times during the whipping, let me up, and asked me if I would tell and when I refused to do so he would put me down and whip me again. He wanted me to tell who the engineer of the party was, and all about the expedition, but I would not do it. I did not tell him anything about it. The engineer was one of our soldiers, who was finally captured with the rest.

Question. Were other persons present when you were flogged?

Answer. Yes, Sir; there was a crowd there. It was right by the side of the railroad, and the people there wanted to hang me. They got a rope and would have hung me, but for a colonel who came up.

Question. Did you have a trial of any sort?

Answer. No, Sir.

Question. Your companion was with you at the time?

Answer. Yes, Sir.

Question. Why was he not whipped?

Answer. I do not know. He told the regiment that he and I belonged to. I suppose, as I was the youngest, they thought that they could make me tell the most; but I would not tell them anything, not even the regiment I belonged to.

Parrott's testimony squares with the accounts of his fellow Ohioans. "Finally, it is said, Robertson sickened at the sight of his comrade's punishment, and seeing his back all gashed and bleeding, told his persecutors that they were United States Soldiers, and that they were in the raid," Dorsey wrote. "This put a stop to the whipping." Nothing in the past of the illiterate farm boy from Kenton, Ohio, would have suggested any native toughness or iron resolve, but to his enduring credit, Parrott was unbreakable under vicious flogging and threats of death by way of mob violence or pistol-shot. The wounds he suffered from his lashing would cause him great pain during the incarceration still to come: Dorsey would describe Parrott's back as "fearfully cut up," and would remember pulling long scabs off of it himself at Parrott's own request. "When asked if he intended to die there among strangers without letting them know who he was," Dorsey recalled, "he said he intended just before he was actually killed—when he thought the end was near—to tell them his name and where he belonged, and let them do their worst."

Parrott would carry the honor and the scars from his flogging for the rest of his life: "I still bear the marks today," he reported in an article more than forty years later.[12]

*B*ack down at Big Shanty, the two oversleepers, Martin Hawkins and John Reed Porter, nearly succeeded in talking themselves out of their predicament. As their comrades were racing up the W&A aboard the *General,* Hawkins and Porter had hiked through the drizzle up the six-mile road from Marietta and reported for enlistment at Camp McDonald. A Confederate colonel, after a cursory interview, directed the two men to report to the commanding officer of the 9th Georgia Battalion. Being shorthanded, one of the battalion's companies was hastily assembled and a vote taken as to whether or not the two strangers should be accepted into the ranks. "The vote was unanimous in our favor," Porter recalled, "and we, after giving fictitious names, were assigned to a certain mess for our suppers." After eating, the two Ohioans enthralled their new Confederate companions with stories of the cruelties then being inflicted by "Yankee hirelings" back home in Kentucky. "Everything went all right with us," Porter wrote, "until in some manner it leaked out among the rebels that the Yankee raiders, by mistake or accident, had left two of their party at Marietta."

Suspicion immediately fell on the new enlistees, whose arrival did seem rather curious, come to think of it, given the commotion over across the way by Lacy's Hotel and the railroad tracks that morning. Hawkins and Porter were sent to headquarters and taken into a room, one at a time, for questioning. Porter identified himself as John Reed, and soon found himself at odds with the presiding officer, a Rebel colonel. "He proceeded in his order of examination as best suited him, and I answered as best suited myself, just the reverse of what they desired," Porter recalled. The six officers became increasingly "menacing and abusive" as the interrogation continued. "On various occasions during nearly four years of army life I experienced some pretty close calls, and run the gauntlet frequently," Porter later said, "but this was a little the closest corner I ever got into."

"Mr. Reed, you stand there thrice damned," the colonel said in concluding the interview, announcing a guilty verdict if not an ultimate sentence. "You may make your peace with your God, but you never can with Jeff Davis, and we ought to hang you without further ceremony."

The two men passed an uneasy night, first under guard at Big Shanty, and then in jail cell back down at Marietta, where they were taken by train. News of the captured spies soon spread through the town, and "in a short time an infuriated mob gathered around the jail and demanded our release, that they might wreak out their vengeance upon us, otherwise they would burn the jail," Porter recalled. The guard was increased and the night passed quietly, though it seemed to Hawkins and Porter that the morning would never come. Shortly after dawn on Sunday, the would-be raiders were taken to the depot, handcuffed, and padlocked together by way of a trace chain around their necks. This time, they succeeded in catching the morning train departing for Chattanooga.[13]

Bill Pittenger likewise came close to escaping by way of a bit of smooth talking and a stated intention to enlist. He had jumped from the left side of the still-moving train at Andrews's direction, tumbling along the railroad bed and coming up unhurt except for some scratches from the tangled briers that inconveniently lined the road at that point. Righting himself and making for the treeline just to the west, he found himself in the exact situation he feared the most—on the run, by himself, in the enemy's country. "I confess for a moment my heart sank within me," he later wrote. He soon came to a swollen stream—probably the Chickamauga—and fought his way through the current to the other side, where a hundred-foot ridge rose in a near-vertical wall. He climbed the steep hill hand-over-hand and collapsed at the top to rest and take stock. The former schoolteacher and newspaper correspondent was alone and exhausted; he had not eaten since the stop at Dalton the night before. His spectacles were streaked with water, the lenses fogged, and the landscape was a blur of greens and browns. The overcast sky blotted the sun completely, and he realized that he did not know whether he was fifteen miles or fifty from Chattanooga. And if all this was not disheartening enough, he soon heard in the distance the baying of a pack of hounds. Pittenger hardly knew what he should do or which way to go, but idleness was plainly no longer an option, so he headed off into the forest, in a direction he believed was perpendicular to the railroad.

He traveled for some time, descending a "wild, solitary valley" and crossing a road. Much to his relief, the sound of the dogs growing fainter as the

Raiders John Wollam, left, and Mark Wood. (*Colonel James G. Bogle Collection*)

day slipped into evening. Pittenger had never much believed the old saw that persons who are lost in the woods tend to travel in a circle, but he soon found himself again crossing a road, back at the same spot he had left an hour before. Frustrated but undaunted, he struck out over a hill, only to wind his way back to the road a third time. Not long after, he was back on the banks of what he was sure was the same river he had crossed before. Pittenger considered himself an educated and resourceful man, despite his limited vision, but in these circumstances, he was overmatched. "I was perplexed beyond measure," he admitted.

The nearsighted corporal continued his wandering throughout the night, hoping to cross the Tennessee River a few miles south of Chattanooga. On two occasions, he was able to inquire of local citizens as to his location: an old man gardening next to a "rude hut" said he was eight miles from the Mountain City, while some horsemen on the road later told him he was only three miles away—but even if the information was accurate, he was too confused to judge which way to go from there. He roamed, backtracked, took random turns, and later admitted following one road "almost regardless of where it should lead." The night sky was completely black and devoid of stars. "Never did I bend a more anxious eye to that darkened firmament, than in my solitary wanderings over the Georgia hills that night," Pittenger wrote a year later in a somewhat melodramatic account of his ordeal. "But all in vain; no North Star appeared to point with beam of hope to the land of the free." Clad in lightweight clothing and shivering from the torrential down-pour, he stumbled on with teeth chattering through much of the night before collapsing in fitful, dream-troubled sleep next to a roadside log.

An equally gray Sunday morning soon dawned, but Pittenger found the Sabbath lacked "the blessed calmness and peace that accompany it in my own sweet Ohio." Hiding in the woods, he saw people making their way to church, and had a strange longing to go with them, if only to make his way out of the wilderness. He wandered throughout the morning before being stopped for questioning just outside of the town of Lafayette, Georgia. As it turned out, he was more than twenty-two miles from Ringgold, and head-ed in exactly the wrong direction. Hoping to head northwest and cross the Tennessee past Chattanooga, he had instead journeyed to the south-south-west, and ended up almost thirty crowflight miles from the banks of the river.

But Pittenger, more so than some of his peers, was a bright young man and a good talker, and he put his persuasive skills to use. Altering the usual story somewhat, he claimed to be from Kentucky and had come south to Chattanooga hoping to enlist and fight against the tyranny of the abolition-ists and Lincolnites. Upon arriving there, he said, he was disgusted with the few poorly armed conscripts in the city and continued south, hoping now to swing through Alabama and join the renowned First Georgia Regiment near Corinth with General Beauregard. The apparent leader of the posse—a "lit-tle, conceited man, who had the epaulets of a lieutenant, but whom they called major"—declared himself satisfied and proposed that they let him go, then and there. Another man, however, sitting on a horse nearby with the brim of his hat pulled down low against the still-falling rain, said in a thick mountain drawl, "Well, y-e-e-s! Perhaps we'd as well take him back to town, and if all's right, maybe we can help him on to Corinth." Brought to the near-by town, Pittenger answered a number of other questions, from his home county—Fleming—to the county seat—Flemingsburg—to the surrounding counties—which he made up out of whole cloth. He then gave a detailed and often entirely fictional narrative of his journey southward, inventing families he had stayed with and describing in detail the country he had supposedly passed through over the past few days. "I still had faint hope that they might be induced to release me, and allow me to continue my journey," Pittenger maintained. But just as his questioners were "deliberating over my case, and could only agree that it needed further investigation," a rider clattered into town on a lathered horse, fresh from Ringgold with news of the capture of the Yankee bridge burners. They had first pretended to be citizens of Kentucky, from Fleming County, he said, but then confessed that they were Ohio soldiers ordered to burn the bridges on the state road. This "produced a marked change in their conduct toward me," Pittenger somewhat dryly recalled. He was searched, his penknife and other articles taken from him, and locked in the county jail.[14]

*F*ive of the raiders, including their leader, came very close to making a clean getaway. Alf Wilson and Mark Wood, who would now and on later occasions prove themselves to be extremely resourceful fugitives, hid for a time in a brush pile just a few hundred yards from the railroad, apparently surrounded on every side. "Several times parties after us passed so close to our hiding place that I could have reached out and touched their legs," Wilson wrote, thinking that the pounding of his heart could have been heard twenty yards away had the searchers not made so much noise themselves. "They were all yelling, swearing and shooting," he recalled, "and on the style of dogs chasing a rabbit in tall weeds—all jumping and looking high, while the game was close to the ground."

The two Ohioans stayed there, buried in the heap of limbs and brush, all Saturday night, through the daylight hours on Sunday, and well into Sunday night. Crawling out of their hiding place in the rain-soaked darkness, Wilson and Wood were so stiff that they had to vigorously rub their arms and legs in order to get moving. They decided to take an opposite course from most of their comrades, thinking the pursuit and suspicion may be less vigilant in that direction, and therefore struck off into the mountains to the northeast. Their goal was to reach the Tennessee River to the east of Chattanooga, and their reasoning was simple. A man traveling in the rough, wooded country, particularly at night, would surely find it hard to keep his direction—as Pittenger and others would demonstrate by their aimless wanderings in the North Georgia mountains. Wilson figured if they could reach the Tennessee, they could travel downstream under cover of darkness and always know they were heading westward, toward General Mitchel and the Third Division in northern Alabama. Strengthened somewhat by a meal of buttermilk and cornbread begged from a country farmhouse, the pair made a "toilsome" journey over the next two days and nights, arriving on Wednesday afternoon at the town of Cleveland, Tennessee, about twenty rugged miles north-north-east of Ringgold. Deciding that they sure could use a map, Wilson walked boldly into the town, found a bookseller, and bought himself a school atlas.

Returning to the woods, the men tore out the pages they needed and continued on their way.

Fortunately, Wilson and Wood were now well into the East Tennessee hills, solid Union country, and they could now hope for help along the way. They found supper at the home of a husband and wife, good Union folks, who warned them to watch out for local cavalry under the command of a man named Snow. Sure enough, they soon encountered the elderly home guardsman, who subjected them to vigorous interrogation and what Wilson called "the most fiery lecture on the subject of Northern rights and Southern wrongs we had ever heard" before returning their pistols to them and letting them go on their way. Following this close call, the two returned to the home of the Unionist couple, where they were hidden and fed through the Easter weekend.

On Monday morning, April 20, the two men were guided to a nearby creek, where they found an unattended canoe. Climbing into the boat—the Englishman Wood no doubt delighted by this change to a naval excursion—they made their way to the Tennessee and paddled downstream in the broad, winding river. They worked their way down the river, traveling intermittently over the next two days and nights, passing Friar's Island, Chattanooga, and Moccasin's Point without being seen. Along the way, they paid three Confederate dollars to a local man, who guided them through the treacherous rapids known to the locals as "the Suck." Late Wednesday night, Alf Wilson and Mark Wood arrived at Bridgeport, Alabama, floating under the railroad bridge and wondering whether they had made it to safety.

The next morning, they abandoned their canoe and struck out on foot, soon hearing from some retreating Rebels that the Yankees were at Stevenson, just four miles away. Arriving in town, they were startled to find it occupied not by friendly bluecoats, but swarming with Confederates. The two men were asked their business in the town and soon found themselves detained, accused by one of the locals of being "one of the rascals that was here with the Federal cavalry." There was little comfort in the fact that this was untrue, and Wilson began secretly destroying his little map, tearing it into small pieces and "chewing up much of it." The pair was taken to Bridgeport, where they were searched and questioned further, when at last, a full twelve days after they abandoned the *General*, their luck ran out. For one among the crowd seemed to recognize Wilson, who had of course been in full view on the engine and tender throughout the engine chase. "I could have killed him without compunction if I had possessed the power," Wilson recalled, "for in the next breath he said: 'I know those fellows. I saw them on the train.'"[15]

As for James Andrews, he had left the faltering engine with the others and joined up with his now-frequent companions, Marion Ross and John Wollam. The three men struck out westward, crossing West Chickamauga Creek at Daffron's Ford south of Graysville and traveling all night through the woods. Andrews was one of the few men among the party who had a compass, and he planned to drive due west. His course would run parallel to and just south of the Tennessee state line, across Missionary Ridge and Lookout Mountain toward Bridgeport, where he supposed the Third Division of the Union Army of the Ohio would be by now. The secret agent and the two Federal soldiers crossed Missionary Ridge at Rossville Gap late Sunday afternoon and spent the night near the foot of the long ridge of Lookout Mountain, at the house of a Union man named Merrick Earpes.

A posse was assembled early Monday morning and soon caught the trail of the three men, with the reluctant help of a local physician, Dr. Thomas Y. Parks, who traveled widely to visit patients and knew the backwoods roads and footpaths of the country. Starting out from McCullough's Mill, the group split up as they made their way across the broad north-south ridge of Lookout Mountain, ten men making their way down the Wauhatchie trail, while a handful of others headed down a blind path pointed out by the doctor. Crossing Lookout Creek at Powell's Ford and inquiring at the home of Mrs. Powell in the valley nearby, the men learned that they were no more than a half hour behind the three suspects, and they spurred their horses into a gallop. They soon came to a meadow and saw the three men disappearing in the distance into a thicket of hawthorn, and they dove pell-mell into the underbrush. John Wollam hid behind an oak tree and sprang out with his revolver cocked, but seeing the armed horsemen, he quickly thought better of it. "There's no sense having two dead men here in the woods," he said, and handed over his weapon. Wollam adamantly maintained that he was down from Kentucky and on his way to join the Confederate army, but the tired story was of no use by now.

Andrews and Ross were rounded up in the woods just ahead, the former claiming rather blithely that they were in fact Rebel soldiers and producing with a flourish a Confederate passport he had used back in his smuggling days. Dr. Parks was no fool, however, and he made his accusation plain. "I know who you fellows are," he said, "you're some of the party that stole the engine at Big Shanty, Georgia, ran it up as far as Ringgold, then left it; you're not looking for the Confederate army."

Andrews replied "in a voice cool and steady, as if speaking to his best friend," and said, "Well, my friend, I am surprised at your information. You're right about it. I see there is no use trying to deceive you." He gave his name and Ross's, and made clear that they were surrendering as prisoners of war, and that they expected to be treated as such. They went along peaceably to join Wollam and the others, though there was a moment of fright for all concerned when Andrews, reaching in his pocket to let down the hammer on his cocked pistol, accidentally discharged the weapon. The doctor was relieved at the otherwise uneventful capture, certain that the three Yankees would have chosen to fight it out had they known the true numbers (only five) and armaments (a rifle, a shotgun, and a butcher knife) of their civilian captors. "All of them were grit to the backbone," Parks said, "but they supposed it was a hopeless fight."

Andrews, Knight, and Wollam were captured just above the hamlet of New England, Georgia, only a dozen or so cross-country miles from the Federal lines near Bridgeport—a single night's journey, in Dr. Parks's estimation. The three men were swung up on horses behind their captors and taken back to the northeast, crossing the series of ridges toward Chattanooga. About ten miles from the city, they were turned over to a company of Confederate cavalry under the command of Lieutenant James Edwards, who took them to General Leadbetter's headquarters for interrogation. Andrews gave his compass to the lieutenant as a souvenir of the occasion, though the young officer later dutifully turned it over to Leadbetter and never saw it again.[16]

William Fuller's dogged continuation of his own personal pursuit of the raiders from the railroad to the North Georgia woods, though admirable, ultimately came up empty. He started off with Fleming Cox and Alonzo Martin, heading at a full run into the trees to the west of the road, and he soon found himself alone in the brush-choked wilderness. About two miles from the railroad, he came upon a farmer plowing his field. The conductor quickly had the man unhitch his plowhorse and dispatched him to nearby Graysville to raise the alarm, later claiming implausibly that "three bridges were saved by the intelligence he bore." He ran another three miles— "uphill and downhill, mostly uphill," he said—fighting through underbrush, fields of wheat, and miry ground he would recall being as "sticky as dough." At one point, he spotted a handful of the raiders at the far side of a muddy field, and he detoured to put several contingents of local horsemen on the trail. He continued searching for the fugitives until darkness fell. "I ran on, and on," he said. "I was, or under ordinary circumstances would have been, broken down. I had not eaten anything since the day before; I had not drunk any water; I was bleeding at the nose, mouth and ears." Though his recollection seems to be seasoned heavily with melodrama, there is no doubt that the railroader had come to the end of a long, exhausting day.

Fuller came at last upon a backwoods farmhouse, whose inhabitants—two men and two women—were "wild with excitement" from the news they had heard, and more than a little suspicious of a stranger showing up on their porch in the thickening dusk. Fuller showed some papers to establish his bona fides with the railroad, and gave the names of some folks he knew in Ringgold, which satisfied the frightened ladies as to his identity. After a welcome drink from a bucket of cold water, the young conductor, stiff and sore and too tired to take another step, asked to be taken back to Ringgold. The two men lifted him up onto an old mule, the only mount they had to offer. Slumped over on a quilt draped across the mule's back, Fuller plodded back toward Ringgold like the Virgin bound for Bethlehem.

Arriving at the stone depot at Ringgold at about half past nine that night, Fuller hobbled into the agent's office and laid down to wait for the next train south to Atlanta. His day was over, but his role in the unfolding drama was not.[17]

Even as the detail of soldiers sent south under his charge were pursued, imprisoned, whipped, and interrogated in North Georgia and Tennessee, General Ormsby Mitchel was receiving the acclaim and appreciation to which, he believed, he was entitled. The crowning grace came on Tuesday, April 15, three days after the Andrews Raid, in the form of a wire from Washington.

> War Department
> Washington, April 15, 1862
>
> Sir:
> I have the honor to propose for your approbation the name of Brigadier-General Ormsby M. Mitchel, of the United States Volunteers, to be major-general by brevet of Volunteers, to date from April 11, 1862, for gallantry and meritorious conduct in the capture of Huntsville, Alabama, and for the Capture of Decatur and Stevenson Junction.
>
> I am, sir, with great respect, your obedient servant,
>
> Edwin M. Stanton
> Secretary of War.

The men in Mitchel's division regarded his promotion to major general as a validation of their actions and a well-deserved honor for Old Stars. "No other man with so few troops has ventured so far into the enemy's country, and accomplished so much," Colonel John Beatty wrote in his diary. "Battles if they result favorably are great helps to the cause, but the general who by a bold dash accomplishes equally important results, without loss of life, is entitled to as great praise certainly as he who fights and wins a victory." And both the soldiers of the Third Division and their general regarded this success as just the beginning. Mitchel's ambition, energy, and experience all seemed to prepare him for great things. "For him, we may almost believe, there was a horoscope," an admirer later wrote, "and that all the planets were conjoined in its composition."[18]

But triumph receded and frustration returned for Old Stars in late April. So recently clamoring to advance, he now found himself cast in the role of the overmatched commander, pleading for reinforcements and struggling to hold what he now held. "I deem the line I occupy one of vast importance, and a heavier force is required for its defense and protection," he wrote to Secretary of War Edwin Stanton on April 17. His division, undersized to begin with, was now dispersed across middle Tennessee and northern Alabama, guarding hundreds of miles of railroad and occupying Shelbyville, Fayetteville, Huntsville, Florence, Decatur, Tuscambia, Bellefonte, and a number of other villages and towns. His men, trains, and supplies were regularly attacked by Rebel cavalry or what he called "straggling bands of mounted men, partly citizens," an annoyance that culminated in early May with the embarrassing capture of his aide and son Edwin.

There was little in the way of help to be had. General Buell, idling the weeks away with General Halleck near Corinth, gave Old Stars no assistance beyond offering suggestions for what position he should occupy if and when he was forced to fall back. Halleck's view of the situation was simple: capturing the important junction at Corinth was the immediate priority in the Department of the Mississippi, and Mitchel was on his own. There would be no reinforcements provided by Buell or Halleck—the latter having rejected out of hand a similar request for reinforcements from Nashville: "We are now at the enemy's throat, and cannot release our great grip to pare his toe nails," he wrote.[19]

By late April, Mitchel's requests for assistance had deteriorated into abject whining in his reports to the War Department. "It is utterly impossible for me, with so small a force, to safely protect and defend so extended a line," he complained to Stanton on April 24. "I have now held my position for two weeks. . . . The deep responsibility resting upon me, added to the fact that I am compelled to be in motion day and night, is too much for my physical health." He concluded, "But for the fact that I have sixteen engines, and cars in proportion, it would be madness to hold my position a single day."

As for the fate of the mission he had sent into North Georgia, Old Stars made no mention of the affair to Washington, to Buell, or to anyone else for that matter; this was no time to dwell on failures. He was busy these days emphasizing his successes and seeking to build upon them. A later hearsay report would suggest that the general told his son and future biographer F.A. Mitchel his belief that all the raiders had been hung. In late April, under orders from Buell, Mitchel's troops burned the long bridge over the Tennessee River at Stevenson. No one in the Union command seemed to give any thought to the raiders, or to threatening Chattanooga, for that matter.[20]

In the end, despite the difficulties imposed on the searchers by foul weather and rough terrain, not a single one of the Yankee raiders escaped. Dorsey, Bensinger, Buffum, and George Wilson, as it turned out, "simply wandered" indeed, finding that they had backtracked in the dense woods just as the wayward Pittenger had. They were rounded up by a local posse only nine miles from Ringgold, even though they had been on the move for almost twenty-four hours. About noon on Sunday, they found themselves surrounded "by an excited crowd of fifty—Bensinger says eighty," Dorsey recalled, with those about barking orders to "Surrender! Surrender, damn you!" George Wilson wisely steered clear of the Flemingsburg, Kentucky, story and spun a tale about having come down from Virginia in pursuit of fugitive slaves, but their captors were unimpressed. Buffum, gutsy as ever, pointed out that they had had nothing to eat for two days, and asked for "a good, square meal before we go over the river." Much to their surprise, the four men were taken to a nearby house and served a fine dinner, "intermingled with numerous questions, and not a little sport and hilarity, much of it at our expense." A chief topic was the issue of reward money—$100 had apparently been offered by William Fuller for the capture of the party—and the Yankee prisoners joined their Southern hosts in debating how the money should be spent, arguing that "widows and needy families of soldiers should have it."

Arriving in Ringgold, the four soldiers were searched again, their money and any trinkets taken from them, and then sent by rail south to Marietta, spending some thirty-six terrifying hours in a basement jail, as "dark as dark could be"—though their fears were doused somewhat by a bottle of whiskey generously supplied by their captors. "We had a reminder of the old fashioned Methodist hell, of which we had heard so much in our childhood, Satan and his chains included," Dorsey remembered. Then it was back up the line to Chattanooga, where they would join their comrades in more permanent quarters. They were marched from the station, handcuffed, and led by trace-chains around their necks through a jeering crowd of locals who had come to the depot to see the show. "Will them houn's hunt?" one among the mob laughed, while others assured the captives, "You all'll make nice ornaments at the end of a rope." The raiders had a standard and defiant response to this taunting. "Hang and be damned!" they said. "Our fellows will hang twenty of you for every one you hang of this party."

For their part, Knight, Brown, Scott, Mason, and Reddick had turned hard to the west from Chickamauga Creek and tried as best they could to head toward Bridgeport, making "poor headway" under cover of darkness over the next six nights. The following day, Mason and Scott were flushed out by a dog and nabbed by Rebel pickets, while Knight, Brown, and Reddick managed to sneak away and spend the night in a nearby cave. The three risked breakfast at a log cabin early the next morning, but the old man there sent his son down the road on a sorrel horse to alert the local cavalry. "Our jig was up!" Knight recalled, and like the others, they were taken to Chattanooga for questioning before General Leadbetter.

The Southern newspapers proudly reported the capture of the "Yankee spies," or "bridge burners," or "engine thieves," as they would come to be called. "Next morning a few stragglers, who had deserted the stolen train, were caught in the swamps, brought to town, and are now in jail," one article said. "Thus ended the invasion of Georgia." The *Daily Intelligencer* soon identified the leader: "a man named Andrews," the paper said, who was found with several thousand dollars on his person and was said to have once lived in Atlanta. (The city's other daily newspaper, the *Southern Confederacy*, would later report the disturbing news that the spy "has often been in our reading room during his peregrinations in the Confederate States.")

"He is an unmitigated Yankee scoundrel, but reckless and daring," the *Intelligencer* said. "He, we learn, confesses nothing."[21]

Part III

Consequences

Chattanooga. (*National Archives*)

CHAPTER ELEVEN

Court-Martial

Chattanooga and Knoxville

THE ENGINE THIEVES.

Twenty-three of these villains have now been captured. They are now undergoing trial before a court-martial in Chattanooga. We know not what progress is being made. We hear that one of the scoundrels proposed to turn state's evidence against the balance, if he can thereby save his neck . . . .

—(Atlanta) *Southern Confederacy*
April 23, 1862

THE JAILER IN CHATTANOOGA was a geezer named Swims, and he was by all accounts a cruel and despicable old man. "If you can form an idea of the personal appearance of Old Satan the devil you can describe old Swims," Wilson Brown wrote decades later. Swims was sixty-two years old but could just as well have been ninety, his wiry form gnarled and stooped like a storm-bent willow. He had a withered, weathered face, bushy brows and thick white hair that would have been snowy had it been clean. A scraggly mustache of sparse, wispy strands hung down over his lip, complemented (if you could call it that) by a smattering of white stubble on his chin that reminded one raider of "porcupine quills sticking in a dog's nose." He wore a coarse homespun suit Brown would describe as "more holy than richous, and well saturated with grease," and addressed his unfortunate guests in a screeching voice somewhere "between the bray of a jackass and the howl of a coyote." Recently promoted to the office of jailer from his prior vocation of public drayman, Swims passed the time by drinking and tormenting his charges, tilting back in a wooden chair to sleep off the effects of copious amounts of whiskey. His sloth and greed were matched, if not exceeded, by a deep and abiding hatred of Negroes and Yankees. It was said that the old man had a Christian name, but nobody cared enough about him to remember it.

If the jailer was the stuff of nightmares, so was the jail itself. "A plain picture of the Chattanooga prison into which the members of the railroad party were thrust cannot be given in all its detail without shocking the sensitive reader," Pittenger wrote. The two-story brick structure was imbedded in a muddy slope at the northwest corner of Fifth and Lookout Streets, mostly hidden from view by a tall wooden fence that surrounded the rock-strewn yard. A local journalist would describe the building as "a queer freak of architecture," which one curious Chattanooga resident would later measure as being some thirty-seven feet long and twenty-three feet wide, with brick walls, barred windows, and a peaked, shingled roof. A rickety exterior staircase on the east side led to the entry on the second floor, which contained a holding cell and meager sleeping quarters for the jailer. One end of the lower floor housed a crude kitchen; while the other end, most of it underground, was used for harsh and hopeless confinement. An iron-banded trap-door in the floor of the upstairs cell led to the dark, putrid dungeon below, its two square windows—one nearly buried in the hillside and the other up under the staircase—covered with thick iron lattice that blotted out light and stifled any whisper of fresh air. Locals called it the Negro jail, as in prewar days it had held mostly recaptured slaves, though the inmates housed there usually called it "the hole." "We added a little to that after a while," William Knight later wrote, "and named it hell hole." At least one Southern official shared this assessment of the place. Colonel H.L. Claiborne, the provost marshal of Chattanooga, reportedly told General Leadbetter that "it would be mercy to those men to take them out and blow their brains out rather than keep them in that hole."[1]

The raiders were reunited there in the black basement of Swims's jail as they were captured, though not before several were taken before General Leadbetter for interrogation, including James Andrews himself. Bill Pittenger was among the first to be ushered into the general's presence, and he would later have nothing but contempt for the Rebel officer. "They said he was a northern man," the Ohio corporal wrote, "but if so, it is very little credit to my section, for he was one of the most contemptible individuals I ever knew." He was "a perfect sot," who was reputed to have "just two states of body . . .

these were, dead drunk, and gentlemanly drunk." Leadbetter made his head-quarters on the second floor of the fine Crutchfield House hotel, just across from the railroad station. There Pittenger was brought before the gray commander, and sure enough, he was "gentlemanly drunk." A lengthy interrogation ensued, and if Pittenger's account can be believed, Leadbetter was even more gullible than he was intoxicated. Pittenger told him that General Mitchel had grand designs indeed—taking Chattanooga and Atlanta and then driving for the coast, with 60,000 or 70,000 men available for the campaign. (This was abject, transparent puffery: Southern newspapers were already reporting—quite accurately—that Mitchel only had between 7,000 and 10,000 men in northern Alabama.) It is unlikely that Leadbetter—an accomplished engineer and an intelligent officer who had graduated third in his class at West Point—put much stock in this false and far-fetched tale, though Pittenger certainly claimed that he did. "Leadbetter seemed profoundly impressed," the former schoolteacher recalled, "[and] said that he had no idea that Mitchel had so many men at his disposal." As for the raid itself, Pittenger gave his name, company, and regiment, but refused to identify the purpose of the mission or the engineer on the train. Leadbetter was undisturbed. He shrugged and said, "Well, I know all about it. Your leader's name is Andrews. What sort of man is he?" Astonished that the Rebel officer knew the identity of their leader, Pittenger smugly replied that he could only tell him one thing, and that was that Andrews was "a man whom you will never catch." Leadbetter smiled broadly at this, and directed that Pittenger be taken on over to "the hole." He found waiting in the hall outside his comrades Marion Ross, John Wollam, and an ironed and shackled James Andrews.[2]

William Knight had a similar experience. Brought to the hotel, he found General Leadbetter seated in a chair, wearing an old-fashioned Dutch knit cap. Somewhat bemused and far from intimidated, Knight thought his inquisitor "looked more like a lager beer sign than like a general." Knight told Leadbetter that he was from Kentucky and had been making his way to Chandler Springs, Alabama. Asked what he planned to do there, the irreverent engineer replied that if he liked the place, he thought he just might buy it. Not at all amused, Leadbetter fired questions at Knight for half an hour and closely examined the wear on his boots, which were considerably scuffed from his days in the rocky North Georgia terrain. (Alf Wilson was subjected to a similar close visual inspection; he claimed that Leadbetter identified him and Mark Wood as Yankees by removing their hats and pointing to their pale complexions as a telltale sign of the round, short-brimmed regulation caps worn by Federal infantry.) Knight was then shown the door, and he too was shocked to find Andrews standing out in the corridor. The engineer managed to keep his composure, he later said, "but I think if I had been struck with seven kinds of lightning, I would not have felt any more streaked than I did just at that moment."[3]

Andrews of course had identified himself to Dr. Parks upon his capture, which was just as well—the Kentuckian was widely known from his contraband business in this part of Tennessee and would have been recognized soon enough in any event. A thorough search before General Leadbetter revealed a large amount of Confederate money, which along with his imposing demeanor and his ivory-handled Colt pistol branded the civilian spy in the minds of the Confederates as the leader of the raid. Following his audience with Leadbetter, Andrews was taken along with Ross and Wollam to the jail, where old Swims greeted them at the gate, jangling his keys. The three were taken into the upstairs cell, where Swims was told to put them "in the hole." Unlocking the trap door, the jailer cried "Look out below!" and slid a ladder down into the gap. The pale, upturned faces of the captives below were barely visible, and a hot, putrid stench rose from the blackness. Andrews, who had faced a myriad of perils in the past and would later meet the hangman without flinching, balked, for once, at the sight of the dungeon below. "That is no place to put a man," he protested. "Let us stay up here for awhile." Swims replied, "It is the best we can do now, but will do better afterwhile," and the three men were forced down the ladder.[4]

The Andrews Raiders would spend nearly three weeks trapped in Swims's hole and would hold frightful memories of the ordeal for the rest of their lives. Wilson and Wood were the last two to be brought in, and Alf would recall the "sepulchral voices and specter-like forms" that greeted them from the gloom below as they descended into the suffocating enclosure. The basement cell was dark and of unlucky dimensions, measuring thirteen feet square and thirteen feet high, and it held nearly two dozen men—several East Tennessee Unionists and a runaway slave by the name of Aleck had been incarcerated there, though they were displaced upstairs one by one as the more notorious "Engine Thieves" arrived. The raiders were kept handcuffed and chained together in pairs by the neck, the heavy chains locked with padlocks one of the upstairs prisoners would describe as being "larger than a man's hand" and weighing nearly two pounds. There was little ventilation, and the daytime heat was oppressive even then, in late April. The place reeked of sweat and offal and was swarming with vermin—"not only rats and mice, but other things smaller and worse," as one raider put it—a particular problem since the handcuffs and trace-chains made swatting and scratching difficult and ineffective. There was not enough room for everyone to lie down to sleep comfortably—they wedged side-by-side in two rows of ten, like rumpled, bent cigars in the foulest of humidors, with a pair of leftover men sleeping longways at the end, between the buckets provided in one corner for water and in the other for their slops. (The water bucket was rarely filled, and the other rarely emptied.)

The prisoners were fed just twice a day, a pitiful offering of spoiled pickled beef or pork, a few crumbling morsels of cornbread, and watery caneseed coffee. Swims delivered these crumbs by way of a hook at the end of a tattered rope, which in its swaying and dangling gave the raiders an uneasy sense of foreboding. Yet the inmates greeted the delivery of their paltry meals with a degree of expectation only one who has been truly hungry can appreciate—"we sat or stood around looking up to old Swims like so many young birds in their nest reaching up to the parent bird to grab the worm she brings in her bill, mouths open, all eager and ready to snatch it—best man forward, first come first served, every fellow for himself, and the devil take the hindmost," Dorsey remembered. It quickly became obvious that this unseemly free-for-all scramble for rations would not do; an agreed-upon authority was needed to fairly distribute the bounty, such as it was. The captives soon established a government, electing Andrews president, "with the full power to appoint assistants, and run things right." Even with the rations shared evenly, feeding themselves was "hard scrabbling," as they had no utensils and most had their hands palm-to-palm in irons, with few if any connecting links. Knight, for one, tried to repel the specter of hunger by making light of the situation: his only wish, he said, was that the Rebels would give him one good square meal before hanging him, so that his body would be heavy enough to break his neck.[5]

Despite the hunger and hardship, the men did not despair and kept themselves busy as best they could. "A very erroneous impression would be given the reader if he imagined that we spent our time here in nothing but hopelessly bemoaning our misery," Pittenger wrote. They passed the time mostly in conversation, the first few days being largely taken up with relating their respective adventures on the run after fleeing the *General*. They spent the long hours thereafter telling stories, or discussing the progress of the war, or the issues of the day. Only two of the Federal soldiers, Pittenger and Buffum, were "out-and-out abolitionists," as they put it—and they soon found they could gain the upper hand in any argument over the question of slavery by appealing to the inhumanity and cruelty of their current circumstances. The raiders talked of hometowns, family, friends, and even future plans, and they grew closer together. No one in the party was permitted to lose his spirit. "Had we been confined in solitude, the dread and foreboding would have been more terrible," Pittenger recalled, "but we made a league against fear and fretting." Dorsey echoed this sentiment. "We were a jolly crew in a bad boat," he said.

At times the aimless discussion gave way to drama—particularly for Robert Buffum, who quoted Shakespeare in his daily life, even when the circumstances called for a tragedy, as they plainly did now. A favorite in those dark days was the Ghost's speech from the first act of *Hamlet*, which the little dark-bearded Massachusetts private would deliver in the dim light with a booming voice, his inflection and gestures recalled by his comrades years later:

> But that I am forbid
> To tell the secrets of my prison-house,
> I could a tale unfold whose lightest word
> Would harrow up thy soul, freeze thy young blood,
> Make thy two eyes, like stars, start from their spheres,
> Thy knotted and combined locks to part
> And each particular hair to stand on end,
> Like quills upon the fretful porpentine:
> But this eternal blazon must not be
> To ears of flesh and blood. List, list, O, list![6]

Though one might suspect that some among the prisoners sought divine assistance, there was in fact little prayer or conversation of a "religious character" in those first days—"that came later," one soldier said—but there was a good deal of language at the other extreme. "If profanity would explode anything, that old dungeon would have blown into a million atoms within the first twenty four hours after we got into it," Dorsey recalled. "I never heard anything like it before nor since," he said—and this was a man who had spent nearly a year in the army. He later found to his surprise (upon emerging from the darkness to a more civilized enclosure) that a few of his comrades—Ross, Porter, Slavens, and Pittenger—did not use profane language at all, though he maintained (perhaps by way of excuse), "that hole was enough to make a preacher swear."[7]

Rather than simply curse their bad fortune, the engineer William Knight, in particular, made special efforts to improve their lot. Had he been in a prison camp in the next century, Knight may well have been known as "the Scrounger." Not only had he managed to hide a substantial sum of money—gold coins, no less—from his captors, but he had also secreted his trusty jackknife—the one he had used to cut the bell-rope on the *General* back at Big Shanty—which was handy for now but would soon become vital. After a few days, he managed to whittle wooden scraps and bones from the rancid meat they were given into serviceable picks for the padlocks. Using Knight's ingenious skeleton keys, the captives were able to free their hands and unhitch from each other, their wrists chafed and swollen and their arms and necks red with rust by now from the cuffs and collars. Knight also was able to make regular purchases of tobacco in large plugs of old navy from Swims or the guards—a true luxury—and this success inspired him to try his hand at supplementing their rations as well. They inquired of the jailer whether they could buy food, and finding no objection—so long as they had the money—engaged in a lengthy debate over what they should purchase, finally settling on an inexpensive but tasty and filling menu of wheat bread and molasses. They handed up a few coins and eagerly awaited "a royal breakfast" next day—but they were disappointed. In the morning, the heartless old warden lowered down their usual fare of spoiled pork and cornbread. In response to the angry complaints from below, Swims stuck his head in the hole and, "in his slowest and most provoking tones," said: "B-o-y-s, I lost that money!"

"The hell you did!" Knight roared. "You damned old scoundrel, you spent it for whiskey! You're drunk now!" A protest to the officer of the guard was summarily denied—he simply laughed and said that if they trusted Swims with their money, they would have to take their chances. From that point forward, the raiders bypassed the old man and appealed directly to the captain on duty for any business matters.[8]

Easing the pain of captivity was all well and good, but the raiders also thought and talked about how they might end it. They considered at length how they might escape, and "the plans for escaping were as numerous as the inmates," Dorsey recalled. Yet the prospects for a successful jailbreak seemed grim indeed. The brick walls of the jail were reinforced here in the hole with oak timbers; the iron in the windows was immovable; the trap door above was kept locked and was well out of reach in any event. Outside, an escapee would have to get past armed Confederate guards, a locked gate, and the high fence, the reward being a swim across the fast-moving current of the Tennessee

River and a cross-country trek over harsh terrain to the west and north toward the Union lines. Some among the captives were injured or sick; all were ill-fed and weak, and any attempt to run would almost certainly require more strength than they could muster. They would keep looking for opportunities, but for now, it seemed they could do little more than bide their time and wait for the inevitable trial to begin.

There was no question that there would be a court-martial, of course. Even though their admirably daring scheme had been thwarted and no lasting damage done, the twenty-two raiders were spies and saboteurs and would have to answer for it. Justice must be done, and lessons given—especially here in East Tennessee—to others who would contemplate similar acts of violence and disloyalty against the South. They were informed that court-martial proceedings would be instituted in short order, and spent long hours of anxious discussion as to what they should and should not say, and what sort of defense they should present to the charges. George D. Wilson and William Pittenger took the lead in outlining their case. Both men felt strongly that any pretense of childlike innocence would be foolish and counterproductive—there were dozens of witnesses who had seen them on the train, and almost all the raiders had already identified themselves by name and regiment. Wilson and Pittenger therefore believed they should embrace their status as United States soldiers and claim the protection of the laws of war. They were enlisted in the service and acting under orders from their superiors, and they must be treated respectfully, as prisoners of war, and not be subjected to the dishonor and the possible capital punishment regularly afforded to traitors and spies. The raid was purely a military expedition, they would argue, and they had not passed a line or outpost of the enemy, and could not be said to be "lurking in and about their camps," a necessary element to convict on the charge of spying. They agreed that they would not reveal Campbell as a civilian; that no one would identify which man or men of the party served as the engineer on the *General*; that they would not disclose the earlier failed attempt to destroy the W&A; and that no one would discuss Andrews's service as a spy for the Union. Pittenger would later assert that all had agreed to this plan, and even appointed him the "spokesman" of the party—though others, especially Dorsey, would claim that many among the Ohioans were "bitterly opposed" to this approach. A confession, however presented, didn't seem to them like much of a plan.

There were, of course, a number of problems with the agreed-upon story in any event: they were soldiers, indeed, but had been disguised in civilian clothes; all had volunteered to undertake a "secret mission" behind the lines, knowing that they would likely be treated as spies if captured; they were in fact hundreds of miles behind enemy lines, and though they may not have "lurked" they certainly commandeered a Southern engine in the midst of a Confederate camp. (Dorsey would adamantly disagree, later arguing that they had captured the locomotive, not stolen it, and that the boundary of the camp was in fact several rods from the railroad tracks at Big Shanty, though the court-martial surely would have had no patience with such trifling distinctions.) Finally, they appeared to be acting under the orders of a civilian smuggler who was not in the army at all—though they planned to disavow his career as a spy and maintain that they all "supposed" he was a Federal officer. At least some of the raiders were far from confident in the legal case—Dorsey and Brown, for example, felt that their only hope was escape, whatever the odds, and they urged Andrews to order and lead an attack on the guards. They would escape, or be killed in the attempt. Wilson and Pittenger objected to this, pointing out the slim chance of success, and Andrews followed their counsel, at least for the time being.[9]

Andrews would be the first tried, and his case would be even more difficult than that of the Union soldiers in his charge. He, too, had been seen aboard the *General*; he was well known as a smuggler; and unlike the others, he could not claim the protection of enlistment or the honors of war. He had in the past rendered service to the South in the course of his contraband trade, and would no doubt emphasize the fact. Apart from that, there seemed little to hope for, though it was whispered among the raiders that the secret agent had connections on the outside, and that money would be liberally spent to influence the court, or effect an escape.

Shortly before the court-martial was to begin, William Pittenger was again removed from "the hole" and taken before an officer—he presumed the president of the upcoming court-martial—for additional questioning. The reason for Pittenger being singled out in this fashion remains in dispute. Dorsey would later contend that Pittenger proposed a plan to induce the authorities to call him as a witness, at which time he would testify that the raiders were not spies, but "regularly detailed soldiers, on a purely military expedition." Another story is that Pittenger feigned sickness in order to be removed so he could talk with the Confederates—probably untrue, as a number of the prisoners were injured or ill, and their captors seemed to have little concern over their physical well-being. The most likely explanation is that the bespectacled corporal had simply been the most articulate, the most forthcoming, or both in prior interviews. Pittenger himself later wrote, "I had to pass a more protracted examination than any of the others, perhaps because I had told General Leadbetter so many of my inferences about war affairs when first taken before him." Upon his return, he was kept apart from the other raiders, at times left outside in the yard and given a New Testament to read. He would be questioned for the next two or three days, and in the future maintained that he strictly adhered to the "plan" suggested by Wilson and him and agreed upon by the entire party. But the isolation and the apparent preferential treatment Pittenger received planted seeds of resentment and distrust that would grow years later into open accusations of betrayal.[10]

Newspapers across the South expressed shock and anger at the theft of the *General*, seasoned heavily with undisguised admiration at the boldness, the nerve, the outright audacity of the raid. As early as April 15, the Atlanta newspaper the *Southern Confederacy* had already christened the affair "THE GREAT RAILROAD CHASE," its subheads proclaiming it "THE MOST EXTRAORDINARY AND ASTOUNDING ADVENTURE OF THE WAR" and "THE MOST DARING UNDERTAKING THAT YANKEES EVER PLANNED OR ATTEMPTED TO EXECUTE." The *Augusta Daily Chronicle & Sentinel*'s headlines echoed the praise from Atlanta: "AN AUDACIOUS ACT"—"A BOLD AND DARING TRICK," the paper pronouncing the raid "one of the most reckless pieces of rascality which it has ever been our lot to hear or read of." An early article in the *Atlanta Commonwealth* called it an "EXTRAORDINARY AFFAIR," saying, "We have to record to-day either one of the most daring robberies or maddest pranks that has ever fallen under our notice . . . certainly one of the most bold and reckless feats of the war."[11]

The facts reported in the early accounts of the raid and the subsequent chase were surprisingly accurate. The *Daily Intelligencer*, for example, obtained the complete reports of William Fuller and Anthony Murphy—which were at that time nearly in full agreement. On April 15, the *Southern Confederacy* ran its dramatic 3,800-word account of the glorious chase (giving "FULL PARTICULARS!") that would provide a foundation for the story's enduring legend and a starting point for historians for years to come. And sadly, despite poor Jacob Parrott's brave silence under the whip, it is apparent from the press reports that some among the raiders were talking to the Confederate authorities—"the captured scoundrels have made 'a clean breast of it,'" the *Intelligencer* said. The press soon described in detail the object of the raid, the name of the leader, the place of origin (Shelbyville) and the size of the party, pegged by one paper as early as Monday, April 14 as being made up of twenty-two men—even though most of the party were still scattered in the forest at that time. As such, it appears that Alf Wilson was sadly mistaken when he wrote, "I am proud to be able to say that not a man of that faithful band was base enough to betray his comrades," though it is unclear who among the raiders may have talked, or when, or why.[12]

There was also outrage among press and populace that such a thing could happen—especially since this was hardly the first time the Southern railroad bridges had been targeted by Union-loyal marauders. (The *Memphis Daily Appeal's* April 15 headline read simply: "MORE BRIDGE BURNERS.") Though the state would be ravaged by war two years hence, Georgians had seen little of the conflict firsthand to this point and were frightened to hear news of armed Yankees sneaking and stealing among them. Excitement and suspicion prevailed for weeks, and citizens in hotel lobbies, barrooms, and railroad depots from Savannah to Knoxville saw in the face of every stranger a saboteur or a spy.

In one well-publicized instance of this irrational suspicion, the misdirected anger of a group of Confederate soldiers resulted in violence committed upon an innocent man. On Saturday about noon, as the raiders were stopped just north of Dalton, they had been approached by one Benjamin Flynn, foreman of the works up at Graysville, who had been "drinking considerably" and was headed back home. He hailed the raiders and asked to hitch a ride northward, but they told him they were running ammunition to General Beauregard. The tipsy foreman waved and hurrahed them onward, calling out, "Hurry her up, boys!" Unfortunately, a company of soldiers under the command of Colonel Jesse A. Glenn witnessed this encouragement, which was later mistaken for complicity. That night, Flynn was dragged from his home, tied to a tree, and beaten "most unmercifully" as a Union sympathizer—a sad episode reported with considerable outrage in the Atlanta papers for weeks to come.[13]

Though this sort of vigilante action was uncalled-for, increased vigilance in guarding the Western & Atlantic certainly was. "Let this be a warning to the railroad men and everybody else in the Confederate States. Let an engine never be left alone for a moment. Let additional guards be placed at our bridges," the *Southern Confederacy* wrote, noting indignantly that it had urged these steps be taken long ago. All agreed that the W&A, the State of Georgia, and the people of the South owed a hefty debt to the railroaders who had chased down the perpetrators. "Great credit is due to Messrs. Kane, Fuller, and Murphy, for the extraordinary exertions which they made to recapture their stolen cars," one paper wrote, noting that the "pursuit was fraught with much danger."[14]

If the days following the raid provided ample time for hysteria and self-congratulation, they also began a still-continuing era of regret, recriminations, and endless speculation as to what might have been. Certainly the Federal raiders, cooped up in Swims's brick-and-iron basement in Chattanooga, had plenty of time to reflect on what went wrong. Pittenger would later catalogue the main reasons for the failure of the mission, ranking Fuller and Murphy's heroic pursuit a distant fourth, behind the one-day delay, the incessant rain, and Andrews's unwillingness to stand and fight. "Andrews, with all his courage, never rightly valued fighting men," Pittenger wrote. "He preferred accomplishing his objects by stratagem and in secrecy rather than by open force." (Pittenger was careful to clarify that he was by no means calling James Andrews a coward—"the term might as well be applied to Julius Caesar!" he said.) Daniel Allen Dorsey speculated that destroying the *Yonah* and the bridge over the Etowah could have been "easily done," snuffing out the pursuit before it even got started. "It is easy to look back and see our mistakes," he admitted. William Knight simply blamed the weather: "We would have been successful," he told audiences years later, "had it not been for the excessive rain which was falling almost in torrents." Others would give their own opinions as to what the raiders should have done differently—better tools, perhaps, or an obstruction at Tunnel Hill, or cutting the wires sooner, an ambush at this point or that. Of course, this sort of empty second guessing is a simple and safe exercise to conduct after-the-fact. But at the time, Andrews had not known that he would encounter extra trains, or that there were no Rebel soldiers at Etowah, or that a relentless pursuit had been behind him from the outset. What the raiders had encountered was not so much "the fog of war," but the cold, stark disconnect between certain plans and uncertain realities. Anthony Murphy may have summed it up best in his account of the chase, written in 1893: "The conception of great and daring deeds is one thing, and their execution is another," he said.

But all concerned, North and South, seemed to agree that the raid was—that is, would have been—a masterstroke for the Union, and that the Confederacy had been spared a grievous blow by its failure. "We now understand it all," the *Southern Confederacy* wrote of the presence of Mitchel's troops in Huntsville. "They were to move upon Chattanooga and Knoxville as soon as the bridges were burnt, and press on into Virginia as far as possible, and take all our forces in that state in the rear. It was all the deepest laid scheme and on the grandest scale that ever emanated from the brains of any number of Yankees combined." Fuller agreed, writing years later that had the raiders succeeded, Mitchel would have taken Chattanooga within five days; all the garrisons from Memphis to Richmond would have been "cut off from all help"; and the battles of Chickamauga and Chattanooga would not have been fought. (Both sides, of course, benefited from this puffing—the raiders were made more heroic by attempting such a daring and valuable mission, and their pursuers made more heroic by foiling it.) Knight thought Fuller and Murphy had done nothing less than save the Confederacy. "If those bridges could of been burned at that time, it would of cut the Southern Confederacy in two," he later argued, vehemently if somewhat inarticulately. "It would of shook them from center to circumference. Our army could of taken Chattanooga. They could of went to Knoxville and struck the Rebel army in the rear at Cumberland Gap or Richmond or wherever they choose."

Pittenger was somewhat defensive about the usefulness of what they had attempted, dedicating an entire chapter of his 1887 book to cataloguing "What Was Actually Accomplished" by the raiders. He argues rather unconvincingly that the raid, although unsuccessful in its object, did result in a diversion of manpower to guarding railroads, a more stringent passport system, and a chilling effect on contraband smuggling, all of which inured to the benefit of the Union cause. But his ultimate conclusion as to the intangible value of the Andrews Raid is worth repeating, because it is in some respects probably true:

> It was especially necessary that in this conflict there should be some unmistakable illustrations of Northern daring; for it had been an accepted tradition, to some extent in the North as well as at the South, that in personal bravery, in dash and enthusiasm, the Southern soldier far excelled the Northern; and up to this time nearly all the daring movements and dashing raids had been displayed on behalf of the South. The idle boast that one Southern soldier was worth five "Yankees" was probably never sincerely made in that extreme form; but there was a firm belief that, man for man, the advantage was on the side of the rebels.
>
> Nothing during the whole war did so much to shake this feeling as our raid. It was beating the enemy at his own game.[15]

The trial of James Andrews was to be held on the second floor of the Old Armory building at Fourth and Market Streets, one block over and two blocks down the hill from the jail. The prosecution's case would be conducted by two respected Confederate officers, both of them Georgians from the recently formed 39th Volunteer Infantry Regiment. Colonel Joseph T. McConnell, the commanding officer of the regiment, had represented his nearby home county of Catoosa at the Georgia convention in January 1861, casting a loud vote in favor of the ordinance calling for the state to secede. His co-counsel, Captain Leander W. Crook, was a prominent lawyer and former superior court judge from Murray County and the leader of Company A of the regiment, the Cohutta Rangers. The two Southern officers made clear their intentions to exact swift justice on the Yankee spy, brushing aside any proffered legal defenses or suggestion of mitigating circumstances. For example, Andrews's recent captor Dr. Thomas Parks soon developed considerable sympathy for the charismatic defendant, finding him to be "a man of prepossessing appearance" and impressed by his "cool and determined manner," and sought to intervene on his behalf. As Captain Crook was a longtime personal friend, Parks pulled him aside just after the trial began. The good doctor told Crook what Andrews had claimed when captured—that he was surrendering as a prisoner of war, that his men were enlisted and in force, and that none could be treated as spies.

The young officer rejected this appeal out of hand. "Enlisted or not enlisted," he said, "they were down there where they ought not have been, and I'll hang every one of them if I can."[16]

With this sort of prosecutorial zeal across the room, Andrews desperately needed formidable defense counsel, and he found it. The Honorable Reese B. Brabson was one of the most famous men in Chattanooga, and rightfully so. Born on a farm in Sevier County in 1817, he was named for his great uncle Reese Bowen, Revolutionary War hero of King's Mountain and Bunker Hill. His farmhouse birth and rural upbringing were by no means rustic— his father owned a huge acreage and a large number of mills and slaves, and the "log cabin" where young Reese was born had no less than fourteen rooms, floored with hardwoods, anchored by a living room fireplace of quarried stone, and finely appointed with mahogany furniture and French china. Gifted even at a young age as an accomplished scholar and an eloquent public speaker, Brabson read law under a relative who was a judge, and in 1851 began his service in the Tennessee General Assembly. It was there in Nashville that he had a public run-in with another prominent Tennessean that would make him famous.

As a young state representative, Brabson gave a fiery speech on the floor of the state house disparaging newspapermen and editors as a class, which was of course promptly and indignantly reported in all the local newspapers.

Felix K. Zollicoffer, the editor of the *Nashville Republican Banner and Whig* (and later an ill-equipped Confederate brigadier general who would be killed at the Battle of Mill Springs), took exception to Brabson's remarks and angrily confronted him outside the St. Cloud Hotel, berating the legislator for spreading falsities and charging that he was not a gentleman. Brabson responded by slapping Zollicoffer full and hard across the face. Never a man for sensible military responses, then or later, Zollicoffer drew his revolver and fired point-blank at the unarmed Brabson—though he somehow missed, the bullet lodging in the front door of the hotel. No harm was done, except perhaps to the pride (and the cheek) of the rebuked Whig editor.

Colonel Brabson conducted himself similarly in all his affairs—self-assured, smart, and bold, refusing to back down even from the most heated confrontation. In 1858, he won a seat in the U.S. House of Representatives, where he would serve until the outbreak of the war, warning his Southern brethren of the danger of walking away from the Union and the constitutional protections it afforded. Though both North and South offered him commissions as an army officer, he chose to sit out the conflict and returned south to Chattanooga. His home was among the most impressive in the city, a red-brick mansion standing farther up East Fifth Street at the top of what was known to the locals as Brabson Hill, surrounded by orchards and gardens and tended by a number of slaves. His elegant wife, the former Sarah Keith, was widely known and well-regarded for her "wit, beauty and graciousness." Now forty-four years old, Brabson was considered an immense legal talent in the prime of his career, "pleasant in his manners" (notwithstanding the occasional abuse of an impertinent newspaper editor), and said to be "especially strong before a jury." One who had heard him speak thought that if Brabson gave a speech on the American Eagle, he would end up soaring out of sight.

"Considerable sympathy had been aroused in Chattanooga by the prisoners' general good appearance, and as the first wrath of the populace wore away, their hardihood and recklessness won favor with the people," a local reporter wrote. After a few days, folks began visiting the jail, no longer mocking or jeering the captives, but instead hoping for a glimpse of or a conversation with the famous Yankee desperadoes. Citizens with Union feeling began to make inquiries about what they could do to help the raiders in their misfortune. Among these well-wishers was Sarah Brabson, whose small kindnesses to the imprisoned soldiers, such as loaning them books from her husband's library, soon offered an opening to seek legal representation. Judge

Brabson gladly accepted the engagement and began preparing for the trial, which was to begin immediately. A lawyer from Holly Springs, Mississippi, was appointed to assist the former congressman, though his name is lost to history.[17]

The ensuing court-martial would last several days spread out over almost three weeks, and unfortunately not a single line of evidence or testimony remains from the event. Andrews was charged not only with spying, but also with treason, based on his prior business with and professed loyalty to the Confederate States. Both charges were considered capital offenses. The star witness was William A. Fuller himself, the hero conductor traveling up from Atlanta to complete his duty by testifying against the Yankee spies. Andrews directed that his Nashville business partner, W.S. Whiteman, be called in his defense, to testify as to the Kentuckian's loyalty to and prior support of the Confederacy. Last would be Pittenger, testifying as "spokesman" for the party—a course that Andrews apparently approved, at least initially. "He seemed to think that while it would not help him—for he had little hope of saving himself—yet he thought it might possibly help us in some way; and he would have done anything to help his men, even though it might make it worse for himself," Dorsey wrote.

Little is known about the details of Andrews's legal and factual defense. "He seems to have sought to make the work that he did appear as small as possible, and his own motive to be only moneymaking, with resulting benefits to the South far greater than the loss," Pittenger suggested. Accordingly, Judge Brabson planned to emphasize Andrews's career as a contraband smuggler, a friend to the South, who ran the blockade many times to the ultimate profit of the Confederacy. Some would suggest that Andrews maintained that he had been offered the opportunity to trade across the lines without interference for a certain amount each month, so long as he would steal a locomotive and bring it northward. (This suggestion—that Andrews's mission was nothing more than an effort to obtain an engine for General Mitchel—was ridiculous. Locomotives were available by the drove in Kentucky and middle Tennessee, and Mitchel had captured more than a dozen when he took Huntsville. It was also inconceivable that a Union general would risk the lives of two dozen soldiers and pay a spy thousands of dollars in exchange for a nine-thousand-dollar engine.)

News accounts of the trial suggest that Andrews claimed that he had been in the Kentucky State Guard "when neutrality was en vogue" and had been "entraped" into the service of the Yankee government. He had no intention to burn bridges, he maintained; he had committed no violence upon soldiers or civilians; and he had only attempted destructive action when he was pursued. His partner Whiteman was called to affirm that he was for the South, but the plan backfired. Whiteman was a loyal Confederate who the year before had advertised in the Nashville papers to offer free lodging to families whose husbands or brothers had left home to serve in the Southern army. The paper mill owner no doubt believed he was helping the Confederate cause by partnering with Andrews; instead, the smuggler had double-crossed him, damaged him financially, and attempted to aid the hated Yankees. Andrews was later said to be "greatly dissatisfied with the conduct of Mr. Whiteman on the trial, thinking that he received far more injury than good from him." Whiteman's testimony only served to emphasize the nature and scope of his covert activities, and Andrews's capture in the presence of Union soldiers while carrying a Confederate passport further affirmed that he was engaged in Yankee mischief. For his part, Pittenger maintained that he stuck to the supposedly agreed-upon story line for his testimony—though Dorsey wrote years later of a telling comment when Andrews returned to Swims's jail one afternoon following the day's adjournment.

"Well, Andrews, how did the trial go today?" Ross asked.

"Well, I hardly know," Andrews replied quietly, nodding at Pittenger, "but I'm afraid that fellow has swatted me."

Judge Brabson did his best to weave a fine defense from the sorry scraps of evidence, and at least was able to do enough to cause hope for the accused and concern on the part of the prosecution. A Chattanooga reporter noted that Andrews's "defense was so ably conducted by Judge Brabson, that that gentleman was notified he was taking too much interest in the man's case, and it might be better for him not to be so much concerned." Andrews's counsel suggested to him that the various interruptions, errors, and informalities in the proceedings may serve to void the trial entirely. The trial concluded without any decision being rendered, the court's finding to be withheld from the defendant and the public until approved by the Secretary of War.

Andrews was returned to Swims's jail to await the verdict.[18]

On the morning of May I—nineteen days after the raid—there was a scrape of the key above and a drunken Swims stuck his face in the trap door opening as he lowered the prisoners' breakfast. He reported in a squeaky, querulous voice that Mitchel had advanced to Bridgeport and was now threatening Chattanooga. The raiders soon extracted from Swims what little he knew about the affair (they were experts by now in drawing the old man into conversation, if only to induce him to leave the trap door open for awhile). A short while later, they could hear the faint booming of cannon in the distance, and they were soon ordered up and out of the jail.

The chained prisoners, weakened from hunger and stiff from confinement, staggered down the stairs and into the yard like drunks at closing time. But the feeling of liberty, however fleeting, and the taste of fresh air was sweet indeed. Squinting in the brightness, they were marched to the depot under heavy guard and loaded on passenger coaches for the ride south. Up front, the train was pulled by the engine *General*, which had been returned promptly to regular service after its recent kidnapping, no worse for wear. The Ohioans noticed some changes along the way—a passport system had been put into effect to confirm the legitimacy and loyalty of travelers on the road, and large bodies of soldiers were now deployed to guard public property, government stores, railroad bridges, and other important points. "We had done some good after all," Dorsey thought, "but it was a hard way to serve the Lord, or our country either, though there was a grain of comfort in the thought."

Word spread down the road that General Mitchel's raiders were traveling on this particular train, and people crowded on the depot platforms and peered in the windows to catch a glimpse of the shackled train thieves. "Northern people can scarcely believe how much curiosity Southern people had to see a Yankee, more especially a Yankee soldier," Alf Wilson wrote. "Some of the Southerners actually seemed to feel a superstitious belief about the Yankees. They imagined them to be some dreadful ogres or incarnate devils, who would steal a 'nigger' as quick as a hawk would a chicken—who would burn houses, ravish women and steal gold watches, but wouldn't fight." He concluded with satisfaction, "I have no doubt that many of them saw more Yankees than they cared to before the end of the Rebellion."[19]

The *Southern Confederacy* reported their arrival in Atlanta, describing the captive soldiers as "sharp, intelligent-looking men, no hard-looking cases like Yankee prisoners and East Tennessee Tories usually are." The raiders' spirits had brightened considerably, and not just because of the fresh air and change of scenery. Everywhere there were rumors of Yankee advances and prisoner exchanges in the works. A friend in the crowd slipped them a newspaper, reporting the capture of New Orleans by United States forces—glorious news indeed. With Mitchel about to take Chattanooga and General McClellan rumored to be threatening Richmond with an overwhelming force, the war surely would be over in a matter of weeks.

The prisoners were taken on to Madison, a lovely community of mansions and oak-shaded streets later made famous as "The Town Sherman Refused to Burn"—though this had more to do with the presence and persuasiveness of Sherman's friend the former U.S. Senator Joshua Hill than it did with the undeniable beauty and charm of the place. Madison was some sixty-seven miles east of Atlanta on the Georgia Railroad and presumably safe, at least for now, from any advancing blue army. Arriving there on May 2, the raiders were placed in the dreary confines of the Morgan County Jail, a small stone building that at first blush seemed little better than "Swims's hotel." Here at Madison was a memorable example of flared tempers among two of the chainmates. John Reed Porter, who had been chained with Daniel Allen Dorsey for nearly three weeks now, jerked Dorsey's neck for what the latter would call "some fancied grievance." Dorsey, as might be expected, "paid it back in kind with interest," as he put it. "And thus it went, jerk, jerk, jerk, back and forth, until each flew at the other, and grabbed his chain around the neck and tried to choke his chainmate," both men hampered by handcuffs and making a clumsy, comic episode of the quarrel. "The other boys set up such a laugh at our folly that we cooled down and became better friends than before," Dorsey recalled.

The raiders' foray to Madison lasted only three days. Nothing came of Mitchel's advance on Chattanooga, which turned out to be just an effort to secure his eastward flank and protect his supply line at Stevenson, and the raiders soon entrained for the return trip northward. The ride was in boxcars this time, but the guards did their best to "render our condition more endurable," as one raider put it. (After all, most of them had ridden in a boxcar before.) They dreaded their arrival back at Swims's jail, a place they had hoped they would never see again. But the provost marshal Colonel Claiborne and their new commander of the guard Captain James Law of the 43rd Georgia, by all accounts a reasonable and kindhearted officer, directed that they be allowed to stay in the upper room. This unfortunately displaced the East Tennessee Unionists back to the dungeon, a sad necessity the raiders justified to themselves by noting that there were only fourteen of the Tennesseans, so the "hell hole" would at least be less crowded.[20]

The ensuing days spent in the upstairs cell were "not so very unpleasant," as one raider put it, though the rations remained hideous and their overall outlook was still rather grim. The light and air from the three large (if barred) windows in the upper room made the confinement much more tolerable and bred a number of new activities to pass the time. Foremost among these was singing. A number of the men in the party were excellent singers—Andrews and Ross had fine voices as well as formal musical training, and Mark Wood and John Porter were said to be "fair assistants" as well. The evening song service, held each night around twilight, soon drew the attention and admiration of the guards and a number of the locals, who crowded into the prison yard to hear the "caged Yankees" sing. Patriotic airs, army songs, and hymns were a regular part of the repertoire, though ballads and odes to sweethearts and home made up the bulk of the program. They opened with "Do They Miss Me At Home?" often followed by "Nettie More" or "The Prairie Queen." Sergeant Major Ross's favorite, strangely enough, was "Kissing Thro' the Bars."

> *'Twas in a grove, I met my love,*
> *One soft and balmy night,*
> *I own'd my flame, she did the same,*
> *And trembled with delight.*
> *When at her gate, we parted late,*
> *I bless'd my lucky stars,*
> *And stole a kiss, to seal our bliss,*
> *Between the wicket bars.*

Then there was "Riding on the Rail" (*Whizzing thro' the mountain/ Buzzing o'er the vale/ Bless me this is pleasant/ A-riding on a rail*), which Andrews sang "with evident glee." The Englishman Mark Wood was particularly fond of "A Life on the Ocean Wave," which seemed to "rouse his naturally jolly spirits to their highest pitch." Andrews's favorite was the melancholy "Carrier Dove," which he sang in a high, crystalline tenor:

> *Fly away to my native land, sweet Dove,*
> *Fly away to my native land,*
> *And bear these lines to my lady love,*
> *That I've traced with a feeble hand.*
> *She marvels much at my long delay,*
> *A rumor of death she has heard,*
> *Or she thinks, perhaps, that I falsely stray;*
> *Then fly to her bower, sweet bird.*
>
> *Oh! Fly to her bower, and say the chain*
> *Of the tyrant is o'er me now—*
> *That I never shall mount my steed again*

With helmet upon my brow!
No friend to my lattice a solace brings,
Except when your voice is heard;
When you beat the bars with your snowy wings,
Then fly to her bower, sweet bird.

I shall miss thy visit at dawn, sweet dove,
I shall miss thy visit at eve;
But bring me a line from my lady love,
And then I shall cease to grieve.
I can bear in a dungeon, to waste away youth,
I can fall by a conqueror's sword,
But I cannot endure should she doubt my truth,
Then fly to her bower, sweet bird.

These songs and many others like them passed the time, entertained the crowds, and lifted the spirits of the chained soldiers. "But the song of songs was the old 'Star-Spangled Banner,'" Dorsey recalled. "We took good care to make that ring in the ear of friends—and we knew we had some friends, though they didn't dare let themselves be known—and foes, at least once nearly every day during our entire imprisonment. If we were to be executed together, we intended to sing 'The Star-Spangled Banner' on the scaffold, and sometimes practiced it with that object in view."

Other pastimes developed as well—reading and card-playing were now more practicable, thanks to plentiful daylight and books and cards donated by visitors or loaned by the guards. (Some among the party, including the future Reverend Pittenger, frowned upon card-playing, but those who engaged in the practice figured they had as much right to do as they pleased in the jail as anyone else.) The raiders shouted to visitors and passersby (they could see over the fence in two directions now) and crowded at the windows to heckle the guards as they drilled nearby. They conducted elaborate mock trials, with William Campbell serving as judge—his ample size deemed to be more than sufficient to keep order in the court and to dole out punishment, usually in the form of good-natured physical abuse, to those found guilty. George Wilson and Bill Pittenger served as counsel for the state and the defense, each making blistering arguments and heaping abuse on the other to the amusement of all. The cases before the court ran the gamut, from imaginary sordid crimes and preposterous claims to actual if usually petty grievances against one's chainmate. Witnesses providing sworn testimony in these disputes often testified of their adventures the previous night in Cincinnati, or Columbus, or Toledo, or on Wall Street, trading stocks. "Anywhere, of course, but the old Swims jail, in Chattanooga."[21]

One day, they had a distinguished visitor in the form of the conductor William Fuller, who had seen Andrews and Pittenger at the leader's recent court-martial but came now to pay his respects to the group as a whole. Fuller remained outside the door of the cell, at first "passing a few words with us in a rather friendly manner," as Dorsey later recalled. But the conductor then seemed to come unhinged, if Dorsey can be believed, and he "got off a speech" Dorsey would never forget: "The trouble with you gentlemen was that you had the wrong man to follow you," he said. "I'm the man that followed you, and by God, I'm not done following you yet! I'll follow you to the scaffold, God damn you! And see you at the end of a rope! Then I'll cease to follow you, and not till then!" Dorsey wrote of this exchange almost apologetically years later, saying, "Maybe I ought not to tell this, but it is a part of the history, and that is what I am writing." There is no corroboration for Dorsey's recollection—none of the other raiders ever mentioned this ugly scene.[22]

The provost marshal Colonel Claiborne soon afforded the imprisoned raiders another indulgence, ordering them brought out into the yard in two shifts for an hour each afternoon. This welcome respite from their cramped quarters afforded the prisoners not only sunlight and exercise, but a greater opportunity to make conversation with guards and locals and gather information. Some neighbors, including a freeman blacksmith named William Lewis, sent food to supplement their rations; others brought small gifts or news of the war. Ross, the only Freemason among the party, made contact with some fellow Masons and received small favors and pieces of intelligence from time to time. Now that a few weeks had passed and the shock of the raid had subsided, the raiders perceived a rising tide of sympathy among the populace that gave them greater hope of surviving their ordeal. There was increasing talk of a prisoner exchange, especially after the capture by Rebel cavalry of General Mitchel's son. The raiders also continued their plans for a possible escape, focusing on two scenarios. The first, proposed by Pittenger, involved releasing their irons and simply rushing the guards when the cell was opened for a meal to be delivered. The formidable statures of Campbell, Ross, and Slavens made a hand-to-hand fight in close quarters an appealing option—and it certainly had the advantage of simplicity—but even if successful, the raiders would then have to contend with as many as thirty armed guards outside the jail. The second proposal, suggested by Andrews, was for the slippery John Wollam to hide under the jailer's bed in the outer room as they returned from the yard; from whence he could sneak out, overpower old Swims, and release the others. They could then make the rush to the gate as a group, under cover of darkness. Although some among the party continued to put their faith in their legal defense or a possible exchange, the raiders set a date to try Andrews's plan.[23]

During the afternoon of the appointed day, however, an order was received to transport twelve of the raiders to Knoxville for trial. The reason for this change of venue is uncertain. Some theorized that the Confederates wanted to divide the large party to make them easier to guard; others thought that the authorities believed that the group had engendered too much sympathy there in Chattanooga and thus should be tried elsewhere. One historian would suggest that Chattanooga had an insufficient number of officers available to serve on a court-martial at the time. George Wilson, who had been ill and allowed to remain in the yard for a longer period, was the first to receive the news, and he was given the privilege of selecting the twelve men to go. Hopeful that the trial might serve to establish their bona fides as prisoners of war and render them eligible for exchange, Wilson selected his comrades from the 2nd Ohio—Bill Pittenger, Marion Ross, and Perry Shadrach—along with friends and former traveling companions from other regiments: William Campbell, John Scott, Samuel Slavens, Samuel Robertson, Robert Buffum, Elihu Mason, Wilson Brown, and William Knight. "When the announcement was made that we must be separated, our spirits ran low, for we all knew that the chances for escape were materially lessened," Dorsey wrote. "This fact, with the uncertainty of our ever meeting again, caused a gloom to fall over us . . . . The parting was painful, especially on Andrews' account, as all felt his days were numbered, though he had had no notice of the fact as yet." It had been several weeks since his trial, and still no word of a verdict, but the same guards that talked of sympathy and exchange to the Ohio soldiers offered no such hope for Andrews. "He bore this like a hero as he was, and continued mild and cheerful as ever," Pittenger recalled, though the parting from the Knoxville twelve had all the markings of a final farewell. Andrews shook the hands of each of the men departing, and said, "Boys, if I never see you here again, try to meet me on the other side of Jordan."[24]

The twelve men departed for Knoxville on the morning of May 31, a Saturday. That same day, as the remaining ten were in the prison yard for their "afternoon airing," Captain Law approached Andrews and handed him an envelope. The Kentuckian "received it coolly," placed it in his pocket, and walked for a short while before climbing the steps along with his chainmate, Martin Hawkins. The rest of the party found them in the cell, reading "a nicely written document," which turned out to be his death warrant. "For once there was a deathlike pallor upon the face of the man who seemed to have no fear," Dorsey recalled. "But the pallor did not last long; Mr. Andrews voluntarily told us of the nature of the document he had received, and as he did so he smiled, but oh! Such a smile. It seemed like the smile of a corpse." The nine soldiers there with Andrews felt anguish, not only for their leader, but for themselves. "We all realized the reality that stared at us," as Alf Wilson put it. "This didn't simply mean the execution of our chief. It was a forerunner of the fate that awaited every man of us."

The order set the date of execution for June 7, one week hence. James Andrews had seven days to live—unless he could escape.[25]

Atlanta. (*Library of Congress*)

CHAPTER TWELVE

The Horrors of the Gibbet

Atlanta and Knoxville

Yesterday evening's train from Chattanooga brought to this place to be executed Andrews, the leader of the Engine Thieves, under sentence of death, convicted by court martial of being a spy. He was carried to Peachtree Street Road, accompanied by three clergymen, and escorted by a guard.

A considerable crowd followed to witness the execution.

—(Atlanta) *Southern Confederacy*
Sunday, June 8, 1862

*T*HE NINE RAIDERS WHO REMAINED in Chattanooga set to work almost immediately on an effort to deliver Andrews from confinement and thus from the noose. Their earlier plans—rushing the guard in a long-odds attempt to win freedom for the entire group by surprise and by force—were abandoned, the focus now on sneaking out a single man, with others to follow if possible. This would by no means be easy, as Andrews had been returned to the basement dungeon below them for extra security. They quickly conceived of a plan for an escape that would be largely vertical—they would bring Andrews up from the dungeon and break through the ceiling of their cell to the attic, where the outer wall of the old jail could hopefully be breached. They had but one asset—Knight's dull penknife, which the engineer (who was one among the recently departed Knoxville twelve) had thoughtfully left behind with his comrades in case they might need it. Moreover, because their plans would necessarily require forcible opening of the trap door and considerable destruction to the ceiling of their cell, the bulk of the work would have to be accomplished in a single night.

The Buckeye soldiers started preparing for Andrews's exodus overnight on Saturday, scoring the oak planking up above to ready the boards for a breakthrough. Their preliminary efforts in this regard went undetected through the day on Sunday, and they resumed after sunset by attacking the lock and latch of the trap door. They drowned out the sounds of their labors with loud conversation, laughter, and singing, a difficult thing to credibly sustain for a long period of time—"our singers and noise-makers were about as weary with the monotony of their efforts as the saw-shovers," Alf Wilson recalled. After a time, the lock was unseated and the trap swung back, and an improvised rope made of twisted blankets and torn clothes lowered down to their leader. They again turned their attention to the two-inch oak boards of the ceiling high overhead, which had been nearly cut through during the similar noisemaking the night before. Three men stood close together to form a scaffold, while a fourth stood on their shoulders and sawed at the planking above until his hand grew tired and the knife was passed to another. It was now after midnight, too late for further singing and noise, and the boards had to be cut through quietly. This was soon accomplished, and Andrews was lifted up to the attic, along with John Wollam, who was to help with the exit and follow if he could.

The two men set to work in the darkness, using the knife and a bone to make an opening, brick by brick, in the gable at the end of the jail. It was slow going; the bricks had to be loosened carefully, pulled inward, and then set gently down, though sounds of chipping and scraping and bits of mortar were unavoidable. At last, as the faintest light began to appear in the sky to the east, Andrews and Wollam whispered down that they were ready. The blanket rope was passed up and secured to a rafter. Andrews removed his boots, holding them in his teeth by the straps. He then slid out through the hole and disappeared.

His exit unfortunately dislodged a loose brick, creating a ruckus outside and alerting one of the Rebel sentries, who cried: "Corporal of the guard! Corporal of the guard! Captain! Oh, Captain! Halt! Halt!" Andrews dropped to the ground and sprinted for the south fence. The guards got off several shots at the fleeing figure, but Andrews was quickly over the high board fence and gone in the darkness of Fifth Street, losing his hat and his boots in the process. Wollam, who one historian would describe as a "thin, wiry, tobacco-chewing scape-grace who would have laughed in the face of Azrael," was entirely undeterred by the hollering guards and whizzing bullets. He slid down just behind Andrews and disappeared over the fence as well.

The eight men remaining all agreed that it would be foolish for another to make the attempt, and the officer of the guard who burst into the cell minutes later found them quiet, innocently pretending to sleep—a laughable fiction, not only because of the shouting and the gunfire, but also because the prisoners strangely lacked blankets, and there was an unexplained hole in the ceiling. Old Swims was "a tower of rage," Dorsey recalled, irate that the raiders had "made merry" last night while cutting his jail all to pieces. He hotly blamed the provost guard and the Confederate sentries for the lenient treatment that had been given the raiders of late, and whined that "he might have known there was some devilment up, the way the damned Yankees were singing hymns." Whatever minimal privileges the raiders had been afforded were now at an end, of course. "It is hardly necessary for me to tell the reader that those of us who failed to make good our escape were now put down in the hole, loaded with heavy irons, and treated with the greatest rigor and severity," Alf Wilson wrote. But the Ohioans were elated with their success. They congratulated each other in the fetid darkness and breathlessly awaited word of the two fugitives.[1]

Andrews and Wollam were separated from the outset, taking disparate routes through the streets as they made for the Tennessee River, racing to beat the coming daylight. Wollam cleverly discarded his coat and vest at the riverbank and waded into the water before returning to the near bank and secreting himself in a canebrake. His pursuers apparently fell for his simple ruse and began searching the other side of the river before concluding that he had been swept away and drowned. At dark, Wollam crept down the bank, found a discarded canoe, and disappeared down the river.

The shoeless Andrews started out with similar plans in mind, but his initial success proved to be fleeting. The spy made his way a short distance outside the city, waded along the riverbank to throw off the dogs, and then climbed a tree to hide and wait out the daylight hours as Wollam had done. He spent the day wedged uncomfortably in the notch of the tree, watching as trains ran along the nearby railroad and armed men scoured the woods and riverbanks around him. Fate again had dark clouds in store for James Andrews—as night fell, a rumbling thunderstorm rolled in and a vigorous wind lashed across the broad, dark surface of the river. Andrews descended and resumed his march, moving gingerly along the bank in his bare feet as a hard rain began to fall. Encountering a high bluff that made further travel down the bank impossible, he decided to swim the river. He removed his trousers, rolling them in a bundle and tying them around his neck, and pulled out into the rushing current. The waters were fast and rough in the storm, and a wave swept Andrews under and dislodged his britches. He finally reached the opposite shore, exhausted and bruised from the rocky bottom of the river, and continued along the bank. He was determined to put as much distance as he could between himself and Chattanooga, but it was hard going in the blackness. He stumbled over rocks and limbs in the dark, briars tearing at his bare legs and feet.[2]

By the time dawn broke on Tuesday, word had spread throughout East Tennessee that the notorious spy Andrews had made good his escape. Newspapers reported the shocking news—"THE ESCAPED TRAIN-STEALERS!" one headline read—and carried a detailed description of Andrews: tall, 180 pounds, short black hair and heavy black beard; "his voice is fine, and his general address good." William Fuller, then in Knoxville to testify in the court-martial proceedings being held there, heard the reports and promptly wired the provost marshal in Chattanooga:

> June 3d, Knoxville
>
> COLONEL HENRY L. CLAIBORNE:
>
> Is it possible that the infamous Andrews escaped? Is he pursued? If not, offer in my name $100 reward for his recapture and reincarceration.
>
> WILLIAM A. FULLER[3]

The conductor might have saved himself the trouble, as Andrews would be arrested before the day was out. Nearly spent from his exertions and unable to find an adequate hideout, he approached a small boy in a dugout Tuesday morning near Moccasin Bend. The poor lad was initially paralyzed with fright at seeing the half-naked, bloody, black-bearded skeleton, but soon recovered and agreed to take Andrews across to Williams Island. Over two miles long and consisting of more than four hundred heavily wooded acres, the island divided the river channel just shy of the entrance to the Tennessee River gorge. The place was owned by and named for Samuel Williams, whose plantation stood just across the river to the east. Williams was a longtime resident of the area and a wealthy storeowner and farmer, referred to by some historians as "the Father of Chattanooga." Like Andrews, the issue of his loyalty was a complicated one: he claimed to be opposed to secession and later would seek compensation for his activities allegedly supporting the Union cause, but he was also known to serve from time to time as a scout for Confederate cavalryman Nathan Bedford Forrest. At any rate, his actions that day would show him to be no friend of the North, or at least no friend of James Andrews.

After hiding again for a time, Andrews at last succumbed to his gnawing hunger and came out in the open (some accounts would have him ultimately discovered in a small boat, others in the branches of a mulberry tree). The boy in the canoe, still shaken by the encounter, had gone straight to Williams's house and informed him of the strange man, who Williams immediately assumed to be one of the escapees. He found Andrews nearby, wearing only his ragged black coat and a "once white" shirt, his feet so swollen and bleeding he could barely walk. Andrews immediately admitted that he was an escaped prisoner; said he had nothing to eat since Sunday; and asked for a meal and some clothes. "The man looked as if everything he said was so," Williams recalled. "His cheek bones stuck out and his face was pinched with hunger."

From here, there is some disagreement about how the capture proceeded. Williams (perhaps wanting to shore up his case after the fact that he was a Union man), claimed that he merely went for food and clothes for the poor fugitive, only to have two visitors, William I. Standifer and a Kentucky doctor by the name of Craig, come upon Andrews and insist on making him their prisoner. On the contrary, the old soldier Captain Standifer—who several weeks before had seen the raiders stepping off the ferry in Chattanooga and thought them "a motley-looking set"—would later maintain that Williams had been an active and conniving participant in arresting James Andrews, and had in fact been sweeping the island and the river looking for the fugitives since the day before.

Whatever the circumstances and conspirators involved in rounding up Andrews, he was taken to Williams's fine colonnaded home, where he was provided with dry clothes and an excellent supper prepared by Mrs. Williams. During his few hours there, he talked openly of his recent escape and wanderings, which Williams would recall as "one of the most pitiful stories I ever listened to." Williams's two daughters, aged nine and fourteen, were quite taken with the handsome stranger and would later remember "his lacerated feet, his handsome countenance, his soft, eloquent voice, and the haunting despair of his eyes," as he spoke of his adventures and the girl he planned to marry. "Andrews had a pleasant voice," Williams recalled, "and could talk the best of any man I ever heard. He was the sort of a person who could make you believe everything he said was the truth. He was an uncommon man, and he showed it."

The younger Williams daughter used a brush to shoo the flies from the table as their mysterious guest finished his meal, and after he hobbled out to rest in a rocking chair on the porch, both girls implored their father not to return him to prison. But return him they did, his captors saddling Andrews on a mule and walking him back to Chattanooga next day. Andrews had made it twelve miles and been free less than thirty-six hours before being snared by Williams and Standifer. Though the source of the hearsay is unclear, tradition holds that Andrews told Williams as they departed, "I am grateful to you for your kindness and hospitality, but you have betrayed me." Certainly the newspapers would see it that way; the *Chattanooga Rebel* ran a story some time later relating the sad story of Andrews's "misplaced confidence," and asked, "Who doubts that if Andrews had applied to one of Sam Williams' negroes, instead of Sam Williams himself, that the negro would have divided his last crust with him and helped him to reach the Federal army?"[4]

A rumor reached the prisoners at Swims's jail on Wednesday that Andrews had been captured, and a short time after, a strong guard and a "rabble of citizens" arrived with the man himself, leaving blood behind him at every step. "Oh, how our hearts and hopes sank down within us beyond the power of expression," Alf Wilson remembered, later vividly describing his despair:

> I have seen those dear to me by ties of kindred called away never to return. I have seen comrades die on the field, and without warning sufficient to speak a parting farewell. I have seen a comrade, endeared to me by long association and friendship amid dangers, chained to me and perishing slowly day by day—his proud spirit broken by disease and hunger, until fever's fitful delirium robbed him of the sense of pain. All this I have seen and felt, yet God, in His inscrutable ways and infinite mercy, never laid upon me the heavy, chastening hand of sorrow and anguish that I felt when I beheld the brutal guards bringing in poor, ill-fated Andrews, bound hand and foot in heavy chains. I could have prayed that death had spared me those painful moments, the most harrowing of my life.

Andrews was placed back in "the hole" with his comrades, and they were shocked at his appearance, which was nothing short of ghastly. "He was the most wretched, pitiable human being I ever saw—a sight which horrified us all, and even drew words of compassion from some of the prison-guards," Wilson recalled. The change was so startling that it hardly seemed possible that it could have taken place in just three days. He was "bloody, bruised, and speechless," his face "pale, haggard, and emaciated," and his eyes "gave forth a wild, despairing, unnatural light." All in all, Wilson thought, "he seemed more dead than alive."[5]

Despite his weakened condition, the provost guard would be taking no further chances with Mr. Andrews. Later that evening, the trap door was opened, and three men descended. First came old Swims, carrying a lantern, followed by an officer wearing a sword, and finally William Lewis, the blacksmith who lived nearby, who had so kindly sent lettuce from his garden to the prisoners. He brought with him a hammer, a pair of crude shackles connected with a heavy chain, and a section of iron to serve as an anvil. One historian would describe Lewis—who everyone called "Uncle Billy"—as "one of the most remarkable negroes in Chattanooga at that time, or any time," and rightly so. Born into slavery in 1813, he had come to Chattanooga as a young man and learned the trade of a blacksmith and ironworker and set out to build a life for himself and his family. After considerable perseverance, he was able to purchase his freedom and that of his wife, for $1,000 each. He then established his own smithy, bought tools and materiel, and hired employees, and soon purchased his six-year-old son, for $400. He next bought freedom for his elderly uncle and aunt ($150 each), then his two brothers ($1,000 each), and finally his sister ($400). He built a handsome two-story home for his growing family, and his blacksmith shop prospered, though he often had to conduct business with a white man serving as his agent. Having so often used his anvil to forge freedom for and improve the lives of others, he was charged tonight with the sad duty of shackling Andrews and ensuring that his life would soon come to an end.

No one spoke as Lewis bent to his work. "Andrews lay prone on the filthy floor, with no blanket, resting on one elbow to watch the proceedings," Dorsey recalled. Lewis knelt next to Andrews as he hammered the shackles around his swollen ankles by the feeble light of Swims's lantern. The other prisoners sat or stood in their chained pairs, silently watching what Dorsey would call "one of the saddest scenes of our lives." When Lewis finished his work, the three men departed—the trap door above closing behind them with a "sickening thud"—and any remaining hope seemed to depart with them.

The next day, a detail of Confederate soldiers began erecting a scaffold near the jail for Saturday's hanging.[6]

*I*n Knoxville, 112 miles away up the East Tennessee & Georgia Railroad, the courts-martial of the rest of the party were by now under way. The twelve raiders had been taken to the old Knoxville jail, a massive stone edifice then used to hold military prisoners, where they were housed in large iron cages, though there was no "crowding and suffocation" like they had experienced in Chattanooga. "This place was a great improvement on any we had endured," William Pittenger recalled, "and we spent the days in comparative pleasure, and in a great degree of hope." Also incarcerated at the Knoxville prison were a number of dangerous East Tennessee Unionists, including G.W. Barlow and Peter Pierce, who had suffered a mighty, cleaving blow to his skull with the barrel of a gun, leaving a permanent vertical scar—more of a trench, really—in his forehead from nose to hairline. His compatriots affectionately called him "Forked-Head," or "Old Gun Barrel," and "he presented the singular combination of great piety and great profanity, singing hymns and cursing the Confederacy with equal zeal," Pittenger remembered. In a neighboring cage, his notoriety earning him a cell of his own, was Captain David Fry, the East Tennessee guerilla leader, who had at last been apprehended by the Confederates and was awaiting a trial of his own. The Andrews Raiders became acquainted with Fry and the other East Tennesseans by writing notes on the margins of newspapers and passing them back and forth. "Afterward he came to be virtually one of our number, to which position we were the readier to admit him, as he also had been a bridge-burner, and far more successful than ourselves," Pittenger recalled.

Again, the defendants managed to come up with capable and perhaps even prominent defense counsel, in the form of a well-respected Knoxville Judge Oliver P. Temple and his law partner John Baxter, future U.S. District Judge for the Eastern District. (Pittenger deserves credit for securing their services, having opened a dialogue by sending a note to Judge Temple asking if he could borrow a book on evidence upon their arrival.) The firm of Temple & Baxter agreed to the engagement for a fee of $150 per case, each defendant giving his note for that sum, to be due and payable upon acquittal. This fee arrangement was in some respects illusory—the two lawyers certainly did not expect to be paid, but given the suspicion and persecution that was often heaped on Union-friendly Tennesseans, it was thought that "their own safety required that their help should appear to be purely professional." The proceedings were convened in the Old Court House, and they were conducted with an air of informality and indifference that would suggest that the outcome was a foregone conclusion. Indeed, at least one Confederate officer posted in Knoxville would later assert that he had refused to serve as a member of what he regarded as a kangaroo court. "The table around which the court sat was covered with bottles, newspapers, and novels, and the members occupied themselves during the proceedings in discussing these," Pittenger wrote. "All this was very well if the object was, as they assured us, merely to put formally on the record our true character as prisoners of war; but it was most heartless if the trial was in earnest, and a matter of life or death."[7]

The court considered testimony from only two witnesses: first, the hero—conductor William Fuller—who testified as to the theft, pursuit, and recapture of the engine—and the raider William Pittenger, who essentially filled in the rest. He would maintain down the years that he had testified only at the request of and in accordance with the wishes and direction of his comrades, seeking to assist the defense—but if this was the goal, he was far from successful. "The impression upon my mind at the time was, that the witness was in the interest of the prosecution, and indeed was," Fuller later wrote, "but from his statement it was by agreement, and that the testimony he gave in was previously agreed upon by all the prisoners as the theory less dangerous." Fuller went on to recount the evidence:

> [Mr. Pittenger] swore to who the prisoners were; that they were United States soldiers; that they, or a part of them, had been detailed, etc., as [later] stated in his book, while I swore to what they did and when, how and where they did it. That they were dressed as citizens when they came on my train at Marietta, and that they claimed to be refugees from Kentucky, and that they were going from Marietta to Big Shanty (then Camp McDonald) to join the Confederate army etc. & etc. I also swore that the defendants took my train and engine in the midst of a military camp—Confederate camp of instruction, and that when they did so they were dressed as citizens and represented themselves to me as such. . . . This was considered by the Confederate side as a good prima-facie case, but they had a good case, beyond doubt, when the character of all the prisoners was given by Pittenger.[8]

The raiders' counsel Judge Temple did not see it that way; in postwar years, he defended the character and testimony of Corporal Pittenger, who he said had testified in the case "under compulsion" and certainly not voluntarily. "In other words," Temple later wrote, "he did not 'turn state's evidence,' but was put on the stand by the prosecuting attorney, with no promise of pardon to him, and when on the stand he testified to such a state of facts as we desired, and which we thought sufficient to acquit you all." Pittenger argued, as planned, that the Ohio soldiers were detailed on a military expedition by General Mitchel and denied that they were spies. Temple noted that he had consulted with the other prisoners every day during the course of the proceedings, and that none complained of Pittenger's conduct. The problem was not the witness but the court itself, which Temple described as "blinded and predetermined to convict." "We believed all the time that you would be convicted, so maddened were men at the time," he wrote. Fuller, too, was willing to take at face value Pittenger's claim that he had by agreement been nominated "the mouth-piece for the whole party of prisoners," concluding that "no improper motive could be imputed to him."

"But I must say that the position assumed by the defense was extremely dangerous," Fuller concluded, "and I can not see how it was hoped to maintain it."[9]

The raiders were tried one at a time, one per day, their request for a consolidation of their cases into one proceeding having been denied at the outset—perhaps due to what one historian would call the "manifest absurdity" of trying a group of a dozen men on charges of secretly lurking and spying. Just as Judge Brabson had for Andrews in Chattanooga, the raiders' attorneys Temple and Baxter put on a spirited defense, their written plea being "an able paper," as Pittenger put it, "and one worthy of their subsequent fame." There was no question, they said, that these were United States soldiers acting under orders on a military mission—though the charges carefully omitted any mention of train-stealing or bridge-burning or any other action that might give the impression of soldiers on a raid. Temple and Baxter asserted that the entire case came down to a complaint that the defendants had been dressed in civilian clothes instead of their uniforms. This was a common tactic employed by the Confederates themselves, the lawyers argued, noting that literally tens of thousands of soldiers in the Southern ranks did not have uniforms at all, and that guerilla bands in homespun clothes regularly attacked Federal supply lines and outposts. They pointed in particular to the celebrated exploits of Confederate General John Hunt Morgan, whose men had donned Federal uniforms, no less, as part of a raid to destroy Northern railroads; some of these Confederates had been captured and treated as prisoners of war. The defendants in the present case, upon their capture, had freely and plainly told the object of their mission, which was "purely military" and as such "authorized by the usages of warfare." The exact course of the argument, and the way in which it was refuted and received by the court, is unclear, as no record exists of the court-martial proceedings themselves. But the defense case was, in the words of the U.S. Judge Advocate who later reviewed the trial, "a just and unanswerable presentation," and the raiders entertained high hopes that they would be acquitted of the charge of spying.[10]

After the trials of seven of the twelve raiders held in Knoxville had been completed, the court-martial was adjourned because of another military threat to Chattanooga, followed by an approach by Union forces under General George W. Morgan to the gates of Knoxville itself. "The first movement stopped the trials; the second rendered our speedy removal necessary," Pittenger recalled. The evidence and arguments of the Knoxville courts-martial would remain unknown for the time being and the subject of bitter debate in the years to come. But if the course of the trials of William Campbell, Samuel Robertson, Marion Ross, John Scott, Perry Shadrach, Samuel Slavens, and George D. Wilson remains in controversy even today, there was no uncertainty about the outcome, which was duly reported and in time approved by the War Department in Richmond:

GENERAL ORDERS, HDQRS. DEPT. OF EAST TENNESSEE

No. 54 Knoxville, June 14, 1862.

At a general court martial, held at Knoxville, by virtue of General Orders, Nos. 21 and 34 (department headquarters, April 15 and May 10, 1862) whereof Lieutenant Colonel J.B. Bibb, of the Twenty-third Regiment Alabama Volunteers, was president, was tried:

William Campbell, private, Company K, Second Ohio Regiment, on the following charge and specifications, to wit:

CHARGE: Violation of section 2 of the one hundred and first article of the Rules and Articles of War.

Specification 1.—In this, that the said William Campbell, private Company K, not owing allegiance to the Confederate States of America, did, on or about the 7th day of April, 1862, leave the Army of the United States, then lying near Shelbyville, Tenn., and with a company of about 20 other soldiers of the U.S. Army, all dressed in citizens' clothes, repair to Chattanooga, Tenn., entering covertly within the lines of the Confederate forces at that post, and did thus, on or about the 11th day of April, 1862, lurk as a spy in and about the encampments of said forces, representing himself as a citizen of Kentucky going to join the Southern army.

Specification 2.—And the said William Campbell, private Company K, Second Ohio Regiment, U.S. Army, thus dressed in citizens' clothes, and representing himself as a citizen of Kentucky going to join the Southern army, and did proceed by railroad to Marietta, Ga., thus covertly pass through the lines of the Confederate forces stationed at Chattanooga, Dalton, and Camp McDonald, and did thus, on or about the 11th day of April, 1862, lurk as a spy in and about the said encampments of the Confederate forces at the places stated aforesaid.

To which charge and specifications the prisoner plead, "Not guilty."

The court, after mature deliberation, find the accused as follows:

Of the first specification of the charge, "guilty."

Of the second specification of the charge, "guilty."

And "guilty" of the charge.

And the court therefore sentence the accused, the said William Campbell, private Company K, Second Ohio Regiment (two-thirds of the members concurring therein), as soon as this order shall be made public, "to be hung by the neck until he is dead."[11]

James Andrews seemed to abandon all hope after his recapture. "His usually mild disposition became more mild, and his voice more plaintive," Dorsey remembered. Though strict security was maintained, Andrews was soon afforded various small liberties and privileges, the markings of a doomed man. He was brought into the upper room of the jail, where there was "more light and less filth," as one raider put it, and allowed to meet with a local minister. He read from a borrowed Bible and spent long hours in silence, apparently "in deep meditation," Dorsey thought, "over his tragic end now so near at hand." The raiders respected this quietude; there was no singing, no jokes or arguments among the prisoners, and little conversation in the small dungeon. Andrews was furnished with a pen, paper, and ink, along with a book to press down on, so that he could write any final correspondence. He wrote a long letter to his friend D. S. McGavic, describing his misfortune and leaving instructions for the disposition of his affairs back in Flemingsburg. (One might think, from these arrangements, that McGavic was a lawyer, or a businessman; in fact, he was a bartender at a local tavern.) The letter and its enclosures would be filed with the court clerk in Fleming County, Kentucky, and duly probated as Andrews's last will and testament.

"Dear Sir," he began, "You will doubtless be surprised to hear from me from this place and more surprised to hear that I am to be executed on the 7th inst., for attempting to run a train of cars from the Western & Atlantic R.R. to Huntsville for the use of General Mitchel." He briefly described the raiders' flight on and from the locomotive, their subsequent capture, and his recent escape and recapture. "The sentence seems a hard one for the crime proven against me," he continued, "but I suppose the court that tried me thought otherwise. I have now calmly submitted to my fate and have been earnestly preparing to meet my God in peace, and have found that peace of mind and tranquility of soul which even astonishes myself. I have never supposed a man could feel so complete a change under similar circumstances." He asked that McGavic "acquaint my friends with my fate"; left regards for his landlord and landlady back home, with hopes that they would meet in heaven someday; and noted that he had written several letters to Flemingsburg, but had received none in return. "What the fate of the balance of the party will be I am unable to say, but I hope they will not share the fate of their leader," he wrote. "Hoping we may meet in that better country, I bid you a long and last farewell." In a postscript, he left instructions for a large lady's trunk left in care of the proprietor of the Louisville Hotel to be retrieved and presented to his fiancée, Miss Elizabeth Layton.[12]

The raiders were roused early on Saturday, June 7, the scheduled date for Andrews's execution, and again escorted to the railroad station to board a train headed south. "Why this change was so suddenly made in the programme I have never been able to discover," Alf Wilson wrote years later. The reason, as it turned out, was that elements of Mitchel's Third Division at last appeared to be advancing on Chattanooga.[13]

Ormsby Mitchel had been trying to hold his own in northern Alabama for the past several weeks, plagued all the while by cavalry raids from without and discipline problems within his own command. "Mitchel's position in

Northern Alabama was at all times precarious," one of his officers later wrote, "he covered too much country; lacked concentration; and was constantly in danger of being assailed in detail; besides, his relations to Buell, his immediate commander, were not cordial." The beleaguered astronomer-general soon found himself accused not only of military incompetence but also "wanton and disgraceful" personal conduct, not to mention outright corruption. Foremost among these criticisms was his handling of—and a public rumor that he had acquiesced in—the infamous sack of Athens, Alabama, by soldiers from the Eighth Brigade under Colonel John Basil Turchin. "I shuts mine eyes for two hours," the Czarist officer had announced in the presence of his troops, who proceeded to plunder the town and terrorize its inhabitants on May 2—"according to the Muscovite custom," as one Union officer put it. Mitchel chastised Turchin over the incident, but refused to punish anyone— he could hardly arraign an entire brigade, he said—and he summarily rejected the aggrieved townspeople's claims for compensation, which totaled what he skeptically called "the very large sum of $54,689.80." He reported that he did order a thorough search of the brigade's baggage and each soldier's knapsack, though not surprisingly, nothing unauthorized was discovered.[14]

"There has not been found in American history so black a page as that which will bear the record of Gen. Mitchel's campaign in North Alabama," Brigadier General and future President James A. Garfield wrote of the "shameful outrages" that had occurred in Athens. But the furor that erupted over this ugly incident—which culminated in a month-long court-martial of Turchin—would not be the only attack made on the character and competence of General Mitchel. Later that summer, one newspaper accused him of speculating in sales of cotton his troops had seized from Southern citizens— though Old Stars promptly refuted the charges by delivering copies of his orders and correspondence over the issue, including his orders from Buell to "encourage the trade in cotton" and his open correspondence with the Secretary of the Treasury over the practice. In some instances, his soldiers had incorporated confiscated cotton bales in fortifications and in one case even used them to construct an ingenious floating bridge. In addition, Halleck and Buell also complained that Mitchel had foolishly burned bridges over the Tennessee River, though Buell himself had ordered that they be torched. ("I spared the Tennessee bridges near Stevenson in the hope I might be permitted to march on Chattanooga or Knoxville, but now am ordered to burn the bridges," Mitchell had written to Chase in late April. "I do not comprehend the order, but must obey it as early as I can.")[15]

These attacks by editors, military rivals, and politicians, although annoying, did not appear to diminish the prominence or the prospects of the Ohio general, at least in his own eyes. Mitchel's star of fame reached the height of its ascendancy on May 10, when his portrait graced the cover of *Harper's Weekly*. The accompanying article—which misspelled his name throughout, adding a superfluous "l" at the end—briefly recounted his "brilliant exploits in Northern Alabama" and described him as "one of our most dashing and splendid generals." No one believed these descriptions more than Mitchel himself. One week later, at a strawberry supper at the home of Union-loyal Judge George W. Lane of Huntsville, Old Stars "monopolized the conversation," Colonel John Beatty recalled, "determined to make all understand that he was the greatest of living soldiers." Despite his continued clashes with his superiors and the absence of railroad bridges between here and there, Mitchel continued to regard the capture of Chattanooga as a laudable and achievable goal. "If the Secretary of War could now bestow sufficient confidence in my ability to execute what I undertake," he wrote his fellow Ohioan Salmon Chase in late April, "let him give me another Division and authorize my advance upon Chattanooga."[16]

That advance, such as it was, was finally in progress even as the doomed Andrews pondered the Gospels and drafted his will. At the end of May, Mitchel ordered Brigadier General James Negley, a Pennsylvania horticulturalist and future U.S. Congressman, to lead an "expedition" from Fayetteville in middle Tennessee and push southeast toward Chattanooga, "with authority to take the town in case he deems prudent." Brushing aside Rebel cavalry along the way through Winchester, Jasper, and Shellmound, Negley arrived at the river opposite Chattanooga on June 7 and commenced a somewhat desultory but nonetheless terrifying artillery bombardment. For three hours that afternoon and six hours on Sunday the 8th, Negley's four-and-a-half-inch Parrott guns lobbed shells into the streets of Chattanooga, "all through Market Street and over the town and far beyond the Crutchfield House," one soldier wrote. According to another Confederate, "The frightful whizzing of the shell, as they fell rapidly near the dwelling of some families near the vicinity of the ferry, produced the greatest consternation among the women and children, who were seen running in every direction, from the river to the centre of the town in the wildest of terror, while the most heart-rending cries and screams of others in the houses frantically illustrated the horrors of war."[17]

The Confederate command in East Tennessee thought the sky was falling, convinced by a combination of the Federal show of force and some faulty intelligence that the action signaled nothing less than the long-awaited "invasion of East Tennessee." Major General E. Kirby Smith got off a panicky wire to Georgia Governor Joseph E. Brown reporting that "Chattanooga is threatened by so superior a force that its evacuation seems almost inevitable," and he gave orders to General Leadbetter to retreat in the direction of Knoxville if he could not hold the town.[18]

Nothing came of Negley's advance in the end—he lacked pontoons or gunboats, carried few supplies, and had no plans for and presently no intention of actually taking and holding the town—but this did not stop him from proclaiming a triumph. His superior General Mitchel did the same, reporting that "The expedition to Chattanooga was a complete success," claiming that Negley "drove the Rebels out of town." The *New York Times* echoed this dispatch, a headline reporting the "Complete Success of the Expedition to East Tennessee." But by June 10, Negley was gone, inflicting negligible damage on the town and leaving the overmatched Confederates in place and for the most part unscathed. (Some would later claim that Negley did more harm than good to the Union cause, due to depredations committed by his troops on the locals in East Tennessee.) Chattanooga remained in Confederate hands and would not be captured by Union forces until Braxton Bragg abandoned the city in the fall of 1863. Some would later glorify Negley's artillery demonstration as the so-called First Battle of Chattanooga, though most histories apply the more realistic and appropriately dismissive title of "Negley's Raid."[19]

Still, the approach of Union troops ignited another panic in the Mountain City, which led to the relocation of Andrews to Atlanta just hours before he was to be hung. "We were soon whirling along on that same, to us, accursed railroad, for it brought no pleasant memories to us," Alf Wilson remembered, noting that Andrews was "reminded and taunted at every station of his approaching doom." The spy, who was not chained to any other prisoner, asked Wilson to go to the coach's water closet and open the window as high as possible. Wilson and Wood, chained together, shuffled down the aisle to the closet and tried to do just that, but the tiny window was shuttered and would only open about six inches. "Andrews received the news with a look of sad disappointment," Wilson recalled. "It was his last hope."

The sharp cry of the train's whistle startled the raiders, though they had been listening for it, and the engine's bell rang out what seemed to Dorsey like a death knell as they slowed for Atlanta. The train pulled into the Car Shed at about four o'clock, the sun still standing high in the June sky. The ten prisoners were taken from the station and marched under heavy guard across Peachtree Street to a three-story building known as the Concert Hall, the still-hobbled Andrews jangling and scraping along in his chains. "The clank, clank of the shackles on Andrews feet as he trudged along on the pavement seem to sound in my ears yet," Dorsey wrote years later. They climbed the stairs to the second floor and were seated on a row of wooden benches, all except for Mark Wood, who was feeling ill and lay down. The men together-er sat in silence, not wanting to disturb Andrews as he sat in mute reflection. The quiet was broken as the sheriff, Colonel Oliver H. Jones, clambered up the stairs, dressed in a fine, funereal black suit. He stood in the open door and spoke gently to the Kentuckian, quite as if he were inviting him to dinner. "Come on, now, Mr. Andrews," he said. Without a word, Andrews stood and firmly shook the hand of each one of his comrades. He then turned and clanked his way out the door and down the steps into the street below, dragging his chains behind him like a Dickensian spook. The nine soldiers watched out the windows as he clumsily pulled himself into an open carriage drawn by two horses. Colonel Jones climbed in beside him, and the carriage—followed by a large detail of mounted soldiers and a "motley crowd" of citizens—rolled away. "That was the last we saw of Andrews, brave, noble true-hearted Andrews! As grand a man as ever gave up his life for the starry flag of the free," Dorsey wrote.[20]

Reverend W.J. Scott, the pastor of Wesley Chapel (later the First Methodist Church of Atlanta), was standing in the broad sunlight at the corner of Decatur and Peachtree Streets when a column of soldiers approached and an open carriage containing Colonel Jones and the famous spy James Andrews pulled up next to him. The colonel asked if Rev. Scott would come along and officiate as chaplain at Mr. Andrews's execution. He politely declined. "I replied that I disliked to witness an execution of the sort and suggested that he procure some other minister," the pastor recalled. But a direct appeal from the condemned man changed his mind. Andrews looked steadily at Rev. Scott and said quietly, "I would be glad to have you go." Feeling that he could not refuse such an earnest request, the preacher climbed in the carriage and sat next to Andrews for the ride to the gallows.

It was a beautiful afternoon for an execution. "How well do I remember that lovely June day!" Mrs. Joseph M. Wustoff would write more than forty years later. A young girl at the time, she stood at her front gate and watched the parade pass by, one of hundreds of Atlantans who came out to witness the grim occasion. "It was quiet—no sound except for the tramp of the soldiers," she remembered. "It was one of our first realizations of the extreme horrors of war, and seemingly a feeling of depression or gloom hung over the city," she remembered. Though some Southerners had in the past days and hours taunted the Yankee captives and called for them to be hanged, those standing along the road seemed respectful, even reverent, now that the moment was at hand. The procession rolled slowly northward up Peachtree Street, taking Andrews outside of the city, a mile and a half from Five Points along the north-south ridge that formed the city's spine then and does so now. "The carriage was escorted by a file of soldiers on either side and followed by a vast multitude of people of all colors, sexes and conditions," Rev. Scott remembered.

The spy looked worn and haggard after his ordeal of the past few days, and he spoke quietly with the pastor about his history and adventures. Andrews said that he was a native of West Virginia, that his parents were strict Presbyterians who were now living in Missouri. "In reply to a question of mine, he said he had no family, although he added, with a slight tremor in his voice, that he was to have been married on the 17th of June," Scott said. "He disclaimed all personal enmity to the Southern people, but said that he was a Union man and he regarded the expedition he conducted as a legitimate military expedition. He was willing, however, to abide his fate."

Like any good man of the cloth, Scott spoke of eternal salvation and inquired about Andrews's readiness for death. Andrews replied that "recently in his great and sore trouble he had tried to seek God." Scott told the prisoner that he would be permitted to make a statement before his execution. Andrews said he would prefer to keep silent and asked that Rev. Scott speak on his behalf.

"Upon our arrival at the place of execution we found a very large assemblage eager to witness the horrors of the gibbet," Scott later wrote. The site of the scaffold, which is today a busy downtown street corner, was in those days largely hidden in the dense woods a few yards from a country road. The gallows, a wobbly platform standing on two posts with a simple trap, had been erected at the center of a natural amphitheater. Guards had cordoned off a perimeter about forty feet from the gallows. The assembled crowd whispered and jostled for position behind the rope, as young men and boys in the rear shinnied up trees to get a better view. The doomed Kentuckian stumbled down from his conveyance—a nice carriage, Mrs. Wustoff insisted, and "no rickety old hack, as has been reported"—and was assisted up onto the platform. "And well do I remember Andrews as he calmly looked around at the crowd—his pale, white face—black hair and long black whiskers," Mrs. Wustoff wrote. A reporter in the crowd thought Andrews "seemed to be very penitent—was composed till he came on the scaffold, when a slight tremor was perceptible." There was a brief delay as Lieutenant James Barnes of the provost guard sent a local boy, fourteen-year-old H.I. McConnell, scampering over to the nearby home of Mr. A.K. Spago to ask for a cloth to cover the prisoner's face. The lad returned moments later, Mrs. Spago having offered up one of her pillowcases. Andrews declined this rather undignified death-mask, asking instead that a simple handkerchief be placed over his eyes.

"Everything being prepared, after a moment's conference with the prisoner, during which I told him I should not remain to see the execution, I ascended the scaffold to address the multitude," Scott said. "There was perfect order—no jeers, no taunts, no unseemly behavior to mar the deep solemnity of the occasion." Rev. Scott spoke as directed on Andrews's behalf, "as nearly as possible in his own words," though neither Scott nor any other witness recorded those words for posterity. A word of prayer was had, and Scott leaned in close to Andrews, softly reminding him that "in God, solely, was his help." With that, the minister bade the condemned man farewell, stepped down from the scaffold and walked back to the city, never turning back.[21]

It was just as well that he did not stay to see the terrible scene that followed, one so grisly that it would have been darkly comical had it not been the stuff of nightmares. The noose was put in place, and Andrews turned and gave his watch and watch-chain to Colonel Jones. The provost marshal gave the signal, and the platform dropped. Andrews fell and the rope snapped taut—but only for a moment. Then the cord began to stretch, swaying and creaking like an old staircase, and Andrews's dangling feet found the ground below him. He kicked desperately in the dust, gurgling, gasping, straining to save his own life. One of the provost guardsmen rushed in and shouldered him to the side, pushing him off the ground and choking him once again, while another guard fell on all fours and began clawing at the dirt beneath Andrews's feet. The gasps of the assembled witnesses gave way to cries for mercy, and ladies and men alike averted their eyes as the horror continued, Andrews a sickly marionette bobbing and jerking on a single string. James Squires, a W&A railroad man who had scaled a hickory tree to see the show that day, was certain that Andrews's neck had not been broken—instead, "he was merely strangled."[22]

His nemesis William Fuller was there in the crowd, playing the role of Javert to Andrews's Jean Valjean to the final curtain, seeing the thing through from the pursuit to the trial in Chattanooga to the hanging. Somewhere along the way, Fuller's initial and admirable determination to recover his engine hardened into a desire for vengeance, and would down the years sour into something dark and unbecoming. "On the scaffold, Andrews did not show much strength of character," Fuller would write as an old man, looking back on that day. "I have never thought he died bravely." The conductor was the only person among the many witnesses that day who ever said such a thing. And although they were not present, the raiders' view of the terrible event was recorded by Daniel Allen Dorsey. "Andrews died without a murmur, like the hero that he was," he wrote. Other witnesses recorded the drama as nothing more than a sad end for a young man who must have exercised bad judgment along the way. "A man was hung here today," Samuel P. Richards wrote in his diary. "His name was Andrews and he was executed as a spy by military authority—poor fellow, he ought to have engaged in a better business."[23]

As the afternoon light faded, Andrews's body was cut down and placed in a crude wooden coffin, his ankles still cuffed and chained by Uncle Billy's shackles. A burial party carried the box some forty yards down the hill to what one Atlantan would call a "ready-made-grave"—a hole under the roots of a pine tree recently knocked down by a storm. For many days thereafter, curiosity-seekers by the dozen came to visit the grave of the notorious locomotive thief. Mrs. Wustoff related the story of one such group of macabre sightseers, one of whom pushed his walking cane down through the still-loose soil until it touched the lid of coffin. "A peculiar sound followed. The young man threw a fit, and had to be carried to his home by his companions," Mrs. Wustoff wrote. "After that sensational episode, it was a deserted grave." And an unmarked grave as well, one that would soon be lost, not only in a snarl of blackberry and wild roses, but also among the thousands of graves of war dead, known and unknown, that would soon come to Atlanta.[24]

The papers reported the execution matter-of-factly next day. The *Southern Confederacy*'s article, for example, simply noted that, after "a feeling prayer" and "a few seasonable words of counsel" from the three ministers present, Andrews was "launched into eternity. Thus ended the life of this daring adventurer, who, according to his own confession, was playing into the hands of both parties in the war to make gain—always, however, in the *confidence* of the enemy; but he was convicted of being a spy." No mention was made of the botched hanging. It was the sort of unfortunate accident, a sad and freakish turn of events, that is best forgotten. After all, such a scene was unlikely to ever happen again.

Word of James J. Andrews's untimely end reached his adopted hometown of Flemingsburg, Kentucky—about 325 crowflight miles due north of Atlanta—within a few days of the execution. The *Southern Confederacy*'s account of the spy being "launched into eternity" was promptly reprinted in a number of Northern newspapers, including the *Cincinnati Commercial*, where it was seen by a relative of Andrews's fiancée, Elizabeth Layton. Her family had heard of Andrews's harrowing adventures and had done their best to keep the news of his peril from young Betsy, but now, just one week before the couple was to have been married, they had no choice but to tell her the truth.

They handed her the newspaper to read for herself. She did so without making a sound, then turned quietly and left the room. She returned hours later, looking drawn and pale, and those present thought "the light had gone out of her eyes." Some weeks later, a large, elegant trunk was delivered from Louisville, just as Andrews had instructed. No one knows what thoughts may have passed through Miss Layton's grieving mind as she stood before the trunk and lifted the lid.

The trunk was empty.

Elizabeth Layton was never the same after that. Once a charming, social young lady, she became morose and withdrawn, and her health rapidly deteriorated. Her family reported that she "took little interest in anything"; her mind, they said, was "obviously shaken." Within two years, she was dead.

Her family insisted ever after that she had died of a broken heart.[25]

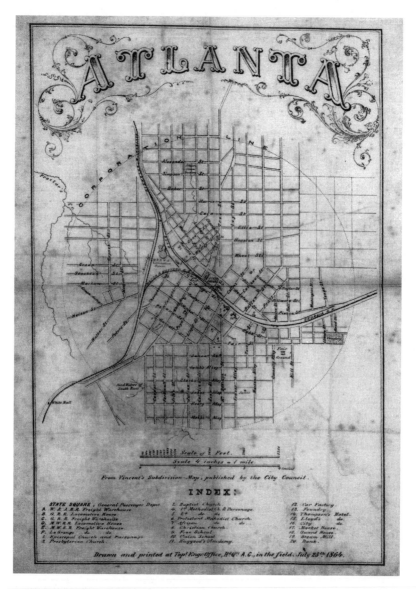

Map of wartime Atlanta. The W&A railroad depot ("the Car Shed") is in the center, with the city limits drawn as a circle one mile in radius from that point. The site of the Fulton County jail at the corner of Fraser and Fair Streets is visible in the lower right quadrant of the map. The site of Andrews's hanging was off the map, about a half mile north of the city limits. (*Hargrett Rare Map Collection, University of Georgia*)

CHAPTER THIRTEEN

Heaven or Cincinnati

Atlanta

Boys, tell them at home, if any of you escape, that I died for my country and did not regret it.

—Sergeant Major Marion A. Ross, 2nd Ohio

*E*VEN AS ANDREWS'S BODY WAS being lowered into its shallow grave, the eight Ohio soldiers who had so recently tried and failed to save his life were taken from the barracks at the Concert Hall and moved to their new quarters. It was nearly dusk. The dirt streets were crowded with horses and wagons, remnants of the depot traffic and the day's commerce, and the sidewalks were bustling with people heading to and from the trains or on their way out to enjoy the warm Saturday evening. Mark Wood was sick with fever and kept holding up the bedraggled column, pleading for stops to rest, until his chainmate Alf Wilson finally picked him up and carried him the rest of the way. They were marched about six blocks southeast to the Fulton County Jail, which stood at the northeast corner of Fraser and Fair Streets (known today as Memorial Drive). The two-story prison was yet another brick-walled edifice, but one the raiders found it to be "a more pretentious structure than we had yet occupied."

Built in 1855, the boxlike jail aspired to be a castle, with a cornice and parapet above giving it the appearance of a squatty, squared-off rook tucked in a fenced-off corner of the chessboard. The first floor, which provided accommodations for the jailer and his family, was bisected by an east-west hallway extending through the building, with locked doors front and rear. A stairway on the right side of the hall led up to a similar central corridor on the second floor. There, four cells, each about sixteen feet by sixteen feet, were used for confinement, two on each side of the hallway. In two of the cells was "a stout iron cage," as Wilson remembered, "similar to that which Barnum used to carry the big rhinoceros in." The cell walls were paneled inside with oak planking spiked to the brick beyond; the windows strongly barred with iron, their lintels and sills made of granite from nearby Stone Mountain; the double cell doors—an inner one of riveted iron bars and an outer one of hardwood—hung on massive hinges and sealed by heavy locks. "From this imperfect description of our prison," Wilson wrote, "the reader will see that the prospect of our *breaking* out was not the best." (Though perhaps not impossible, as we shall see.) The eight men were placed in the southwest cell and shortly thereafter were given one welcome accommodation. The authorities, with apparent confidence in the sturdy construction of the jail and the alertness and ability of the guards, removed the handcuffs, collars, and trace-chains the Ohioans had worn for more than six weeks. "This was a great relief," Wilson recalled. "We had worn them so long in couples that we would find ourselves involuntarily, at times, following each other about as if still compelled to do so by chains."[1]

The raiders were housed in the open part of the cell by day and confined to the "rhinoceros cage" at night. They slept in a tight circle with their heads in the center, resting on a single bed tick of straw. Although it was summer, they lacked blankets and on some nights found the iron floor of the cage painfully cold. Again their rations were meager and disgusting: spoiled bacon, cornbread (often with the cob ground right in), "negro peas" liberally seasoned with tiny insects—"almost enough to convulse the stomach of a hungry dog," Wilson said. But they ate every morsel. Speaking from experience, Wilson later recorded his observation that "man, when forced to it, is as ravenous, reckless, unreasonable and brutish in his appetite as the lowest form of animal creation."

Mark Wood, his thin body wracked with illness and fever, suffered much in their first days in the jail. Some among the party later admitted to wondering whether it would be a "merciful kindness" to let him die of disease rather than survive only to suffer a more hideous fate. They tried to rally the poor Englishman by needling him relentlessly. "Mark, if I were you, I would not try to get well," they told him. "You can, by dying, save the rebels the trouble of hanging you." In response, Wood would cackle wildly, and say he was determined to recover, just to spite them.[2]

A few days after Andrews's hanging, the eight soldiers received word that their comrades who had been sent to Knoxville for trial had arrived in Atlanta and would soon be joining them. The Knoxville contingent, consisting of the twelve men from Andrews's party and a number of the East Tennessee loyalists, including Captain David Fry, arrived at the Car Shed on a "delightful" afternoon and were met by what one historian would describe as "a curious if not hostile mob," though one among the assembled throng seemed hostile indeed. A man who supposedly identified himself as the mayor of Atlanta, but who they later determined to be Colonel Jones, "began to insult Captain Fry, telling him that he knew him well, that he was a great rascal, and that he hoped soon to have the pleasure of hanging him," Pittenger recalled. "Then turning to us, he boasted that he had put the rope around Andrews's neck, and was waiting and anxious to do the same for us!" After this unsettling welcome, the prisoners left the depot and were marched to the jail. "The insulting mob did not follow us," Pittenger recalled, "and as we looked upon the beautiful residences which we passed, everything seemed so calm and peaceful that it was difficult to realize our perilous position."[3]

The Knoxville dozen, along with David Fry, were placed in the northeast cell; the remainder of the East Tennesseans, including G. W. Barlow and "Old Gun Barrel" Pierce, were locked up across the hall. The Fulton County jailer was a kindly older gentleman named Turner, who Pittenger recalled as a "Union man at heart" who sympathized with the Northern prisoners. His assistant, in contrast, was an "odious old man" known to the raiders as Thor or Thoer, who saw to it that the Federals were given scanty rations and few privileges. Still, they passed their first week in their new surroundings in comparative ease and with cautious hope for the future. Certainly their day-to-day surroundings had improved since Swims's underground dungeon, and the guards were now talking openly of their belief that Andrews was the only one to be executed and that the remainder would be spared and exchanged. "There was no word of any further court-martialing," Pittenger later wrote, "and those of our number who believed our lives would be spared made converts seemingly of all the rest."

This was true with certain exceptions, foremost among them being Marion Ross. The sandy-haired sergeant-major exhibited none of the optimism or spirit so prevalent in his companions of late; instead, he was ever mournful and pessimistic—so much so that his fellow soldiers feared that he had suffered some injury of mind in the course of their recent hardships. Others later surmised that Ross, being a Freemason, may have along the way received some secret intelligence from one of his Masonic brethren, warning him of the trouble ahead.

Their new companion Fry likewise held no illusions as to what was in store. Al Dorsey, who was always seeking to convince the others that escape was their only hope, seemed to sense this, and he asked the East Tennessee guerilla what he thought their chances were if they remained in the hands of the Rebels. "With a broad smile," Dorsey recalled, "the captain replied that he thought we would surely be executed unless we could by some means break our confinement and escape." His listeners put a good deal of stock in this answer—Fry was an intelligent man, and a Southerner himself, after all, and should know his own people. But others, especially George D. Wilson, were absolutely incredulous at the idea that the raiders could possibly face execution for spying. "Why, the possibility that we could be treated as spies seemed to him so absurd that he was all out of patience to those who took the opposite view," Dorsey said.[4]

Wednesday, June 18 dawned warm and clear in Atlanta—"a bright and lovely day," Dorsey recalled. The Andrews Raiders—now twenty in number, with their leader eleven days in the grave and John Wollam either still at large or dead himself—passed the morning hours engaged in their customary entertainments, playing games and arguing over the course of the war and the enemy's intentions. Several among the party had been troubled by bad dreams the night before, especially George Wilson and a few of the others who had been tried at Knoxville. Though no one among the party was particularly superstitious, they related their nightmares to their comrades as they flipped cards from a borrowed, dog-eared deck. "They had dreamed of being in muddy sloughs, in mirey places," Dorsey remembered. "Some had seen great piles of fresh dug earth, where great trenches had been opened in the ground."[5]

It was early afternoon, perhaps two o'clock, when the card playing and checkers were interrupted by a clatter in the street outside heralding the arrival of a body of cavalry. Presently a group of officers clomped up the stairs, sabers clanking, along with the jailers Turner and Thor and an ominous gaggle of black-gowned ministers hovering behind. Turner unlocked the door of the cell across the way and ushered the group of East Tennessee loyalists held there out into the corridor. Then the northwest cell was opened, and the names of the seven men tried at Knoxville were called to account: William Campbell, Samuel Robertson, Marion A. Ross, John Scott, Perry G. Shadrach, Samuel Slavens, and George D. Wilson. The six Union soldiers and their giant civilian companion Campbell stepped forward, though Robertson was ill, laid low by a blazing fever, and had to be helped to his feet.

The seven were taken to the vacated cell across the hall and the intervening doors slammed shut. "All was silent for a moment," Dorsey said, "then we heard a voice as if someone were reading in a rather subdued or solemn tone, or perhaps praying." The muffled voice they heard was, of course, the announcement of the judgment of the court-martial and the sentence to be imposed. The order provided that the executions were to take place between the 15th and the 22nd day of June, but the Confederate authorities had apparently learned their lesson from the one-week warning that had been given to Andrews and his subsequent escape. There would be no delays this time, now that the order was received. The provost marshal had scarcely finished reading the sentence—"to be hung by the neck until he is dead"—when the arms of the seven men were bound before them.[6]

Leading the group of ministers was the Rev. W. J. Scott, who again found himself summoned by the authorities to take part in bearing what he called "unwelcome tidings" to the unsuspecting condemned. He had brought with him his friend Rev. G. N. McDonnell, the pastor of Trinity Church, who also did not care for executions—he came along on the sole condition (a rather peculiar one for a spiritual counselor to require) that Scott would agree to do all the talking. (Some accounts suggest that a third minister was also present, though his identity is unknown.) The ministers had an initial exchange with the always-outspoken George Wilson, who again protested that the raiders should be treated as prisoners of war, and complained of the method of execution. "We would not care so much to be shot as soldiers, but to be hanged like a dog is a burning shame," he said.

"Young gentlemen," Rev. Scott replied, "we are not here to discuss the justice or injustice of the court's action. That is a matter over which we have no control. We have visited you, as ministers of the gospel, for the sole purpose of helping you by our prayers and counsels to prepare for death, and it is my painful duty to tell you that the hour is at hand."

The Methodist pastor was impressed with the handsome appearance of the seven—"They struck me at once as a body of remarkably fine-looking men," he said—though upon the announcement of their sentence, "every cheek blanched to the lily's whiteness." His spiritual work was cut out for him that day—none among the doomed men identified themselves as church members, and only one said he prayed: "sometimes, but not regularly." Nevertheless, Rev. Scott had reassuring words for all. "I then remarked that we were all forgetful of God and duty, but that He was merciful and long-suffering, and while the time for preparation was short, if they were truly penitent God could save them as well in an hour as in a twelvemonth," he remembered. The minister recited a few passages of Scripture "applicable to their condition" and then all knelt in prayer.[7]

They were returned across the hall to their comrades, already "pale as death," as Dorsey recalled. "We are to be executed immediately," George Wilson whispered. He took advantage of the few moments he had left to deliver words of warning and hard realization to his friends. He had been completely deceived, he said, utterly mistaken in ever thinking that they would be released or exchanged. The rest of you will go the same way, he said. He also had a word for Pittenger. Like most of the raiders, Wilson was a "professed unbeliever" and had often debated with his friend the truth of the Christian religion. "Pittenger, I believe you are right now," he said. "Try to be better prepared when you come to die than I am."

"God bless you," Pittenger offered.[8]

The seven men handed off trinkets and keepsakes to their comrades for safekeeping or promised delivery to loved ones back home. Wilson removed the gold pin he wore and pinned it to the inside of his vest, close to his heart. He then gave a copy of his death warrant to William Knight, who folded it in an inside pocket and would later deliver it to a Union officer, from whence it would find its way into the archives in Washington. A few took advantage of Rev. Scott's offer to mail any final letters or messages, scratching out a few parting words on scraps of paper—though none of these sentiments were ever received by family or friends, and in fact were never sent in the first place, "due to some technical objection from the War Department," Scott later explained. Again, he declined to witness the execution itself, and he took his leave from the unlucky seven. "We did what we could for them and saw them start on their last journey," the reverend wrote.[9]

"Then came the final, choking farewells," Alf Wilson remembered. Though the wrenching scene borders on melodrama in the written recollections of those present, several of the surviving raiders catalogued the reactions of their unfortunate friends. Stout, black-bearded Samuel Slavens's thoughts were of his wife and his three little boys. "Wife—children—tell them—" he said, but that was as far as he got, his eyes welling and his voice choked with emotion. His April 6 letter would stand as his final goodbye to Rachel. "I don't want you to give yourself any uneasiness, any more than you can help, about me," he had written just before leaving camp in Shelbyville, "but if anything happens to me that we never meet again on earth, I hope we will meet in heaven." The once merry and mischievous Perry Shadrach was solemn, despairing that the hour had come. "Boys, I'm not prepared to meet my Jesus," he said. His comrades, many of whom were crying by now, tried to reassure him and encouraged him to think of heavenly mercy. "I'll try, I'll try," he told them, "but I know I'm not prepared." His giant friend William Campbell wore a grim half-smile "with no light in it," Pittenger recalled. "Yes, boys, this is Goddamned hard," he said, adding an eleventh-hour sin just before his final reckoning. John Scott shook hands with his friends in silence, probably thinking of his young wife or his little brother back in the ranks, both of whom would now have to fend for themselves. Sammy Robertson, who had just passed his nineteenth birthday while incarcerated in Swims's jail, wept as he spoke of his mother. He was by then so dazed by the ravaging fever that Dorsey was certain he would have died in a few days in any event. Robert Buffum would later testify that Robertson was literally carried out by the guards to be loaded onto the death-cart and taken to the gallows.

Marion Ross, above all, seemed to rise to meet his fate head-on. Perhaps he had simply steeled himself for this eventuality more than the others, prepared for the worst—"he had his lamps trimmed and burning," as Dorsey put it. The gloom that had hung over him the past few weeks seemed to fall away, and the former flute player from Antioch College, who no one seemed to think was sergeant material, who even the scrawny Pittenger once thought would be of little account on a mission behind enemy lines, showed himself to be a hero that day. "Others were bitterly and terribly disappointed; he was not," Pittenger remembered. "He was perfectly erect, with easy grace; there was not a sign of dread, while his eye beamed and his whole face became radiant with the martyr's joy." Ross told his comrades, in a firm, unwavering voice: "Boys, tell them at home, if any of you escape, that I died for my country and did not regret it."[10]

Alf Wilson was awed by the quiet courage of his friends, later expressing his "proud admiration for their noble, manly fortitude in that trying moment." He wrote: "A true man, in the mad excitement of strife on the battle-field, can march with his comrades to meet death without faltering, but for an innocent man to bravely and calmly meet the fate of a murderer on the scaffold, is a test of courage for a soldier, which few men can realize until commanded to prepare for the halter." Wilson Brown, too, carried the hard memory of that day for the rest of his life. "The boys were brave under this trying ordeal, but that was a time that tried men's souls," he wrote in a letter in 1904. "Brave men wept. When I recall this incident, I cannot suppress my feelings, for it was an awful scene. Is it not a wonder that our reason is not dethroned? Who can read a recital of this event from the pen of one of the participants and not have a feeling of sympathy in their hearts?"[11]

The seven men were led from the cell, down the stairs, and out to the gate onto Fraser Street, their arms nearly pinioned with ropes from hands to elbows. They emerged from the prison yard and climbed onto a sideless, flat-bottomed cart, their feet dangling over the sides like farm boys riding off to town in daddy's wagon. Accompanied by a cavalry escort, the cart left the prison, turned left onto Fair Street, and rolled eastward toward a distant grove of trees that marked the city cemetery. In their second-floor cell, their friends strained to watch the procession through the tiny holes in the iron-latticed windows. "They were soon out of sight forever," Dorsey remembered. Conductor William Fuller walked along behind the wagon, seemingly making good on his promise to follow the raiders all the way to their graves. There had been no public notice of the day's unfolding drama, but word traveled quickly through the bustling streets, and store windows were shuttered and offices locked as hundreds of citizens rushed to witness what one would later describe as "the biggest execution of white men ever held in Atlanta, or perhaps anywhere in the South."[12]

"It was a hot June afternoon in 1862," Private John W. Woodruff said, recalling the scene years later. "Back of us was Atlanta, busy and noisy with her warlike industries. Around us the green trees were vocal with the music of twittering birds, and beneath our feet stretched patches of daisies and other wild flowers. The sun glared like a red ball of fire through the dust which hung over the bustling city, and altogether the scene was a memorable one." Woodruff was a soldier in the 9th Georgia Artillery Battalion, commonly known as Leyden's Battery, recently organized there in Atlanta. He served as a courier to Major Leyden and thus was free that day to watch the execution, sitting astride a horse that gave him a capital view of the gallows over the hats and bonnets of the gathering throng of Atlantans.

The gardenlike city cemetery, known in those days as the Atlanta Graveyard or City Burial Place, had been established by the town fathers in 1850. The resting place was less than a mile from the Zero Mile Post that marked the city center and was a favorite destination for Atlantans on carriage rides or Sunday picnics. Carpeted with lush grass and wildflowers and dotted with oaks, the well-kept graveyard covered six acres on a gentle rise east of town. The South's heroic fallen sons would soon demand more space, however, and the cemetery would expand to eighty-eight acres by 1872, when it would be renamed Oakland Cemetery. In later years it would become an exclusive final destination, reserved for the privileged dead, but in its early days, the cemetery gates were open to all comers, welcoming the fortunate and unfortunate alike.[13]

The seven doomed men surely found the three-quarter mile ride to the grove of oak trees near the graveyard's southwest corner to be all too brief. The crowed parted and quieted as the prisoners were led from their conveyance and each moved into place on the rickety scaffold. "I watched them closely, and not one flickered from first to last," Woodruff said. William Fuller agreed. "They were brave, fearless men, and met their fate as all true Americans do," he recalled. "They stood erect on the rude platform, and faced death with apparently no regrets, save the manner in which they were to die." (The raiders had asked for the generous privilege of being shot, so they could die like soldiers, but this request had of course been denied.) The gallows was "a rough affair," according to Woodruff, seven nooses strung along a thick crossbar supported by stout uprights—some witnesses would remember the beam resting in the forks of two trees. The doomed men stood side-by-side on a thick plank, hinged at each end and sawed through in the middle, where it was supported for the time being by a thick post—Fuller later would describe the scaffold as "a hurriedly and horribly constructed death-trap." A broad, shallow trench had been dug in the dusty clay just behind the structure. "The spectators looked on with breathless interest, and the Confederate soldiers detailed to conduct the hanging wore serious faces," Woodruff observed. "It was a terrible piece of work for them to do—to hang seven brave young fellows like dogs, and they hated the job."[14]

All was quiet as the nooses were put in place. If any of the Yankees remembered their earlier bluster—that they would sing "The Star-Spangled Banner" on the scaffold when the end came—no one mentioned it now. The soldiers were informed, however, that they would be permitted to say a few words if they would like.

George D. Wilson accepted the opportunity to speak, and he addressed the gathering in ringing tones, like a preacher at a summer revival, seemingly unfazed by the rope around his neck. He did not believe, he said, that he and his comrades should be treated as spies. They were not spies, and all there assembled knew it. They were soldiers doing the duty assigned to them by their officers. They had been captured and convicted having done nothing more than what many Confederates had done themselves: gone into the enemy's country. "True," he admitted, "we were disguised; so were Confederates who had been captured within the Union lines. But, it is now too late to discuss that question."

"We are here to die as Union soldiers, who undertook to do in one day, that which will cost the country millions of dollars and thousands of lives to accomplish in years," he said. He told the crowd that he and his comrades held no grudge or ill will against the people of the South. They were not to blame for this war—their leaders were responsible. But he predicted that many would yet live to regret this tragedy. "Some of you will live to see the American flag flying and waving over the spot where we, as soldiers, are about to offer up our lives," he said in closing. "This seems hard, but if it be the will of Him, who doeth all things well, 'so mote it be.' We are ready."[15]

Wilson's eloquent speech entranced and moved many of the assembled witnesses, and it seemed for a moment like his words might sidetrack the entire proceeding. "Why don't they stop him? What do they allow such talk for?" one Confederate officer reportedly grumbled, and a black man in the crowd later remarked, "Massa, if that man had only spoke a few minutes longer, they never could have hung him in the world." But if his patriotic remarks tugged at the hearts of the Southern ladies and gentlemen, it did nothing to dissuade the newly-appointed provost marshal, Captain G.J. Foreacre. He gave the signal with a wave of his sword, and the center post was yanked from beneath the platform.[16]

The seven men dropped in unison with a *snap!* of the ropes, and five were left bobbing and dangling, departed souls all. But two of them—the pair on the end, the big men, Campbell and Slavens—proved more weight than the nooses could handle. Amazingly, their ropes broke, and both fell heavily to the ground, "half-strangled," as Woodruff put it. Several guards rushed forward and removed the handkerchiefs from their eyes, finding the two men alive and partly conscious. Each was sat up and given a drink of water, still in the shadow of the swaying corpses of their friends. Perhaps an hour passed as the bodies of the five dead men were cut down and placed in their wooden coffins—meanwhile, the guards collected two thick ropes from the necks of nearby cavalry horses and fashioned them into nooses. Campbell and Slavens begged for more time to prepare themselves, but their appeals were denied by Captain Foreacre, whose orders left no room for such discretion. The prisoners were to be hung by the neck until dead, and if it took two successive hangings to get them there, so be it.

William Campbell and Samuel Slavens were placed back up on the plank. Again the signal was given and the support pulled from under the platform. This time the ropes proved sufficient, and it was a good thing, too. Several of the guards, who were more than a little spooked after the bungled execution and the horrible re-hanging of Campbell and Slavens, were heard to remark that if the ropes broke a second time, they would have nothing more to do with the assignment. In fact, some folks in the crowd had opposed the second attempt entirely, having heard somewhere before that the breaking of a rope on the gallows was evidence that the accused was not guilty.

The excitement finally over, the crowd dispersed, most of them walking back westward down Fraser Street toward the slanting late afternoon sun and the spires of the city. The surviving raiders watched as the empty death-cart returned to the yard of the jail. Conductor Fuller lingered after the hangings, watching as the coffins were moved to their unmarked grave. (He later explained that, as a fellow Mason, he had promised Sergeant Major Ross to mark the burial place.) He also kept a macabre souvenir of the occasion—Captain Foreacre gave him the rope that had hung Samuel Slavens, and Fuller would keep it as a prized possession for the rest of his life. But in later years, Fuller would insist that, though mistakes were made, there was no undue or intentional cruelty in the way the executions were carried out. "The poor fellows were decently executed, and by *Americans*, who had souls and manly principles," he wrote in a letter to his son-in-law. "We would not have tolerated any sort of inhumane treatment of the soldiers."[17]

For the people of Atlanta, who would see much death and destruction in the months and years to come, the hangings were "the first thing that happened in our midst to give us a realization of the sad things of war," Atlanta diarist Sallie Clayton wrote in her memoirs. Having turned out in droves to experience the dark thrill of watching other men die, many of the witnesses instead found themselves deeply saddened and disturbed by what they had seen. One such person was James Crew, who worked as a general ticket agent for the Georgia, Atlanta & LaGrange, and Macon & Western Railroads, who penned a letter to his wife back home in Madison that same afternoon. "Seven more of the bridge burners were hung here this evening," he wrote. "The rope broke & let two of them to ground and a new rope procured and again put upon the scaffold. Is this not awfull? Men in the prime of life landed into Eternity without an hour's warning and what for? Would to God I was out of this town until this war is over."

John Woodruff, too, was profoundly affected by what he had seen that day. "It made a boy as I was a deep impression on my mind and God grant I may never see another such," he later wrote. He turned his horse away from the lingering guards and gravediggers and trotted off to rejoin his battalion. "I had seen enough," he recalled, "and mounting my horse I rode back to camp with all horrors trouping through my young brains, never to be forgotten."[18]

Private Woodruff's was not the only impressionable mind shaken by the day's events. Also present at the hanging that Wednesday afternoon were four young boys, Smith and Tom Clayton of Atlanta and their cousins, Andrew and Tom Semmes, the twin sons of Confederate Brigadier General Paul J. Semmes, who was then fighting in Virginia and would later be mortally wounded in the Wheatfield at Gettysburg. The boys, who ranged in age from eight to ten years, had taken a break from an ingenious summer enterprise— collecting leeches for sale to local physicians—to come out and watch the execution of the hated Yanks. The Clayton boys' older sister Sallie tried to dissuade them, warning that the hangings may well create what she called "a lasting mental picture, that might probably never leave them; but, they turned deaf ears to all that was said and away they went." The two young Toms lost their nerve, turning their backs and covering their eyes and ears as the unlucky seven were led onto the scaffold. But Smith Clayton and Andrew Semmes watched wide-eyed as the trap was sprung and the men hanged. That night about midnight, these two young witnesses "sent up howls that were loud enough to have brought out the entire police department," Sallie Clayton recalled. "One poor little fellow insisted that all seven of the men were sitting on the foot of his bed. No one could comfort them and it was ever so long before they could be sufficiently made to sleep." The boys learned their lesson, according to Sallie, "for the sight of that hanging caused a complete loss of taste for executions."[19]

The summary hangings of their seven comrades shook the surviving raiders to the core. Word of the two botched executions and the suffering of their friends horrified and disgusted the survivors. "The thought of being decently executed (if such a thing as decency can be applied to such horrible work) was terrible enough, but the thought of being hanged twice, or being strangled to death with our feet on the ground, made our pending doom a sickening nightmare," Dorsey remembered. The kindly jailer Mr. Turner allowed the five Knoxville survivors to move across the hall to join their eight comrades, reuniting the raiders in the inauspicious number of thirteen, with Wollam still missing.

Among the reactions to the death of their friends was a newly kindled interest in religious matters, which did not come easily to the soldiers in the group, poor sinners all, none of whom except John Porter and Bill Pittenger had any established faith to fall back on. Singing resumed in the jail, but now the program was filled with "Rock of Ages," "Jesus, Lover of My Soul" and other hymns instead of patriotic songs and homesick ballads. Yet even the hymns themselves—which included mournful verses like "Plunged in a Gulf of Dark Despair" and "Hark! From the Tombs a Doleful Sound"—seemed to reflect a growing hopelessness and despondency among the survivors. Pittenger felt the evil that had befallen their comrades required a certain cleansing—whether to establish themselves as good souls worth sparing or to prepare for heavenly Judgment—and he led an almost Puritan revival, declaring that gambling and games of chance should be forbidden, going so far as to throw their borrowed playing cards out the jail window. Those who disliked the nearsighted corporal before truly resented him now that they were reduced in their entertainments to marathon games of checkers on a board scratched on the floor with a nail.[20]

For what it was worth (and some thought it wasn't worth much), all among the party devoted time to earnest prayers, beginning with a solemn prayer service held just after the executions under the leadership and guidance of Captain Fry. Alf Wilson bowed his head like all the others, though he wasn't sure it would do any good. "I believe in the efficacy of earnest Christian prayer, but prayer in a Confederate prison seemed to have less effect than in any place I have ever before or since been," he later wrote. At times, he thought that "God, in his anger, had stricken that part of Rebeldom from Heaven's court calendar, as unworthy of representation in His kingdom of peace, justice and good will, and only fit for the fate of Sodom and Gomorrah." On later occasions they were at times assisted in spiritual matters by local ministers, including Rev. McDonnell, who began by asking the Lord that the poor prisoners' lives be spared—but only if it was in the best interests of the Confederacy. "This prayer did not suit us exactly," Wilson remembered.[21]

Robert Buffum, too, placed little stock in the power of prayer. "Pittenger! Say, Pittenger!" he would tease. "Pray in one hand and spit in the other and see which will get full the soonest!" But even the irreverent Bay State private had been rattled by the abrupt hangings of his companions, and he prayed as best he could. He knelt with the others, his bony legs crossed behind him at the ankles, and he bowed his dark, heavily-bearded head as he prayed. "Lord, we are taught to pray for our enemies," he said, "therefore we pray Thee to have mercy on these god damned Rebel sons of bitches, for they know not what they do."

Dorsey participated in the religious services, though he found them nothing more than a way to pass the time. "My heart was not in it," he admitted. The prayers and hymns, in his mind, did nothing more than serve to reconcile the prisoners to their fate—convincing them that "a haven of rest, peace and happiness awaited us"—and thereby lessening their resistance and muffling any plans to escape. "I believe all men have a religious faith of some kind, a belief as to the life and destiny of mankind," he wrote years later, "but soldiers situated as we were had far better have devoted their attention to fighting their way out than to have resorted to any form of religious entertainment or pastime." If they believed in anything at all in those dark days, Al Dorsey and an ever-increasing number of his companions believed in the maxim that God helps those who help themselves.[22]

Having taken their appeal "to the Throne of Grace," the desperate prisoners decided they might as well exhaust all possible avenues for relief and seek a pardon from the man many Northerners considered to be the devil himself. Their request would be directed to Confederate President Jefferson Davis, explaining to him the facts of their case and asking for his mercy. The author of the letter, perhaps not surprisingly, was William Pittenger, though he claimed that someone else had suggested it, and that he did not like the idea. (Al Dorsey would argue that the whole thing was Pittenger's idea, while Alf Wilson merely said that Pittenger acted as scribe.) A lengthy and sometimes heated debate erupted over the proposed letter writing, though most seemed to think that it was worth a try and could hardly make things worse. Pittenger's first draft was discarded as "too servile in tone," as Dorsey put it, though Pittenger would claim that others wanted more pleading—"Put it on a good deal stronger," Wilson Brown supposedly urged. "Get right down and beg to him." Whatever process of joint authorship took place, a second version was generated that was apparently acceptable to all. (The letter was dated June 18, the day of the executions, but was probably written a day or so later.)

> June 18, 1862
> To His Excellency, JEFFERSON DAVIS
> President of the Confederate States of America
> SIR:
> We are the survivors of the party that took the engine at Big Shanty, on the 12th of April last. Our commander, Andrews, and seven of our comrades have been executed. We all (with the exception of Andrews) were regularly detailed from our regiments in perfect ignorance of where we were going, and what we were to do. We were ordered to obey Andrews, and everything we did was done by his order, he only telling his plans when he wished us to execute them. In this we are no more to blame than any northern soldiers,

for any one of them in our circumstances would have been obliged to do just as we did. For fuller details we refer to the evidence in the cases that have been tried. No real harm was done, and as far as thought and intention is concerned, we are perfectly innocent.

O! it is hard to die a disgraceful and ignominious death; to leave our wives, our children, our brothers and sisters, and our parents without consolation. Give this matter your most kind and merciful consideration. Give us that mercy you yourself hope to receive from the judge of all. We will all take an oath not to fight or do anything against the confederacy. If this can not be done, at least spare our lives until the war is closed, if we have to remain in prison until that time.

Wilson W. Brown, 21st OV, Co F		Wm. Pittenger, 2nd Ohio, Co. G	
Wilson W. Brown, 21st OV, Co F		Daniel A. Dorsey, 33d OV, Co H	
William Bensinger, " "	Co G	Jacob Parrott, " "	Co K
Elihu H. Mason, " "	Co K	Wm. Reddick, " "	Co B
John A. Wilson, " "	Co C	M. J. Hawkins, " "	Co A
John R. Porter, " "	Co G		
Mark Wood, " "	Co C		
Robert Buffum, " "	Co H		
William Knight, " "	Co E		

Robert Buffum, an irrepressible soul even when pleading for his life, wanted to tweak the Confederate chief executive by adding (after the words "we are perfectly innocent") Davis's own famous phrase: "All we ask is to be let alone." This proposal was sensibly rejected, and all thirteen soldiers signed below. Dorsey had to sign for the illiterate Jake Parrott, and Wilson Brown was apparently so shaken by recent events that he signed his name twice.

It was a remarkable letter indeed. The Andrews Raiders, renowned for their daring, their courage, and their selfless dedication to the Union cause, had reached a point where desperation seemed to eclipse those former virtues entirely. They lied about their knowledge of Andrews's plan and their complicity in the raid; they claimed not only that no harm was done, but that none was intended; and they pitifully invoked the images of mourning wives and inconsolable families in an effort to spark sympathy. Most notably, the letter sought to invoke the protection of their status as United States soldiers and at the same time offered to compromise their loyalty by going so far as to take an oath not to fight against the Confederacy.

If this apparent loss of courage and abdication of duty ever troubled the authors of the letter, none of them said so, then or later.[23]

Nothing came of the survivors' letter writing, at least not at first. As the long, hot summer days passed and the calendar turned from June to July, their terror and grief inevitably subsided, replaced by the drudgery of imprisonment. The raiders found ways to pass the time, thanks in large part to the kindness of Rev. McDonnell, who not only offered them spiritual comfort now and then but also sent over volumes from his shelves. The loaned books included travel, adventure, history, biography, even theological dissertations—everything but fiction. As reading these books aloud to those interested required some measure of silence, two hours of (comparative) quiet were set aside in the morning and two in the afternoon for reading.

One of the borrowed books contained a sermon by the famous bishop and orator John Bascom on "The Joys of Heaven." Pittenger read the sermon to the group one sultry afternoon, magnificently describing the heavenly rewards and divine peace that awaited each and every one of them. After he finished, the party sat reflecting on the inspirational text, when Wilson Brown suddenly proposed a possible alternative: "Well, boys, that is very good; but I would like to know how many of this party would rather be there now, safe from all harm, or back in Cincinnati?" Up to heaven or back to Ohio—now this was an intriguing topic for discussion, indeed, and the prisoners debated it at length, and "with great animation." The argument was ultimately resolved by a vote, with a clear majority holding for Cincinnati.[24]

Just as they had done in Chattanooga, the raiders haggled, pleaded, and improvised to gather small comforts and necessities. At the top of the list of desired goods was tobacco. Most of the prisoners were tobacco chewers or smokers or both and went to great ends to obtain even the smallest amounts of the leaf, which many said they valued more than their daily bread. They begged for tobacco from just about everyone: from the guards, from the black servants who brought their food, even from the jailer himself—if the Right Reverend McDonnell had chewed, they would have pleaded with him too. Often, they were successful, touching on that universal and inexplicable spirit of sympathy and sharing which all users of tobacco seem to have for one another. The tobacco thus obtained was then used to its utmost, chewed until all hint of flavor was gone and then dried and smoked in corncob pipes.

The raiders also found that they could barter to improve their situation,

Mr. Turner being a much more honest broker than the hated Swims. They sold off what they could spare to the guards—handkerchiefs, vests, and other unnecessary articles, and bought food or other goods with the proceeds. Knight, who found himself heir to Andrews's previously fine Prince Albert coat, sold it off and invested his returns in apples, onions, and (of course) tobacco. Pittenger sold his vest and empty pocketbook and had Turner purchase for him three additional books: *Pilgrim's Progress, Pollock's Course of Time,* and *Paradise Lost.* He spent hours memorizing the latter, and in the months to come would make "considerable progress" in doing so.[25]

In addition to fighting despondency, the raiders battled the oppressive Georgia summer. They spent most days shirtless and sometimes shed their trousers as well, both to cool themselves and to preserve their ragged clothing in case of future escape. William Knight borrowed a pair of shears and one day opened a barber shop of sorts, giving haircuts to all comers in return for trinkets and favors. He soon felt unappreciated for the hot, itchy work. After cutting half of William Reddick's hair close to the scalp, Knight refused to complete the job and "went on a strike for higher wages, and let poor Bill go for several days in this odd manner."[26]

The monotony of incarceration was broken along toward the end of June by a question from the jailer Mr. Turner, who asked the raiders if any of them knew a man by the name of John Wollam (he pronounced it "Woo-lam"). The Yankee captives initially demurred, not wanting to compromise a friend if he was still at large or being questioned, when Wollam strode into view and said in a hearty voice, "Boys, don't go back on me now!" He walked through the open cell door, shaking hands with his friends, an ear-to-ear grin yanked leftward by a fist-sized chaw of tobacco wedged in his jaw. He was quite a spectacle, shirtless in a straw hat, black trousers held up by suspenders running over his bare shoulders, and a heavily abused pair of boots. He was sunburned from nose to waist, his skin "as black as his trousers," Knight remembered, and his face as "slick as a peeled onion." The wayward private was welcomed by his comrades like the prodigal son returned, and Knight thought that Wollam "seemed almost as glad to return to prison with the boys as he would have been to have returned home."

Wollam had floated down the Tennessee in his "borrowed" canoe and soon was clear of Chattanooga. He made slow progress, hiding himself and his dugout by day and traveling only under dark of night. At one point, he passed safety by without knowing it—General Mitchel had converted a captured barge into a gunboat of sorts, and Wollam, assuming it to be a Rebel craft, had crept past it carefully, hugging the opposite bank. He traveled this way for days until he was sure he was safely in friendly territory and then abandoned his former precautions, rowing along boldly in broad daylight—hence the sunburn. He was soon confronted by Confederate soldiers and taken to a nearby camp, where he had the unbelievably bad fortune of being recognized by one of the same officers who was involved in his original capture back in early April.

The raiders were pleased to see their friend but were terribly disappointed by his recapture, as they had hoped he would reach the Federal lines and save them in some way—inspiring renewed military action, perhaps, or pressing the Union command to arrange for an exchange—but it was not to be. For his part, Wollam wanted to know which one of the boys had turned state's evidence. Someone in the group tried to explain to him what Dorsey called "Pittenger's witness business," but he did not seem to credit the information. "Yes, but, by God, they say outside he turned state's evidence," he said.

"There was no use to talk to Wollam about good faith," Dorsey later wrote. "From what he had heard outside his mind was made up, and no amount of persuasive eloquence ever changed it. He lived and died believing Pittenger had played false."[27]

Another memorable occasion in the hot, dreary weeks of confinement in the Fulton County Jail was Independence Day, recognized even in Southern newspapers as "the Glorious Fourth." Dorsey remembered seeing a Confederate flag on that day on a staff to the east of the jail. "The day was warm and sultry," he wrote years later, and the Rebel flag "hung lifelessly down from its perch as if drooping its head in acknowledgment of guilt, as if in fact it were weighed down with the blood of the innocent, and ashamed to flaunt its guilty face before the world." The raiders sang "The Star-Spangled Banner" with special attention, but the festivities in Atlanta were otherwise sparse and unenthusiastic. "The boys cracked torpedoes in the streets," the *Southern Confederacy* reported, and one of the local fire companies had its annual dinner and parade, but "otherwise there was not the slightest indications . . . of its being the anniversary of the birth-day of a great nation."[28]

The raiders crowded up to the iron-laced windows to watch the meager celebration. Meanwhile, a small party of Confederate officers arrived outside the cell door, another delegation of curious Southerners who wanted to see the notorious train stealers. William Knight, swept up in a holiday mood, addressed the visitors with a mocking request: "Say, Mister," he said to one of the officers, a colonel. "Can't you let me go down the street and see the parade? I'm patriotic and want to help celebrate."

"Well, hardly!" the officer replied, plainly not amused.

Knight was undaunted. "I intend to celebrate the next Fourth of July at home," he said.

"You'll celebrate it in hell," the colonel growled, his comment haunting the Yankee engineer for weeks to come. For what it is worth, Knight would look back on this exchange with satisfaction: he would, indeed, spend July 4, 1863, on leave at home.[29]

*T*he remainder of the summer passed with no further incidents and no response to or acknowledgment of their letter to President Davis. In August, someone conceived of the notion of trying again, this time directing their request through proper military channels in hopes of reaching "a humbler person" than the Confederate president. Again a heated debate ensued, not only of the efficacy of such a plea, but also as to the wisdom of sending the request at all. Some felt that the Confederate authorities had simply forgotten about them, or perhaps assumed (given the crowds and publicity that had accompanied the earlier executions), that the engine thieves had all been hanged and the matter concluded. Sending a letter now, two months after their seven comrades were killed, may only serve to call unwelcome attention to themselves.

Those in favor of a second appeal prevailed in a vote, and a second letter was written by Pittenger and addressed to Confederate Major General Braxton Bragg (an officer who one would hardly call a "humbler person," by the way). The letter read:

Atlanta Jail, August 17, 1862.

RESPECTED SIR:

We are United States soldiers, regularly detailed from our command to obey the orders of Andrews. He was a stranger to us and we ignorant of his design, but of course we obeyed our officers. You are no doubt familiar with all we did, or can find it recorded in the trials of our comrades. Since then Andrews himself and 7 of us have been executed, and 14 survive. Is this not enough for vengeance and a warning to others? Would mercy in our case be misplaced? We have already been closely confined for more than four months. Will you not, sir, display a noble generosity, by putting us on the same footing as prisoners of war, and permitting us to be exchanged, and thus show that in this terrible war, the south still feels the claim of mercy and humanity?

If you will be so good as to grant us this request we will ever be grateful to you.

Please inform us of your decision as soon as convenient.

W.W. Brown,	Wm. Pittenger,
Wm. Knight,	Second Ohio Regt.
Elihu Mason,	
Jno. R. Porter,	Wm. H. Reddick,
Wm. Bensinger,	Jno. Wollam,
Robt. Buffum,	D.A. Dorsey,
Mark Wood,	M.J. Hawkins,
Alfred Wilson,	Jacob Parrott,
Twenty-first Ohio Regt.	Thirty-third Ohio Regt.

All of Sill's brigade, Buell's division.

The raiders' appeal was handed to the provost marshal, G.W. Lee, who dutifully sent it on to General Bragg. Knowing nothing at all about the case, Bragg forwarded the petition on to Adjutant General Jasper S. Whiting at Richmond, who indorsed it to G.W. Randolph, Confederate Secretary of War. Randolph, in turn, respectfully submitted it to President Jefferson Davis on September 2, along with his recommendation: that the surviving raiders be "respited until further orders and detained as hostages for our own people in the hands of the enemy." The cold, dyspeptic Davis, apparently not at all feeling "the claim of mercy and humanity," ignored Randolph's suggestion and replied:

> Inquire whether there is anything to justify a discrimination between these and others who were executed for the same offense.
>
> J.D.[30]

Davis posed a good question, come to think of it—if eight of the Yankee spies had deserved to be executed—if they "needed killin'," to use the Southern phrase—seems like all of them would. The various endorsements to the letter, including the president's comment, were forwarded back down the line to Captain G.W. Lee, the new provost marshal in Atlanta charged with guarding the prisoners. He replied that he had inherited the task of holding and punishing the Andrews Raiders when he took over as provost marshal in late June, shortly after the seven poor Ohio boys had been hanged. As for the status of the others, he did not know. He supposed that the only reason that the remaining raiders had not been hung was that they had not been tried as yet. He promised to contact his predecessor, Captain G.J. Foreacre, and find out "why fourteen of the engine thieves were respited while the others were executed, and whether or not there is anything to justify a discrimination in their favor."

Foreacre responded to Lee's inquiry promptly though not very helpfully. He had received orders back in June that seven men were to be hung, he replied, and he had attended to the executions as ordered. "The remaining fourteen," he said, "were reported to this office only for safe-keeping, some having been tried, but not sentenced, and others, not tried." The only officer who could answer the provost marshal's question and solve the conundrum was presumably General E. Kirby Smith, who had signed the execution order. (Lee chose not to inquire with General Smith, who presumably had bigger problems to contend with those days.)

Frustrated by now and perhaps concerned that he not be viewed as failing to effectuate the orders of those above him, Captain Lee went to the jail to ask the raiders firsthand why seven were hanged and fourteen were not. Knight responded by claiming that the prominent members of the party, including the ringleader and the engineer, were chosen for execution, and the court had not considered the surviving fourteen to be as guilty as the rest. Capt. Lee seemed unimpressed by this suggestion. Still, he stayed for a spell and talked "very pleasantly" with the raiders, sharing with them his belief that they would be put on the same footing as other prisoners of war. As he departed, he promised to return with word on how the matter had been decided in Richmond. "Some thought we had made a favorable impression on the provost marshal, and that he would use his influence to have us treated as ordinary prisoners of war," Dorsey recalled, "but others were not so sanguine."

Whatever the views and influence of the new provost marshal, it was clear that Confederate authorities were now asking questions and trying to figure out what to do with them. Sending those letters might have been a mistake, after all.[31]

Union blockade vessels offshore. (*Library of Congress*)

CHAPTER FOURTEEN

"A Damned Long Ways from Camp"

Escape from Atlanta

It was clear that our only hope was in our own resources. We must escape
if we were to live.

—Corporal Daniel A. Dorsey, 33rd Ohio

*A*TLANTA REMAINED UNTOUCHED and unthreatened as 1862 wore on, and
the city went about its business, prosperous and naïve. Despite the lack
of any apparent military danger, its citizens soon began to feel the pain and
the pinch of the distant conflict. Business still boomed, of course; the town's
arsenals and other industries could hardly keep up with the ceaseless demand
of the hungry gray armies to the north and west. In a plea that embodied the
increasingly desperate need, Captain J.T. Montgomery of the Jeff Davis
Flying Artillery signed an advertisement in the Atlanta papers asking local
houses of worship to donate their church bells to be melted down for cannon. (Apparently, few churches responded to this call for ecumenical ammunition.) All manner of goods were manufactured or harvested and shipped to
the front, with precious little left for the everyday needs of the locals. Dry
goods and foodstuffs grew scarce due to the needs of the army and the tight
grip of the Union blockade. Prices swelled and then skyrocketed, first
because of merchants who merely reflected the limited supply, and later due
to opportunistic speculators who descended on the city like crows to a car-
cass. The price of flour, sugar, salt, butter, bacon, and other provisions rose
sharply and continually from 1861 through 1863, the only inexpensive com-

modity being cotton—and even then, most finished goods, such as a lady's fine calico dress that had run the Union blockade, would sell for five or six times the price of a year ago. The prohibitive cost of living resulted in widespread scarcity and want and then inspired increasing crime and theft among the city's ever-growing population, which included soldiers, skulkers, slaves, runaways, refugees, and other transients and desperadoes. "Prostitution, disease, robbery, murder, and a persistent, unnerving rowdyism worried Atlantans and added to the disruption and chaos the war brought," one prominent historian wrote of the period. "Throughout 1862, Atlanta verged on chaos."

All in all, it was enough to make even the wealthy merchants long for simpler times. "Our sales continue good and our profits also good," S.P. Richards wrote of his thriving paper store in September 1862, "but yet I would willingly go back to old trade and moderate profits if we could only have peace and independence."[1]

The railroads, too, strained to meet expectations, carrying foodstuffs, ordnance, and other supplies as freight and passenger rates doubled and regular schedules were for the most part discarded entirely. At times, northbound trains on the W&A ran so close together that the line of cars on the tracks between Atlanta and Marietta was nearly continuous. Trains carried nervous, grass-green volunteers north as reinforcements, while inbound cars brought the wounded and the sick from the battlefields and bivouacs of Virginia and Tennessee. Refugees, off-duty train crews, and other traveling civilians fought for space in the crowded, often reeking coaches and sometimes wedged themselves in boxcars next to merchandise, sacks of grain, or sides of meat. Occasionally the stiff bodies of dead soldiers were transported here or there for burial, their rough coffins stacked in with the baggage and carried free of charge by the responsible railroad company.[2]

It was this commerce—the trade in and transport of what one local historian would call "the quick, the dead, and those in between"—that began to affect the people of Atlanta most deeply. The papers regularly carried the grim reports of Confederate casualties and long lists of names, often simply headlined "THE DEAD," of the many who had passed away in the city's hospitals. Throughout the summer and fall, the war raged on and the list of bloody battles lengthened: Gaines Mill, Frayser's Farm, Malvern Hill, Second Manassas, Ox Hill, and Sharpsburg, which the Yankees called Antietam. For many Georgians, the losses became deeply personal—the city marshal Oliver H. Jones, for example, lost his brother Robert, a chaplain killed in Virginia on June 28. The once-faraway war became close and sharp and very real, no longer just something one read about in the newspapers. And the fighting showed no signs of slacking off. In the face of the hardship and the dying, the previous fascination with the months-ago engine heist by a handful of Yankee soldiers—a flamboyant spectacle where no military result of any moment had been achieved and where not a soul had been killed—might have seemed mere folly.[3]

The Andrews Raiders appeared to have been forgotten, locked away in the county jail with Confederate deserters, Tennessee loyalists, and accused murderers and thieves. There was no further word of the famous train-stealers in the Atlanta newspapers, whose narrow columns were now crowded with battle news and casualty lists. The constant flow of curious visitors to the jail dwindled to almost nothing. (Pittenger recorded one notable visit by Mr. Turner's adult daughter, who brought along her infant son. Sergeant Elihu Mason was permitted to touch the child between the bars of the cell door, and he wept at the thought of his own children as he held and kissed the baby's hand.) In the meantime, the Ohio soldiers had no definite news of any further court-martial proceedings, nor of any planned release or prisoner exchange. They had received no response from their appeals to President Davis or General Bragg, and by now did not expect one—not a positive one, in any event.

Back in the Union ranks, the missing raiders were presumed to be long since dead. Most of the unit records merely reflected their absence—muster rolls of Company H of the 21st Ohio, for example, listed Private Robert Buffum as assigned "on special duty," and sometimes as "on secret service by order of Genl O.M. Mitchell." Some of their officers, however, had by now assumed the worst. Captain Thaddeus A. Minshall, who was then in command of Company H of the 33rd Ohio and later would become a justice on the Ohio Supreme Court, wrote in the company book next to D.A. Dorsey's name: "Executed by Confederate authority. The exact date of this execution is not known." (Some months later, Dorsey would happily see to the correction of this entry himself.) For the long months after they went missing, the raiders' wives and families back home were left to wonder what had happened to their loved ones, why the letters had stopped, why inquiries sent to Washington or to camp were quietly but firmly rebuffed.[4]

As August crept into September, the Atlanta captives focused on developing additional diversions to fend off boredom and bouts of melancholy while continuing the ever-present endeavor of planning their escape. They formed a debating society of sorts, with a sharp divergence of views being expressed and argued on a number of topics—"except capital punishment, about which there was no chance for argument, as we were all opposed to it," Dorsey said. Reading and storytelling continued each day, along with religious services composed of Bible-reading, singing, and prayer.

While thus feeding their minds and spirits, the soldiers also did their utmost to keep themselves physically fit under the circumstances. They exercised as best they could in the confined space, hoping for a chance to put their strength to use in the coming weeks. They drew marks on the floor to measure progress in broad-jumping, and the former circus performer Martin Hawkins tutored the others in performing handsprings, tumbling, and other gymnastic feats. Boxing matches were popular as well, with each participant encouraged to imagine that his opponent was a Rebel, which at times caused the friendly sparring to deteriorate into serious violence. One of the most feared opponents was Buffum and his "little bony arms, which were more like handspikes than human arms," as Dorsey remembered it. Wollam and Bensinger created their own rough game, a "bulldog tussle" whereby each would dig his teeth into the other's shoulder as they fought to determine who could endure the most punishment. These and other sports occupied participants and spectators alike, and kept the raiders as fit and strong as their confinement and their short rations would permit. Still, despite the range of activities, Dorsey noticed a slow but unmistakable change in himself and his companions, their voices weaker, their bodies thinner, their eyes glassy and increasingly distracted. "We were dying by inches," he said.[5]

Over time, the raiders found they had friends and allies in the two black servants, John and Kate, who brought their food and water. Twice a day, the pair also served up along with their meals whispered information overheard from guards or masters, and soon were smuggling in newspapers concealed in the bottom of the raiders' food trays. "They assisted us by every means in their power, and seemed willing to take any personal risk on our behalf," Pittenger recalled. The two slaves also inspired the captive soldiers with their unshaken optimism and their firm belief in the Union cause. "They believed all Northern soldiers were unselfish, fighting only for the rights of men, and considered it a privilege to help us in any possible way," Pittenger said. "I never talked with a negro yet who seemed to have the slightest doubt of the victory of the Union troops, and in their own freedom as the result of the war."

That freedom seemed nearer at hand in late September, when word of emancipation reached the Fulton County Jail. On September 22, in the wake of the vicious battle on the banks of Antietam Creek in Maryland that forced the withdrawal of Robert E. Lee and his Army of Northern Virginia, President Lincoln had announced his preliminary Emancipation Proclamation. On the first day of January 1863, all slaves within any state or district then in rebellion against the United States would be "then, thenceforth, and forever free." The raiders heard of the proclamation from new prisoners brought into the jail. "The Negroes . . . seemed to take a lively interest in the Proclamation, and were never so pleased as when they could speak to us on the sly about it," Alf Wilson recalled. But the news caused "great commotion among the Rebels, and brought down bitter maledictions upon the President's head." In fact, the event had kindled widespread controversy in the North and an explosion of fury among many Southerners, including the Confederate government.[6]

The raiders may have sensed this new hostility as they continued to wait for word of their own emancipation. All signs, however, suggested that circumstances were shifting the other way. In addition to poring over smuggled newspapers and hearing whispered tidbits from the servants, the raiders gathered intelligence from the prisoners in the adjacent cells. A stovepipe in the corner of their room shared a chimney with a similar stovepipe in the cell next door, and they had discovered that they could remove the pipe elbow and speak through the hole to their neighbors next door. In addition, they passed information to and fro with the inmates held across the hallway, tying a note to a stick on a string, which they would then throw across the hall and through the one-inch gap under the doorway. "Our telegraph system," they called it. (The string allowed them to pull the stick back to receive a reply or to reel in the projectile in the event of a wayward toss.) Through these mechanisms, the Ohio soldiers found, as the Indian summer arrived and the leaves began to turn, that "the evidence was increasing daily that something was in the wind that boded no good to us." Some time after provost marshal Lee's disturbing mid-September visit to the jail, two prisoners of war in the next cell overheard him telling the officer of the guard that he expected to receive an order at any time for the execution of "those raiders." This was soon corroborated when the message stick arrived under the door with a scrap of paper tied to it bearing disturbing news. It seemed that Mr. Turner—who the raiders thought had been showing an unusual degree of compassion in recent days—had given orders to the guards to keep a closer watch over the train stealers. "Those Ohio men will be executed in a short time," he had reportedly told the sentries before adding his own personal regrets. "There are some fine men in that room," he had said.

Just like that, the prisoners' days of idle confinement and uncertainty as to their future and their ultimate fate were over. "After sifting and weighing closely all the information we had, it stood in about this way," Wilson said. Nothing more than "a little formality—Confederate red tape—was all that now stood between us and the scaffold. If we had any hope of getting beyond those prison walls, except on a death-cart to the gallows, the blow must be struck at once." Dorsey agreed. "Our time had come and everything went to prove it," he wrote. "There was no longer any doubt of the proper course to pursue."[7]

The raiders made hasty preparations for their departure. They used a borrowed needle and lengths of thread liberated from the bed-ticking to mend their clothing; patched and reinforced their tattered shoes from the limited materials at hand; struggled to come up with makeshift weapons, such as a club of sorts fashioned from a piece of wood worked free from the wall near the doorframe. Captain Fry, the highest ranking man present and undeniably the most physically imposing (now that poor William Campbell was gone) and the one with firsthand experience in taking violent action, was placed in command of the escape attempt. Energized by the consensus appointment, he worked out a detailed plan of attack and gave directions on the role each man would play as they moved on the jailer and the guards. They would attack just after evening mealtime, when the jailer and the servants came to remove their empty trays. Fry would subdue the jailer, and Buffum would take his keys and open the other cells. Then the group would descend the stairs and divide into two parties to rush from the doors, front and rear, overpower the guards outside, and head for the fence and then for the woods.

All the raiders were to participate in the escape attempt, along with Fry and a handful of the other inmates. One of the East Tennesseans, G.W. Barlow, wanted to take the risk and join the effort. He was given permission by the unsuspecting jailer to move across the hall and join his fellow Tennessean Captain Fry. (The other East Tennessee Tories, including "Old Gun Barrel" Peter Pierce, would decide not to make the attempt.) Another inmate pleaded to be included in the breakout as well, a Georgia boy in the next cell who faced trial on charges of desertion and probably a firing squad. Yet another cell contained a number of civil prisoners, including a convicted murderer; the Ohioans agreed that they would not unlock that cell at all.

The raiders planned to go out that very night, October 15, but a soft, soaking rain that afternoon gave them pause. Dorsey believed, rightly or wrongly, that the wet leaves and ground would allow dogs to track them more easily, so they postponed until the next evening after supper. The next twenty-four hours was "a day of awful suspense—the longest I ever put over in my life," Dorsey remembered. There were no games and few songs that day; instead, the prisoners passed the daylight hours of October 16 in a self-taught class on escape, evasion, and wilderness survival. They discussed and debated such topics as what direction they should take, how to throw dogs off the scent, how to approach a house in search of food, how to cross rivers and streams, and the likely whereabouts of Union forces. Meanwhile, they kept an eager watch out the barred windows, fearful that the regular guard detail would be increased or the routine changed, signaling an imminent court-martial or a hasty execution. They marked the afternoon hours and the approach of evening by watching the shadow of the jail as it lengthened and spread across a knoll just to the east.

At last the supper hour arrived, and to their relief, the guard had not been reinforced. The usual detail was posted in the yard outside—a sergeant and six men. The prisoners would have the advantage of numbers, and hopefully of surprise, but they would face locked doors and armed guards, and all were in an admittedly weakened condition. "We felt that it was probably the last day on earth for some of us," Dorsey recalled. "Some would surely be killed in the fight with the guards and who it would be no one could tell." They shook hands warmly and traded farewells and best wishes all around. Each man left a message in the hands of a couple of different comrades, to be passed along to family and friends if they were killed in the attempt or left behind, so that their loved ones might know what had become of them. Captain Fry led the group in a word of prayer, closing the benediction just as Mr. Turner and the two servants came shuffling up the stairs bearing their supper trays.[8]

The doors were unlocked and the cells served one by one, just like always. The raiders divided their small meals, eating a bite or two for strength and pocketing the rest so they would have a morsel to consume later on. After a time, Turner returned to the northeast cell and unlocked the door. The servants John and Kate came into the cell to clear out the supper dishes and to give the prisoners fresh water for the night. Just after they passed in, Fry, Knight, Brown, and the others stepped quickly through the door into the narrow hallway, blocking the cell door so it could not be closed. The rest of the party followed, surrounding a confused Turner in the corridor. He was alone. No guards had accompanied him up the stairs, and the old watchman Thoer was nowhere in sight. This was lucky for Mr. Thoer, one raider later wrote, as he surely would have received a bottle over the head had he been present.

"Good evening, Mr. Turner," Captain Fry said kindly, a warm smile on his face.

"Good evening!" Turner replied, startled by the quiet but persistent advance through the doorway.

"A pleasant evening," Fry continued, stalling for time as more men sidled into the hallway around him.

"Yes," Turner agreed.

"Mr. Turner," Fry said, "we feel like taking a little walk this evening."

"What! How? Where?" Turner said, his surprise giving way to puzzlement.

"Well, we have been in here long enough, and you know that we will all be hanged soon if we remain, and we are going out."

"Yes," said Turner, still in disbelief, protesting weakly, "but you will have the guards to contend with."

A rumble of low, confident voices around him assured the old warden that they would take care of the guards. Then Buffum stepped forward and reached for his keys. "Oh, yes, Mr. Turner, let us have those keys; those boys want to go out too," the little private said, gesturing toward the northeast cell. This seemed to shake the befuddled jailer out of his initial daze and spark a deep-seated sense of responsibility. "No," he said, "you can go out, but you cannot interfere with the other prisoners."[9]

Fry suddenly seized the wiry jailer in an iron grip from behind, clapping a hand over his mouth to muffle his cries. (Pittenger would later assert that it was he who had hushed the struggling Turner, receiving from him a bitten finger in return.) Buffum snatched the ring of keys and moved to open the other cells even as the rest of the party skittered quietly down the stairs. "Buffum stayed like a man and unlocked our doors," one prisoner said admiringly years later. Pittenger would remember that their sometime allies, the two black servants John and Kate, kept perfectly silent as they watched the Federal prisoners wrestle the jailer and then flee for the exits, "only beginning to scream when the noise outside convinced them that they might as well contribute their share."[10]

A number of the raiders would later describe in great detail the exciting jailbreak and the melee in the prison yard that followed. Perhaps not surprisingly, no two of these accounts are alike, and no amount of comparison could possibly reconcile them. "It all happened in a twinkling," Dorsey said. The fourteen surviving Andrews Raiders, along with Captain Fry, the desperate Rebel deserter, and perhaps a handful of others, descended the stairs and burst out of the building and into the yard. One party of guards had been passing the late afternoon engaged in a card game, their muskets leaning against the building nearby. Knight got between them and their weapons and they scrambled away in a flutter of diamonds and spades. William Bensinger, still powerful even after months of captivity, subdued another guard, seizing him by the throat as John Porter wrested away his musket. Alf Wilson recalled the jailyard skirmishes as a free-for-all scrap wherein several guards were "knocked down and roughly handled"; none of them seemed to be able to get a shot off in the confusion. Wilson, Wollam, and Hawkins grabbed bricks and bottles from a trash pile and hurled them toward the sentries as they ran for the gate, screaming "Murder!" and hollering for the captain of the guard.

Sensing that their opportunity was slipping away as the alarm was spread, Knight told the others, "Boys, if we want to get away, we've got to get out of this." The soldiers cast aside their makeshift weapons and ran for the perimeter. The fence was high and topped with pickets, but three horizontal stringers nailed inside were as good as a stepladder. The men scrambled over and scattered into the unfamiliar streets of the city, heading for the woods about a mile away in any direction. They ran pell-mell through yards and gardens, tearing through brush and hurdling pickets as the ruckus faded behind them and cool evening air burned at the back of their throats. "That was the hardest race I ever ran," Dorsey recalled. As he passed one house, a lady emerged and asked what was the matter. "Oh, nothing," one of the escapees replied. "Just some prisoners escaped." Still no shots were fired until the fugitives were nearly to the treeline, and those fell short or whizzed by harmlessly in the failing light. (Alf Wilson would later claim he was hit while going over the fence, though the wound must have been superficial, as it seemed to give him little trouble during the hundreds of miles he traveled thereafter.)

Back at the jail, those who failed to make it out of the yard in the first chaotic seconds soon found themselves trapped by the guards and a number of arriving reinforcements. Jacob Parrott and William Reddick were slow out of the blocks and were nabbed before they got to the fence. Robert Buffum made it out to the streets, but he had lingered too long opening the other cells. He had fled just a few hundred yards when a fleet-footed Rebel ran him down. Bill Pittenger bounced from point to point around the prison yard, squinting through his spectacles at the chaos and searching in vain for an opening. "At no time in all my Southern experience did I find my defective vision to be such a misfortune as just now," he recalled sadly. It soon was obvious even to Pittenger's weak eyes that the initial panic had dissipated and that any chance for surprise and escape was gone. He returned to the building of his own accord and made his way up the stairs to watch the pursuit out one of the second-floor windows. "It was a wild and exciting spectacle," he remembered. "Company after company of soldiers came up. The bells of the city were ringing, and shots were being fired rapidly, while loud commands and screams were mingled. I feared that many of our number were or would soon be killed."[11]

Pittenger soon found that his fears in this regard were happily unfounded. Ten of the fourteen surviving Andrews Raiders made it out of the city and off into the shadows of the forest—Bill Bensinger, Wilson Brown, D.A. Dorsey, Martin Hawkins, William Knight, Elihu Mason, John Reed Porter, Alf Wilson, Mark Wood, and John Wollam. (Two of these, Mason and Bensinger, were rounded up within forty-eight hours—the former weakened by illness and the latter exhausted by pursuing men with bloodhounds and then caught by a local planter as he tried to approach his slave quarters in search of sanctuary.) The desperate Confederate deserter got away as well and soon separated from the rest; the raiders later heard that the young man was eventually recaptured and hanged. David Fry also made good his escape, eventually returning to his hometown of Greenville, Tennessee, before returning to active service. His fellow East Tennessean G.W. Barlow was not so lucky. He hurt his leg going over the fence and was quickly collared and dragged back to the jail. All in all, ten men had escaped—eight raiders, Fry, and the Confederate deserter; the only known casualty was the injury to the limping young Barlow. In the minds of a number of the raiders, this was an excellent showing for an escape attempt many had regarded as all but suicidal.

Back in the jail, the recaptured raiders were locked in their cells, fearing for the retribution they were sure would come. They spent the remainder of the "doleful night" pondering their fate as they listened to the bragging of the guards outside. "Generally they lauded their own bravery to the skies, telling how they had served the prisoners who had broken out upon them," Pittenger recalled. "Occasionally, one who had not been present then, would suggest that it did not show a great deal of bravery to let unarmed men snatch their guns from them, but such hinted slanders were always received with the contempt they deserved, and the work of self-praise went on."

Provost Marshal G.W. Lee was in a "towering passion" at the breakout, riding to and fro on his horse as he directed a widespread and merciless search for the fugitives. He ordered nearby river ferries and key crossroads picketed, railroad lines guarded, and he showed no sign of the cordiality he had exhibited in earlier visits to the jail. "Don't take one of the villains alive," Pittenger heard him say. "Shoot them down and let them lie in the woods." His anger and embarrassment were certainly understandable, as it would be his unfortunate duty to explain the escape to the War Department and the adjutant general in Charleston. In his report of the incident (which he would somehow manage to delay until mid-November), he complained of the inadequate force at his disposal and the carelessness of the elderly jailer, who had acted contrary to his instructions in opening the cell while alone and unarmed. Interestingly, Lee would attribute the escape to "outside influences" and his failure to recapture the fugitives to the "great number of sympathizers" found outside the jail. There were indeed Yankee sympathizers in the city, some of whom had extended small kindnesses to the Federal prisoners during their stay, but there is no evidence that any Atlantans were complicit in planning or aiding the dramatic escape.

The morning after the jailbreak, an angry gaggle of local authorities arrived at the jail to interrogate the remaining inmates, roughly demanding that they reveal the course their comrades planned to take. The Ohio soldiers replied that the escapees had said only that "Atlanta was in the middle of what was left of the Confederacy, and that they planned to travel toward the outside."[12]

The *Southern Confederacy* reported the startling "ESCAPE OF THE BRIDGE-BURNERS!" in its second edition the next day—though the story focused not on the engine thieves but instead on the actions of Captain David Fry, "the notorious and daring leader of the tory band in the bridge-burning enterprise." Still, the raiders' return to the news columns was no small accomplishment, as the papers these days were largely preoccupied with reports of the ongoing campaign in Kentucky, an atrocious murder in Marietta, and the arrival of five Northern locomotives recently captured at Warrenton and Manassas, including an engine named "Old Abe," which the *Southern Confederacy* observed was "pretty well battered up, and has about as ill-favored a look as the arch-traitor after whom it was named." As for the escape, the papers blamed the guards, "who have so long stood and lain around there night and day that they had ceased to be on the alert," but initially expressed confidence that the escapees would be quickly recaptured. "Final escape we should consider impossible," the story concluded.

But a week later, with the majority of the band still at large, the local editors would pronounce themselves entirely mystified at the unaccountable disappearance of the fugitives. "The escape of these men is the most mysterious thing in the history of this section," the *Confederacy* wrote on October 25. "Their escape from the jail was known, and men were after them in less than half an hour. Mounted men were quickly beyond any point they could have reached; and the most ceaseless activity and vigilance has been displayed by Col. Lee. Men have been out constantly, night and day, scouring the country and watching in every direction, and no trace whatever of them has been found."[13]

The escaped prisoners scattered and scurried into the countryside like hares flushed from a thicket, each man striking out into the Georgia wilderness (for most of the state was still wilderness in those times) with a prearranged partner. Despite their jailhouse consultations on which course to pursue, each duo had a different view of the best way to go about reaching the Union lines. It was just as well that they did not know just how far they would have to travel to reach the safety of the blue armies, for Federal troops were no longer at the gates of Chattanooga, or holding Huntsville, or even garrisoned in Nashville. After the fall of Corinth, Mississippi, General Don Carlos Buell had been given instructions in early June to move eastward through northern Alabama along the Memphis & Charleston Railroad, finally coming to the aid of Old Stars, who had been pleading for meaningful support since his initial conquest in April. Much to the delight of President Lincoln, Buell moved his column—three divisions totaling 35,000 men— east to Huntsville, poised to join up with Mitchel's 10,000-man division near Bridgeport, along with Morgan's 9,000 at Cumberland Gap. The Army of the Ohio was on the move and would soon be united. They could capture Chattanooga and then make a prompt lefthand turn to Knoxville or a right toward Atlanta. The railroad was open, the troops in good spirits, Chattanooga still thinly defended, the weather perfect for campaigning. It seemed that the end of the war was in sight.

Buell, however, saw nothing but problems. His supply lines were plagued by cavalry raids and sniper fire. Rolling stock for the railroad was scarce, resulting in interruptions in supply and ordnance and short rations for the men. Up ahead there was rugged terrain, swollen rivers, burned bridges, guerilla activity. As a result, the initial march to Huntsville was followed by a month of idleness and fretting as Buell wrestled with difficulties, both real and imagined. In Washington, Lincoln's delight again soured to disappointment. "The President telegraphs that your progress is not satisfactory and that you should move more rapidly," General Halleck wrote to Buell on July 8. Don Carlos was so stunned by this rebuke that he made no reply for three days. In the meantime, even Buell's own officers and men became increasingly frustrated with their cautious commander, as they marked time in the summer heat, transformed, as Shelby Foote put it, from "happy-go-lucky soldiers into ill-fed railroad workers." Buell, one subordinate wrote in disgust, was an "amiable idiot," governed by the deliberate, cordial military policy of a dancing master: "By your leave, my dear sir, we will have a fight; that is, if you are sufficiently fortified. No hurry; take your time." An Indiana soldier writing in his diary had a starker and more pessimistic view of the situation: "This war will last 400 years," he wrote.[14]

In early August, Buell sent a wire to Washington with a litany of excuses for the delay—"I know I have not been idle or indifferent," he insisted. He promised that he would "march upon Chattanooga at the earliest possible day"—though he added a qualifier: "unless I ascertain certainly that the enemy's strength renders it imprudent." Twelve days later, with Buell still immobile, a substantial Confederate column under the command of General Braxton Bragg was reported crossing the river in force at Chattanooga. In what would come to be recognized as the largest Confederate railroad movement of the war, Bragg had moved his 30,000-man force via a 776-mile circuitous route from central Mississippi through Mobile and Atlanta before appearing in Chattanooga. Buell's predictable reaction to the news of this threat was initially to pull back northwest up the Nashville & Chattanooga Railroad to Decherd, Tennessee, and four days later to order an all-out withdrawal. His entire army, Mitchel's men included, retreated back to Nashville, firing the newly rebuilt railroad bridges in their wake. By mid-September he was all the way up in Bowling Green, Kentucky, 150 crowflight miles from Chattanooga and 250 from Atlanta. Thanks to a forward push by the harsh, irascible Bragg—whose Rebel force was about half the size of Buell's reinforced army—and to an appalling lack of nerve by Buell himself, the Confederates had driven the Union army from its hard-won positions in North Alabama and East Tennessee without firing a shot.[15]

Whatever the eventual strategic implications of these moves and countermoves in the summer and fall of 1862, the practical result for the escaped Andrews Raiders was a drastic lengthening of the road to safety. Rather than facing a hundred-or-so-mile trek to their comrades in north Alabama, the raiders would have to go north all the way to Kentucky, or west to Mississippi, scrounging for food and avoiding pursuers, Rebel soldiers and unfriendly civilians every step of the way. This they would have to accomplish though all were weakened by six months of imprisonment, with ragged clothes, tattered shoes, no provisions, no maps, no weapons, no transportation, and no friends. Incredibly, all eight would rise to meet the challenge.

John Reed Porter paired up for the journey from Atlanta with John Wollam, who was assembling considerable experience by now in the business of breaking out of prison and running for his life. "Everybody was wild with excitement," Porter said of the escape, "women screaming, men running, bells ringing, drums beating, dogs barking, in fact a regular stampede." The pair stopped running early on and covered themselves with leaves and brush to wait for full darkness. They were still close enough to hear the city's church and courthouse bells, tolling the news of their escape.

Because Wollam had come so close to reaching the Federal lines the last time he had fled, he saw little reason to change from his previous route. He and Porter struck out to the northwest, hoping to find their way to the winding avenue of the Tennessee River. The morsels they had saved from their last few meals would be their only food for the first twelve days out from Atlanta. As the country grew rugged and homesteads few and far between, they began to cautiously approach cottages and cabins from time to time in search of supplies. On two occasions they broke into homes where the families were absent, finding cornbread and meat for their trouble. They slept by day in caves or thickets, huddling together to keep warm as November arrived.

After twenty-two days of sneaking and scrounging, they reached the Tennessee River, perhaps thirty miles below Bridgeport. They had no way of knowing it, of course, but the Federal Army was no longer occupying the majority of the hills and towns of northern Alabama. The two men found a canoe and soon were floating westward toward freedom. They traveled for three nights without food before securing a meat-and-cornbread dinner fried up by a kind woman, supplemented by pots of delicious honey collected from some beehives near the riverbank. The river was low this time of year, and they eventually had to abandon their canoe and travel on foot for nearly forty miles. They finally were able to return to the river and secure an abandoned skiff, which they floated until they were less than twenty miles from Corinth.

On November 18, 1862—a month and two days after the jailbreak in Atlanta—Porter and Wollam spotted several wagons and teams, driven by soliders in *blue coats*. They emerged from the woods, just four miles now from

Corinth, and identified themselves to the Federal soldiers. "We were soon in the midst of a squad of the Ninth Iowa, but we still bore the resemblance of dilapidated rebels," Porter recalled. The pair was taken to an officer, who accused the Union infiltrators of being Confederate spies. From there they appeared before a lieutenant of the 20th Ohio, who seemed less skeptical, and then the provost marshal in Corinth, who remained unconvinced by their wild story but directed that they be sent to the headquarters of Brigadier General Grenville Dodge.[16]

Only thirty-one years old, General Dodge was an officer of growing promise and reputation and a favorite of Sherman and Grant, who had just three days before appointed him to command the newly established Department of Corinth. A native of Massachusetts and now the pride of his adopted hometown Council Bluffs, Iowa, Dodge had proven himself back in March at the Battle of Pea Ridge, Arkansas, where he had three horses shot from under him and was wounded in the right side. As the new commander of Union forces in the area, he was charged with guarding, repairing, and improving a 150-mile stretch of the Mobile & Ohio Railroad. (In postwar years, Dodge would secure enduring fame as the chief engineer of the Union Pacific and a central designer and financier of the Transcontinental Railroad.) He also happened to be an opportunistic and clever spymaster who employed slaves, freemen, and Union-loyal white Southerners to gather intelligence for his superior, General Grant. If any commander in the Union army was likely to believe the farfetched tale of espionage and escape spun by Wollam and Porter, it was Dodge.

"After a short interview, he recognized our true character and received a full detail of our adventures," Porter recalled. Not only did Dodge believe the two strangers, he had deep respect for their courage and demonstrated immediate concern for their well-being. Dodge ordered his quartermaster to furnish the escaped heroes with a full complement of clothing and blankets. He then gave them orders for transportation to their regiments, along with a personal gift of five dollars apiece. "We went to the Quarter-Master's department, drew our clothing, took a general clean up, robed ourselves in army blue," Porter wrote. "[We] felt that we were no longer fugitives and wanderers, but free men."[17]

*D*aniel Allen Dorsey and Martin Hawkins, too, would reach safety that same November 18, though their route, their experiences, and their endpoint were entirely different. Instead of heading west toward Mississippi,

Dorsey and Hawkins struck out to the northeast, hoping to reach Union-loyal East Tennessee and then Kentucky. In many respects their story is like that of Porter and Wollam—five weeks of toil through forest and brush, marked by desperate close calls and debilitating hunger. But Dorsey and Hawkins would benefit—in fact their lives were probably saved—by a veritable Underground Railroad of slaves and loyalists who helped them on their way.

The pair's first such encounter came eight days out, when they cautiously approached a pair of black men with hunting dogs, who promptly agreed to ferry them across the Chattahoochee River. One of the men went for provisions and returned with a feast of boiled pork, beans, Irish and sweet potatoes, and cornbread. Dorsey remembered the generous offering as "the first food worthy of the name we had eaten for six long months!" This was a rugged region of caves and abandoned mines, their Samaritans told them, and they offered to hide the fugitives nearby. Hawkins and Dorsey declined; they wanted to keep moving. The two men gave them a broken-off butcher's knife to use on their journey, along with directions to the Hiawassee River and the name of a slave there who would ferry them across.

They resumed their northward flight—traveling at night and resting by day, finally reaching the Hiawassee, where they hailed the dark-skinned ferryman and found him to be the same man who had been recommended to them. The young man persuaded them to hide with him for a couple of days until he could help them along downriver to the junction of the Hiawassee and the Tennessee. "He treated us royally, shared his scanty allowance of food with us, for he had only a slave's rations, doctored my ankle, kept us in his best bed—a *feather* one . . . and, on starting, gave us a bottle of molasses and a piece of pork," Dorsey said. Their host then found them a dugout canoe and sent them off downriver to the Tennessee—though the Ohioans would decline to follow the great river west for the dangerous run past Chattanooga. Instead, they steered to the north bank and then struck out on foot north into the Cumberland Mountains.

At times, they almost enjoyed the peaceful solitude: "The lofty peaks, the wide landscape, the rising and setting sun were doubly solemn in the profound silence, and amid the mighty forest of that region," Dorsey recalled. "I can never forget the beauty of nature associated with so much peril." But for every such moment, the pair spent miserable hours, days, and nights in what Dorsey would describe as "very prosaic toil"—struggling on hands and knees through a quarter-mile wide mass of vicious briars, or stumbling from weakness and lack of sleep, or finding themselves so hungry that they dropped to the ground and felt in the darkness for fallen persimmons to eat. They forded the Sequatchie River and for two days thereafter "traveled and rested alternately in the mountains, hungry, wet with the rain that now began to fall, and as solitary as if we were the only inhabitants of the globe."

Desperate for food and so weak they repeatedly fell as they made their way along the rocky ground, Dorsey and Hawkins descended a steep slope and approached a group of men chopping wood to beg for something to eat. They told the woodsmen they were Confederate soldiers who had taken sick and been left behind in a hospital and now were trying to return to their regiments. They found their story coolly received and their request for assistance firmly rejected. Further conversation revealed that they were now in a so-called "Lincoln district"—it was said that only two votes in the entire county had been cast in favor of secession. At this, Dorsey and Hawkins revealed their true identities, and to their relief "the hospitality which had been denied before was now readily extended."

The two soldiers soon found themselves not only fed, but again aided by a secret network of Federal sympathizers, who passed them safely along from one Lincolnite household to the next as they continued northward. In one such home, they met an old gentleman, ninety years old, an "enthusiastic Union man" who "declared his intention to use his old rifle if the Rebels ever bothered him or his neighbors," Dorsey fondly recalled. "The old gentleman literally forced upon us a dollar—the last one he had." That same day marked the first time in seven months they had eaten three straight meals in succession.

The pair made their way northward through Jamestown, Tennessee, and resuming travel on their own crossed into Kentucky, arriving in Monticello in mid-November. There, a Union-friendly host gave them the name of his son-in-law, a Dr. McKinney in Somerset, who would find them transportation. The next day, the good doctor obtained passage for the two men on wagons that were going to Lebanon for salt, and Dorsey and Hawkins found their journey afoot "suddenly and very happily ended."

"I would like to tell how the old Star Spangled Banner looked to me as we saw it floating grandly in the evening breeze at Lebanon on that day—the 18th of November, 1862—but language fails me," Dorsey wrote. Their initial reception was similar to that experienced by Porter and Wollam. "We were not very cordially received by the officers in charge, as we bore a very striking resemblance to the parolled Confederates," Dorsey recalled. Though the commanders doubted their story, they were sent on to the local barracks, where they soon met soldiers from their own company. "Dorsey—is that you?" one soldier cried out in amazement. "From these friends we learned all about our comrades in arms: who had fallen in battle, who had been wounded, who discharged, something about friends at home," Dorsey recalled. He would later rejoin his full regiment at Murfreesboro, Tennessee, just thirty miles from Shelbyville, and just in time for the bloody year-end battle that would take place there.[18]

Just as they had been the first men to climb aboard the *General* on that gray April morning, the two engineers William Knight and Wilson Brown were the first to rush from the county jail and attack the guards and the first to reach the shelter of the woods. They made slow progress the first four days, however, as they half-carried along with them Sergeant Elihu Mason, the latest of the raiders to be crippled by illness. Brown and Knight ignored the sergeant's pleas that they leave him to die in the woods and save themselves, instead seeking help at a farmhouse just a few miles from Atlanta. There they were given food and a night's rest, but their breakfast the next morning was interrupted by three men searching for the Yankee fugitives. Brown and Knight had no choice but to abandon their sick friend and make a run for it. One of the pursuers turned his hounds loose after the fleeing pair, who fended the dogs off with rocks at close range and then again took to the woods. "As the Southerners used to say after a battle," Knight recalled, "we won the victory, but we evacuated the ground."

From there, the two engineers began an incredible odyssey. The basic facts of their escape are simple to establish: they traveled more than 300 grueling miles through the Blue Ridge and Great Smoky Mountains (probably following a route some distance east of that traveled by Dorsey and Hawkins), arriving at the Federal lines near Somerset, Kentucky, in late November. Wilson Brown summarized the ordeal in a letter: "How we subsisted 47 days and nights on chestnuts, roots, and green corn—how we traveled by the north star as a guide—how we waded swamps, swam rivers, climbed mountains and how we were pursued by Blood hounds and Bloodthirsty Rebels— how we were secreted in a cave by East Tenn. patriots—how we finally reached the Union lines in a rude condition—every word true but it reads like a romance."

The story read like a romance indeed when Brown wrote his tale for a public audience nearly thirty years later. In 1890, no doubt aware of the numerous successful books published by his comrades William Pittenger and Alf Wilson and openly jealous of the fame enjoyed by his former friend Will Knight, who Brown felt unfairly took all the credit as the engineer of the raid, Wilson Brown undertook to write his own version of their escape. "MITCHEL RAIDERS—THRILLING INCIDENTS NEVER BEFORE PUBLISHED," he called his story, which ran as a series of articles in the *North Baltimore Ohio Weekly Beacon*. His latter-day narrative of their adventure is one so plainly and heavily embroidered and embellished that it is difficult to discern truth from fiction.

To hear Brown tell it, not only did he and Knight travel hundreds of miles and escape from many close scrapes with wild animals, gray soldiers, and local vigilantes, but they also were a formidable military force in their own right along the way. Using knives, clubs, and stolen or borrowed muskets, they killed numerous Rebel bushwackers outright—one they merely frightened to death—and took down a number of bloodthirsty Southern hounds. On one occasion, Brown asserted, they encountered an almost-mythical "monster" of a brown snake "six inches through the middle" that Brown believed to be twenty feet long (Knight, he said, thought it was "only" eighteen). At another point, Knight was supposedly recaptured and taken to a Confederate encampment, where he was to be burned at the stake, no less. Brown, of course, claimed that he rescued his helpless friend just in the nick of time.

Knight fails to corroborate any of these wild encounters, and a number of the Andrews Raiders would later cast aspersions on their comrade Brown's credibility as well. (Indeed, just as he made an uncorroborated claim that he had a personal interview with General Mitchel in Shelbyville back in April, Wilson Brown would also make an unverified claim that he was the first to receive a personal audience with Abraham Lincoln.) Although it is impossible to either confirm or entirely discredit Brown's story, it is not difficult to appreciate just how outlandish his tale is—one simply has to read the entire ten-month weekly newspaper serial to (dis)believe it. One historian of the Andrews Raid dismisses Brown's narrative entirely, calling it "the wildest damn thing you ever read."

Not surprisingly, William Knight's many public lectures, written accounts, and letters made no mention of these adventures—on the contrary, Knight's account is much more consistent with Brown's unpublished and presumably unembellished letter ("How we subsisted 47 days and nights . . .") described previously. Leaving Atlanta behind them, the two soldiers struck out to the northeast through the rough terrain of North Georgia, reaching the

Chattahoochee River after ten days of hard travel, "without a bite to eat save what the woods furnished, such as nuts, bark, buds, &c." According to Knight, apart from the rock-throwing duel with the dogs when they left their friend Mason, the only violence committed by the two Ohioans was when they captured a defenseless wild goose and, some days later, a wild pig, which provided rations all the way to the Hiawassee River in North Carolina. The country was high, the air thin, and the terrain imposing—"mountains it took two men and a boy to see to the top of," Knight recalled. Contrary to Brown's rip-roaring tale of bloody battles in the woods with gray marauders, they met no Confederate soldiers at all, and the only armed encounter, according to Knight, was anticlimactic and thankfully resulted in no violence at all. "In a deep mountain valley beside a river we met two men armed to the teeth," he said. "We all stopped as if we had been shot, but quickly moved on again. We simply spoke when we met, and all seemed glad to get by without anything more to do with each other."

Passing through the northeast corner of Tennessee, they came upon a riverside cabin and after a cautious exchange with two men sitting on the porch found that the family were friends of the Union. One of the men said that "for his part he was opposed to the war," Knight recalled. "We were too!" He and Brown revealed themselves as Union soldiers and engine thieves, and their hosts, who had heard of their exploits in Georgia, gave them dinner, along with soap and water for a good wash, and offered to hide them for several days. That afternoon, the father led them to a nearby cave and supplied them with torches, quilts, and enough food to last them nearly a week. "There was a good sized room in the cave," Knight recalled, "and he said we could have all the fire we wanted, and halloo as loud as we pleased without danger."

Knight and Brown ate and rested for five days in the relative comfort and safety of their mountain retreat. A guide then took them upriver to another old house in the woods, where another group of Union-friendly East Tennesseans provided them with another guide, ten dollars apiece to help along the way, and, for the first time in a year, a complete suit of fresh clothes. From there they were taken across the Tennessee River and passed along from house to house as they moved northward. "This was comparatively easy traveling, and we passed rapidly and safely on till we reached our own lines," Knight remembered. "We had spent forty-seven days and nights, passing over some of the roughest country that ever laid out of doors!"[19]

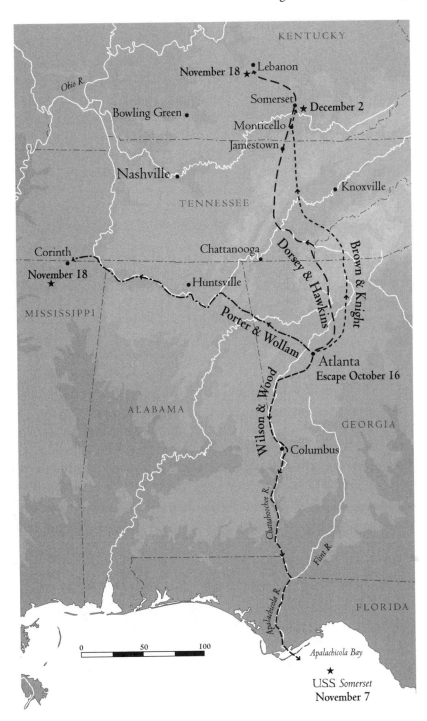

Escape routes of the Andrews Raiders, October to November 1862.

The story of Alf Wilson and Mark Wood's journey to safety was even more remarkable, and unlike Brown's odyssey, it also happened to be (at least mostly) true. Wilson was nothing if not creative, and his plan to reach the protection of the United States military was so counterintuitive as to be brilliant. Alf proposed that, rather than striking out northward or westward toward the Federal lines, he and Wood should escape Dixie by heading *almost due south*. They would make for the nearby Chattahoochee River, he told his English-born friend, and then find a boat and float down to the Gulf of Mexico. This would be easier than traveling by land and trying to keep their bearings at night in unfamiliar country, and it would also be exactly the opposite direction from the expected route where the Rebels would be searching for them. The plan seemed then and seems now to be more than a little crazy, though in the end Wilson and Wood not only would make it, but would reach safety more than a week earlier than their north- and westbound overland comrades.

The two men spent a harrowing first night dodging Rebel cavalry on the roads and then concealing themselves in thick brush as search parties were formed to scour the woods on foot. At one point, they crawled on their bellies to slip through a line of sentries posted no more than thirty paces apart. They pressed on through the night until they collapsed from exhaustion, unable to proceed a single step further. Despite their fatigue, both experienced a "wild, almost childish joy" at being free from the gloom of prison, with the bright though still distant prospect ahead of seeing family, friends, and home.

But they had a long way to go and many trials ahead. What was more, they had little hope of encountering anyone without raising immediate suspicion, due to their ragged clothes and their unmistakable "jail-bird look." Wilson realized this that first morning out, as he looked over his friend Wood as they rested under a great tree and ate their last crumbs of bread left over from the jail. "The miserable garments he wore did not cover his nakedness. His face was begrimed with dirt almost set in the skin. He had become thin and emaciated with fever, and had a ravenous appetite; his eyes were sunken in his head and seemed to have the wild, unnatural glare of a madman, which, at times, almost made me shudder," Wilson recalled. "And I suppose my own appearance was no more prepossessing than his." The pair concluded from this self-inspection that it would be unsafe to approach any house and agreed that they would do the best they could to avoid being seen by any human being.[20]

Wilson's plan first required that they locate the Chattahoochee River—by no means a foregone conclusion, since neither man knew the country or the location of the river and had no map, compass, or other means of finding it. Wilson knew only that the river "flowed by west of Atlanta" and eventually reached the waters of the gulf. He presumably obtained this paltry information through the lengthy jailhouse consultations about potential escape routes, as his own knowledge of Southern maps and terrain, as he later admitted, was limited to "a slight general idea I had of it from the school geographies." From its trickling headwaters in the Blue Ridge Mountains, the Chattahoochee follows a diagonal northeast-to-southwest course as it slashes through north central Georgia, passing at one point within ten miles of the jail. But Wilson and Wood, navigating by the stars, set out on a course "slightly south of west," perhaps even running parallel to the river for a time, and therefore lengthened the distance and the time to reach the river. Passing through rough, heavily forested country, they soon came upon the northeast-to-southwest running line of the Atlanta & West Point Railroad and felt reassured that their course was about right.

Their confidence soon faltered, however, as they traveled for four days and nights without finding the river they had thought to be nearby. Along the way, they ate nothing but raw ears of corn and soon found themselves so weak from hunger and their feet so bruised and sore they could hardly continue. At one point, Mark Wood crawled along on his hands and knees for a considerable distance in order to spare his blistered feet. "Alf," he said to his friend, "what's a fellow's life but a curse to him when he has to drag it out in this way? I would rather be dead and be done with it." Wilson felt much the same way. "I sometimes wondered, like Job of old, why my afflictions were so great," he later wrote.

After several more hours of this creeping progress, they heard off to the right the welcome sound of rushing water, and soon found themselves standing on the banks of the Chattahoochee. Here was hope, and inspiration to continue. "De Soto did not feel more joy when he first discovered the Mississippi," Wilson recalled. They waded out into the water, cooling their blistered feet and drinking their fill. A short distance downstream, they located a skiff and in minutes were gliding quietly down the green-brown current. "I doubt if two more joyful mortals ever navigated a canoe than we two, with that stolen little craft," Wilson remembered.

Alf Wilson and Mark Wood spent the next three weeks traveling down the Chattahoochee, paddling for hours each night and resting during the day, though sleep was hard to come by thanks to their gnawing hunger and swarms of gnawing mosquitoes. Their hunger even haunted them as they slept—"I could, while sleeping, see in my dreams, tables spread and groaning with loads of good things to eat: bread, meat, cheese, coffee, biscuit and butter were all within my reach," Wilson recalled. But the waking reality was all too different—nothing but the ears of hard corn they found almost indigestible. They soon broke their initial pledge to avoid other people at all costs, and made their way from the river to the isolated home of a "couple of quite intelligent, but unsophisticated old people, in comfortable circumstances," where they claimed to be hungry soldiers in search of the nearby ferry and, if possible, something to eat. "I had been in Dixie so long that I had acquired, from the guards and citizens, their vernacular of speech quite perfectly," Wilson said; "besides this, we had learned the names of officers and the number of different regiments, such as the Eighth Georgia Cavalry, Fifth Tennessee Infantry, etc., until we were able to tell quite a plausible story, if not too closely questioned," Wilson recalled. The couple invited them in and told them they were welcome to such food as they had. As they devoured everything the woman put before them, the man told them the latest news from Atlanta: a number of the Yankee raiders had overpowered the guards and escaped from jail, he said, and had not yet been caught. "We expressed great surprise that such a piece of audacity could be made successful in Atlanta," Wilson said.

Reinvigorated by the meal, Wilson and Wood returned to their little boat and resumed their southward cruise, though they soon discovered that river travel was not always quiet paddling on glassy water. On one occasion, Wilson suddenly found himself flat on his back in the cold river, frightened by the shock and suddenness of the blow. "What on earth had happened I did not know, the accident had been so sudden," he recalled. "I thought of earthquakes, whales, sharks, torpedoes and many other things." Wood fished him out of the water, and they found the cause to be much less dramatic: he had been knocked back by a ferry-boat wire stretched across the river, just low enough to catch him as he sat high in the stern of the boat. Another night, as they made their way further south, the river sped faster, with ledges, rocks, and rapids to contend with, and later a mill-dam, which they ran past "with the velocity of an express-train." The churning river soon grew so rough that they had no choice but to abandon their craft and take up again on foot.

For three more nights, the two privates hobbled through the rocky terrain. The next morning, dawn revealed the spires and smokestacks of the city of

Columbus, the head of commercial navigation for the Chattahoochee, still almost 200 winding river miles north of the Gulf of Mexico. With much of the cotton trade choked off by the blockade, Columbus had been transformed from a cotton port to a manufacturing center, arsenal, and shipyard working in support of the Confederate army and navy. Wilson and Wood kept to the treeline as they circled wide around the town, hearing all the while "a constant clattering sound, as of a hundred workmen with hammers." As they drew back close to the river early the next morning, they saw the cause of the ruckus—construction was proceeding on a powerful gunboat, its decks and its sloping hull swarming with workmen sheathing it with iron. Wilson would later come to believe that the ship was the fearsome Rebel ironclad *Chattahoochee*, which was being outfitted at Columbus to pose single-handedly a deadly threat to the Union blockade in the Gulf. (Nothing would come of this plan—the *Chattahoochee* would explode and sink near the mouth of the Flint River in May 1863.)[21]

Wilson and Wood stayed hidden in the piney woods outside Columbus for two additional days and nights, as the still-ailing Wood nursed his sore feet and Wilson prowled up and down the riverbank in search of another boat. They eventually discovered one—"a leaky old concern" that required constant bailing as well as paddling; and later swapped it out for a flatboat farther downstream. "Thus we progressed, traveling by boat at night, and laying by in the daytime," Wilson wrote. They crept in the darkness past upbound steamboats and tiny riverbank settlements with names like Egypt and Fowlstown and Argyle. They floated by countless creeks, runs, inlets, and tributaries as the Chattahoochee wound its way southward and eventually joined with the Flint to form the Apalachicola River. The river scenery became "particularly monotonous" as the landscape flattened and mountains and rocks gave way to fields and marshes. Hunger remained their principal enemy, and they subsisted for nearly two weeks on nothing more than corn, roots, raw pumpkins, and pumpkin seeds. "When I look back and think of those long, painful, hungry nights and days, I wonder how it was possible that we kept up," Wilson later wrote. "I do not think I could withstand the same deprivation again, although a man does not know what he can endure until he tries it."

As they moved from woodland to swamp, Mother Nature threw additional terrors and torments at the two desperate fugitives. First, there were the omnipresent, bloodthirsty mosquitoes, which swarmed over the wide patches of skin left bare by their torn clothing. Wilson and Wood covered themselves with mud and "great skeins of moss" from the marshy banks, worsening their already grimy appearance—though amazingly, the moss seemed effective in fending off the skeeters and protecting them from the sun. They also saw large numbers of moccasin snakes, coiled on the banks or swimming in the brown river. But their greatest terror was the alligators, a strange and fearsome species Wilson would remember as a "ferocious, hungry, dangerous looking beast." They would wake from a daytime nap only to find every hammock and log around them covered with gators, watching them "listlessly and lazily, with eyes almost shut, looking hungrily and quizzically out of one corner of their wicked peepers." The superstitious Englishman Wood worried that these creatures posed not only a great physical danger, but were also a bad omen—like the sharks he had heard in seafaring legend would follow in the wake of a doomed ship.

Their prospects improved considerably when, while out scrounging for food, Wilson found some lines and fishhooks in a vacant cabin near the river. They soon enjoyed a dinner of raw catfish, which seemed at the time a great improvement over raw corn. What was more, the widening river and other signs indicated that they were nearing the gulf. Inquiring at a nearby cabin, Alf learned that they were just five miles from Apalachicola and that the Federal blockading squadron held the bay beyond the town. Meanwhile, Wood had collected an armload of sweet potatoes. Stopping in a cane-brake, the two men cooked up their first decent meal in weeks. "Here we secreted ourselves and built a little fire, roasted fish and potatoes, parched corn, and dined in right royal style, although we felt the need of a little salt," Wilson remembered.

After another night's travel, they awoke to find themselves on a sandy shore lined with orange, lemon, and palm trees. Knowing nothing of the rising and falling of tidewater, Wilson was dumbfounded to see their boat high and dry, two hundred yards from the edge of the water where they had left it. After an hour of sweating and tugging to drag their little craft back to the water's edge, the two men paddled out toward an island with a smattering of dead trees, at one point stopping alongside a bar, where Wood reached down and appeared to crack open a muddy stone and eat from it. Wilson thought his hungry comrade had finally lost his mind completely. "Taste this," Wood said to his land-lubbing friend Alf, who lapped up from the shell the sweet, plump flesh of an oyster. "I think I never tasted anything so delicious," he later said.

Their feast on raw oysters was cut short, however, as slow realization dawned that the dead trees they had seen were not trees at all, but instead were the spindly masts of a number of ships anchored in the sound just beyond the island. They rowed back out into the bay at a lively rate, and Wilson would later describe their approach to the flotilla:

> We were now nearing the ships very fast, and were a little anxious to see their colors, as we had become so suspicious of everybody and everything that we half feared running into the clutches of our enemies. But we were not long in suspense, for suddenly a little breeze sprang up, and I shall never, no, never, forget my joy on seeing the old flag, the glorious old stars and stripes, as they unfolded to the ocean breeze and seemed to extend their beneficient protection over us, after nearly eight months of terrible bondage. We could see the field of blue, studded with golden stars, and the stripes of white and red! Yes, it was our flag, old *E Pluribus Unum!*
>
> We threw down our paddles in the boat and stood up and yelled and screamed and cried like a couple of foolish boys lost in the woods. We could not restrain ourselves.

They manned their paddles with newfound strength and steered a course for the nearest of the three ships visible. As they drew closer, they could see the portholes, the muzzles of the cannons, officers and men crowded near the deck-rail in clean, blue uniforms.

The ship was the U.S.S. *Somerset*, a 521-ton side-wheel steamer, with 110 souls and six guns aboard. The converted ferryboat was one of dozens of ships belonging to the U.S. Navy's East Gulf Blockading Squadron, assigned to seal off the Florida coast from Cape Canaveral all the way around to Pensacola. Her skipper was Lieutenant Commander Alexander F. Crosman, a St. Louis-born, Pennsylvania-raised graduate of the U.S. Naval Academy, who though only twenty-four years old somehow managed not only the demeanor but also the appearance of a crusty old sea-dog. Crosman regarded his present orders—guarding St. George's Sound and Apalachicola Bay—as particularly important to the Union cause. Not only was it necessary to choke off river access up to Columbus, which he described as "one of the grand depots and sources of strength of the Confederacy," but also the city of Apalachicola itself was in his eyes "an important strategic point, inasmuch as its possession insures a base for any operations upon the interior of Georgia and Alabama."[22]

Now here were Wilson and Wood, paddling up like a pair of forlorn Crusoes, castaways from a faraway and very landlocked Atlanta jail, as if to

give dramatic proof to Crosman's point about the accessibility of the interi-
or of Georgia. "Come to, there!" Crosman barked. "Who in hell are you, and
what are you paddling under my guns in this manner for?" Wilson, taken
aback by this angry interrogation, stood and meekly replied that they were
two men trying to get back to God's country, among friends. It was only then
that he again became conscious of his strange appearance. "We had been so
overjoyed and excited, that we had forgotten to pull off the old moss, which
covered our nakedness and protected us from the sun, from our backs, and
we must have looked like scare-crows or swamp-dragons." Crosman demanded additional explanation, whereupon Wilson told him that he and Wood
were enlisted Federal soldiers from the command of General O.M. Mitchel
in Tennessee.

"You're a damned long ways from camp," Crosman growled, an accurate
observation indeed. They had traveled more than 400 miles from Atlanta,
most of that distance on the winding river, and they were more than 600
miles from the present encampment of the Third Division.

Wilson explained that they were fugitives from a Confederate prison, that
they were famished, and that they had traveled through mountains and forest and then down the river to seek protection under the Old Flag. At this,
the young/old sea-dog seemed to soften and reached out a hand to help the
two men up the ladder and over the rail himself. The sailors aboard were horrified at the appearance of the two castaways, and their commander's sympathy for them soon gave way to sulfurous anger at the damned Confederates
who would do such a thing to good Union men. "He raved and swore as he
paced up and down, and stamped the deck until the air seemed fairly blue
with brimstone," Wilson recalled. "I think if he could have gotten hold of
old Jefferson Davis, or some other first-class rebel, about that time, he would
have hung him, and then tried him afterwards."

Wilson and Wood were taken to Crosman's cabin, where they were first
fortified with a few swallows of brandy before being sent aft for their first
wash with soap in more than seven months. They were, Wilson said, shown
the utmost kindness, their wounds and sores treated and dressed. They were
given sailor's clothes and then returned to the commander's quarters for dinner. As they ate, Crosman told them they were welcome to stay and recuper-
ate as long as they wanted, but both soldiers expressed a desire to get back to
some part of the Federal lines where they could report and hopefully do
something to save their imprisoned comrades in Atlanta. Arrangements were
made for the men to be transferred to a nearby cruiser bound for the

blockading squadron's base at Key West, Florida. As they prepared to depart, Crosman handed them letters of introduction he had written to the commandant at Key West, along with a generous supply of his best tobacco. He saw them off with a hearty farewell handshake and wishes for a safe voyage and better fortune in the future.

Wilson and Wood climbed down into a boat to be rowed across to the steamer anchored nearby. They took note of her name stenciled on the dark wood of her hull: *Stars and Stripes*. A short time later, the ship weighed anchor and was underway for the four-day journey to Key West.

Alf Wilson climbed up to the upper deck and stood alone at the rail. He was clean, well-fed, wearing fresh clothes, and most of all, safe from any danger. His mind was filled with gratitude and amazement at the change in his present condition and his future prospects. Tears welled up in the young Ohio soldier's eyes as, for the first time in his life, he gazed out on the ocean.

Part IV

Valor

The War Department. (*Chicago Historical Society*)

CHAPTER FIFTEEN

The Medal of Honor

The War Department and the White House

> The expedition itself, in the daring of its conception, had the wildness
> of a romance, while in the gigantic and overwhelming results which it
> sought, and was likely to accomplish, it was absolutely sublime.
> —Joseph Holt, Judge Advocate General, U.S. Army
> Report to Hon. Edwin M. Stanton, Secretary of War
> March 27, 1863

THE UNITED STATES OF AMERICA HAD no military medals at the outset of
the Civil War. Some eighty years before, the young nation's
Revolutionary leaders, hoping to shore up morale as the struggle for independence ground to a close and unreliable funding left many soldiers unpaid,
had sown the seeds of such awards, but none of these early efforts had taken
root. In 1782, General George Washington issued from his headquarters at
Newburgh, New York, a field order establishing a decoration known as the
Badge of Military Merit to recognize those members of the Continental
Army who performed "any singular meritorious action." The author of such
an action, Washington's order said, "shall be permitted to wear on his facings,
over his left breast, the figure of a heart in purple cloth or silk edged with
narrow lace or binding." Only three of these citations are known to have ever
been awarded, however, and the badge quickly fell into disuse. In 1932, this
oldest of American decorations would be revived by the War Department
and reconstituted as the Purple Heart, honoring the sacrifice of soldiers and
sailors who literally shed blood in service of their country. But in the mid-
nineteenth century—with the exception of a "Certificate of Merit" briefly

awarded during the Mexican War—the United States military had no means for recognizing gallantry or valor by the soldiers in its ranks.

Perhaps there was little perceived need for such an award in those days, as the scattered, undersized and largely unappreciated U.S. Army manned far-flung forts and outposts and skirmished now and then with Indian tribes. The epic scale and the high stakes of the Civil War would change the reputation of the American military and engender newfound esteem and national affection for the men who marched in its ranks. In the weeks and months after Fort Sumter, not only the nation's professional soldiers, but men and boys from all walks of life—farmers and millworkers, lawyers and university professors, shopkeepers and longshoremen, neighbors and family members—would be fighting for the Union, carrying with them the hopes and pride of their communities. What was more, many of these volunteers would prove themselves to be not only local but actual heroes, committing acts of bravery and self-sacrifice on battlefields across the land.

The idea for creating a medal to recognize and reward the extraordinary courage often demonstrated by American soldiers originated with forty-four-year-old Lt. Col. Edward Davis Townsend, Assistant Adjutant General in the War Department. Born to a prominent Boston family, Townsend was a graduate of Harvard and West Point and a brave and brilliant man in his own right. He had served in the army since his graduation from the Academy at the age of twenty and was a third-generation American soldier—his grandfather was an army surgeon during the Revolution, and his father lost a leg at the Battle of Crysler's Farm in the War of 1812. He had risen through the ranks steadily but slowly over the course of his twenty-four-year army career, and after Fort Sumter was posted in Washington as chief of staff to the legendary general-in-chief of the army, Lieutenant General Winfield Scott. His interests and his talents extended far beyond the realm of military administration, however, and he spent his spare hours as a respected Biblical scholar, publishing catechisms on the Pentateuch and the Old Testament books of Judges and Kings. Though he did most of his soldiering behind a desk, Townsend's energy and imagination would leave an enduring mark on the nation's history: not only was he instrumental in creating the Medal of Honor, but would also help to establish a permanent and soon-to-be-famous military prison at Fort Leavenworth, Kansas.[1]

In the fall of 1861, as the early months of the war passed by without a substantial victory or even a meaningful advance by Union forces, Townsend (like many other rear-echelon planners in Washington) found himself searching for methods great and small to inspire the troops and the nation. As he walked along the wooden sidewalks near the War Department and Willard's Hotel, he was struck by the gaudy, proliferate ribbons and medals worn by European soldiers-of-fortune and foreign military delegates to the city. He also noted the awe and respect that the decorations seemed to engender among those who saw them. Military medals were a well-established tradition in Europe by that time—Napoleon established the Légion d'honneur, a chivalric order, in 1802; King Friedrich Wilhelm III of Prussia introduced the Iron Cross in 1813; and Britain began awarding the Victoria Cross in 1856, honoring redcoat heroes from the Thin Red Line in the Crimean War. As a student of military history, Townsend was well aware of these decorations, and it troubled him that the United States had nothing even remotely comparable. Commissioned officers in the Union army who demonstrated particular merit could be rewarded by brevet promotions—an honorary increase in rank with no commensurate adjustment in pay—and if these brevets were often tainted by politics, conniving and favoritism, they were nonetheless desired and respected in the officer corps. Yet no similar reward, however imperfect, was available to the vast numbers of enlisted men then fighting for flag and country.

Townsend believed that a new battlefield decoration, one that could be awarded to soldiers of all ranks and would become widely known and highly regarded, would serve to encourage the common soldiers of the army and inspire them to great and gallant conduct. Accordingly, he penned a memorandum in the fall of 1861 suggesting that the United States Army follow the example of the nations of Europe and establish a medal for valor. General Scott firmly rejected the suggestion, condemning not only the specific proposal but the general concept of such an award as being "contrary to the spirit of American institutions." The United States was a republic, after all, decidedly and deliberately lacking in aristocracy and blueblood orders, knighthoods, and the like. Scott not only believed that the idea smacked of Old World vanity, elitism, and snobbery, he also thought that such an award was entirely unnecessary—surely volunteer soldiers fighting for the Union could be counted on to do their duty without such incentives. (In General Scott's defense, Queen Victoria had much the same reaction with regard to the cross that bore her name. The medal had originally been inscribed "For Bravery," but the queen thought that implied that only recipients of the Victoria Cross were brave. She had the legend changed to read "For Valour.")

There was some irony and no little hypocrisy in General Scott's position. The elderly commander was famously known as "Old Fuss and Feathers," fond of all manner of affected glory and military foppery. Antebellum photographs of the great general show his stern visage scowling above a huge neck and shoulders adorned with epaulettes and tassels and a massive chest fairly rampaging with buttons, medals, ribbons, tassels, and gold embroidery. The seventy-five-year-old Scott was well past his prime and soon to be supplanted as general-in-chief, and due to his departure in the first act of the unfolding drama, his role in the Civil War is often minimized today. But at the time, he was an American icon—a great hero of a fifty-year career that spanned the War of 1812, the Black Hawk War, the Second Seminole War, the Mexican War, and the Civil War—so much so that the astounded interjection "Great Scott!" appears to have been inspired by the legendary general. He had served every president from Thomas Jefferson to Abraham Lincoln, and his views were given considerable weight at the time. There would be no medal of honor so long as General Scott had anything to say about it.

Soon, however, two events would clear the way for the creation of what would come to be the Army Medal of Honor. First was Scott's retirement in October 1861, and second was the United States Navy's adoption of its own Medal of Honor in December. General Scott may have had his entrenched ideas about the broad social implications of military decorations, but Secretary of the Navy Gideon Welles held no such qualms. What was more, Welles was continually in search of ways to encourage young men to sign on or reenlist for the hard, solitary, and too often short life of a sailor in the U.S. Navy. Having heard of Townsend's proposal, either from seeing his memorandum or through hallway conversations at the White House or the Navy Department, he adopted the idea of establishing a decoration to recognize and honor distinguished service in the seafaring ranks. On December 21, 1861, President Lincoln signed into law an otherwise unremarkable bill to promote the efficiency of the Navy, which included within it a provision for a Navy Medal of Valor, "to be bestowed upon such petty officers, seamen, landsmen, and Marines as shall most distinguish themselves by their gallantry and other seamanlike qualities during the present war." Not to be left behind, and freed of the formidable obstacle of General Scott, the Army soon followed suit. In July 1862, Lincoln signed a bill creating the Army Medal of Honor, which would similarly be awarded "to such noncommissioned officers and privates as shall most distinguish themselves by their gallantry in action, and other soldier-like qualities, during the present insurrection." In early 1863, Congress amended the original legislation in a number of respects: first, it dropped the limitation to "the present insurrection," making the Medal of Honor a permanent decoration that could be awarded beyond the

Civil War; second, it clarified that the medal could be awarded retroactively, for acts dating back to the start of the war; and third, it broadened eligibility to include commissioned officers as potential recipients as well.[2]

The medal was originally designed by Christian Schussel and its prototype created by assistant engraver Anthony C. Paquet at the United States Mint in Philadelphia. "The medal of honor is bronze, of neat device, and is highly prized by those on whom it has been bestowed," Townsend wrote in an 1864 report. Its original design, embodied first in the Navy Medal, was an inverted, five-pointed star—each point containing leaves of oak (representing strength) and laurel (representing achievement)—faced with a circle of thirty-four stars, one for each of the United States. Within the circle is the figure of Minerva, the Roman goddess of civic strength and wisdom, her left hand holding an axe bound with fasces and her right holding a shield emblazoned with the arms of the United States. The goddess stands triumphant, firmly repulsing a cowering, serpent-entwined figure representing Discord, or as one Unionist said, "the foul spirit of Secession and Rebellion." The Navy medal was suspended from a flag-like ribbon with a field of blue above and thirteen red and white stripes below, with an anchor at the lower clasp. The Army medal would have a similar ribbon and pendant, but substituted an eagle and crossed cannons for the Navy's anchor.

Notwithstanding the provision in the legislation that allowed the medal to be bestowed retroactively, and despite the bloody struggles and acts of personal gallantry on dozens of fields from Manassas to Shiloh to Antietam to Stones River, as of March 1863, the War Department had not awarded a single Medal of Honor. Congress had passed legislation appropriating funds for the medals, to be purchased from the manufacturer William Wilson and Sons of Philadelphia at a cost of two dollars each. The Navy Department initially ordered just two hundred medals. The Army, apparently having a different view of how lavishly the decoration was to be awarded, ordered two thousand.

Shortly thereafter, the War Department had received its first shipment of medals, stacked in silk-lined wooden cases in the office of Secretary of War Edwin M. Stanton. The Secretary had his medals—now all he needed was a soldier or soldiers worthy of the award.

*B*ack in Atlanta, the Andrews Raiders, once twenty-four in number as they met under the gathering storm outside Shelbyville, had been reduced to a mere half-dozen by their comrades' successive departures to the gallows and then to the woods. The eight escapees all returned promptly to active duty—Brown, Knight, Porter, Wilson, and Wood to the 21st Ohio Regiment and Dorsey, Hawkins, and Wollam to the 33rd, which was then recovering from hard knocks suffered at the Battle of Perryville. Both Buckeye regiments would in the months to come be exposed to vicious fighting on fields from Murfreesboro to Missionary Ridge to Chickamauga. "Our old comrades received us almost as two who had come to them from the dead," Alf Wilson remembered. Considering their lengthy confinement in Southern prisons and their respective treks to freedom, the returned soldiers showed remarkable resiliency in their eagerness to return to their companies and share the hardship of the winter and early spring campaigns. "After a few days rest, I was again ready for duty," Porter said simply.[3]

The six Yankee soldiers left behind in the Fulton County Jail—William Bensinger, Robert Buffum, Elihu Mason, Jacob Parrott, William Pittenger, and William Reddick—spent the days just after the jailbreak in fearful apprehension of being tried and executed themselves, or at least of suffering retaliatory treatment and new humiliations in the name of tightened security. On the contrary, however, after the provost marshal Colonel Lee's initial irritation at the escape wore off, they enjoyed what one described as "the mildest and most humane treatment we received during our whole sojourn in the Confederacy." Colonel Lee, understandably disappointed in the lackadaisical security provided by the civilian county jail, had the prisoners moved to a Rebel barracks two blocks from the depot, where they would be kept under constant watch by a company of gray soldiers. Along with a handful of prisoners of war and ten of the East Tennesseans, they were placed in a large upstairs room with tall windows, an open fireplace, and a gas burner that was kept lighted all night. Their diet also improved considerably—meals of bread and meat, sometimes served at a rude wooden table in an adjacent common mess room. The food was still doled out in modest quantities, to be sure, but was supplemented with soup and an occasional treat: sweet potatoes, which the inmates roasted in the ashes of the open fire. They were also granted the luxury of a daily opportunity to wash themselves, which improved not only the appearance and the odor but also the morale of the entire party. After suffering through the pit in Chattanooga, the iron cages and hard confinement of the county jail, and the ever-present specter of the gallows, the prisoners found these new quarters to be "a blessed relief—a place where we could rest for a little time from the storms that had swept over us."[4]

The raiders' previous interest in religious matters admittedly waned as comforts increased and peril receded. Rev. McDonnell made no more visits to the jail, and the soldiers' hymns and religious services became more infrequent. "A few of our number seemed to think that now that we were not in a dark cell, and were treated more as regular prisoners, there was no need of so much prayer," Pittenger observed. "But the majority clung to the good resolutions made in dark hours."[5]

The burden of Pittenger's own confinement was further lightened when the commander of the barracks, Major Jack Wells, spotted him making shorthand notes in the margin of a book. "What kind of crow-tracks are you making there?" the officer asked as he stood peering over Pittenger's shoulder. The young corporal replied that he was only writing to pass the time, and he did his best to explain the method behind his seemingly mad penmanship. Suitably impressed by this, Wells soon had him working in his office as a clerk, filling out requisitions and writing daily reports. Pittenger felt that no harm could come to the United States by his assisting a Southern officer in such menial tasks, and he drew a careful though illusory distinction between working for Major Wells as requested and working for the benefit of the Confederacy, which he steadfastly refused to do. He also justified his new "trusty" position as a means to observe the workings of the Rebel post and gather intelligence for his comrades.[6]

Apart from that, there is little to tell of the remaining weeks the remnant of Andrews's party spent languishing in Atlanta. The excitement and danger of the summer and early fall gave way to a dull, repetitive daily haze of claustrophobia and mind-numbing *ennui*. Raiders who would later fill volumes recording their adventures on the raid and the ordeal of the first months spent in the Chattanooga and Atlanta jails would make little comment on and describe but few anecdotes as the year 1862 neared its end. "Few things occurred worthy of note," Pittenger wrote, adding: "The same monotony which makes prison life so dreadful robs it of interest when recorded."[7]

All this would change at the beginning of December. Without warning, a delegation of Confederate officers arrived at the barracks, called the prisoners into line "with great manifestations of friendliness," and announced: "You have all been exchanged, and all that now remains is for us to send you out of our territory." It was not quite as simple as that, as the raiders would learn—they would first be sent to Richmond for further processing before the final exchange. Major Wells directed his clerk Pittenger to write out a requisition for rations for them to take along on their trip northward, but the Ohio corporal's hands were shaking so badly that he had to pass the task along to someone else. They were to depart that same evening, and they spent the afternoon preparing for the trip (though they found they had little to pack). The order that would enable and accompany their transfer enclosed a list of the six raiders plus fourteen other prisoners slated for eventual exchange and warned the brigadier general commanding in Richmond that the transferred prisoners "have been confined here some time and are many of them a desperate, bad set of men." They were marched to the depot in the sharp chill of the December evening, accompanied by Major Wells—who was "drunker than usual," Pittenger recalled—and the ten-man escort that would see them to Virginia. Wells "hiccoughed an affectionate farewell" and the prisoners took their last look at Atlanta—though some among them would return to the city two years later in the company of General Sherman.[8]

Prisoner exchanges in the Civil War were intermittent, inconsistent, and often arbitrary. At the start of the war, the United States had refused to consider a system of exchange at all, fearing that such formal arrangements with the enemy would lend an air of legitimacy or even sovereignty to the newly established Confederate government. This prohibition of exchanges was soon to be honored more in the breach than the observance, however, as front-line commanders, both blue and gray, negotiated unofficial exchanges on the battlefield due to practical necessity or the "dictates of humanity." What was more, by late 1861 the unkind fortunes of war and the reality of the relative numbers of captured men weighed heavily on Washington to establish an exchange, as the jails and camps of the undersized Confederacy held far more Federal prisoners than the Union held Rebels. After months of negotiations, limited exchanges, and official reluctance, a cartel was finally reached in July 1862. The months that followed were plagued with problems on both sides and accusations of dishonesty, unfair treatment, and fraud. Still, thousands of prisoners were exchanged under the cartel, facilitated by an agreed-upon system of military mathematics that held all men far from equal—one brigadier general, for example, could be exchanged for twenty privates.

The precarious system of exchange was threatened again in the fall. Jefferson Davis retaliated against Lincoln's preliminary Emancipation Proclamation by issuing a proclamation of his own: any white Union officer captured while leading black soldiers in battle would be charged with leading a slave insurrection and would be subject to the penalty of death. Union Secretary of War Stanton responded by immediately suspending the exchange of all commissioned officers—though to the ultimate good fortune of the surviving Andrews Raiders, the exchange of enlisted men under the cartel would continue through the spring of 1863.[9]

The six raiders arrived in Richmond after a frigid, halting three-day box-car trip by way of Dalton, Cleveland, Knoxville, and Lynchburg. "Richmond is a beautiful city, but we saw little of its attractions on this first visit," Pittenger wrote. They were marched from the station and first taken to Libby Prison, a three-story brick warehouse confiscated from and named for its former owner, Luther Libby. This initial billet was, the raiders thought, an encouraging sign: they had heard that Libby Prison was the place where prisoners were taken on their way to City Point, where exchanges were completed. They took further comfort in their fellow inmates at Libby, which included a large number of prisoners of war—for the first time in months, the raiders saw men in dark blue United States uniforms. Their hopes were dashed again next morning, however, when they were called out of line and marched down the street to more fearsome and seemingly more permanent quarters: Castle Thunder, "the Bastille of the South," Richmond's most notorious wartime prison.

Castle Thunder was a three-building complex anchored by the former Gleanor Tobacco Factory, a large brick building at the corner of Cary and 18th Streets that had been opened and christened the previous summer. The *Richmond Daily Enquirer* had pronounced the new prison's name "as good as any other than could be chosen," believing it appropriately "indicative of Olympian vengeance upon offenders against her laws." The brutality of the prison was none too mythical, with widespread cruelty practiced both upon and among the prison's 1,400 inmates—a criminal menagerie that included "every kind of offender," as one Virginia historian noted, "with little segregation between a soldier and a sociopath." The commandant of the prison was Georgia-born Captain George W. Alexander, a thirty-two-year-old hard case who had been captured by Federal authorities in Maryland and sentenced to death for treason, whereupon he escaped from Fort McHenry and made his way to Richmond. He had been given command of Castle Thunder in November, and he ruled his grim domain like a dastardly storybook villain. Dressed in black from head to boots, he clattered about prison grounds and city streets on a great black horse, his long black beard flowing behind him. His constant companion was the prison's most famous and most feared guard: a vicious Bavarian boar hound named Nero. The dog was legendary—it was said that he had fought three battles with full-grown wild bears and won each time, and that he was trained to attack anyone wearing blue. As a jailer, Alexander was a far cry from the cruel, drunken bumbler Swims in Chattanooga and the well-meaning but inept warden Turner in

Atlanta. He imposed rigorous, heartless security, his sentries always watchful for a chance to shoot any inmate who moved too close to one of the building's windows. The Richmond papers praised Alexander for the "faultless" system he employed at the prison; everything was in "apple-pie order," the *Enquirer* said, its editors fond of referring to new inmates at the jail as being "Thunder Struck." The *Richmond Whig* noted in December: "A man who once gets in there has little disposition to try it a second time; for, however much care may be bestowed upon its management; no human effort could make a Paradise of such a place as that."[10]

The raiders, huddling for warmth and wary of their new cellmates, found Castle Thunder far from a paradise, indeed. Gaslights were used for illumination and water was generally available, but the rooms were frigid, the floors filthy, the latrines open and putrid, and the enclosed yard used not for exercise but for executions by firing squad. "In this cheerless place our party, six in number, and the nine remaining Tennesseans—fifteen in all—were confined during the months of December and January," Pittenger recorded. "We did not suffer from crowding or lack of air as in the Swims dungeon; but other evils endured, especially cold and hunger—were scarcely less tormenting than the inflictions of that vilest of all dens."

In early February, the raiders were moved from their initial cell into a large upper floor with the general population, one so spacious that for a time it seemed like freedom by comparison. What was more, the great room had a stove, and the constant torture of cold could now be held at bay. They spent another six weeks in this confinement, their only pleasures being a daily opportunity to read the Richmond newspapers, followed in the evening by a gathering around the stove of a gang of unpredictable ruffians by day who turned to enthralling storytellers after dark. "I would sometimes join them, and listen for a great part of the night to some of the finest fairy tales and most romantic legends it has ever been my fortune to hear," Pittenger remembered. In these last weeks of imprisonment, the six raiders survived an outbreak of smallpox, continued deprivation and despondency, hours of menial labor (devised more for pain and demoralization than for any actual result), as well as nightly robberies and fistfights among their less reputable peers.[11]

Finally, on March 17, 1863, as the many Irish-born prisoners at Castle Thunder marked St. Patrick's Day, an officer abruptly entered and barked an unusual order: "All who want to go to the United States, fall into line, and come into the office." (It occurred to some of the raiders that, in their view, they were already in the United States, but now was certainly not the time to raise such trifling political distinctions.) "There was a rush and a scramble to the middle of the floor, and no line was ever formed more promptly," Pittenger recalled. Names were taken, lists checked and rechecked, individual paroles signed, and arrangements made for the prisoners' departure the next morning. After a night of fitful sleep and fearful suspense, the Andrews Raiders, along with more than 300 other prisoners, were marched from the yard of Castle Thunder and taken by train to City Point for exchange. The *Richmond Dispatch* made note of their departure. Included in the group of exchanged prisoners, the paper reported, were "a number of renegades from Tennessee and Kentucky, some of whom were arrested for bridge-burning, engine-stealing, and similar crimes in the states named. The departure of these prisoners will relieve the Confederate Government of a considerable item of expense." The bulk of the exchanged prisoners were taken to Annapolis, Maryland, to complete processing for their parole and release, but the raiders convinced the Federal authorities that they had been detailed on a special mission, that lives were still in danger, and that they must proceed directly to Washington to report to the War Department.[12]

The liberated Yankees arrived in Washington on Thursday, March 19, where they were given shelter and, much to their chagrin, were initially placed under guard. William Reddick suggested that "as we looked like poor people from the country, they had only employed these guards to protect us from city sharpers!" They were given ample blankets for the night, and were fed generous quantities of soft bread, boiled beef, and strong, hot coffee. The raiders' East Tennessee companion Peter "Gun Barrel" Pierce, who had taken particular offense at the presence of the guards, grumbled appreciatively, "Well, if Uncle Sam does shut a fellow up, he feeds well, which is more than Jeff. does." An influential friend, the Honorable J.C. Wetmore of the Ohio Military Agency, intervened to procure a small allowance of funds for the soldiers and obtain lodging with a wealthy and patriotic woman named Mrs. Fales. Restrictions on their movements were soon lifted, and they spent the next few days in leisure and comfort, eating, resting, attending church services, and walking the muddy streets of the young capital city.

On one of these perambulations, the raiders visited the Smithsonian Museum, where they noticed a tall, striking bearded gentleman near the prehistoric skeletons who exchanged words with them "in a kind, sad way." Pittenger insisted that the man was none other than Abraham Lincoln. Buffum and the others disagreed. "We'll go and see him at the White House soon," Pittenger replied, "and then you can judge."[13]

*I*n the meantime, the raiders still had some official business to take care of during their visit to the capital. Upon hearing of their arrival in Washington, Secretary of War Edwin M. Stanton directed the Judge Advocate General of the Army, Joseph M. Holt, to investigate this curious matter of the failed railroad raid in Georgia and prepare a comprehensive report. After a fairly informal initial meeting with Judge Holt, Bensinger, Buffum, Parrott, Pittenger, and Reddick returned the next day and found a justice of the peace there to swear them in and a phonographer prepared to take down their testimony. (Mason, perhaps suffering a recurrence of whatever ailment had struck him back in October, had fallen ill and was unable to give a deposition—thus leaving no firsthand account whatsoever of his participation in and impressions of the raid.) After being sworn, each man gave a deposition summarizing the raid—though unfortunately for historians seeking different points of view, Pittenger went first and the others merely confirmed much of what he had said, adding only a few brief anecdotes of their own. The exception was Jacob Parrott, who described in detail his lashing at the hands of his Confederate captors.

Judge Holt was well impressed by the six soldiers and their story, and his report reflected both his admiration and his conclusion that the failure of the mission had been unavoidable. "The expedition thus failed from causes which reflected neither upon the genius by which it was planned, nor upon the intrepidity and discretion of those who had engaged in conducting it," he concluded. "But for the accident of meeting the extra trains, which could not have been anticipated, the movement would have been a complete success, and the whole aspect of the war in the South and Southwest would have been at once changed." Holt also praised Jacob Parrott for his firm refusal to betray his country or his comrades despite the "horrible flogging" he endured. "His subdued and modest manner, while narrating the part he had borne in the expedition, showed him to be wholly unconscious of having done anything more than perform his simple duty as a soldier. Such Spartan fortitude, and such fidelity to the trusts of friendship and to the inspirations of patriotism, deserve an enduring record in the archives of the Government, and will find it, I am sure, in the hearts of a loyal people."[14]

Parrott's bravery was also noted in an unofficial visit to the Union League Club, where four of the raiders appeared at a meeting of the pro-Republican organization on the evening March 23. A reporter present at the occasion pronounced the raiders' description of their adventure "very interesting," though he misstated the end, the means, the route, and even the direction of the raid—an effort to run a train *down* the Nashville & Chattanooga Railroad into Georgia, he incorrectly wrote, becoming one of the first of many to misreport the circumstances of the Andrews Raid. Yet here, too, the young private was singled out for a special word of admiration. "One of them, Parrott, bears on his back the scars of one hundred lashes, inflected by these scions of chivalry, and his denunciations of those in the North who are apologists and friends of a system and a cause which has such a savage and brutal spirit as he saw in Secessia were truly forcible and eloquent," the reporter wrote.[15]

Two days later, having completed their testimony before the judge advocate and with Mason now on the mend, the six raiders reported to the War Department for an audience with the Secretary of War. The headquarters of the War Department stood at the corner of 17th Street and Pennsylvania Avenue just west of the White House. A department clerk described the grim, unimpressive edifice as "a dingy, old-fashioned brick building, with dimensions and interior finish reflecting the severe and economical tastes of Federal officials half a century or more ago." Originally built as a two-story structure, a third floor had been hastily added in the early days of the war, its flues and chimneys so poorly constructed that "incessant care was necessary to prevent the department from being burned out." From the halls of this rickety building, described by the same clerk as "a hive of industry day and night," the War Department directed the operations of the Union armies and navies. In a rear corner of the second story, its windows facing the Executive Mansion next door, was the office of the Secretary of War.[16]

Abraham Lincoln sometimes referred to his Secretary of War Edwin McMasters Stanton as "Old Mars," and if his powers were something less than godlike, he was without question the second most powerful man in the Union. Stanton had served on Lincoln's cabinet for more than a year now, having succeeded the ineffectual and corrupt (or at least corruptible) Simon Cameron in January 1862. Like most of the Andrews Raiders, Stanton was a native Ohioan, hailing from the same hometown as William Pittenger and Perry Shadrach—the Ohio valley hamlet of Steubenville. Balding and nearsighted, with tiny oval spectacles and a broad black beard riven by a streak of silver-gray, Stanton was soft and thick in form, but hard-edged and hard-driving in philosophy and in presentation. A reporter meeting with him shortly after his appointment had been impressed with his energy, noting that "Force—undaunted Force—Stanton's indisputable characteristic—streamed from the eye, hair, whiskers, and very garments of the new Secretary of War." This native fierceness was the product of his successful prewar career as a prosecutor and corporate lawyer; or perhaps it was the successful career that had resulted from the ferocity. Described by the *Atlantic Monthly* as a man of "intense patriotism, sleepless vigilance, and tireless activity," Stanton's seriousness and drive often manifested itself as rudeness, disdain, or even anger to whatever unfortunate subordinate, colleague, or visitor might find himself in the Secretary's field of fire.

Notwithstanding his tendency to render harsh judgments and his unwillingness to suffer fools, Stanton nonetheless was accessible not only to the army and its commanders but to the public, devoting at least an hour each morning to general business, come what may, in an effort to keep his later hours free from interruption. A great mass of visitors regularly took advantage of this opportunity to speak directly with Stanton each day, all of whom he disposed of quickly and decisively—and sometimes harshly. "Contractors, claimants, sick, wounded, cranks, chaplains, crooks, kickers, spies, politicians, constitution-savers, office-seekers, Cyprians after passes, sorrowing widows, broken-hearted fathers, convicts, deserters, dismissed or suspended officers—everybody came cocked and primed for a bout with the Secretary— and got it," an early biographer wrote. Charles F. Benjamin, a War Department subordinate who witnessed a number of these public audiences, described the Secretary at work: "The glittering of the eyes through the polished glasses; the breadth and quivering of the nostrils; the projecting, compressed lips; the icy, deliberate voice; the slow movement of the body, and the steady, seemingly defiant gaze, gave to the Secretary an air of reserve and haughtiness which made the first approach to him embarrassing," Benjamin wrote. "Nothing was more common or more amusing than to see some pompous or arrogant personage ushered into his presence, only to emerge from the room in a state of collapse, crushed by the manner rather than by the words of the lion at bay within."[17]

The Andrews Raiders could certainly expect a more kindly reception from the Secretary than many of the others who would call on him at the War Office on that early spring day. This was because of their status as heroes, of course, but also because of the boldness and initiative they had displayed. Above all, Secretary Stanton valued action. He had spent much of his time over the past fifteen months dealing with a stagnant army led by recalcitrant generals who seemed far more adept at making excuses than making war. With the background of this experience, he was certainly predisposed to admire and applaud daring efforts like the one undertaken by the Andrews Raiders the previous April. Indeed, his appreciation of their exploit may well have been magnified by looking back at his own struggles at the time. In the spring of 1862, he had spent months arguing with and prodding the then-general-in-chief George McClellan to move his army forward against the main Confederate army near Richmond. At the time, he had famously said of McClellan and his idle force of 100,000 men, "This army has got to fight or run away. And while we are striving nobly in the West, the champagne and oysters on the Potomac must be stopped." Meanwhile, in pleasant contrast, he had watched with approval as Ormsby Mitchel drove his men southward toward and into Alabama. Now here to see him were six soldiers from Mitchel's own Third Division, all of whom had not only "strived nobly" but had volunteered for a dauntless behind-enemy-lines strike at the heart of the Confederate war machine, and had heroically endured great hardships since that time.

The six raiders were ushered through an anteroom and past a number of other waiting callers, including two Union major generals, and into Stanton's office, a sun-soaked room with tall windows and a large, high table heaped with books, maps, letters, and other papers. Stanton rose and skirted the table to greet them, shaking the hand of each man and asking them to sit. His guests would see no sign that day of the rudeness or irascibility he was famous for; instead, the six soldiers enjoyed a "very delightful interview."

"We talked for a considerable time," Pittenger remembered, "not so much on the subject of our expedition—for I took it for granted that, lawyer-like, he had looked over the evidence in the case and made up his mind about it—as upon general topics, such as our impressions of the South and the Union men in it, and of our hope and feeling about the war." Stanton told his visitors that he had been aware of their mission at the time, but had received no accurate reports as to the fate of those involved. He had assumed for some time that all involved had perished in the effort. Upon learning in October that some among the party still survived, he said, he had threatened retaliation if any more men were hanged and had since done all within his power to secure their safe exchange.

"You will find yourselves great heroes when you get home," Stanton told the raiders warmly, adding "many kind words about the high appreciation of our services by the government." Pittenger noted that the offering of these thanks and compliments, "coming from the Secretary of War of a great nation, to private soldiers, was most flattering."

Stanton seemed especially pleased with Jacob Parrott. By far the youngest man present, the former farm boy was comparatively reserved during the interview with the Secretary, humble and, as Pittenger would put it, "of very quiet and simple manners." Stanton offered him a complete education—Pittenger interpreted this to mean an appointment to the United States Military Academy at West Point—but Parrott, still unable to read or write, politely declined. As long as the war lasted, he said, he "did not wish to go to school, but would rather go back and fight the Rebels who had used him so badly." At this, Stanton broke into a broad, approving smile—a fairly infrequent occurrence for the intense cabinet secretary—and told the young private, "If you want a friend at any time, be sure to apply to me."

Stanton then excused himself for a moment and stepped out of the office to retrieve half a dozen of the newly minted Medals of Honor. It is unclear whether he had intended all along to award these decorations to the Andrews Raiders, or whether the thought only occurred to him as he sat and talked with the six men of their adventures. Returning to the office, he presented the first of the medals to Private Jacob Parrott. "Congress has by a recent law ordered medals to be prepared on this model, and your party shall have the first," Stanton said. "They will be the first that have been given to private soldiers in this war." The other five then received their medals: Sergeant Elihu Mason, Corporal William Pittenger, Corporal William Reddick, Private William Bensinger, and Private Robert Buffum. Stanton also gave each man a present of $100—appropriated from the secret service fund, for "pocket money," Pittenger said—and ordered that they be reimbursed for all expenditures and compensated for the value of any arms and property taken from them by the Confederates.

With the medal ceremony, such as it was, now complete, the Secretary inquired of the party about their future plans. All six expressed their desire to return as soon as possible to the ranks of the army. Stanton voiced his approval of this sentiment, but thought that, at a minimum, promotions were in order. He offered each of the raiders a commission as a lieutenant in the regular army. Grateful for the commission, the raiders nonetheless expressed their preference for a comparable appointment in the volunteer service of their home state, as none were career soldiers and all hoped to leave the army and return to peacetime pursuits once the war was over. Stanton promised that he would request of Governor Tod of Ohio equivalent commissions in their own regiments. "We left his presence profoundly convinced that republics are not always ungrateful," Pittenger wrote. Closing the interview, the Secretary bid a hearty goodbye to his six visitors and sent them next door to the White House, where they had been invited to meet with the President of the United States.[18]

Private Jacob Parrott's Medal of Honor, the first ever awarded. (*Colonel James G. Bogle Collection*)

*M*arch 25, 1863, a Wednesday, was a busy day for Abraham Lincoln. As always, he consulted with Stanton and Halleck and anxiously awaited news from the Federal armies, east and west—especially any update on the progress of the determined but painfully slow campaign by General Grant directed toward cracking the Confederates' Mississippi River stronghold at Vicksburg. But the commander-in-chief also devoted attention to other matters, from military to political to mundane. He spent a good part of the day in correspondence: among other things, responding to a request from General William S. Rosecrans that he renominate Brigadier General Robert B. Mitchell for the rank of major general; commuting the death sentence of James S. Pleasants of Montgomery County, Maryland, who had been convicted of feeding and harboring the enemy, and forwarding a donation from a British subject to the United States Christian Commission for the purchase of Bibles. With these and other tasks disposed of in the morning, the crowded waiting room outside his office promised a busy afternoon of conferences with and personal requests from a variety of military and civilian callers. Lincoln was no doubt looking forward to later that evening, when he planned to attend a performance of *Hamlet* starring Edward Loomis Davenport at Grover's Theatre—a rival of nearby Ford's. One among his visitors that afternoon was his friend, the reporter Noah Brooks. Lincoln asked him to "tarry for a while," as a party of Ohio soldiers who had lately been exchanged were coming to see him.

The raiders took their leave from Secretary Stanton and walked the short distance east amid the late March blooms to the White House. There, they ascended to the second floor and passed through a vestibule and waiting room, where they bypassed an impatient throng of callers waiting their turn for an audience, and entered the President's office. As they were ushered in, they were struck by the plain furnishings of the long, rectangular room—scarcely more than a broad oak table stacked with books and papers and an unpretentious smattering of sofas and comfortable chairs. The upholstery and the drapes echoed a sweet whisper of tobacco from pipes and cigars smoked by predecessors or subordinates of the current president. A number of maps were tacked side-by-side along the left-hand wall, directly opposite a portrait of Andrew Jackson that frowned down upon them from over the marble fireplace. They had only an instant to take in this background as the imposing figure of Abraham Lincoln strode forward to receive them "with great warmth of feeling," reported the next day's *Washington Chronicle*, as they entered the room.

William Bensinger, Robert Buffum, Elihu Mason, Jacob Parrott, William Pittenger, and William Reddick were introduced to Lincoln by their escort, Major General Ethan Allan Hitchcock, then serving as the lead commissioner for prisoner of war exchange. "Their names were given to the President, and, without missing the identity of a single man, he shook hands all around with an unaffected cordiality and good-fellowship difficult to describe," the reporter Brooks wrote of the meeting. "He had heard their story in all its details, and as he talked with each, asking questions and making his shrewd comments on all they had to say, it was evident that for the moment this interesting interview was to him of supreme importance." This deep personal engagement with the "common soldier" was customary and heartfelt for President Lincoln, as Brooks also noted. "Mr. Lincoln's manner toward enlisted men, with whom he occasionally met and talked, was always delightful in its bonhomie and its absolute freedom from anything like condescension," he observed.

The raiders found his manner just so, as they engaged in lively and familiar conversation with the chief executive. "I remember telling him that we were very glad to see him, though we had been hearing a great many things not complimentary about him for the past year," Pittenger recalled. "He smiled, saying, 'Indeed, there are a good many people up here that say about as bad things of me.'" All remained standing for the brief visit, the President circulating easily from one man to the next, addressing each with warmth and courtesy. He finally came to rest with an elbow propped against the mantel, his long frame folded like a black umbrella leaning in a stand, his creased face animated as he spoke. "He has a face like a hoosier Michael Angelo," Walt Whitman famously wrote of the president in a letter to a friend just a week before, "so awful ugly it becomes beautiful, with its strange mouth, its deep cut criss-cross lines, and its doughnut complexion." The poet had also spoken approvingly of Lincoln's "idiomatic western genius, careless of court dress or court decorums."

It was this casual frankness and familiarity that came to the fore as the president talked with sergeants, corporals, and privates about their adventures, as well as the military situation and the political winds of the day. "He asked them many questions and treated them with great cordiality," Brooks recorded. Pittenger remembered one of Lincoln's comments in particular, brought about when one among the party expressed satisfaction at the recent promise of Union advances after the setbacks of the year before. "Yes," President Lincoln responded, "if we could only have a little luck with the battles now, all would soon be right and the war be over." The meeting ended shortly thereafter, and Lincoln grasped the hand of each man in both his own as they departed, telling each how thankful he was that their lives had been spared. "We left him, exceedingly proud of the honor the greatest man in the nation (or the world) had conferred upon us," Pittenger wrote.

"The stories of these long-suffering men, and the cheerful lightness with which they narrated their courageous and hazardous deeds, impressed Mr. Lincoln very deeply," Brooks wrote of the meeting. "Speaking of the men afterward, he said, with much feeling, that their bearing, and their apparent unconsciousness of having taken their lives in their hands, with the chances of death all against them, presented an example of the apparent disregard of the tremendous issues of life and death which was so strong a characteristic of the American Soldier."[19]

Although they certainly enjoyed and appreciated the medals and the money and the officers' commissions and the official thanks of their government, the Ohio soldiers were also given a much more welcome gift, practically speaking: a sixty-day furlough and an order for government transportation to their homes. With no further business to bind them to Washington, the six men returned to their quarters and began packing their few belongings and preparing to depart for Ohio. In the meantime, they received a welcome visitor themselves. Some weeks before, hearing word that his son may be alive and in Richmond, William Henry Harrison Reddick's father, George Washington Reddick, had boarded a train for parts east. He arrived in Washington just before the six raiders left for Ohio, and "his surprise and joy in finding his boy free and safe were indescribable"—though it was said that Mr. Reddick hardly recognized his own son due to the lad's pitiful physical condition. He and young Reddick traveled for a time with the others, who were finding joy of their own each day in the small freedoms of life—sleeping in a bed, ordering a restaurant meal, taking a leisurely walk down the street, making a purchase with their own money. "The freshness of liberty had by no means worn off, and each change was a delight in itself, yet the hours that intervened between us and *home* seemed all too long," Pittenger recalled. "Mr. Reddick insisted on buying for the whole party everything we could possibly eat along the way, and in the delight he took in the presence of his son we could see reflected what was in store for the rest of us."[20]

And so the Andrews Raiders boarded another train, this time on the Baltimore & Ohio Railroad, headed west. They had been gone for well more than a year now, their lives in peril for much of that time. They had never fought a battle of any kind, yet they could claim a daring adventure that they would remember for the rest of their lives, one that would remember them to the world long after they were gone. They had endured eleven months of incarceration and depravation in Southern jails in Chattanooga, Knoxville, Atlanta, Madison, and Richmond. They had seen eight comrades and friends marched away to be executed, and had watched and prayed as eight others pulled off a daring escape. They had pleaded with Jefferson Davis to spare their lives, and nine months later accepted the congratulations and thanks of Abraham Lincoln. And they had become the first men in American history to be awarded the Medal of Honor, which would later become the most highly respected and perhaps the most rarely awarded military decoration in the world.

Now, at least for awhile, they were going home.

The eight escaped raiders would get their medals too, though geographic dispersion and bureaucratic snarls would delay the awards for several months. The largest batch of medals was doled out to the five members of the 21st Ohio, thanks to the efforts of their commander, Colonel J.M. Neibling. Within three weeks of the War Department medal ceremony in late March, he forwarded up the chain of command the story of the men in his command and noted the awards, promotions, and furloughs given to their comrades. Along the way, Neibling's report received the endorsements of Major Generals George S. Thomas and William S. Rosecrans before crossing Edward Davis Townsend's desk on its way to Stanton's office. The Secretary of War ordered that the five members be "placed upon the same footing as the other members of their party." Accordingly, in September 1863, Wilson Brown, William Knight, John Reed Porter, Alf Wilson, and Mark Wood were awarded the Medal of Honor, along with Daniel Dorsey and Martin Hawkins of the 33rd. (It appears that no one pointed out to the War Department the embarrassing fact that Hawkins and Porter had overslept and missed the morning train and the ensuing heroics that day.) For some reason, or perhaps for no reason at all, one escapee—the indomitable John Wollam—was left off the list, but the oversight was remedied and his medal appropriately bestowed the following July.

The War Department, which by the summer of 1863 was handing out Medals of Honor by the dozen, was not as generous in bestowing the award on the honored dead of the Andrews Raid. In the end, only one-half of the eight men who had forfeited their lives in the aftermath of the Andrews Raid would be awarded the Medal of Honor. The families of Marion Ross and Samuel Robertson were presented with posthumous awards in September 1863, apparently the result of the same process that had given medals to their surviving comrades. John Scott was awarded the medal in 1866, and his father wrote a letter to Washington acknowledging receipt. Samuel Slavens was overlooked for nearly twenty years. In 1883, the Medal of Honor was delivered to his wife Rachel, the recipient of his foreboding letter from Shelbyville twenty-one years before.

But the names of the other four men would never be listed on the roll of Medal of Honor recipients. James Andrews and William Campbell, both being civilians, were simply not eligible for the award. George Wilson and Perry Shadrach, for whatever reason, would never receive the Medal of Honor, and in fact it appears that they were never seriously considered. Perhaps it was that no one ever requested the medal on their behalf. Indeed, poor Shadrach was treated just the opposite. Back home in Steubenville, Ohio, the fallen private's name was omitted from being inscribed on a court-house-square monument to the town's war dead. Apparently, some folks figured he did not deserve to be there, listed among the fallen blue-uniformed heroes.

After all, Shadrach had been hanged as a spy. No honor in that.[21]

Reuniting for the first time in more than two decades, the Raiders and Pursuers pose with the *General* at the Grand Army of the Republic Encampment, Columbus, Ohio, in 1888. J. Alfred Wilson stands on the tender, William J. Knight and Wilson W. Brown are in the cab, Elihu H. Mason and William H. Reddick stand at left, John Wollam, Daniel A. Dorsey, and William Pittenger are seated in front, William Bensinger and Jacob Parrott stand behind the cowcatcher. Leaning on the post at far right is William A. Fuller. (*Colonel James G. Bogle Collection*)

CHAPTER SIXTEEN

The *General* Rides Again

When the actors in the bloody drama of the Rebellion shall all have
passed away, and personal jealousies and sectional animosities have died
out, then will history make an impartial award of merits to the actors in
that great struggle. Much that was real and dreadful will then read like
fiction and romance, as if it had occurred in the days of miracles and
wonders.

Introduction, *The Adventures of Alf Wilson* (1880)

T HE TIDE OF THE WAR BEGAN TO TURN in the summer of 1863, and
President Lincoln finally got, as he wished, "a little luck with the battles." On the Fourth of July, Union forces under Major General Ulysses S.
Grant captured the Mississippi River stronghold of Vicksburg, while in
Pennsylvania the day before, the Army of the Potomac shattered a desperate
attack by Confederate forces on the rock-strewn hills just south of a little
college town called Gettysburg. Of course, the war was far from over, and
over the next twenty months it would take a great deal of blood and courage
and far more than "a little luck" to turn things for the Union. Superior
resources and manpower, economic strength, and the emergence of capable,
relentless commanders—Ulysses S. Grant, William Tecumseh Sherman,
Winfield Scott Hancock, Philip Sheridan, George H. Thomas—ultimately
positioned the Union for victory. Railroads continued to play a pivotal role
in the war, and Federal commanders planned strategic advances in the East
and West with railroad routes in mind, as raiders in blue and gray directed
considerable efforts toward breaking up railroad lines, bridges and depots.

The Western & Atlantic Railroad in Georgia was targeted again by Union
soldiers in the spring of 1863, this time in a raid so poorly conceived and

thoroughly botched that it would make Andrews's effort seem all the more dashing and brilliant by comparison. In April, just days after the six raiders received their medals in Washington, Colonel Abel D. Streight led an Indiana regiment of sixteen hundred mounted infantrymen—mounted on mules, that is, as there were too few horses available—with orders to break up the W&A and destroy the foundries and mills on the banks of the Coosa River at Rome. The unlucky Streight's plodding, braying column drew the attention of Confederate General Nathan Bedford Forrest, already famous as "the Wizard of the Saddle," whose cavalry fretted the sluggish Federals in a series of running battles across north Alabama, from Day's Gap to Blountsville to Gadsden to Turkeytown to Gaylesville. For the slow-moving bluecoats, it was the military equivalent of being repeatedly struck by lightning. Surrounding the frazzled Union riders just west of Rome, the heavily outnumbered Forrest met with Streight under a flag of truce and convinced the Northern commander that his mule-mounted cavaliers were hopelessly overmatched. The down-home Georgia columnist Bill Arp described Forrest's bluff as a high-stakes game of poker played under a cedar tree. "The Yankees had a Streight, which would hav tuk Forrest and raked down the pile, but he looked on rite in the eye and sed he would see 'm, and '4,000 better,'" he wrote. "The raid looked at him and he looked at the raid, and never blinked."

On May 3, 1863, Streight surrendered his 1,466 remaining men, along with their mules, arms and equipment, to Forrest's 400 troopers. The citizens of Rome, happily delivered from the Yankee hordes, expressed their gratitude by throwing a festive Saturday afternoon picnic for the Confederate cavalrymen—though the Romans magnanimously fed the prisoners as well. "Then begun the ovashun of fair women and brave men to Gen. Forrest and his gallant boys," Arp wrote of the occasion. "Bokays and tears were all mixed up promiskous, and big chunks of cake and gratitude were distributed generally and frequent." Streight's Raid had been foiled just as the Andrews Raid had, with no harm to the railroad and no loss to the Confederates. The W&A would remain secure for another year. "Howsumever," Arp warned his readers, "I supposed that Mr. Linkhorn will keep 'peggin' away.'"[1]

The Union army would indeed keep peggin' away at north Georgia, and the third and final threat to the State Road could not be avoided. In the spring of 1864, Major General William T. Sherman's 100,000-man army descended into Georgia like a great blue spider clinging to the iron thread of the W&A. Chattanooga had been occupied at last by Union troops in the fall of 1863, and a breakout victory over the Confederate Army of Tennessee at Missionary Ridge in late November opened the door for invasion. Locations made famous two years before by the Andrews Raid—Ringgold, Tunnel Hill, Dalton, Allatoona, Big Shanty, Kennesaw Mountain—would soon have their pictures in *Harper's Weekly* and *Leslie's Illustrated* and their names in the newspapers once again, as Sherman moved steadily southward through the north Georgia mountains toward Atlanta. Sherman's army marched into the railroad yard at Kingston on May 19, 1864, and set up its headquarters and a supply depot at Big Shanty just over three weeks later. On July 3, General Sherman briefly established his headquarters in Fletcher House, the Marietta hotel overlooking the railroad tracks, where the majority of the Andrews Raiders had slept for a few fitful hours twenty-seven months before.

Atlanta would fall in early September, and first the retreating Confederates and then Sherman's own columns ravaged the city and the railroad as they embarked on their March to the Sea. Along the way, the southbound Yankees tore up, heated and twisted hundreds of rails into useless iron curlicues known to the troops as "Sherman's neckties." "The car shed, the depots, machine shops, foundries, rolling mills, merchant mills, arsenals, laboratory, armory, etc. were all burned," an officer of the Georgia State Militia reported to Gov. Joseph E. Brown, noting further that "every species of machinery that was not destroyed by fire was most ingeniously broken and made worthless in its original form—the large steam boilers, the switches, the frogs, etc. Nothing has escaped." On November 14, back up the road a ways at Big Shanty, departing Union cavalrymen burned to the ground Mr. and Mrs. Lacy's pretty white trackside hotel.

Sherman's Atlanta Campaign and his subsequent March to the Sea was, in a very real sense, the greatest railroad raid of them all. But the havoc and devastation wrought by Sherman's army, though crippling to the state of Georgia and to the Confederate cause, would in the end be a temporary setback for the resurgent city of Atlanta. Within three months of Robert E. Lee's surrender at Appomattox, the Western & Atlantic was back in service—with the city's other radiating lines—the Georgia Railroad, the Macon & Western, the Atlanta & West Point—fully operational as well, soon to be followed by a new railroad between Atlanta and Charlotte under construction by 1869. This renewed transportation and commerce picked up Atlanta's growth and economic fortune right where it had left off, and the 1870 census would show a population of 21,789, nearly three times the city's prewar total. Atlanta was not only born of, but was in the end resurrected by the railroad.

As for Sherman, he would in postwar years acknowledge the critical role of the W&A in his historic march through Georgia. "The Atlanta Campaign of 1864 would have been impossible without this road," he wrote in an 1886 letter to former W&A executive and future governor of Georgia Joseph M. Brown, "and the Western & Atlantic Railroad of Georgia should be the pride of every true American, because by reason of its existence the Union was saved."[2]

Other Northern generals did not fare so well, fading into the footnotes of history at the same time Grant and Sherman were writing their names in bold. Don Carlos Buell, perhaps not surprisingly, dragged his feet one too many times and lost his command and his military career as a result. So recently the savior of the Union Army at Shiloh—at least in his own mind—and thereafter firmly ensconced with his blue force as far south as Alabama, Buell had been forced to fall back northward all the way to the Ohio River to respond to Confederate General Braxton Bragg's autumn counteroffensive into Kentucky. On October 8, the two armies clashed amid the Chaplin Hills in the sanguinary but indecisive Battle of Perryville, with Buell holding the field but suffering more than 4,000 dead, wounded or missing. Bragg's Confederates then slipped away and Buell was slow to get after them, offering a litany of excuses: that the bluegrass countryside ahead was "almost a desert;" that "there is but one road and that a bad one;" and that while his adversary was "moving back on his supplies . . . we must bring ours forward." Over the next two weeks, General-in-Chief Halleck and President Lincoln repeatedly prodded Buell to abandon his customary hesitation and pursue the retreating Rebels into the Tennessee hills. "The capture of East Tennessee should be the main object of your campaign," Halleck wrote, stating plainly that the president "does not understand why we cannot march as the enemy marches, live as he lives, and fight as he fights, unless we admit the inferiority of our troops and of our generals." But Buell did nothing more than begin an erratic crabwalk—not to the southeast, after Bragg, but to the southwest, abandoning the pursuit entirely. Lincoln had had enough. On October 24, sixteen days after Perryville, he relieved Buell from command.[3]

Buell spent most of the next year in Indianapolis, awaiting the outcome of a court of inquiry looking into whether he had been unduly dilatory and hoping to obtain another assignment. He had some prominent supporters, including U.S. Grant, who urged that Don Carlos be given another chance.

"General Buell was a brave, intelligent officer, with as much professional pride and ambition of a commendable sort as I ever knew," Grant wrote in his memoirs. "No one who knew him ever believed him capable of a dishonorable act," he continued, noting that "Buell commanded the confidence and respect of all who knew him." But many who had been along with him during the recurring frustrations of the 1862 campaign would have disagreed with General Grant. "No words were too harsh to apply to Buell," an Ohio war correspondent wrote the day after the general was relieved. "None differed in the general opinion about him. Major generals and privates talked alike." Whichever of these opinions about him was correct, and despite Grant's plea to restore him to duty, Buell was finished. New orders never came, and on June 1, 1864, he resigned his commission and left the army for good.[4]

Buell's ambitious and flamboyant subordinate Ormsby MacKnight Mitchel saw his fortunes turn sour as well in the months following the Andrews Raid. His drive into Alabama had given him national fame and applause from Washington, and as the early summer campaign against Chattanooga stalled under Buell and Halleck, he pleaded with the War Department to be assigned to "more active duty." For a time, Lincoln strongly considered him for more active duty, indeed, as Mitchel's friends Stanton and Chase urged the President to place Old Stars in command of the Army of the Potomac or of the expedition down the Mississippi River against Vicksburg—an assignment that would later propel U.S. Grant into military and political immortality. "It would also gratify me very much to have your eminent military genius employed actively in the East," Stanton wrote to Old Stars in late June, "but the President regards the advance on East Tennessee as only second in importance to Richmond, and that you cannot be safely withdrawn from that field, so that at present the Department cannot gratify your wishes."[5]

So Mitchel remained stuck in northern Alabama, and it was all downhill for him from there. As the summer wore on, he was increasingly plagued by scandal, including allegations of profiteering from cotton speculation and criticism for the depredations committed by soldiers in his command. In the meantime, he continued to butt heads not only with General Buell but also with the ascendant and often conniving General Halleck, who regarded Mitchel as a loose cannon and a possible rival to his own plans for power. On July 2, no longer able to stomach Buell's refusal to support his plans for a drive in force to the east and south, Mitchel resigned his command and asked to be reassigned. He passed the next several weeks in Washington, under consideration for more important work but also under attack by newspapers and politicians for his alleged inattention and malfeasance in Alabama.

In mid-September, Mitchel was reassigned to command of the Department of the South, headquartered at Hilton Head Island, South Carolina. Here Old Stars again displayed his imagination and his thirst for action, devising within days of his arrival a thrust against the Charleston & Savannah Railroad some twenty-five miles west of Hilton Head at Pocotaligo and Coosawhatchie. The expedition was foiled in dramatic fashion by a small Confederate force under General P.G.T. Beauregard—the supposed beneficiary of Andrews's fictional "ammunition train"—who reported dramatically to Richmond: "Charleston Railroad uninjured. Abolitionists left dead and wounded on the field."

But General Mitchel would leave a deeper mark on South Carolina history than the memory of yet another failed attempt to sever a Southern railroad artery. Following his arrival at Hilton Head, Mitchel—perhaps thinking of the thousands of cheering slaves who had lined the dirt roads in Alabama to welcome his triumphant Third Division back in the first glad days of April—was disgusted by the treatment and the living conditions of local black residents, many of them former slaves left behind when whites abandoned the island to the Federal navy in 1861. The Cincinnati general ordered that a "Negro village" be established for their benefit, in a cotton field on the former Drayton Plantation, close by the Federal encampment. The result, in distinct contrast to slave quarters or a contraband shantytown, was a source of pride and a model for future communities. The town featured orderly streets lined with single-family homes on quarter-acre lots, each built on a pier foundation with wood floors, shingled roofs, stoves or chimneys, and glass-paned windows. The residents elected their own government—the first black city councilmen in America—established churches, passed laws, collected taxes, and required that all children between the ages of six and fifteen attend school—the first compulsory education law in South Carolina. Mitchel gathered together the heads of seventy former slave families and advised them that they had the right to have not only a first name but also a family name, and suggested that they adopt the surnames of their former owners—whereby the Sea Islands were soon filled with freedmen bearing distinguished names of the landed Carolina gentry—Trenholms, Rhetts, Barnwells, Beauregards, and Ravenals. (According to African-American historian Benjamin Quarles, some among the freed slaves preferred to go without a family name than take the name of their former master: "I'se had nuff o' ole massa," one said.)

The following spring, the townsfolk would honor their founder by naming their little village Mitchelville, which by 1865 would be home to 1,500 self-sufficient, self-governing blacks. The town would endure for decades but would vanish in the 1930s, its population dwindling and its land ultimately carved up in estate disputes and sold off to Northern investors. Though efforts are under way to preserve the barren acreage where it once stood, Mitchelville is now lost to history and to Hilton Head, most of its vacationers and residents unaware that their million-dollar homes and resort hotels surround the site of the nation's first town established for and governed by freed slaves.[6]

Although the community he founded would endure for generations, Mitchel's stay at Hilton Head—and his life, as it turned out—would come to an end in a matter of weeks. When the chaplain of a New York regiment asked what had brought him to the Carolina Lowcountry, General Mitchel, disconsolate over what he regarded as being relegated to a backwater of the war, answered grimly: "I came to be buried." About this, he turned out to be right. On September 20, 1862, three days after the bloodbath at Antietam, Old Stars reported to Washington a small outbreak of yellow fever among his new command near Hilton Head. But there was no cause for alarm: "The medical director does not anticipate at present that the disease will spread," Mitchel assured the War Department. The following week, he despaired in a letter to a friend: "I am doing nothing here, and shall *die* (yes, *die* is the word) of inaction."

Five weeks later, Old Stars died of yellow fever. His death was mourned throughout the North as the loss of what the *New York Evening Post* called "one of its truest and noblest citizens, one of its ablest and most brilliant defenders." Cincinnati journalist Whitelaw Reid eulogized the astronomer-general and his truncated career: "Amid the stumblings of those earlier years, his was a clear and vigorous tread. While the struggling Nation blindly sought for leaders, his was a brilliant promise. But he never fought a battle, never confronted a respectable antagonist, and never commanded a considerable army. Yet what he did had so won the confidence of his troops, and the admiration of the country, that his death was deplored as a public calamity, and he was mourned as a great general."

Mitchel's body was carried North for burial—but not before a reunion of sorts, by remarkable coincidence, with two of the volunteers he had sent behind enemy lines. Alf Wilson and Mark Wood, taken by the *Somerset* from Apalachicola Bay to Key West in early November, soon made their way up the coast to Port Royal and then Hilton Head, South Carolina. There, they boarded another steamer, the 208-foot transport *Star of the South*, departing for New York. The two soldiers were shocked and saddened to learn that a coffin containing the body of their former commander General Mitchel had been taken aboard for the trip northward to his final resting place, Green-Wood Cemetery in Brooklyn. "I believe he died in the thought that our lives had all been sacrificed," Wilson later wrote. "And if he did die, so believing, it was a cause of pain and sorrow to him, for his was a noble, humane and sensitive nature—a soul of honor."[7]

Remarkably, every one of the Ohio volunteers who survived the ill-fated Andrews Raid also survived the Civil War. All would return to the Union ranks, at least for a time, and most would see combat before the war's end. Their regiments, the 2nd, 21st, and 33rd Ohio Infantry, reorganized in the course of their long absence and folded into the newly formed Army of the Cumberland in the wake of Buell's departure, would participate in some of the hardest fighting of the Western Theater. More than half of the surviving raiders were engaged in the Federal defeat at Chickamauga in September 1863, where their new commander Major General William S. Rosecrans believed he was pursuing the fleeing Rebels but instead found his army the victim of a mugging on a creekbank in northwest Georgia. Timely reinforcements and stalwart leadership by Major General George H. Thomas, thereafter known as "the Rock of Chickamauga," saved the blue army from disaster—but not from defeat and retreat, and not before it suffered galling casualties and an unusually high number of soldiers captured—nearly 5,000—as entire regiments were cut off or left behind in the frantic withdrawal. Foremost among these units was the valiant 21st Ohio, which ran out of ammunition and saw 116 men captured—including Wilson Brown, Elihu Mason, John Porter, and Mark Wood. John Wollam of the 33rd Ohio was rounded up in the course of the rout as well.

Brown (who gave a false name for fear he would be tried on the old spying charge) and Wood, both wounded in the battle, were released in an exchange of the injured a few days later. Their comrades, however, would not be so fortunate. Elihu Mason, who had been shot in the hip as the 21st made its courageous stand, would hobble through another fourteen painful months of imprisonment before being exchanged in December 1864. Porter and

Wollam, too, seemed destined for another long stay behind bars, but the two would instead prove their talent as escape artists once again. Wollam was identified as one of the Andrews Raiders and returned to prison in Atlanta, where he was forced to wear a ball and chain throughout the ensuing winter. His stoic endurance of the trying circumstances drew the admiration of his fellow inmates. "Comrade Wollam was a man of few words, but a braver or more patriotic soldier never enlisted in the cause of humanity and country," a prisoner of war from the 3rd Ohio Cavalry later wrote. In late February, Wollam managed to work his way out of his irons and again escaped from Atlanta. He rejoined his regiment in Chattanooga in April and in the months to come returned to Atlanta yet again—this time in the company of General Sherman.[8]

Though it would take him a little longer, Wollam's friend John Porter, still thin as a rifle barrel, would also make it back to his regiment, and he would along the way demonstrate a knack for getting out of whatever enclosure the Rebels chose to put him in. Porter was taken east from Chickamauga and held over the winter in a prison in Danville, Virginia, where he survived a smallpox epidemic and participated in efforts to escape by tunneling. In May 1864, while en route to the notorious Southern prison at Andersonville, Georgia, Porter managed to escape from a train of cars at Black Stock Station, South Carolina. Three days later, he was recaptured and imprisoned at Columbia—where he again tried tunneling out. At the end of June, he and a number of other prisoners were again entrained for Andersonville. Shortly after passing through Augusta, Porter and his companions cut their way out by sawing a board in the bottom of the locked boxcar, using a table knife they had filed down to make a saw. Porter headed west, making for the advancing Yankee army in North Georgia. After twenty-six days on the run, he struck the Western & Atlantic Railroad near Big Shanty, where he jumped aboard a southbound train for General Thomas's headquarters near Marietta. He was soon safe with his old regiment at the gates of Atlanta, after a ten-month absence.

Following a brief furlough, Porter again joined the 21st just in time to take part in the March to the Sea, where he was placed in charge of a foraging party. Having survived without a scratch the Andrews Raid, months of hard imprisonment, the harrowing battle at Chickamauga, and the desperate life of a fugitive, Porter finally suffered his first war wound near Bentonville, North Carolina, when he was thrown from a mule. He mustered out of the service ten days before the surrender at Appomattox.[9]

Other veterans of the Andrews Raid would travel their own separate military roads, missing Chickamauga and the Atlanta Campaign for various reasons, as they compiled service records that ran the gamut from distinguished to disgraceful. William Bensinger was promoted to captain and assigned to command of Company C of the 13th United States Colored Volunteers, where he would serve with distinction. His commanding officer recorded in his official report of action near Nashville in December 1864 that Captain Bensinger had led his company of black soldiers in battle "in the most gallant manner," noting that the enlisted men of his command had exhibited "great bravery" as well. Ironically, Bensinger's new regiment was detailed shortly thereafter for service as railroad guards in Tennessee. While posted there, he met and married seventeen-year-old Sarah Harris of Charlotte, Tennessee, a pretty and headstrong girl who had held true to the Union despite the two brothers she had serving in the Confederate ranks.[10]

In marked contrast to Captain Bensinger, Robert Buffum's military career following the raid was far from commendable, and his life would become increasingly unraveled after the war's end. After obtaining his commission as a second lieutenant as directed by Secretary Stanton, Buffum returned to the ranks after his furlough and then immediately sought a medical leave of absence. The regimental surgeon of the 21st Ohio recommended that Buffum be permitted more time to convalesce, first at home in Salem, Massachusetts, and thereafter in camp at Murfreesboro, finding that "he is suffering from chronic gastritis, the result of long captivity and starvation of the Rebels." After repeated extensions of this leave, Buffum disappeared for a time—reportedly in the company of another officer of "doubtful character"—and drew the ire of the post commander at Murfreesboro. "The within named Lieut. Buffum has not been at his post since I came here," Col. John Coburn reported on November 21. "In a word, he has left in bad odor with all my military predecessors who are here and should be closely watched hereafter if he ever turns up."[11]

He did turn up eventually, a bad penny indeed, as company returns showed him present in January and February 1864 but "In arrest—awaiting charges" by early March. "On several occasions said Lieut. Buffum has been intoxicated and is now absent from his command without authority," Captain S.F. Cheney reported from Chattanooga on March 9. "He did not report with the Regiment at this Post and has not been seen or heard from since its arrival here. His actions cannot longer be tolerated being such a disgrace to the name and bearing of a soldier." Colonel James M. Neibling, the regimental commander of the 21st Ohio, agreed and recommended that Buffum be dismissed from the service for "conduct unbecoming an officer and a gentleman."

Buffum's infractions were repeated and well documented—yet his military superiors struggled with what to do with him. The recommendation that he be brought up on charges and dismissed was referred all the way up the chain of command to General Thomas, with a copy sent to John Brough, the newly elected Governor of Ohio. Brough called the matter to the attention of General-in-Chief Halleck in Washington, noting pointedly that the allegations against Buffum were counterbalanced by "other facts known at this department"—presumably referring to the fact that Buffum was a well-regarded hero of the secret service, medaled and commissioned an officer, who had only recently returned from a debilitating illness brought on by his long imprisonment. In the end, largely to spare his family any embarrassment or disgrace, Buffum was permitted to resign quietly, "for the good of the service"—his superiors noting that "his resignation will rid the service of a miscreant and a bother."[12]

The army soon lost Lieutenant William Pittenger as well, on account of poor health rather than poor conduct. On August 14, 1863, just four months after receiving the Medal of Honor and less than sixty days after returning from his furlough—and five weeks before the scrap at Chickamauga—Pittenger received a medical discharge and left the army. "I was unable to endure the hardships of the campaign," he said.

Two months later, in October, William Pittenger published his first book on the Andrews Raid.[13]

*T*he rival engines of the Great Locomotive Chase also saw active service—along with their share of violence—before the war's end, and some of the iron horses involved that day would inevitably fare better than others. Though she managed to survive the destruction of the Cooper Iron Works in the spring of 1864, the little switch engine *Yonah* was headed for a mundane existence and an inglorious end. She was modified and used as a stationary engine in the Atlanta shops for a brief period after the war—from there, she went the way of most broken-down locomotives of the era, disappearing into obscurity (no photograph was ever made of the little yard engine) and the eventual terminus of the scrapyard.

The *Texas* was the beneficiary of a fortuitous transfer, loaned for use on the East Tennessee & Virginia Railroad in early 1863, which removed her from the path of Gen. Sherman and saved her from suffering any serious damage in the war. Wiley Harbin's Rome railroad engine *William R. Smith*, too, was moved from North Georgia, but the result was far less fortunate—her lease to the Muscogee Railroad running from Columbus to Macon placed her in harm's way. On Easter Sunday, April 16, 1865—one week after Lee's surrender at Appomattox and one day after the death of Abraham Lincoln— Federal cavalry raiders under General James H. Wilson captured Columbus and destroyed the city's naval works, bridges, railroad shops, and fifteen locomotives, including the *Smith*.[14]

The *General* would nearly suffer the same fate. Despite the recklessness of her April 12, 1862, adventure, the engine came through the chase without a scratch and was within days back in service on the State Road. The *General* would log thousands of miles on the W&A in 1863 and 1864, used primarily to move supply trains in support of the increasingly threatened Rebel forces in North Georgia and Tennessee. On June 27, 1864, the *General* ran ammunition to the Confederate lines during the Battle of Kennesaw Mountain, carrying the butternut wounded from the field down to hospitals in Atlanta later that afternoon.[15]

At the end of August 1864, with the Battle of Atlanta lost and the surrender of the city seemingly inevitable, the *General* and a sister engine the *Etowah* made a desperate attempt to escape the Federal vise by running south out of the city along the Macon & Western Railroad with a train of guns and ammunition. But Union forces had blocked the road south of town at a station called Rough & Ready, and the two locomotives with their trains were forced back to the yard of the Georgia Railroad near Oakland Cemetery. Confederate General John Bell Hood ordered his army to evacuate the city and to destroy military installations, public stores, and railroad stock. On the night of September 1, the departing Rebels set ablaze eighty-one railroad cars, many of them loaded with supplies and ordnance, and then set to work wrecking the five locomotives in the yard by the light of the flames. The *General* was run backward and smashed into the locomotive *Missouri* and her train of cars set afire. General Sherman, unable to sleep at his headquarters twenty miles away at Jonesboro, stood with a local farmer and listened to the distant rumble of the exploding ammunition trains. The next morning, September 2, 1864, just as George D. Wilson had defiantly predicted as he stood on the gallows, the Stars and Stripes was raised over the city of Atlanta.[16]

The sad state of the fallen *General* was recorded a few days after the fall of Atlanta by Northern photographer George N. Barnard. His image showed

The *General* photographed by George N. Barnard in September 1864. The engine suffered considerable damage upon the Confederate abandonment and Union capture of Atlanta. Note the missing cab and headlamp and the large holes in the smokestack. (*Library of Congress*)

the wrecked engine's light, bell, sand dome, and the entire cab gone and two ragged holes in the balloon stack. Barnard described his subject as the hero of the Andrews Raid, which led to the picture being incorrectly captioned as an image of the Confederate locomotive "Hero." The U.S. Military Railroad Service, apparently considering the battered engine not worth fixing, returned the *General* to the W&A after the close of the war. In October 1865, the road's master mechanic listed the *General* on his report to the superintendent with the notation: "Needing General Repairs."[17]

On April 9, 1865—three days shy of the third anniversary of the Andrews Raid and the fourth anniversary of Fort Sumter—General Robert E. Lee and the proud remnant of the Army of Northern Virginia surrendered near Appomattox Court House, and the Civil War for all practical purposes came to an end. The Ohio veterans, like hundreds of thousands of soldiers and sailors around the broken country, returned to peacetime endeavors and scattered to the four winds—though the strongest gust would blow toward a handful of counties in northwestern Ohio, where most of the men were born and where most would die. There, they focused on building careers and families and new lives for themselves until, in September 1888, ten of the eleven raiders then remaining gathered for a reunion right in their respective backyards: at the National Encampment of the Grand Army of the Republic in Columbus, Ohio. More than a quarter-century had passed since the Andrews Raiders had last been together as a group in the Fulton County Jail on October 16, 1862, the night that eight had made their escape to freedom.

The 1888 GAR Reunion was a massive spectacle that threatened to overwhelm the city of Columbus: 70,000 veterans marched in the Grand Parade, and an estimated 250,000 visitors, dignitaries, and other spectators attended the festivities, including General Sherman and former President Rutherford B. Hayes. Ten out of the original two dozen men who constituted the Andrews Raiders were present for the festivities: William Bensinger, Wilson Brown, Daniel Dorsey, William Knight, Elihu Mason, Jacob Parrott, William Pittenger, William Reddick, Alf Wilson, and John Wollam. Although they had once shared a common mission, a defining adventure, and a great and noble cause, they found that they had traveled widely divergent roads thereafter. Most had simply returned home to Ohio and picked up their lives more or less where they had left off. Bill Bensinger worked for a time as a railroad employee at Lima and St. Mary's before settling down to a quiet life of farming near Deweyville. Wilson Brown and Elihu Mason were businessmen in Dowling and Pemberville, respectively. Jacob Parrott had overcome his limited education and was a successful contractor and gravel quarry operator in Kenton. Alf Wilson had opened a grocery store in Perrysburg.

A few, in addition to the absent Porter, had strayed from the Buckeye State: Al Dorsey, for example, had moved to Illinois and thence to Kearney, Nebraska, where he settled down for good. He farmed awhile and later passed the bar, focusing his frontier practice on the booming real estate business. William Knight lived for a time in California and then in Indiana before returning to Ohio and his former occupation as an engineer—though he traded locomotives for stationary engines and ran a wood processing plant in Stryker, Ohio. Bill Reddick had moved to Iowa, where he displayed little direction or ambition. "I have since the war fished a little in all kinds of labor, from farming to chopping cord-wood, making railroad ties, peddling notions, book agencies, and township clerk, back to honest clod-hopping, which latter I hope will furnish me my daily bread for the remainder of my life," he wrote to his friend Pittenger shortly before the reunion. "I am a living encyclopedia to all the aches and pains that flesh is heir to—a used-up man, from the treatment received in that abominable hole of Swims', in Chattanooga."[18]

None among the reunited raiders had to ask what Bill Pittenger had been up to—they had read about it. For one thing, it was Reverend Pittenger now. Citing a promise he had made to God in his hour of trouble, Pittenger was admitted to the ministry in March 1864. Over the next two decades, he built a successful career as a pastor in the Methodist church in Pennsylvania, Ohio, and New Jersey. Always a good talker, he joined the faculty at the National School of Elocution and Oratory in Philadephia and published a number of successful volumes on extemporaneous speaking. All the while, he kept up investigatory correspondence with former friends and foes alike, and turned out new and longer accounts of his adventures, spreading the gospel of the Andrews Raid.

In 1887, just a few months before the reunion, Pittenger's new account of the raid was published—*Daring and Suffering*, it was called—and though it corrected earlier errors and in many respects shared the glory all around, it also continued to gloss over certain aspects of the story. As one historian noted, "the most careful reader would still have had difficulty learning that Pittenger had appeared as a witness against eight of his fellow raiders, and Pittenger's role as a leader in plans for resistance and eventual escape had been magnified rather than increased." The book sold well, however, and was widely praised in the Northern press. "A romance as thrilling as any exploit in the days of Chivalry," the *Cleveland Leader* gushed; "Reminds us of Tolstoy," the *Brooklyn Eagle* wrote; while the *Philadelphia Times* predicted that Pittenger's book "will have as lasting qualities as *Uncle Tom's Cabin*." Two years later, the *Chillicothe Leader* would note that *Daring and Suffering* "was in half the old soldier households in the country."[19]

Even as they renewed old friendships at the grand reunion, the ten Third Division veterans also no doubt reflected on those who by then had been lost. One surviving raider had apparently missed the Columbus gathering by choice—the perpetual wanderer John Porter was tumbling around the American West at the time and lacked either the means or the inclination to attend. But other absences were more solemn, and more permanent. Mark Wood's jailhouse illnesses were compounded by the wounds he received in battle, first at Chickamauga and later in a mountain pass near Dalton called Buzzard's Roost. He was discharged on grounds of disability in late 1864. The Englishman returned to his adopted home of Toledo, Ohio, and died of pneumonia in July 1866, an illness some attributed to the persistent fever that struck him during his long imprisonment and his flight through the swamps of Georgia and Florida.[20]

Robert Buffum, too, was gone by then. Following his ignoble resignation, Buffum had returned to his family and seemed for a time to settle down. But he continued a losing battle with his demons, spiraling down into alcoholism and apparent mental illness. Always volatile, he turned increasingly violent. In Minerva, Ohio, he shot a man in the face who had dared to insult Abraham Lincoln—the victim miraculously survived—and in 1870, he shot and killed fifty-two-year old John S. Seaverns in the town of Newburgh, Orange County, New York. Buffum and his wife and son were houseguests of the Seaverns, and Buffum apparently believed that Seaverns had abused his wife the night before. He walked up behind Seaverns as he sat in his parlor drinking tea and shot him in the back of the head with a double-barreled pistol.

The notorious, cold-blooded crime—"The Newburgh Murder"—was a local sensation, and the ensuing trial was covered in detail in the *New York Times*. A great throng of spectators turned out for the proceedings. The sheriff provided extra security at the Orange County Courthouse, as folks there had talked openly of lynching the accused for what many believed had been a premeditated act. The slate of trial witnesses was a diverse cast of characters worthy of a mystery novel—the chief of police, a gunsmith and locksmith, a carpenter, a barber, two doctors, and the star witness, a servant girl named Kate Kelly, who had served poor Mr. Seaverns his steaming cup of tea just moments before he was shot. A physician named Dr. Lee had examined the defendant and found him sluggish and indolent, but concluded that he could not pronounce Buffum insane—"his eyes indicated more of the result of debauchery than anything else," the doctor said. The *Times* reporter, watching the proceedings and the accused from a seat in the crowded gallery, seemed to detect something more sinister. "Buffum did not speak, and only nodded his head, but exhibited ill-concealed but intense emotion. His villainous expression of countenance was generally remarked," the paper said. The jury returned that same afternoon with a verdict of guilty, and the defendant was sentenced to life imprisonment.[21]

Robert Buffum would spend only six days in the state prison at Sing Sing before being consigned to an insane asylum in Auburn, New York. There he committed suicide, cutting his own throat on June 20, 1871.[22]

Though his tale was not as dramatic and his end far less ghastly, bad luck had continued for Martin Hawkins, the experienced engineer who had overslept and missed the April 12 adventure. Once physically agile and mechanically adept, he had suffered mightily from the ugly head wound he received at Chickamauga. Although he bravely continued in army service through the balance of the war, he was in many ways never the same again. After the war, he moved to Illinois and, when able, found work as an engineer until his death in 1886.[23]

The last two volunteers missing from the 1888 Reunion had missed the raid in the first place—these were the two wayward would-be raiders James Ovid Wellford Smith and Samuel Llewellyn, who had enlisted in the Confederate army to avoid suspicion near Jasper and did not participate in the theft of the *General* at all. This inconvenient fact did nothing to deter one of the two from seeking to share in the resulting honors: seemingly untroubled by his son's lack of involvement in the operation, Smith's father had actively lobbied the War Department for his son to receive the Medal of Honor. In June 1864, Brigadier General Edward Canby, at the direction of Secretary Stanton, directed that Private Smith be placed "on the same footing as the other men of his party, as regards compensation and medal." (Presumably, the Secretary of War received information that Smith was a member of the by-now renowned party of volunteers, without realizing that the young private had not actually taken part in the raid itself.) Young Smith was understandably delighted with the award and even wrote a giddy letter acknowledging receipt:

> E.D. Townsend, Asst. Adjt. Genl.
> Washington, DC
> Parkersburg, Oct. 15th/64
>
> Sir:
> I was made happy yesterday by the receipt of the medal which the secretary of war was pleased to award to me for services rendered and which I hope to wear long and honorably.
>
> I am doubly happy to have received this mark of distinguished appreciation during the administration of that gentleman, scholar and patriot A. Lincoln: long may he wave.
>
> Very respectfully
> Your Obt. Servt.
>
> James Smith

Smith would wear his Medal of Honor honorably enough, but he would not do so for long. He died of pneumonia in 1868 at the age of twenty-three.[24]

Smith's companion in early capture Samuel Llewellyn returned to the 33rd Ohio after his unwilling stint as a Rebel artilleryman and was wounded in the chin and captured at Chickamauga in September 1863. He was paroled the following May and discharged from the service at Villenou, Georgia, in October. In the years to come, he would serve two terms in the Ohio General Assembly and lived a long life in Sandusky, Ohio, where he died at the Ohio Soldiers and Sailors Home in 1915.

But even though he had served honorably in the blue ranks and was a wounded veteran with a long and distinguished public life ahead, Sam Llewellyn did not attend any of the reunions of the Andrews Raiders, apparently because he did not consider himself to be a member of the party. And he was never awarded the Medal of Honor—for the refreshingly honest and humble reason that he did not believe he deserved it.[25]

The various allies and antagonists of the Ohio volunteers had each come to the end of their own personal lines by that time as well. Marietta hotelier and Union spy Henry Greene Cole continued his intelligence gathering and espionage as the war proceeded. In the fall of 1863, he learned that a large Confederate force under General Longstreet was moving to reinforce Bragg near Chickamauga, and had the news sent to Union Major General George Thomas. "The General always gave me a great deal of credit for that act," he wrote after the war, "and said that what was saved at Chickamauga was saved by that means." Cole was eventually found out and arrested by Confederate authorities in the spring of 1864, charged with attempting to pass to advancing Federal forces a plan of Snake Creek Gap near Dalton. "They always had suspected me," Cole said. He was held in Atlanta for several weeks before being moved to Charleston, South Carolina, where he was imprisoned on Sullivan's Island for eight months before being released. In the meantime, Cole's elegant hotel—which he took pride in as the "finest house in Georgia"—was used by Union commanders as a headquarters as they directed the final stages of the campaign against Atlanta.[26]

On July 31, 1866, in exchange for a nominal payment of five dollars, Cole transferred to the United States Government twenty acres on a hill just east of the town square in Marietta, to be used as a cemetery for fallen Federal and Confederate troops. Cole's idealistic attempt to effect an eternal reconciliation of sorts between North and South was rejected, as local citizens were outraged at the idea of burying Dixie's heroes side-by-side with Yankee invaders. Accordingly, a burial place for Rebel dead was established nearby, making Marietta one of the few towns in America with both a Union and a Confederate cemetery. Cole died on April 18, 1875, and was buried in a plot set aside for his family in the National Cemetery. His large estate, which included property he owned in twelve Georgia counties, was not finally settled by the Cobb Probate Court until January 1941, sixty-six years after his death.[27]

Captain David Fry, the notorious ringleader of the East Tennessee bridge burners, made good his escape from Atlanta and returned to the Tennessee hills, where he continued in active service fighting the Rebels through raids, sabotage, and violent intimidation of pro-Confederate citizens. Alf Wilson by chance ran into Fry shortly after returning to his regiment near Nashville. He was not only surprised to find the dauntless Tennessean alive—Wilson thought that Fry had been shot down and killed during the hectic skedaddle from the Atlanta jail—but also was amazed by the transformation in his appearance. Once "bareheaded, starved, ragged and bony" after months of imprisonment, within weeks of his return to the blue ranks, Fry was "a robust, well-fed, soldierly, noble-looking man, but in heart, courage, manliness and nobility of character, the same man who had been our faithful comrade in prison." Fry was wounded several times in the war and in time was promoted to colonel in recognition of his leadership and his exploits.

After the war, David Fry returned to a quiet life at home in Greeneville, Tennessee. On August 21, 1872, he was struck by a train and died a few days later. "As a soldier, possessing great rugged qualities of mind and heart, he would have been a fit associate for Frederick the Great," Alf Wilson wrote. "I know of few men for whom I entertain greater respect than Captain David Fry."[28]

Confederate Brigadier General Danville Leadbetter's success in securing East Tennessee and his proven skill and experience as an engineer led to important assignments as the war continued. He served for a time as chief engineer of the Army of Tennessee, worked on Longstreet's siege of Knoxville, laid out Bragg's lines at Chattanooga, and eventually returned to his adopted hometown of Mobile, Alabama, to design the city and bay defenses there. He vanished for a time at the close of the war—official biographies indicate that no record of his final capture or parole was found. He fled for a time to Mexico and thence to Canada, where he died in the town of Clifton on September 26, 1866. He was laid to rest in the Magnolia

Cemetery in Mobile. Despite his eventful tenure in Chattanooga, his service as an engineer under Longstreet, Johnston, and other Confederate heroes, and his enduring legacy of antebellum work on the U.S. Coast Survey— Leadbetter Point and Leadbetter State Park in the state of Washington are named in his honor, for example—the Maine-born Confederate officer remains a little-known figure of the Civil War.

The newspapers in East Tennessee reported a few weeks later the news that the villain Leadbetter had died, reportedly "leaving a considerable sum of money and valuable effects." One editor no doubt expressed the views of many Tennesseans on the passing and the final judgment of their former oppressor. "If Leadbetter has not received his due compensation of reward within the confines of the lost—then we infer, there is no hell, and the Word of God is a cunningly devised fable," he wrote. "The purest blood of East Tennessee's loyal sons cries from the ground against this foul murderer who has gone to his final account."[29]

Though the raiders devoutly wished for him a miserable end, their jailer Old Swims survived the war, fleeing south in the fall of 1863 as Federal armies at last occupied the Mountain City. The jail at Fifth and Lookout Streets was torn apart by Union soldiers who had heard of the suffering of their comrades there, its lumber burned in Federal campfires and its bricks used to construct fireplaces and chimneys for the bluecoats' tents.

The old jailer returned to Chattanooga shortly thereafter—Dorsey claimed to have found him there in the spring of 1864, "a feeble old man, tottering on the verge of the grave." Swims died of smallpox three years later. "His remains rest in the Citizens' cemetery," a local reporter wrote in 1898, "marked with a discolored headstone, which time will soon blot beyond recognition."[30]

The reunited raiders no doubt spoke of Old Swims and General Leadbetter and Captain Fry as they gathered for the reunion, and they took a careful accounting of the fates of each of their absent comrades. Yet those who later wrote of the 1888 Reunion recalled little in the way of melancholy reminiscence there at Columbus; instead, the ten veterans spent time posing for photographs, sharing proud reflections on their expedition, and engaging in warm conversation, catching up on the postwar exploits of the still-living. They also welcomed two honored guests from down south: William A. Fuller, who was reportedly "well-received and kindly treated," and the majestic, flag-draped *General*, which had made the trip up to Ohio under her own steam.

The Confederate government had awarded no official decoration or other honors to William Fuller, or to any of the pursuing party, for that matter— first of all, because they were civilians, and second, because the Confederate States of America never had military medals in any event. For a time, it looked as though the State of Georgia—no doubt grateful for the heroic protection of the state railroad—would bestow public honors on the pursuers. On November 6, 1862, Georgia Governor Joseph Brown, addressing the state legislature at Milledgeville, declared that "the conduct of Mr. Fuller, the Conductor, and some others . . . deserves the highest commendation" and recommended that "medals or other public acknowledgment" be awarded. Nothing ever came of the governor's suggestion, as the state legislature found itself swamped with wartime business and crises. (Fuller's family would finally obtain a specially designed commemorative medal from the State of Georgia in 1950, thanks to the efforts of his son-in-law Wilbur Kurtz.) On February 23, 1864, Governor Brown bestowed what honor he could on his own, commissioning William A. Fuller as a captain in what he called the "Independent State Railroad Guards in the Regiment of Infantry of the Volunteers for the State of Georgia." Fuller continued to work in service on the State Road through and beyond the end of the war, held in high regard in Atlanta as nothing less than a war hero, widely referred and deferred to as Captain Fuller. In fact, a number of accounts of the Andrews Raid would identify Fuller throughout as "Captain Fuller," though he held no such rank at the time of the chase. According to the *Atlanta Constitution*, the former conductor, who in the late 1870s had left the railroad and entered the mercantile business, "was one of the prominent citizens of Atlanta and was identified with the upbuilding of the place as much almost as any man in it."[31]

Fuller had no sooner arrived in Columbus, shaking hands all around as he was introduced to the surviving raiders and their families, when he came face-to-face with Mrs. Rachel Slavens, the widow of the executed Samuel. It was the most poignant encounter of the reunion, a moment reported by an article in the *Columbus Dispatch* next day. Daniel Dorsey found the meeting "especially pathetic," and the *Dispatch's* correspondent, who had introduced the pair, observed of Mrs. Slavens that "the years of sorrow lingered on her brow." He continued:

> No one can ever tell the thoughts of this woman as she took the hand of the man who was responsible for her husband's death. When I mentioned her name I seemed to observe a perceptible, but momentary feeling in the nature of a slight shock come into

Captain Fuller's strong frame. He spoke so gently, however, and kindly, that the lady was deeply touched.

They sat down beside each other and conversed in undertones. What they said they alone know, though the house was silent, and we were all in the room. It was a touching scene, and one which those present will never forget. When they had finished their talk, Captain Fuller was introduced to the remainder of the party.

Mrs. Slavens was a changed woman after her meeting with Captain Fuller, for she said she felt all right now toward the men who captured, tried and hanged her husband. I have no doubt but that it made her life happier.

Some among the party were not so forgiving as the Widow Slavens—John Wollam, for example, at first refused to shake Fuller's hand, but he came around before the close of the proceedings. Others thought their former adversary stacked up well at least by comparison to others—Bill Knight was reportedly heard to say that he thought more of Fuller than he did of his fellow Ohioan Pittenger.[32]

Those among the party who were still alive and able would convene again in Chattanooga three years hence—this time for the dedication of a monument to their fallen comrades.

The Andrews Raiders who had not survived, including James Andrews himself, would eventually have a reunion of their own. For a time, there seemed to be little chance that the executed raiders would be remembered as heroes, or even remembered at all, for that matter. They were buried in an unmarked grave that would soon become one of thousands of unmarked graves in and around Atlanta, and their passing was given the slightest mention by the local press, again without any suggestion that the hanging had in any way been mishandled. "HUNG," the *Southern Confederacy*'s headline read on June 19, 1862. "Yesterday afternoon, seven more of the engine thieves were hung near this city," the paper said. "They were a portion of the party of twenty-four that arrived here [from Knoxville] in strings a few days ago. They were all Ohioans. We have not learned their names."[33]

Their names were William Campbell, Samuel Robertson, Marion A. Ross, John M. Scott, Perry Shadrach, Samuel Slavens, and George D. Wilson, and they were not at all forgotten, at least not back home. In February 1866, the Ohio legislature passed a resolution formally requesting that the quartermaster of the army require that the seven Buckeye soldiers executed at Atlanta be removed to and reinterred at the "Cemetery for U.S. Soldiers at Chattanooga or Murfreesboro, Tenn." Two months later, the chief quartermaster of the Military Division of Tennessee dispatched a man named Jonas Drury to Atlanta, where he "commenced a search and general enquiry for the bodies of seven Ohio soldiers hung by Rebels near the woods on or about the 22nd of June 1862." Directed to the spot by the locals, he found them buried in rough coffins next to a little creek bed, about twelve rods from where they were executed. "In one hole, six lay side by side, and the seventh lay across at their feet," Drury reported. Unable to identify the men by name, he numbered their new coffins and described their remains, one by one:

> No. 1. Was six feet high. Very large round head with a few gray hairs—Teeth sound, dress, Black Satin Vest, New Kip Boots, Black satin self adjusting Neck Tie, other clothes too much decayed to be described.
>
> No. 2. Five feet 8? inches high, light built—Dress—Black Satin Vest and Neck tie, Gaiter shoes, feet small—
>
> No. 3. Five feet ten inches high. Dress—A Confederate Army Jacket, Gray pants and Cavalry Boots—
>
> No. 4. Five feet eight inches high. Dress, Black Satin Vest, striped flannel shirt, Cavalry Boots, The head enclosed in a black Silk Handkerchief, on his bosom was a Gold Pin, with the likeness of a Lady and in the pocket of the Vest a Gold Ring—
>
> No. 5. Five feet eleven inches high. Dress, Cavalry Boots, Black ribbed Kersey Vest double breasted with Gutta Percha buttons—
>
> No. 6. Five feet eight inches high, Black Vest, White Cotton Shirt, Cavalry Boots—
>
> No. 7. The coffin was all to pieces as I had to shovel up the remains and can give no description, except that he had on Cavalry Boots—

The coffins were loaded on a train car for the trip north up the old State Road, and on April 25, 1866, the seven soldiers were reburied at the National Cemetery in Chattanooga.[34]

More than twenty years later, their leader would join them. In April 1887, an Atlanta resident named John H. Mashburne directed a party of searchers to Andrews's grave—about twenty paces southeast of the intersection of Juniper and Third Streets, in a shallow depression filled with leaves and choked with a tangle of blackberry bushes. Three feet down in the clay, they found the remains of a large man, approximately the size of James Andrews. William Fuller later claimed that he had directed the searchers to the spot where Andrews was buried—and perhaps the gravedigging delegation had inquired of the old conductor in addition to Mashburne. But however they managed to locate Andrews's resting place, Fuller had his doubts as to whether the remains they unearthed actually were those of the Kentucky spy—no trace of Andrews's manacles were found with the body, though numerous witnesses to the hanging and the burial had insisted they were never removed. "I pointed out as nearly as I could *where we laid him,* and there we found *bones,*" Fuller wrote. "I can only hope they were those of Andrews." The remains were taken north to Chattanooga, where Andrews would be reunited with his seven volunteers in the National Cemetery.[35]

The 1888 reunion of the surviving veterans of the chase had given new life to a proposal to erect a suitable memorial to honor the Andrews Raiders. The following spring, the Ohio General Assembly passed a bill appropriating $5,000 for a monument to be constructed at the National Cemetery in Chattanooga. Among the supporters of the measure was Captain William Fuller of Atlanta, who had said in his address at the reunion, "I desire to say to the Grand Army of the Republic and especially to the people of Ohio that, though you have ample opportunity and abundance of wealth, you are unable to do too much for the surviving members of this expedition, nor can you do too much in memory of the dead."[36]

On Memorial Day, May 30, 1891, the monument was unveiled at a grand ceremony, attended by raiders, pursuers, family members, representatives of veterans' groups, and all manner of notable citizens of Tennessee, Georgia, and Ohio. Of the survivors, Bill Bensinger, Daniel Dorsey, Elihu Mason, William Pittenger, John Porter, and Alf Wilson were present. (Conspicuously absent from the dedication was the irrepressible raider and serial escapee John Wollam, who had been present at the GAR Reunion but had passed away in Topeka, Kansas, on September 25, 1890.) Mrs. Rachel Slavens was there with her grown sons, as were a number of other relatives of the fallen raiders. William Fuller and Anthony Murphy represented the pursuers, along with White Smith, the local man whom Fuller had sent north from Acworth on horseback in the course of the pursuit. Rev. Pittenger gave the invocation, and former Ohio Governor and soon-to-be U.S. Senator Joseph B. Foraker—who despite the difference in spelling happened to be first cousin to the wartime Atlanta provost marshal G.J. Foreacre—gave a "lengthy and very able address" to mark the occasion. Marion R. Ross, the young nephew of the heroic sergeant-major, did the honors and pulled the cord to unveil the statue: a large pedestal of Vermont marble, inscribed with the names and military units of each of the raiders and topped with a bronze miniature of the locomotive *General* and its tender. The monument itself was "literally buried under a profusion of rich floral tributes," including a large bouquet sent by President and Mrs. Benjamin Harrison.

Anthony Murphy was touched by the unveiling and the sentiments expressed by his former adversaries. "The kindness shown me while there, by all that I met, after twenty-nine years had passed, touched a tender cord, and forced me to ask the question: 'What country?—under what flag?—aye, what people, but Americans meet and shake hands and forgive the past, each retaining their self-respect, yet according to each other the highest praise for the courage in the performance of their duty?'"

James Andrews and his seven volunteers, their duty done, lie in eternal rest on a green hill in Chattanooga, their modest white headstones set in a gentle arc in the shadow of the Ohio monument.[37]

*T*he Andrews Raiders would join together one last time, in September 1906, more than forty-four years after their expedition, though by then only a handful would remain. John Porter, William Knight, Jacob Parrott, William Bensinger, and Daniel Dorsey were present, along with their former adversary Anthony Murphy, who attended along with Captain Fuller's son, William A. Fuller. Two solemn group portraits were made of the white-haired gathering—one in front of the Ohio monument, with the likeness of the *General* and rows of white grave markers standing behind them, and a second in front of the *General* herself, with William Knight standing proudly on the engine next to the smokestack. Yet even as the ever-dwindling party of raiders were reunited, the story of the raid itself was still being shaped and defined for the public, and for history. Friendships were being tested, controversy growing, jealousy emerging among the former comrades.[38]

Time and illness had again taken their toll since the raiders were last together, fifteen years before, and a number of friends were missing. The quiet, sometimes despondent sergeant and devoted father Elihu Mason died in 1896 in Pemberville, Ohio, at the age of sixty-five, leaving behind him a great deal of silence as to his part in the Andrews Raid. Indeed, Sergeant Mason, unique among the raiders who survived for many years after the war, appears never to have written of his experiences or spoken of them publicly. His role in the entire adventure, accordingly, remains largely unknown. And though he had sought no glory for his exploits, he was quietly proud of his participation in the raid, as evidenced by his faithful attendance at the Columbus reunion, as well as by his tombstone, in a small cemetery near Pemberville, which reads: "A soldier slumbers here. Captain Elihu H. Mason, Mitchel Raider."[39]

William Reddick had passed away as well. The former corporal, who later found himself "a used-up man" as a result of his wartime ordeal, made it to the first reunion but never saw his comrades again after that. He settled in Seventy-six Township, near Letts, Iowa, where he died on November 8, 1903.[40]

The following year, the party had lost two of its most prominent members, each of them renowned authors for their exciting accounts of the Great Locomotive Chase. J. Alfred "Alf" Wilson, the fireman and brakeman on the captured *General* and who had since become a small-town grocer, published in 1880 his account of the Andrews Raid, the immodestly titled *The Adventures of Alf Wilson*. Although it is riddled with minor inaccuracies, and portions rely almost verbatim on William Pittenger's earlier accounts (a fact acknowledged by Wilson in the preface), Alf's book illuminates two key aspects of the adventure—first, his vivid descriptions of the chase from his perspective aboard the *General*, and second, his account of the harrowing river escape to the Gulf of Mexico. Though there is some puffing and some unverifiable encounters—Wilson, too, claimed to have met separately with President Lincoln—the book overall is humble in tone. "This is the story of a private soldier who aspires no literary honors, who claims no credit for martyrdom, whose deeds didn't change the tide of a single battle," he wrote. "All I can claim for myself in the expedition is that I did all in my power to carry out the orders of my general, tried to serve my country faithfully, and believe I cheated the Rebels out of the pleasure of hanging me."[41]

But despite the pride he expressed in his adventures and the modesty and wit of his narrative, the raid in fact would haunt Alf Wilson for the rest of his life. "On the subject of his many startling adventures, his perilous hardships, and hairbreadth escapes, he is usually reticent," an acquaintance observed years after the war. "When he is induced to speak of them, the dark hours of his imprisonment seem to harrow up his feelings to their utmost tension. His eyes dance with an unnatural light, he grows excitedly nervous over the recollections of that terrible summer, and his every action indicates that of a tempest-tossed spirit over the bitter memories of the past." In the end, for Wilson, the tale of the raid was not one of heroism and adventure,

Last Reunion of the Andrews Raiders and Pursuers, National Cemetery, Chattanooga, September 19, 1906. Front left to right: John Reed Porter, William J. Knight, Jacob Parrott, Anthony Murphy, Daniel Allen Dorsey. Rear left to right: William Bensinger and Henry Haney. (*Colonel James G. Bogle Collection*)

but one of sorrow and of suffering. My story, he wrote, "is a cloud without a silver lining." Alf Wilson died on March 18, 1904, in Perrysburg, Ohio.[42]

The raid's most famous and controversial scribe passed away just a few weeks later. In 1890, Rev. William Pittenger had moved his ministry and his family west to San Diego County, California, where he purchased a twenty-acre homestead and for the next fourteen years served as pastor of the newly constructed Methodist church in the town of Fallbrook. There he died on April 25, 1904. He was buried in the Odd Fellows Cemetery in Fallbrook, where his gravestone reads: "Sergeant Wm. Pittenger, Co. G, 2 Ohio Inf - One of the Andrews Raiders." A local chapter of the Sons of Union Veterans is named in his honor.

Yet the peace of Rev. Pittenger's later years had been disrupted by controversy, his honesty and his honor vigorously challenged by his former friend and comrade, Daniel Allen Dorsey, who nurtured a festering, almost obsessive belief in postwar years that Pittenger had sold out his fellow soldiers in order to save himself. Shortly after the 1888 reunion, Dorsey began to think of writing his own story of the raid, going so far as to copyright the title for a play: "Andrews the Spy," he called it. About the same time, his views of

Pittenger for some reason began to harden. Dorsey no longer thought his bespectacled compatriot merely guilty of irritating behavior and bad decisions, but of willful and self-interested treachery. He began to write letters— to the raiders' former counsel, Judges Baxter and Temple, to the War Department, to his former enemy Captain Fuller—seeking incriminating information. He came up empty in this effort, and Fuller, who had been portrayed rather well in Pittenger's most recent book, warned Dorsey to leave well enough alone. "Pittenger has made heroes of us all, and we ought to be satisfied," he wrote to Dorsey.[43]

The conductor's warning went unheeded, and Dorsey wrote a letter to the *Chillicothe Leader* that "more than intimated that Pittenger had turned traitor when the hour of danger came," a charge the newspaper pronounced to be "a terrible one, almost too terrible for belief." In 1893, Dorsey wrote a series of articles for a veterans' newspaper, *The Ohio Soldier*, which gave a detailed and dramatic narrative of the raid. But again, his account was leavened heavily with accusations of disloyalty and self-dealing.[44]

Several of the surviving raiders came swiftly to Pittenger's defense. William Reddick believed a great injustice had been done to Pittenger and pronounced Dorsey's attack to be entirely unwarranted. "I never saw where Pittenger received any favor from the Rebels," he said. John Porter did this one better, noting that Dorsey himself had "talked quite differently two years ago." If any man was diminished in Porter's eyes by the accusations, it was Daniel Dorsey. "I would like to know what members of the party, if any, will be influenced by a man who will falsify and vilify men who have been his best friends," Porter said. "Dorsey's attitude against Pittenger is not popular," Wilson Brown wrote years later. "Dorsey thinks Pittenger testified to things before the court at Knoxville detrimental to the Party—but it is all imagination." William Knight, asked by an interviewer about the possibility that Pittenger had sold his comrades south, "poo-poo'd the mere idea of it," calling the accusation "one of Dorsey's fool notions." Even William Fuller defended Pittenger, writing a long letter to the editor of the *Columbus Dispatch*, which concluded: "I am firmly of the belief that Dr. Pittenger was at all times and under all circumstances true to his comrades and loyal to his cause."[45]

Of course, Pittenger was certainly capable of defending himself as well, and he wrote a series of lengthy rejoinders to the "bitterly abusive attack" that had been made against him, his honor, and his reputation. His letters were for the most part an evidentiary presentation, citing the sworn, corroborating testimony already on the record and the many friends, foes, and counselors that supported him; while Dorsey was, he said, "an unscrupulous enemy [who] does not hesitate to make utterly baseless assertions." He also intimated that Dorsey's motive was nothing more than anger and envy over his success: "Had I agreed to share the anticipated profits of the new edition of my book with Mr. Dorsey and agreed with him politically, his tirades would never have been written," Pittenger suggested.[46]

At the end of the day, the record suggests that William Pittenger—despite Dorsey's accusations and the enduring suspicion of others—was not a traitor to his country or his comrades. There is no hard evidence, for example, to suggest that Pittenger had any *quid pro quo* agreement with the Confederate prosecutors to give testimony against the others, and the strong supporting endorsements from the raiders' Tennessee defense attorneys weigh heavily in his favor. Pittenger's strategy at the court-martial appears to be the product of honest misjudgment (either by himself or defense counsel or both) rather than any sinister plan to sell out his friends. The sad fact remains, however, that Pittenger gave key testimony confirming the identification and the culpable conduct of six United States soldiers and two civilians who were subsequently convicted and executed for their actions. He was also undeniably a man smart enough and resourceful enough to make the best of a bad situation—as the special treatment he received while in jail both in Chattanooga and in Atlanta plainly demonstrates.

In addition, while he was every bit as brave as his comrades in volunteering for the raid and seeing it through, Pittenger also revealed himself to be something of a braggart and a shameless self-promoter. According to his books—all of them well-written, detailed, compelling accounts—Pittenger was not merely one enlisted man among twenty-two enlisted men on the mission, he was a key player, leader, decision maker, and man of action throughout. To hear Pittenger tell it, he was the first and only soldier who actually volunteered for the raid; he led Campbell, Shadrach, and Wilson safely behind enemy lines; he bravely urged Andrews to stop and fight the pursuers rather than cut and run; he planned a brilliant legal defense that was defeated only by the blatant prejudice and predetermined judgment of the court-martial members; he suggested the plans for the successful prison break; and he personally stifled the cries of the struggling jailer, allowing his comrades to escape. (And of course, though he would not emphasize the fact, he penned the letters to President Jefferson Davis and General Braxton Bragg.)

Pittenger's ultimate victory in shaping popular history would not be complete until more than fifty years after his death, with Walt Disney's release of his new motion picture *The Great Locomotive Chase* in 1956. In the climactic medal ceremony scene of the Disney film—which was advertised as "A Remarkable *True* Spy Story!"—it is Bill Pittenger, not Jake Parrott, who becomes the first American soldier to be awarded the Medal of Honor.[47]

Unpersuaded by Pittenger's evidence and indifferent to the considerable anguish that his defamatory claims caused Rev. Pittenger and his wife Winnie in their later years, Dorsey continued his campaign even after Pittenger's death and apparently believed until his own dying day—May 10, 1918, in Wadsworth, Kansas—that Pittenger had manipulated and ultimately betrayed his fellow soldiers. "Those who have read *Tom Sawyer* and *Huckleberry Finn* will recognize the striking characters in our party," Dorsey wrote, summing up his view of the controversy. "Pittenger was Tom Sawyer, while all the rest of us were Hucks."[48]

*D*uring the same time period, another petty dispute had developed between the two Yankee engineers. William Knight had always taken fierce and very public pride in his role as the engineer of the famous *General*. During the 1870s and 1880s, he toured the Midwest giving lectures on the subject, which newspaper ads described as "the most thrilling incident in American warfare." Knight's speech was complemented by a series of panoramic oil paintings—today preserved at the Ohio Historical Society— which he rolled across a screen from a great scroll to illustrate his narrative. His sparse written accounts—"An Engineer's Story," an interview in a small-town Ohio newspaper, and "How I Ran the '*General*'," published in *The Railroad Man's Magazine*—emphasized his interactions with Andrews in the cab and his work at the throttle of the *General*. Knight presented himself as the engineer on the run up the W&A—"next to Andrews," announcements for his lectures said, "[he] was the most important member of the expedition." He described his fellow engineer Brown as "my assistant," and regularly repeated his claim that he was the first one on the engine that day, and the last one off.[49]

His fellow engineer Wilson Brown bristled at what he viewed as Knight's intimations that he had been "the whole push of the raid." Brown insisted in letters to the editors of various Ohio newspapers that he was the one whom General Mitchel had selected as the engineer on the mission, concluding: "It is a fact, well understood all over the country, that I was on that engine when she made that run, and did officiate at the throttle of the '*General*.'" This struggle for credit and recognition became intimately personal and was vigorously argued between the two engineers, but as is often the case in such disputes, the truth appears to lie somewhere in between. Both Knight and Brown stood at the throttle of the *General* at various times on that April morning, and both shared in the numerous other tasks involved in running a locomotive flat-out under less than ideal conditions. Historian Wilbur Kurtz summed up the rivalry in his notes from a 1904 interview with Knight. "The facts will stand undenied by anyone," he said: "that Knight was the first man on the *General* and the one who pulled the throttle—that both Brown and Knight were on the locomotive—that both had had experience with locomotives prior to the war, and both had a goodly share in sending the grand old machine on its mad career up the road."[50]

Wounded in the knee and the hand at Chickamauga, Wilson Brown never ran a locomotive again. He settled down to a life of farming and fathered seven children, one of whom—his daughter Gertrude—went on to marry John Parrott, son of fellow raider Jacob Parrott. After the turn of the century, Brown lived on his meager pension and in later years was reduced to begging correspondents for money and postage stamps. "I am a poor man and you will not be surprised when I tell you that I sacrificed my all on the altar of my country," he told one correspondent. Even in the twilight of his life, his letters are filled with lingering resentment toward his old friend Knight, as well as desperate pleas to be recognized and remembered as the raid's chief engineer. "I want Exact Justice," he demanded. "Let honor be given to whom honor is due." Having been born on Christmas Day, 1839, Wilson Brown died at his home in Toledo on Christmas Day, 1916, at the age of seventy-seven. His fellow engineer Bill Knight died earlier that same year at age seventy-nine.[51]

Other veterans seemed to step easily clear of postwar squabbles and made no effort to trade on their past exploits at all. William Bensinger, for example, lived a long and contented life with his wife Sarah, working his family farm near Deweyville, Ohio. He died on December 18, 1918, just a few weeks shy of his seventy-ninth birthday.[52]

Jacob Parrott, too, seemed almost disinterested in past glories. The first recipient of the Medal of Honor was discharged from the army at Savannah on January 2, 1865, just days after Sherman presented the historic Georgia city to President Lincoln as a Christmas present. Parrott got married a year later, settled in Kenton, Ohio, and despite his illiteracy found success in his contracting business. As he grew older, Parrott became a confirmed Spiritualist, so much so that an observer at the 1906 reunion noted that he seemed to be more interested in Spiritualism than in the Andrews Raid. On December 22, 1908, while walking down South Main Street in Kenton, the sixty-five-year-old veteran collapsed and died. He was buried in nearby Grove Cemetery, where his marker records that "Lieut. Parrott was honored by Congress with the first medal issued for distinguished bravery."[53]

John Reed Porter spent the better part of three decades roaming across Kansas, Idaho, Oregon, California, and Arkansas before finally returning to Ohio and a life of what he described as "mercantile pursuits." He was the last of the Andrews Raiders to pass away, dying at his home in Dayton, Ohio, on October 15, 1923.[54]

*A*part from the honorary commission Fuller had received back in '63, the Georgia railroad men who had chased down the *General* never did receive any public honors or monetary reward. For the most part, that suited them just fine. Engineer Peter Bracken did not care a whit about getting a medal—or any other recognition for that matter—for his role in driving the *Texas*; on the contrary, his family would later recall that he was sensitive about not having served in the Confederate army during what some Southerners would refer to as the War Between the States, or the War of Northern Aggression, or even the Second American Revolution. "I do not want any unnecessary notoriety about the chase," he insisted in an 1895 letter to Bill Fuller, and he limited his postwar bragging to the yarns he told to his grandchildren. Still, Bracken firmly believed that he had been the right man, perhaps the only man, for the job of running down the stolen *General*. Even thirty-three years after the fact, it made the old railroader nervous to think of the breakneck speed, the dropped boxcars, and the crossties thrown on the track ahead of the *Texas*. "If I had not been running myself," he told Fuller, "I would not have rode on her with anyone else running as I would not have taken the chances or run the risk we run that day with anyone else handling the engine." Bracken, who showed himself time and again as a man who did not give up easily, continued running engines on the W&A until the bitter end: by the summer of 1865, he was one of only nineteen employees left on the railroad's payroll. After the war, he worked as an engineer, machinist, and superintendent on the Macon & Brunswick Railroad, and in the 1890s moved to Savannah to work for a lumber company.

Pete Bracken died on May 26, 1909, and was buried in an unmarked grave at Rose Hill Cemetery in Macon. In 1971, historian James Bogle arranged for the placement of a proper headstone, which features a fine engraving of the *Texas* and remembers Bracken as the "Engineer of the Locomotive *Texas* during the Great Locomotive Chase on the Western & Atlantic Railroad, April 12, 1862."[55]

Oliver Wiley Harbin, the engineer of the *William R. Smith*, spent another twenty-nine years running trains on the Rome Railroad. He settled in Tunnel Hill, Georgia, and died in 1910 at the age of seventy-six.[56]

Edward Henderson would spend another forty years as a telegraph operator, moving first to Florida, where he married the former Miss Fanny Ross, and then to New York, where he worked in the main office of the Western Union Telegraph Company. He and Fanny raised two sons, Tally and Ed, Jr., both of whom became operators as well. Henderson eventually returned south and settled in Smithville, Georgia, where he died in 1894. "Ed was one of the first to receive messages by sound," his sister proudly wrote, "and at the time of his death was considered by all who knew him, one of the best operators in the South."[57]

Henry P. Haney, the fifteen-year-old fireman on the *Texas*, went from stoking fires to putting them out. He spent another twenty years working in various posts on the W&A before leaving in 1885 to join the Atlanta Fire Department, where he put in thirty-four years and rose to the post of First Assistant Chief. He died in 1923.[58]

Jeff Cain, the assigned engineer of the *General* as she left Atlanta early on April 12, continued with the Western & Atlantic Railroad and despite his "frail and tubercular" condition lived to be nearly seventy. He died of consumption on February 10, 1897, and is buried at Oakland Cemetery in Atlanta. There, his error-filled epitaph reads: "Jeff Cain. The historic engineer of the W&ARR manned the famous *General* on the thrilling wartime run. It was he who drove the locomotive in the historic chase of the Andrews raders May 12, 1862." Of course this is incorrect—Cain certainly did not man the *General* on its thrilling run—he had it stolen right out from under him. And he had no part in the "historic chase" except running through the mud and abandoning the effort just after Kingston. But Cain was not the only pursuer to inflate his contributions, up to and beyond the grave.[59]

As precise recollections of who did what began to fade and the story of the Great Locomotive Chase grew in national prominence—thanks in large part to the success of Pittenger's books—Fuller increasingly emphasized his role as the chief pursuer and captor of the intrepid raiders. His speech at the GAR Reunion in Columbus, for example, had focused on the first person singular and centered on what one observer called "the theme that he led the pursuit and was himself responsible for its success." In a letter to one of the raiders, Fuller acknowledged the role of unexpected delays in foiling the Yankee plot, but noted the greatest cause as a simple one: "you had the wrong man behind you in the race," he wrote. "Am I immodest in saying so?"[60]

For his part, Anthony Murphy remained largely silent in the face of this one-sided battle for credit, as he rose in postwar years to become one of the city's foremost citizens in his own right. Murphy served as president of the Atlanta waterworks, was elected to the city council, and worked as a successful railroad financier and cotton trader. In 1891, he finally spoke publicly of his role in the chase in a letter written at the request of D.A. Dorsey, who had the account published in an Ohio newspaper. But the minor discrepancies between Murphy's newly submitted story and Fuller's earlier version drew little attention from the public or the participants themselves.

All that would change in 1895, when the *Atlanta Journal* ran what seemed like a fairly innocuous article praising the aging locomotive *Texas*, which Murphy regarded as "the real heroine of the day." Touching only briefly on the circumstances of the chase itself, the paper quoted Murphy as saying of the pursuit, "Mr. Fuller was with me all the way, Mr. Cain part of the distance." This characterization drew a prompt and venomous response from Fuller, who was irritated at the article's focus on Murphy and downright furious about Murphy's intimation that made the conductor seem like a sidekick. "In your article, you say '*Mr Fuller was with me all the way*,'" he wrote. "Now I was not *with you*, at all. The while you went along, *you were with me. I,* not you, was in full charge." A few weeks later, Fuller had published in the *Atlanta Constitution* a full rebuttal, complete with affidavits from Peter Bracken and Henry Haney that minimized Murphy's role in running the *Texas*. Pained by this attack, Murphy wrote a letter to the editor—which he either never sent or was never published—complaining of his depiction as a mere "on looker" and noting of the article, "There is animus all through it unworthy of anyone." If anything, however, Fuller's animus towards the former foreman Murphy would only increase, his attacks sharper and more frequent in the years to come. "Murphy had absolutely nothing to do with the chase or pursuit one way or the other," he insisted in an 1896 letter published in the *Columbus Dispatch*. "Murphy did none of the work and none of the planning. He is entitled to none of the honors or sins of the pursuit."

Fuller's greatest effort to hoard the honors of the pursuit took place a year later, when he read a chapter devoted to the story of the Andrews Raid in a new history book penned by Joel Chandler Harris, already famous by then for his Uncle Remus stories. Again, Fuller was incensed at the prominence given to Anthony Murphy. He wrote angrily to the author, claiming that the foreman "had absolutely nothing to do with pursuit or re-capture" and "had no right to even have his name mentioned." Harris, apparently chastened by this criticism, promised to revise the chapter and even sent a new manuscript to Fuller for approval. Still, the angry former conductor went so far as to threaten to sue the book's publisher if it did not withdraw the earlier version from the shelves. The new edition of *Stories of Georgia* was released in 1898 and apparently soothed Fuller, as it increased his role in the adventure, always listed his name first (referring to him as "Captain" Fuller, though that rank had not yet been bestowed), and slighted Murphy by describing him not as foreman but as merely "an employee of the road." In issuing this new edition, Harris apparently never consulted with Anthony Murphy.[61]

The comparative vanities of William Fuller and Anthony Murphy are embodied for all time at their respective burial places. Fuller died in 1905, and Murphy followed four years later. Both men were buried in Oakland Cemetery, just a few hundred yards from the hollow where the seven Ohio soldiers were hung in June 1862. A tall granite obelisk marks Fuller's grave, these days tangled with encroaching weeds and dandelion. The inscription reads:

> Captain William Allen Fuller
> Born April 15, 1836
> Died Dec. 28, 1905
> Captain Independent State Troops of Ga. C.S.A.
>
> On April 12, 1862, Captain Fuller pursued and after a race of 90 miles, from Big Shanty northward on the Western & Atlantic Railroad, re-captured the historic War-Engine "General" which had been seized by 22 Federal soldiers in disguise, thereby preventing the destruction of the bridges of the railroad and the consequent dismemberment of the Confederacy.

Viewing Fuller's epitaph on a recent visit to the cemetery, one venerable Atlanta historian said wryly: "You known damn well he wrote that thing himself."

Just a few paces to the south down a cracked brick footpath, Anthony Murphy rests in his large family plot. His epitaph says only:

Anthony Murphy
Born Nov. 29, 1829,
In County Wicklow, Ireland
Died Dec. 28, 1909[62]

In the end, despite their rivalry, both men deserve substantial commendation and a fairly equal share of credit for the foiling of James Andrews's plot. Fuller has been widely recognized down the years as the hero of the day—just as his tombstone attests—yet Murphy, and the other Georgia railroad men, too—Harbin and Haney, Bracken and Henderson—each earned his own share of praise for the pursuit as well. Murphy stayed with Fuller every step of the way, and his presence and authority on the road no doubt assisted in pressing others into service during the chase. There is no question that William Fuller, for all his heroics—some real, and some imagined—did not and could not have recovered the *General* and captured the Yankee raiders on his own.

Even so, again without question, it was Fuller's initiative and determination that not only kicked off the chase—it is doubtful whether anyone would have taken off on foot after the fleeing engine if Fuller had not led the way—but also sustained it against the odds and despite all manner of obstacles. Though he had little in the way of transportation, arms, or military support, and though he faced repeated interruptions, harsh terrain, broken track, and the possibility of an ambush, Fuller remained undaunted. The raiders, indeed, had the wrong man behind them in the race.

And even as he clamored for exclusive credit as the war receded in time, Fuller also showed himself to be gracious and friendly to his former adversaries, the surviving Andrews Raiders—and perhaps this is how he deserves to be remembered, most of all. As the wounded nation struggled to heal itself, and as memories faded, rivalries emerged, and beards grew long and gray, the old conductor reached out to his former foes and did some healing of his own. He corresponded with a number of the Ohio veterans, lauded them publicly for their fortitude and boldness, faithfully attended their reunions and dedications, wrote in earnest support of monuments and state pensions, and even expressed words of comfort to the relatives of the fallen. In doing so, Fuller found redemption for whatever sins of pride he had committed in after-years, and along the way achieved some measure of peace with the fact that in doing his duty he had sent eight men to the gallows.

In June 1882, Al Dorsey wrote to Captain Fuller seeking information on the court-martial of his comrades, and a good-natured exchange between the former adversaries ensued. Dorsey thanked Fuller for the "loan" of his engine on the day of the raid, and took the former conductor to task "for being so suspicious of his neighbor's intentions and running after the borrowed property to bring it back before we had done with it." On that day, Dorsey said, "all we asked was to be let alone."

Fuller promptly sent a warm reply, responding in kind to Dorsey's teasing. "You gentlemen are certainly very welcome to any little courtesies of mine on the occasion of your next visit," he wrote. "Next time you come to see me, don't be so awful hasty about your goodbye. 'Spend the day with me.' 'Bring your knitting.' Don't rush off without your breakfast, and by the way, cause me to lose mine, as well as dinner and supper."

Then, all jesting aside, the old railroader's sentiment turned sincere. "You were all good boys," he said. "My very heart was made sick by the sad fate of some of your comrades. But how could I avoid the part I took? I would have died in one moment and you know it, for the cause I loved. Don't you know it?"

"It is past now, and we all live in one great country common to us all," he closed. "Let us give each to the other his just dues."[63]

The *General* arriving at Kennesaw during the Centennial celebrations, April 1962. (*Colonel James G. Bogle Collection*)

Caboose

*T*HE STORY OF THE ANDREWS RAID endures even today, not only in the archival collections and memorials and tombstones of the participants—and the many books and films they inspired—but also in the landmarks and the landscape of North Georgia. Thanks to Sherman, nothing is left of the antebellum railroad buildings of Atlanta—but the Zero Mile Post that marks the city's geographic and historic center still remains, hidden beneath the Central Avenue viaduct in Underground Atlanta. The little hollow where seven Ohio volunteers were hanged is a wood-fenced, oak-shaded backyard behind a house on Woodward Avenue, just south of Oakland Cemetery. From downtown Atlanta all the way north to Chattanooga, a busy railroad line runs today along the original route of the Western & Atlantic Railroad. Moving north, five historic depot buildings still stand along the line, at Cartersville, Adairsville, Dalton, Tunnel Hill, and Ringgold. At Marietta, the former Fletcher House hotel where the raiders slept and Sherman headquartered today houses the Marietta Museum of History, overlooking the railroad tracks. Massive twin granite monuments—each inscribed with the heading "GENERAL"—stand trackside at Kennesaw and north of Ringgold, marking the exact locations where the Chase began and ended.

Priceless relics remain from the episode as well, most notably the two rival locomotives. As the victor of the Great Locomotive Chase, the *Texas* arguably should be the more revered of the two engines, but the pursuing locomotive for whatever reason did not receive the acclaim of the *General* in postwar years. In the early 1870s, the *Texas* was overhauled and converted to a coal burner, her balloon smokestack replaced by a more efficient and far less handsome diamond stack. Little is known of the engine's service over the next three decades. By 1903, the *Texas* had been demoted to periodic use as a switch engine on a branch line near Emerson, Georgia—a far cry from her glory days as a powerful workhorse and the pride of the State Road.

Retired from service shortly thereafter, the *Texas* would travel a much less glamorous road than its former rival—no fancy reunion appearances, no full-color lithographs commissioned, no bronze statues cast. By 1895, the old iron horse sat on a weed-choked siding, "unhonored and unsung," as the *Atlanta Journal* put it. "With the name of *Cincinnati* on her sides and her smoke stack gone, the old engine *Texas* is half buried in the dirt in the 'bone yard' at Vinings," the paper reported. Anthony Murphy was quoted in the article lamenting the fate of the old engine, which seemed to him to be "wounded and bleeding." "I have often thought it strange," he observed, "that so much should be said about the *General* and nothing about the *Texas*, the real heroine of the day."

Still, there seemed to be little interest in restoring and preserving the locomotive, which was by that time "a solid sheet of rust." The *Texas* was initially offered to the state of Georgia, but in marked contrast to the battle it would later wage for possession of the *General*, the state declined—either thinking little of the rusty engine (which was named in honor of another state, after all) or simply having no funds to fix it and no place to put it. The city of Atlanta accepted the locomotive and in 1911 placed it in Grant Park, where for sixteen years it stood outside among the oaks, before finally being moved into the basement lobby of the Atlanta Cyclorama building, where it remains today. Visitors to the Cyclorama—a spectacular 358-foot circular depiction of the Battle of Atlanta that claims the distinction of being the largest oil painting in the world—first pass by the restored *Texas* on their way upstairs. Having played second fiddle to the *General* ever since Civil War days, the magnificent locomotive *Texas* remains today nothing more than an opening act.[1]

The recaptured *General*, in contrast, went on to lead a charmed if controversial life. Despite the extensive damage she had suffered as Atlanta burned, the *General* was quickly repaired and refitted after the war by Georgia's still-thriving and resourceful railroad companies. As early as 1866, the locomotive was listed on the W&A's Annual Report as being in "Good Order" and would run thousands of miles each year for the rest of the decade. In the early 1870s, she too was converted to burn coal, advancing in technology but losing her large Radley & Hunter stack and with it some of the magic of the Age of Steam. By 1892, more than thirty-five years after her construction, the old engine was retired from service and placed on a siding near Vinings Station, where she seemed destined, like the *Yonah*, for the scrap heap. There in the Vinings boneyard she may have remained, but for an enterprising young lecturer and photographer named E. Warren Clark, who suggested that the *General* be refurbished and displayed at the World's Columbian Exposition in Chicago the following year. The Nashville, Chattanooga & St. Louis Railway, which had recently taken over the lease of the W&A, agreed to the project, and the *General* was entirely refurbished, her balloon stack returned, her finish gleaming, and her boiler festooned with flags and bunting. The famous locomotive was one of sixty-two engines displayed in the Transportation Building Annex at the great fair in Chicago and thereafter was returned to what all assumed would be her permanent home, on display under the vaulted brick arches of the Union Depot in Chattanooga. In the years to come, the *General* would make appearances at the Cotton States and International Exposition in Atlanta in 1895, the Tennessee Centennial Exposition in Nashville in 1897, and the Chicago Railroad Fair and the New York World's Fair in 1939. When the centennial of the Civil War arrived, the *General* was again reconditioned and in 1962 began a 23,000-mile national tour, including a year on display at the 1964 New York World's Fair. At the close of her centennial tour, the engine was brought to the shops of the Louisville & Nashville Railroad in Louisville, Kentucky, for repairs. In the meantime, a custody battle was brewing.[2]

Ownership of the *General* rested with the L&N Railroad by way of a merger that brought the Nashville, Chattanooga & St. Louis Railway, the lessee of the W&A, into the L&N system. In April 1968, the Georgia General Assembly formally requested of L&N that the *General* be returned to the state and directed that the engine would be permanently displayed at Kennesaw, formerly known as Big Shanty. The railroad's president agreed to the request, and five months later, the *General* departed Louisville headed for Georgia. As the train passed through Chattanooga on the night of September 12, Mayor Ralph Kelly, who had obtained a writ of attachment to seize the engine, had sheriff's deputies block the railroad and took possession of the famous locomotive. The *General* may not have reached Chattanooga on April 12, 1862, but the mayor thought she sure as hell had become a permanent resident since then, by virtue of her continuous display in the city's Union Station for more than sixty years. The *Saturday Evening Post*, after all, had referred to the vaunted *General* as "The Original Chattanooga Choo-Choo"—the city had gone so far as to adopt a likeness of the locomotive on its official seal—and Mayor Kelly planned to keep her right where she was.[3]

"In this lawsuit, the pursuit of the *General* continues," U.S. District Judge Frank W. Wilson wrote of the dispute. "While the capture of the ancient and historic steam locomotive known as the *General* remains the object of the pursuers in this lawsuit, unlike on that fateful day of April 12, 1862, life and death does not hang in the balance. Rather here the pursuers and the pursued vie with each other as to the more appropriate manner to preserve and do honor to the men and the traditions which are bound up in the story of the *General.*" The three-year litigation involved two separate cases—one brought by the City of Chattanooga against the L&N Railroad and the other brought by the State of Georgia, which claimed that Chattanooga's seizure of the state's property was nothing less than unconstitutional, constituting an unlawful burden on interstate commerce. Meanwhile, Chattanooga argued strenuously in favor of its right of attachment and fought for possession of the *General* under a slew of legal theories, including charitable trust, prescriptive interest, implied contract, and estoppel. By agreement of the parties, the famous locomotive was returned to neutral ground—back to the L&N shops at Louisville—to await the court's decision.

On January 4, 1969, Judge Wilson issued a lengthy written opinion that shot down each of the city's claims and ordered that the writ of attachment be released and the case dismissed. Possibly thinking of the criticism he would hear from his neighbors, the East Tennessee judge noted that "the issue before this court is not the appropriateness or inappropriateness of the display of the *General* in Chattanooga, Tennessee or in Kennesaw, Georgia," but rather whether under Tennessee law Chattanooga was entitled to maintain an action for attachment and injunction. The defeated city appealed, but the U.S. Court of Appeals for the Sixth Circuit affirmed Judge Wilson's ruling in May. Chattanooga took the case all the way to the United States Supreme Court, which on November 9, 1970, refused to hear the city's appeal. The *General* would return to the state of Georgia and stay there for good.[4]

In February 1972, the *General* was loaded on a flatcar in Louisville for her final journey. Taking no chances this time, her route would bypass Chattanooga, looping around past Cincinnati and thence through Knoxville, Cartersville, and Atlanta. On Friday morning, February 18, 1972, standing in a cold drizzle, Governor Jimmy Carter accepted the historic engine on behalf of the people of Georgia. Four and a half years after she was seized by Mayor Kelly at Chattanooga, the *General* arrived at Kennesaw. There she remains today, perhaps the most famous steam locomotive in the world, on permanent and glorious display at the Southern Museum of Civil War and Locomotive History—just a few feet from the spot where James Andrews and his men first swung aboard her on April 12, 1862.[5]

*T*he Medal of Honor, too, remains with us today, though it too was refurbished and transformed. Since that first ceremony in Stanton's office at the War Department in March 1863, the Medal of Honor has been awarded 3,461 times to 3,441 American men—and one woman (nineteen men have won the decoration twice). Recipients of the medal have served in the United States Army, the Navy, the Marines, the Air Force, and the Coast Guard; they fought in the Civil War, the Indian Wars, the Spanish-American War, the First and Second World Wars, Korea, Vietnam, Somalia, and Iraq. The medal commemorates deeds of valor performed on hallowed fields from Gettysburg to Omaha Beach, from Belleau Wood to Wounded Knee, from Ia Drang Valley to Mogadishu, and on waters from Mobile Bay to the Coral Sea. The roll of Medal of Honor recipients reads like a Valhalla of legendary American heroes. The list includes Joshua Lawrence Chamberlain, William F. "Buffalo Bill" Cody, Eddie Rickenbacker, Theodore Roosevelt, Gregory "Pappy" Boyington, James Doolittle, Douglas MacArthur, Audie Murphy, Charles Lindbergh, Alvin York, and hundreds more lesser known but no less courageous soldiers, sailors, and Marines. The Medal of Honor is rarely awarded, deeply admired, and often coveted. "I'd give my immortal soul for that decoration," General George S. Patton said, watching the presentation of the medal to a soldier at Casablanca in 1943.

The Medal of Honor was awarded to 1,522 soldiers for actions in the Civil War, many of these the result of battlefield heroics committed before and since the Andrews Raid, from Bull Run to Petersburg—but there was something singular, something uniquely compelling about the valor and the volunteer spirit of the Andrews Raiders that enthralled Secretary Stanton and President Lincoln. For here were nearly two dozen men who stepped up for a mission behind enemy lines, risking their lives and the inglorious death of a marauder and a spy in a cause "above and beyond the call of duty," to borrow from the modern criteria for the Medal of Honor. "They were simply typical, volunteer Ohio boys, barely out of their teens, without name, family, influence or station, to cause them to be remembered and honored as they are remembered and honored today," Governor Foraker said of the raiders at the dedication of the Andrews monument in 1891. And it was not only their selflessness in volunteering and their actions in the frantic hours of the chase, but their fortitude in the months that followed that proved themselves heroes and worthy recipients of the nation's highest decoration.

The Andrews Raiders would not be the last soldiers to win the Medal of Honor without fighting a battle, killing an enemy combatant, storming a beach, or rescuing a comrade. Sadly, for a time at least, the Medal was threatened with the taint of politics and personal ambition, and the price of gallantry and the commensurate worth of the decoration was diminished. In later years, the roll of Medal of Honor winners would include such characters as the twenty-nine honorary pallbearers who accompanied the remains of President Lincoln from Washington to Springfield, Illinois; all 864 members of the 27th Maine Regiment, who were given the medal as an incentive to reenlist (though only 309 signed on for extended duty); and a Navy ensign who in 1923 saved a woman from a burning hotel in Yokohama, Japan. In addition, though James J. Andrews and William Campbell were never considered for the award because of their civilian status, some of the Medal's most famous recipients were also civilians, including Dr. Mary Edwards Walker, the only woman to receive the award, Charles Lindbergh—who received what one retired officer called "a Medal of Honor by public acclamation"—and Buffalo Bill Cody, who was, like James Andrews, a civilian scout acting in conjunction with the United States military. The low point came in 1872, when the Medal of Honor was doled out to a retired lieutenant colonel, who wrote to the War Department by way of application: "I understand there are a number of bronze medals for distribution to soldiers of the late War, and request I be allowed one as a souvenir of memorable times past."[6]

Such careless awards of the Medal of Honor were brought to an end under President Theodore Roosevelt. During his administration, the criteria for the decoration were clarified and strengthened, a panel of retired generals appointed to review past awards, and a new design approved and patented. (Interestingly, Roosevelt's own personal pursuit of the Medal of Honor for his heroics at the Battle of San Juan Hill would not bear fruit until 2001, when he was awarded the Medal of Honor posthumously, eighty-two years after his death. Though a number of military heroes have occupied the White House—including Ulysses S. Grant, John F. Kennedy, Dwight D. Eisenhower, and George H. W. Bush—TR is the only president to receive the Medal of Honor.) Since 1918, the Medal of Honor has been awarded only to a person who, "while a member of the armed forces, distinguishes himself or herself conspicuously by gallantry and intrepidity at the risk of his life above and beyond the call of duty while engaged in an action against any enemy of the United States." Meanwhile, due to its origins in federal legislation and the traditional award of the Medal of Honor by the President of the United States "on behalf of the Congress," the medal over the years came to be widely known as the Congressional Medal of Honor—a technically erroneous but perfectly understandable designation. Indeed, in its early years, the reverse of the medal was inscribed from "The Congress to" the honored recipient. Groups affiliated with the decoration have chosen to embrace rather than to painstakingly correct the misnomer—including the Congressional Medal of Honor Society (an organization comprised of all living recipients of the decoration) and the Congressional Medal of Honor Foundation.[7]

Military men and women often refer to the decoration, briefly though reverently, as "the CMH"—though some of the more cynical in the ranks maintain that the acronym stands for "casket with metal handles." To them, it seems that a fellow has to get himself killed to merit consideration for the award, and there is considerable evidence to support this view. In recent years, more often than not, the medal has been presented to grieving widows, sons, and daughters—since 1918, 60 percent of all Medals of Honor have been awarded posthumously. "The time when the Medal was a decoration primarily for live heroes [is] long in the past," one historian wrote.[8]

Most recently as of this writing, the medal was awarded to Sergeant First Class Paul R. Smith of Tampa, Florida, killed in Iraq on April 4, 2003. Sergeant Smith, his unit surrounded and outnumbered by Republican Guard troops near Baghdad Airport, climbed aboard an armored vehicle under "withering enemy fire" and manned a .50 caliber machine gun, covering the evacuation of wounded Americans and killing as many as fifty enemy soldiers before being mortally wounded. In so doing, according to his Medal of Honor citation, Smith displayed "extraordinary heroism and uncommon valor without regard to his own life," and thereby became the latest posthumous recipient of the Medal of Honor.

The first posthumous recipient was Sergeant Major Marion A. Ross.[9]

*D*espite the many breathless assessments of the Andrews Raid at the time and down the years—"the boldest adventure of the war," the "Most Extraordinary Exploit in American History," "The Most Daring Undertaking that Yankees ever Planned," "absolutely sublime,"—the enduring question of the strategic wisdom and the tactical feasibility of the expedition remains. If Andrews and his men had succeeded, would the raid have been effective in isolating Chattanooga and providing for its ready investment and capture? Could the raid have actually worked, if the fickle winds of fortune—wet weather, railroad traffic, one-day delays, oversleeping engineers—had shifted and if things had turned out differently? If the raiders had burned, say, five bridges on the W&A, would Ormsby Mitchel have captured Chattanooga and sliced the South in two?

The answer to this question turns on the capability of Mitchel's under-sized division to successfully undertake aggressive action against an unknown Confederate force occupying a strong natural position. A number of observers, civilian and military, thought Chattanooga susceptible to capture in the spring of 1862, and some believed that Mitchel was the man to do it. Horace Greeley, the editor of the *New York Tribune*, later wrote of Mitchel: "Had he been even moderately rëenforced, he would have struck and proba-bly could have destroyed the great Rebel armories and founderies in Georgia, or have captured Chattanooga." Greeley's qualifications—that Mitchel *proba-bly* could have captured his objective *if reinforced*—undermine his assertion entirely. Mitchel had already divided his 10,000-man force into three parts in capturing Huntsville, with a large portion of his division strung out along the Memphis & Charleston Railroad from Decatur to Bridgeport. With his already small command thus dispersed along more than a hundred miles of railroad in Rebel territory, if Mitchel were going to capture Chattanooga in April 1862, he would have required the support of General Buell—which was not forthcoming.[10]

The man who may have lamented Mitchel and Buell's failure to move on Chattanooga the most was General Ulysses S. Grant. In his memoirs, Grant expressed sincere regret at Buell's slow eastward movement along the M&C, creeping forward and repairing the railroad as he advanced, only to have the line destroyed by guerillas as soon as the bluecoats moved out of the way. Grant concluded:

> If he had been sent to Chattanooga as rapidly as he could march, leaving two or three divisions along the line of the railroad from Nashville, he could have arrived with but little fighting and would have saved much of the loss of life which he afterwards incurred in gaining Chattanooga. Bragg would not then have had time to raise an army and contest the possession of middle and east Tennessee and Kentucky; the battles of Stones River and Chickamauga would not necessarily have been fought; Burnside would not have been besieged in Knoxville without the power of helping himself or escaping; the battle of Chattanooga would not have been fought. These are the negative advantages, if the term negative is applica-ble, which would probably have resulted from prompt movements after Corinth fell into the possession of the National forces. The positive result might have been: A bloodless advance to Atlanta, to Vicksburg, or to any other desired point south of Corinth in the interior of Mississippi.[11]

This is not to say, of course, that James Andrews and his men necessarily held the key that could unlock an alternate history that would bypass subsequent battlefields and bloody sieges and campaigns. Notwithstanding General Grant's wishful scenario of what might have been, in the end, Ormsby Mitchel simply lacked the means and the command support to take Chattanooga in the spring of 1862, and his superior, General Buell, lacked the initiative and the will to do so. As a result, even if Andrews had succeeded in reducing several bridges on the W&A to smoldering ruins, he may have found himself caught in the same fix the East Tennessee Tory bridge burners had faced the previous November—their own mission accomplished, the damage done to the railroad as planned, but an unresponsive Union force nearby unwilling or unable to move to take advantage of the interruption. That said, the city of Chattanooga was unquestionably vulnerable. The rugged terrain and the winding river that protected the junction town also served to isolate it, and its few defenders were untrained, ill-equipped, and for the most part all alone—as the two great armies of the Confederacy were fully occupied, wrestling with problems of their own far to the east and west. In short, if the Mountain City had been cut off, a committed Federal assault could indeed have taken the town—as Grant himself recognized.

Yet even if staggering military results had been achievable during that rainy April week, the attempt to sever the W&A was compromised in any event. In some ways, the tactical effort was simply jinxed with sorry luck, much as Andrews's earlier attempt had been, with the rain and the interminable delay at Kingston hurting the raiders' chances most of all. Then, of course, there was the relentless pursuit of a small party of Georgia civilians, who robbed the raiders of the luxury of time and ultimately made their escape impossible. But some observers would later question the planning and the execution of the raid as well. James Andrews has been romanticized as a dauntless adventurer and the boldness and initiative of the raiders for generations has been justly praised, but the mission suffered from a lack of military leadership in its most critical moments. Intrigued by Andrews's plan and mesmerized by his appearance and demeanor, General Mitchel had after all placed two dozen of his soldiers under the sole direction of a civilian who had no military background and no railroad experience whatsoever. No officer from the Third Division was dispatched to accompany and direct the soldiers, and neither the regimental sergeant major, Marion Ross, nor the two sergeants Elihu Mason and John Scott appeared to exercise any authority over the privates and corporals along the way. Not a single one of the surviving raiders ever spoke of any order being issued by these three men;

on the contrary, many of the key decisions made that day—whether to stop and fight, whether to destroy the *Yonah*, whether to abandon the engine— appeared to be considered and made either by Andrews alone, with or without the advice of others, or by various *ad hoc* committees. The Andrews Raid was a military operation that at times was run more like the governance of a country church.

In hindsight, many who claimed to know better how to run a secret mission—historians, veterans, even some of his own men—would later criticize Andrews for these and other failings. But even though he held no commission and wore no badge of rank, there was no question that James Andrews led the raid with vigor and panache. The contraband runner devised a creative and workable plan of sabotage, safely conducted twenty men more than 120 miles behind enemy lines, stole a Southern locomotive in the middle of a Confederate camp (wearing an Abe Lincoln hat, no less)—and he damn near pulled the whole thing off. "The objective would have been worth regiments," one historian concluded, "and the agent called Andrews and his hastily picked party of twenty-one came astonishingly close to achieving it on their own." And even in failure, Andrews and his men not only won the admiration of citizens up to and including Abraham Lincoln, but also shocked the Confederacy and foreshadowed the great invasion of Georgia two years hence—as well as other daring, medal-winning raids by the United States military still to come. As to whether the Andrews Raiders could have enabled an early Federal occupation of Chattanooga and caused a meaningful change in the storms of the Civil War, the facile but honest answer is that no one will ever know.

"Now, my braves," Andrews had told his gathered volunteers in their initial meeting outside Shelbyville, "there is little doubt that we will burn the bridges, and that General Mitchel will occupy Chattanooga, the most important strategic point in the Confederacy. . . . Our work is the entering wedge to more important movements which will result in a speedy suppression of the rebellion, the restoration of the peace, and our return to our homes and peaceful pursuits."[12]

If only it had been so.

The Great Locomotive Chase endpoint marker, north of Ringgold. (*Author*)

Notes

PREFACE.

1 Wayne Snow, "Georgia to Honor Yankee Spy," United Press International, April 4, 1982 (LEXIS/NEXIS); *Ohio Boys in Dixie: The Adventures of Twenty-Two Scouts Sent by Gen. O.M. Mitchell* [sic] *to Destroy a Railroad, With a Narrative of Their Barbarous Treatment by the Rebels and Judge Holt's Report* (New York: Miller & Matthews, 1863), p. 8.

2 Joel Chandler Harris, *Stories of Georgia* (New York: American Book Co., 1896, 1898), p. 296.

3 Letter from Wilbur Kurtz to Walt Disney, Feb. 1, 1952, p. 2, Wilbur G. Kurtz Collection, Margaret Herrick Library, Academy of Motion Picture Arts and Sciences, Los Angeles; David J. Eicher, *The Longest Night: A Military History of the Civil War* (New York: Touchstone, 2001), p. 237.

CHAPTER ONE. THE BRIDGE BURNERS

1 Ralph Waldo Emerson, "The Young American," *Ralph Waldo Emerson: Essays and Lectures* (New York: Library of America, 1983), p. 213; George Edgar Turner, *Victory Rode the Rails: The Strategic Place of the Railroads in the Civil War* (Lincoln: University of Nebraska Press, 1992), p. 16.

2 David M. Stokes, "Railroads Blue and Gray: Rail Transport in the Civil War, 1861-65: A Bibliography," *National Railway Bulletin,* 65, no. 5 (2000), p. 5; James M. McPherson, *Battle Cry of Freedom: The Civil War Era* (New York: Oxford University Press, 1988), pp. 11-12 (discussing development of United States rail network and its profound effect on American life). For an excellent overview of the role of railroads in the war, see Turner, *Victory Rode the Rails.*

3 Gary Gallagher, Introduction, in Turner, *Victory Rode the Rails,* p. 1. Gallagher notes: "Railroads made possible the strategic concentration of soldiers from widely separated areas, provided logistical arteries for Federal forces moving into the Confederacy, and acted as lifelines for the principal southern armies in the field." Ibid. George B. McClellan to Abraham Lincoln, Aug. 2, 1861, in *The War of the Rebellion: A Compilation of the Official Records of the Union and Confederate Armies,* 128 vols. (Washington, D.C., 1880-1901), vol. 5, pt. 1, p. 7 (hereinafter cited as OR; all references are to series 1 unless otherwise noted). These and other episodes and strategic movements involving railroads in the early days of the war are recounted in Turner, *Victory Rode the Rails,* pp. 48, 86-88.

4 Stokes, "Railroads Blue and Gray," p. 5; Turner, *Victory Rode the Rails,* p. 18.

5 The trunk lines and their intersection in Chattanooga are described in Frank M. Gregg, *Andrews Raiders: or the Last Scenes and Final Chapter of the Daring Incursion into the Heart of the Confederacy* (Chattanooga: Republican Job Print, 1891), pp. 8-9; William Pittenger, *Daring and Suffering: A History of the Andrews Railroad Raid* (New York: War Publishing Co. 1887; 3rd ed. reprint, Cumberland House, 1999), p. 15; Stan Cohen and James G. Bogle, *The General and the Texas* (Missoula, Mont.: Pictorial Histories Publishing Co., 1999), p. iv.

6 David Herbert Donald, *Lincoln* (New York: Simon & Schuster, 1995), p. 45 (quoting *The Collected Works of Abraham Lincoln,* Roy Basler, ed. [New Brunswick, N.J.: Rutgers University

Press, 1953], 1:509-10); ibid., p. 329; Abraham Lincoln, July 23-27, 1861, Memoranda on Military Policy After Bull Run, Abraham Lincoln Papers, Library of Congress (hereinafter AL-LOC). In the Civil War, the Eastern Theater was considered the area between the East Coast and the Appalachian Mountains, with the Western Theater defined as the land from Appalachia to the Mississippi River. Hence, in Civil War terms, Georgia, Tennessee, Alabama, and Mississippi are considered a part of "the West," while Virginia, Maryland, and Pennsylvania were in "the East."

7 Richard Nelson Current, *Lincoln's Loyalists: Union Soldiers from the Confederacy* (Boston: Northeastern University Press, 1992), p. 60; David Madden, "Unionist Resistance to Confederate Occupation: The Bridge Burners of East Tennessee," *East Tennessee Historical Society's Publications*, 52-53 (1980-81), p. 22; E. Kirby Smith to W.W. Mackall, March 14, 1862, *OR*, vol. 10, pt. 2, p. 325; A.G. Graham to Jefferson Davis, Nov. 12, 1861, *OR*, series 2, vol. 1, pt. 1, p. 842.

8 Current, *Lincoln's Loyalists*, pp. 33-40; Alf Wilson, *The Adventures of Alf Wilson: A Thrilling Episode of the Dark Days of the Rebellion* (Toledo, Ohio: Blade, 1880), p. 149 ("a man of fine stature . . ."); Pittenger, *Daring and Suffering*, p. 265 ("one of the noblest men in the world"); John C. Inscoe and Gordon B. McKinney, *The Heart of Confederate Appalachia: Western North Carolina in the Civil War* (Chapel Hill: University of North Carolina Press, 2000), p. 107.

9 Oliver Temple, *East Tennessee and the Civil War* (1899; reprint ed., Johnson City, Tenn.: Overmountain Press, 1999), p. 388; Isham G. Harris to Jefferson Davis, Nov. 12, 1861, *OR*, series 2, vol. 1, pt. 1, p. 841. Benjamin reassured the president of the East Tennessee and Virginia Railroad: "Troops are now moving to East Tennessee to crush the traitors. You shall be amply protected." J.P. Benjamin to John R. Branner, Nov. 13, 1861, *OR*, series 2, vol. 1, pt. 1, p. 843. For a detailed account of the various attacks on the East Tennessee bridges, see Madden, "Unionist Resistance to Confederate Occupation," pp. 30-34.

10 Ezra Warner, *Generals in Gray: Lives of the Confederate Commanders* (Baton Rouge: Louisiana State University Press, 1964), pp. 176-77. General Leadbetter for the most part lacks an unbiased biographer—virtually all the contemporaneous descriptions of the man are by his adversaries, all of whom regarded him as a drunken incompetent at best and the devil incarnate at worst. See, e.g., W.G. Brownlow, *Sketches of the Rise, Progress and Decline of Secession; with a Narrative of Personal Adventures Among the Rebels* (Philadelphia: George W. Childs, 1862), pp. 353, 360 (describing Leadbetter as "that prince of villains, tyrants, and murderers," a man who "never had a gentlemanly emotion of soul in his life"); William Pittenger, *Daring and Suffering: A History of the Great Railroad Adventure* (Philadelphia: J.W. Daughaday, 1864), pp. 123-24 (calling Leadbetter a drunken coward, and "one of the most contemptible individuals I ever knew"). Some Southerners added their own criticisms of Leadbetter's courage and military acumen. See, e.g., Mary Chadick, Diary, May 10, 1862, quoted in "A Housewife's Perspective on the Occupation of Huntsville," *Huntsville Historical Review*, 16, nos. 1 and 2 (Spring-Fall 1989), p. 17 (claiming that Gen. Leadbetter "acted cowardly" at Bridgeport); Wilson, *Adventures of Alf Wilson*, p. 94; J.P. Benjamin to G.B. Crittenden, Nov. 13, 1861, *OR*, series 2, vol. 1, pt. 1, pp. 855-56; Brownlow, *Sketches of the Rise, Progress and Decline of Secession*, p. 420.

11 D. Leadbetter to S. Cooper, *OR*, series 2, vol. 1, pt. 1, p. 853.

12 Current, *Lincoln's Loyalists*, p. 36; Judah P. Benjamin to W.B. Wood, Nov. 25, 1861, *OR*,

series 2, vol. I, pt. I, p. 848 ("executed on the spot"); Brownlow, *Sketches of the Rise, Progress and Decline of Secession*, pp. 420-21.

13 Charles Kendall O'Neill, *Wild Train: The Story of Andrews' Raiders* (New York: Random House, 1956), p. 34; Wilson, *Adventures of Alf Wilson*, p. 149 ("left to his fate almost unaided").

14 Benjamin to Wood, Nov. 25, 1861, *OR*, series 2, vol. I, pt. I, p. 848; Current, *Lincoln's Loyalists*, p. 39; D. Leadbetter Proclamation "To the Citizens of East Tennessee," Nov. 30, 1861, *OR*, series 2, vol. I, pt. I, pp. 851-52; Leadbetter to S. Cooper, Dec. 8, 1861, *OR*, vol. 7, p. 748 ("the happiest effect").

15 Current, *Lincoln's Loyalists*, p. 38. Lincoln's concern and support for the Union-loyal citizens of East Tennessee was earnest and unwavering throughout the war. More than a year later, he would tell two petitioners from the region, quite accurately, "I do as much for East Tennessee as I would, or could, if my own home and family were in Knoxville." Lincoln to Robert Morrow and John M. Fleming, Aug. 9, 1863, AL-LOC. And Lincoln's view of Chattanooga as a critical strategic point never changed as well. In October 1863, he wrote to Major General William S. Rosecrans, "If we can hold Chattanooga, and East Tennessee, I think the rebellion must dwindle and die." Lincoln to Rosecrans, Oct. 4, 1863, *Collected Works*, 6:498.

16 Stephen D. Engle, *Don Carlos Buell: Most Promising of All* (Chapel Hill: University of North Carolina Press, 1999), pp. 24-28, 40-41, 59-61. On Buell's service in the Mexican War, Engle quotes a fellow junior officer who opines that Buell, shot in the chest while scaling a redoubt at Churubusco, was "the bravest man it was ever my fortune to know." Ibid., p. 41. Another fellow officer well impressed with Buell was William Tecumseh Sherman, who told his stepbrother Philemon Ewing, "Buell is our best soldier." W.T. Sherman to Philemon B. Ewing, July 13, 1862, in *Sherman's Civil War: Selected Correspondence of William T. Sherman*, Brooks D. Simpson and Jean V. Berlin, eds. (Chapel Hill: University of North Carolina Press, 1999), p. 253. Buell's participation in the unfolding drama at Forts Moultrie and Sumter is described in David Detzer, *Allegiance: Fort Sumter, Charleston, and the Beginning of the Civil War* (New York: Harcourt, 2001), pp. 80-82.

17 George B. McClellan to D.C. Buell, Nov. 27, 1861, *OR*, vol. 7, pt. I, p. 450 ("unless it is impossible"); McClellan to Buell, Dec. 3, 1861, *OR*, series 2, vol. I, pt. I, p. 896 ("brighter laurels"); Andrew Johnson and Horace Maynard to Buell, Dec. 7, 1861, *OR*, series 2, vol. I, pt. I, pp. 897-98.

18 Buell to McClellan, Nov. 27, 1861, vol. 7, pt. I, p. 451 ("I have studiously avoided"); see also Gerald Prokopowicz, *All for the Regiment: The Army of the Ohio, 1861-1862* (Chapel Hill: University of North Carolina Press, 2001), p. 67; Buell to McClellan, Dec. 10, 1861, *OR*, series 2, vol. I, pt. I, pp. 898-99 ("I have by no means been unmindful"); John Beatty, *The Citizen-Soldier; or, Memoirs of a Volunteer* (Cincinnati: Wilstach, Baldwin & Co., 1879), p. 89; Lincoln to Buell, Jan. 4, 1862, *OR*, vol. 7, pt. I, p. 530; Buell to Lincoln, Jan. 5, 1862, *OR*, vol. 7, pt. I, pp. 530-31.

19 Lincoln to Buell, Jan. 6, 1862, *OR*, vol. 7, pt. I, pp. 927-28.

20 McClellan to Buell, Jan. 6, 1862, *OR*, vol. 7, pt. I, p. 531; Mitchel letter, February 1862, quoted in F.A. Mitchel, *Ormsby MacKnight Mitchel, Astronomer and General* (Boston: Houghton Mifflin, 1887), p. 242.

21 Lincoln to Buell, Jan. 7, 1862, *OR*, vol. 7, pt. I, p. 535; Halleck to Lincoln, Jan. 6, 1862, *OR*, vol. 7, pt. I, pp. 532-33.

22 Edwin M. Stanton to Thomas A. Scott, March 8, 1862, *OR*, vol. 10, pt. 2, p. 20 ("The President is much pleased with the cautious vigor of General Buell . . ."). Buell's occupation of Nashville and his policy of conciliation are recounted in detail in Engle, *Don Carlos Buell: Most Promising of All*, pp. 183-200.

23 Buell describes his mid-March arrangements after he was ordered to join with Grant in Don Carlos Buell, "Operations in North Alabama," *Battles and Leaders of the Civil War* (New York: Century Co., 1887), vol. 2, p. 701; see also Propokowicz, *All for the Regiment*, p. 95; Buell to Mitchel, *OR*, vol. 10, pp. 71-72.

24 Beatty, *Citizen Soldier*, p. 118. Beatty writes in his diary on March 18, 1862: "Toward evening we went into camp on the plantation of a widow lady, and here for the first time in my life I saw a field of cotton; the old stalks still standing with many bulbs which had escaped the pickers."

CHAPTER TWO. OLD STARS

1 "Mitchel, General Ormsby McKnight," in *Biographical Encyclopaedia of Ohio* (Cincinnati: Galaxy Publishing Co., 1876), p. 312; "Biographical Notice," in O.M. Mitchel, *Astronomy of the Bible* (New York: Albert Mason, 1874), p. 14. Unless otherwise noted, the discussion of Mitchel's early life is based upon F.A. Mitchel, *Ormsby MacKnight Mitchel, Astronomer and General* (Boston: Houghton Mifflin, 1887); Kevin J. Weddle, "Old Stars: Ormsby Macknight Mitchel at the Gates of the Confederacy," *Blue & Gray*, July 1987, pp. 28-29; and Kay Cornelius, "Old Stars in Alabama: General Ormsby M. Mitchel," *Alabama Heritage*, 34 (Winter 1994), pp. 18-20. His friendship with Jefferson Davis is noted by Whitelaw Reid, *Ohio in the War: Her Statesmen, Her Generals and Soldiers* (Cincinnati: Moore, Wilstach & Baldwin, 1868), vol. I, p. 592.

2 Mitchel's career as an astronomer is recounted in Mitchel, *Ormsby MacKnight Mitchel, Astronomer and General*, pp. 49-204; and Kevin J. Weddle, "Old Stars: Ormsby Mitchel," *Sky and Telescope* (January 1986), pp. 14-16. Weddle describes in detail Mitchel's efforts to raise funds for the new Cincinnati observatory and his quest to locate and procure a fine telescope for the facility. The Mountains of Mitchel on Mars, incidentally, are not a snowy mountain range (as Mitchel surmised) at all; rather, the formation is a rift or detachment near the Martian polar ice cap. Frederic W. Taylor, *The Cambridge Photographic Guide to the Planets* (Cambridge: Cambridge University Press, 2001), p. 160.

3 Mitchel's lectures are described in Whitelaw Reid, *Ohio in the War*, vol. I, pp. 594-98; and are quoted extensively in Mitchel, *Ormsby MacKnight Mitchel, Astronomer and General*, pp. 159-99; and P.C. Headly, *The Patriot Boy: The Life and Career of Major-General Ormsby M. Mitchel* (New York: W.H. Appleton, 1865). Among those noting the connection between Mitchel and Whitman's famous poem are Cornelius, "Old Stars in Alabama," *Alabama Heritage*, p. 19 ("it is tempting to speculate that Mitchel may have had the dubious honor of being the inspiration for Whitman's poem 'When I Heard the Learn'd Astronomer'"); and Timothy Steifel, "O.M. Mitchel," in *Walt Whitman: An Encyclopedia*, J.R. Lemaster and Donald D. Kummings, eds. (New York: Garland, 1998), p. 434. Whitman's poem says, in part: "When I, sitting, heard the astronomer, / where he lectured with much applause in the lecture-room, / How

soon, unaccountable, I became tired and sick; / Till rising and gliding out, I wander'd off by myself, / In the mystical moist night-air, and from time to time, / Look'd up in perfect silence at the stars." Walt Whitman, *Leaves of Grass* (New York: Bantam, 1983), p. 219.

4 Reid, *Ohio in the War*, vol.I, pp. 593-94 (Little Miami Railroad); Mitchel, *Ormsby MacKnight Mitchel, Astronomer and General*, p. 45 (railroad experience); O'Neill, *Wild Train*, p. 11 ("inexhaustible Roman candle").

5 Mitchel to Lincoln, July 27, 1861, AL-LOC.

6 Joseph Warren Keifer, *Slavery and Four Years of War: A Political History of Slavery in the United States, Together With a Narrative of the Campaigns and Battles of the Civil War in Which the Author Took Part: 1861-65* (New York: G.P. Putnam's Sons, 1900), pp. 264-65; Beatty, *The Citizen-Soldier*, p. 132.

7 William Vocke, "The Military Achievements of Major-General Ormsby MacKnight Mitchel," in Commandery of the State of Illinois, Military Order of the Loyal Legion of the United States (MOLLUS-IL), *Military Essays and Recollections*, vol. 4, p. 84 ("not over five feet six inches tall . . ."); Beatty, *The Citizen-Soldier*, pp. 96-97 ("never drinks and never swears"); Diary, May 1, 1862, H.C. Patton Papers, Indiana Historical Society, quoted in Prokopowicz, *All for the Regiment*, p. 122 ("Gen. Mitchell is the man . . ."); Reid, *Ohio in the War*, vol.I, p. 616 ("nervous excitability . . .").

8 The Third Division's repair of the two spans over the Duck River are recounted in Mitchel, *Ormsby MacKnight Mitchel, Astronomer and General*, pp. 268-70; Pittenger, *Daring and Suffering*, pp. 19-20; and Reid, *Ohio in the War*, vol.I, p. 606. Pittenger, *Daring and Suffering*, p. 20 ("stimulating them by word and example"); William Pittenger, *Capturing a Locomotive: A History of Secret Service in the Late War* (Philadelphia: J.B. Lippincott & Co., 1881), p. 10 ("worked like a beaver").

9 Buell to Mitchel, March 27, 1862, *OR*, vol. 10, pt. 2, pp. 71-72.

10 Craig Angle, *The Great Locomotive Chase: More on the Andrews Raid and the First Medal of Honor* (Rouzerville, Pa.: C. Angle, 1992), pp. 16-17 (history of Shelbyville); *Cincinnati Commercial*, April 13, 1862, reprinted in *Brooklyn Daily Eagle*, April 25, 1862 (describing warm reception by Unionists at Shelbyville); Vocke, "Military Achievements," MOLLUS-IL, *Military Essays and Recollections*, vol. 4, p. 88; Mitchel to George S. Coe, April 2, 1862, quoted in Mitchel, *Ormsby MacKnight Mitchel, Astronomer and General*, pp. 270-71.

11 McClellan's advance on the Peninsula is described in Stephen Sears, *To the Gates of Richmond: The Peninsula Campaign* (New York: Houghton Mifflin, 2001), p. 7 ("Napoleon himself . . ."). For an excellent account of the Battle of Shiloh and its context, see Larry J. Daniel, *Shiloh: The Battle that Changed the Civil War* (New York: Simon & Schuster, 1997).

12 William Haines Lytle to Josephine Lytle Foster and Elizabeth Lytle Broadwell, April 6, 1862, in William Haines Lytle, *For Honor, Glory & Union: The Mexican & Civil War Letters of Brig. Gen. William Haines Lytle*, Ruth C. Carter, ed. (Lexington: University Press of Kentucky, 1999).

13 No witnesses were present at the meeting between Mitchel and Andrews, and the exact content and duration of their discussion are uncertain. See Pittenger, *Daring and Suffering*, pp. 25, 35; (Atlanta) *Southern Confederacy*, April 19, 1862 ("most extraordinary adventure" and "most daring undertaking").

14 O'Neill, *Wild Train*, pp. 21-28, 382-89. O'Neill notes, "The man known as James J.

Andrews was nearly thirty before presently available history places him as even being alive." See also J.J. Andrews to "Ladies Soldiers Aid Society of Flemingsburg," Dec. 6, 1861, Fleming County Library Collection, Flemingsburg, Kentucky; Mrs. W.T. Lindsay, quoted in O'Neill, *Wild Train*, p. 22; J.J. Andrews to D.S. McGavic, June 5, 1862, James J. Andrews Papers, William P. Palmer Collection, Western Reserve Historical Society Archives.

15 Gary L. Miller, "Historical Natural History: Insects and the Civil War," *American Entomologist*, 43 (1997), pp. 227-245 (discussion of quinine smuggling in the Civil War).

16 The known facts and some informed speculation on Andrews's background are recounted in O'Neill, *Wild Train*, pp. 21-28, 382-89. O'Neill theorizes, based on certain misspellings in Andrews's letters, that he was born and educated in Europe, and that his ancestry was Finnish, Estonian, or Swedish. I would note, however, that none of the raiders who spent many weeks traveling and in prison with James Andrews would ever make a similar suggestion or note so much as a trace of a foreign accent. See also Jacob Parrott and Frank C. Dougherty, "The Andrews' Railroad Raid," *McClure's*, Sept. 1903, p. 498 ("I didn't know Andrews, but I had heard of him"); William A. Fuller, "Battle of the Locomotives," *Atlanta Journal Magazine*, March 16, 1930 (parenthetical question mark in original); William Knight, Interview with Wilbur G. Kurtz, in Andrews Raid Notebook I, Wilbur G. Kurtz Collection, Atlanta History Center (hereinafter Kurtz-AHC), pp. 79-80 (making the "surprising statement" that Andrews was in the spy business for the money); Buell, "Operations in North Alabama," *Battles and Leaders of the Civil War*, vol. 2, p. 716. Raider William Pittenger recounts the rumor that Andrews provided "a complete account of the Confederate forces" at Fort Donelson, along with a sketch of their defenses. Pittenger, *Daring and Suffering*, p. 61.

17 Andrews's first attempt to break the Western & Atlantic Railroad is described somewhat disdainfully by Buell's adjutant James B. Fry, in "Notes on the Locomotive Chase," *Battles and Leaders*, vol. 2, p. 716, concluding: "In relation to the merits of this scheme it may be said that at the time it was of sufficient importance to offset the probabilities of failure and the risk to the men engaged. But at best the undertaking was hardly commendable." See also Pittenger, *Daring and Suffering*, pp. 14, 16-19, 21-24; Pittenger, *Capturing a Locomotive*, p. 22 ("Never!"); Dorsey, "The Mitchel Raiders," *The Ohio Soldier*, May 20, 1893, p. 322 ("as though he had a rope around his neck").

18 Brig. Gen. J.H. Trapier, CSA, Dec. 26, 1861, quoted in Robert C. Black III, *The Railroads of the Confederacy* (Chapel Hill: University of North Carolina Press, 1998), p. 137 ("legs and stomach"). There is considerable uncertainty about what sort of monetary reward was to be paid to Andrews for the raid. See W.J. Scott, "An Episode of the War: Andrews and His Scheme," in *From Lincoln to Cleveland: and Other Short Studies in History and General Literature* (Atlanta: J.P. Harrison, 1886), p. 154 (Andrews was to receive "a large sum" and the privilege to trade across the lines); Pittenger, *Daring and Suffering*, p. 262 (noting that "it pleased [Andrews] to represent [the raid] to the enemy as a purely financial transaction, and as of little military importance. He never made any such representation to us when alone"). See also Scott, *From Lincoln to Cleveland*, p. 151 ("picked men, chosen because of their soldierly qualities").

19 Dorsey, "The Mitchel Raiders," *The Ohio Soldier*, Feb. 25, 1893, p. 226.

20 Ibid., pp. 226-27; deposition of Jacob Parrott, *Ohio Boys in Dixie*, p. 39; deposition of William Bensinger, *Ohio Boys in Dixie*, pp. 45-46.

21 William J. Knight, quoted in Pittenger, *Daring and Suffering*, pp. 36-37.

22 O'Neill, *Wild Train*, p. 17; Cohen and Bogle, *The General and the Texas*, p. 13.

23 Brown, quoted in Pittenger, *Daring and Suffering*, pp. 36-37. Brown's account of his meeting with the commanding general is entirely uncorroborated and should be viewed with skepticism, given the inaccurate statements and farfetched claims he would make on other matters related to the raid.

24 Keifer, *Slavery and Four Years of War*, p. 268 ("a farmer boy . . ."); Pittenger, *Daring and Suffering*, p. 41.

25 Dorsey, "The Mitchel Raiders," *The Ohio Soldier*, Feb. 25, 1893, p. 227.

26 Samuel Slavens to Wife Rachel, April 6, 1862, quoted in O'Neill, *Wild Train*, pp. 60, 373; Dorsey, "The Mitchel Raiders," *The Ohio Soldier*, March 11, 1893, p. 241.

27 Pittenger, *Daring and Suffering*, p. 43; Dorsey, "The Mitchel Raiders," *The Ohio Soldier*, March 11, 1893, p. 241 ("more as a newspaper correspondent than as a soldier"), p. 386 (Pittenger's talking).

28 The location of the initial meeting of the Andrews Raiders is marked by a Tennessee State historical marker, some two miles east of Shelbyville on present day State Highway 64 (Tennessee Historical Marker 3G 16). Biographical sketches of each of the raiders are included in Cohen and Bogle, *The General and the Texas*, pp. 2-13; see also Keifer, *Slavery and Four Years of War*, p. 268 ("Never before . . ."); Deposition of William Reddick, *Ohio Boys in Dixie*, p. 44 ("unacquainted"). In all, twenty-three men were detailed to join Andrews, though many would later suggest that the mission was to include a twenty-fourth volunteer. "The twenty-fourth was never heard of," William Pittenger wrote, "whether he tried to reach us and failed, or whether some one of the captains who was to furnish a man was unable to induce any one to accept the dangerous honor, is uncertain." Pittenger, *Capturing a Locomotive*, p. 40. Andrews Raid historian Parlee C. Grose suggests that the twenty-fourth volunteer may have been Sgt. Robert F. Bonham of Company F, 21st Ohio, but ultimately he concedes: "As to the twenty-fourth volunteer, . . . we know nothing. We do not know his name, nor do we know which of Sill's three Ohio regiments he was from. Nor do we know what adventures may have befallen this soldier if (as Pittenger admits was possible) he started out alone to overtake the others after they had departed." Parlee C. Grose, *The Case of Private Smith and the Remaining Mysteries of the Andrews Raid* (McComb, Ohio: General Publishing Co., 1963), pp. 113-14.

29 Pittenger, *Daring and Suffering*, pp. 40, 42; Dorsey, "The Mitchel Raiders," *The Ohio Soldier*, Feb. 25, 1893, p. 227.

30 Parrott and Dougherty, "The Andrews' Railroad Raid," pp. 498-99; Pittenger, *Daring and Suffering*, p. 48.

31 Andrews is quoted at length by Dorsey, "The Mitchel Raiders," *The Ohio Soldier*, Mar. 11, 1893, pp. 241-42; Parrott and Dougherty, "The Andrews' Railroad Raid," pp. 499-500; and Pittenger, *Daring and Suffering*, pp. 47-51. As Pittenger notes, it is impossible to recount the instructions and discussion word for word. As a result, these eyewitness accounts of the meeting differ in certain respects as to the exact words spoken, but all are consistent on the overall mission, the warnings given to the raiders, the contingency plans for enlisting in the Southern army, and the plans to coordinate with the southward advance of General Mitchel.

32 Parrott and Dougherty, "The Andrews' Railroad Raid," p. 499; Frank M. Gregg, *Andrews Raiders: or the Last Scenes and Final Chapter of the Daring Incursion into the Heart of the Confederacy* (Chattanooga: Republican Job Print, 1891), pp. 14-15; Pittenger, *Daring and Suffering*, pp. 50-51.

33 Pittenger quotes a longer version of these final instructions in *Daring and Suffering*, p. 51. See also Wilbur G. Kurtz, "The Andrews Raid," *Atlanta Historical Bulletin* 13 (Dec. 1968), p. 14 (ten days of rain); James G. Bogle, "The Great Locomotive Chase or The Andrews Raid," *Blue & Gray* (July 1987), p. 11 (same).

CHAPTER THREE. THE HEART OF DIXIE

1 Pittenger, *Daring and Suffering*, p. 64; Knight, quoted in Jim Leeke, "Always Very Daring and Reckless: Private William J. Knight and the Andrews Raid," *Timeline* (Nov.-Dec. 2003), p. 6; Dorsey, Personal Diary, quoted in Angle, *Great Locomotive Chase*, p. 32.

2 William M. Kerr to Wilbur G. Kurtz, Jan. 3, 1905, Wilbur G. Kurtz Collection, Kurtz-AHC (describing Campbell's great strength ["he was called a giant"] and weight ["at least 250 pounds"]); Wilbur G. Kurtz, "The Andrews Raiders in the Fulton County Jail," unpublished manuscript, 1966, Kurtz-AHC, p. 12 ("a hulking, fairly good-natured bullying type of man . . ."); Pittenger, *Daring and Suffering*, pp. 67-68 (description of Campbell).

3 Shadrach information in MSS 132, Box 6, Folder 2, Kurtz-AHC; Pittenger, *Daring and Suffering*, p. 67 (description of Shadrach); Kurtz, "Andrews Raiders in the Fulton County Jail," Kurtz-AHC, p. 14; Dorsey to Wilbur G. Kurtz, July 30, 1904, Kurtz-AHC ("he had no special accomplishments"); Kerr to Kurtz, Jan. 3, 1905, Kurtz-AHC ("in every way unfitted").

4 Pittenger, *Daring and Suffering*, pp. 66-67 (description of G. Wilson); Cohen and Bogle, *The General and The Texas*, p. 13; O'Neill, *Wild Train*, p. 16.

5 William Knight, description of John Wollam, as related to Wilbur G. Kurtz, Kurtz-AHC, Box 6, Folder 2; C.W. Evers, Foreword, in *Adventures of Alf Wilson*, p. xi (description of Wilson); Wilson, *Adventures of Alf Wilson*, p. 136 (description of Wood).

6 Cohen and Bogle, *The General and the Texas*, pp. 2, 10, 8 (descriptions of Smith, Robertson, Parrott); Parrott and Dougherty, "The Andrews' Railroad Raid," p. 500.

7 Dorsey to Wilbur G. Kurtz, July 30 and Sept. 5, 1904, Kurtz-AHC (description of Buffum); Col. John Coburn, indorsement regarding Robert Buffum, Nov. 21, 1863, Robert Buffum Papers, Bowling Green State University ("jayhawker, fillibuster and guerila, with a sprinkle of the horse thief"); O'Neill, *Wild Train*, p. 18. Buffum was a member of the second New England Emigrant Aid party, a group of antislavery migrants from the northeast who traveled to Kansas in 1854. Buffum's cousin David was shot and killed by proslavery forces in 1856. See Joseph Savage, *Recollections of 1854*, No. 8 (1870) (describing Buffum as "small and wiry and full of activity, but inclined to be a little fast and rather uncertain," and noting incorrectly that "in the late war [he] . . . was hung by the rebels as a spy"); see also Shelly Hickman Clark, "Lawrence in 1854: Recollections of Joseph Savage," *Kansas History*, 27 (Spring–Summer 2004); Dale E. Watts, "How Bloody Was Bleeding Kansas? Political Killings in the Kansas Territory 1854-1861," *Kansas History: A Journal of the Central Plains*, 18, no. 2 (Summer 1995), p. 128 (noting killing of David C. Buffum). The progress of the

Andrews/Dorsey group is recounted in Dorsey, "The Mitchel Raiders," *The Ohio Soldier*, March 11, 1893, pp. 242-43.

8 Dorsey, "The Mitchel Raiders," *The Ohio Soldier*, March 11, 1893, p. 242.

9 Wilson, *Adventures of Alf Wilson*, pp. 20-21.

10 Knight, quoted in Pittenger, Great Locomotive Chase, p. 80; Dorsey, "The Mitchel Raiders," *The Ohio Soldier*, March 11, 1893, pp. 242-43.

11 Dorsey, "The Mitchel Raiders," *The Ohio Soldier*, March 11, 1893, p. 243.

12 William Bensinger, quoted in O'Neill, *Wild Train*, p. 81; Dorsey, "The Mitchel Raiders," *The Ohio Soldier*, March 25, 1893, p. 258; Cohen and Bogle, *The General and the Texas*, pp. 4, 7; O'Neill, *Wild Train*, pp. 8-9, 19 (descriptions of Bensinger, Porter).

13 Pittenger, *Daring and Suffering*, p. 74.

14 Dorsey, "The Mitchel Raiders," *The Ohio Soldier*, March 25, 1893, p. 257; Pittenger, *Daring and Suffering*, p. 76.

15 Pittenger, *Daring and Suffering*, p. 88.

16 "Gossip About Our Generals," in *Harper's New Monthly*, 35, no. 206 (July 1867), pp. 212-13.

17 Mitchel, Ormsby MacKnight Mitchel, Astronomer and General, p. 280; *Cincinnati Commercial*, quoted in *Brooklyn Daily Eagle*, April 25, 1862, p. 2; ibid., May 5, 1862, p. 2 ("clock-work"); Beatty, *The Citizen-Soldier*, p. 101.

18 Mitchel, *Ormsby MacKnight Mitchel, Astronomer and General*, p. 281. Mitchel's plan to cut the railroad east and west of Huntsville and take the city by surprise is described in Conduce H. Gatch, "General O.M. Mitchel and his Brilliant March Into the Heart of the Southern Confederacy," Iowa Commandery, Military Order of the Loyal Legion of the United States, War Sketches and Incidents (MOLLUS-IA) (Des Moines: Kenyon Press, 1898), vol. 2, pp. 121-22; Vocke, "Military Achievements of Major-General Ormsby MacKnight Mitchel," MOLLUS-IL, vol. 4, p. 91.

19 The odyssey of Privates Llewellyn and Smith is examined in detail in Parlee C. Grose, *The Case of Private Smith and the Remaining Mysteries of the Andrews Raid* (McComb, Ohio: General Publishing Co., 1963). Their capture is also discussed in Cohen and Bogle, *The General and the Texas*, pp. 14-15.

20 Dorsey, "The Mitchel Raiders," *The Ohio Soldier*, March 25, 1893, p. 257; William J. Knight, Narrative transcription (unpublished), original handwritten version in Box 13, M1997-000099, VFM Collections, Ohio Historical Society (hereinafter Knight Narrative, OHS); see also Knight, quoted in Pittenger, *Daring and Suffering*, p. 81. The exact location of Clepper's home is marked on a map of Jasper and vicinity in the *Atlas to Accompany the Official Records of the Union and Confederate Armies* (Washington, D.C.: Government Printing Office, 1891-95), Plate 35, Map 5.

21 The suspicions cast upon the Andrews Raiders at Jasper are described by Chattanooga reporter Frank Gregg, who attempted to trace the path of the raiders by interviewing citizens of Tennessee who lived along the eastward route years later. Frank M. Gregg, *Andrews Raiders: or the Last Scenes and Final Chapter of the Daring Incursion into the Heart of the Confederacy*,

(Chattanooga: Republican Job Print, 1891), pp. 14-15; Dorsey, "The Mitchel Raiders," *The Ohio Soldier*, March 11, 1893, p. 243.

22 Dorsey, "The Mitchel Raiders," *The Ohio Soldier*, March 25, 1893, p. 257; Bensinger, quoted in ibid., p. 258.

23 *Atlas to Accompany the Official Records of the Union and Confederate Armies*, Plate 35, Map 6. A number of the guests who spent the night at Widow Hall's later wrote of the experience, including Dorsey and Pittenger. Chattanooga reporter Frank Gregg has noted that members of the Hall family remembered the episode decades after the war's end. Gregg, Andrews Raiders, p. 15.

24 Pittenger, *Daring and Suffering*, p. 73; Parrott and Dougherty, "Andrews' Railroad Raid," p. 500.

Chapter 4. An Uncompromising and Violent Union Man

1 F.A. Mitchel, quoted in Gatch, "General O.M. Mitchell," MOLLUS-IA, vol. 2, p. 121; Reid, Ohio in the War, vol. 1, p. 607.

2 Harrison Millard, "The Battle of Perryville," *National Tribune*, Aug. 8, 1889, p. 1; "Huntsville," in *Encyclopedia of the American Civil War: A Political, Social and Military History*, p. 1022; *Brooklyn Daily Eagle*, April 12 and 15, 1862 (reporting Mitchel's capture and occupation of Huntsville and providing detailed description of the city); Mary Jane Cook Chadick, Diary, April 12, 1862, quoted in "A Housewife's Perspective on the Occupation of Huntsville," *Huntsville Historical Review* 16, nos. 1–2 (1989), p. 11; John Withers Clay to C.C. Clay, Jr., May 15, 1862, quoted in "A Journalist's Perspective on the Invasion of Huntsville," *Huntsville Historical Review* 16, nos. 1–2 (1989), pp. 23-25.

3 Reid, *Ohio in the War*, vol. 1, p. 607; OR, vol. 10, pt. 2, pp. 439-41 (exchange of Confederate correspondence regarding Larcombe and the telegraph office at Huntsville).

4 The men and materiel captured at Huntsville is fairly consistently described in a number of Army and newspaper sources, although there are minor variations in the total numbers of prisoners and rail cars, for example. See Mitchel to OR, series 1, vol. 10, p. 641 (fifteen locomotives, 200 prisoners, and "a large amount of passenger, box and platform cars"); Reid, *Ohio in the War*, p. 607 (seventeen locomotives, 150 cars, 170 soldiers); Vocke, "Military Achievements," MOLLUS-IL, vol. 4, p. 91 (fifteen locomotives, 80 cars, "several hundred Confederate officers and soldiers"); *Brooklyn Daily Eagle*, April 12, 1862, p. 3 (fifteen locomotives, 200 prisoners, and "a large amount of rolling stock"). The captured Beauregard-Lee dispatch is discussed in Edwin C. Fishel, *The Secret War for the Union: The Untold Story of Military Intelligence in the Civil War* (New York: Houghton Mifflin, 1996), p. 184, and Mitchel, Ormsby MacKnight Mitchel, Astronomer and General, pp. 304-5. The dispatch, dated Corinth, April 9, 1862, read, in part: "General S. Cooper, Richmond, Va.: All present probabilities are that whenever the enemy moves on this position he will do so with an overwhelming force of not less than 85,000 men. We can now muster only about 35,000 effectives. . . . If defeated here, we lose the Mississippi Valley and probably our cause; whereas we could even afford to lose for a while Charleston and Savannah for the purpose of defeating Buell's army, which would not only insure us of the valley of the Mississippi but our independence. P. G. T. Beauregard."

5 William Haines Lytle to My beloved Sisters, May 6, 1862, in *For Honor, Glory & Union*, p. 114.

6 *Cincinnati Commercial*, quoted in *Brooklyn Daily Eagle*, April 25, 1862, p. 2; Mary Chadick, Diary, April 12, 1862, *Huntsville Historical Review* 16, nos. 1–2 (1989), pp. 12-15 (meeting with Mitchel; "sentinels on every corner").

7 *OR*, vol. 10, pt. 1, p. 641.

8 Buell, "Operations in North Alabama," *Battles and Leaders*, vol. 2, p. 707. Buell continues: "The most trivial occurrence is reported [by General Mitchel] with the flourish of a great battle; an old flat-boat in which he had rigged the machinery of a saw-mill, incapable of harming anything or resisting anything, is called a gun-boat and named the Tennessee, which he reports he has extemporized, and hopes will arrive in time to take part in the fight at Chattanooga, where he hopes also to receive 600 prisoners."

9 Dorsey, "The Mitchel Raiders," *The Ohio Soldier*, March 25, 1893, p. 258; Pittenger, *Daring and Suffering*, p. 82; Parrott and Dougherty, "Andrews' Railroad Raid," p. 500. Lookout Mountain's name in the Cherokee language is O-tullee-ton-tannâ-ta-kunnâ-ee, which means "mountains looking at each other." Gilbert E. Govan and James W. Livingood, *The Chattanooga Country, 1540-1976: From Tomahawks to TVA*, 3rd ed. (Knoxville: University of Tennessee Press, 1977), p. 12.

10 Wilson, *Adventures of Alf Wilson*, p. 24 ("little, crazy, frail affair"); Parrott and Dougherty, "Andrews' Railroad Raid," p. 501; Gregg, *Andrews Raiders*, pp. 15-16 (Standifer quote).

11 "Chattanooga," in *Encyclopedia of the American Civil War*, pp. 415-17; Benjamin F. Taylor, *In Camp and Field*, quoted in John Wilson, *Chattanooga's Story* (Chattanooga: Chattanooga News-Free Press, 1980), p. 96; Dr. Thomas Jefferson Eaton, quoted in Govan and Livingood, *The Chattanooga Country*, p. 157; Wiley Sword, *Mountains Touched with Fire: Chattanooga Besieged, 1863* (New York: St. Martin's Press, 1995), pp. 83-84 (quoting John Y. Simon, ed., *The Papers of U.S. Grant*, vol. 9, pp. 334-35).

12 Porte Crayon, quoted in Govan and Livingood, *The Chattanooga Country*, p. 154; Gregg, *Andrews Raiders*, p. 16; Knight, quoted in O'Neill, *Wild Train*, pp. 110-11; Pittenger, *Daring and Suffering*, p. 84; Dorsey, "The Mitchel Raiders," *The Ohio Soldier*, March 25, 1893, p. 258.

13 E. Kirby Smith to Adjutant and Inspector General S. Cooper, March 23, 1862, *OR*, vol. 10, pp. 355-56; *Mobile Daily Advertiser and Register*, June 10, 1862; Knight, quoted in Leeke, "Always Very Daring and Reckless," *Timeline* (Nov.-Dec. 2003), p. 6.

14 Henry David Thoreau, quoted in James A. Ward, *Railroads and the Character of America, 1820-1887* (Knoxville: University of Tennessee Press, 1986, p. 37); Wilson, *Adventures of Alf Wilson*, p. 24; William Knight, "How I Ran the General," *The Railroad Man's Magazine*, March 1911; Pittenger, *Daring and Suffering*, p. 85. Even later in the war, a reporter would describe the South's passport system "a perfect humbug. On leaving any of our cities for a train of cars, you find, generally, an ignorant, illiterate boy with a musket in his hand stationed at the doors of the cars, who asks you if you have a passport; on answering 'yes,' you are at once admitted, without the document being demanded for inspection." Sam Reid, *Mobile Daily Advertiser and Register*, June 10, 1862, quoted in J. Cutler Andrews, *The South Reports the Civil War* (Princeton: Princeton University Press, 1970), p. 234.

15 *Map of the country embracing the various routes surveyed for the Western & Atlantic Rail Road of Georgia, under the direction of Lieut. Col. S.H. Long, Chief Engineer* (U.S. Topographical Bureau, M.H. Stansbury, Del., 1837), Library of Congress Geography and Map Division,

Washington, D.C.; Lee Kennett, *Marching Through Georgia: The Story of Soldiers and Civilians During Sherman's Campaign* (New York: HarperCollins, 1995), p. 9 (quoting Illinois soldier); Pittenger, *Daring and Suffering*, p. 85.

16 Black, *Railroads of the Confederacy*, p. 32 (sixteen miles per hour); Pittenger, *Capturing a Locomotive*, p. 73 (same); Freeman H. Hubbard, *Railroad Avenue: Great Stories and Legends of American Railroading* (New York: McGraw-Hill, 1945), p. 338 (passenger complaints regarding the cowcatcher).

17 Pittenger, *Capturing a Locomotive*, p. 64; Dorsey, "The Mitchel Raiders," *The Ohio Soldier*, March 25, 1893, p. 258.

18 Dorsey, "The Mitchel Raiders," *The Ohio Soldier*, March 25, 1893, p. 258; Pittenger, *Capturing a Locomotive*, p. 64.

19 Not one of the detailed eyewitness accounts of Andrews's various briefings to the raiders suggests that he warned the Ohio volunteers that there was a large Confederate encampment at Big Shanty. See, e.g., Pittenger, *Daring and Suffering*, pp. 47-51; Parrott and Dougherty, "Andrews' Railroad Raid," pp. 499-500; Dorsey, "The Mitchel Raiders," *The Ohio Soldier*, March 11, 1893, p. 242. Perhaps the Kentucky spy felt that such a disclosure would cause his recruits to decide the risks were too great. One historian suggests that Andrews himself may have been unaware of the presence of the recently established Camp McDonald, but this seems unlikely given his previous trips south on the W&A and the detailed intelligence he possessed about other aspects of the railroad and the station. See James G. Bogle, "The Great Locomotive Chase or The Andrews Raid," *Blue & Gray* (July 1987), p. 13. At least some among the raiders believed the rebel base had been established since Andrews's last visit to the area. See Dorsey, "The Mitchel Raiders," *The Ohio Soldier*, March 25, 1893, p. 259 (describing establishment of Camp McDonald as a "material change" that had occurred "since Andrews' last trip over this line").

20 For the history of Marietta, Georgia, see generally James B. Glover, V et al., *Marietta 1833-2000* (Charleston, S.C.: Arcadia Publishing, 1999); Joseph M. Brown, *Marietta: The Gem City of Georgia* (1887, reprinted by Cobb Landmarks and Historical Society); Sarah Blackwell Gober Temple, *The First Hundred Years: A Short History of Cobb County in Georgia* (Atlanta: Walter D. Brown, 1935). Oliver Otis Howard, *Autobiography of Oliver Otis Howard, Major General, United States Army* (New York: Baker and Taylor, 1907), vol. I, p. 293.

21 Temple, *The First Hundred Years*, p. 123; Mimi Jo Butler, "Cole-Fletcher Families," *Cobb County, Ga. Geneological Society, Inc. Quarterly* (Dec. 1992), p. 146; *Savannah Republican*, June 11, 1863, p. 2; Records of the Southern Claims Commission (Allowed Claims), Cobb County, Georgia, RG 217 (217.8.7), National Archives, Washington, D.C. (claim of Henry G. Cole, claims 13312 and 19724).

22 Records of the Southern Claims Commission (Allowed Claims), Cobb County, Georgia (claim of Henry G. Cole, claims 13312 and 19724); Thomas G. Dyer, *Secret Yankees: The Union Circle in Confederate Atlanta*, (Baltimore: Johns Hopkins University Press, 1999), p. 151. As Dyer notes, "So fragmentary is the historical record left by Civil War Atlantans—even more so Atlanta Unionists and federal spies—that it is impossible to know the extent of connections with and support of Union agents." Ibid., p. 153.

23 Wilson, *Adventures of Alf Wilson*, p. 26; Dorsey, "The Mitchel Raiders," *The Ohio Soldier*, March 25, 1893, p. 259; Pittenger, *Daring and Suffering*, p. 86. Pittenger consistently and

inexplicably refers to the hotel in Marietta as the "Tremont House." There was no Tremont House hotel in Marietta, then or later. A large number of sources confirm that most of the Andrews Raiders stayed at the Fletcher House, with a handful of the party nearby at the Marietta Hotel.

24 Andrews Raid historian Craig Angle suggests that "there is credible evidence that, after directing his men to local hotels, [Andrews] entrained for Atlanta." Angle, *The Great Locomotive Chase*, p. 108. After considering this theory, and the considerable evidence to the contrary, I respectfully disagree (as does prominent historian James G. Bogle). A number of accounts confirm that Andrews stayed with the Third Division soldiers at Fletcher House in Marietta that night. See, e.g., Dorsey, "The Mitchel Raiders," *The Ohio Soldier*, March 25, 1893, p. 259 (noting that "Andrews was at the hotel with the rest of us," sharing a room with William Knight and Wilson Brown); Pittenger, *Daring and Suffering*, p. 86 ("Andrews was with the larger party in the hotel near the railroad station . . ."). Moreover, had Andrews traveled down to Atlanta and taken the 4:00 A.M. train back north to Marietta, he would have had no rest whatsoever, and no time to convene the "council of war" that was to take place in his own hotel room in Marietta the next morning.

Chapter Five. All Aboard

1 William Fuller is pictured and described in Cohen and Bogle, *The General and the Texas*, p. 17; O'Neill, *Wild Train*, pp. 124-25. Fuller described his own appearance and dress that day in a letter to Wilbur Kurtz dated April 3, 1905, recounted in Kurtz Notebook No. 2, pp. 3-4. Note that Lloyd Street, the site of Washington Hall, is sometimes spelled "Loyd."

2 O'Neill, *Wild Train*, pp. 124-25 (describing Fuller as "a born partisan, of quick and stubborn convictions"); N.J. Bell, *Southern Railroad Man: Conductor N.J. Bell's Recollections of the Civil War Era*, James A. Ward, ed. (DeKalb: Northern Illinois University Press, 1994), pp. 10, 12 (quotes on exemption of railroad men and long hours of railroading).

3 Stephen H. Long, quoted in James Michael Russell, *Atlanta, 1847-1890: City Building in the Old South and the New* (Baton Rouge: Louisiana State University Press, 1988), p. 25. Other early railroad men agreed with Colonel Long's assessment, including Richard Peters, a director of the Georgia Railroad, who wrote of Marthasville in 1846: "The thing is all out for the present, all deadflat. . . . The place can never be much of a trading city, yet may be of some importance in a small way." Richard Peters to Lemuel P. Grant, July 26, 1846, quoted in Russell, *Atlanta, 1847-1890*.

4 There are a number of competing stories on the origin of the name Atlanta, recounted in Franklin M. Garrett, *Atlanta and Environs: A Chronicle of Its People and Events* (New York, 1954), vol. I, pp. 224-27; see Richard Peters to W.R. Hanleiter, May 9, 1871 (describing Thomson's letter suggesting the name Atlanta), ibid. at 225; Russell, *Atlanta, 1847-1890*, p. 25 n. 24 ("The principal reason for changing the name to Atlanta was that railway ticket agents complained they had trouble getting 'Marthasville' on one ticket"); Angle, *Great Locomotive Chase*, pp. 335-36 n. 5; Gary M. Pomerantz, *Where Peachtree Meets Sweet Auburn* (New York: Penguin Books, 1996), pp. 35-36, 557-58; *Atlanta Constitution*, Dec. 30, 1870. See also Kenneth K. Krakow, *Georgia Place-Names: Their History and Origins*, 3rd ed. (Macon, Ga.: Winship Press, 1975), pp. 8-9 (available online at http://www.kenkrakow.com/gpn/georgia_place-names.htm).

5 Russell, *Atlanta, 1847-1890*, pp. 100-104 (growth of wartime industry in Atlanta), 108-9 (crimes, proceedings in the Mayor's Court), 257 (Table I, "Population of Atlanta, 1850-1890"); *Columbia Daily South Carolinian*, reprinted in (Atlanta) *Southern Confederacy*, May 23, 1863 ("goaheadativeness"); *Mobile Register and Advertiser*, June 10, 1862 ("slight perceptible odor of Yankeedom").

6 Russell, *Atlanta, 1847-1890*, pp. 91-115 (describing wartime Atlanta); see also Wilbur Kurtz's fascinating bird's-eye painting of Atlanta in 1864, in Wilbur G. Kurtz, *Atlanta and the Old South: Paintings and Drawings* (Atlanta: American Lithography Company, 1969), p. 20; *Mobile Register and Advertiser*, Sept. 24, 1863, p. 2 ("Atlanta! ha!"); U.S. Census, Fulton County, 1860, recounted in Garrett, *Atlanta and Environs*, pp. 489-91 (fifty-nine locomotive engineers versus twenty-six blacksmiths).

7 Matthias N. Forney, *The Railway Gazette*, quoted in Henry B. Comstock, *The Iron Horse: An Illustrated History of Steam Locomotives*, 2nd ed. ([Sykesville: Md.]: Greenberg Publishing, 1993), p. 92 ("melodies cast and wrought in metal"); see also John H. White, Jr., quoted in David Ross, *The Encyclopedia of Trains and Locomotives* (San Diego: Thunder Bay Press, 2003), p. 9 (describing the steam locomotive as "self-reliant and unafraid. Its only bad habits were drinking and smoking"). The General's specifications are recorded by former Rogers drafts-man Louis L. Park and reprinted in O'Neill, *Wild Train*, p. 127; and in Cohen and Bogle, *The General and the Texas*, p. 40. Most modern images of the General show its later red-and-black coloration. The original green, silver, and brass version is depicted in the carefully researched artwork of Wilbur G. Kurtz, which is reproduced in full color in Cohen and Bogle, *The General and the Texas*, pp. 130-34. There is some uncertainty as to whether the General bore the number 39 at the time of the raid. Wilbur Kurtz's meticulously researched illustrations of the General in its "wartime character" depict the numeral stenciled on the dome; however, historian James G. Bogle indicates that locomotives on the W&A were not numbered until after the Civil War. Raymond B. Carneal and James G. Bogle, "Locomotives of the Western & Atlantic Railroad," *Atlanta Historical Bulletin*, 15 (Spring 1970), pp. 26-27.

8 O'Neill, *Wild Train*, p. 127 (General's history); Black, *Railroads of the Confederacy*, pp. 16-17 (naming of Southern locomotives); Carneal and Bogle, "Locomotives of the Western & Atlantic Railroad"; David Bright, *Confederate Railroads*, www.csa-railroads.com (W&A locomotive usage, 1861-62); Cohen and Bogle, *The General and the Texas*, p. 16 (description of Cain).

9 Anthony Murphy, "Pursuit of Andrews' Raiders," *Atlanta Journal Magazine*, Nov. 8, 1931, p. 1; Angle, *Great Locomotive Chase*, p. 156; Black, *Railroads of the Confederacy*, p. 21. Angle notes that the General averaged 37 miles per cord of wood in the prior fiscal year, where Black, citing the October 1861 annual report of the W&A, puts the engine's average mileage per cord at less than 33. Either way, these numbers confirm Black's characterization of steam locomotives as "voracious consumers of fuel and supplies." Ibid.

10 Wallace Putnam Reed, "Hero of the Famous Engine Chase," *Atlanta Constitution*, July 15, 1899; see also O'Neill, *Wild Train*, pp. 125-26; Angle, *Great Locomotive Chase*, p. 126.

11 Angle, *Great Locomotive Chase*, p. 127 et seq. Here and elsewhere in the course of recounting the General's path northward, Angle does an excellent job retracing and describing the various uphill and downhill grades, curves, and landmarks along the route. For scenes and images of wartime Atlanta, see generally Kurtz, *Atlanta and the Old South*; as well as photos of Atlanta in the American Memory collection of the Library of Congress.

12 Pittenger, *Daring and Suffering*, pp. 99-101; Pittenger, quoted in O'Neill, *Wild Train*, pp. 129-31.

13 Ross's eleventh-hour objection to proceeding further and Andrews's response are recounted in Pittenger, *Daring and Suffering*, pp. 100-101. Interestingly, none of the other raiders (except Parrott, whose account is an outright copy of Pittenger's in many respects) ever mentions this early morning meeting, either in deposition testimony, correspondence, or their own later published writings on the war. William Knight would firmly deny that such a meeting ever took place. Knight interview with Wilbur G. Kurtz, Sept. 30, 1903, Kurtz-AHC. This direct conflict and puzzling lack of corroboration of Pittenger's description does not mean that the meeting did not happen (why would Pittenger make it up?) but it should give rise to skepticism as to the accuracy of and the motive behind Pittenger's account.

14 Parrott and Dougherty, "The Andrews' Railroad Raid," p. 501; Wilson, *Adventures of Alf Wilson*, p. 28; Murphy, "Pursuit of Andrews' Raiders," *Atlanta Journal Magazine*, Nov. 8, 1931, p. 1; Fuller, quoted in O'Neill, *Wild Train*, p. 132.

15 Several raiders' accounts mention that they immediately noticed the presence of the three boxcars, including Parrott and Dougherty, "The Andrews' Railroad Raid," p. 501; Pittenger, *Daring and Suffering*, p. 101; Atlanta *Daily Intelligencer*, April 12, 1862, p. 2.

16 Porter, "John R. Porter's Account," in *Adventures of Alf Wilson*, pp. 229-30; Wilson, *Adventures of Alf Wilson*, p. 27 ("a serious loss").

17 See Kennesaw Mountain National Battlefield Park Travel Guide, National Park Service (Online reference available at www.nps.gov/kemo/pphtml/print.html); Wilson, *Adventures of Alf Wilson*, p. 28; Knight, quoted in Leeke, "Always Very Daring and Reckless," *Timeline* (Nov.-Dec. 2003), p. 8; Dorsey, "The Mitchel Raiders," *The Ohio Soldier*, March 25, 1893, p. 259; Fuller, quoted in O'Neill, *Wild Train*, p. 32.

18 Pittenger, *Daring and Suffering*, p. 58; Wilson, *Adventures of Alf Wilson*, p. 28.

19 Dorsey, "The Mitchel Raiders," *The Ohio Soldier*, March 25, 1893, p. 259 (sentries so close you could hear "the rattle of their tin cups and bayonets"). An excellent contemporary map of the layout of Camp McDonald, showing the railroad at Big Shanty and Lacy's Hotel, is reprinted in Bowling C. Yates, *Historic Highlights in Cobb County*, (Cobb Landmarks and Historical Society, 2001), pp. 32-33. Recollections differ as to exactly "who did what when" in the few seconds following the General's arrival at Big Shanty. Most accounts agree that Andrews and Knight stepped off the train first—though some indicate that engineer Wilson Brown went with them as well—and the other soldiers left the train shortly thereafter on a quiet signal from Andrews.

CHAPTER SIX. "SOMEONE IS RUNNING OFF WITH YOUR TRAIN!"

1 *Mobile Register and Advertiser*, Sept. 24, 1863, p. 2 ("one of the pleasantest places in all Georgia . . ."); *Southern Confederacy*, July 2, 1861 ("You will find in some squads . . ."); Krakow, *Georgia Place-Names*, p. 19; Sarah Blackwell Gober Temple, *The First Hundred Years: A Short History of Cobb County in Georgia* (Atlanta: Walter D. Brown, 1935), pp. 236-40, 249-55 (quoting soldiers' letters and describing Camp McDonald).

2 Temple, *The First Hundred Years*, p. 240.

3 Bogle, "The Great Locomotive Chase or The Andrews Raid," *Blue & Gray*, p. 14.

4 Wilbur G. Kurtz, "The Andrews Railroad Raid," *Civil War Times Illustrated*, 5 (April 1966), pp. 11-12.

5 William J. Knight to Wilbur G. Kurtz, March 9, 1904, Kurtz-AHC; Pittenger, *Daring and Suffering*, p. 103; Parrott, "Great Locomotive Chase," pp. 275-76. Wilson Brown would later insist that he, not Knight, was the one who pulled the pin to sever the train.

6 Dorsey, "The Mitchel Raiders," *The Ohio Soldier*, March 25, 1893, p. 259; Pittenger, *Daring and Suffering*, p. 105; Wilson, *Adventures of Alf Wilson*, p. 29. The Confederate sentries on guard that day may have been Private Henry Whitley and Corporal Robert F. Webb of Company F, 56th Georgia Infantry Regiment. Whitley was interviewed at a reunion years after the war and claimed that he and Webb were standing post at Big Shanty that morning. Speaking of the theft of the train, Whitley recalled that "it all happened so quickly" that he and Webb "didn't know what to make of it." Whitley also claimed to be present at Andrews's subsequent execution. Account of Henry Whitley, in Kurtz Notebook No. 3, pp. 134-35, Kurtz-AHC.

7 Knight to Kurtz, March 9, 1904, Kurtz-AHC; Turner, *Victory Rode the Rails*, p. 39 (describing lack of braking mechanism on war-era locomotives); Knight Narrative, p. 25.

8 "Mrs. Seawell Tells of War," in Wilbur G. Kurtz, "Strong Plea Made for Grant Park Museum," *Atlanta Constitution*, May 7, 1911.

9 Murphy, quoted in Gregg, *Andrews Raiders*, pp. 19-20; see also "Pursuit of Andrews' Raiders," *Atlanta Journal Magazine*, Nov. 8, 1931, p. 1; William A. Fuller, "Mr. W.A. Fuller's Statement," quoted in *Daily Intelligencer*, April 15, 1862 ("something was wrong with the engine"). On a later occasion, Fuller would claim that he actually saw through the front window of the dining room as the strangers who had boarded at Marietta mounted the engine. See William A. Fuller, Pursuit and Capture of the Andrews Raiders (unpublished manuscript, 1906), p. 32; O'Neill, *Wild Train*, p. 137. For a comprehensive analysis of the conflict between Murphy and Fuller's accounts of their respective roles in the Locomotive Chase, see Stephen Davis, "The Conductor Versus the Foreman: William Fuller, Anthony Murphy, and the Pursuit of the Andrews Raiders," *Atlanta History*, 34, no. 4 (Winter 1990-91), pp. 39-55.

10 Murphy, "Pursuit of Andrews' Raiders," p. 1; Fuller, 1888 Address at GAR Encampment, Columbus Dispatch, Jan. 1, 1889, reprinted in *North Georgia Citizen*, Sept. 19, 1900, p. 9. (The page numbers indicated for this source refer to the transcription in Kurtz-AHC.)

11 Murphy, "Pursuit of Andrews' Raiders," p. 1; Fuller, *Pursuit and Capture*, p. 33.

12 Pittenger, *Daring and Suffering*, p. 105; Knight to Kurtz, March 9, 1904, Kurtz-AHC; Wilson, *Adventures of Alf Wilson*, p. 29. Years later, Knight would steadfastly deny that he had mishandled the engine and pulled the throttle too hard. "When I pulled that throttle," he declared in a 1903 interview, "I did not jerk it, but drew it easy, and we started out slowly. There was no sudden hiss of steam or grinding of wheels!" Knight interview, Sept. 30, 1903, Kurtz-AHC. A number of eyewitness accounts and later analyses suggest that in fact, no shots were fired at the retreating train by Rebel soldiers at Big Shanty. See, e.g., Pittenger, *Daring and Suffering*, p. 105 ("without a shot fired").

13 Pittenger, *Capturing a Locomotive*, pp. 71 ("a pull, a jar, a clang") and 73 ("This engine gave us wings"); Dorsey, "The Mitchel Raiders," *The Ohio Soldier*, March 25, 1893, p. 259. A detailed discussion of the *General's* early loss of power is found in Angle, *Great Locomotive Chase*, pp. 140-41.

14 Angle, *Great Locomotive Chase*, p. 141 (describing Moon's Station); "Narrative of L. Jackson Bond," Andrews Raid Notebook No. 2, Kurtz-AHC, pp. 84-85. Bond insists that the raiders did not stop here at Moon's Station, but his recollection is directly contrary to a number of other accounts. One historian theorizes that the raiders may have borrowed their tools from John Landers's section gang, at work farther up the line. Angle, *Great Locomotive Chase*, p. 339, n. 14.

15 Pittenger, *Daring and Suffering*, p. 106; Cohen and Bogle, *The General and the Texas*, p. 3 (profile of John Scott); Wilson, *Adventures of Alf Wilson*, p. 145 ("one of the best men in our party"). Among the accounts of Scott's cutting of telegraph wires are Wilson, *Adventures of Alf Wilson*, p. 30; Pittenger, *Daring and Suffering*, p. 106.

16 A number of historians of the raid discuss Andrews's early reliance on the W&A's regular schedule to pass trains and avoid suspicion, including Gregg, *Andrews' Raiders*, p. 18; Wilbur G. Kurtz, "The Andrews Raid," *Atlanta Historical Bulletin*, 13 (Dec. 1968), p. 17; and Bogle, "The Great Locomotive Chase or The Andrews Raid," p. 17. See also Dorsey, "The Mitchel Raiders," *The Ohio Soldier*, April 8, 1893, p. 225 ("awful storm gathering around us"); Pittenger, *Daring and Suffering*, p. 107.

17 Fuller, *Pursuit and Capture*, p. 72 (discussing the effort to organize pursuit from Marietta and Big Shanty); Franklin Crawford, interview with Wilbur Kurtz, Andrews Raid Notebook No. 2, Kurtz-AHC; Porter, quoted in *Adventures of Alf Wilson*, p. 229.

18 Angle, *Great Locomotive Chase*, pp. 148-49 (describing stretch from Acworth to Allatoona). Note that the various accounts of the "engine thieves" and their pursuers disagree on when the raiders first pried up a rail, and when and where this was done later in the chase. Some recall a rail being taken up at the first deliberate stop of the train; others not until after Allatoona. Compare Wilson, *Adventures of Alf Wilson*, p. 30; Pittenger, *Capturing a Locomotive*, pp. 76-78; Dorsey, "The Mitchel Raiders," *The Ohio Soldier*, April 8, 1893, p. 225. This confusion is probably an inevitable byproduct of having several eyewitness accounts of an exciting episode, most of which were not written until many years after the fact. "There is considerable discrepancy in the many published accounts of the following chase, which the author has not in every case been able to perfectly reconcile," William Pittenger wrote in 1882. "Some of the incidents of the chase, such as the number of times the track was torn up, and whether we were fired on by pursuing soldiers, allow some room for a conflict of memory. But the variations are not material." Pittenger, *Capturing a Locomotive*, p. 76.

19 Knight to Kurtz, March 9, 1904, Kurtz-AHC (describing red flag); Angle, *Great Locomotive Chase*, p. 149. Other raiders would state that the party also affixed a red flag to the back of the last boxcar. E.g., Pittenger, *Daring and Suffering*, p. 108.

20 Jim Miles, *Fields of Glory: A History and Tour Guide of The War in the West, The Atlanta Campaign, 1864*, 2nd ed. (Nashville: Cumberland House, 2002), p. 96 (Etowah River Bridge); William T. Sherman, Diary, May 23, 1864, quoted in ibid. at 83 ("Rubicon of Georgia"); Fuller, *Pursuit and Capture*, p. 35; Mark Cooper Pope, III with J. Donald McKee, *Mark Anthony Cooper:*

Iron Man of Georgia (Atlanta: Graphic Publishing Company, 2000), pp. 85, 93-94, 172; Carneal and Bogle, "Locomotives of the Western & Atlantic Railroad," *Atlanta Historical Bulletin*, 15, p. 29 (No. 10, the *Yonah*); Bright, www.csa-railroads.com (noting that *Yonah* compiled a respectable 7,680 miles from October 1860 to September 1861). The former town of Etowah now lies under manmade Lake Allatoona.

21 Pittenger, *Daring and Suffering* (1863), p. 60 ("unforeseen contingencies"); Knight, quoted in Leeke, "Always Very Daring and Reckless," *Timeline* (Nov.-Dec. 2003), p. 8; see also Pittenger, *Daring and Suffering*, p. 110.

CHAPTER SEVEN. THE CROOKEDEST ROAD UNDER THE SUN

1 Fuller, Address at GAR Encampment, *North Georgia Citizen*, p. 8 ("I mean run"); Fuller, "Battle of the Locomotives," *Atlanta Journal Magazine*, March 16, 1930, p. 11.

2 Fuller, Address at GAR Encampment, North Georgia Citizen, p. 9 (arrival at Moon's, "Yankee trick"); Fuller, *Pursuit and Capture*, pp. 33-34; "Narrative of Jackson Bond," Andrews Raid Notebook No. 2, Kurtz-AHC, p. 85.

3 Ibid., pp. 85-86. Compare Fuller's description of his individual actions, Fuller, "Battle of the Locomotives," *Atlanta Journal Magazine*, March 16, 1930, pp. 11, 26; Fuller, *Pursuit and Capture*, pp. 34 et seq.; Fuller, Address at 1888 GAR Encampment, reprinted in North Georgia Citizen, Sept. 19, 1900; with Murphy's discussion of what "we" did in pursuit, Murphy, "Pursuit of Andrews' Raiders," *Atlanta Journal Magazine*, Nov. 8, 1931, p. 1.

4 Fuller, "Battle of the Locomotives," *Atlanta Journal Magazine*, March 16, 1930, pp. 11, 26.

5 "Narrative of Jackson Bond," Andrews Raid Notebook No. 2, Kurtz-AHC, pp. 85-86; Murphy, "Pursuit of Andrews' Raiders," *Atlanta Journal Magazine*, Nov. 8, 1931, p. 1. Fuller minimizes the contribution of Jackson Bond and his section gang. He would later maintain that only Murphy, Cain, and himself pushed the pole-car from Moon's to Etowah ("Thus all along we pressed forward, one resting and two pushing"). Fuller, Address at GAR Encampment, *North Georgia Citizen*, p. 10; Fuller, *"Pursuit and Capture,"* pp. 34-35. Murphy records that two of the section gang assisted aboard the pole-car, along with two other volunteers picked up at Allatoona, "making about seven men on our little pole-car, pretty well crowding it." Murphy, "Pursuit of Andrews' Raiders," p. 2.

6 Fuller, *Pursuit and Capture*, pp. 35-36; "Narrative of Jackson Bond," Andrews Raid Notebook No. 2, Kurtz-AHC, pp. 85-86. Another minor discrepancy in the various accounts occurs here—Fuller and other accounts maintain that the pursuers obtained their shotguns at Acworth; while Murphy and some other sources state that this happened at Allatoona. Compare Fuller, Address at GAR Encampment, *North Georgia Citizen*, Sept. 19, 1900, p. 10; with Murphy, "Pursuit of Andrews' Raiders," *Atlanta Journal Magazine*, Nov. 8, 1931, p. 2; and Gregg, *Andrews Raiders*, p. 20 (pursuers secured arms at Allatoona).

White Smith, the man dispatched on horseback, later maintained that he rejoined the pursuers at Allatoona and stayed on until the end of the chase, but Fuller and others reject this claim. See Fuller to Kurtz, Aug. 8, 1904, Kurtz-AHC ("When I reached Acworth, 7 miles north of Big Shanty, I put young Smith on a horse and ordered him to make all speed he could to Allatoona, 5 miles up the road and give the alarm of the capture if the raiders had not already passed when he got there—supposing he could make better time on horse back than I could afoot and on a hand car. . . . But I made better time on the hand car than Smith did on the horse, and passed Allatoona before he arrived and saw him no more—so much for Smith").

7 Fuller, *Pursuit and Capture*, p. 43; Fuller, quoted in Gregg, *Andrews Raiders*, p. 20 ("We pushed with a vim").

8 Fuller, *Pursuit and Capture*, pp. 43-44. The identity of the *Yonah*'s engineer that day remains uncertain—Fuller recalls it was Marion Hilly, while Bond and others state that it was Frank Gober. See "Narrative of L. Jackson Bond," Andrews Raid Notebook No. 2, Kurtz-AHC, p. 86.

9 "Wilson Lumpkin (1783-1870)," *New Georgia Encyclopedia*, www.georgiaencyclopedia.org; James Houstoun Johnston, *Western and Atlantic Railroad of the State of Georgia* (Atlanta: Stein Printing, 1932), pp. 5-6.

10 Johnston, *Western and Atlantic Railroad of the State of Georgia*, pp. 19-20, 24; J.F. Cooper, *Map of the Country Embracing the Various Routes Surveyed for the Western & Atlantic Rail Road of Georgia, under the direction of Lieut. Col. S.H. Long, Chief Engineer* (Stansbury, Del.: U.S. Topographical Bureau, M.H., 1837), Library of Congress Geography and Map Division, Washington, D.C.; James G. Bogle, "Western & Atlantic: Crookedest Road Under the Sun," Southeastern Railway Museum, www.srmduluth.org/Features/wanda.htm; John W. Lewis, *Annual Report of the Western & Atlantic Railroad*, Sept. 30, 1860, p. 5. For an excellent overview of the W&A and its role in the 1864 Atlanta Campaign, see James G. Bogle, "The Western & Atlantic Railroad in the Campaign for Atlanta," in *The Campaign for Atlanta and Sherman's March to the Sea*, Theodore P. Savas and David A. Woodbury, eds. (Campbell, Calif.: Savas Woodbury, 1994), pp. 313-42.

11 Pittenger, *Capturing a Locomotive*, p. 72.

12 Pittenger, *Daring and Suffering*, p. 111; Parrott, "The Great Locomotive Chase," *Battles and Leaders*, vol. 5, p. 276.

13 Krakow, *Georgia Place-Names*, p. 36; see Lucy Cunyus, *History of Bartow County, Georgia—Formerly Cass* (1933, reprint ed., Greenville, S.C.: Southern Historical Press, 1994). In another ill-advised local government action, the citizens of Cassville voted in 1861 to change the name of their town to Manassas, in honor of the great Confederate victory there. The new name never stuck, however—Federal postal authorities simply refused to recognize the change. In the end, some folks said that the only effect of the name change was to provoke Union troops into burning the town when they came through in 1864. Krakow, p. 36.

14 Knight, "How I Ran the General," *Railroad Man's Magazine*, March 1911 (recounting dialogue with Russell); *Southern Confederacy*, April 19, 1862; Pittenger, *Daring and Suffering*, pp. 111-12; Wilson, *Adventures of Alf Wilson*, p. 31; Parrott, "The Great Locomotive Chase," *Battles and Leaders*, vol. 5, p. 277. Some sources, including Anthony Murphy, put this encounter and dialogue with the tank tender at Roger's Station (three miles away), not Cass. I am inclined to credit the Cass story, in part because it is corroborated by the newspaper accounts just after the raid. See *Southern Confederacy*, April 15, 1862 (describing the raiders' encounter at Cass Station with the "attentive and patriotic tank-tender, Mr. William Russell").

15 Pittenger, *Daring and Suffering*, p. 112.

16 A.L. Waddle, *Three Years with the Armies of the Ohio and Cumberland* (Chillicothe, Ohio: Scioto Gazette Book and Job Office, 1889), p. 14; Pittenger, *Daring and Suffering*, p. 93.

17 Private Jacob Adams, Diary, Ohio Historical Society, quoted in Grose, *The Case of Private Smith*, p. 22; Waddle, *Three Years*, p. 15.

18 Reid, *Ohio in the War*, pp. 607-8 (capture of Decatur); Mitchel to S.P. Chase, April 20, 1862, in John Niven, ed., *The Salmon P. Chase Papers* (Kent, Ohio: Kent State University Press, 1997), vol. 3, p. 180; *Brooklyn Daily Eagle*, April 28, 1862, p. 2.

19 O.M. Mitchel to J.B. Fry, April 11, 1862, *OR*, vol. 10, pt. 1, pp. 641-42; Waddle, *Three Years*, p. 15 (destruction of Widden's Creek bridge); see also Pittenger, *Daring and Suffering*, pp. 95-96. Some sources refer to the tributary as Widow's Creek. See Keifer, *Slavery and Four Years of War*, p. 275.

20 The depot, the layout of the intersection, and circumstances of the confusing traffic snarl at Kingston are examined and described in detail in Wilbur G. Kurtz, "Harbin's Narrative" (unpublished manuscript, based on interview with Oliver Wiley Harbin, 1907), Kurtz-AHC. Kurtz, working from eyewitness descriptions by Oliver Wiley Harbin, engineer of the Rome train, prepared a detailed diagram of the scene, reprinted in Cohen and Bogle, *The General and the Texas*, p. 28. A handwritten note on the diagram corrects the drawing and indicates that the main line and parallel sidings ran east-west, not north-south (ibid.). A diagram reflecting this east-west configuration is found in Angle, *Great Locomotive Chase*, p. 169.

21 Kurtz, "Harbin's Narrative," pp. 2-6.

22 Ibid., pp. 6-7; Pittenger, *Daring and Suffering*, p. 113.

23 Kurtz, "Harbin's Narrative," pp. 7-8; Dorsey, "The Mitchel Raiders," *The Ohio Soldier*, April 8, 1893, p. 273; Wilson, *Adventures of Alf Wilson*, p. 32.

24 Pittenger, *Daring and Suffering*, p. 114.

25 The dialogue between Andrews and the conductor of the train pulled by the *New York* is recounted by Pittenger in *Daring and Suffering*, p. 115. Pittenger's source for the story is unclear, though it is possible that Andrews described the exchange to him sometime later. In addition, there is considerable uncertainty as to whether the station men were aware of the capture of Huntsville on the morning of April 12.

26 Parrott, "The Great Locomotive Chase," *Battles and Leaders*, vol. 5, p. 277; Dorsey, "The Mitchel Raiders," *The Ohio Soldier*, April 8, 1893, p. 273.

27 Wilson, *Adventures of Alf Wilson*, p. 33. Alf Wilson's account of this section of the chase is tremendously confused. He jumbles together events at different stops along the route, and then describes many of them as happening at a nonexistent station he calls "Marengo." (This is probably a mangled recollection of the depot at Ringgold, farther up the line.) See Wilson, pp. 30-33; Charles O'Neill to Wilbur G. Kurtz, Nov. 2, 1955, Kurtz-AHC (suggesting that Wilson "made a double mistake: splicing actions that happened elsewhere and mistakenly placing them at Ringgold; then turning Ringgold into Marengo").

CHAPTER EIGHT. THE *Texas*

1 Pittenger, *Capturing a Locomotive*, p. 80.

2 Pittenger, *Daring and Suffering*, p. 114.

3 There is some dispute as to the accuracy of the accounts of this encounter with the "old switch tender" at Kingston. Wiley Harbin, the Rome engineer, would later maintain that there was no switchman in the yard at Kingston, and that he did not recall Andrews having a dispute with anyone that day. However, Harbin was "not at all enthusiastic about the reliability of his memory" when he was interviewed in detail in August 1907—more than forty-five years after the fact. Kurtz, "Harbin's Narrative," Kurtz-AHC, pp. 3, 8. I have therefore included the story here, in part because a number of the raiders corroborate the altercation. See Pittenger, *Daring and Suffering*, pp. 120-21; Parrott, "The Great Locomotive Chase," p. 278; Dorsey "The Mitchel Raiders," *The Ohio Soldier*, April 8, 1893, pp. 273-74.

4 Fuller, *Pursuit and Capture*, p. 44. There is conflicting testimony as to whether the *Yonah* made the run from Etowah to Kingston facing forward (cowcatcher in front, pulling tender and flatcar behind) or running in reverse (with the flatcar in the lead). Bond would distinctly recall that the *Yonah* ran backward on this stretch. "Narrative of L. Jackson Bond," Andrews Raid Notebook No. 2, Kurtz-AHC, pp. 86-87. Others disagree, however, and with a turntable readily available at Etowah Station, there seems to be no reason—other than sheer haste—why the *Yonah* would not have been turned "right-way-round." Andrews Raid historians such as Wilbur Kurtz note this discrepancy but do not resolve it.

5 Fuller, *Pursuit and Capture*, p. 44; Murphy, "Pursuit of Andrews' Raiders," *Atlanta Journal Magazine*, Nov. 8, 1931, p. 2.

6 Fuller, Address at GAR Encampment, *North Georgia Citizen*, Sept. 19, 1900, p. 11.

7 Murphy, "Pursuit of Andrews' Raiders," *Atlanta Journal Magazine*, Nov. 8, 1931, p. 2.

8 Compare Pittenger, *Daring and Suffering* (suggesting two trains); *Daring and Suffering* (three trains); Parrott, "The Great Locomotive Chase," *Battles and Leaders*, vol. 5, pp. 277-78 (three trains); Angle, *Great Locomotive Chase*, pp. 163-70 (two trains). See also Kurtz, "Harbin's Narrative," pp. 9, 18 (concluding, as to the specifics of the traffic jam at Kingston, that "all the persons who were present, speaking with unquestionable authority, simply do not agree"). Kurtz notes that "This time element in the story simply cannot be reconciled to the various accounts: stop-watches were not used by close, calculating eyewitnesses, and two men's recollections of any event are never the same."

9 Fuller, *Pursuit and Capture*, p. 46.

10 Anthony Murphy to W.G. Kurtz, Dec. 12, 1907, transcribed in "Harbin's Narrative," pp. 18-21; Murphy, "Pursuit of Andrews' Raiders," *Atlanta Journal Magazine*, Nov. 8, 1931, p. 2.

11 Pittenger, *Daring and Suffering*, p. 123; Parrott, "The Great Locomotive Chase," *Battles and Leaders*, vol. 5, p. 278.

12 Pittenger, *Daring and Suffering*, p. 124.

13 Ibid. For years to come, Pittenger would be puzzled about how the pursuers managed to cross this break in the rails. His confusion was the result of a belief that this rail was broken north of Adairsville—after Fuller and Murphy had boarded the *Texas*. Fuller compounded the confusion by claiming in early years that his engine had actually jumped over a gap in the rails. Pittenger, who was then researching a new edition of his book *Daring and Suffering*, resolved the confusion in an exchange of letters with Anthony Murphy in 1887-88. These letters are transcribed in Wilbur Kurtz's Andrews Raid Notebook No. 2, Kurtz-AHC, pp. 9-19.

14 Pittenger, *Daring and Suffering*, p. 125.

15 Ibid., pp. 125-26; see also Parrott, "The Great Locomotive Chase," *Battles and Leaders*, vol. 5, p. 278.

16 *Augusta Chronicle & Sentinel*, April 18, 1862 (reporting fatal derailment on Atlanta & West Point Railroad south of Newnan); Ken Dornstein, *Accidentally on Purpose: The Making of a Personal Injury Underworld in America* (New York: St. Martin's Press, 1996), p. 219 (quoting *Harper's Weekly* and discussing rise in railway accidents and fatalities in Civil War era); David Detzer, *Donnybrook: The Battle of Bull Run, 1861* (New York: Harcourt, 2004), p. 10 (citing statistics on frequency of railroad accidents in the United States).

17 Pittenger, *Daring and Suffering*, p. 126; see also Dorsey, "The Mitchel Raiders," *The Ohio Soldier*, April 8, 1893, p. 274 ("During the last half of this ten mile stretch the whistle on our engine kept up a continual screaming and tooting as a warning to the south bound train if it should be on the main track").

18 Wilson, *Adventures of Alf Wilson*, pp. 34-35.

19 Pittenger, *Daring and Suffering*, p. 126; Parrott, "The Great Locomotive Chase," *Battles and Leaders*, vol. 5, p. 278; Dorsey, "The Mitchel Raiders," April 8, 1893, p. 274.

20 Knight, quoted in Leeke, "Always Very Daring and Reckless," *Timeline* (Nov.-Dec. 2003), p. 8; Pittenger, *Daring and Suffering*, p. 131.

21 Kurtz, "Harbin's Narrative," p. 11. Both Harbin and Fuller recall a collision with one cross-tie obstruction and the removal of another. Again, Fuller's account suggests he acted alone. Fuller, *Pursuit and Capture*, p. 59 ("Fortunately, a stop was made in time, and I removed the obstructions"). See also *Southern Confederacy*, April 22, 1962 (including Cicero Smith among the men receiving praise for their role in the "pursuit of the engine-stealing bridge burners").

22 Fuller, *Pursuit and Capture*, p. 46; Murphy, "Pursuit of Andrews' Raiders," *Atlanta Journal Magazine*, Nov. 8, 1931, p. 2.

23 Kurtz, "Harbin's Narrative," p. 12.

24 Bracken is pictured and described in Cohen and Bogle, *The General and the Texas*, p. 17; William A. Fuller to Wilbur G. Kurtz, March 21, 1905, Andrews Raid Notebook No. 2, Kurtz-AHC, p. 7; Murphy, handwritten note quoted in Davis, "The Conductor Versus the Foreman," p. 47 (discussing suspicion of Bracken). For a fuller discussion of Bracken's background and role, see Eugene Alvarez, "Peter James Bracken: The Forgotten Engineer of the 'Great Locomotive Chase'," *Atlanta Historical Journal*, 24, no. 4 (Winter 1990), pp. 41-50.

25 The history and postwar story of the *Texas* is recounted in detail in James G. Bogle, "The Texas," *The Landmarker* (Cobb County Landmarks Society) 4, no. 3 (Winter 1979-80), pp. 3-14. For those who want a firsthand look, the *Texas* remains on display at the Atlanta Cyclorama in Grant Park. See also Gregg, *Andrews Raiders*, p. 22 ("God-send"); Murphy, "Pursuit of Andrews' Raiders," *Atlanta Journal Magazine*, Nov. 8, 1931, p. 2; Fuller, *Pursuit and Capture*, p. 59.

26 Alvarez, "Peter James Bracken," p. 46; Fuller, *Pursuit and Capture*, pp. 59-60.

27 See Cartersville-Bartow County Convention and Visitors Bureau,

www.notatlanta.org/adairsville.html (promoting Adairsville as "home of the Start of the Great Locomotive Chase"). To commemorate the adventure, the town of Adairsville hosts an annual Great Locomotive Chase Festival each autumn.

CHAPTER NINE. A TRIAL OF SPEED

1 Wilson, *Adventures of Alf Wilson*, p. 34; Fuller, *Pursuit and Capture*, p. 60.

2 Gregg, *Andrews Raiders*, p. 23 (Watts quote). Henderson's background is discussed in correspondence with his family, collected in Kurtz, "Harbin's Narrative," pp. 21-31, and discussed in Andrews Raid Notebook No. 2, Kurtz-AHC, p. 9. Edward Henderson is pictured and profiled in Cohen and Bogle, *The General and the Texas*, p. 19. Again, there is a conflict here between Fuller, who claims that he swung Henderson up onto the tender, see Fuller, Address at GAR Encampment, p. 13 ("As we ran past the station, I took him by the hand and lifted him into the tender"); and Murphy, who said he pulled the boy up onto the engine. Murphy, "Pursuit of Andrews' Raiders," *Atlanta Journal Magazine*, Nov. 8, 1931, p. 2 ("I helped him up on the '*Texas*' and moved on").

3 Fleming Cox is described in Andrews Raid Notebook No. 2, p. 9, and profiled in Cohen and Bogle, *The General and the Texas*, p. 16; see also O'Neill, *Wild Train*, p. 164.

4 Randall W. McBryde, The Historic "General" (Chattanooga: McGowan & Cook, 1904), quoted in O'Neill, *Wild Train*, p. 163; W.J. Whitsitt to Wilbur G. Kurtz, March 23, 1907, Kurtz-AHC; Andrews Raid Notebook No. 2, pp. 57, 126, Kurtz-AHC (Whitsitt correspondence and narrative).

5 Krakow, *Georgia Place-Names*, p. 167.

6 Parrott, "The Great Locomotive Chase," *Battles and Leaders*, vol. 5, p. 280; Pittenger, *Daring and Suffering*, p. 133 ("a thousand thunders"); Pittenger, *Capturing a Locomotive*, p. 101.

7 Pittenger, *Daring and Suffering*, pp. 136-37.

8 Murphy, "Pursuit of Andrews' Raiders," *Atlanta Journal Magazine*, Nov. 8, 1931, p. 2; Fuller, *Pursuit and Capture*, p. 63.

9 Fuller to Kurtz, January 21, 1904, Kurtz-AHC, cited in Angle, *Great Locomotive Chase*, p. 187 (finding discarded boxcar); Wilson, *Adventures of Alf Wilson*, p. 35.

10 Dorsey, "The Mitchel Raiders," *The Ohio Soldier*, April 22, 1893, p. 290 (assuming pursuers were "numerous and well-armed"); Andrews Raid Notebook No. 1, p. 36 (notes of Murphy's description of position and roles of the individuals on the *Texas*); Fuller, Address at GAR Encampment, *North Georgia Citizen*, Sept. 19, 1900, p. 12 ("It is impossible for me . . ."); Fuller, "*Pursuit and Capture*," pp. 61-62 ("a little pale" and "fine-tooth comb").

11 Pittenger, *Capturing a Locomotive*, pp. 103-4; Dorsey, "The Mitchel Raiders," *The Ohio Soldier*, April 8, 1893, p. 274; Parrott, "The Great Locomotive Chase," *Battles and Leaders*, vol. 5, p. 281.

12 The legend of the *Texas* jumping over a space in the rails first appears in Pittenger, *Capturing a Locomotive*, pp. 103-4, and has been repeated in numerous other accounts over the years. The controversy over the missing rail was eventually sorted out in a lengthy exchange of correspondence between William Pittenger and Anthony Murphy in 1887. Pittenger to Murphy, Jan. 6, 17, 27, Feb. 14, March 18, 19, 1887, Andrews Raid Notebook No. 1,

Kurtz-AHC; see also Pittenger to Murphy, Jan. 10, 1888 ("I could do nothing else than leave out the 'engine jump' after you convinced me that it did not take place"). Murphy suggested two explanations—first, that it was the rail the raiders were prying with, and not the one spiked to the railbed, that had broken; and second, that Pittenger was simply mistaken about where the rail was taken up. See also *Southern Confederacy*, April 15, 1862.

13 The flaming-boxcar-on-the-bridge story appears in Parrott, "The Great Locomotive Chase," *Battles and Leaders*, vol. 5, p. 282; Pittenger, *Capturing a Locomotive*, pp. 112-13; and is shown in the panoramic paintings that accompanied William Knight's postwar lecture tour. See Leeke, "Always Very Daring and Reckless," *Timeline* (Nov.-Dec. 2003), p. 9 (painting depicting burning boxcar on covered bridge). The story was contradicted or debunked by Dorsey, "The Mitchel Raiders," *The Ohio Soldier*, April 8, 1893, p. 274; by Fuller, Fuller to Kurtz, Jan. 21, 1904, Kurtz-AHC ("Neither of the three (3) cars were afire, or burning when I coupled to them—Neither the two I took between Calhoun and Resaca, nor the one attached to the tender of the General when I recaptured her"), as well as by Anthony Murphy and Henry Haney, who rejected the story at the Andrews Raid reunion in Chattanooga in 1906. Andrews Raid historian Wilbur G. Kurtz dissected the burning boxcar incident in a letter to Parlee C. Grose, calling the episode "a bit of inspired invention," and concluding: "Do you suppose, for one minute, that Fuller, Murphy and Haney would have denied that burning-car-on-the-bridge thing, if it had actually happened? Here was a climactic situation: Fuller and the *Texas*, in hot pursuit find a blazing box-car on the bridge; the mounting levin bites into the shingle roof of the cover and the plank or weather-boarded siding; the lurid flame and smoke spell imminent peril, yet the gallant Fuller and the *Texas* crew plunge forward and push the burning car off the bridge, and still forward, to the siding at Ringgold! Real movie stuff. Fuller et al. are the heroes of this episode—why would they—all three, Fuller, Murphy and Haney—deny it? Simply because it didn't happen. Had it happened, the three of them would have gone around taking bows the rest of their lives" (Kurtz to Parlee C. Grose, March 9, 1954, Kurtz-AHC).

14 Murphy, "Pursuit of Andrews' Raiders," *Atlanta Journal Magazine*, p. 2. Dorsey would later suggest, somewhat wistfully, that had Martin Hawkins not overslept and been along aboard the General, "we no doubt would have been better advised on the manner of obstructing our pursuers." Dorsey, "The Mitchel Raiders," *The Ohio Soldier*, April 8, 1893, p. 274.

15 Wilson, *Adventures of Alf Wilson*, p. 37; Pittenger, *Daring and Suffering*, pp. 139-40 ("However we did not wait for them to get close enough to use their shotguns—at least not to any effect, though Wilson, in his published account, is quite positive that some guns were fired"); Knight, "How I Ran the General," *Railroad Man's Magazine*, March 1911 ("some of them tried to pick us off with their rifles").

16 Pittenger, *Daring and Suffering*, pp. 140-41; Parrott, "The Great Locomotive Chase," *Battles and Leaders*, vol. 5, p. 282.

17 Pittenger, *Daring and Suffering*, p. 134 (first feeling of despondency); Gregg, *Andrews Raiders*, p. 24 ("the turning point of the contest"); Fuller, Address at GAR Encampment, *North Georgia Citizen*, Sept. 19, 1900, p. 14; Murphy, "Pursuit of Andrews Raiders," p. 3; Parrott, "The Great Locomotive Chase," *Battles and Leaders*, vol. 5, p. 280. Originally known as Dublin, the town of Resaca was renamed by Georgia soldiers returning from the Mexican

War in honor of their victory at Resaca de la Palma. The townsfolk initially misspelled the name with two c's, incorporating as "Resacca" in 1854. The error was corrected and the town reincorporated as Resaca in 1871. Most Civil War histories consistently spell the town with one "c"; to avoid confusion, I have done the same.

18 Wilson, *Adventures of Alf Wilson*, pp. 35-37; Gregg, *Andrews Raiders*, p. 24.

19 Pittenger, *Daring and Suffering*, p. 142; Knight, Interview with Wilbur G. Kurtz, Sept. 30, 1903, p. 14, Kurtz-AHC; Dorsey, "The Mitchel Raiders," *The Ohio Soldier*, April 8, 1893, p. 274.

20 Johnston, *Western and Atlantic Railroad*, pp. 39-42. Chief tunneler Charles Linton was presented with a cash bonus of thirty-five dollars, "in testimony of his skill, courage, and fidelity as Chief Tunneler." Ibid. The tunnel was closed in 1928 when a new and larger passage was dug through the ridge nearby. The original tunnel, however, has been restored and preserved. For a description of the restoration, see www.edwinbradyconstruction.com/tunnelhill.html.

21 Parrott, "The Great Locomotive Chase," *Battles and Leaders*, vol. 5, p. 282; Pittenger, *Daring and Suffering*, p. 143; Fuller, *Pursuit and Capture*, p. 66; Murphy, "Pursuit of Andrews' Raiders," p. 27.

CHAPTER TEN. "EVERY MAN FOR HIMSELF!"

1 Fuller to Leadbetter, quoted in O'Neill, *Wild Train*, p. 175. Some sources assert that a diverging telegraph wire, running up the East Tennessee & Georgia line from Dalton to Cleveland, assured the delivery of Fuller's message even if the line along the W&A had been cut. See, e.g., Gregg, *Andrews Raiders*, p. 24; Pittenger, *Capturing a Locomotive*, pp. 110-11.

2 *Southern Confederacy*, April 18, 1862 (column of "News and Gossip" from "Our Special Chattanooga Correspondent"); Pittenger, *Daring and Suffering* (1863), p. 70 ("general massacre").

3 Wilson, *Adventures of Alf Wilson*, p. 37; Pittenger, *Daring and Suffering* (1864), p. 70; Parrott, "The Great Locomotive Chase," *Battles and Leaders*, vol. 5, p. 282. Pittenger spells out his case for why it would have been better for the raiders to stay together in a single body and fight it out in a number of his books. See, e.g., *Capturing a Locomotive*, pp. 116-17; *Daring and Suffering*, pp. 148-50.

4 The quote in the text embodies the substance of Andrews's last command, though the many eyewitnesses remember his exact words differently. Compare Knight, "How I Ran the *General*," *Railroad Man's Magazine*, March 1911 ("Stop her, Knight! Scatter boys! It's every man for himself now!"), with Dorsey, "The Mitchel Raiders," *The Ohio Soldier*, April 8, 1893, p. 274 ("Every man for himself! Engineer, reverse your engine! Send her back and jump for your life!"), with Wilson, *Adventures of Alf Wilson*, p. 39 ("Every man for himself now"), with Pittenger, *Daring and Suffering*, p. 150 ("jump off and scatter"). See also Gregg, *Andrews Raiders*, p. 25; Murphy, "Pursuit of Andrews' Raiders," *Atlanta Journal Magazine*, Nov. 8, 1931, p. 27.

5 Here again is a factual conflict, perhaps important only to the participants themselves. Brown and Knight would each claim to be at the throttle as the chase ended—"I will say that I was the first on the engine and last off," Knight said, claiming that he had reversed the

engine; while Brown would for years complain of Knight's efforts to overshadow him and that he pulled the reverse lever before jumping off. See Dorsey, "The Mitchel Raiders," *The Ohio Soldier*, May 20, 1893, p. 321 (Knight's account); Wilson W. Brown, Correspondence, MSS 132, Box 6, Folder 6, Kurtz-AHC (numerous letters seeking recognition as the "chief engineer" of the raid). Dorsey, an apparently impartial observer, states that it was Brown who reversed the engine and "stuck to her until just as the last of us jumped off." Dorsey, "The Mitchel Raiders," *The Ohio Soldier*, April 8, 1893, p. 274.

6 Fuller, *Pursuit and Capture*, p. 68; Gregg, *Andrews Raiders*, p. 27 (noting Whitsitt's initial pursuit and the accidental wounding of one of his men).

7 Murphy, "Pursuit of Andrews' Raiders," *Atlanta Journal Magazine*, Nov. 8, 1931, p. 27. There is some uncertainty as to the comment, "Those damned Yankees; they can run an engine as good as any of us," as it was first provided by White Smith. Although Smith joined the pursuit back down at Acworth and gave detailed descriptions of the end of the chase, several men aboard the *Texas*, including Fuller, Murphy, and Haney, confirm that Smith was not on the pursuing engine at the end of the chase. Several Andrews Raid historians quote Smith's account in any event, see Gregg, *Andrews Raiders*, p. 26; O'Neill, *Wild Train*, p. 183, and Anthony Murphy made a very similar comment, writing of the Yankee engineer in his report of the incident: "Whoever he was, he knew how to run her." "Mr. Murphy's Statement," *Daily Intelligencer*, April 15, 1862.

8 "Mr. Murphy's Statement," *Daily Intelligencer*, April 15, 1862. The distance the Andrews's raiders ran the General is commonly but inaccurately reported as being 87 miles. In fact, the 87-mile figure is the distance between Big Shanty and Ringgold; the distance of the entire chase is about 89 miles. For mileage charts for the W&A (each with slight differences), compare Richard E. Prince, *Nashville, Chattanooga & St. Louis Railway: History and Steam Locomotives* (Bloomington: Indiana University Press, 2001); V.T. Barnwell, *Barnwell's City Directory* (Atlanta: Intelligencer Book and Job Office, 1867), p. 107; David Bright, "CSA Railroads," www.csa-railroads.com.

9 It is unclear who first raised the alarm at Ringgold. Fuller claimed he sent the *Texas* back to spread the news, while Murphy said he sent the *Catoosa* back as soon as it arrived. As the *Catoosa* was behind the *Texas* on the single-line road, and since Fuller quickly left the *General* and headed into the woods while Murphy stayed behind, the latter's account is more plausible. Compare Fuller, *Pursuit and Capture*, p. 68; with Murphy, "Pursuit of Andrews' Raiders," *Atlanta Journal Magazine*, Nov. 8, 1931, p. 27. See also Pittenger, *Daring and Suffering* (1863), p. 92.

10 Knight, quoted in Dorsey, "The Mitchel Raiders," *The Ohio Soldier*, May 20, 1893, p. 321 ("flock of quail"); Dorsey, "The Mitchel Raiders," *The Ohio Soldier*, April 22, 1893, p. 291 (Dorsey, Wilson, Buffum, and Bensinger's flight).

11 Pittenger, *Daring and Suffering*, pp. 181-83.

12 Deposition of Jacob Parrott, *Ohio Boys in Dixie*, p. 39; Dorsey, "The Mitchel Raiders," *The Ohio Soldier*, May 6, 1893, p. 307; Parrott, "The Great Locomotive Chase," *Battles and Leaders*, vol. 5, p. 283 ("I still bear the marks today").

13 Porter's account is quoted in full in Wilson, *Adventures of Alf Wilson*, pp. 229-33; and is described in Pittenger, *Daring and Suffering*, p. 184.

14 The description of Pittenger's flight from the *General* and his eventual capture is largely based on his initial 1864 account in *Daring and Suffering*—the first of four books he would write on the raid. *Daring and Suffering* (1864), pp. 93-111. He would write yet more detailed narratives of his flight in his later books. See *Capturing a Locomotive*, pp. 120-40; *Daring and Suffering*, pp. 161-80; *The Great Locomotive Chase*, pp. 161-80.

15 Wilson describes his and Wood's twelve-day odyssey in detail in *Adventures of Alf Wilson*, pp. 53-90.

16 Andrews's route of flight from the General is recounted in Gregg, *Andrews Raiders*, pp. 30-34. Gregg quotes Dr. Parks at length, pp. 31-34.

17 Fuller, *Pursuit and Capture*, pp. 68-71. Fuller was no doubt exhausted, though he overstates his case. Not only does he claim he was bleeding from nose, mouth, and ears, but he also asserts that he "had already been on foot for more than thirty miles that day," an obvious exaggeration.

18 Beatty, *The Citizen-Soldier*, p. 133; "Biographical Notice," *Astronomy of the Bible*, p. 17 ("there was a horoscope").

19 Mitchel to Stanton, April 17, 1862, *OR*, vol. 10, pt. 2, p. 111; Mitchel to Stanton, May 4, 1862, *OR*, vol. 10, pt. 2, p. 161 ("straggling bands of mounted men"); Halleck to Stanton, April 26, 1862, *OR*, vol. 10, pt. 2, p. 129 ("We are now at the enemy's throat").

20 Mitchel to Stanton, April 24, 1862, *OR*, vol. 10, pt. 2, p. 124; Pittenger, *Daring and Suffering*, p. 236 (discussing Mitchel's comment to his F.A. Mitchel that the raiders had been hanged); see also Mitchel, *Ormsby MacKnight Mitchel, Astronomer and General*, p. 299 (noting report that reached Mitchel indicated that Andrews and his men had been hanged).

21 *Southern Confederacy*, April 18 and 30, 1862; *Daily Intelligencer*, April 18, 1862.

CHAPTER ELEVEN. COURT-MARTIAL

1 Wilson W. Brown to Wilbur G. Kurtz, Jan. 13, 1904 (describing Swims), Kurtz-AHC; Pittenger, *Capturing a Locomotive*, p. 171; Gregg, *Andrews Raiders*, p. 37 ("queer freak of architecture"); Knight, quoted in Dorsey, "The Mitchel Raiders," *The Ohio Soldier*, May 20, 1893, p. 322; Claiborne, quoted in Dorsey, "The Mitchel Raiders," *The Ohio Soldier*, May 6, 1893, p. 307. Based upon their recollection of the basement "hole" as a thirteen-by-thirteen-foot cell, the raiders uniformly recalled the jail's overall dimensions as considerably smaller than twenty-three feet by thirty-seven feet. The traditional spelling of Swims's name, employed by the raiders themselves as well as most histories, may in fact be an error. The 1860 Hamilton County (Chattanooga) census lists a John Swaim, male, age sixty, profession "Jailor." 1860 Hamilton County, Tennessee Census, p. 115; see also Wilson, *Chattanooga's Story*, p. 67 (describing "Swaim's Jail" and its naming its proprietor, John Swaim). Because the raiders knew him as Old Swims, I have used that spelling in the text. The former location of the jail is commemorated by a Tennessee historical marker, no. 2A 77, near the corner of Fifth and Lookout Streets in Chattanooga.

2 Pittenger, *Daring and Suffering* (1863), pp. 123-26; *Daring and Suffering*, pp. 212-14.

3 Knight, quoted in Dorsey, "The Mitchel Raiders," *The Ohio Soldier*, May 20, 1893, p. 322; Wilson, *Adventures of Alf Wilson*, pp. 91-92.

4 Gregg, *Andrews Raiders*, pp. 34-35 (interrogation of Andrews).

5 James A. Pike, "Prison-Experience of a Union Spy," in *Annals of the Army of the Cumberland*, John Fitch, ed. (Philadelphia: J.B. Lippincott & Co., 1864), pp. 620-21 (describing his encounter with the Andrews Raiders in the Chattanooga jail); Wilson, *Adventures of Alf Wilson*, p. 98; Dorsey, "The Mitchel Raiders," *The Ohio Soldier*, May 6, 1893, pp. 306-7. For further description of Swims's jail, see Pittenger, *Daring and Suffering*, pp. 217-21.

6 Pittenger, *Daring and Suffering*, pp. 228-29 (conversations in the hole); Dorsey, "The Mitchel Raiders," *The Ohio Soldier*, May 20, 1893, p. 324 ("jolly crew in a bad boat"); Parrott to Wilbur G. Kurtz, in Kurtz handwritten notes, MSS 132, Box 6, Folder 2, p. 10, Kurtz-AHC (Buffum's dramatics); see also Brown to Kurtz, July 11, 1904, Kurtz-AHC; William Shakespeare, *Hamlet*, act I, scene v.

7 Dorsey, "The Mitchel Raiders," *The Ohio Soldier*, May 6, 1893, p. 307.

8 Ibid.; see also Pittenger, *Daring and Suffering*, pp. 226-27.

9 The dispute over Pittenger and Wilson's plan for the raiders' legal defense is one of the great controversies of the Andrews Raid. Pittenger details his version of events in his various accounts (with a slightly different explanation given in each book). Compare Pittenger, *Daring and Suffering* (1863), pp. 136-37; Pittenger, *Capturing a Locomotive*, pp. 211-12; Pittenger, *Daring and Suffering*, pp. 229-32. In his 1863 book, Pittenger claims that "no amount of persuasion, threatening or promises, could induce any of the party to betray one of our reserved secrets," but he also omits entirely the fact that he testified at the trials of Andrews and seven of his comrades. Ibid. at 139-40, 173 ("The only evidence they had was of the men who pursued us on the train, and also of those who afterward arrested us; but of course none of these knew anything of our lurking around the camps"). Pittenger's greatest critic in later years was Dorsey, who at first believed Pittenger's plan to be "a great mistake," but later came to view him as a traitor who turned state's evidence and deliberately betrayed his comrades. See generally Dorsey, "The Mitchel Raiders," *The Ohio Soldier*, May 20, June 3, July 1, 1893; see also Dorsey, "Trial of Andrews' Raiders" (unpublished manuscript), Western Reserve Historical Society (noting that Pittenger's plan seemed to be to "give it all away").

10 Dorsey, "The Mitchel Raiders," *The Ohio Soldier*, May 20, 1893, p. 323; Pittenger, *Daring and Suffering*, pp. 232-33.

11 *Southern Confederacy*, April 15, 1862; Augusta *Daily Chronicle & Sentinel*, April 14, 1862; *Atlanta Commonwealth*, April 14, 1862.

12 *Daily Intelligencer*, April 15, 1862; *Southern Confederacy*, April 15, 1862; *Augusta Daily Chronicle & Sentinel*, April 14, 1862 ("On Saturday morning, eight of the party were arrested and after being soundly whipped, confessed that they had been sent out from Shelbyville by the Federalists for the purpose of burning the bridges and tearing up the track of the railroad so as to prevent reinforcements. . . . They state that the party numbered 22"); Wilson, *Adventures of Alf Wilson*, p. 114.

13 The beating of Benjamin Flynn is discussed in Gregg, *Andrews Raiders* (erroneously referring to "John A. Flynn"), and Pittenger, *Daring and Suffering*, p. 144. The incident was initially reported in the *Daily Intelligencer*, April 18, 1862, and the *Southern Confederacy*, April 20, 1862.

14 Memphis Daily Appeal, April 15, 1862; Southern Confederacy, April 15, 1862; Augusta Daily Constitutionalist, April 15, 1862.

15 Pittenger, Capturing a Locomotive, p. 116 ("Andrews never rightly valued fighting men . . ."); Southern Confederacy, April 15, 1862; Fuller, Pursuit and Capture, pp. 73-76; Knight, quoted in Leeke, "Always Very Daring and Reckless," Timeline, Nov.-Dec. 2003, p. 4; Murphy, "Pursuit of Andrews' Raiders," Atlanta Journal Magazine, p. 27; Pittenger, Daring and Suffering, pp. 154-55.

16 Gregg, Andrews Raiders, pp. 36-37.

17 Wilson, Chattanooga's Story, pp. 55-56; Gregg, Andrews Raiders, p. 36.

18 Dorsey, "The Mitchel Raiders," The Ohio Soldier, May 20, 1893, p. 324 ("He seemed to think that it would not help him . . ."); Pittenger, Daring and Suffering, p. 232; Nashville Daily Union, April 15, 1862 (republishing April 22, 1862, advertisement placed by W.S. Whiteman); Dorsey, "The Mitchel Raiders," The Ohio Soldier, June 3, 1893, p. 337 (Andrews "that fellow has swatted me"). Dorsey claimed that both John Reed Porter and William Knight heard Andrews's comment about Pittenger and confirmed it at the raiders' reunion in 1887. Ibid. See also Gregg, Andrews Raiders, p. 36 (Brabson "taking too much interest in the man's case").

19 Dorsey, "The Mitchel Raiders," The Ohio Soldier, June 3, 1893, p. 338; Pittenger, Daring and Suffering, pp. 237-40; Wilson, Adventures of Alf Wilson, p. 108.

20 Southern Confederacy, May 3, 1862; Dorsey, "The Mitchel Raiders," The Ohio Soldier, June 3, 1893, p. 338; see also Wilbur G. Kurtz, "Andrews Raiders in Madison" (unpublished manuscript), MSS 132, Box 3, Folder 2, Kurtz-AHC. The captain of the guard in Chattanooga is identified by the raiders as "Capt. Lawes" of the 43rd Georgia; rosters suggest this individual is actually Capt. James F. Law of Company F of the 43rd.

21 Dorsey, "The Mitchel Raiders," The Ohio Soldier, June 3, 1893, p. 339 ("not so very unpleasant"). The raiders' songs and mock trials are recounted by a number of survivors, including Dorsey, Wilson, and Pittenger. See ibid.; Pittenger, Daring and Suffering, pp. 242-44; Wilson, Adventures of Alf Wilson, p. 121 (noting that singing "was a very common pastime with us in the evening").

22 Dorsey, "The Mitchel Raiders," The Ohio Soldier, June 3, 1893, p. 339.

23 Pittenger, Daring and Suffering, pp. 246-47; Dorsey, "The Mitchel Raiders," The Ohio Soldier, June 3, 1893, p. 339. Again, Pittenger ascribes to himself a great deal of leadership and nerve in claiming to be the author of this escape plan. It is somewhat difficult to believe that the corporal was on the one hand constructing a complex legal defense and on the other urging that the party attempt a violent jailbreak. Dorsey claims that Wilson and Pittenger actually opposed an escape attempt, but that Brown, Dorsey, and others convinced Andrews that it was their only chance.

24 Gregg, Andrews Raiders, p. 39; Pittenger, Daring and Suffering, pp. 247-48; Dorsey, "The Mitchel Raiders," The Ohio Soldier, June 17, 1893, pp. 353-54. Dorsey maintained that George Wilson was told that Pittenger had to be included in the Knoxville party (presumably to testify), and that Wilson was to select the other ten.

25 Dorsey, "The Mitchel Raiders," The Ohio Soldier, June 17, 1893, p. 354; Wilson, Adventures of Alf Wilson, p. 120.

Chapter Twelve. The Horrors of the Gibbet

1 Dorsey, "The Mitchel Raiders," *The Ohio Soldier*, June 17, 1893, pp. 354-55; Wilson, *Adventures of Alf Wilson*, pp. 121-24; Wilbur G. Kurtz, "James J. Andrews at Williams Island," *Atlanta Constitution* Magazine, June 15, 1930 ("tobacco-chewing scape-grace"). In addition to Andrews, the nine raiders left in Chattanooga were William Bensinger, Daniel Allen Dorsey, Martin Hawkins, Jacob Parrott, John Reed Porter, William Reddick, Alf Wilson, John Wollam, and Mark Wood.

2 Andrews told the story of his flight to his eventual captor Samuel Williams, who related it in turn to reporter Frank Gregg. Gregg, *Andrews Raiders*, pp. 41-43; see also Dorsey, "The Mitchel Raiders," *The Ohio Soldier*, June 17, 1893, p. 355.

3 *Knoxville Whig*, June 4, 1862.

4 The two eyewitness accounts of Andrews's capture—one from Samuel Williams and one from William Standifer—sharply contradict each other in describing the role played by Williams. Both are quoted in full in Gregg, *Andrews Raiders*, pp. 41-45. The conflicting stories are thoroughly presented in Kurtz, "James J. Andrews at Williams Island," *Atlanta Constitution Magazine*, June 15, 1930, pp. 5-6; see also *Chattanooga Rebel*, April 1, 1864 (describing Williams's "betrayal" of Andrews).

5 Wilson, *Adventures of Alf Wilson*, pp. 126-27. Andrews's recapture and return to Swims's jail are also described in Dorsey, "The Mitchel Raiders," *The Ohio Soldier*, June 17, 1893, pp. 355-56.

6 Kurtz, "James J. Andrews at Williams' Island," p. 5; Dorsey, "The Mitchel Raiders," *The Ohio Soldier*, June 17, 1893, p. 355.

7 Pittenger, *Daring and Suffering*, pp. 265-67; *Capturing a Locomotive*, pp. 207-8 (description of Pierce, Fry) and 212-13 (Temple and Baxter fee arrangement; court proceedings). Unfortunately, though he was a prolific author and published a number of books, Judge Temple never wrote of the court-martial of the Andrews Raiders. In his well-regarded 588-page history *East Tennessee and the Civil War*, he only mentions the fact of the representation in a footnote. Temple, *East Tennessee and the Civil War*, p. 400, n. 1. Oliver P. Temple to Wilbur G. Kurtz, July 18, 1904, Kurtz-AHC ("I never did write or publish an article dealing with the Court Martial of the Andrews Raiders. . . . It is possible that I have the notes executed by such of the defendants as were tried, but if so they are among the rubbish of a lawyer of forty years standing"); see generally Oliver Perry Temple, O.P. Temple Papers, 1832-, Special Collections Library of the University of Tennessee, Knoxville (containing Temple's correspondence with Dorsey, Pittenger, and Kurtz).

8 Fuller to Dorsey, Oct. 31, 1884, William P. Palmer Collection, Western Reserve Historical Society. Pittenger spends most of a chapter describing the Knoxville court-martial proceedings without mentioning that he testified in the trial. Pittenger, *Daring and Suffering*, pp. 264-72.

9 Temple, quoted in Dorsey, "The Mitchel Raiders," *The Ohio Soldier*, July 29, 1893, p. 402; Fuller to Dorsey, Oct. 31, 1884, quoted in Dorsey, "Trial of the Andrews Raiders" (unpublished manuscript), 1899, Western Reserve Historical Society.

10 Wilbur G. Kurtz, "The Andrews Raiders in the Fulton County Jail" (unpublished manu-

script, 1966), Kurtz-AHC, p. 4 ("manifest absurdity"); Pittenger, *Daring and Suffering*, pp. 271-72 (describing defense case as argued by Temple); Report of Judge-Advocate-General Holt to the Secretary of War, March 27, 1863, in *Ohio Boys in Dixie*, p. 15 ("a just and unanswerable presentation").

11 *OR*, vol. 10, pt. 1, pp. 637-38. Historian Wilbur Kurtz once called the trial of the seven men at Knoxville, Tennessee, "one of the blind spots in the story." Kurtz to Parlee C. Grose, March 9, 1954, Kurtz-AHC. Daniel Dorsey wrote a number of letters to the War Department and various archives after the war to try to obtain copies of any records of the proceedings, and came up empty. See Robert T. Lincoln, Secretary of War, to D.A. Dorsey, Jan. 13, 1882, Palmer Collection, WRHS (advising that the court-martial proceedings in the Andrews raid case do not appear on file at the War Department). More recently, Civil War court-martial expert Dr. Thomas Lowry of the The Index Project, Inc. confirmed that apparently no official record remains from any of the trials of the Andrews Raiders. Thomas Lowry to the author, Jan. 4, 2006.

12 Dorsey, "The Mitchel Raiders," *The Ohio Soldier*, June 17, 1893, p. 356; Andrews to D.S. McGavic, June 5, 1862, Andrews Papers, WRHS. Andrews's letter to McGavic is also quoted in *OR*, series 2, vol. 5, pp. 417-18.

13 Wilson, *Adventures of Alf Wilson*, p. 131.

14 Keifer, *Slavery and Four Years of War*, p. 283 ("Mitchel's position . . . precarious"); Cincinnati Gazette, July 22, 1862 ("wanton and disgraceful"); James A. Garfield to his brother, July 9, 1862, in Frederick D. Williams, ed., *The Wild Life of the Army: Civil War Letters of James A. Garfield* (Lansing: Michigan State University Press, 1964), p. 121 ("according to the Muscovite custom"); Mitchel to General George S. Hunter and others, Committee, Athens, May 24, 1862, *OR*, vol. 10, pt. 2, pp. 212-13 (noting aggregate losses at $54,689.80 and stating "I cannot arraign before a court, civil or military, a brigade . . ."). For more on the sack of Athens, see Mark Grimsley, *The Hard Hand of War: Union Military Policy Toward Southern Civilians, 1861-1865* (Cambridge: Cambridge University Press, 1995), pp. 81-85; Roy Morris, Jr., "The Sack of Athens," *Civil War Times Illustrated* 24 (Feb. 1986), pp. 26-32.

15 Garfield to his brother, July 9, 1862, in Williams, ed., *The Wild Life of the Army*, p. 121 ("so black a page" . . . "shameful outrages"). The allegations regarding Mitchel's alleged speculation in the cotton trade were printed in the *Louisville Courier* and are described in Grimsley, *Hard Hand of War*, pp. 82-84. Later that summer, Mitchel submitted to Stanton a vigorous and unapologetic defense to the various charges against him, including no less than thirteen supporting enclosures. Mitchel to Stanton, July 19, 1862, *OR*, vol. 10, pt. 2, pp. 290-95. For accusations and discussions related to Mitchel's burning of the Tennessee River bridges, see Halleck to Lincoln, June 7, 1862, *OR*, vol. 10, pt. 1, p. 670 ("Mitchel's foolish destruction of bridges embarrassed me very much, but I am working night and day to remedy the error"); cf. Buell to Mitchel, April 19, 1862, *OR*, vol. 10, pt. 2, p. 114 ("I telegraphed you several days ago in regard to the importance of destroying the bridge over the Tennessee River beyond Stevenson and also the Decatur bridge . . ."); Mitchel to Chase, April 19, 1862, *OR*, vol. 10, pt. 2, p. 115 ("I spared the Tennessee bridges . . ."); see also Prokopowicz, *All for the Regiment*, p. 118 (noting that "the destruction of the bridges had no effect on the Confederate war effort but impeded Union operations in the area for

months"). Mitchel's concluding comment on the matter came in September, when he said of Halleck, "His talk about bridge burning shows either his meanness or his utter stupidity." Mitchel to George S. Coe, Sept. 26, 1862, quoted in Mitchel, *Ormsby MacKnight Mitchel*, p. 361.

16 *Harper's Weekly*, May 10, 1862; Beatty, *The Citizen-Soldier*, p. 143 (describing strawberry supper at Judge Lane's); Mitchel to Chase, April 20, 1862, in *The Salmon P. Chase Papers*, vol. 3, p. 181.

17 Mitchel to Buell, June 7, 1862, *OR*, vol. 10, pt. 2, p. 271 (noting Negley's authority to take Chattanooga "in case he deems it prudent"); David M. Key to wife Elizabeth, quoted in Dr. James B. Jones, Jr., "Negley's Raid, June 2-9, 1862," www.historic-battles.com; Frank Moore, ed., *The Rebellion Record: A Diary of American Events, with Documents, Narratives, Illustrative Events, Poetry, etc.* (New York: G.P. Putnam, 1861-68), vol. 5, pp. 189-90 ("The frightful whizzing of the shell . . .").

18 Asst. Adj. Gen. H.L. Clay to Brig. Gen. C.L. Stevenson, June 7, 1862, *OR*, vol. 10, pt. 2, pp. 598-99 (reporting that "there seems to be no doubt that the enemy contemplate an attack in large force upon Chattanooga, and probably the invasion of East Tennessee. . . ."); Smith to Gov. Joseph E. Brown, June 6, 1862, *OR*, vol. 10, pt. 2, p. 596 ("Chattanooga is threatened," etc.).

19 Mitchel to Halleck, June 10, 1862 ("complete success"); *New York Times*, June 13, 1862 ("Complete Success").

20 Wilson, *Adventures of Alf Wilson*, pp. 131-32; Dorsey, "The Mitchel Raiders," *The Ohio Soldier*, Aug. 26, 1893, p. 270. Sources disagree over the party's arrival time in Atlanta. Dorsey puts it at 4 o'clock, and newspaper accounts report the raiders arrival on the "evening" train; but other accounts put it at 11 A.M. (Given the typical seven-hour train ride from Chattanooga, the afternoon arrival seems more plausible.)

Alf Wilson attributes an extra amount of cruelty to the Atlanta authorities, claiming that Andrews was told to "be damned quick about it" when he asked for a moment to say farewell to his comrades. Wilson, Adventures, at 132. Numerous sources refer to Oliver H. Jones as the provost marshal in Atlanta; in fact he was the sheriff or "city marshal."

21 Scott, "An Episode of the War: Andrews and His Scheme," in *From Lincoln to Cleveland*, pp. 153-56; Mrs. Joseph M. Wusthoff, quoted in "Raider Andrews Was Hanged in Georgian Terrace Block," *Atlanta Journal*, April 13, 1913; *Southern Confederacy*, June 8, 1862 ("He seemed to be very penitent . . ."). Mrs. Wustoff was the sister-in-law of Anthony Murphy, who apparently did not attend Andrews's execution. For a thorough description of the hanging and a careful analysis of the site of the gallows, see Kurtz, "The Execution of James J. Andrews," *Atlanta Constitution Magazine*, March 8, 1931.

22 Kurtz, "The Execution of James J. Andrews," *Atlanta Constitution Magazine*, March 8, 1931; see also Gregg, *Andrews Raiders*, p. 46. The grisly hanging of Andrews has been vividly described by a number of people who were not there. See, e.g., Dorsey, "The Mitchel Raiders," *The Ohio Soldier*, July 1, 1893, p. 370; Wilson, *Adventures of Alf Wilson*, pp. 132-33; *Ohio Boys in Dixie*, p. 8. It is difficult to confirm the bungled execution, however, through eyewitness accounts. Rev. Scott did not stay to watch the hanging; and Mrs. Wustoff saw the processional and later saw the grave, but did not witness the execution itself. Squires's

description is one of the few eyewitness accounts to describe the terrible "strangling." James Squires interview with Wilbur G. Kurtz, Dec. 22, 1908, Andrews Raid Notebook No. 2, p. 96; but see Ward S. Greene, "Romance of the Rails: Fifty Years of Railroading As Seen By 'Uncle Jim' Squires, the Oldest Engineer of the W. & A. Railroad," *Atlanta Journal*, March 9, 1913 (describing hanging of Andrews without mention of the incident).

23 Fuller, *Pursuit and Capture*, p. 85. Fuller's unfeeling statement regarding Andrews's courage in the face of death is puzzling, especially since he said exactly the opposite in a speech in 1888. ("Early in June, 1862, all the prisoners were taken to Atlanta and Andrews was at once hung. He died bravely.") See also Dorsey, "The Mitchel Raiders," *The Ohio Soldier*, July 1, 1893, p. 370; Diary of Samuel Pierce Richards, June 7, 1862, quoted in Garrett, *Atlanta and Environs*, p. 524.

24 "Raider Andrews Was Hanged in Georgian Terrace Block," *Atlanta Journal*, April 13, 1913; Gregg, *Andrews Raiders*, p. 46 (describing unmarked grave lost under blackberry bushes and wildflowers).

25 The empty trunk sent by James Andrews to his fiancée has never been explained. Some have suggested that an explanatory letter to Miss Layton must have been lost; others theorized that he had purchased the trunk to carry their wedding presents. Miss Layton's reaction to the news of Andrews's execution is described by William Pittenger, who investigated that aspect of the story years after the war. Pittenger, *Daring and Suffering*, p. 263.

CHAPTER THIRTEEN. HEAVEN OR CINCINNATI

1 Dorsey, "The Mitchel Raiders," *The Ohio Soldier*, July 1, 1893, p. 370; Wilson, *Adventures of Alf Wilson*, p. 155 ("a stout iron cage"; description of jail), 135 ("a great relief . . ."). The history, design, and construction of the jail are recorded in Wilbur G. Kurtz, "Fulton County's First Jail," *Atlanta Journal*, Nov. 6, 1932.

2 Dorsey, "The Mitchel Raiders, *The Ohio Soldier*, July 1, 1893, p. 370; Wilson, *Adventures of Alf Wilson*, pp. 136-37.

3 Kurtz, "The Andrews Raiders in the Fulton County Jail," p. 6 ("curious if not hostile mob"); Pittenger, *Daring and Suffering*, p. 277.

4 Pittenger, *Daring and Suffering*, pp. 277-78. The cruel jail guard referred to by the raiders as Thor or Thoer was in fact fifty-nine-year-old Atlantan Benjamin Thrower. See 1867 Atlanta City Directory (listing jail guard Benjamin Thrower); Kurtz, "The Andrews Raiders in the Fulton County Jail," p. 8.

5 Dorsey, "The Mitchel Raiders," *The Ohio Soldier*, July 29, 1893, p. 404.

6 Pittenger, *Daring and Suffering*, pp. 279-80; Dorsey, "The Mitchel Raiders," *The Ohio Soldier*, July 29, 1893, p. 404. Dorsey notes the reason for the speedy execution: "But you see they had learned a lesson by Andrews' attempt to escape, and thought they would have no more of that kind of work, or perhaps, and I think quite likely, they were afraid that if it should become known that seven more of the raiders were to be put to death, public sentiment would condemn it, and the people might protest." Ibid.

7 Scott, *From Lincoln to Cleveland*, pp. 156-59. Scott also records that following the prayer, Sergeant Major Ross gave him a Masonic sign of distress. After confirming that Ross was a fellow member of the order, he spoke with him alone. Ross asked Scott to try to obtain a

delay of the execution, and Scott promised to do all he could. When he spoke with the provost marshal, however, his request was denied. Ibid.

8 Dorsey, "The Mitchel Raiders," *The Ohio Soldier*, July 29, 1893, p. 404; Pittenger, *Daring and Suffering*, p. 284.

9 Kurtz, "The Andrews Raiders in the Fulton County Jail," p. 22; Scott, *From Lincoln to Cleveland*, pp. 160-61.

10 Dorsey, Pittenger, and Wilson all describe in detail the farewells of their doomed comrades. Dorsey, "The Mitchel Raiders," *The Ohio Soldier*, July 29, 1893, p. 404; Pittenger, *Daring and Suffering*, p. 284; Wilson, *Adventures of Alf Wilson*, pp. 143-45.

11 Wilson, Adventures, p. 143; Brown to Kurtz, Feb. 27, 1904, Kurtz-AHC.

12 Kurtz, "The Andrews Raiders in the Fulton County Jail," pp. 22-23; John W. Woodruff, quoted in Wallace Putnam Reed, "When Atlanta Saw Seven Men Hanged," *Atlanta Constitution*, July 28, 1902.

13 Woodruff, quoted in Reed, "When Atlanta Saw Seven Men Hanged," *Atlanta Constitution*, July 28, 1902; Tevi Taliaferro, *Historic Oakland Cemetery* (Charleston, S.C.: Arcadia Publishing Co., 2001), p. 7; see also www.oaklandcemetery.com/AboutOakland.htm.

14 Woodruff, quoted in Reed, "When Atlanta Saw Seven Men Hanged," *Atlanta Constitution*, July 28, 1902; see also Woodruff to D.A. Dorsey, May 5, 1904, Palmer Collection, WRHS; Fuller, *Pursuit and Capture*, p. 85 ("They were brave, fearless men. . ."); Fuller, "Epitome of the Andrews Raid," p. 17 ("hurriedly and horribly constructed death-trap").

15 Wilson's speech on the gallows is recounted by a number of eyewitness accounts and other sources, including Fuller, *Pursuit and Capture* of the Andrews Raiders, pp. 85-86; Woodruff, quoted in Reed, "When Atlanta Saw Seven Men Hanged," *Atlanta Constitution*, July 28, 1902; Pittenger, *Daring and Suffering*, pp. 286-88; Dorsey, "The Mitchel Raiders," *The Ohio Soldier*, Aug. 12, 1893, p. 3; Wilson, *Adventures of Alf Wilson*, pp. 145-46. The last comment, referring to the "will of Him, who doest all things well," was reported by Fuller, who witnessed the speech firsthand, and it is a curious remark given Wilson's professed atheism.

16 Pittenger, *Daring and Suffering*, p. 288.

17 The botched hanging of Campbell and Slavens is recorded by John Woodruff, in Reed, "When Atlanta Saw Seven Men Hanged," *Atlanta Constitution*, July 28, 1902; Fuller, *Pursuit and Capture*, p. 86; and further described by Dorsey, "The Mitchel Raiders," *The Ohio Soldier*, Aug. 12, 1893, p. 2; Pittenger, *Daring and Suffering*, pp. 288-89; and Wilson, *Adventures of Alf Wilson*, pp. 146-47. Fuller writes of his strange souvenir of the occasion (Slavens's rope) in *Pursuit and Capture*, p. 86; see also Fuller to Kurtz, April 8, 1904 ("The poor fellows were decently executed . . .").

18 Sarah Conley Clayton, *Requiem for a Lost City: A Memoir of Civil War Atlanta and the Old South*, Robert Scott Davis, Jr., ed. (Macon, Ga.: Mercer University Press, 1999), p. 47; James R. Crew to Dear Wife, June 18, 1862 (probable date), James R. Crew Collection, AHC; Woodruff to Dorsey, May 5, 1904, Palmer Collection, WRHS.

19 Clayton, *Requiem for a Lost City*, pp. 47-48.

20 Dorsey, "The Mitchel Raiders," *The Ohio Soldier*, Aug. 26, 1893, p. 17. Pittenger gives his side of the story on the excommunication of the playing cards in *Daring and Suffering*, p. 299.

21 Wilson, *Adventures of Alf Wilson*, p. 157.

22 Dorsey, "The Mitchel Raiders," *The Ohio Soldier*, Aug. 26, 1893, p. 18. Dorsey offered some excuse for Buffum's curse-filled prayers: "He was all right until he thought of the enemy, then he unconsciously gave vent to his feelings." Ibid.

23 Kurtz, "The Andrews Raiders in the Fulton County Jail," p. 28. The raiders' letter to Jefferson Davis is quoted in full and its text pictured in Pittenger, *Daring and Suffering*, pp. 291-94; see also Wilson, *Adventures of Alf Wilson*, p. 152 (describing the writing of the letter); Dorsey, "The Mitchel Raiders," *The Ohio Soldier*, Aug. 26, 1893, p. 18 (same).

24 Pittenger, *Daring and Suffering*, pp. 300-304.

25 Ibid., pp. 304-5.

26 Dorsey, "The Mitchel Raiders," *The Ohio Soldier*, Sept. 23, 1893, p. 34.

27 Wollam's return to prison is vividly described by Knight in interview notes by Wilbur Kurtz, MSS 132, Box 6, Folder 2, Kurtz-AHC, and is also noted by Dorsey, "The Mitchel Raiders," *The Ohio Soldier*, Aug. 26, 1893, pp. 18-19; and Pittenger, *Daring and Suffering*, p. 297.

28 Dorsey, "The Mitchel Raiders," *The Ohio Soldier*, Aug. 26, 1893, p. 19 (remembering Rebel flag on the Fourth of July); *Southern Confederacy*, July 5, 1862; see also S.P. Williams Diary, July 4, 1862, quoted in Garrett, *Atlanta and Environs*, p. 542 ("Friday 4th. The once 'Glorious Fourth' has passed by very quietly this year. A Fireman's Dinner and a few faint poppers being all the celebration vouchsafed to it").

29 Knight interview, quoted in Kurtz, "The Andrews Raiders in the Fulton County Jail," p. 29.

30 *OR*, vol. 10, pt. I, pp. 635-36.

31 The raiders' August 17 letter, its endorsements, and its aftermath are discussed in Pittenger, *Daring and Suffering*, pp. 307-12; Dorsey, "The Mitchel Raiders," *The Ohio Soldier*, Aug. 26, 1893, p. 20, and Sept. 23, 1893, pp. 33-34; Kurtz, "The Andrews Raiders in the Fulton County Jail," pp. 30-32.

CHAPTER FOURTEEN. "A DAMNED LONG WAYS FROM CAMP"

1 Russell, Atlanta, 1847-1890, pp. 96-99; Garrett, *Atlanta and Environs*, pp. 533 (quoting ad seeking church bells) and 533-35 (discussing price inflation and speculators); Dyer, *Secret Yankees*, p. 97 ("Atlanta verged on chaos"); S.P. Richards Diary, September 6, 1862, quoted in Garrett, p. 535.

2 Garrett, *Atlanta and Environs*, pp. 533-34 (discussion of burden on railroad, rate increases, traffic between Atlanta and Marietta).

3 Bell, *Southern Railroad Man*, p. 10 (describing transportation of troops, provision and equipment); Garrett, *Atlanta and Environs*, p. 534 ("the quick, the dead, and those in between"), 531 (newspaper listings of the dead), 542 (death of O. Jones's brother).

4 Muster Rolls, Company H, 21st Ohio, May 31 to Aug. 31 and Aug 31. to Dec. 31, 1862, copies in Robert Buffum Papers, Ohio Historical Society; Dorsey, "The Mitchel Raiders," *The Ohio Soldier*, Nov. 4, 1893, p. 82 (quoting Minshall's entry in 21st Ohio Company H records).

5 Dorsey, "The Mitchel Raiders," *The Ohio Soldier*, Sept. 23, 1893, p. 34.

6 Pittenger, *Daring and Suffering*, p. 297; Dorsey, "The Mitchel Raiders," *The Ohio Soldier*, Oct. 7, 1893, p. 50 (servants' names were John and Kate); Wilson, *Adventures of Alf Wilson*, p. 156.

7 Wilson, *Adventures of Alf Wilson*, p. 56; Dorsey, "The Mitchel Raiders," *The Ohio Soldier*, Oct. 7, 1893, p. 49.

8 Dorsey, "The Mitchel Raiders," *The Ohio Soldier*, Oct. 7, 1893, p. 49.

9 Fry's dialogue with Turner is quoted by Pittenger, *Daring and Suffering*, pp. 316-17; Dorsey, "The Mitchel Raiders," *The Ohio Soldier*, Oct. 7, 1893, p. 50; and Wilson, *Adventures of Alf Wilson*, pp. 160-61. Pittenger claims that he clapped his hand over the jailer's mouth to muffle his cries; while Wilson and Dorsey both say it was Fry who did so.

10 Narrative of Isaac A. Coleman, in Kurtz, Andrews Raid Notebook No. 3, p. 56 ("Buffum stayed like a man"); Pittenger, *Daring and Suffering*, p. 320.

11 The various accounts of the raiders' jailbreak in Atlanta are found in Wilson, *Adventures of Alf Wilson*, pp. 159-65; Dorsey, "The Mitchel Raiders," *The Ohio Soldier*, October 7, 1893, pp. 50-51; Pittenger, *Daring and Suffering*, pp. 316-26.

12 G.W. Lee to Clifton H. Smith, Nov. 18, 1862, *OR*, vol. 10, pt. 1, p. 639; Pittenger, *Daring and Suffering*, p. 327.

13 *Southern Confederacy*, Oct. 17, 19, and 25, 1862.

14 Shelby Foote, *The Civil War: A Narrative* (New York: Random House, 1958), vol.I, pp. 558-66; H.W. Halleck to Don Carlos Buell, July 8, 1862, *OR*, vol. 16, pt. 2, p. 104; Beatty, *The Citizen-Soldier*, pp. 117-18 (describing Buell's dancing-master policy); John W. Switzer Diary, July 20, 1862, Indiana Historical Society, quoted in Engle, *Don Carlos Buell*, p. 272.

15 Buell to Halleck, August 6 and 7, 1862, *OR*, vol. 16, pt. 2, pp. 265-66, 278; McPherson, *Battle Cry of Freedom*, pp. 512-17 (describing Buell and Bragg's movements in the Chattanooga campaign); Foote, *The Civil War: A Narrative*, pp. 564-65.

16 John Reed Porter, "Down the Tennessee—Escape of Porter and Wollam," in Pittenger, *Daring and Suffering*, pp. 342-47.

17 Porter, in Pittenger, *Daring and Suffering*, p. 346 (describing interview with General Dodge). For background on General Grenville M. Dodge, see David Haward Bain, *Empire Express: Building the First Transcontinental Railroad* (New York: Penguin Putnam, 2000), pp. 157-60; see generally Stephen Ambrose, *Nothing Like It In the World: The Men Who Built the Transcontinental Railroad 1863-1869* (New York: Simon & Schuster, 2000).

18 Dorsey, "The Mitchel Raiders," *The Ohio Soldier*, Oct. 7, Oct. 21, and Nov. 4, 1893; see also Dorsey, "The Loyal Mountaineers," in *Daring and Suffering*, pp. 334-41.

19 Wilson W. Brown to Wilbur G. Kurtz, undated letter (possibly 1904), in Kurtz-AHC, Box 6, Folder 6 ("How we subsisted 47 days and nights . . ."). For Knight's account of the escape, see "In Cave and Mountain," in *Daring and Suffering*, pp. 327-33; and Knight, quoted in Ralph R. Miller, "Daring Raid of Andrews and His Brave Men," *Findlay Republican Jeffersonian*, April 17, 1906. Brown's preposterous saga appears in "Mitchell Raiders: Thrilling Incidents Never Before Published," *North Baltimore Daily Beacon*, Jan. 17, 24, 31, Feb. 7, 4, 21, 28, March 7, 14, 21, 28, April 11, 18, 25, May 2, 9, 16, 23, 30, June 6, 13, 20, 27, July 4, 11, 18, 25, Aug. 1, 8, 15, 22, 29, Sept. 5, 12, 19, 26, Oct. 3, 10, 1890. Its primary pur-

pose, in addition to spinning an entertaining yarn, seems to be to emphasize the heroism, ruthlessness, resourcefulness, and fighting prowess of the author Wilson Brown, while continually slighting his comrade William Knight, who is depicted as a weak tag-along who repeatedly expresses amazement at his friend Brown's abilities. Knight was one of several raiders who viewed Brown's recollections as completely unreliable. See Knight to Kurtz, March 9, 1904, Kurtz-AHC ("I would not believe Brown on oath"). See also James G. Bogle, Interview with the author, Jan. 12, 2006 ("wildest damn thing you ever read").

20 Wilson and Wood's adventure is recounted in three sources: first, they told their story to the *Key West New Era* upon their arrival there on Nov. 10, 1862 (this account is reprinted in *Ohio Boys in Dixie*, pp. 3-10); second, they gave a "plain and unvarnished statement" of the raid, their imprisonment, and the escape to Lieutenant A.C. Spafford, Company C, 21st Ohio upon their return to their regiment in February 1863, *OR*, vol. 52, pt. I, pp. 347-49; and finally, Alf Wilson wrote extensively of their odyssey in *Adventures of Alf Wilson*, pp. 160-211.

21 The C.S.S. *Chattahoochee* was actually constructed in the summer of 1862 at David S. Johnston's shipyard at Saffold, Georgia. The ship suffered from chronic mechanical problems and was stationed at various points up and down the river during late 1862 and early 1863. Although she was not under construction as Wilson and Wood supposed, it is possible that the *Chattahoochee* was undergoing repairs and refitting in Columbus at the time the two escapees saw her in late October. See generally Maxine Turner, *Navy Gray: Engineering the Confederate Navy on the Chattahoochee and Apalachicola Rivers* (Macon, Ga.: Mercer University Press, 1999), pp. 50-107. Historian James Bogle asserts that the ironclad at Columbus was not the *Chattahoochee*, but was instead the equally ill-fated Confederate ironclad ram C.S.S. *Muscogee*. James G. Bogle, Introduction, in Wilson, *Adventures of Alf Wilson*, (Marietta, Ga.: Continental Book Co., reprint ed. 1972), p. vii.

22 A.F. Crosman to Gideon Welles, Dec. 17, 1862, *Official Records of the Union and Confederate Navies in the War of the Rebellion* (Washington, D.C.: Government Printing Office, 1903), ser.I, vol. 17, pp. 347-48; see also "United States Vessels of War Serving in the East Gulf Blockading Squadron from February 22, 1862 to July 17, 1865," ibid., pp. xviii-xix (providing data on *Somerset*). Crosman would figure in another Medal of Honor story upon his death. On April 12, 1872, Crosman was drowned at Greytown, Nicaragua, following an explosion aboard the U.S.S. *Kansas*. Six of the doomed ship's crew were awarded the Navy Medal of Honor for displaying "coolness and self-possession" and "by heroism and personal exertion, prevent[ing] greater loss of life."

CHAPTER FIFTEEN. THE MEDAL OF HONOR

1 The origin of the Medal of Honor is recounted in detail in Joseph L. Schott, *Above and Beyond: The Story of the Congressional Medal of Honor* (New York: G.P. Putnam's Sons, 1963), pp. 21-26; see also "Medal of Honor," in Byron Farwell, *The Encyclopedia of Nineteenth Century Land Warfare: An Illustrated World View* (New York: W.W. Norton, 2003), pp. 543-44; Michael P. Musick, "The Only Medal," *Prologue*, 27, no. 3 (Fall 1995); Mark C. Mollan, "The Army Medal of Honor: The First Fifty-Five Years," *Prologue*, 33, no. 2 (Summer 2001); see also Angle, "Prologue," Great Locomotive Chase (noting that "The American Nation, which had given little thought to its Army in time of peace, now found it to be the focal point of attention").

2 12 Stat. L. 329-330, Dec. 21, 1861 (Navy bill); 12 Stat. L. 623-24, July 12, 1862 (Army medal); 12 Stat. L. 744-754, March 3, 1863 (amendments).

3 Wilson, *Adventures of Alf Wilson*, p. 223; Porter, quoted in *Daring and Suffering*, p. 347.

4 Pittenger, *Daring and Suffering*, p. 360.

5 Ibid., p. 366.

6 Ibid., p. 363.

7 Ibid., p. 368.

8 Ibid., pp. 369-71. The order effecting the raiders' transfer is found in the Official Records. See G.W. Lee to Brig. Gen. Winder, Commanding, Richmond, Dec. 3, 1862, *OR*, series 2, vol. 5, pt. 1, pp. 777-78 (enclosing list of transferees, including Bensinger, Buffum, Mason, Parrott, Pittenger, and Reddick).

9 Lonnie R. Speer, *Portals to Hell: Military Prisons in the Civil War* (Mechanicsburg, Pa.: Stackpole Books, 1997), pp. 97-105 (Civil War prisoner exchange).

10 Pittenger, *Daring and Suffering*, pp. 374-77; *Richmond Enquirer*, Aug. 12, 1862; Speer, *Portals to Hell*, pp. 89-91 (describing Libby Prison) and 93-95 (describing Castle Thunder and its commandant George Alexander); James I. Robertson, Jr., *Civil War Virginia: Battleground for a Nation* (Charlottesville: University Press of Virginia, 1991), p. 99 ("soldier and a sociopath"); *Richmond Enquirer*, Aug. 21, 1862; *Richmond Whig*, Dec. 27, 1862.

11 Pittenger details his experiences in Castle Thunder in *Daring and Suffering*, pp. 377-96.

12 Ibid., pp. 398-99; *Richmond Dispatch*, March 1863, quoted in Pittenger, *Daring and Suffering*, p. 402.

13 Pittenger, *Daring and Suffering*, pp. 406-9. It is uncertain whether the man the raiders saw at the Smithsonian was indeed President Lincoln. Pittenger strongly implies that he was in his books, but there is no record of Lincoln being at the Smithsonian during the week of March 19-26, 1863.

14 Holt, *Ohio Boys in Dixie*, pp. 12-14.

15 Noah Brooks, "Returned Prisoners from Richmond" (March 24, 1863), in *Lincoln Observed: The Civil War Dispatches of Noah Brooks*, Michael Burlingame, ed. (Baltimore: Johns Hopkins University Press, 1998), pp. 29-30.

16 Charles F. Benjamin, "Recollections of Secretary Stanton by a Clerk of the War Department," *The Century*, 33, no. 5 (March 1887), p. 758 (description of War Department, Stanton's office).

17 Louis M. Starr, *Bohemian Brigade: Civil War Newsmen in Action* (New York: Knopf, 1954), pp. 82-83, quoted in Stephen M. Sears, *Landscape Turned Red: The Battle of Antietam* (New York: Houghton Mifflin, 1983), p. 6 ("Force—undaunted Force . . ."); Henry Wilson, "Edwin M. Stanton," *Atlantic Monthly*, 25, no. 148 (Feb. 1870), p. 237; Frank Abial Flower, *Edwin McMasters Stanton: The Autocrat of Rebellion, Emancipation, and Reconstruction* (Boston: Geo. M. Smith & Co., 1905), p. 142 ("Contractors, claimants . . ."); Benjamin, "Recollections of Secretary Stanton," p. 758 ("The glittering of the eyes . . .").

18 Pittenger describes the interview with Stanton in *Daring and Suffering* (1864), pp. 287-88; *Capturing a Locomotive*, pp. 339-40; *Daring and Suffering*, pp. 411-13; and *The Great Locomotive*

Chase, pp. 411-13. There appears to be no question that Parrott received the first Medal of Honor. See Pittenger, *Daring and Suffering* (1864), p. 287 ("Jacob Parrott, the boy who endured the terrible beating, received, as he deserved, the first one"). It is unclear in what order the remaining five medals were awarded that day, though tradition holds that Sergeant Elihu Mason, the ranking member of the party, was the second to receive the decoration. Some suggest that the medals were awarded in alphabetical order. Due to the informality of the proceeding, however, it is possible that the medals were awarded in no particular order at all.

19 The raiders' audience with President Lincoln on March 25, 1863, was reported in several newspapers, including the *Washington Chronicle*, March 26, 1863, the *New York Tribune*, March 26, 1863, and the *Philadelphia Inquirer*, March 26, 1863. The meeting is described in detail in Noah Brooks, "Glimpses of Lincoln in War Time," *The Century*, 49, no. 3 (Jan. 1895), pp. 466-67; Brooks, "The Returned Prisoners from Rebeldom" (March 26, 1863), in *Lincoln Observed*, pp. 30-32; and Pittenger, *Daring and Suffering*, pp. 413-15. See also Walt Whitman to Fred Gray, March 19, 1863, quoted in Daniel Mark Epstein, *Lincoln and Whitman: Parallel Lives in Civil War Washington* (New York: Ballantine Books, 2004), p. 133 ("Hoosier Michael Angelo"). Pittenger was the only raider present who ever wrote or spoke of their meeting with the President, a regrettable omission in the record. Buffum's reaction to his conversation with Lincoln, for example, was never recorded, though the little soldier might have appeared to some like a miniature version of his commander-in-chief. Though six inches in height and a frontier versus a Bay State upbringing separated the two men, both were dark-complected, with thick brown hair and beard, and an abiding melancholy often kept at bay with a sharp and irreverent wit. (Buffum, who like the president was a great admirer of the Bard, no doubt would have been envious of Lincoln's engagement to see *Hamlet* later that night.)

20 Francis Willis McIntosh II, "William Henry Harrison Reddick in the Civil War," in *Reddick: The Descendants of George Washington Reddick*, Emmer Tex Reddick II, ed. (unpublished), Southern Museum of Civil War and Locomotive History Archives, p. 373 (noting that William Reddick "had suffered with rheumatism, scurvy and hemorrhoids and had lost quite a lot of weight" and that his father "did not know him"); Pittenger, *Daring and Suffering*, p. 415.

21 Parlee C. Grose to Wilbur G. Kurtz, Sept. 12, 1965, Kurtz-AHC.

CHAPTER SIXTEEN. THE *General* RIDES AGAIN

1 Foote, *The Civil War*, vol. 2, pp. 179-86 (Streight's raid); George Magruder Battey, Jr., *A History of Rome and Floyd County* (Atlanta: Webb and Vary Co., 1922), vol. 1, pp. 161-64; "Bill Arp" (aka Charles Henry Smith), *Southern Confederacy*, quoted in Battey, pp. 166-68.

2 W.P. Howard to His Excellency Joseph E. Brown, Governor of Georgia, Dec. 7, 1864, quoted in Garrett, *Atlanta and Environs*, vol.1, pp. 653-55 ("The car shed, the depots . . ."). For the Atlanta Campaign, see generally Albert Castel, *Decision in the West: The Atlanta Campaign of 1864* (Lawrence: University Press of Kansas, 1992), and Lee Kennett, *Marching Through Georgia: The Story of Soldiers and Civilians in Sherman's Campaign* (New York: HarperCollins, 1996); see also Lesa Campbell, "Atlanta: Destiny, Destruction and Determination," Southern Railway Museum, www.srmduluth.org/Features/destiny.htm (describing resurgence of Atlanta and its railroads). Letter from W.T. Sherman to Jos. M. Brown, Esq., Jan. 18, 1886,

reprinted in Jos. M. Brown, *Mountain Campaigns in Georgia, or War Scenes on the W. & A.* (Buffalo, N.Y., 1886) (internal quotations omitted).

3 Buell to Halleck, Oct. 16, 1862, *OR*, vol. 16, pt. 2, p. 619 ("almost a desert"; "there is but one road"; "moving back on his supplies"); Halleck to Buell, Oct. 19, 1862, *OR*, vol. 16, pt. 2, pp. 626-27 ("The capture of East Tennessee . . ."); see Foote, *The Civil War*, vol. 2, pp. 739-44.

4 Grant, *Personal Memoirs*, p. 193 ("General Buell was a brave, intelligent officer . . ."); Whitelaw Reid, Oct. 25, 1862, in *A Radical View: The "Agate" Dispatches of Whitelaw Reid* (Memphis: Memphis State University Press, 1976), vol. 1, p. 102 ("No words were too harsh to apply to Buell"). After the war, Buell settled in Indiana and thereafter in Kentucky, where he entered the mining business and became president of the Green River Iron Company. Later in life, he served fourteen years as a government pension agent and in 1890 became a member of the newly created Shiloh National Park Commission. He died in 1898 at the age of eighty, with his stormy Civil War career destined to become the subject of enduring debate among historians, who disagree to this day as to whether the gruff Ohioan was overcautious, underrated, or perhaps some mixture of both. Buell's life in postwar years is described in Engle, *Don Carlos Buell*, pp. 345-63.

5 Mitchel to Stanton, June 21, 1862, *OR*, vol. 16, pt. 2, p. 46 ("more active duty"); Stanton to Mitchel, June 21, 1862, ibid. ("eminent military genius," etc.).

6 Beauregard to S. Cooper, Oct. 23, 1862, *OR*, vol. 14, pt. 1, p. 179 ("Charleston Railroad uninjured . . ."); see Foote, *The Civil War*, vol. 1, p. 795. Mitchelville is described by Whitelaw Reid, *After the War: A Southern Tour, May 1, 1865 to May 1, 1866* (London: S. Low, Son & Marston, 1866), pp. 89-91; Benjamin Quarles, *The Negro in the Civil War* (Boston: Little, Brown, 1953), pp. 287-88 (describing Mitchel's suggestion that black families adopt surnames); see also "Mitchelville," Wikipedia, http://en.wikipedia.org/wiki/Mitchelville. For recent preservation efforts, see Tim Donelly, "Mitchelville on the Mind," *Island Packet*, Jan. 3, 2006, and "Mitchelville preservation Taking Shape," *Island Packet*, June 5, 2006. All that is left of Mitchelville is a historical marker along Beach City Road.

7 Rev. Dr. Strickland, Chaplain, 48th N.Y. Volunteers, quoted in Mitchel, *Ormsby MacKnight Mitchel, Astronomer and General*, p. 360 ("Why, General! What brought you here?" "I came to be buried."); Mitchel to George S. Coe, Sept. 26, 1862, quoted in Mitchel, p. 361 ("I am doing nothing here"); *New York Evening Post*, Nov. 5, 1862; Reid, *Ohio in the War*, pp. 612, 616. Reid observed further: "Two years before Sherman, Mitchel showed how armies might depend on single lines of railroad through great tracts of the enemy's country for supplies. As early as Butler, he showed how Rebels should be made to support the war. Eighteen months before Rosecrans, he fastened upon [Chattanooga], the strategic point of the whole central half of the Southern States. Almost three years before Sherman, he showed how the shell of the Confederacy might be pierced, and how little resistance was to be expected once this shell was passed. Much of his success, doubtless, he owed to the utter surprise which his movements proved to an enemy not then accustomed to expect such energy and auda-cious boldness. Many of his movements, doubtless, at another stage of the war, or under other conditions, would have been impracticable. But it was his sagacity which perceived that to be the time for audacious movements." Ibid. Wilson, *Adventures*, pp. 212-16 (Wilson and

Wood aboard the *Star of the South* with Mitchel's coffin). In addition to Mitchelville, Old Stars' other notable legacies were Fort Mitchell, Kentucky—named in his honor despite the misspelling—and a descendant, Lt. Ormsby M. Mitchel, Jr., who was awarded the Navy Cross for extraordinary heroism in 1943 after his gunboat was torpedoed and sunk by a German U-Boat off the coast of Virginia.

8 On Chickamauga, see generally Peter Cozzens, *This Terrible Sound: The Battle of Chickamauga* (Urbana: University of Illinois Press, 1992); W.O. Johnson, *National Tribune*, Nov. 13, 1890, quoted in Dorsey, "The Mitchel Raiders," *The Ohio Soldier*, Nov. 18 1893, p. 98 ("Comrade Wollam was a man of few words . . ."); Pittenger, *Daring and Suffering*, Supplement, p. 6.

9 Porter recounts his escapes and adventures in a letter quoted in Pittenger, *Daring and Suffering*, Supplement, pp. 9-10.

10 Report of Col. John A. Hottenstein, 13th U.S. Colored Troops, of operations Nov. 30, 1864-Jan. 15, 1865, *OR*, vol. 45, pt. I, p. 549 ("in the most gallant manner"); O'Neill, *Wild Train*, p. 359.

11 William J. Nash, M.D., certificate regarding Lieut. Robert Buffum, June 24, 1863, Robert Buffum Papers, Bowling Green State University; Col. John Coburn, indorsement, Nov. 21, 1863, in ibid.

12 Company Muster Roll and Returns, 21st Ohio, in Buffum Papers, Bowling Green State University; various indorsements regarding Robert Buffum, ibid. After the war, Buffum was instrumental in obtaining a special pension for the Andrews Raiders, to compensate them for the extraordinary hardships they had endured. Buffum wrote a personal letter to the interim Secretary of War U.S. Grant, who referred the matter on to the speaker of the House for legislative action. "The long imprisonment, exposure and cruelty with which we were treated while in the hands of the enemy, has so impaired my health and mind that I am in no condition to earn a livelihood for myself," Buffum wrote. "I have a wife and three small children dependent upon me for support, and have no home or means of caring for them." Unfortunately, no legislative action was taken on the measure despite Grant's support, and the pension bill—granting each of the raiders $24 per month—was ultimately passed by Congress and signed by the president in 1884, long after Buffum's death. Robert Buffum to General U.S. Grant, Secretary of War ad interim, Dec. 18, 1867, in U.S. Congress, House, Robert Buffum: Letter from Secretary of War Ad Interim, 40th Cong., 2d Sess., Ex. Doc. No. 74; Pittenger, *Daring and Suffering*, Supplement, pp. 11-12.

13 Pittenger, *Daring and Suffering*, Supplement, pp. 10-11 ("I was unable to endure . . .").

14 Kurtz, "The Andrews Raid," *Atlanta Historical Bulletin*, p. 29 (describing the fate of the *Yonah* and the *William R. Smith*). Among those wounded in Wilson's Raid on Columbus was a Georgia home guard colonel named John Stith Pemberton, who would twenty years later invent Coca-Cola. Mark Pendergast, *For God, Country and Coca-Cola* (New York: Basic Books, 2000), pp. 18-19.

15 Bogle, "The Locomotive General," *The Landmarker* (Cobb County Landmarks Society), 5, no. I (Fall 1980), p. 6.

16 Ibid.; see also Edison H. Thomas, "The Night They Burned the Train," *L&N Magazine*, Sept. 1964, pp. 18-19; William T. Sherman, *Memoirs of General W.T. Sherman* (New York: Library of America, 1984), p. 581.

17 Bogle, "The Locomotive General," pp. 6-8. The destruction of the Atlanta railroad mills and cars and the near destruction of the *General* are recounted in detail in Edison H. Thomas, "The Night They Burned the Train," *L&N Railroad Magazine*, Sept. 1964, pp. 18-19. It is unlikely that the U.S. Military Railroad Service repaired the *General* and used her in Federal military service after her near-destruction in September 1864. See Bogle, "Locomotive General," *Landmarker*, p. 8.

18 Ed Lentz, *Columbus: The Story of a City* (Charleston, S.C.: Arcadia Publishing, 2003), pp. 92-94 (describing the 1888 GAR Encampment); O'Neill, *Wild Train*, pp. 390-91 (summarizing postwar vocations of the surviving raiders); Reddick letter, quoted in Pittenger, *Daring and Suffering*, Supplement, p. 9.

19 O'Neill, *Wild Train*, p. 403 ("the most careful reader would still have had difficulty . . ."); newspaper reviews quoted in *Daring and Suffering*, inside back page.

20 Cohen and Bogle, *The General and the Texas*, p. 9. Both Pittenger and Dorsey blamed Wood's death on diseases he contracted during his imprisonment. Dorsey, "The Mitchel Raiders," *The Ohio Soldier*, Nov. 18, 1893, p. 99; Pittenger, *Daring and Suffering*, Supplement, p. 7.

21 "The Newburgh Murder," *New York Times*, Sept. 1, 1870. The *Times* misspelled the defendant's name as "Buffern."

22 Buffum's suicide is noted in many sources, including Dorsey, "The Mitchel Raiders," *The Ohio Soldier*, Nov. 18, 1893, pp. 98-99; Pittenger, *Daring and Suffering*, Supplement, p. 7; O'Neill, *Wild Train*, p. 390.

23 Dorsey, "The Mitchel Raiders," *The Ohio Soldier*, Nov. 18, 1893, p. 98; Pittenger, *Daring and Suffering*, Supplement, p. 8; Cohen and Bogle, *The General and the Texas*, p. 13.

24 Smith to E.D. Townsend, Oct. 15, 1864, quoted at "Medal of Honor," www.medalofhonor.com/AndrewsRaid.htm; see also "The Case of Private James Smith," in Cohen and Bogle, *The General and the Texas*, pp. 14-15; and Parlee C. Grose, *The Case of Private Smith and the Remaining Mysteries of the Andrews Raid* (McComb, Ohio: General Publishing Co., 1963).

25 Cohen and Bogle, *The General and the Texas*, p. 5.

26 Testimony of Henry G. Cole, Feb. 12, 1873, in Claim of Henry G. Cole (nos. 13312 and 19724), Records of the Southern Claims Commission (Allowed Claims), Cobb County, Georgia, RG 217 (217.8.7), National Archives Southeast Region, East Point, Georgia. See also Dyer, *Secret Yankees*, pp. 151 and 354 n. 35.

27 Butler, "Cole-Fletcher Families," *Cobb County Genealogical Society Quarterly*, 2, no. 4 (Dec. 1992). Cole's complicity in the Andrews Raid, if any, remains a mystery, though his unstinting allegiance and daring service to the Union cause is beyond dispute. Three years after his donation of the plot for the National Cemetery, Union General George H. Thomas praised the transplanted New Yorker in a letter from Willards Hotel, Washington, D.C.: "Mr. H.G. Cole of Georgia has always been known as a most uncompromising friend of the Union. He rendered the Government most valuable assistance by sending information through the lines of movements of the enemy, which movements might not have been known but for the information communicated by Mr. Cole. His information regarding the roads and resources of Georgia were of inestimable value to the army operating against Atlanta. From my first

knowledge of Mr. Cole I have entertained for him the highest respect on account of his well-known loyalty and friendship for the Government. / Signed / Geo. H. Thomas, Maj Genl U.S.A." Letter of Geo. H. Thomas, Apr. 6, 1869, in Claim of Henry G. Cole, Records of the Southern Claims Commission, National Archives.

28 Wilson, *Adventures of Alf Wilson*, p. 224; Pittenger, *Daring and Suffering*, Supplement, p. 5.

29 Warner, *Generals in Gray*, pp. 176-77; Lash, "A Yankee in Gray," *Civil War History*, 38, no. 3, p. 217; "Death of a Rebel," *Jonesborough Whig*, Oct. 5, 1866, quoted in Donahue Bible, "Their Eyes Have Seen the Glory: East Tennessee Unionists in the Civil War, 1861-1865," reprinted online at www.rootsweb.com/~tngreene/pbb012.html ("If Leadbetter has not received . . .").

30 Dorsey, "The Mitchel Raiders," *The Ohio Soldier*, Nov. 4, 1893, p. 83 ("a feeble old man"); Gregg, *Andrews Raiders*, p. 38 ("marked with a discolored headstone").

31 Dorsey, "The Mitchel Raiders," *The Ohio Soldier*, Dec. 2, 1893 (Fuller "well received and kindly treated"); Gov. Jos. E. Brown, Address to Georgia Senate and House of Representatives, Nov. 6, 1862, quoted in James G. Bogle, "A Postscript: Three Letters and a Medal," *Atlanta Historical Bulletin* 13 (Dec. 1968), p. 35; Commission of W.A. Fuller as a Capt. of the Independent State Railroad Guards in the Regiment of Infantry of the Volunteers for the State of Georgia, Feb. 23, 1864, Kurtz-AHC, Box 4, Folder 3; "Death of Capt. W.A. Fuller Removes Gallant Veteran," *Atlanta Constitution*, Dec. 29, 1905 (describing Fuller as "one of the prominent citizens of Atlanta," etc.).

32 Stephen B. Porter, *Columbus Dispatch*, Sept. 1888, quoted in Dorsey, "The Mitchel Raiders," *The Ohio Soldier*, Dec. 2, 1893, p. 114; see also Pittenger, *The Great Locomotive Chase*, p. 482; Gregg, *Andrews Raiders*, pp. 86-87; O'Neill, *Wild Train*, pp. 404-5.

33 *Southern Confederacy*, June 19, 1862.

34 Jonas Drury to Capt. W.A. Wainwright, April 20, 1866, quoted in Bogle, "The Andrews Raid: A Sequel," *Atlanta Historical Bulletin* 16 (Summer 1971), pp. 36-37.

35 Bogle, "The Andrews Raid: A Sequel," pp. 41-42; Fuller to Kurtz, April 8, 1904 ("I pointed out as nearly as I could . . .").

36 Bogle, "The Andrews Raid: A Sequel," p. 42; Fuller, Sept. 1888, quoted in Pittenger, *The Great Locomotive Chase*, p. 481 ("I desire to say to the Grand Army of the Republic. . .").

37 Dorsey, "The Mitchel Raiders," *The Ohio Soldier*, Dec. 2, 1893, p. 116 (describing dedication ceremony for Ohio monument); Murphy, quoted in Dorsey, p. 116.

38 The 1906 Reunion is described and pictured in Cohen and Bogle, *The General and the Texas*, pp. 93-94. Notably, William Fuller's son-in-law Wilbur G. Kurtz attended the reunion as well, taking extensive notes of his impressions and interviewing a number of the surviving raiders.

39 Ibid., p. 6.; Bogle, "The Andrews Raid: A Sequel," p. 41.

40 Cohen and Bogle, *The General and the Texas*, p. 8.

41 O'Neill, *Wild Train*, p. 390; Wilson, *Adventures of Alf Wilson*, pp. iii-iv.

42 Wilson, *Adventures of Alf Wilson*, pp. xi ("On the subject of . . .") and 236 ("cloud without a silver lining"); Cohen and Bogle, *The General and the Texas*, p. 11.

43 Dorsey's public campaign against Pittenger is recounted in detail in O'Neill, *Wild Train*, pp. 390-464. Fuller letter to Dorsey, quoted in ibid., p. 404 ("Pittenger has made heroes of us all . . .").

44 Chillicothe Leader, Feb. 9, 1889, quoted in O'Neill, *Wild Train*, pp. 408-9; see generally Dorsey's series of articles in *The Ohio Soldier*, Feb.-Nov. 1893, quoted extensively herein.

45 Reddick, quoted in O'Neill, *Wild Train*, p. 413; Porter, quoted in ibid.; Brown to Kurtz, undated letter, Kurtz-AHC, MSS 132, Box 6, Folder 6; Kurtz to Grose, March 9, 1954, Kurtz-AHC (Knight "poo-poo'd the mere idea of it"); Fuller to the Editor, *Columbus Dispatch*, Nov. 15, 1888, quoted in O'Neill, *Wild Train*, p. 413.

46 Pittenger to the Editor, *The Ohio Soldier*, Aug. 26, 1893.

47 Walt Disney and Lawrence Edward Watkin (Producers) and Francis Lyon (Director), *The Great Locomotive Chase* (Walt Disney Pictures, 1956).

48 Dorsey, quoted in O'Neill, p. 428 ("Pittenger was Tom Sawyer").

49 Knight's lectures are described in detail and many of his panoramic paintings reproduced in Jim Leeke, "Always Very Daring and Reckless: Private William J. Knight and the Andrews Raid," *Timeline* (Nov.-Dec. 2003); see also Bogle, "The Andrews Raid: A Sequel," pp. 39-40; Cohen and Bogle, *The General and the Texas*, p. 5.

50 Wilson Brown, quoted in "Captain W.W. Brown says a few words," Findlay (Ohio) *Morning Republican*, Sept. 23, 1890 ("I have no desire to raise a controversy on the subject, but when Mr. Knight assumes to be the whole push on that raid, I emphatically deny the asser- tion and stand ready to prove what I say in defense of my claims. . . . it is a fact, well under- stood all over the country, that I was on that engine when she made that run, and did offici- ate at the throttle of the 'General'"), quoted in Kurtz Notebook No. 3, pp. 226-27; see also "The Andrews Raid: W.J. Knight's Claim is Disputed by W.W. Brown," *Democratic Messenger* (Fremont, Ohio), March 14, 1895; Wilbur G. Kurtz, interview notes with William J. Knight, Sept. 30, 1903, Kurtz-AHC, Box 2, Folder 2.

51 Cohen and Bogle, *The General and the Texas*, p. 12; Brown to Kurtz, Jan. 13, 1904 ("I am a poor man"); Brown to Kurtz, Aug. 5, 1904 ("I want Exact Justice").

52 Cohen and Bogle, *The General and the Texas*, p. 4.

53 Cohen and Bogle, *The General and the Texas*, p. 2; Kurtz note, Kurtz-AHC, MSS 132, Box 5, Folder 4 ("Parrott was a confirmed Spiritualist; he seemed to be more interested in this than in the Andrews Raid").

54 Porter, quoted in Pittenger, *Daring and Suffering*, Supplement, p. 10 ("mercantile pur- suits"); Cohen and Bogle, *The General and the Texas*, p. 7.

55 Alvarez, "Peter James Bracken," *Atlanta Historical Journal* 24 (Winter 1980), pp. 45-47; Bracken to Fuller, Oct. 7, 1895, quoted in Cohen and Bogle, *The General and the Texas*, p. 72 ("I do not want any unnecessary notoriety . . ." and "If I had not been running myself . . .").

56 Kurtz, "Harbin's Narrative," Kurtz-AHC; Cohen and Bogle, *The General and the Texas*, p. 18.

57 Kurtz, "Harbin's Narrative," Kurtz-AHC, pp. 21-28; Mrs. W.M. Boswell to Kurtz, Jan. 1, 1908, quoted in ibid., pp. 26-27.

58 Cohen and Bogle, *The General and the Texas*, p. 16.

59 Ibid., pp. 16, 92.

60 Stephen Davis, "The Conductor Versus the Foreman: William Fuller, Anthony Murphy, and the Pursuit of the Andrews Raiders," *Atlanta History*, 34, no. 4 (Winter 1990-91), p. 44 ("the theme that he led the pursuit . . ."); Fuller to unnamed raider, quoted in Dorsey, "The Mitchel Raiders," *The Ohio Soldier*, Dec. 2, 1893, p. 113.

61 Murphy, quoted in "The Story of Texas," *Atlanta Journal*, Oct. 1, 1895 ("Mr. Fuller was with me all the way. . ."); Fuller, in "Fuller on History: The Man Who Chased the General Gives the Facts," *Atlanta Constitution*, Nov. 3, 1895, p. 4. The conflict between Fuller and Murphy over credit for the chase and the recapture of the General is described in detail in Davis, "The Conductor Versus the Foreman." For the full story of Fuller's interactions with Harris, see Stephen Davis, "Joel Chandler Harris's Version of the Andrews Raid: Writing History to Please the Participant," *Georgia Historical Quarterly*, 74, no. 1 (Spring 1990), pp. 99-116.

62 I am indebted to Dr. Stephen Davis for pointing out the juxtaposition of and contrast between Fuller and Murphy's epitaphs, and to Col. James G. Bogle for pointing out the gravestones in person. See Davis, "The Conductor Versus the Foreman," *Atlanta History*, pp. 50-51; James G. Bogle, Interview with the author, April 18, 2006 ("You know damn well he wrote that thing himself").

63 Dorsey, "The Mitchel Raiders," *The Ohio Soldier*, Dec. 2, 1893, p. 114 (quoting exchange of correspondence between Dorsey and Fuller).

CABOOSE

1 "The Story of Texas," *Atlanta Journal*, Oct. 1, 1895.

2 Kurtz, "The Andrews Raid," pp. 26-28; Bogle, "Locomotive General," *Landmarker*, pp. 8-9, 17-20. Notably, the *General* made no appearance in either of the major motion pictures based on the Andrews Raid: Buster Keaton's classic comedy *The General* and Walt Disney's adventure *The Great Locomotive Chase*. The former was filmed in Oregon using western 4-4-0s as stand-ins for the W&A locomotives; and Disney's movie, though filmed on the Tallulah Falls Railroad in North Georgia, used the B&O engine *William Mason* to play the part of the *General*. Bogle, "Locomotive General," *Landmarker*, pp. 22, 26.

3 Bogle, "Locomotive General," *Landmarker*, pp. 35-36; Joe F. Head, *The General: The Great Locomotive Dispute* (Cartersville, Ga.: Bartow History Center, 2d ed. 1997), pp. 34-35.

4 City of Chattanooga, Tennessee v. Louisville & Nashville Railroad Co., 298 F. Supp. 1 (E.D. Tenn. 1969), affirmed, 427 F.2d 1154 (6th Cir.), cert. denied, 400 U.S. 903, 91 S. Ct. 141 (1970); State of Georgia v. City of Chattanooga, Tennessee, 406 F.2d 830 (6th Cir. 1969). Writing for the Sixth Circuit panel, Senior U.S. Circuit Judge Clifford Patrick O'Sullivan pointed out that "The General would be little seen if returned to its wonted stall in the Union Station at Chattanooga," which by that time stood empty. "Only the birds that twitter in the upper, and now rusted, supports of the silent train shed would see it," he wrote. 427 F.2d 1156, n.2. The litigation over possession of the General is described in detail in Bogle, "Locomotive General," *Landmarker*, pp. 35-38, and in Head, *The General: The Great Locomotive Dispute*, pp. 34-42.

5 Cohen and Bogle, *The General and the Texas*, p. 69.

6 See generally Schott, *Above and Beyond*; Lyle F. Padilla and Raymond J. Castagnaro, "History, Legend and Myth: Hollywood and the Medal of Honor," http://www.voicenet.com/~lpadilla/lindbergh.html ("Medal of Honor by public acclamation"). The full texts of the citations of all Medal of Honor recipients are made available online by the U.S. Army Center for Military History, at http://www.army.mil/medalofhonor.htm.

7 The full criteria for the Medal of Honor, as amended by acts of Congress in 1918 and 1963, limits the award to "a person, who, while a member of the armed forces, distinguishes himself or herself conspicuously by gallantry and intrepidity at the risk of his life above and beyond the call of duty while engaged in an action against any enemy of the United States; while engaged in military operations involving conflict with an opposing foreign force; or while serving with friendly foreign forces engaged in an armed conflict against an opposing armed force in which the United States is not a belligerent party. The deed must have been one of personal bravery or self-sacrifice, an action that conspicuously distinguished the individual above his comrades. Incontestable proof of the performance of service is exacted and the recommendation for award of this decoration is considered on the standard of extraordinary merit. Eligibility is limited to members of the armed forces of the United States in active military service."

8 Schott, *Above and Beyond*, p. 272.

9 For more on SFC Paul Smith, see Eric Schmitt, "Slain Sergeant to Get Medal of Honor," *New York Times*, March 30, 2005; Alex Leary, "Iraq hero joins hallowed group," *St. Petersburg Times*, Feb. 2, 2005.

10 Horace Greeley, *The American Conflict: A History of the Great Rebellion in the United States of America, 1861-65* (Hartford: O.D. Case & Company, 1866), p. 72.

11 Grant, *Personal Memoirs*, p. 207.

12 O'Neill, *Wild Train*, p. 469; Dorsey, "The Mitchel Raiders," *The Ohio Soldier*, March 11, 1893, p. 242 (quoting Andrews).

Bibliography

Participants' Accounts and Papers

Andrews, James J. Papers 1862-63. Ohio Historical Society.

————. Letter to Ladies' Soldiers Aid Society of Flemingsburg, Kentucky, December 6, 1861. Fleming County Public Library, Flemingsburg, Kentucky.

Bensinger, William. Correspondence and questionnaire responses, Wilbur G. Kurtz, Sr. Collection, Atlanta History Center. (MSS 132, Box 5, Folder 5.)

Brown, Wilson W. Correspondence and questionnaire responses, Wilbur G. Kurtz, Sr. Collection, Atlanta History Center. (MSS 132, Box 6, Folder 6.)

————. "Mitchell's Raiders: Thrilling Incidents Never Before Published." Series of articles appearing in the *North Baltimore (Ohio) Weekly Beacon*, Jan. 17-Oct. 10, 1890.

Buffum, Robert. Papers, 1861-1864. Center for Archival Collections, Bowling Green State University, Bowling Green, Ohio.

Dorsey, Daniel A. "Andrews' Raiders: A Thrilling Story of the Civil War by a Participant, Mr. D. Dorsey, Now a Citizen of Enid." *Weekly Enid Eagle*, Sept. 10, 1903.

————. "The Mitchel Raiders: History of a Secret Military Expedition in Southern Tennessee and Northern Georgia, April, 1862." *Ohio Soldier and National Picket Guard*, Feb. 25-Dec. 2, 1893. Western Reserve Historical Society, Cleveland, Ohio.

————. Correspondence and questionnaire responses, Wilbur G. Kurtz, Sr. Collection, Atlanta History Center. (MSS 132, Box 5, Folder 1.)

————. Daniel A. Dorsey collection of Civil War memorabilia and scrapbook, 1862; 1881-1909. Western Americana Manuscript Collection, University of the Pacific, Stockton, California.

————. "Trial of the Andrews' Raiders." Unpublished manuscript. William P. Palmer Collection, Western Reserve Historical Society, Cleveland, Ohio.

Fuller, W.A. "Battle of the Locomotives." *Atlanta Journal Magazine*, March 16, 1930, pp. 11, 26 (furnished for posthumous publication by his son, William A. Fuller).

————. Correspondence. Wilbur G. Kurtz, Sr. Collection, Atlanta History Center. (MSS 132, Box 4, Folders 1-2.)

————. "Epitome of the Andrews Raid." *Jacksonville (Fla.) Times-Union*, May 8, 1904. Wilbur G. Kurtz, Sr. Collection, Atlanta History Center.

————. Interview in "Muscle vs. Steam," *Sunny South*, Feb. 16, 1878.

————. Pursuit and Capture of the Andrews Raiders. Unpublished manuscript, 1906. Wilbur G. Kurtz, Sr. Collection, Atlanta History Center. (MSS 132, Box 4, Folder 9.)

————. Speech to GAR Reunion, Columbus, Ohio, *Columbus Dispatch*, Jan. 1, 1889, reprinted in North Georgia Citizen, Sept. 19, 1900.

————. "Mr. W.A. Fuller's Statement," quoted in *Atlanta Daily Intelligencer*, April 15, 1862.

"Fuller on History: The Man Who Chased the General Gives the Facts." *Atlanta Constitution*, Nov. 3, 1895, p. 4.

Haney, Henry P. Correspondence. Wilbur G. Kurtz, Sr. Collection, Atlanta History Center.

Harbin, Oliver Wiley. Correspondence and questionnaire responses. Wilbur G. Kurtz, Sr. Collection, Atlanta History Center. (MSS 132, Box 3, Folder 7.)

Knight, William J. Correspondence and questionnaire responses, Wilbur G. Kurtz, Sr. Collection, Atlanta History Center. (MSS 132, Box 6, Folder 7.)

———. "An Engineer's Story." *Chillicothe (Ohio) Leader*, Feb. 9, 1889.

———. "How I Ran the 'General.'" *The Railroad Man's Magazine*, March 1911.

———. Narrative transcription (unpublished). (Original handwritten version in Box 13, M1997-000099, VFM Collections.) Ohio Historical Society.

Murphy, Anthony. Correspondence and questionnaire responses, Wilbur G. Kurtz, Sr. Collection, Atlanta History Center. (MSS 132, Box 5, Folder 7.)

———. "Mr. Murphy's Statement," quoted in *Atlanta Daily Intelligencer*, April 15, 1862.

———. "Pursuit of Andrews' Raiders." *Atlanta Journal Magazine*, Nov. 8, 1931, pp. 1-2, 27.

Ohio Boys in Dixie: The Adventures of Twenty-Two Scouts Sent by General O.M. Mitchell to Destroy a Railroad: With a Narrative of Their Barbarous Treatment by the Rebels and Judge Holt's Report. New York: Miller & Matthews, 1863. (Contains deposition testimony of Bensinger, Buffum, Parrott, Pittenger, Reddick.)

Parrott, Jacob. Correspondence and questionnaire responses, Wilbur G. Kurtz, Sr. Collection, Atlanta History Center. (MSS 132, Box 5, Folder 4.)

———. "The Great Locomotive Chase." *Battles and Leaders of the Civil War*. Vol. 5. Peter J. Cozzens, ed. Champaign: University of Illinois Press, 2002, pp. 272-83.

Parrott, Jacob, and Frank C. Dougherty. "The Andrews' Railroad Raid." *McClure's*, Sept. 1903, pp. 498-508.

Pittenger, William. *Capturing a Locomotive: A History of Secret Service in the Late War.* Philadelphia: Lippincott, 1882.

———. Correspondence and questionnaire responses, Wilbur G. Kurtz, Sr. Collection, Atlanta History Center. (MSS 132, Box 6, Folder 3.)

———. *Daring and Suffering: A History of the Great Railroad Adventure.* Philadelphia: J. W. Daughaday, 1863.

———. *Daring and Suffering: A History of the Andrews Railroad Raid.* New York: War Publishing Co., 1887; 3rd ed. Republished by Cumberland House, 1999.

———. *The Great Locomotive Chase: A History of the Andrews Raid into Georgia in 1862,* 3rd ed. New York: John B. Alden, 1889.

———. "The Locomotive Chase in Georgia." *Battles and Leaders of the Civil War* (1887). Vol. 2, pp. 709-16.

———. "The Locomotive Chase in Georgia." In *Famous Adventures and Prison Escapes of the Civil War.* New York: Century, 1917.

Porter, John Reed. Correspondence and questionnaire responses, Wilbur G. Kurtz, Sr. Collection, Atlanta History Center. (MSS 132, Box 5, Folder 5.)

———. John R. Porter Papers, 1861-1921. Atlanta History Center.

Reddick, William H. Correspondence and questionnaire responses, Wilbur G. Kurtz, Sr. Collection, Atlanta History Center. (MSS 132, Box 5, Folder 5.)

Wilson, John A. *The Adventures of Alf Wilson: A Thrilling Episode of the Dark Days of the Rebellion.* Toledo, Ohio: Blade, 1880.

Wood, Mark, and John A. Wilson, Report to Lieut. A.C. Spafford, Company C, 21st Ohio Volunteers, February 1863. *The War of the Rebellion: A Compilation of the Official Records of the Union and Confederate Armies*, Series I, Vol. 52, pp. 347-49.

OTHER MEMOIRS, DIARIES, CORRESPONDENCE, AND PERSONAL PAPERS

Abraham Lincoln Papers. Library of Congress.

Beatty, John. *The Citizen-Soldier; or, Memoirs of a Volunteer*. Cincinnati: Wilstach, Baldwin & Co., 1879.

Brownlow, W.G. *Sketches of the Rise, Progress and Decline of Secession; with a Narrative of Personal Adventures Among the Rebels*. Philadelphia: George W. Childs, 1862.

Chase, Salmon P. *The Salmon P. Chase Papers*. John Niven, ed. 5 vols. Kent, Ohio: Kent State University Press, 1997.

Clayton, Sarah Conley. *Requiem for a Lost City: A Memoir of Civil War Atlanta and the Old South*. Robert Scott Davis, Jr., ed. Macon, Ga.: Mercer University Press, 1999.

Crew, James R. Correspondence, including Letter to Dear Wife, June 18, 1862 (probable date). James R. Crew Collection, Atlanta History Center (MSS 79F).

Fletcher, Louisa Warren. *Journal of a Landlady*. H. Higgins and C. Cox, eds. Chapel Hill, N.C.: Professional Press, 1995.

Grant, Ulysses S. *Personal Memoirs*. New York: Penguin, 1999.

Keifer, Joseph Warren. *Slavery and Four Years of War: A Political History of Slavery in the United States, Together with a Narrative of the Campaigns and Battles of the Civil War in Which the Author Took Part, 1861-1865*. New York: G.P. Putnam's Sons, 1900.

King, John M. *Three Years with the 92nd Illinois: The Civil War Diary of John M. King*. Mechanicsburg, Pa.: Stackpole Books, 1999.

Kurtz, Wilbur G. Letter to Walt Disney, Feb. 1, 1952, Wilbur G. Kurtz Collection, Margaret Herrick Library, Academy of Motion Picture Arts and Sciences, Los Angeles.

Kurtz, Wilbur G. Correspondence. Wilbur G. Kurtz Collection, AHC.

Lytle, William Haines. *For Honor, Glory, and Union: The Mexican and Civil War Letters of Brig. Gen. William Haines Lytle*. Ruth C. Carter, ed. (Lexington: University Press of Kentucky, 1999).

Mitchel, O.M. Correspondence. University of Cincinnati Library.

———. Papers, 1823-1862. Cincinnati Historical Society.

Nolan, Warren. Letter to Wilbur G. Kurtz, December 23, 1926. Wilbur G. Kurtz Collection, Margaret Herrick Library, Academy of Motion Picture Arts and Sciences, Los Angeles.

Richards, Samuel P. Diary. S.P. Richards Collection, Atlanta History Center.

Scott, W.J. "An Episode of the War–Andrews and His Scheme." In *From Lincoln to Cleveland: and Other Short Studies in History and General Literature*. Atlanta: J.P. Harrison, 1886, pp. 148-62.

Sherman, William T. *Memoirs of General W. T. Sherman*. New York: Library of America, 1984.

Temple, Oliver Perry. O.P. Temple Papers, 1832- . Special Collections Library of the University of Tennessee, Knoxville.

Waddle, Angus L. *Three Years with the Armies of the Ohio and the Cumberland*. Chillicothe, Ohio: Scioto Gazette Book and Job Office, 1889. (Letters originally published in *The Ohio Soldier*, over the signature of "Adjutant," Jan. 21–Oct. 13, 1888.)

Ward, James A., ed. *Southern Railroad Man: Conductor N.J. Bell's Recollections of the Civil War Era.* DeKalb: Northern Illinois University Press, 1994.

Wusthoff, Mrs. Joseph M. "Raider Andrews Was Hanged in Georgian Terrace Block." Eyewitness account, reprinted in *Atlanta Journal*, April 13, 1913.

BOOKS AND COMPILATIONS

Abbott, John S.C. *The History of the Civil War in America.* New York: Henry Bill, 1864.

Abdill, George B. *Civil War Railroads: A Pictorial Story of the War Between the States, 1861-1865.* Bloomington: Indiana University Press, 1999.

Aiken, Gene. *The Great Locomotive Chase As Told By Men Who Made It Happen.* Gatlinburg, Tenn.: Historic Press/South, 1994.

Andrews, J. Cutler. *The South Reports the Civil War.* Princeton: Princeton University Press, 1970.

Angle, W. Craig. *The Great Locomotive Chase: More on the Andrews Raid and the First Medal of Honor.* Rouzerville, Pa.: By the Author, 1992.

Armstrong, Zella. *The History of Hamilton County and Chattanooga, Tennessee.* 2 vols. Chattanooga, Tenn.: Lookout Publishing Co., 1931.

Barnwell, V.T. *Barnwell's City Directory and Stranger's Guide.* Atlanta: Intelligencer Book & Job Office, 1867.

Beyer, W.F., and O.F. Keydel, eds. *Deeds of Valor: How America's Civil War Heroes Won the Congressional Medal of Honor.* Detroit: Perrien-Keydel Co., 1903; reprint, Stamford, Conn.: Longmeadow Press, 1992.

Black, Robert C., III. *The Railroads of the Confederacy.* 1952; reprint, Chapel Hill: University of North Carolina Press, 1998.

Brooks, Noah. *Lincoln Observed: Civil War Dispatches of Noah Brooks.* Michael Burlingame, ed. Baltimore: Johns Hopkins University Press, 1998.

Brown, Joseph M. *Marietta: The Gem City of Georgia.* 1887. Reprinted by Cobb Landmarks and Historical Society.

————. *The Mountain Campaigns of Georgia, or, War Scenes on the W. & A.* Buffalo, N.Y.: Matthews, Northrup & Co., 1886.

Buell, Don Carlos. "Operations in North Alabama." *Battles and Leaders of the Civil War* 2 (1887), pp. 701-8.

Buell, Thomas B. *The Warrior Generals: Combat Leadership in the Civil War.* New York: Crown, 1997.

Castel, Albert. *Decision in the West: The Atlanta Campaign of 1864.* Lawrence: University Press of Kansas, 1992.

Catton, Bruce. *This Hallowed Ground: The Story of the Union Side of the Civil War.* New York: Doubleday, 1956.

Chicoine, Stephen. *John Basil Turchin and the Fight to Free the Slaves.* Westport, Conn.: Praeger, 2003.

Clark, John E., Jr. *Railroads in the Civil War: The Impact of Management on Victory and Defeat.* Baton Rouge: Louisiana State University Press, 2001.

Cohen, Stan, and James G. Bogle. *The General and The Texas.* Missoula, Mont.: Pictorial Histories Publishing, 1999.

Comstock, Henry B. *The Iron Horse: An Illustrated History of Steam Locomotives.* 2nd ed. [Sykesville, Md.]: Greenberg Publishing, 1993.

Cunyus, Lucy Josephine. *The History of Bartow County, Formerly Cass.* Bartow County, Ga.: Tribune Publishing, 1933.

Current, Richard Nelson. *Lincoln's Loyalists: Union Soldiers from the Confederacy.* Boston: Northeastern University Press, 1992.

Daniel, Larry J. *Days of Glory: The Army of the Cumberland, 1861-1865.* Baton Rouge: Louisiana State University Press, 2004.

————. *Shiloh.* New York: Simon & Schuster, 1997.

Danley, W.L. *The Story of the "General," 1862.* Nashville, 1906(?).

Detzer, David. *Allegiance: Fort Sumter, Charleston, and the Beginning of the Civil War.* New York: Harcourt, 2001.

————. *Donnybrook: The Battle of Bull Run, 1861.* New York: Harcourt, 2004.

Donald, David Herbert. *Lincoln.* New York: Simon & Schuster, 1995.

Dyer, Thomas G. *Secret Yankees: The Union Circle in Confederate Atlanta.* Baltimore: Johns Hopkins University Press, 1999.

Engle, Stephen Douglas. *Don Carlos Buell: Most Promising of All.* Chapel Hill: University of North Carolina Press, 1999.

Epstein, Samuel, and Beryl Williams. *The Andrews Raid or The Great Locomotive Chase.* 2nd ed. New York: Coward-McCann, 1955.

Farwell, Byron. *The Encyclopedia of Nineteenth-Century Land Warfare: An Illustrated World View.* New York: W.W. Norton, 2003.

Faulkner, William. *The Unvanquished.* New York: Random House, 1938.

Feuerlicht, Roberta S. *Andrews' Raiders.* New York: Crowell-Collier, 1967.

Fisher, Noel C. *War at Every Door: Partisan Politics and Guerrilla Violence in East Tennessee, 1860-1869.* Chapel Hill: University of North Carolina Press, 1997.

Fitch, John. *Annals of the Army of the Cumberland.* Philadelphia: J.B. Lippincott & Co., 1864.

Flower, Frank Abial. *Edwin McMasters Stanton: The Autocrat of Rebellion, Emancipation and Reconstruction.* Boston: Geo. M. Smith & Co., 1905.

Foote, Shelby. *The Civil War: A Narrative.* 3 vols. New York: Random House, 1958.

Fry, James B. *Military Miscellanies.* New York: Brentano's Press, 1889.

————. "Notes on the Locomotive Chase." *Battles and Leaders of the Civil War* 2 (1887), p. 716.

Garrett, Franklin M. *Atlanta and Environs: A Chronicle of Its People and Events.* 4 vols. New York, 1954. Vol. I.

Gatch, Conduce H. "General O.M. Mitchel and his Brilliant March Into the Heart of the Southern Confederacy." Iowa Commandery, Military Order of the Loyal Legion of the United States, *War Sketches and Incidents.* MOLLUS-IA, vol. 2. Des Moines: Kenyon Press, 1898, pp. 110-28.

Glover, James Bolan V, et al., *Marietta 1833-2000.* Charleston: Arcadia Publishing, 1999.

Govan, Gilbert E., and James W. Livingood. *The Chattanooga Country, 1540-1976: From Tomahawks to TVA.* 3rd ed. Knoxville: University of Tennessee Press, 1977.

Gregg, Frank M. *Andrews Raiders: or the Last Scenes and Final Chapter of the Daring Incursion into the Heart of the Confederacy.* Chattanooga: Republican Job Print, 1891.

Grimsley, Mark. *The Hard Hand of War: Union Military Policy Toward Southern Civilians, 1861-1865.* Cambridge: Cambridge University Press, 1995.

Grose, Parlee C. *The Case of Private Smith and the Remaining Mysteries of the Andrews Raid.* McComb, Ohio: General Publishing Co., 1963.

Harris, Joel Chandler. *Stories of Georgia.* New York: American Book Co., 1896, 1898.

Head, Joe F. *The General: The Great Locomotive Dispute.* Cartersville, Ga.: Etowah Historical Foundation, 1990.

Headley, P.C. *Old Stars: The Life and Military Career of Major-General Ormsby M. Mitchel.* Boston: Lee and Shepard, 1864.

————. *The Patriot Boy: The Life and Career of Major-General Ormsby M. Mitchel.* New York: W.H. Appleton, 1865.

Henry, Robert Selph. *The Story of the Confederacy.* Indianapolis: Bobbs-Merrill, 1931.

————. *Trains.* Indianapolis: Bobbs-Merrill, 1954.

Hubbard, Freeman H. *Railroad Avenue: Great Stories and Legends of American Railroading.* New York: McGraw-Hill, 1945.

Johnston, James Houstoun. *Western and Atlantic Railroad of the State of Georgia.* Atlanta: Stein Printing Company, 1932.

Jones, Robert C. *Kennesaw (Big Shanty) in the Nineteenth Century.* Kennesaw, Ga.: Kennesaw Historical Society, 2000.

Judd, Cameron. *The Bridge Burners: A True Adventure of East Tennessee's Underground Civil War.* Johnson City, Tenn.: Overmountain Press, 1996.

Kennett, Lee. *Marching Through Georgia: The Story of Soldiers and Civilians During Sherman's Campaign.* New York: HarperCollins, 1996.

Krakow, Kenneth K. *Georgia Place-Names: Their History and Origins.* 3rd ed. Macon, Ga.: Winship Press, 1975. Available online at http://www.kenkrakow.com/gpn/georgia_place-names.htm.

Kurtz, Wilbur G. *Atlanta and the Old South: Paintings and Drawings.* Atlanta: American Lithography Co., 1969.

————. *Historic Atlanta: A Brief Story of Atlanta and Its Landmarks.* Atlanta: Conger, 1929.

McBryde, Randell W. *The Historic "General": A Thrilling Episode of the Civil War.* Signal Mountain, Tenn.: Antiques Research Publications, 1967.

McPherson, James M. *Battle Cry of Freedom: The Civil War Era.* New York: Oxford University Press, 1988.

Mitchel, F.A. *Ormsby MacKnight Mitchel, Astronomer and General.* Boston: Houghton Mifflin, 1887.

Mitchel, O.M. *The Astronomy of the Bible.* New York: Albert Mason, 1874.

————. *The Planetary and Stellar Worlds: A Popular Exposition of the Great Discoveries and Theories of Modern Astronomy.* New York: Baker & Scribner, 1848.

Miles, Jim. *Fields of Glory: A History and Tour Guide of The War in the West, The Atlanta Campaign, 1864.* 2nd ed. Nashville: Cumberland House, 2002.

Nicolay, John G., and John Hay, eds. *The Complete Works of Abraham Lincoln.* New and enl. ed. New York, F. D. Tandy Company, [1905].

O'Neill, Charles Kendall. *Wild Train: The Story of Andrews' Raiders.* New York: Random House, 1956.

Pope, Mark Cooper, III, with J. Donald McKee. *Mark Anthony Cooper: The Iron Man of Georgia, A Biography.* Atlanta: Graphic Publishing Company, 2000.

Prokopowicz, Gerald J. *All for the Regiment: The Army of the Ohio, 1861-1862.* Chapel Hill: University of North Carolina Press, 2001.

Reid, Whitelaw. *Ohio in the War: Her Statesmen, Her Generals, and Soldiers.* Cincinnati: Moore, Wilstatch & Baldwin, 1868.

Russell, James Michael. *Atlanta, 1847-1890: City Building in the Old South and the New.* Baton Rouge: Louisiana State University Press, 1980.

Schott, Joseph L. *Above and Beyond: The Story of the Congressional Medal of Honor.* New York: Putnam's, 1963.

Schult, Dain. *Nashville, Chattanooga and St. Louis: A History of the Dixie Line.* Motorbooks International, 2003.

Sears, Stephen W. "The Great Locomotive Chase." *The Civil War: The Best of American Heritage.* New York: Houghton Mifflin, 1991, pp. 73-88.

———. *Landscape Turned Red: The Battle of Antietam.* New York: Houghton Mifflin, 1983.

———. *To the Gates of Richmond: The Peninsula Campaign.* New York: Mariner Books, 2001.

Simpson, Brooks D., and Jean V. Berlin, eds. *Sherman's Civil War: Selected Correspondence of William T. Sherman, 1860-1865.* Chapel Hill: University of North Carolina Press, 1999.

Smith, Mark H. *History of Kennesaw.* Kennesaw Gazette, 1980-81.

Sword, Wiley. *Mountains Touched with Fire: Chattanooga Beseiged, 1863.* New York: St. Martin's Press, 1995.

Temple, Oliver P. *East Tennessee and the Civil War.* Cincinnati: R. Clarke Company, 1899 (reprint Johnson City, Tenn: Overmountain Press, 1995).

Temple, Sarah Blackwell Gober. *The First Hundred Years: A Short History of Cobb County in Georgia.* Atlanta: Walter D. Brown, 1935.

Turner, George Edgar. *Victory Rode the Rails: The Strategic Place of Railroads in the Civil War.* Indianapolis : Bobbs-Merrill, 1953; reprint Lincoln: University of Nebraska Press, 1992.

Van Horne, Thomas B. *History of the Army of the Cumberland.* Wilmington, N.C.: Broadfoot Publishing Co., 1988 (1875), vol. I.

Vocke, William. "The Military Achievements of Major-General O. McKnight Mitchel." In Commandery of the State of Illinois, Military Order of the Loyal Legion of the United States (MOLLUS-IL), *Military Essays and Recollections,* 4: 83-121.

Ward, James A. *Railroads and the Character of America, 1820-1887.* Knoxville: University of Tennessee Press, 1986.

Warner, Ezra. *Generals in Blue: Lives of the Union Commanders.* Baton Rouge: Louisiana State University Press, 1959.

———. *Generals in Gray: Lives of the Confederate Commanders.* Baton Rouge: Louisiana State University Press, 1964.

White, John H., Jr. *A History of the American Locomotive: Its Development, 1830-1880.* New York: Dover, 1979.

Williams' Atlanta Directory, City Guide and Business Mirror, Vol. 1, 1859-60. Atlanta: M. Lynch, 1859.

Williams, Kenneth P. *Grant Rises in the West: The First Year, 1861-1862.* Lincoln: University of Nebraska Press, 1997.

Wilson, John. *Chattanooga's Story.* Chattanooga: Chattanooga News-Free Press, 1980.

Yates, Bowling C. *Historic Highlights in Cobb County.* Cobb Landmarks and Historical Society, 2001.

ARTICLES

Abbott, John S.C. "Heroic Deeds of Heroic Men VII—A Railroad Adventure." *Harper's New Monthly Magazine,* July 1865, pp. 164-74.

Alvarez, Eugene. "Peter James Bracken: The Forgotten Engineer of the 'Great Locomotive Chase'." *Atlanta Historical Journal,* 24 (Winter 1980).

Benjamin, Charles F. "Recollections of Secretary Stanton by a Clerk of the War Department." *The Century,* 33, no. 5 (March 1887), pp. 758-68.

Bible, Donahue. "Shattered Like Earthen Vessels." *Civil War Times Illustrated,* 36, no. 6 (Dec. 1997), p. 48.

Bogle, James G. "The Andrews Raid: A Sequel." *Atlanta Historical Bulletin,* 16 (Summer 1971), pp. 26-46.

———. "Civil War Railroads—Georgia and Tennessee." *Atlanta Historical Bulletin,* 12, no. 3 (Sept. 1967), pp. 23-37.

———. "The General." *The Landmarker* (Cobb County Landmarks Society), 5, no. 1 (Fall 1980), pp. 3-46.

———. "The Texas." *The Landmarker* (Cobb County Landmarks Society, Inc.), 4, no. 3 (Winter 1979-80), pp. 3-14.

———. "The Great Locomotive Chase or The Andrews Raid." *Blue & Gray,* July 1987.

———. "A Postscript: Three Letters and a Medal." *Atlanta Historical Bulletin,* 13 (Dec. 1968), pp. 30-35.

———. "The Western & Atlantic Railroad in the Campaign for Atlanta." In *The Campaign for Atlanta and Sherman's March to the Sea,* Theodore P. Savas and David A. Woodley, eds. Campbell, Calif.: Savas Woodbury Publishers, 1994, pp. 313-42.

Brooks, Noah. "Glimpses of Lincoln in War Time." *The Century,* 49, no. 3 (Jan. 1895), pp. 466-67.

Butler, Mimi Jo. "Cole-Fletcher Families." *Cobb County, Ga. Geneological Society, Inc. Quarterly* (Dec. 1992), p. 146.

Carneal, Raymond B., and James G. Bogle. "Locomotives of the Western & Atlantic Railroad." *Atlanta Historical Bulletin,* 15 (Spring 1970), pp. 6-42.

Carter, Chip. "At Home with the General." *Civil War Times Illustrated,* 30 (Jan.–Feb. 1992), pp. 10, 12-13, 74.

Chadick, Mary. "A Housewife's Perspective on the Occupation of Huntsville." *Huntsville Historical Review,* 16, nos. 1–2 (1989).

Clay, John W. "A Journalist's Perspective on the Invasion of Huntsville." *Huntsville Historical Review,* 16, nos. 1–2 (1989).

Cornelius, Kay. "Old Stars in Alabama: General Ormsby M. Mitchel." *Alabama Heritage,* 34 (Winter 1994).

Davis, Stephen. "The Conductor Versus the Foreman: William Fuller, Anthony Murphy, and the Pursuit of the Andrews Raiders." *Atlanta History*, 34, no. 4 (Winter 1990-91), pp. 39-55.

———. "Joel Chandler Harris's Version of the Andrews Raid: Writing History to Please the Participant." *The Georgia Historical Quarterly,*. 74, no. 1, (Spring 1990), pp. 99-116.

Engle, Stephen D. "Don Carlos Buell: Military Philosophy and Command Problems in the West." *Civil War History*, 41, no. 2 (June 1995), pp. 89-115.

Gabel, M.G. "General O.M. Mitchel's Occupation of Huntsville." *Huntsville Historical Review*, 1, no. 3 (July 1971).

Gibbons, Robert. "Life at the Crossroads of the Confederacy—Atlanta 1864-65." *Atlanta Historical Bulletin*, 23 (1979).

Greene, Ward S. "Romance of the Rails: Fifty Years of Railroading As Seen By 'Uncle Jim' Squires, the Oldest Engineer of the W&A Railway." *Atlanta Journal*, March 9, 1913.

Howell, Elmo. "William Faulkner and the Andrews Raid in Georgia 1862." *Georgia Historical Quarterly*, 49, no. 2 (1965), pp. 187-92.

Hughes, Brent. "Yankee Spies and Rebel Pursuers in 'The Great Locomotive Chase.'" *Washington Times National Weekly Edition*, Sept. 28-Oct. 4, 1998, p. 28.

Kurtz, Henry H., Jr. "Hijack of a Locomotive: The Andrews Raid Revisited." *Atlanta History*, 34, no. 3 (Fall 1990), pp. 5-14.

Kurtz, Wilbur G. "The Andrews Raid." *Atlanta Historical Bulletin*, 13 (Dec. 1968), pp. 9-29.

———. "The Andrews Railroad Raid." *Civil War Times Illustrated*, 5 (Apr. 1966), pp. 8-16, 38-43.

———. "The Execution of James J. Andrews." *Atlanta Constitution* Magazine, March 8, 1931.

———. "Fulton County's First Jail." *Atlanta Journal Magazine*, Nov. 6, 1932, pp. 10, 21.

———. "Harbin's Narrative." Unpublished manuscript, based on interview with Oliver Wiley Harbin at Tunnel Hill, Georgia, Oct. 28, 1907. Wilbur G. Kurtz Collection, Atlanta History Center. (MSS 132, Box 3, Folder 7.)

———. "James J. Andrews at Williams' Island." *Atlanta Constitution* Magazine, June 15, 1930, pp. 5-6, 14.

———. "Motives and Locomotives of the Andrews Raid." *Chattanooga Times*, Sept. 18, 1938.

———. "The Andrews Raiders in The Fulton County Jail." Unpublished manuscript, 1966. Wilbur G. Kurtz, Sr. Collection, Atlanta History Center. (MSS 132, Box 2, Folder 10.) 37 pgs.

———. "Last Moments of the Andrews Raid." Unpublished manuscript. Wilbur G. Kurtz, Sr. Collection, Atlanta History Center. (MSS 132, Box 2, Folder 7.)

Lash, Jeffrey N. "A Yankee in Gray: Danville Leadbetter and the Defense of Mobile Bay, 1861-63." *Civil War History*, 37 (Sept. 1991), pp. 187-218.

Littell, E., ed. "The Federal Bridge-Burning Expedition." *Littell's Living Age*, 85, no. 1091 (April 29, 1865), pp. 144-51.

Madden, David. "Unionist Resistance to Confederate Occupation: The Bridge Burners of East Tennessee." *East Tennessee Historical Society's Publications*, 52-53 (1980-81), 22-39.

Mancini, John. "The Bold and Bloodless Raid." *Civil War*, 8 (Nov.–Dec. 1990), pp. 26-32, 34.

Mollan, Mark C. "The Army Medal of Honor: The First Fifty-Five Years." *Prologue*, 33, no. 2 (Summer 2001).

Morris, Roy Jr. "War Crime? Colonel Turchin and the Sack of Athens, Alabama." *Civil War Times Illustrated*, 24 (Feb. 1986), pp. 26-32.

Musick, Michael P. "The Only Medal." *Prologue*, 27, no. 3 (Fall 1995).

Reed, Wallace Putnam. "When Atlanta Saw Seven Men Hanged." *Atlanta Constitution*, July 28, 1902.

Robbins, Peggy. "Audacious Railroad Chase." *America's Civil War* (Sept. 1991), pp. 22-29.

Secrist, Philip L. "Aftermath of Adventure: The Andrews Raiders." *Civil War Times Illustrated*, 12 (June 1973), pp. 12-22.

Snow, Wayne. "Georgia to Honor Yankee Spy." United Press International, April 4, 1982 (LEXIS/NEXIS).

Stokes, David M. "Railroads Blue and Gray: Rail Transport in the Civil War, 1861-65: A Bibliography." *National Railway Bulletin*, 65, no. 5 (2000), pp. 4-11, 32-39.

Thomas, Edison H. "James J. Andrews Slept Here, . . . And Here, . . . And Here!" *Marietta Daily Journal*, Dec. 19, 1971.

———. "From *Yonah* to *Smith* to *Texas*." *L&N Magazine*, Feb. 1963, pp. 10-11, 26-27.

Weddle, Kevin J. "Obstacles Frustrated Union's Rising Star; Officer Loved Astronomy, Hated Delays." *Washington Times*, July 23, 1994, p. B3.

———. "Old Stars: Ormsby Macknight Mitchel at the Gates of the Confederacy." *Blue & Gray*, July 1987, pp. 28-29.

MAPS, SURVEYS, COURT DECISIONS AND OFFICIAL REPORTS

Annual Report, Western & Atlantic Railroad, October 1861.

Atlanta, from Vincent's Subdivision Map, published by the City Council, Drawn and printed at Topl. Engr. Office, H.Q. A.C., in the field, July 25th, 1864. Hargrett Rare Map Collection, University of Georgia.

Atlas to Accompany the Official Records of the Union and Confederate Armies. Washington, D.C.: Government Printing Office, 1891-95.

Birds-eye map of the Western & Atlantic R.R., the great Kennesaw Route from Atlanta to the north and north-west, 1864. New York: Fleming, Brewster & Alley (July 1887). Library of Congress Geography and Map Division, Washington, D.C.

City of Chattanooga, Tennessee v. Louisville & Nashville Railroad Co., 298 F. Supp. 1 (E.D. Tenn. 1969), *affirmed,* 427 F.2d 1154 (6th Cir.), *cert. denied,* 400 U.S. 903, 91 S. Ct. 141 (1970).

Map of the country embracing the various routes surveyed for the Western & Atlantic Rail Road of Georgia, under the direction of Lieut. Col. S.H. Long, Chief Engineer. U.S. Topographical Bureau, M.H. Stansbury, Del. (1837). Library of Congress Geography and Map Division, Washington, D.C.

Official Records of the Union and Confederate Navies in the War of the Rebellion. Washington, D.C.: Government Printing Office, 1903.

Records of the Southern Claims Commission (Allowed Claims), Cobb County, Georgia, RG 217

(217.8.7), National Archives, Washington, D.C. (claim of Henry G. Cole, claims 13312 and 19724).

Report of the Treatment of Prisoners of War by the Rebel Authorities During the War of the Rebellion . . . Washington, D.C.: Government Printing Office, 1869, pp. 885-86 (testimony of Anderson L. Scott).

Reports of the Superintendent, Treasurer, and Chief Engineer of the Western & Atlantic Rail-Road, 1846, quoted in James M. Russell, "Atlanta: Gate City of the South, 1847-1885" (Ph.D. diss., Princeton, 1971), revised and published as Russell, supra.

Reunion of the Survivors of the "Andrews' Raiders": Held at Chattanooga, Tenn. and Chickamauga Park, September 18-20, 1906. Nashville, Tennessee: Nashville, Chattanooga & St. Louis RR (1906).

State of Georgia v. City of Chattanooga, Tennessee, 406 F.2d 830 (6th Cir. 1969).

Statement of Miss Carrie King, April 27, 1864, in "Scouts, Guides, Spies and Detectives." Shandly, Ed and Scott, Jas, Office of Provost Marshal General 1861-66, RG 110, box 3, National Archives, Washington, D.C.

The War of the Rebellion: A Compilation of the Official Records of the Union and Confederate Armies. 128 vols. Washington, D.C.: Government Printing Office, 1880-1901.

NEWSPAPERS

Atlanta Constitution

Atlanta Journal

Augusta Daily Chronicle & Sentinel

Augusta Daily Constitutionalist

Brooklyn Daily Eagle

Chattanooga Daily Rebel

Chattanooga News-Press

Chattanooga Times

Cincinnati Commercial

Cincinnati Gazette

Cleveland Plain Dealer

Daily Intelligencer (Atlanta)

Harper's Weekly

Huntsville Times

Key West New Era

Marietta Daily Journal

Mobile Daily Advertiser and Register

New York Tribune

Perrysburg (Ohio) Journal

Philadelphia Inquirer

Richmond Daily Enquirer

Richmond Dispatch

Richmond Whig

Savannah Republican

Southern Confederacy (Atlanta)

Steubenville (Ohio) Herald
Sunny South (Atlanta)
Washington Chronicle

WEBSITES AND ONLINE REFERENCES

Stan Cohen and James G. Bogle, www.andrewsraid.com

David L. Bright, www.csa-railroads.com

The New Georgia Encyclopedia, www.georgiaencyclopedia.org

MUSEUMS, LIBRARIES, AND HISTORICAL SITES

Atlanta Cyclorama (Home of the *Texas*)

Atlanta History Center

Chattanooga National Cemetery, Chattanooga, Tennessee

Cincinnati Historical Society

Cobb County Public Library (Georgia Room), Marietta

Fleming County Public Library, Flemingsburg, Kentucky

Georgia Department of Archives and History

Margaret Herrick Library, Academy of Motion Picture Arts and Sciences, Los Angeles

Huntsville-Madison County Public Library

Library of Congress

Marietta Museum of History

Nashville Public Library

National Archives and Records Administration

Oakland Cemetery, Atlanta

Ohio Department of Archives and History

Ohio Historical Society, Columbus

Ohio State University Library

Southeastern Railroad Museum, Duluth, Georgia

Southern Museum of Civil War and Locomotive History, Kennesaw (Home of the *General*)

Tennessee State Library and Archives, Nashville

University of Cincinnati Library

University of Georgia Library

Robert W. Woodruff Library, Emory University

Western Reserve Historical Society, Cleveland

Sources and Acknowledgements

A NY HISTORY OF THE GREAT LOCOMOTIVE CHASE rests upon the foundation of the firsthand accounts of the men who participated in the event. Eleven of the sixteen surviving Andrews Raiders published works, wrote extensive correspondence, or gave sworn testimony, detailed interviews, and/or public lectures on the raid, and I have, of course, relied heavily upon these accounts, published and unpublished, in reconstructing the episode. I examined these recollections carefully, reconciling conflicting versions where possible, removing embellishments, and sifting out retroactive self-promotion. (In many instances, there are direct clashes of memory that cannot be entirely resolved, and I have noted these discrepancies in the text or in the notes.)

Much of my effort in this regard has been necessarily directed toward the recollections of one man: William Pittenger. I have concluded after four years of extensive examination of sources and accounts of the Andrews Raid that its history has benefited greatly but also suffered mightily from an overdose of Pittenger. The former schoolteacher and future minister published four full-length books on the raid: *Daring and Suffering: The Great Railroad Adventure* (1863), *Capturing a Locomotive: A History of Secret Service in the Late War* (1882), *Daring and Suffering: A History of the Andrews Railroad Raid* (1887), and *The Great Locomotive Chase: A History of the Andrews Raid into Georgia in 1862* (1889), as well as several shorter accounts, including an article in the classic compilation *Battles and Leaders of the Civil War* (1887). His admittedly engaging narrative and dramatic description of events soon overwhelmed all other accounts and became widely accepted as definitive. Other participants writing their own accounts, such as Alf Wilson and Jacob Parrott, frankly acknowledge their reliance on—and in some instances, outright copying of—Pittenger's descriptions. Other supposedly more objective histories and accomplished historians likewise rely disproportionately on Pittenger's books. Railroad historian George Edgar Turner devoted a chapter to the Andrews Raid in his definitive history of Civil War railroads, *Victory Rode the Rails*, with the entire chapter—including melodramatic "facts" and a blistering criticism of General Mitchel—sourced entirely to Pittenger.

This is not to say, of course, that I have excluded Pittenger or disregarded his invaluable contribution to the historical record. On the contrary, I quote him extensively—in part because of his vivid characterizations and the

careful research he did in his own right, and in part because for some portions of the story (such as the Knoxville court-martial proceedings) his is the
only eyewitness account. I have, however, corroborated his recollections as
best I could, balanced Pittenger's viewpoint with other accounts, and, whenever in doubt, favored accuracy over drama and self-glorification. (And in
Pittenger's defense, I should note that he was far from the only one who
described himself a hero. For example, Pittenger's rival and critic Daniel
Allen Dorsey, when asked what portion of the raid he found most exciting,
responded: "I felt just like any man would feel in the discharge of an important duty which he was extremely anxious to accomplish. I was not excited at
all—calm and self-possessed from start to finish.")

Similar skepticism was required in reviewing the military career of Major
General Ormsby MacKnight Mitchel. Apart from the *Official Records* of the
war and a few items of personal correspondence, there is little in the way of
contemporaneous sources on Old Stars. The only biographies of Mitchel are
a biased account written by his son, Frederick A. Mitchel, and an 1862
hagiography written to inspire young boys, P.C. Headley's *The Patriot Boy: The
Life and Career of Major-General Ormsby M. Mitchel*. Yet because he lacks an objective biographer and died long before the war ended, Mitchel has no defend-
er of his actions and was never able to explain them himself. As a result,
reviews of Mitchel's conduct and command decisions are strongly slanted
against him, including an article by Don Carlos Buell in *Battles and Leaders* containing a scathing attack on the defenseless Mitchel, who had by then been
dead for twenty-five years. Modern judgments of Old Stars, such as they are,
range from the dismissive to the unduly harsh, such as George Edgar Turner's
conclusion that Mitchel was nothing more than a "vain poseur." I have relied
predominantly on the *Official Records* and contemporaneous letters and documents written by and about Old Stars and made my own judgments about
the accomplishments and shortcomings of General Mitchel. I invite the reader to do the same.

*M*y debts are deep and extensive. Like all modern researchers of the
Great Locomotive Chase, I am indebted above all to the late Wilbur G.
Kurtz, the son-in-law of William Fuller, who spent decades investigating
every aspect of the Andrews Raid and its consequences. His voluminous
research on the raid—from his maps, sketches, and meticulous illustrations
of events to extensive correspondence, notes, questionnaires, and in-person
interviews with raiders and pursuers alike—were an indispensable resource

and a delight to explore. The staff of the Archives of the Atlanta History Center was patient and supportive of my review of these valuable materials. I also relied heavily on the writings, both published and unpublished, of other historians of the raid, including Charles O'Neill, Parlee C. Grose, Frank Gregg, and Craig Angle.

I owe deepest thanks to Atlanta railroad historian and author James G. Bogle. Colonel Bogle, like Wilbur Kurtz, has devoted many years of his life not only researching the Andrews Raid but ensuring its remembrance as well. He is responsible for the erection of numerous historical markers related to the raid—including the James Andrews marker described at the beginning of this book—and in 1982 supervised the restoration of the locomotive *Texas*. Colonel Bogle spent countless hours answering questions and sharing with me his unparalleled knowledge of the raid, the locomotives, and the characters involved. He offered detailed comments and gentle corrections on each chapter of the manuscript; generously loaned treasured original photographs for reproduction; and, on a lovely mid-April afternoon, gave me a personal tour of Oakland Cemetery. I would have been lost without his insights and lacking for critical unpublished sources. I was delighted to find in him not only a resource and a mentor but also a new friend.

I am grateful to other historians as well, especially Harper Harris of the Southern Museum of Civil War and Locomotive History, the home of the *General*, who gave enthusiastic guidance and encouragement and showed me around the cab of the world's most famous locomotive. Thomas G. Dyer of the University of Georgia shared his extensive knowledge of Union spies in wartime Atlanta and provided original source material on Henry Greene Cole. Colonel Kevin J. Weddle of the U.S. Army Military History Institute at Carlisle Barracks, perhaps the leading authority on Ormsby MacKnight Mitchel, gave invaluable insight on Old Stars and helped shape my impression of the good general. Dan Cox, director of the Marietta Museum of History, shared his considerable knowledge of local history, including his conspiracy theories regarding Henry Greene Cole. Accomplished historian and Civil War cavalry expert Eric Wittenberg provided helpful advice and recommended a terrific publisher. Dr. Stephen Davis shared his opinions on the raid, the strategic context, and the personalities involved.

Many others helped with elusive manuscript sources, including Connie Hammond of the Western Reserve Historical Society; Pat Cates at the Archives of the Southern Museum of Civil War and Locomotive History; Beverly Cooper of the Fleming County Public Library in Flemingsburg,

Kentucky, who provided materials on James Andrews; Debbie King of Colorado, who shared documents and information regarding her ancestor, Marion Ross; Jim Leeke, who shared materials from his excellent article on engineer William Knight; and David Simmons of the Ohio Historical Society, who provided a transcript of Knight's postwar lecture on the raid.

I am also indebted to a number of friends and colleagues. My friend Michael Kline endured long conversations over this book and gave thoughtful suggestions from the perspective of an experienced writer and a general reader and suggested the title. My boss Ben Garren at The Coca-Cola Company was encouraging and accommodating throughout. Tom Curvin, Tammy Harden Galloway, Ken Glazer, and Frank Whitaker each deserve special thanks as well for their assistance and support.

At Westholme, my publisher Bruce H. Franklin believed in this story as I did and worked closely with me to strengthen this book every step of the way. I appreciate his vision, his passion, and his confidence. Copyeditor Noreen O'Connor improved the narrative throughout. Joe Clark produced informative maps, and John Hubbard's design made me hope that people would, at least at first, judge the book by its cover.

Finally, I owe a great debt to my family. My father, lost to us three years ago now, was my hero. This book is dedicated to him, though it seems too late, and not enough, to show how much he meant to me. My mother, Nancy Bonds, instilled in me a love of reading and let me check out as many books as I wanted from the Marietta library as a kid. Throughout this effort, as in all my endeavors in life, she has been enthusiastic and unfailingly supportive. Thanks to my sister Holly Bonds Pipkey for her love and support as well. My daughters Caroline, Sophie, and Ava interrupted the writing just when I needed it (and even if I didn't) with love and a constant reminder of what is important in life. They also endured numerous trips to museums, libraries, and old depots, with only an occasional visit to the gift shop in meager recompense.

Most of all, I owe deepest thanks and love to my wife Jill—my first reader, staunchest supporter, and best friend. She endured many lonely hours and tolerated a dining room table that was for months piled high with books, maps, and documents, all the while offering nothing but ready assistance, insightful advice, and unwavering reassurance. Jill has always believed in me—and for that, and for her, I am profoundly grateful.

Index